BASIC
CAR CARE
ILLUSTRATED

2nd Edition

W9-BLC-516

BASIC CAR

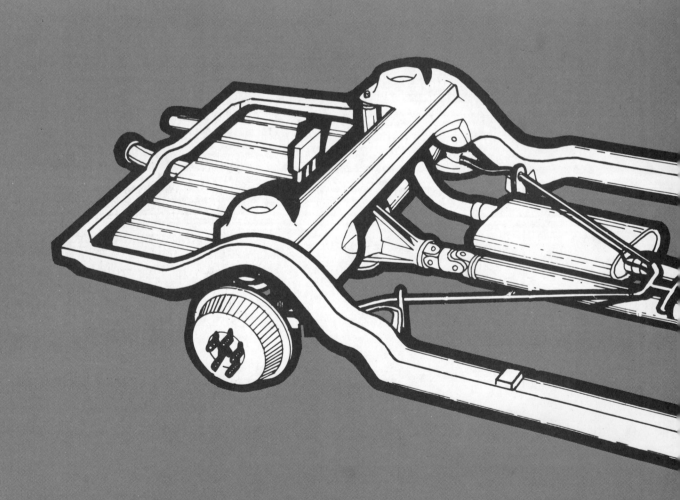

Hearst Books
The Hearst Corporation
New York, New York

CARE ILLUSTRATED

2nd Edition

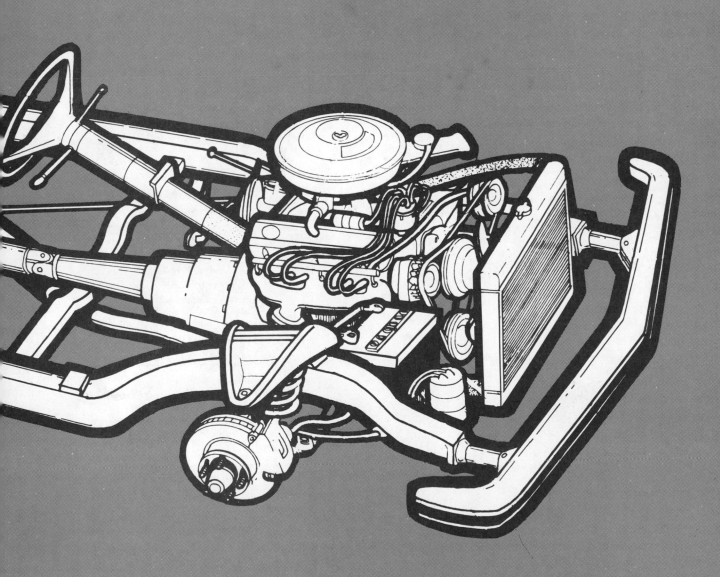

Other titles from

SATURDAY MECHANIC

Tuneup & Troubleshooting
Bodywork & Painting
Car Care Guides

Chevy
Nova
Chevelle
Vega
Ford
Torino
Pinto
Valiant
Dart
Cutlass
VW Beetle
VW Rabbit
Toyota
Datsun
Honda

BASIC CAR CARE ILLUSTRATED
2nd EDITION

Hard Cover Edition
Library of Congress
Catalog Card No. 79-63092

ISBN No. 0-87851-523-2

Soft Cover Edition

Library of Congress
Catalog Card No. 78-58662

ISBN No. 0-87851-520-8

Printed in the United States of America

Copyright © 1980, 1978 The Hearst Corporation

All Rights Reserved

Published by the Hearst Corporation, New York, New York.

No part of the text or illustrations in this work may be used without written permission by The Hearst Corporation.

The information herein has been compiled from authoritative sources. While every effort is made by the editors to attain accuracy, manufacturing changes as well as typographical errors and omissions may occur. The publisher and the editors cannot be responsible nor do they assume responsibility for such omissions, errors, or changes.

10 9 8 7 6 5 4 3 2 1

BASIC CAR CARE ILLUSTRATED, 2ND EDITION

Editor	*Allen D. Bragdon*
Text Editor	*Hannah K. Selby*
Art Editor	*Michael Eastman*
Technical Editor, Second Edition	*Miles Schofield*
Technical Writers	*William Flerx*
	Michael Labella
	Nicholas Marino
Copy Editor	*Deborah E. Perlmutter*
Contributing Artist	*Jeff Mangiat*
Contributing Photographers	*Jack Abraham*
	John B. Miller
Specifications Editor, Second Edition	*Cliff Gromer*
Technical Advisors	*Louis C. Forier*
	Lucien L. A. Garvin
	Joe Oldham
Project Coordinator	*Claude Milot*
Composition and Film	*Publishers' Design and Production Services, Inc.*
Editorial Design	*Allen D. Bragdon, Publishers, Inc.*

Acknowledgments

The editors are grateful for the assistance provided by the following individuals, manufacturers, and organizations.

AC Delco Division
General Motors Corporation

American Motors Corporation

Louis Auerbach, Principal,
Automotive High School, Brooklyn, N.Y.

Buick Division
General Motors Corporation

Cadillac Division
General Motors Corporation

Champion Spark Plug Company

Chevrolet Division
General Motors Corporation

Chrysler Corporation

Dayton Tire & Rubber Company

E.I. Du Pont, de Nemours & Company

Loretta Elbert

Firestone Tire & Rubber Company

Ford Division
Ford Motor Company

Gabriel Division
Maremont Corporation

General Tire & Rubber Company

B.F. Goodrich Tire Company

Goodyear Tire & Rubber Company

Holley Carburetor Division
Colt Industries

Helen Kessler

Lincoln-Mercury Division
Ford Motor Company

Michelin Tire Corporation

Monroe Auto Equipment Company

National Bureau of Standards
US Department of Commerce

National Tire Dealers and
Retreaders Association

Oldsmobile Division
General Motors Corporation

Frank Pelosie, Operating Superintendent,
*Sears Automotive Center, Hicksville,
New York*

Pirelli Tire Corporation

Pontiac Division
General Motors Corporation

George R. Quarles, Chief Administrator,
*Center for Career and Occupational
Education, New York City Board of
Education*

Rubber Manufacturers Association

Michael Ruvolo, Assistant Principal,
Automotive High School, Brooklyn, N.Y.

John Samanich

Glen Sperle, Public Relations
Department, *Sears, Roebuck, and
Company*

Automotive Department
Sears, Roebuck & Company

Speedway Auto Radiator

Tire Industry Safety Council

Union Carbide Corporation

Uniroyal Inc.

CONTENTS

BASIC CAR CARE ILLUSTRATED, 2ND EDITION

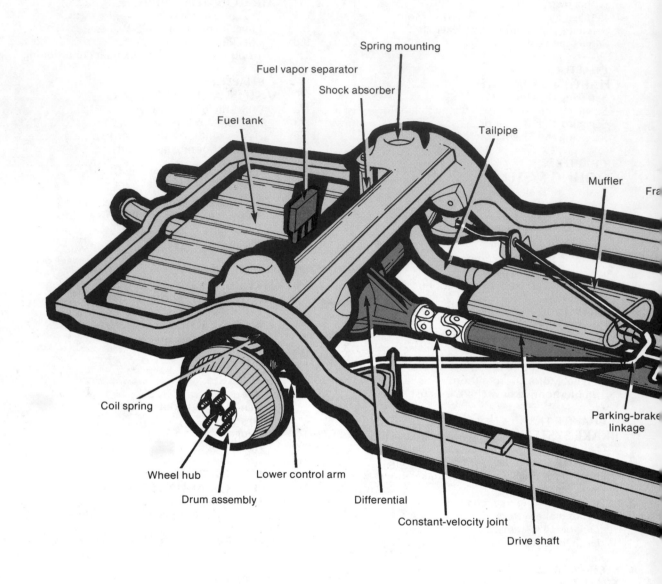

Spring mounting

Fuel vapor separator

Shock absorber

Fuel tank

Tailpipe

Muffler

Fra

Coil spring

Parking-brake linkage

Wheel hub

Lower control arm

Drum assembly

Differential

Constant-velocity joint

Drive shaft

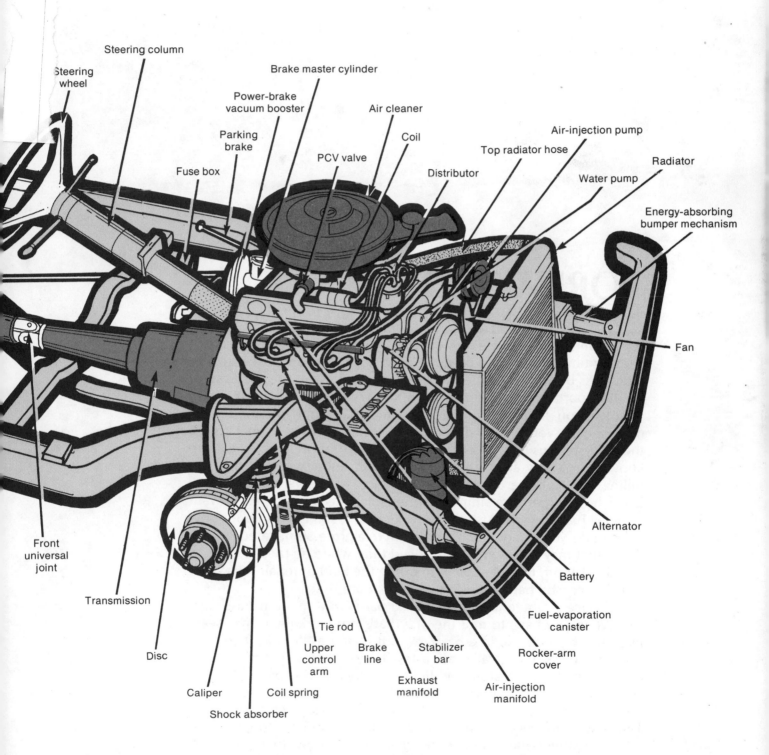

Steering wheel

Steering column

Brake master cylinder

Power-brake vacuum booster

Parking brake

Fuse box

PCV valve

Air cleaner

Coil

Distributor

Top radiator hose

Air-injection pump

Water pump

Radiator

Energy-absorbing bumper mechanism

Fan

Alternator

Battery

Fuel-evaporation canister

Rocker-arm cover

Air-injection manifold

Stabilizer bar

Exhaust manifold

Brake line

Tie rod

Upper control arm

Coil spring

Shock absorber

Caliper

Disc

Transmission

Front universal joint

FOREWORD

BASIC CAR CARE ILLUSTRATED, 2ND EDITION

If you can afford to buy a new car every year and take it to a mechanic every time it hiccups, you don't even have to know how it works, much less be able to fix it. But if you are trying to get the most out of the transportation you already own, it pays to find out what makes your two-ton, mile-a-minute investment tick. Even if you don't make most repairs yourself, it doesn't hurt to know what is making all those mysterious ticking sounds, clunks, roars, hums, and squeals; to know where they are coming from; and to know whether they are telling you to make an adjustment or not. At the very least, if you know how to perform simple maintenance checks, you can prevent or delay breakdowns. Also, if you understand something about how a car works you can describe a problem to a professional mechanic in a way that may save some high-priced time while he tries to trace it. The big pay-off, though, comes in doing the kind of repair jobs yourself that can be handled safely in your spare time.

Let's face it, there are about 15,000 parts on a modern passenger car. When you have to find the one that's not working, it may seem like locating a needle in a haystack. But it isn't as hard as it sounds. All those parts fit logically into a few basic systems that make your car start, move, turn, stop, and light up. Once you know something about how these systems work—which the first part of this book will tell you—finding a defective part in a system becomes a lot easier. The how-to instructions in this book will tell you how to take apart the component that's not working correctly; how to replace the faulty part; and how to reassemble it so you can be on your way again with a few dollars saved and the satisfaction of having done the job right and having learned something new.

Some jobs are better left to a professional

There are many reasons for this. No matter how much you develop your mechanical skills some jobs can be done more accurately, and less expensively in the long run, by a professional with specialized equipment. For instance, given a compressed air system and tire mounting machines, a service station or tire shop can change a tire in a couple of minutes. Trying to do it yourself with hand tools, a rubber-faced hammer, and sweat simply isn't worth it. Even some jobs you could do yourself with a set of basic tools when everything goes right may not be worth sweating over if you hit a snag that only specialized tools can overcome. Replacing a muffler that has become fused to the exhaust pipe, for instance, may be an insurmountable problem unless you can find someone with an acetylene torch to cut it off (which is what most commercial muffler shops do anyway).

When you are looking for a commercial auto repair shop, sometimes it is difficult to determine ahead of time how competent the mechanics are. A non-profit organization called the National Institute for Automotive Service Excellence was founded in 1972 to certify professional auto mechanics. Professionals who have passed NIASE's written examinations wear or display a round blue and orange patch that looks like a gear with cogs around the outside and the NIASE name in the center. This program is still fairly new though, and many well-qualified mechanics have not taken the NIASE certifying exams.

How this book is organized

The first chapter of this book, Know Your Car, is a short course in how a car works. It is well worth reading before getting into the how-to instructions for specific maintenance and repair jobs that make up the bulk of the book. It explains what each system does, what its component parts are called, where to look for them in your car, and how they relate to each other. This information will help you spot problems early, then diagnose and trace them to a specific malfunction so you will be less likely to waste time and money looking for the real problem or fixing the wrong thing.

The how-to instructions are contained in subsequent chapters under the title of each system. Before you start a specific job, it is a good idea to at least skim over the full chapter to be sure your repair will not affect a related component in the system.

To find the page on which instructions for a repair job appear in this book, look in the table of Contents in the front, the individual table of Contents which precedes each chapter, or the Index in the back. A Glossary of automotive terms is provided in the back of the book, if you want to learn the meaning of a technical word in non-technical language.

An Appendix, located in the back of the book just before the Glossary, contains the manufacturer's specifications for each make and model of domestic car by year from 1975 through 1980. These provide tune-up specifications, cooling system and capacity data, for each engine and make. The Appendix also gives the manufacturer's recommended periodic maintenance checks by make, model, and year.

Most of the job entries in the chapters of how-to instructions contain a list or discussion of the tools and parts that will be required for that job. Cautions about potentially hazardous or tricky procedures are printed in italic type. Here and there throughout this book you will find boxes called "Pro Shop" with useful tips from a professional mechanic that might help a beginner save time or frustration. "Quick Fix" suggestions for repairing some minor breakdowns that can be fixed temporarily, until you can find the time, tools, or parts to repair them permanently, also appear throughout the book. And the 20 "Econotips," fuel-saving tune-up and driving recommendations, should help you save money on that ever more precious commodity, gas.

Some friendly advice

If you are a car enthusiast and like machinery, chances are you already have a pretty good box of tools and a setup in your garage where you can handle most of the do-it-yourself jobs in this book. If you don't, but want to start saving some money by doing the simple maintenance jobs your service station has been doing for you, think about where you can work on your car. A quick oil change in the driveway is one thing; trying to complete a tune-up during an unexpected thunderstorm with a wrench that won't reach the spark plugs can dampen anybody's enthusiasm, to say the least. A commercial, do-it-yourself, car repair shop may be the answer. These operations will rent a service bay, hoist, tools, manuals, parts—sometimes at discount prices—and usually have a professional mechanic around to help a beginner get unstuck should problems develop. The money saving may be minor compared with having the job done professionally, but the practical experience can pay off later. Also, this chance to work with various brands of tools and equipment will help a beginner when the time comes to buy his own.

A word about safety. This book gives a great deal of attention to safety hazards and the proper procedures to minimize them. Anyone who works on a piece of machinery as large, as powerful, and as complex as a car must realize that he or she alone carries two big responsibilities. The first is for his or her own safety while making a repair; the second is for the safety of the people who will be riding in the car or others on the road after the repair is attempted.

If you don't find instructions anywhere in this book for a repair job you want to tackle, in the judgment of the experts who prepared the technical material it is probably too difficult for a do-it-yourself mechanic to handle without coming to grief—given the tools, equipment, and experience available to him or her. Whatever job you get into, from an oil change to new brake shoes, work slowly and carefully, keep the work area and parts clean, be alert for the safety of yourself and others around you while you are working, and stay relaxed enough to enjoy the job you are doing. Good luck.

CONTENTS

KNOW YOUR CAR

To protect what is probably the second-largest single investment you'll ever make, it is worth some effort to familiarize yourself with the basic systems that make a car run. In this way, you should be able to identify and correct problems before they become costly and possibly dangerous. But even when you cannot make a repair yourself, your knowledge may help you get better service or lower repair charges, or both, from a professional because the quality of information you are able to provide will help him in diagnosing the source of the problem quickly and accurately. The aim of this chapter, then, is to explain in non-technical language how a modern family car works.

Your car is composed of a variety of systems, each with many operating parts. Through normal usage, many of the 15,000 total parts in your car gradually deteriorate. Some wear out sooner than others because they work harder (spark plugs, for example), while many can last the lifetime of the car. The performance of each system, such as brakes, steering, suspension, ignition, and carburetion, depends not only on the condition of all of its own parts, but also on the proper functioning of other related systems. If, for example, a hose breaks in the cooling system, the overheating that results can damage the engine, electrical, and lubrication systems. For safety's sake, you should become sensitive to the earliest warnings in each system and check them out immediately.

As systems begin to fail, your driving attitude probably changes. Most drivers tend unconsciously to adjust their driving habits. When the brakes show signs of going soft, do you begin to pump them? Or, if the car is pulling to one side, are you correcting for it by steering differently? Keep in mind that you are dealing with a potentially hazardous condition that needs to be corrected by adjustments to the car, not by adjusting your driving habits.

Some trouble signs are visible; others give warning through changes in sound, sudden or gradual, or can be detected by the way the car handles. After reading this chapter, you will be better able to tune your senses to symptoms of failure and locate the problem. You can then decide whether to do your own troubleshooting or to take your car in for service. If you do nothing else, just following the regular maintenance procedures as prescribed in this book will not only help you achieve maximum car performance and safety, but may also spare you the expense of avoidable repairs.

The Internal Combustion Engine

Just as the human body converts the calories in the food it consumes to produce energy, the internal combustion engine converts fuel and air to power. The systems which support the internal combustion engine can also be compared in their functioning to systems of the body. Respiration enables us to bring in oxygen and rid the body of carbon dioxide. The car also has an intake and exhaust system, and one of the waste products of the engine's cycle is carbon monoxide. When we run fast, we breathe harder. Similarly, as a car's speed increases so does its air intake. The lubricating system has a network which reaches all parts of the engine just as the human circulatory system nourishes every organ and limb; and the cooling system is as necessary to the car as sweating is to humans.

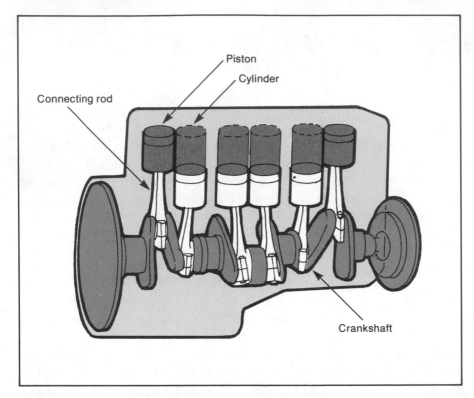

The internal combustion engine burns fuel within the cylinders. The expansion of the burning fuel pushes the pistons downward in the cylinders, activating the crankshaft through the use of connecting rods.

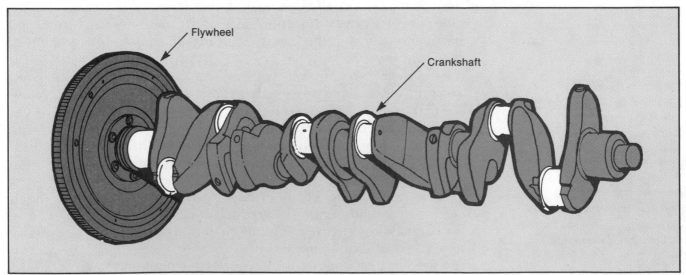

The crankshaft, which handles all of the engine's power output, changes the reciprocating, or up-and-down, motion of the pistons into rotary motion. Attached to the rear of the crankshaft is a heavy disc, known as a flywheel, whose momentum keeps the crankshaft running smoothly and assists the pistons through their cycles.

The four-stroke-cycle engine

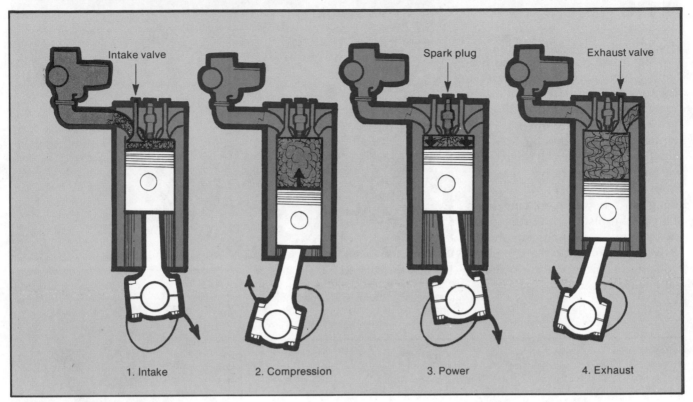

Intake valve · Spark plug · Exhaust valve

1. Intake   2. Compression   3. Power   4. Exhaust

Intake. The intake valve opens and the piston, moving downward, draws the fuel-and-air mixture into the cylinder.

Compression. With both valves closed, the rising piston compresses the mixture.

Power. At the upper limit of piston movement, both valves are closed and the mixture is ignited. The resulting explosion forces the piston downward on the power stroke.

Exhaust. The exhaust valve opens as the piston pushes spent gas from the cylinder.

The diesel engine has a simplified ignition and carburetion system. At the intake stroke, for example, there is no diesel fuel carburetor to mix fuel and air. The diesel also does away with the throttle valve which governs the amount of air entering the cylinders. Fuel is injected during the compression stroke and is ignited by the heat of the compressed air. For a further discussion of the diesel engine, see Chapter 4.

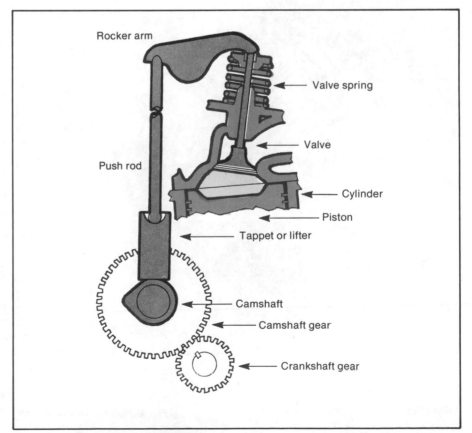

Rocker arm · Valve spring · Push rod · Valve · Cylinder · Piston · Tappet or lifter · Camshaft · Camshaft gear · Crankshaft gear

The valve train is a precisely-timed mechanism which opens and closes the intake and exhaust valves at the top of the cylinders in synchronization with the pistons. It governs the inflow of the fuel-and-air mixture and expels the burned gases.

The engine lubrication system

The lubricating oil in the engine has five major functions. It reduces friction by lubricating moving parts in the engine, thereby minimizing power loss. It assists in cooling by flowing between the internal moving parts, carrying much of the destructive heat away. It cleans by washing away abrasive materials from friction surfaces. It seals by filling gaps between moving parts such as the pistons, the rings, and the cylinders. And it absorbs shocks between bearings and other parts, reducing engine noise and extending engine life.

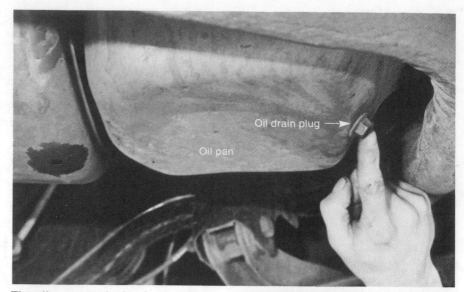

The oil pan, attached to the underside of the engine block, serves as a storage container for the oil and allows heat dissipation.

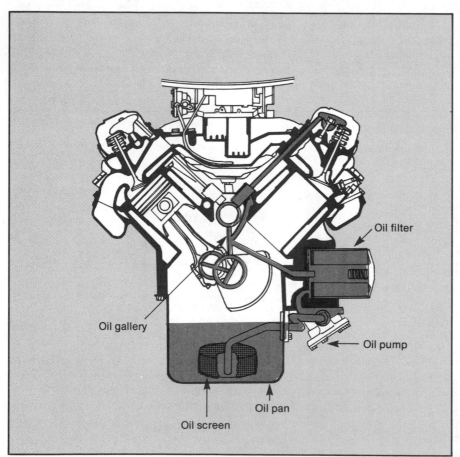

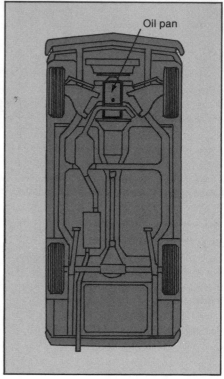

The oil pump circulates oil, under pressure, to all internal moving parts. Through a screen, the pump picks up oil from the pan, and the oil flows through a filter for cleaning. From this point, it flows through the main oil gallery to all of the moving parts of the engine.

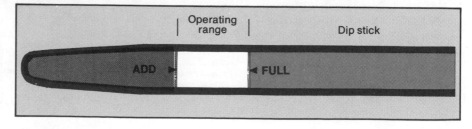

A dip stick is used to check the amount of oil in the pan. The oil-pressure indicator, located in the dashboard, indicates the oil pressure in the lubricating system. It does not measure the amount of oil in the pan.

The cooling system

The heat generated in the combustion chamber of the engine's cylinders may exceed 4,500°F. A temperature this high can destroy the engine's lubrication system and its internal moving parts. Approximately one-third of the engine's heat is used to produce power, one-third leaves through the exhaust system, and the remaining one-third must be dissipated through the cooling system. The coolant used in the modern car engine is a mixture of water and permanent antifreeze, a solution which has a lower freezing point and a higher boiling point than water.

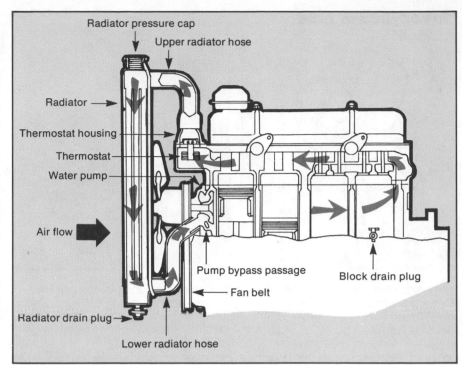

The flow of the coolant. The water pump, driven by a belt attached to the crankshaft pulley, moves the coolant through the engine block, radiator, and heater.

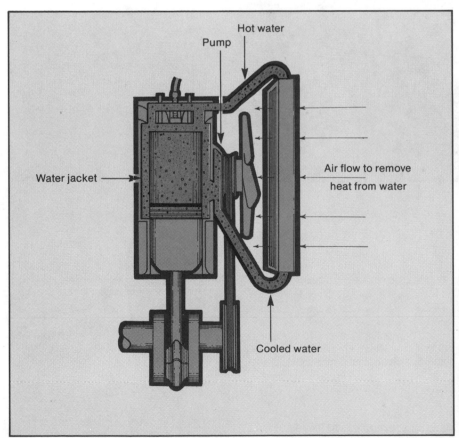

The radiator sends the heat absorbed by the coolant into the atmosphere. Additionally, in many modern cars, it cools the automatic transmission fluid by allowing it to flow through a cooler which is built into one of the radiator tanks. Cool air is drawn through the radiator by means of the fan.

The thermostat, located in a housing at the lower end of the upper radiator hose, is designed to maintain proper coolant temperature by controlling the flow of coolant to the radiator.

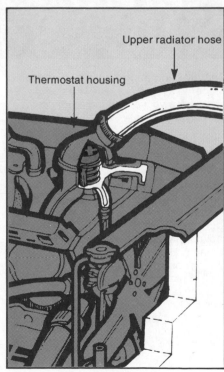

Three types of fans

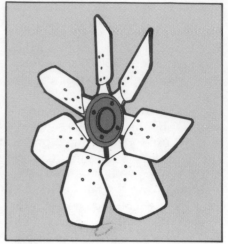

The flexible fan. The pitch of the individual blades of the flexible fan varies with the speed of the engine. At high speed the blades flatten out to produce less airflow and less noise.

The thermostatically controlled fan. The speed of the thermostatically controlled fan varies according to the temperature of the air being drawn through the radiator core.

The standard fan. The number of blades (four to seven) on the standard fan determines the amount of air passing through the radiator.

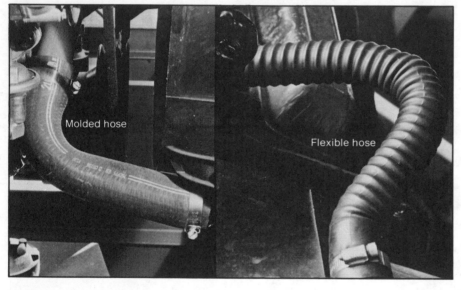

Molded hose

Flexible hose

Radiator and heater hoses are made of rubber to allow for engine vibration. There are two types of radiator hoses, molded and flexible.

The radiator pressure cap. The high coolant operating temperature of the modern car engine, approximately 225°F, is made possible by the use of a radiator pressure cap. A typical 15-pound pressure cap will increase the boiling point of the coolant approximately 45°F. *Caution: The radiator pressure cap can be removed only when the engine is cold.* The temperature indicator light or gauge mounted on the dashboard indicates the temperature of the coolant only, not the amount of coolant in the system. This must be done by eye

as follows: remove the radiator cap and look into the radiator. You should see the top of the fluid. If not, add coolant. Your car may have an overflow recovery system, a clear plastic tank marked "full" and "empty," which you will find on the side of the radiator.

A coolant level indicator is installed on some cars, in addition to the temperature gauge or temperature light. The level indicator lamp will light if the coolant level is low.

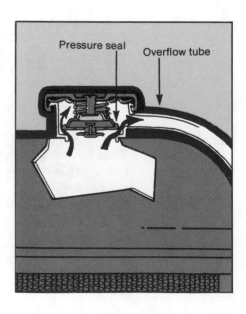

Pressure seal

Overflow tube

The fuel system

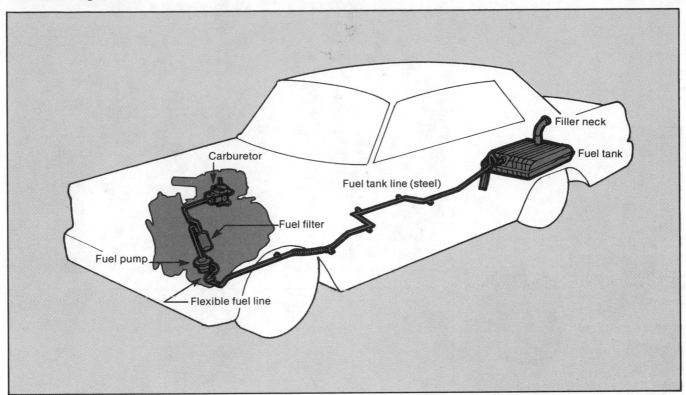

The fuel system supplies fuel to the carburetor, which mixes it with air for engine combustion. The system consists of
the fuel tank, the gas cap, fuel lines, the
fuel pump, the filter, and the carburetor.
The fuel line runs along the chassis and
is connected to the tank and pump by a
system of rigid steel and flexible hoses
usually made of neoprene.

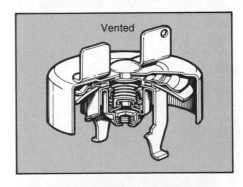

Vented

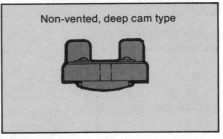

Non-vented, deep cam type

Gas caps. Today's fuel systems use two
different types of gas caps—vented and
non-vented. The correct cap must be
used. If the wrong cap is used, it may
cause lowered fuel delivery or allow
vapors to escape.

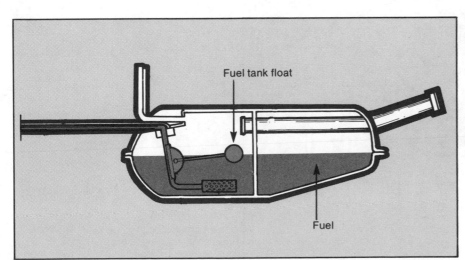

The fuel tank is a container made of
sheet metal usually located at the rear of
the car. Inside the fuel tank is a float unit
which is electrically connected to the
gas gauge on the dashboard. As the gas
level and float move up or down, the
gauge registers the amount of gasoline
in the tank.

The fuel pump is usually powered by the engine's camshaft. The pump draws fuel from the tank and delivers it to the carburetor under pressure. Some late-model automobiles have an electrically-operated pump inside the tank.

Fuel pump

Outlet

Inlet

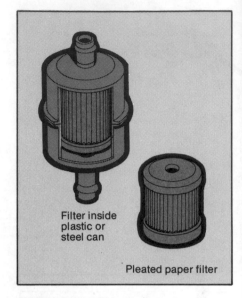

Filter inside plastic or steel can

Pleated paper filter

The fuel filter is located between the fuel pump and the carburetor. There are several different types of filters.

Ceramic and paper filters are located in the carburetor's inlet.

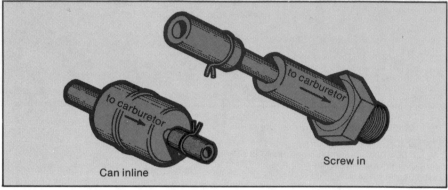

to carburetor

Can inline

to carburetor

Screw in

External-type filters are either screwed into the carburetor's inlet nut or they are cut into the fuel line between the fuel pump and the carburetor.

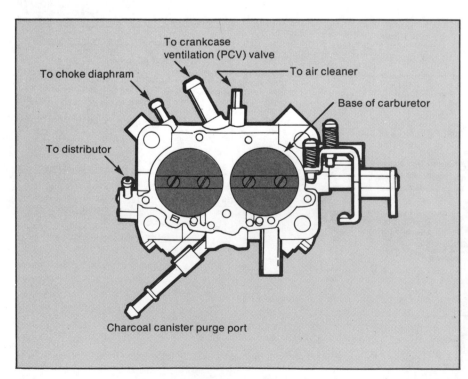

To crankcase ventilation (PCV) valve

To choke diaphram

To air cleaner

Base of carburetor

To distributor

Charcoal canister purge port

The carburetor, mounted on the intake manifold, mixes the proper amounts of fuel and air to produce a combustible mixture for all engine operating conditions. It may have one, two, or four barrels depending upon the number and arrangement of cylinders.

Turbochargers

A turbocharger is a high speed fan, or blower, that blows the fuel-and-air mixture into the compression chamber. Because of the blowing action, more fuel and air is packed into the chamber, giving greater power. Turbochargers are driven by the exhaust gases. The exhaust passes over a turbine wheel and spins it at high speed. The blower is attached to the same shaft as the turbine wheel. The faster the exhaust drives the turbine, the faster the blower packs the fuel-and-air mixture into the combustion chamber. At idle, or cruising at small throttle openings, there is not enough flow to the exhaust gas to drive the turbine. The engine then draws the mixture past the blower wheel and the wheel spins from the force of the incoming airflow.

With open throttle

Turbochargers only boost the horsepower an appreciable amount at high engine RPM and wide throttle openings. When the throttle is wide open at high RPM, the exhaust flow increases. This increases the force turning the exhaust turbine, which then spins the blower faster to pack in more mixture. Opening the throttle at low RPM will not boost the horsepower, because the exhaust flow is not great enough. A turbocharger results in much faster acceleration, but only in the hands of a knowledgeable driver. The engine must be kept wound up at high RPM so the turbocharger can work.

A bypass system

When the turbocharger is in operation, the intake passageways between the blower and the compression chamber are under pressure, instead of vacuum. The blower is actually pressurizing the intake system. If allowed to go too high, this pressure can pack so much mixture into the compression chamber that the engine might be damaged. To prevent this, a pressure actuated diaphragm is connected by a hose to the intake manifold. When the pressure rises to the set value, the diaphragm opens a wastegate. The wastegate allows some of the exhaust to go around the exhaust turbine. This reduces the force against the turbine and also reduces the pressure produced by the blower.

Turbochargers are ideal for boosting the horsepower of smaller engines. If the engine is driven normally, the turbo will idle along, contributing nothing, but restricting the intake very little. When the throttle is opened at high RPM, the turbo boosts the horsepower to equal that of a larger engine. The effect is the economy of a small engine, with the horsepower of a larger engine, when needed.

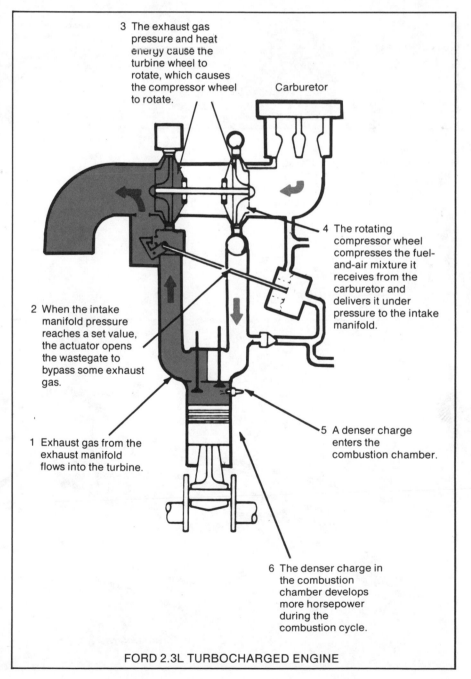

3 The exhaust gas pressure and heat energy cause the turbine wheel to rotate, which causes the compressor wheel to rotate.

Carburetor

4 The rotating compressor wheel compresses the fuel-and-air mixture it receives from the carburetor and delivers it under pressure to the intake manifold.

2 When the intake manifold pressure reaches a set value, the actuator opens the wastegate to bypass some exhaust gas.

1 Exhaust gas from the exhaust manifold flows into the turbine.

5 A denser charge enters the combustion chamber.

6 The denser charge in the combustion chamber develops more horsepower during the combustion cycle.

FORD 2.3L TURBOCHARGED ENGINE

The exhaust system

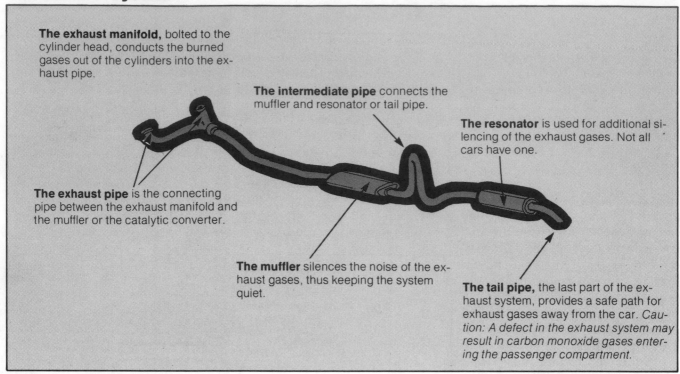

The exhaust manifold, bolted to the cylinder head, conducts the burned gases out of the cylinders into the exhaust pipe.

The intermediate pipe connects the muffler and resonator or tail pipe.

The resonator is used for additional silencing of the exhaust gases. Not all cars have one.

The exhaust pipe is the connecting pipe between the exhaust manifold and the muffler or the catalytic converter.

The muffler silences the noise of the exhaust gases, thus keeping the system quiet.

The tail pipe, the last part of the exhaust system, provides a safe path for exhaust gases away from the car. *Caution: A defect in the exhaust system may result in carbon monoxide gases entering the passenger compartment.*

The exhaust system expels burned gases from the engine into the atmosphere. The system consists of an exhaust manifold, an exhaust pipe, a muffler, an intermediate pipe, a resonator, and a tail pipe.

The catalytic converter, an emission control device, is installed between the exhaust pipe and the muffler on late-model cars.

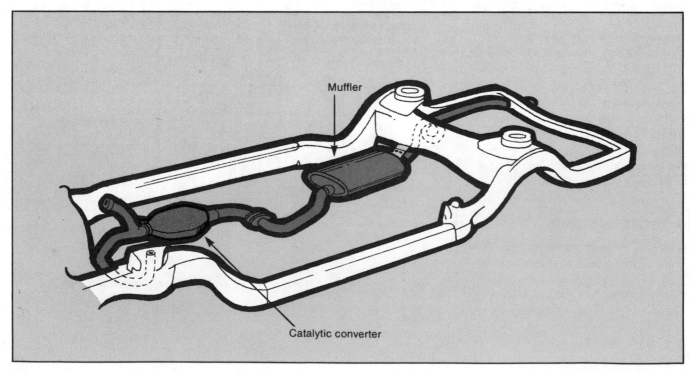

Muffler

Catalytic converter

Emission control system

Fiberglass filter

Bottom of canister

CARBON CANISTER

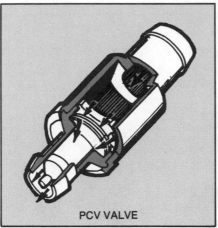

PCV VALVE

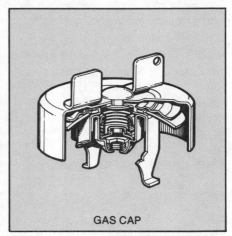

GAS CAP

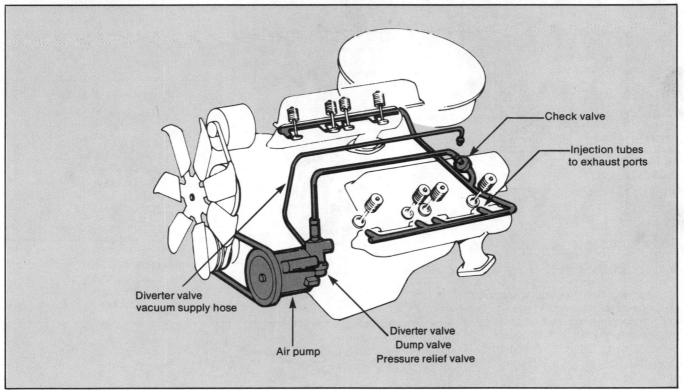

Check valve

Injection tubes to exhaust ports

Diverter valve vacuum supply hose

Air pump

Diverter valve
Dump valve
Pressure relief valve

Harmful gases, including unburned fuel (hydrocarbons), burned fuel (carbon monoxide), and high combustion temperatures which produce oxides of nitrogen are emitted by the car and cause pollution. The hydrocarbons are controlled by the carbon canister, the positive crankcase ventilation valve (PCV), the catalytic converter, the air injection reaction system (AIR), the gas tank filler cap, and the ignition spark control system.

The exhaust gas recirculating valve (EGR) and an ignition spark control system limit the emissions of nitrogen oxides and hydrocarbons. Carbon monoxide is controlled primarily by a well-tuned engine and a catalytic convertor.

Getting Started

Three electrical systems act collectively to start your car and keep it running: the cranking circuit, the charging circuit, and the ignition circuit. Although each of these systems can function independently, they share some common parts, the ignition switch and the battery, for example.

Starter solenoid

Starter motor assembly

The cranking system

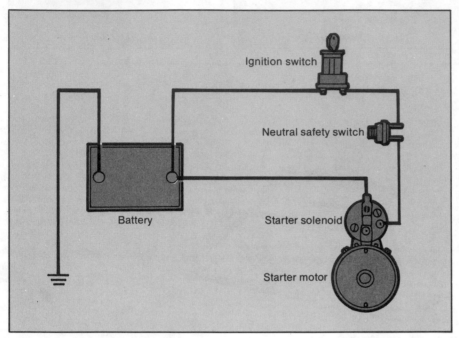

Ignition switch

Neutral safety switch

Battery

Starter solenoid

Starter motor

The starter solenoid and motor. The solenoid, an electromagnetic switch mounted on the starter, serves a dual purpose. It connects the battery to the starter motor, and it engages the starter motor to the engine's flywheel, just as a switch in your home connects the power plant in your community to the bulb in your lamp. The starter motor is a small, powerful, electric motor designed to crank the engine.

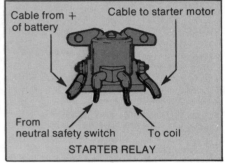

Cable from + of battery

Cable to starter motor

From neutral safety switch

To coil

STARTER RELAY

The starter relay is an electromagnetic switch that connects the battery to the starter motor. It is usually mounted on the fire wall or the inner fender pan.

The purpose of the cranking circuit, or starting system, is simply to get an internal combustion engine turning over so that it can begin running on its own. It consists of the battery, battery cables, the starter relay or starter solenoid, the ignition switch, the neutral safety switch, and the starter motor.

The ignition switch, which is activated by the car key, starts the flow of electricity from the battery to the cranking circuit and the charging system as well as to car accessories.

The neutral safety switch, which is usually mounted on the steering column below the dashboard, or on the transmission or clutch linkages, is a safety device that automatically prevents cranking of the engine when the transmission is in gear.

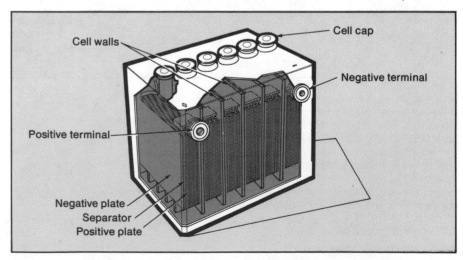

Cell walls

Cell cap

Negative terminal

Positive terminal

Negative plate
Separator
Positive plate

The battery, which converts chemical energy into electrical energy, is the car's basic source of electrical power. It is connected to the electrical system by means of cables attached to the battery's terminals, or posts. The posts may be on the top or, on some more recent models, on the side. The negative post, marked "NEG." or with a minus sign (−), is grounded to the engine or chassis. The positive post, "POS." or (+), is connected to the starter solenoid or starter relay. The negative post is always the smaller of the two.

The charging circuit

ECONOTIP

 # 1

Why check mileage?

Does it seem like a lot of trouble to fill the tank every time you get gas and figure the mileage? It may be easier to just dash into a station without a line and pump in a few gallons. But that technique may ultimately consume more gas. If the mileage is checked every tankfull, it will be obvious when something goes wrong with the engine and the mileage starts to fall off. You may not even notice that the car is running differently, but the falling mileage will prove that something is wrong. If you are really serious about getting the best mileage, check it with every fill-up, and also check the engine (or the driver) whenever the mileage gets worse.

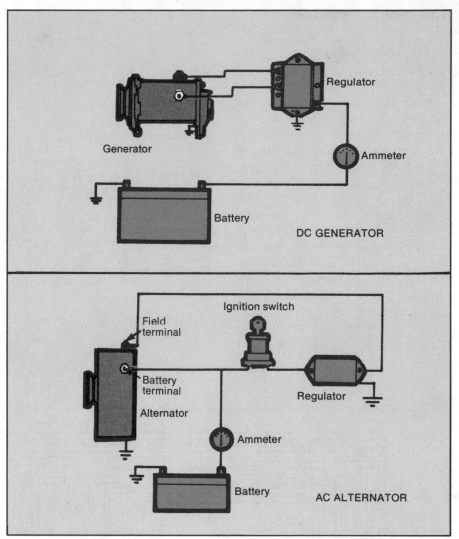

The charging circuit maintains the battery in a fully charged condition, and provides power for the car's electrical systems. It consists of an alternator or a generator; a voltage regulator; an ignition switch; a charging indicator, which is either an ammeter or an indicator light, mounted on the dashboard; and a battery and battery cables.

The alternator supplies the electrical needs of today's highest performance cars. Introduced by auto companies in 1960, it has replaced generators in all cars built since 1965.

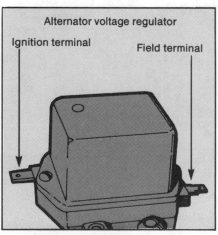

The voltage regulator controls the electrical output of the alternator or generator, and is located in the engine compartment (on the fire wall, inner fender pan, or radiator support), or, in some cases is built into the alternator unit itself.

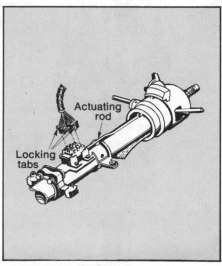

The ignition switch, as used in the alternator charging circuit, electrically connects the battery to the voltage regulator.

The ignition system

The function of the ignition system is to produce a high voltage, and to deliver it to the spark plugs at a precise instant to ignite the compressed fuel-and-air mixture in the cylinders. The system consists of a primary and a secondary circuit.

The primary circuit is composed of the battery, the alternator or generator, the ammeter or indicator light, the ignition switch, the ignition by-pass wire or ballast resistor, the ignition coil, the ignition points, and the condenser. The points and condenser are located in the distributor. The secondary circuit is composed of the ignition coil, the high-voltage coil wire, the distributor rotor, the distributor cap, the spark plug wires, and the spark plugs.

The ignition switch starts the circuit in two ways. It engages the starting circuit for engine cranking, and at the same time, it supplies battery voltage, through a wire that by-passes the resistor, to the positive (+) side of the coil.

The ballast resistor or resistor wire goes from the ignition switch to the positive side of the ignition coil. The purpose of the resistor is to reduce current flow through the coil and points so they will last longer.

The ignition coil is basically a "step-up" transformer. It raises primary battery voltage to secondary voltage, which is necessary to ignite the fuel-and-air mixture in the cylinders. A high voltage of 8,000 to 15,000 volts is required to jump the spark plug gap.

The resistor by-pass wire is used to eliminate the ignition resistor during engine cranking (starting). The available battery voltage to the primary side (+) of the coil will produce a higher secondary voltage which is necessary to ignite the richer fuel mixture needed for starting. During engine cranking, the battery voltage is reduced because of the drain caused by the starter motor. To compensate for this, the resistor must be by-passed.

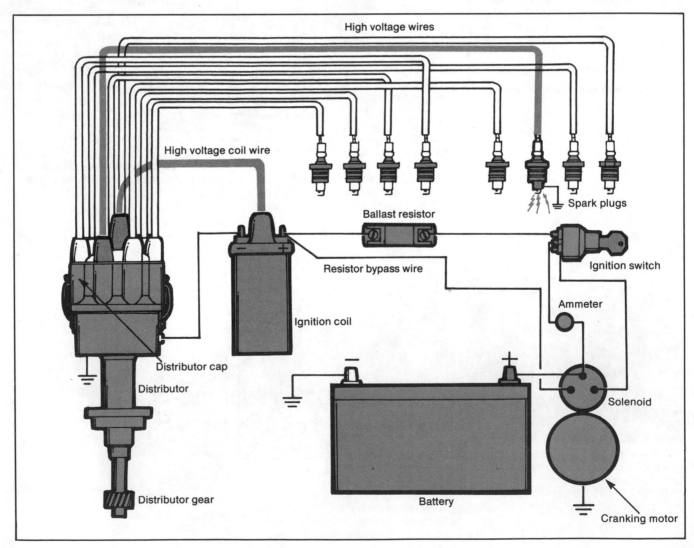

High voltage wires

High voltage coil wire

Spark plugs

Ballast resistor

Resistor bypass wire

Ignition switch

Ignition coil

Ammeter

Distributor cap

Distributor

Solenoid

Distributor gear

Battery

Cranking motor

The ignition points and condenser are located in the distributor assembly. The points are comparable to a light switch. They "make," or close, the circuit, and "break," or open it. The opening action of the points builds up a high secondary voltage in the coil secondary circuit and creates the spark. The points open, breaking the circuit, when the distributor cam turns and a lobe comes in contact with the rubbing block of the points. There is one lobe for each cylinder. A spring closes the points, making the circuit, as the cam turns. The cam is turned by the rotation of the camshaft. As with engine valve timing, this is a precisely-timed procedure.

The condenser is connected to the point spring with a strip of wire. Its housing is grounded to the distributor with a bracket and screw. The condenser assists in the quick collapse of the magnetic field in the coil which produces the spark.

The distributor assembly. The rotor is keyed to the distributor cam in such a way that it is in position to transfer the high voltage from the coil to the distributor cap towers when the points begin to open. The cap, made of molded, highly insulated material, provides a separate path for the high voltage from the coil through the rotor to each of the distributor cap towers. The spark plug wires, made of the same material as the high-voltage coil wire, carry the high voltage from the distributor cap towers to the spark plugs.

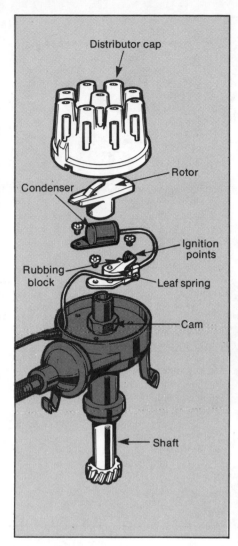

The high-voltage coil wire delivers high voltage from the coil to the center tower of the distributor cap. There are two types of wire. The resistor wire (carbon-nylon core), known as TVRS (Television-Radio Suppressor), is the more popular because it prevents radio and television interference. The conductor wire (metal core) is not commonly used.

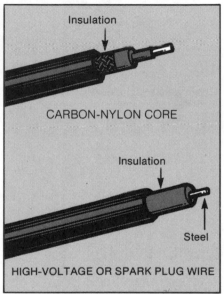

Spark plugs provide the gap across which the spark jumps, igniting the compressed fuel-and-air mixture in the cylinder. The two most popular spark plug sizes used today are 14mm and 18mm. These designations refer to thread diameter.

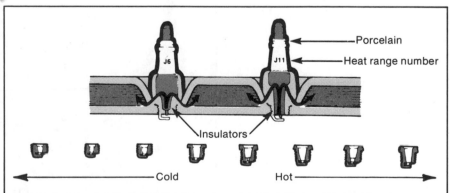

The spark plug's heat range. In order to achieve maximum engine performance, spark plugs have various operating temperatures or heat ranges. The heat range is determined by the length of the insulator and designated by a number printed on the porcelain. The higher the number, the hotter the plug.

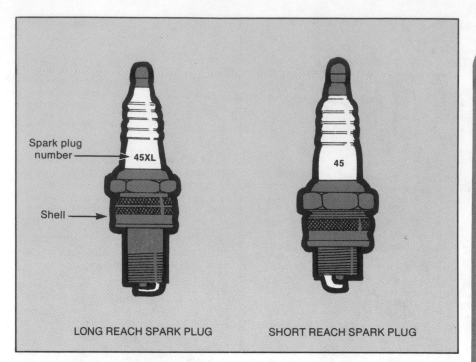

LONG REACH SPARK PLUG   SHORT REACH SPARK PLUG

Spark plug number

Shell

45XL

45

ECONOTIP

#2

Do you have a nervous foot?

The biggest cause of poor gas mileage is unnecessary movement of the gas pedal. Some drivers have a nervous foot. They find it impossible to keep their foot steady on the pedal for more than a few seconds. And they may be doing it unconsciously.

To find out if you have a nervous foot, get someone to take a ride with you and watch for unnecessary foot movement. Have the person shine a flashlight on your foot, if necessary, for good observation. If it turns out that you have a nervous foot, you may not be able to break the habit, but at least you will know why your gas mileage is not better.

Spark plug reaches are measured from the base of the shell to the end of the thread, and they vary. *Caution: Never interchange spark plugs of differ-* *ent reaches. A long-reach spark plug installed in an engine that requires a short-reach spark plug will damage the pistons or valves.*

Ignition timing

As engine speed increases, the piston moves through the compression stroke more rapidly, but the burning rate of the fuel-and-air mixture remains almost the same. To compensate for the increased piston speed, the spark must occur earlier in the compression stroke. This is accomplished by the centrifugal advance mechanism in the distributor.

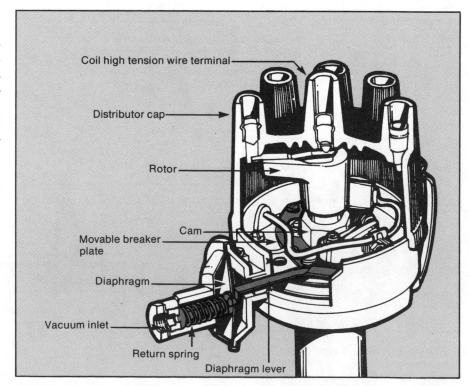

Coil high tension wire terminal

Distributor cap

Rotor

Movable breaker plate

Cam

Diaphragm

Vacuum inlet

Return spring

Diaphragm lever

The vacuum advance Engine vacuum decreases as engine load increases, and vice versa. Idling, for example, produces a higher engine vacuum. The vacuum unit advances ignition timing as engine load decreases by turning the distributor plate, to which the points are connected.

The centrifugal advance mechanism advances the ignition spark as engine speed increases. This is accomplished by two weights attached to the cam. As the engine's speed and that of the distributor shaft increase, the weights move outward by centrifugal force, thereby turning the cam and causing the ignition to advance.

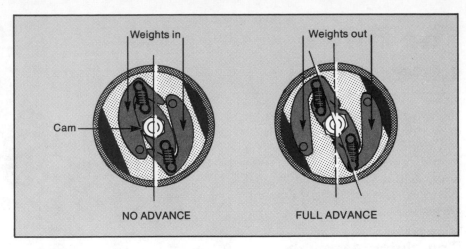

Weights in   Weights out

Cam

NO ADVANCE   FULL ADVANCE

Electronic ignitions

The conventional ignition system, with ignition contact points and condenser, although adequate, has been taxed to its capacity. One major difficulty is its inability to maintain constant ignition timing because the contacts cause wear which changes the point gap. This problem was solved with the introduction of the electronic ignition system.

In electronic ignition systems the points, condenser, and distributor cam are replaced by a magnetic pick-up assembly. A reluctor, attached to the distributor shaft, replaces the cam, and a magnetic pick-up assembly replaces the points and condenser. The rotating reluctor is never in contact with the magnetic pick-up, so they are not subject to wear. The pick-up assembly sends an electrical signal to the electronic control module, where a transistor (an electronic switch with no moving parts) makes

and breaks the primary circuit allowing the ignition coil to produce a high, or secondary, voltage, as high as 40,000 volts in many systems. Understandably, heavier gauge and more heavily insulated high-voltage coil and spark plug wires must be used. All other ignition components—the mechanical advance unit, the vacuum advance unit, the rotor, the distributor cap, and the spark plugs—function essentially the same as in the conventional system.

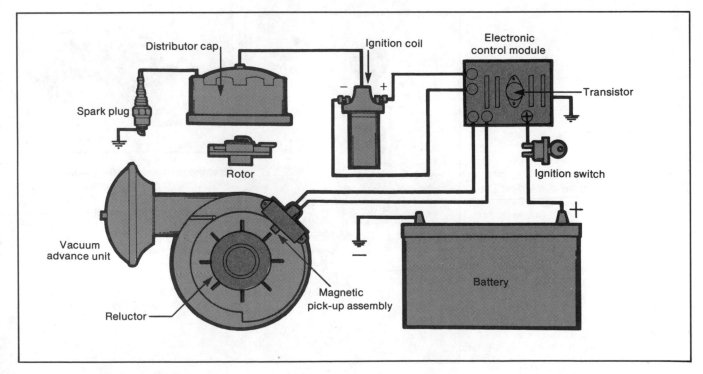

Distributor cap   Ignition coil   Electronic control module

Spark plug

Transistor

Rotor

Ignition switch

Vacuum advance unit

Magnetic pick-up assembly

Battery

Reluctor

The Drive Line

The drive line makes the car go by delivering power to the wheels. It consists of a clutch assembly or a torque convertor, a transmission, a drive shaft assembly, a differential assembly (rear end), rear axles, and wheels.

The clutch assembly

The clutch assembly, as used with a standard transmission, mechanically engages and disengages the engine and the transmission. The clutch assembly is attached to the flywheel, and consists of the following elements: a clutch disc (with friction material on each side) which is splined onto the transmission input shaft; a pressure plate made of heavy steel with coil springs or diaphragm release fingers or levers, and a cover which is bolted to the flywheel; a release bearing which slides on the transmission input shaft; and the clutch release fork that is connected to the foot pedal.

Flywheel — Clutch disc — Pressure plate — Clutch release fork — Release bearing

Pedal down, clutch disengaged

Pedal up, clutch engaged

Function of clutch parts. When the clutch pedal is released (in upward position) the clutch disc is sandwiched, under pressure, between the flywheel and pressure plate, connecting the engine directly to the transmission. When the driver depresses the clutch pedal, the clutch release fork moves the release bearing into contact with the pressure plate's fingers, thereby releasing the pressure on the clutch disc. This disconnects the engine from the transmission input shaft and permits the gears to shift smoothly.

The torque converter, which is generally used with automatic transmissions, serves as a hydraulic clutch. In addition, it steps-up engine torque (turning ability) under various operating conditions: idling, passing, or hill climbing for example.

Elements of the torque converter. The torque converter is made up of three major elements: an engine-driven pump or impeller, a fluid-driven turbine, and a stator. The impeller, which is attached to the flywheel, forces the transmission fluid against the vanes of the turbine causing the turbine to rotate. The turbine is attached to the transmission input shaft. The stator redirects the fluid flow to boost impeller action, thereby multiplying engine torque. These three elements work together in a sealed, fluid-filled housing.

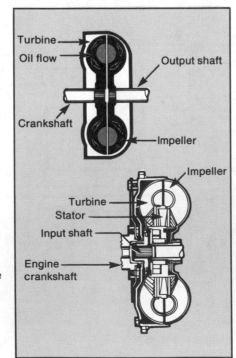

Turbine — Oil flow — Output shaft — Crankshaft — Impeller

Impeller — Turbine — Stator — Input shaft — Engine crankshaft

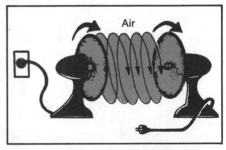

Air

How the torque converter works. To understand the basic operating principle of the torque converter, imagine two fans positioned close together with the blades facing each other. One fan is plugged in and turned on. The air flow from the plugged-in fan will cause the blades of the second to turn. In this case, air is the medium of power transfer, whereas in the torque converter, transmission fluid is the medium.

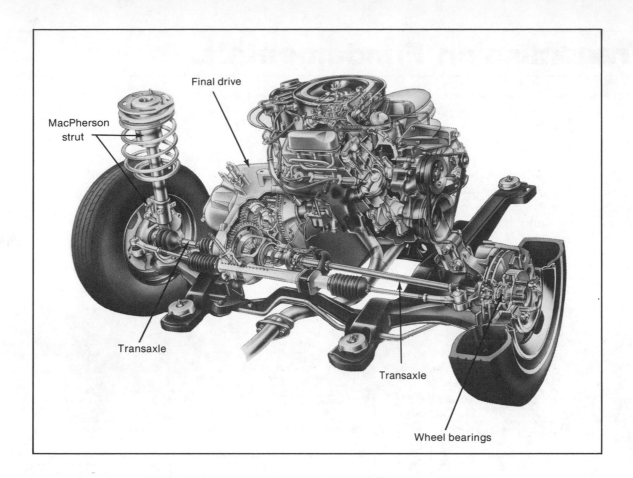

Final drive

MacPherson strut

Transaxle

Transaxle

Wheel bearings

General Motors 1980 X-Body Cars

The 1980 Chevrolet Citation, Buick Skylark, Oldsmobile Omega, and Pontiac Phoenix are all built on the same basic front-wheel drive chassis-body combination. The engine is mounted in the front, with the cylinders in line across the car. The transmission and final drive are bolted to the engine in the conventional way at the engine bellhousing. The final drive sits slightly to the rear, so the driveshafts can connect to both front wheels.

Easy to service

Transverse-engine, front-wheel drive cars have traditionally had cramped engine compartments and were difficult to service. The X-body cars have been designed for easy service. The removal and repair of the cylinder head, oil pan, water pump, rear main seal, and engine front cover are all possible without removing the engine. The engine or the transaxle can be removed separately, or both together as a unit. This is made possible by a unique engine cradle that can be unbolted and split in half for service.

Maintenance-free parts

Several parts that are normally serviced over the life of a car have been designed without any need for adjustment or service. The clutch is designed with no free play and constant tension. Clutch free play adjustments are not required. An automatic adjuster, similar to an automatic brake adjuster, keeps the clutch adjusted throughout its life. The clutch throwout bearing is always against the clutch fingers, which eliminates free play. However, the pressure against the bear-

ing is minimal, reducing wear.

Both front and rear wheel bearings are sealed and lubricated for life. Also, there is no adjustment required on the front wheel bearings. Dexron II automatic transmission fluid is used in both automatic and manual transaxles. Dexron II is much thinner than the usual 90 weight. The result is less drag from the heavy oil and better gas mileage.

Strange but nice

Spark plugs, even on the V-6, are easy to remove and replace, and all belts are easily adjusted. Although the transverse engine looks different, it takes very little time to get used to it. Servicing in many instances is much easier than on a conventional rear-drive car.

Transmission Fundamentals

The transmission, a box containing gears, varies the speed and torque of the rear axle in relation to the speed and torque of the engine. Getting the auto to move from a complete standstill requires the greatest torque, or turning power, from the engine. This is first or low gear. Once the auto is underway, less torque is required to keep it moving. Therefore, the transmission can be shifted into lower torque, greater speed gears, second, third, and sometimes fourth speed. In addition, there are two other gears: reverse for backing up, and neutral for complete disengagement of the engine from the drive shaft and rear wheels.

Operation of standard transmissions

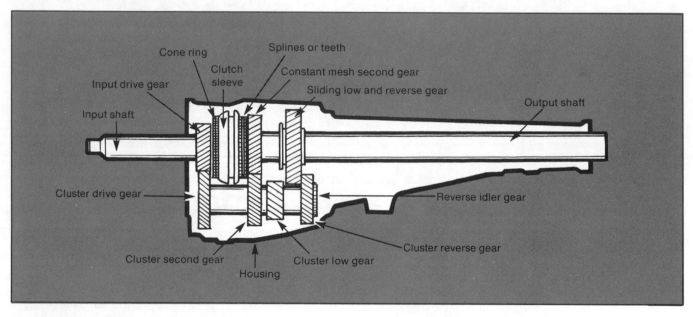

The torque and speed of the drive shaft in the standard transmission are regulated by different gear ratios in the transmission box.

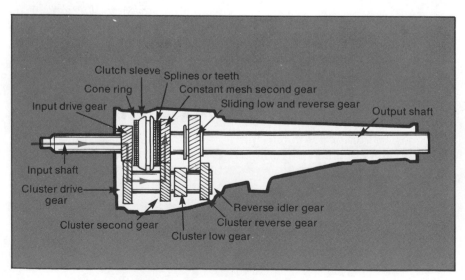

In neutral, the input drive gear, which is in constant mesh with the cluster drive gear, turns at the same speed as the engine. The cluster drive gear turns at a slower speed than the input drive gear because the cluster drive gear is larger. The constant mesh second gear, which is in mesh with the cluster second gear, rotates freely on the transmission output shaft. This prevents the delivery of power to the output shaft, hence, "neutral."

In first gear, the sliding low and reverse gear meshes with the cluster low gear. This provides high torque and less speed to the transmission output shaft. The gear ratio in "low" is approximately 2.8:1. This means that the engine makes 2.8 turns for each turn of the transmission output shaft.

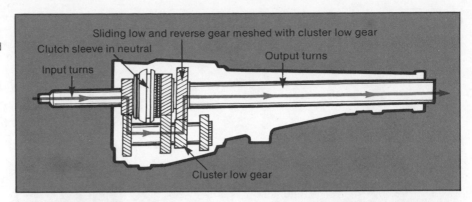

In second gear, the clutch sleeve, which is splined to the transmission output shaft, locks with the constant mesh second gear. Since this gear and the cluster second gear are always in mesh, power is now delivered to the transmission output shaft. The ratio in "second" is approximately 1.7:1.

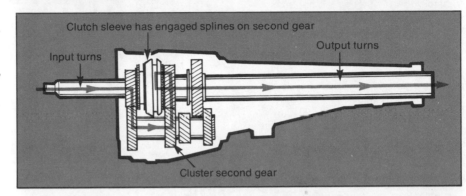

In third or high gear, the clutch sleeve connects the input shaft of the transmission to the output shaft of the transmission, producing a 1:1 direct drive ratio. One turn of the engine delivers one turn of the transmission output shaft. The operation of a four-speed transmission is basically the same, except that there is less difference in ratios from one gear to the next.

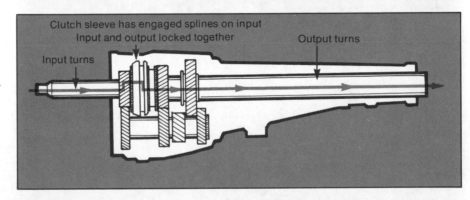

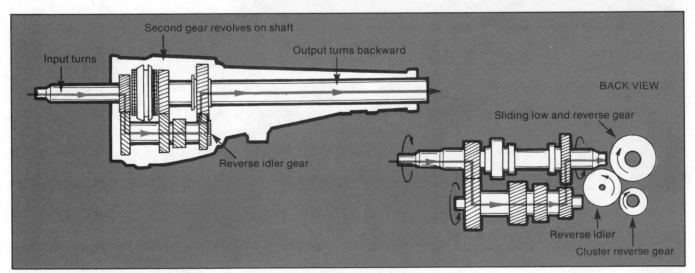

In reverse, the sliding low and reverse gear meshes with the reverse idler gear, which is in constant mesh with the cluster reverse gear. In "third" or "high," three gears are used in order to reverse the direction of the transmission output shaft. The gear ratio in reverse is approximately 3.8:1, the highest of all the gears.

Operation of automatic transmissions

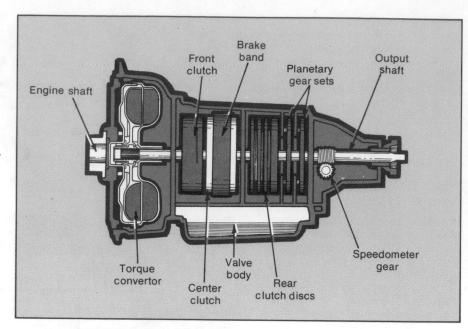

Front clutch

Brake band

Planetary gear sets

Output shaft

Engine shaft

Torque convertor

Valve body

Center clutch

Rear clutch discs

Speedometer gear

Like the standard transmission, the automatic transmission shifts into its various speeds to provide a smooth transmission of torque and speed from the engine to the drive shaft. The automatic transmission is a box which contains clutches, bands, planetary gearsets, valve body, and a torque convertor.

The clutch assembly ensures a smooth engagement and disengagement of the planetary gear carrier and the output shaft of the transmission. In addition, it creates a neutral gear.

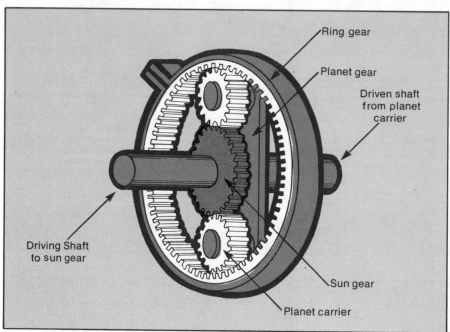

Ring gear

Planet gear

Driven shaft from planet carrier

Driving Shaft to sun gear

Sun gear

Planet carrier

The planetary gearset is so called because of its similarity to the solar system. The sun gear is the center of the planetary gearset and the planetary gears revolve around it. Just as our solar system has a gravitational field which keeps the planets in their orbits, the gearset has a ring gear surrounding the planetary gears keeping them in mesh. Indeed, the components of the planetary gearset are in constant mesh. They never shift in or out. The sun gear is attached to the input shaft of the transmission and is driven by the torque convertor. The

planetary gears rotate on pins, which are attached to the carrier. The carrier, in turn, is connected to the output shaft by a clutch assembly. The ring gear provides direct drive between input and output by allowing the entire system to rotate as one unit. It provides for gear reduction (more torque, less speed), by means of a brake band which holds the ring gear in place, forcing the planetary gears to travel around inside the ring. Reverse gear in the automatic transmission requires a second planetary gearset.

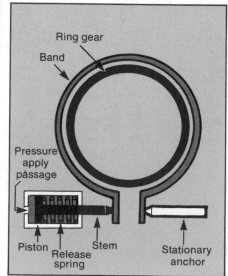

Ring gear

Band

Pressure apply passage

Piston

Release spring

Stem

Stationary anchor

The brake band surrounding the ring gear is operated by a hydraulic servo which applies the band for gear reduction.

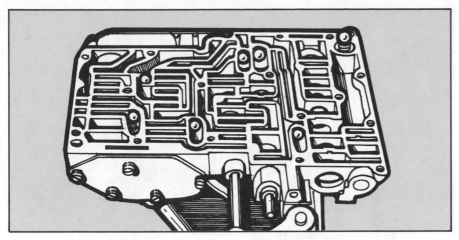

The valve body directs the flow of oil, under pressure, to various parts of the transmission.

At low speed, it directs oil to the servo applying the band around the ring gear. To shift into a higher gear, oil is directed through the valve body to the clutch assembly, locking the carrier and the output shaft, and simultaneously releasing the band.

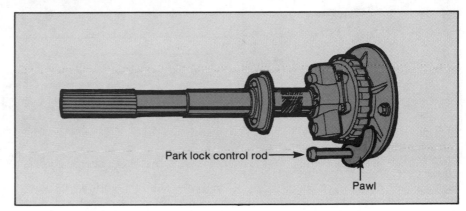

Park lock control rod

Pawl

In "park," the transmission mechanically locks the output shaft, preventing it from turning. This is done by means of a pawl engaging a gear attached to the output shaft.

The drive shaft assembly

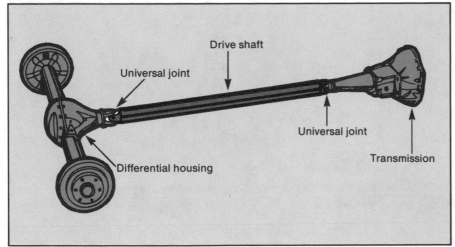

Drive shaft

Universal joint

Universal joint

Transmission

Differential housing

The drive shaft assembly transmits power from the transmission to the differential. The shaft itself is a length of tubular steel. Because of the up-and-down movement of the differential, and the fixed position of the transmission, a drive shaft with flexible joints (universal joints) must be used.

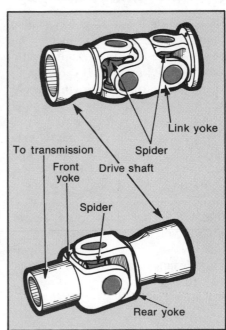

Link yoke

To transmission

Spider

Front yoke

Drive shaft

Spider

Rear yoke

The universal joint assembly enables the drive shaft to transmit the power evenly to the differential. A universal joint consists of two yokes, a cross member, and four bearings.

The constant velocity universal joint, generally used on heavier cars, provides a smoother power transfer with less vibration than the conventional universal joint. It typically consists of a slip yoke, a centering ball stud yoke, a link yoke, a ball stud support yoke, a ball stud assembly, two cross members, and eight bearings.

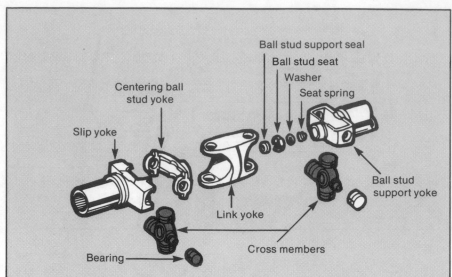

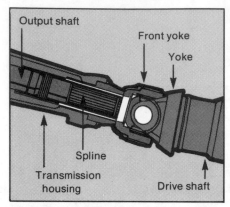

The drive line changes length. The distance between the transmission and the differential changes as the rear end moves up and down. To compensate, the front yoke is splined to the output shaft of the transmission, allowing the yoke to slide in and out on the output shaft.

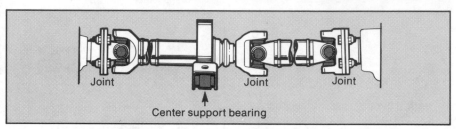

The center support bearing. The number of universal joints used on a drive shaft varies from model to model. Some use two, one at the front and one at the rear. Others use a third universal joint in the center of the drive shaft which requires the use of a center support bearing.

The differential assembly

The differential assembly, also called the rear end, transfers the power from the drive shaft to the two rear driving axles. It is designed to allow the outside driving wheel to turn faster than the inside wheel when the car is making a turn. Without this device, the rear wheels would skid or slide around turns causing tire damage. This action is similar to a line of skaters making a turn. The inner skater moves very little while the last or outer skater must travel fast to stay in line.

There are various differential gear ratio designs and these will affect such things as economy and pulling power.

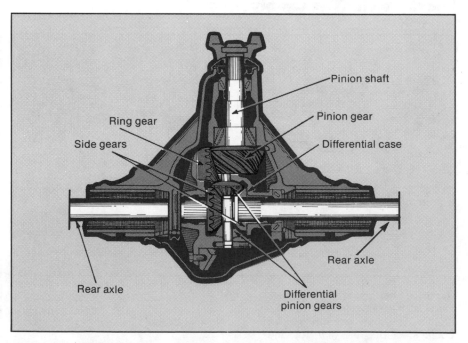

The differential assembly consists of a pinion shaft, attached to the drive shaft; a pinion gear, attached to the pinion shaft; a ring gear, geared to the pinion gear; a differential case, to which the ring gear is bolted; two differential pinion gears, pinned to the case; and two side gears, into which two rear axles are splined.

How the differential operates.

When the car is moving straight ahead, the power from the engine is transmitted through the drive shaft to the pinion shaft, which, with its pinion gear, turns the ring gear and differential case. The side gears, which are mounted in the case, turn the two rear axles. At this point, both rear wheels will be turning at the same speed.

When a car turns a corner, both wheels are turning, but one is going faster than the other. The inside wheel—and thus the differential gear on its axle shaft—is revolving more slowly than the differential case. The differential gear is turning more slowly than the pinion is being carried around, so the pinion must turn on its own shaft. It will turn more slowly than when the car was going straight ahead, and in a direction which adds to the speed of the opposite differential gear. It adds to it exactly the amount taken away from the slower gear and wheel. For example, suppose the differential case is being driven at 500 revolutions per minute. Then if the inside wheel is turning 400 revolutions per minute (RPM), the outer one must be turning 600 RPM. If one is turning 490 RPM, the other is at 510 RPM. That is the way a differential must work—what is subtracted from one side must be added to the other. The ring gear speed always splits the difference between the two.

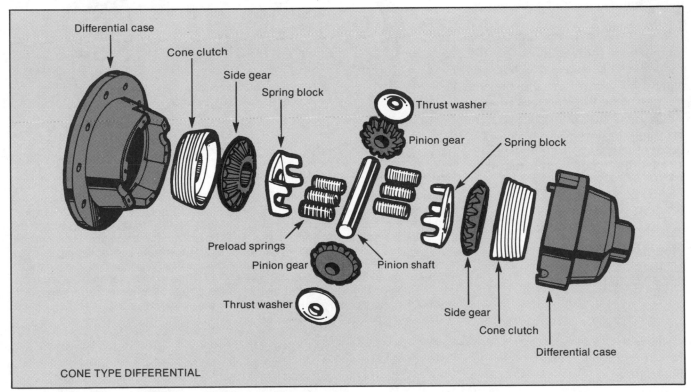

CONE TYPE DIFFERENTIAL

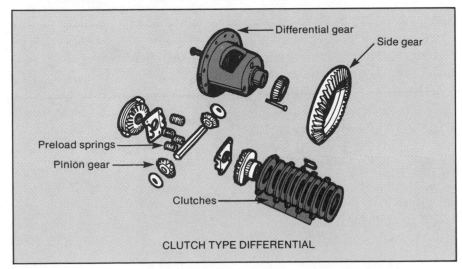

CLUTCH TYPE DIFFERENTIAL

The non-slip differential assembly.
Manufacturers use various trade names for this type of differential, but the basic operating principles are very similar. The construction of the ordinary differential is such that one rear wheel spins freely on ice, snow or mud, while the other rear wheel remains stationary, so that the car can't move. This means that the wheel meeting the least resistance will turn. To help overcome this problem, the non-slip differential assembly was designed. While the operation of this assembly is basically the same as the conventional differential, in the non-slip system, when one rear wheel begins to spin freely, a series of clutches or cones built within the differential case locks both axles to the case allowing both rear axles to turn equally.

The Brakes

The modern car is equipped with a four-wheel hydraulic braking system which exerts pressure on all four wheels, enabling the car to stop in a straight line.

In the past, the four-wheel drum brake shoe system was adequate, but it has one major drawback. Because of excessive heat build-up, the brakes fade or lose their power to stop the car. To overcome this problem, disc brakes were introduced. The disc brake is superior because it deals with heat more effectively.

When you step on the brakes, momentum throws most of the car's weight forward. Approximately 60 percent of the braking force is exerted by the front wheels. Since for balanced braking, it is necessary to have more braking capacity there, the front brakes are ideally disc-type, with drum-type brakes in the rear.

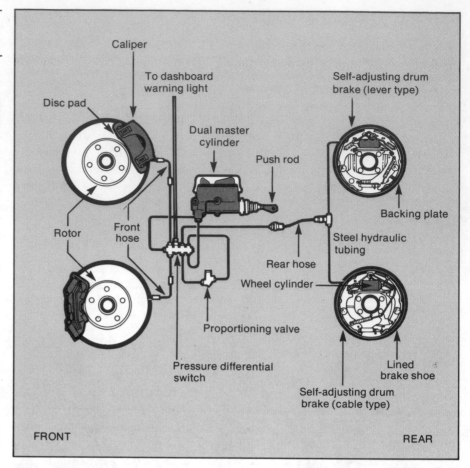

FRONT

REAR

How brakes work. As the driver applies pressure to the brake pedal, which is attached to the push rod, the master cylinder piston moves the brake fluid through the steel lines and brake hoses to each of the wheel cylinders or calipers. At this point, the calipers or wheel cylinder pistons push the disc pads or brake shoes against the rotors or brake drums. The friction developed by the pads against the rotors or the brake shoes against the brake drums stops the wheel from turning. A flexible brake hose is connected to each front wheel to allow for up-and-down movement and for turning. A third flexible hose is connected to a junction "T" fitting mounted on the rear axle housing to allow for up-and-down movement in the rear.

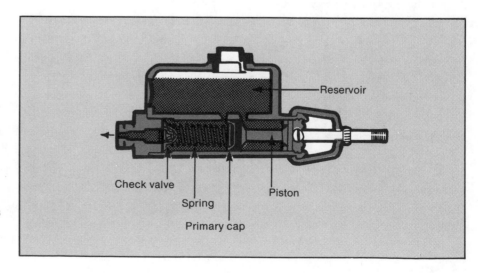

The single piston master cylinder was used until the late 60's. If a leak occurred anywhere in the hydraulic system, the entire braking system failed.

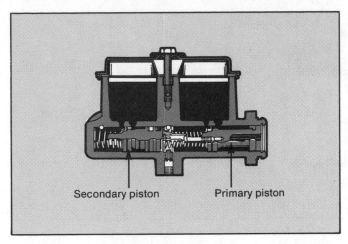

Secondary piston   Primary piston

The double piston, dual master cylinder was designed to prevent complete brake-system failure. The dual master cylinder moves fluid, under pressure, separately but simultaneously to the front wheels and the rear wheels, so that if a leak occurs in one section of the system, the other section continues to operate.

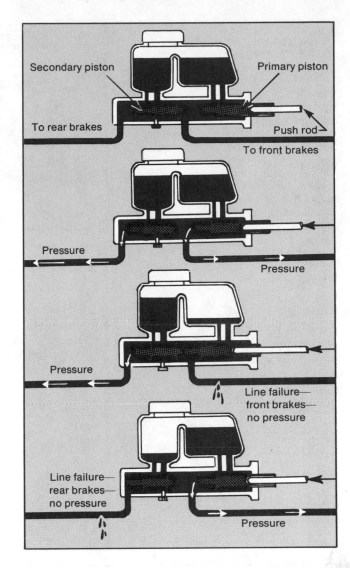

Secondary piston   Primary piston

To rear brakes

Push rod

To front brakes

Pressure

Pressure

Pressure

Line failure—front brakes—no pressure

Line failure—rear brakes—no pressure

Pressure

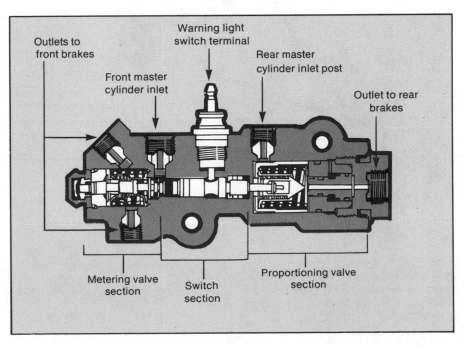

Outlets to front brakes

Warning light switch terminal

Front master cylinder inlet

Rear master cylinder inlet post

Outlet to rear brakes

Metering valve section

Switch section

Proportioning valve section

The three-way valve is used on cars equipped with disc brakes in front and drum brakes in the rear. The metering section delays the application of the front discs so both front and rear brakes come on at the same time. Delaying the front disc application gives the rear shoes time to expand and take up the clearance between the shoe and the drum. The proportioning section limits the hydraulic pressure to the rear wheels so they won't lock up during hard braking. The warning light switch turns on the light if there is a loss of pressure in either system.

The power booster unit increases the pressure on the master cylinder push rod when the brake pedal is depressed. The booster unit is attached to the master cylinder and consists of two separate chambers divided by a diaphragm or piston which is connected to the master cylinder's push rod. One chamber contains a valve which can be opened to the atmosphere, and the second chamber is connected to the engine's vacuum. When the brake pedal is depressed, the valve in the atmosphere chamber opens allowing atmosphere pressure to move the dividing diaphragm toward the vacuum chamber, applying additional pressure on the master cylinder push rod. A spring returns the diaphragm to its original position when the brake pedal is released.

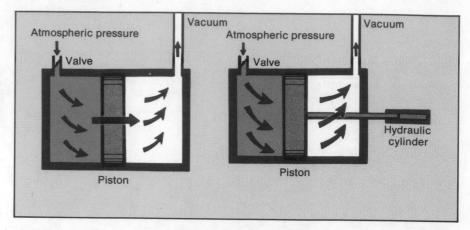

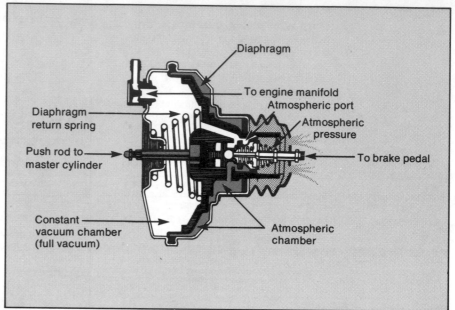

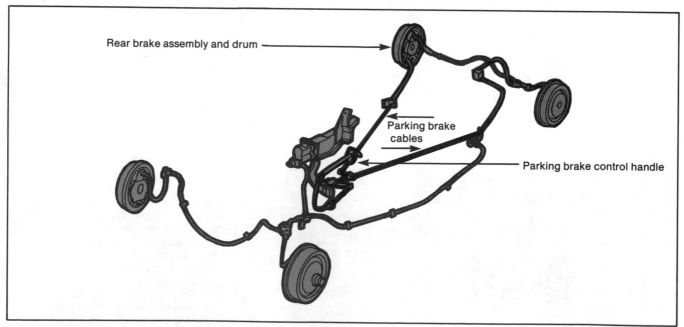

The parking brake is a mechanically-operated system designed to prevent the car from rolling when parked. In case the hydraulic system completely fails, the parking brake system may be used to slow down the auto. When the foot lever or hand lever is applied, a cable mechanically expands the brake shoes against the brake drums.

The Suspension System

The suspension system is designed to permit the front and rear wheels to move up and down independently so that your car remains level and steady. The suspension system gives the car roadability.

The front suspension consists of the upper and lower control arms, the upper and lower ball joints, the coil springs or torsion bars, the shock absorbers, and a stabilizer bar assembly.

The upper and lower control arms are attached to the frame and are designed to move up or down without changing the vertical position of the front wheels. In some cases the coil springs are supported between the upper control arms and the frame as shown.

The upper and lower ball joints, attached to the outer ends of the control arms, permit the control arms to move up or down, and the front wheels to turn right or left.

The stabilizer bar, or sway bar assembly, is attached to the frame and to the lower control arm. It dampens road shock, smooths out a rough ride, and minimizes sway in turns.

Front suspension

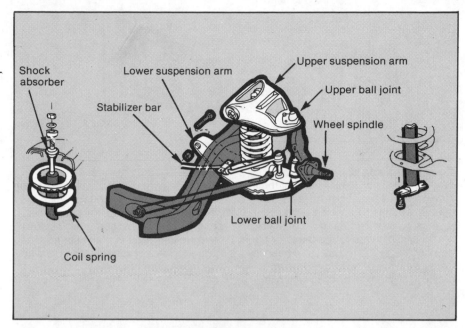

Shock absorber · Lower suspension arm · Upper suspension arm · Upper ball joint · Stabilizer bar · Wheel spindle · Lower ball joint · Coil spring

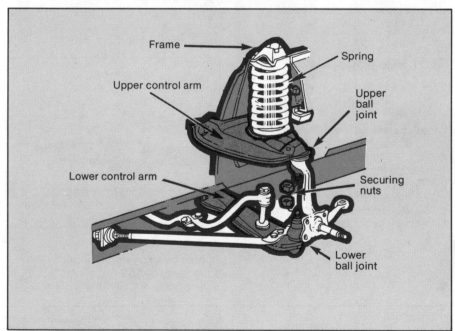

Frame · Spring · Upper control arm · Upper ball joint · Lower control arm · Securing nuts · Lower ball joint

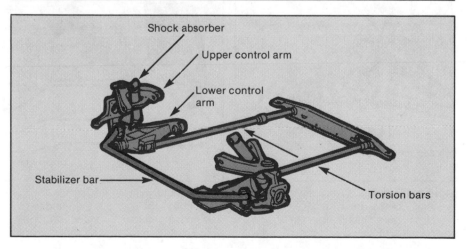

Shock absorber · Upper control arm · Lower control arm · Stabilizer bar · Torsion bars

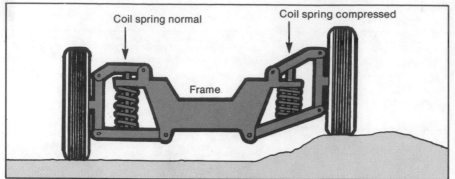

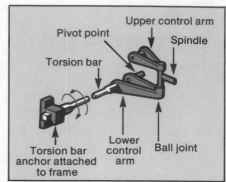

Coil springs and shock absorbers.
The frame supports the weight of the engine, transmission, body, and passengers. It is in turn supported by the springs, which keep the front of the car level if a front wheel hits a bump or pothole. As the bump forces the wheel upward, the coil spring begins to compress. The shock absorber, which is mounted between the frame and the lower control arm, slows down the compressing action of the spring. When the wheel clears the bump, the spring expands. The shock absorber slows down the expanding action of the spring. The spring action is reversed when the wheel rolls into a pot-hole.

Torsion bars. Some manufacturers prefer to use a torsion bar in place of a front coil spring. Although the purpose of the torsion bar is the same as that of the coil spring, the action is different. The torsion bar is attached between the frame and the lower control arm. As the wheel moves up or down, the arm pivots and twists the torsion bar. This twisting action serves the same purpose as the coil springs. An advantage of torsion bars is that the riding height of the front of the car is adjustable.

Rear suspension

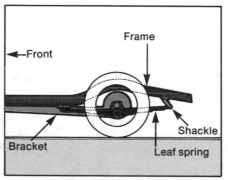

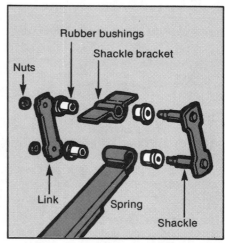

The rear springs. The center of the leaf spring is mounted to the rear axle housing. The front eye of the spring is mounted to the frame with a supporting bracket and bolt. The rear eye of the spring is attached to the frame with a spring shackle that permits the spring to flex as the wheels move up and down.

Rubber bushings are installed in the spring eyes and the frame brackets to reduce noise and vibration.

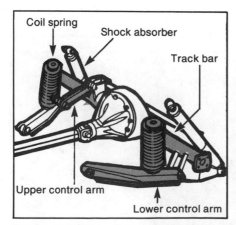

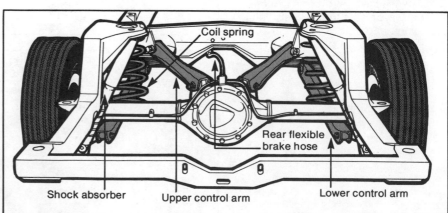

Rear coil springs. On cars with rear coil springs, control arms, stabilizer arms, and track bars must be used to let the rear wheels move up and down, and to keep them in line with the frame. The lower coil of the spring is mounted to the axle housing or lower control arm. The upper part fits into a spring seat built into the frame. The control arms and/or track bar are attached to the frame and to the rear axle housing to minimize side-to-side movement of the housing.

Steering, Front Wheel Alignment, and Tires

Whether your car has manual or power steering, the function of the system is the same: to allow you to turn your car easily and safely. The steering and alignment systems minimize road shock, the tendency of the front wheels to shimmy when going over bumps. In addition, if they are operating properly, wear on your front tires is reduced.

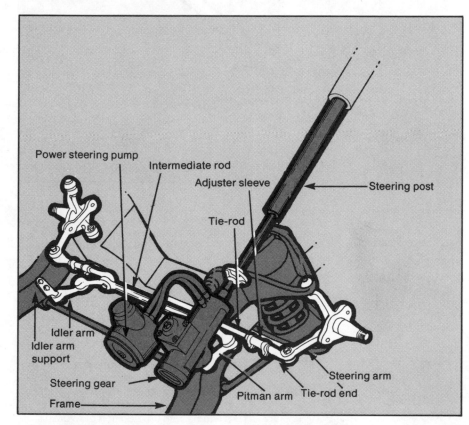

Power steering pump
Intermediate rod
Adjuster sleeve
Tie-rod
Steering post
Idler arm
Idler arm support
Steering gear
Frame
Pitman arm
Tie-rod end
Steering arm

Steering system components. The typical steering system is composed of the steering wheel, the steering post, a manual or power steering gear, the power steering pump, the power cylinder assembly, and the steering linkage, which connects the steering system to the front wheels. The linkage consists of the Pitman arm, the intermediate rod, the idler arm, tie-rods, and the steering arms or knuckles.

Manual steering systems

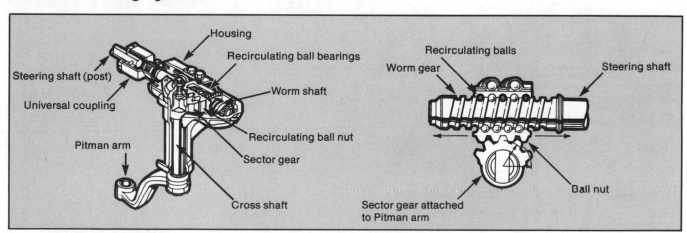

Housing
Recirculating ball bearings
Steering shaft (post)
Universal coupling
Worm shaft
Pitman arm
Recirculating ball nut
Sector gear
Cross shaft

Recirculating balls
Worm gear
Steering shaft
Ball nut
Sector gear attached to Pitman arm

The recirculating ball system. As the steering wheel is turned, the worm gear on the end of the steering shaft rotates, causing the recirculating balls to move the ball nut up or down along the worm. The movement of the ball nut is transferred to the sector gear, which is geared to its side, permitting the Pitman arm shaft to pivot. This turning action of the shaft moves the steering linkage.

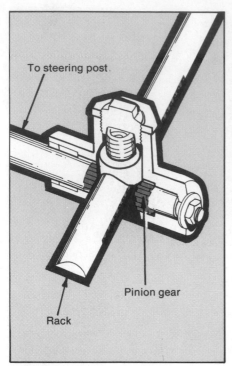

To steering post.

Pinion gear

Rack

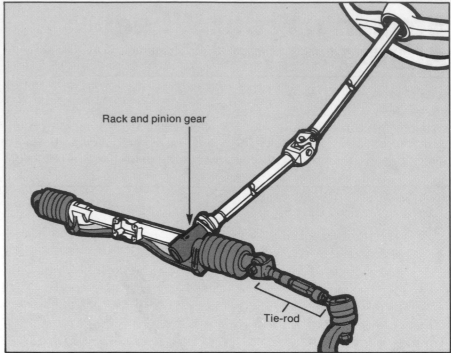

Rack and pinion gear

Tie-rod

The rack and pinion steering gear system. As the steering wheel is turned, the pinion gear, which is connected to the steering post, rotates, causing the rack, which is geared to it, to move laterally, pushing or pulling the front wheels simultaneously.

Power steering

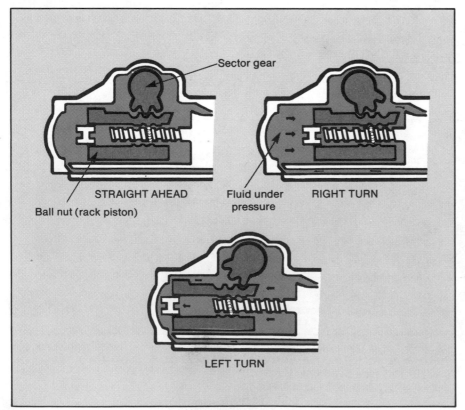

Sector gear

STRAIGHT AHEAD

Ball nut (rack piston)

Fluid under pressure

RIGHT TURN

LEFT TURN

Power steering-integral type. The two types of power steering systems—integral and linkage or booster—operate under the same principles as manual systems with the addition of hydraulic assistance. The power steering system incorporates a pump which is belt-driven by the engine. The pump builds pressure when the engine is operated. The fluid, under pressure, is delivered to the control valve. As the driver turns the steering wheel, hydraulic fluid, under pressure, is directed to the front or rear of the ball nut, now enclosed in a moveable piston called a "rack piston," causing the ball nut to turn the sector gear. As a result the driver is relieved of most of the steering effort.

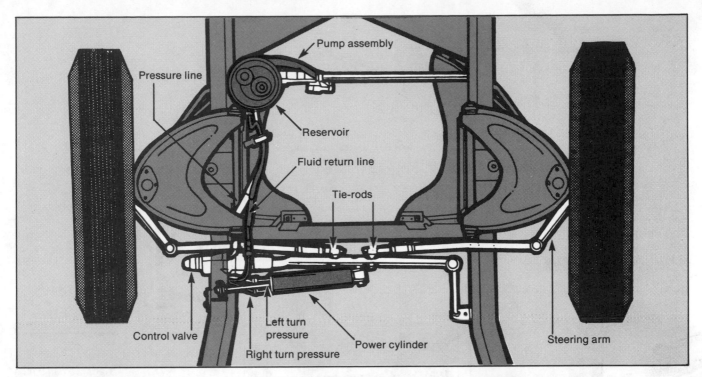

Pump assembly

Pressure line

Reservoir

Fluid return line

Tie-rods

Control valve

Left turn pressure

Right turn pressure

Power cylinder

Steering arm

Linkage-booster type. Once again, as the driver turns the steering wheel, fluid under pressure is directed by the control valve to one or the other side of the power cylinder assembly, which sits between the frame and the intermediate arm. As pressure is exerted against the piston in the cylinder assembly, it pushes or pulls the arm. This "push-pull" action turns the front wheels to the right or left. Once again, hydraulic pressure takes care of most of the steering effort.

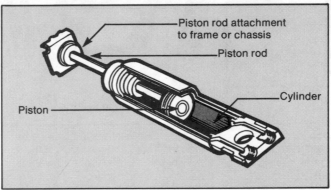

Piston rod attachment to frame or chassis

Piston rod

Cylinder

Piston

Front wheel alignment

Front wheel alignment is so highly sophisticated that adjustments should be made only by a fully qualified wheel alignment mechanic. Incorrect adjustment will cause steering difficulties and excessive tire wear. In the chapter, "Front End and Steering," steering difficulties will be discussed. Below are some definitions that will help you discuss front wheel alignment with your mechanic.

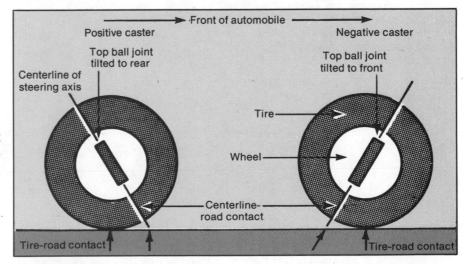

Front of automobile

Positive caster

Negative caster

Top ball joint tilted to rear

Top ball joint tilted to front

Centerline of steering axis

Tire

Wheel

Centerline road contact

Tire-road contact

Tire-road contact

Caster is the backward or forward tilt of the upper ball joint, which permits the car to lead the front wheels in a straight path. Caster is adjusted either positive or negative. Positive, the backward tilt of the upper ball joint (top of wheel), tends to force the front wheel to travel straight ahead. Negative caster, the reverse of positive caster, is used to ease the turning of the front wheels and to reduce road shock.

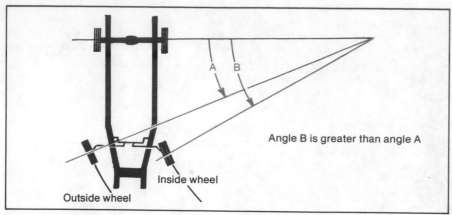

Angle B is greater than angle A

Inside wheel

Outside wheel

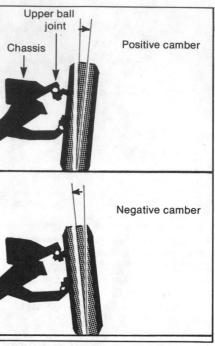

Upper ball joint

Chassis

Positive camber

Negative camber

Toe-out on turns is not adjustable. Built into the steering arms, it allows the inside front wheel to turn at a greater radius than the outside front wheel when making a turn. This prevents front tire scuffing.

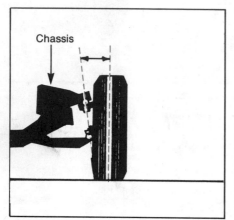

Chassis

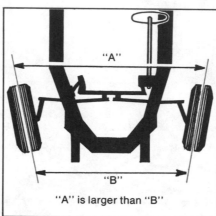

"A"

"B"

"A" is larger than "B"

Steering axis inclination is a non-adjustable setting, built into the knuckle support or spindle arm, which assists in returning the front wheels to a straight ahead position after completing a turn. You might compare it to a swinging garden gate. The top of the post is tilted toward the gate so that the weight of the gate tends to return it to the closed position. The weight of the front end of the car helps return the wheels to a straight ahead position.

Toe-in is the difference in distance between the fronts and the rears of the front wheels. It keeps the front wheels parallel when the car is going forward. In addition, toe-in helps prevent front tire wear.

Camber is the inward (toward the chassis) or outward (away from the chassis) tilt of the upper ball joint. Like caster, camber can be adjusted either positive or negative. Positive is the tilt of the upper ball joint outward, negative is the inward tilt. Camber assists in keeping the front wheels in a straight ahead path, helps reduce tire wear, and combined with steering axis inclination, eases steering.

Tires

A few years ago, about all you needed to know when buying tires was the right size. Today, tire construction, body cord materials, belt materials, tread design, and performance characteristics, must be considered before you buy.

In the last few years, new concepts in design, new cord materials—polyester, fiberglass, and steel —and a whole new vocabulary—78 series, 70 series, bias-belted—have introduced complications into the process of choosing the right tire. However, these new designs and materials give you the wider choice necessary for getting the best tire for your car in today's sophisticated automotive market.

For a fuller discussion of tires— construction fundamentals, size designations, and materials used— see Chapter 18.

Air Conditioning and Heating Systems

The car's air conditioning and heating systems work to keep the temperature in the passenger compartment comfortable. The air conditioner transfers heat from the passenger compartment to the atmosphere and removes humidity. The heating system transfers heat from the engine into the passenger compartment. Both systems use the same blower motor.

Functions of the air conditioner's parts

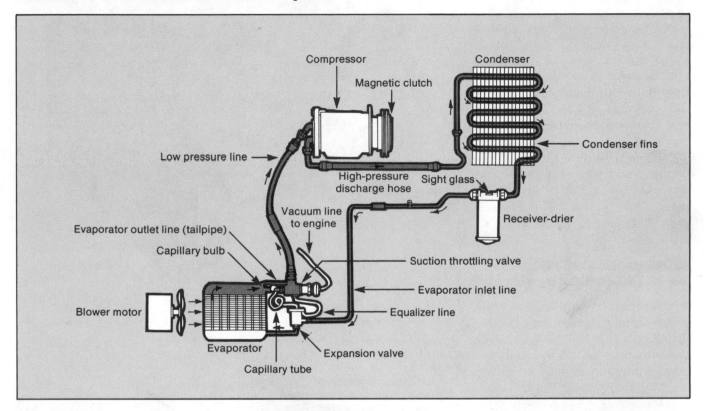

The compressor, a pump driven by a belt or belts from the engine, draws the low pressure gas from the evaporator and compresses it into a high-pressure, high-temperature gas. The compressor then delivers this high-pressure gas to the condenser.

The expansion valve limits the high pressure liquid coming from the receiver-drier into the evaporator core, causing the high pressure liquid to change into a low-pressure, low-temperature gas. The valve is connected in the inlet tubing of the evaporator, and is controlled by a capillary tube or bulb that senses the temperature of the evaporator core outlet (tailpipe), and an equalizer line connected to the suction throttling valve.

The evaporator core is a radiator-like container connected between the expansion valve and the suction throttling valve. The evaporator core carries the low-pressure gas from the expansion valve, absorbing the heat from the passenger compartment.

The receiver-drier is designed to store refrigerant, keep it clean, and remove moisture. It is located between the condenser and the expansion valve of the system and is usually mounted on the radiator support for cooling purposes.

The suction throttling valve is designed to maintain a pressure of from 28 to 29 psi (pounds per square inch) in the evaporator core. There is a direct ratio between the pressure and the temperature of the refrigerant, R-12. That is, if the pressure of the R-12 is 29 psi, then the temperature of the refrigerant will be approximately 29 degrees. The evaporator core will be 29 degrees, but the evaporator core fins will be about five degrees higher, or 34 degrees. This prevents freezing of the evaporator core. If the pressure of the refrigerant drops below 29 psi, the suction throttling valve uses engine vacuum to activate the expansion valve, thereby flooding the evaporator core with refrigerant, raising the pressure and the temperature.

The magnetic clutch, which is attached to the belt end of the compressor, engages or disengages the compressor in order to control the circulation of the refrigerant through the system. The magnetic clutch is controlled manually, by a switch on the dashboard, or by a temperature-sensing device attached to the evaporator core.

The condenser dissipates the heat picked up by the refrigerant from the evaporator core located in the passenger compartment. In addition, the condenser allows the compressed high-pressure, high-temperature gas to cool, changing the gas into a high-pressure, high-temperature liquid before the refrigerant enters the receiver-drier. The condenser is mounted in front of the car's radiator or in a location that will expose the condenser to the outside air for maximum heat dissipation.

A sight glass is sometimes mounted on the outlet port of the receiver-drier to indicate whether or not the system is fully charged with refrigerant.

Air conditioning

The air conditioner works on the thermodynamic principle that heat will travel from a hotter to a colder body. A hot-liquid refrigerant, R-12, is slowly released from pressure, changing it to a gas and lowering its temperature. This low-pressure, low-temperature gas travels through a series of coils, drastically cooling them. A fan then circulates the air to be cooled over the coils. The coils are the cooler body, and so they draw the heat, and moisture, out of the air. This cooled air now circulates in the passenger compartment.

Because your car is built primarily of metal and glass, a high-capacity air conditioning unit, rated at 36,000 Btu's (British thermal units), or more, is needed to heat and cool it.

What makes up the air conditioning system?

Different manufacturers use a variety of controls, valves, and devices for their models. There are basic components, however, that are common to all car air conditioning systems: the receiver drier; the expansion valve; the evaporator core; the suction throttling valve; the compressor and magnetic clutch; the condenser; the hoses and tubing; the blower motor, or fan; and the refrigerant (R-12).

The heating system

The basic heating system consists of heater hoses, a heater core, a blower motor, an air- or coolant-flow control device, and duct work.

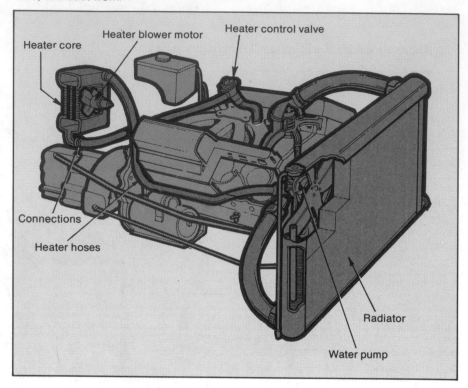

How the heater works. The engine's coolant is directed through hoses to a heater core, a small radiator located in the passenger compartment. Outside air is directed through openings provided in the engine cowling. This air passes through ducts leading to the heater core. A blower fan draws this air across the heater core. The air is then heated and directed to the passenger compartment or windshield defroster ducts. Dashboard controls, including the blower motor switch, duct direction doors, and a control lever, are driver-operated.

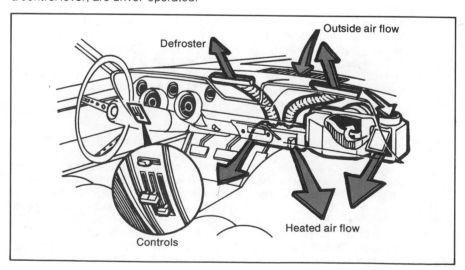

JACKING AND SUPPORTING

In this chapter you will learn the various methods of raising and supporting your car safely so that you can get under it to perform many of the jobs described in this book.

Unless you have access to a hydraulic floor jack like the ones used in service stations and repair shops, you should not attempt to raise both front and rear wheels off the ground simultaneously.

You can safely use a heavy duty scissor jack to raise one corner of the car at a time. This type will raise it high enough to place a metal jack stand under the car's frame or chassis to support it while you are working under it.

The bumper jack that comes with the car is designed only to lift one corner of the car high enough to service one wheel. It should be used only to change tires. It is not strong enough or stable enough to raise an automobile safely if you are going to get underneath it.

The safest and most convenient device for raising your car so that you can work underneath it is the kind of lift used in service stations and repair shops. There are four basic types of these lifts: drive-on, frame contact, double post, and single post rail. Establishments in some areas rent space, including the lift, where you may work on your own car. Full instructions for the safe operation of these lifts should be posted in the lift area.

Here are some of the most useful items you should have on hand (in addition to tools and the necessary parts) before getting under the car to work on it.

- **A creeper.** You may have seen one in action at your local service station or repair shop. It's a small-wheeled board that the mechanic lies down on, on his back, and uses to roll himself under the car. If you can't rent one, a creeper can be purchased for a reasonable price at an auto parts supply store.
- **Good lighting.** Since you will almost certainly want to have both hands free, an ordinary cylindrical flashlight is likely to be more frustrating than useful. A battery pac-type lamp with a head that tips up and down points the light where you need it, and stays put. It is also a handy item to carry in the trunk of your car in case of emergency breakdowns at night. Better still, get a droplight with a long extension cord and a wire cage covering the bulb to protect it and prevent you from burning yourself on the hot bulb.
- **Hand cloths. Collect a supply of rags for wiping dirt off the parts you are working on and for clean-up after the job is done.**
- *Caution: Never leave any cloths soaked with grease, oil, or gas lying around. They can catch fire spontaneously, especially in sunlight through a window. Dispose of soiled cloths in a closed metal can.*
- **Eye protection.** Wear safety eyeglasses or goggles and a cap while working under your car to protect your eyes and hair from loose bits of greasy dirt, drops of oil or gas, and falling parts or tools.
- *Caution: Always park on level ground.*

CONTENTS

The great and the small

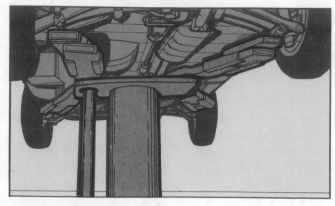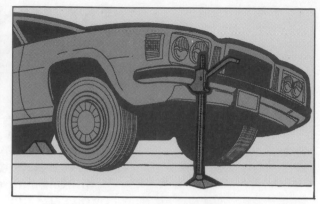

The hydraulic lift, found in professional garages, is the ideal way to raise your car safely and fast. There may be a garage near you where such lifts are available when you rent their space and facilities to work on your car. However, if you cannot avail yourself of this luxury, you can still get your car off the ground fairly easily by using the jacks and stands described in this chapter. Be sure to heed the safety tips for each type; they may save you from the awkward experience of having your car roll over you.

Use the bumper jack supplied with your car to raise only one wheel just long enough to change a tire. You will find instructions on a decal attached to the inside of the trunk lid. At no time should the bumper jack be used to raise both front or both rear wheels. Above all, never get under a car which is supported only by a bumper jack.

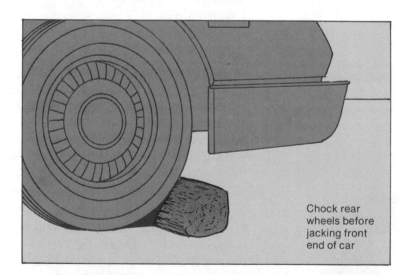

Chock rear wheels before jacking front end of car

How to chock the wheels. Even if you have set the parking brake before you start jacking up the car, you must also place chocks against the tires at the other end of the car. The parking brake may not hold when one end is raised. If the car rolls off the jack, you or the car or both can be seriously harmed. A car can roll off metal support jack stands even if only one end is raised, especially if the auto is not on level ground. When jacking the rear wheels, place chocks in front of the front wheels. When jacking up the front wheels, chock the back of the rear wheels. Use anything handy for a chock: a block of wood, a brick, a large stone, or even your spare tire.

Chock front wheels before jacking up rear end of car

Hydraulic Floor Jacks

A hydraulic jack, with at least 1½ ton capacity, is the safest and easiest to use for raising the entire front or rear of a passenger car. Under no circumstances should you try to work under a car which is supported only by the jack. The car could roll, the hydraulic cylinder in the jack could leak, or someone could accidentally lower it while you are still working underneath.

Jacking up the rear

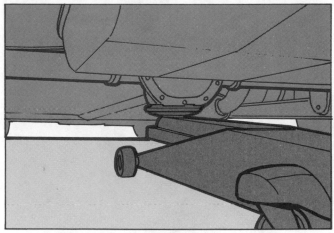

1 **Position the jack** under the rear of the car until the saddle is directly below the rear end housing.

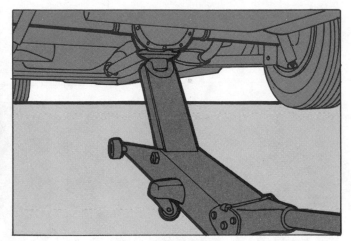

2 **Raise the car** high enough to slide jack stands under the rear axle housing or chassis. If your car has front wheel drive and hence no axle, you will have to put the stands under the chassis.

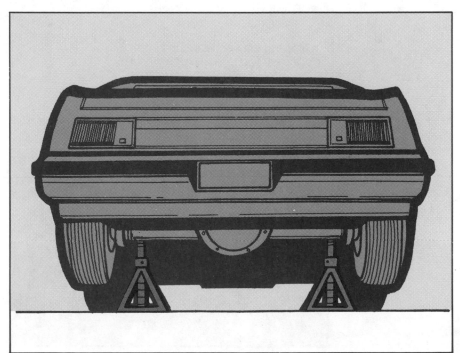

3 **Positioning the stands.** Place one jack stand on each side. If you support the car by the rear axle housing, slide each stand as close as possible to the inside of each rear wheel. You can also safely support the car by placing one stand on each side under the frame. The frame is the heavy square-shaped steel beams that run along the bottom of the car inside the wheels.

4 **Removing the jack.** Slowly lower the car onto the jack stands and remove the jack. Before you get under it, rock the car gently from side to side to make sure that it cannot be knocked off the stands if someone leans against the car or climbs into it.

Jacking up the front

1 **The safest jacking point.** Before attempting to raise the front of the car, locate the front suspension cross member of the frame. This is the best jacking point. Be sure the saddle of the jack will not make contact with the oil pan, radiator, or steering linkage.

If your car has no front suspension crossmember, look for a lift pad. Some cars have unibody construction instead of exposed frames, and they have lift pads—flat pieces of metal welded under the car—which are the proper lifting points.

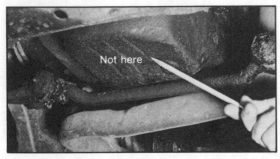

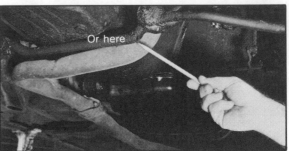

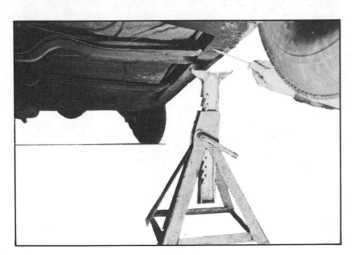

2 **The supporting points.** Locate the supporting points for jack stands on each side of the frame. Check to be sure the frame or supporting member is not rusted out. Then place the stands in position. Slowly lower the car onto the stands and remove the jack.

3 **Lowering the car.** Lower the front end of the car first to achieve better stability. Jack the car up off the stands, remove the stands, and lower it slowly to the ground. Lower the rear of the car in the same way.

Rock the car from side to side to be sure it will remain securely on the stands while you are working under it.

Bumper and Single-Piston Jacks

Bumper jacks and the small single-piston hydraulic jack with a 1½-ton lifting capacity are not sturdy enough for any job except changing a tire. These types aren't designed to raise more than one corner of a car just high enough to get the wheel off and the spare back on. Don't expect the bumber jack or single-piston jack to raise even a corner of your car high enough to position a jack stand. And by no means should you mistake one of these lightweights for the floor jack described earlier, which can easily handle one end of a car.

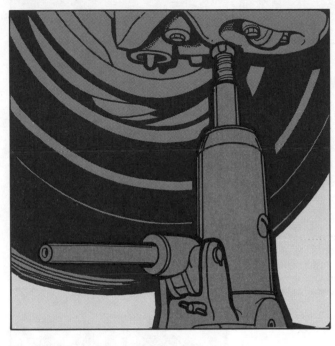

To raise a front wheel using a single-piston jack, place the jack under the lower control arm as close to the ball joint as possible. Raise the wheel high enough to remove it.

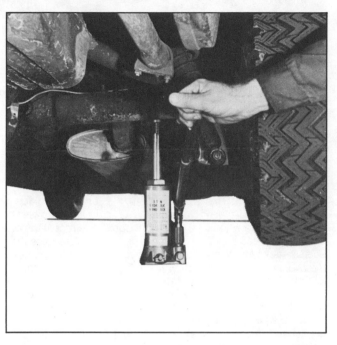

To remove a rear wheel, place the single-piston jack directly under the center of the spring-support pad.

Locating the jack

- Support front-engine, rear-drive cars at the rear axle, the differential housing, the suspension arms, or the front chassis cross-member if your car has one.
- If your car is equipped with a bumper jack, you can also support it at the bumpers or bumper brackets.

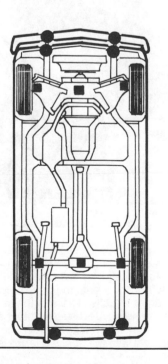

Make your own blocks

A set of wheel blocks will frequently come in handy when you're performing certain maintenance operations. You can make a set easily and inexpensively.

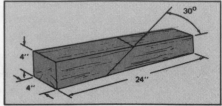

1 **Cut a 2-foot length** of 4 x 4-inch hardwood in half diagonally, at an angle of 30°.

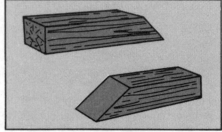

2 **Flip one piece over** and you have two wheel blocks, as shown.

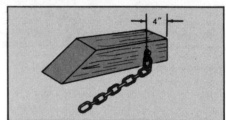

3 **Buy a 26-inch length** of inexpensive sash chain and attach the ends of the chain four inches from the square end of each block with a long roofing nail.

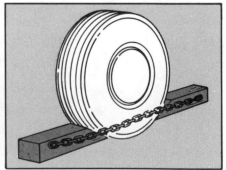

4 **You can now block** the front and rear of a wheel with the one set of blocks. When not using the blocks, you can store them by hanging the chain over a hook in your garage or, preferably, keep them in your luggage compartment in case you must change a tire on the road.

The scissor jack. This is an inexpensive, mechanical-type jack that will safely raise one wheel at a time. The one in this photo has a two-ton capacity. Scissor jacks are not designed to raise the two front or the two rear wheels simultaneously. They are operated by turning a crank handle to raise or collapse the jack's diamond-shaped frame. To raise the front, place the jack under one wheel's lower control arm close to the ball joint. Raise the wheel high enough to place a jack stand under the chassis. Lower the car onto the stand and repeat the operation on the opposite side. To raise the rear, place the jack under the center of the spring-support pad or the rear axle housing on one side. When the car is high enough, position the jack stand under the rear axle housing or frame. Lower the car onto the stand and repeat the operation on the opposite side.

Drive-on ramps

Drive-on ramps should be used with extreme care. If possible, a second person should be stationed in a safe position to guide the driver onto the ramps. Position the ramps directly in front of the front wheels and slowly drive up onto them in first gear. If the ramps are not in perfect alignment with the front wheels, the car can fall off the ramps as you attempt to drive onto them. Secure the car by putting the transmission in "Park," setting the parking brake, and chocking both rear wheels. If the car is equipped with a standard transmission, switch off the ignition and put the transmission in gear.

CONTENTS

PREVENTIVE MAINTENANCE

If you visit your dentist before you get a toothache, you will save yourself a lot of pain, inconvenience, and expense. The same principle applies to your car. Regular inspection and routine maintenance can prevent major—and expensive—repairs. Preventive maintenance means performing certain service jobs on a car on a regularly-scheduled basis, before there is any sign of trouble.

There are several good reasons for preventive maintenance, but the most important is to prevent accidents. According to the Motor and Equipment Manufacturers Association, more than 60 percent of the cars in the country are running inefficiently, and inefficient cars waste time, money, and gas. But more importantly, they are a major cause of highway accidents. More than one out of eight accidents involves a vehicle that is not in proper working order, resulting in over 5,000 deaths and 200,000 serious injuries annually.

There are additional reasons for preventive maintenance. It allows you to uncover and immediately correct mechanical deficiencies while they are still minor; it helps you to prepare your car to meet extreme weather conditions; and it is generally required to keep a car's warranty in effect.

The engineers who designed your car spent many hours in laboratories and on proving grounds to find out how long each part would perform before it needed lubrication, adjustment, or replacement. The service recommendations in your owner's manual and in this chapter are based on those tests.

If most of your driving is local, the engine never really warms up, so condensation and unburned fuel do not get hot enough to boil off and escape through the crankcase ventilation system. Instead, they just dilute the engine oil. That is why car makers recommend that oil should be changed every four to six months when the car is driven less than 1,000 miles per month.

Most joints in the steering and suspension systems are sealed and require lubrication only at infrequent intervals. However, there are exceptions, even in late-model cars. Some parts may need lubrication as often as every 4,000 miles. Check the recommendations in your owner's manual or in this chapter.

Remember that time is just as important as mileage. Some materials, such as rubber, deteriorate from exposure to the elements even when the car is not in use.

How and where you drive also influences service requirements. Most car manufacturers specify more frequent changes of transmission fluid and adjustment of the transmission when the car is used to tow a trailer. And if you drive in dusty territory, the air cleaner should be serviced at shorter intervals than those specified for normal use.

Before the development of lubricants and coolants suitable for year-round use, it was necessary to change to a winter-grade oil and add antifreeze when the weather turned cold. Now, in most sections of the country, you can use a multi-grade oil, such as 10W-30, at all times. The 10W-30 designation means the oil flows as freely at low temperatures as a 10W (winter-grade) oil, and yet holds its body at high temperatures just as well as a 30 (summer-grade) oil. If, however, you encounter extremely high or low temperatures, seasonal changes may still be necessary.

The same coolant should be used throughout the year and changed once a year. Fall is the best time of year to change it to be sure you have maximum protection against freezing. Normally, no seasonal changes of transmission or rear axle lubricants are necessary. However, some manufacturers recommend the use of winter lubricants in manual transmissions for easier shifting in cold weather.

This chapter is organized into two sections. The first is a series of checklists you should use as a guide to the services your car needs daily, weekly, monthly, seasonally, and before a long trip. The second section covers the step-by-step procedures necessary to perform the various preventive maintenance operations. Refer to the Appendix for the manufacturer's recommended maintenance schedules for all four major US automakers. The tables cover all models from 1975 to 1980. Generally, the recommended service schedules must be met or exceeded to keep a car's warranty in effect, so these maintenance schedules are very important if you have a late-model car still under warranty. If your car is no longer under warranty, the manufacturer's recommended service intervals are a useful guide for minimum periodic maintenance on your car. Our own recommendations are somewhat more extensive than those of the manufacturer.

Checklists for Preventive Maintenance

DAILY CHECKS

These basic and simple checks should really be done every day. If, however, you find you must sometimes skip a day, be sure you add this list to the list of weekly checks.

Check:
1. Lights.
2. Horn.
3. Windshield wiper operation.
4. Windshield washer operation.
5. Outside rearview mirror(s).
6. Front windshield cleanliness.
7. Rear windshield cleanliness.
8. Side window cleanliness.
9. Tires (visual check).

WEEKLY CHECKS

With the car stationary and engine cold, Check:
1. Engine oil level.
2. Battery fluid level.
3. Radiator coolant level.
4. Windshield washer reservoir fluid level.
5. Power steering reservoir fluid level.
6. Automatic transmission fluid level.
7. Tire air pressure.
8. Tires for cuts and tire wear patterns.
9. Brake pedal action.
10. Fan belts and cooling system hoses.

With the engine running at operating temperature, Check:
1. Automatic transmission level.
2. Refrigerant charge in air conditioner.
3. Fluid leaks.

On the road, Check:
1. Brake performance and pedal height.
2. Automatic transmission performance.
3. Manual transmission and clutch performance.
4. Steering.
5. Engine performance.
6. Instrument operation.
7. Any unusual rattles or noises.

MONTHLY CHECKS

Brakes, Check:
1. Brake pedal action.
2. Master cylinder fluid level.
3. Parking brake action.

Steering, Check:
1. Steering action.
2. Power steering reservoir fluid level.

Signals, Check:
1. Horn.
2. Turn signal operation.
3. Hazard warning flasher light operation.

Shock absorbers, Check:
1. Shock absorber action.
2. For possible leakage.

Seat belts, Check:
1. Hardware for firm latching.
2. Belts for cuts and wear.

Tires, Check:
1. Inflation.
2. Wear patterns.
3. For possible cuts.

Exhaust system, Check:
1. For possible leaking exhaust system components.
2. For leaks by looking for graying or blackening of joint locations.

Visibility, Check:
1. Glass, for chips and cracks.
2. Window operation.
3. Mirrors, for looseness.
4. Windshield washer fluid level.
5. Windshield wiper blades, for wear.
6. Defroster action.

Door locks and latches, Check:
1. Door lock and latch performance.
2. Hood latch.

Ignition system, Check:
1. Spark plugs.
2. Distributor points.
3. Distributor cap and rotor.
4. Ignition coil and wires.
5. Spark plug wires.
6. Point dwell and ignition timing.

SEASONAL CHECKS

Some services need to be performed only once or twice a year, if you drive under normal conditions and cover about 10,000 to 12,000 miles a year. These are often referred to as seasonal checks, and many of them are necessary because of varying climatic conditions in different parts of the country.

Winterizing

Cooling system

1. Drain and flush system.
2. Inspect hoses and connections.
3. Add fresh coolant.
4. Check strength of coolant to make sure it meets the temperature needs of your area.
5. Test radiator pressure cap.
6. See that drive belts are in good condition and properly adjusted.

Battery
1. Inspect and test battery.
2. Clean cable terminals and battery posts.
3. Make sure cables are in good condition.

Ignition System
1. Remove and inspect spark plugs.
2. Check distributor points.
3. Inspect distributor cap and rotor.
4. Visually check ignition coil and wires.
5. Check spark plug wires.
6. Check point dwell and ignition timing.

Fuel system
1. Check condition of carburetor air cleaner filter element. Replace if dirty.
2. Check automatic choke operation.
3. Add dry gas to fuel tank.

Lubrication
1. Change oil and oil filter.
2. Lubricate chassis.
3. Lubricate body points.

Tires
1. Mount snow tires after inspecting them for adequate tread, general condition, and pressure.
2. Check front tires for tread, general condition, and pressure.
3. If snow tires are unnecessary in your area, rotate your regular tires.

Brakes
1. Check fluid level in master cylinder. Top off, if necessary.
2. Check system for leaks.
3. Inspect linings for excessive wear.
4. Be sure brakes are adequately adjusted.

Suspension and steering
1. Check steering linkage for tightness.
2. Check power steering reservoir fluid level. Top off, if necessary.
3. Check power steering pump drive belt for wear and adjustment.
4. Check shock absorbers for leakage and operation.

Visual equipment
1. Check windshield wiper blades for condition and adjustment.
2. Check windshield wipers for proper operation.
3. Check windshield washer system for proper operation.
4. Check fluid or solvent in windshield reservoir. Top off, if necessary.
5. Check front windshield defroster for proper operation.
6. If your car has a rear windshield defroster, check its operation.

Other important inspections
1. Check exhaust system. No leaks should be detectable and all parts should be firmly suspended by hangers and clamps.
2. Check automatic transmission fluid level.
3. Check heater for proper operation.
4. Lubricate manifold heat control valve.

Summerizing

Cooling system
1. Check system for leaks.
2. Test radiator pressure cap.
3. Check drive belts for wear and proper tension.
4. Check thermostat operation.
5. Check all hoses and clamps for signs of wear, and make sure clamps are tight.
6. Add rust-inhibitor water pump lubricant.

Exhaust system
1. Check muffler and pipes for rusted-through spots.
2. Check clamps for tightness.
3. Lubricate manifold heat control valve.

Brakes
1. Check brake linings for wear.
2. Check fluid level in master cylinder. Replenish, if necessary.
3. Check system for leaks.
4. Check brake adjustment.

Lubrication
1. Change oil and oil filter.
2. Lubricate chassis.
3. Lubricate body points.
4. Check positive crankcase ventilation (PCV) valve.

Battery
1. Inspect and test battery.
2. Clean cable terminals and battery posts.
3. Make sure cables are in good condition.

Ignition system
1. Remove and inspect spark plugs.
2. Check distributor points.
3. Inspect distributor cap and rotor.
4. Visually check ignition coil and wires.
5. Check spark plug wires.
6. Check point dwell and ignition timing.

Tires
1. Remove snow tires.
2. Inspect tires for adequate tread and general condition. Discard questionable tires.
3. Rotate tires and have wheels balanced.
4. Inflate tires to recommended pressure.

Suspension and steering
1. Check steering linkage for looseness.
2. Check power steering fluid level. Top off, if necessary.
3. Check power steering pump drive belt for wear and adjustment.
4. Check shock absorbers for operation and leakage.
5. Have front end alignment checked.

Visual equipment
1. Check windshield wiper blades for condition and proper adjustment.
2. Check windshield wipers for proper operation.
3. Check windshield washer system for proper operation.
4. Check fluid in windshield washer reservoir. Top off, if necessary.
5. Check lights and all warning signals for proper function.

Many motorists use the seasonal changes as a reminder to make other checks. Please remember that these are only guidelines. If, for instance, your car begins to show symptoms of needing a tune-up in the middle of December, you should not wait until spring to have the tune-up done.

TRIP CHECKS

If you follow a regular maintenance schedule, your car should be ready for either short or long hauls at any time. However, for longer trips it is a good idea to make a few special checks.

1. Have wheel alignment and balance checked. Wheels that are out-of-line or unbalanced often go unnoticed when you are just driving around town, but they can cause severe vibration at high speed or create uneven tire wear in just a few hundred miles of turnpike travel.
2. Check oil level. Note condition of oil and change it if it is dirty or if a change is due.
3. Check coolant level in radiator and inspect radiator hoses. Replace hoses if they show any sign of wear.
4. Check automatic transmission fluid level.
5. Check level of power steering fluid in power steering reservoir.
6. Check brake fluid level in master cylinder and look for signs of fluid leakage.
7. Check all tire pressures including spare, when tires are cold. Inflate tires four pounds extra if you are going to carry a full carload or if you will be driving at high speed. Check depth of tire tread and see that tires are not damaged.
8. Clean headlights and windshield.
9. Fill windshield washer reservoir with fluid.
10. Check windshield wiper blades and replace them if they are worn or brittle.
11. Inspect fan belts for fraying and looseness. Replace them if they are damaged. Adjust to proper tightness.
12. Check battery electrolyte level and battery charge.
13. Check operation of turn signals, hazard warning flasher lights, stoplights, taillights, and backup lights.
14. Get and store your on-the-road emergency kit.
15. Fill gas tank.

Pro Shop
Unlocking the locks

In winter, car locks may become frozen. There are several ways to free a frozen lock. You can use a deicing fluid, available in spray cans. This is the same fluid you use to remove ice from your windshield. Spray it directly into the lock opening. Note: You may have to insert your key part-way to do this. Or try heating the key with a cigarette lighter after inserting it into the lock. *Caution: Keep the flame away from the body finish. Do not use the heat-* *ing method if you have already sprayed the lock with deicing fluid, because the fluid will burn. Do not grasp the hot key with your bare hands.*

In summer, all locks should be maintained with a lock graphite lubricant. If lubricated correctly, a lock will work easily and will not freeze in winter. If your locks do not work easily after lubrication, they may need to be repaired by a mechanic.

ON-THE-ROAD EMERGENCY KIT

1. Copy of a troubleshooting guide and the owner's manual for your particular car.
2. Flares.
3. Lug wrench and jack.
4. Jumper cables.
5. Screwdrivers, pliers, and wrenches.
6. Strong tow rope or chain.
7. Old blankets.
8. Folding camp shovel.
9. Fire extinguisher.
10. Rags or strong paper towels.
11. Cream hand cleaner.
12. First aid kit.
13. Pencils and notebook.
14. Spare coins for meters and phone calls.
15. Flashlight.
16. Road maps.
17. Extra electrical fuses.
18. Pocket tire pressure gauge.
19. Extra fan belt.
20. In winter only: windshield de-icer spray; windshield scraper brush; small snow shovel; bag of sand; extra blankets and coats.

Alignment of the front wheels should be checked before a long trip. If they are out-of-line, the steering will be unstable and the tires will wear unevenly, hence requiring replacement earlier than they normally would with the same number of miles on them. Wheel alignment can be measured and adjusted only with special equipment, so take your car to a shop that provides this service rather than trying to do it yourself.

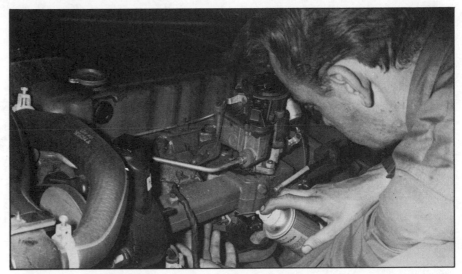

During long, hard driving the heat valve in the manifold sometimes sticks in the heat position. This makes the manifold too hot, which cuts down both fuel economy and engine power. Before you leave, give the valve a couple of shots of a spray lubricant while holding the valve open with your fingers when the engine is cool.

If you have to use jumper cables during your trip, be sure you hook them up so that one cable connects the positive terminal (usually marked with a + sign) on the live battery to the positive terminal on the dead battery—and the other cable connects the negative terminal (usually marked with a − sign) of the good battery to a ground on the engine with the dead battery. If you cross the terminals, you can permanently damage the ignition system and both batteries.

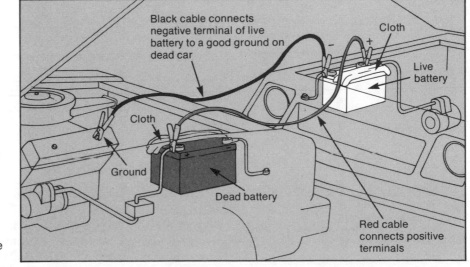

Black cable connects negative terminal of live battery to a good ground on dead car

Cloth

Live battery

Cloth

Ground

Dead battery

Red cable connects positive terminals

How to Push and Tow Automatic Drive Cars

A disabled car must not be towed on the rear wheels with the transmission in any of the driving gears because unnecessary damage to the transmission may result. Unless otherwise indicated in the following chart, it may be towed for short distances only, with the control lever or push button in neutral (N) at a speed not in excess of 25 miles per hour.

If for any reason the transmission is locked up, the car must not be towed on its rear wheels or serious damage to the transmission will result. If the car is to be towed for any extended distance, it should be done with the rear wheels off the ground or with the propeller shaft removed. Note: Beginning with 1969 General Motors cars (1970 for others), except Corvair, if the ignition key is not available it will be necessary to tow the car with the front wheels off the ground and the rear wheels on a dolly or vice versa, since the steering and shift mechanisms are also locked.

As indicated in the following chart, a number of transmissions cannot be started by pushing. The oil circuits in these transmissions are such (no rear pump) that the engine cannot be driven through the transmission. If the battery will not crank the engine, a fully-charged battery should be installed or a "jumper" circuit should be used from another charged battery.

Alternator-equipped cars cannot be push-started when the battery is completely dead because, unlike a generator, there is no residual magnetism in the rotor (which corresponds to the field coils in a generator).

When using jumper cables on alternator-equipped cars, be sure to connect positive to positive and negative to negative to prevent damage to the alternator.

Pushing and towing cars with automatic transmissions

Car	Transmission	Push Starting				Towing	
		Start pushing in	Ignition on at MPH	Shift at MPH	Shift to	Hold speed at or below MPH	Maximum distance miles
American Motors	Flashomatic[9]	Neutral	15-20	15-20	L	40	[1]
	Shift Command	[3]	[3]	[3]	[3]	35	50
	Torque Command	[3]	[3]	[3]	[3]	35	50
Chrysler Corporation	Powerflite	Neutral	0	25	L	35	100
	Torqueflite, aluminum[8]	Neutral	0	15	L	30	[1]
	Torqueflite, cast iron	Neutral	0	15-20	L	35	100
Ford Motor Company	C3, C4, C6, CW, FMX & Jatco	[3]	[3]	[3]	[3]	30	15
	3 speed[10]	Neutral	30	30	L	40	12
	2 speed	Neutral	25	25	L	30	15
General Motors Corporation	Buick Dual Path Drive	[3]	[3]	[3]	[3]	25	[1]
	Buick Twin Turbine	Neutral	0	15	L	35[2]	[1]
	Corvair Powerglide	Neutral	0	20-25	L	50	[1]
	Dual Coupling Hydra-Matic	Neutral	30-35[6]	30-35[6]	D[6]	5	[1]
	F-85 Hydra-Matic, 1961-63	[3]	[3]	[3]	[3]	30	[1]
	Jetaway Hydra-Matic	[3]	[3]	[3]	[3]	35	[1]
	Roto Hydra-Matic	[3]	[3]	[3]	[3]	30	[1]
	Turbo Hydra-Matic "200," "250," "350" & "375B"	[3]	[3]	[3]	[3]	35	50
	Turbo Hydra-Matic "375," "400" & "425"	[3]	[3]	[3]	[3]	35	50
	Powerglide, aluminum[9]	Neutral	0	25-30	L	35	50
	Powerglide, cast iron	Neutral	0	25-30	L	30	[1]
	Super Turbine "300"	[3]	[3]	[3]	[3]	35	50
	Super Turbine "400"	[3]	[3]	[3]	[3]	35	50
	Tempestorque, 1961-63	Neutral	0	20-25[7]	L	30	[1]
	Tempestorque, 1964	[3]	[3]	[3]	[3]	25	[1]
	Turboglide[6]	Neutral	25	25-30	HR or GR	30[4]	[1]
Studebaker	Flightomatic	Neutral	0	20	L	40	[1]

[1] See towing precautions.
[2] 25 MPH with air suspension.
[3] Not possible to start by pushing. See Push starting above.
[4] 10 MPH with air suspension.
[5] Do not tow.
[6] Not possible to push start after 1958. See Push starting note above.
[7] Not possible to push start after 1962. See Push starting note above.
[8] Not possible to push start after 1965. See Push starting note above.
[9] Not possible to push start after 1966. See Push starting note above.
[10] Not possible to push start after 1967. See Push starting note above.

Tire Service

Tires should be inspected regularly for excessive or abnormal tread wear, fabric breaks, cuts, or other damage. A bulge or bump in the sidewall or tread may indicate that it has separated from the tire body. If so, get rid of the tire.

As for worn tires, surveys show that while tires are to blame for less than one percent of all highway accidents, in more than half of these cases the tires are bald to the cords. Bald tires are also up to 44 times more likely to go flat than new tires. And the risk of skidding, which is five to ten times higher on wet roads as on dry ones with normal tires, is twice that on bald tires.

Inflation pressure

Proper inflation is the key to maximum performance from any tire. Underinflation causes excessive wear at the outer edges of the tire, and also makes it generate excessive heat—one of the greatest causes of tire wear and failure. Overinflation causes faster wear in the center groove area, and in addition makes the tire more susceptible to damage from objects or holes in the road. The proper air pressure for your tires is listed in the owner's manual for your car. Tires should always be checked when they are cool, because pressure will build up after they have been in motion. Never reduce built-up pressure when the tires are hot; and, remember to check the pressure in your spare.

You may want to add four pounds of pressure when traveling long distances at turnpike speeds, or pulling a trailer, or carrying a heavy load, but do not exceed the maximum cold pressure specified on the tire's sidewall, normally 32 pounds for a passenger car tire.

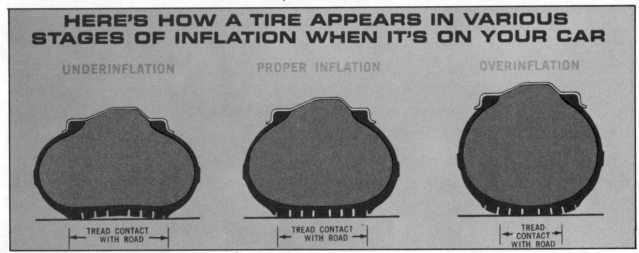

HERE'S HOW A TIRE APPEARS IN VARIOUS STAGES OF INFLATION WHEN IT'S ON YOUR CAR

UNDERINFLATION — PROPER INFLATION — OVERINFLATION

TREAD CONTACT WITH ROAD

Tire replacement

Tread or sidewall cuts, cracks, or snags deep enough to expose tire ply cords or fabric mean you need new tires.

Measuring tread depth

About $^{11}/_{32}$ of an inch is the optimum tread depth for a new tire. The reason deeper treads aren't used is heat. The deeper the tread, the hotter the tire runs, and a tread of over $^{11}/_{32}$ generates enough heat to cause excessive tire wear.

When the tread is worn down to $^{2}/_{32}$, the tire is no longer capable of delivering the traction you need for safety. In other words, it is bald. And in many states, anything less than $^{2}/_{32}$ is illegal. There are two simple ways of telling whether you have enough tread for safe driving.

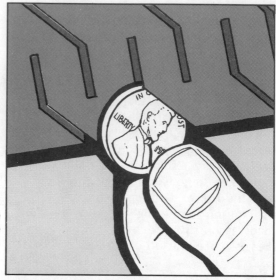

Lincoln-head penny trick. A penny inserted into a groove in the tread, with the top of Lincoln's head pointing toward the tire, can tell you if it is unsafe. If you can see all of the head, it is time to replace the tire.

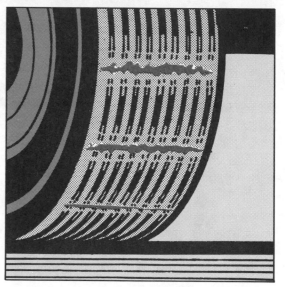

Tread-wear bars have been built into all new tires produced since 1969, when the Department of Transportation came into being. Once the tread is worn down to $^{1}/_{16}$ of an inch, they appear as smooth bands running across the tread area. When bands appear in two or more adjacent grooves, replace the tire.

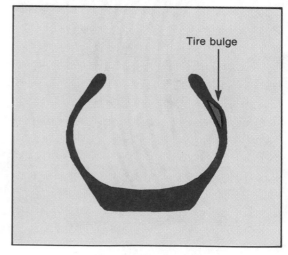

Tire bulge

Bumps, bulges, or knots indicate possible separation of the tread or sidewall from the tire body and should be examined by an expert to see if replacement is necessary.

Tire wear patterns

Tire wear patterns are indicators of a variety of problems with inflation and front wheel alignment.

Camber. Tread with one side worn off on a front tire is caused by improper camber setting. This also requires a front end specialist.

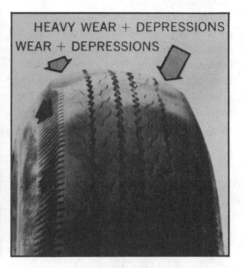

Toe-in. Tiny feathered edges on one side of the tread block indicate excessive toe-in. If you place the palm of your hand on the tread and move your hand inward, toward the chassis, the tire will feel smooth. As you draw your hand outward, toward yourself, you will feel sharp edges. Take the car to a front end specialist for correction.

Toe-out. The wear pattern resulting from toe-out is the reverse of the wear pattern caused by toe-in. See a front end specialist.

Out-of-balance wheels. Uneven or spotty tread wear, which sometimes takes the form of cupping, scalloping, or bald spots around the tire, may be caused by out-of-balance front wheels or faulty wheel alignment. In either case, see a front end specialist.

Overinflation causes the center of the tread to wear more rapidly than the edge. Reduce the tire pressure to the manufacturer's specifications.

Underinflation causes the edges of the tread to wear more rapidly than the center. Inflate the tires to the manufacturer's specifications.

Tire rotation

Rotation equalizes normal tire wear. Tires do wear normally, and while nothing lasts indefinitely, by equalizing tire wear over the entire tread surface, you extend tire life. According to one tire company, rotating your tires every 5,000 miles provides you with 20 percent more mileage from each tire. With rear-end-drive, front tires undergo normal wear primarily on their outer shoulders, as a result of cornering maneuvers, whereas rear tires wear mainly in the center, because of the power thrust from the rear axle.

Rotation plans. The systematic movement of tires and wheels from one position to another depends upon the kind of tires you have—bias, bias-belted, or radial—and whether or not you plan to rotate four or five tires. If you have five new tires, as with a new car, it is preferable to choose a five-tire rotation plan. Note: Preventive maintenance should keep you from getting a flat tire. But if you do, follow the instructions for rotating tires to change your flat.

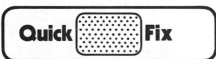

Lost lug nuts

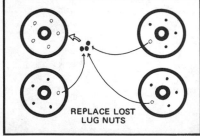

REPLACE LOST LUG NUTS

If you ever find yourself short of lug nuts after changing a flat tire on the road, there is a way for you to safely get to a service station to replenish your supply of nuts. Remove one nut from each of the other three wheels and use these nuts to fasten the wheel back on your car. The vehicle can now be driven at a moderate speed to a service station or auto supply store.

Tools and equipment:
Jack.
Safety stands.
Lug wrench.
Large screw driver.
Rubber mallet.
Hand cloth.

Caution:

Radial-ply tires should never be cross-switched. Move them front to rear or rear to front on the same side of the car.

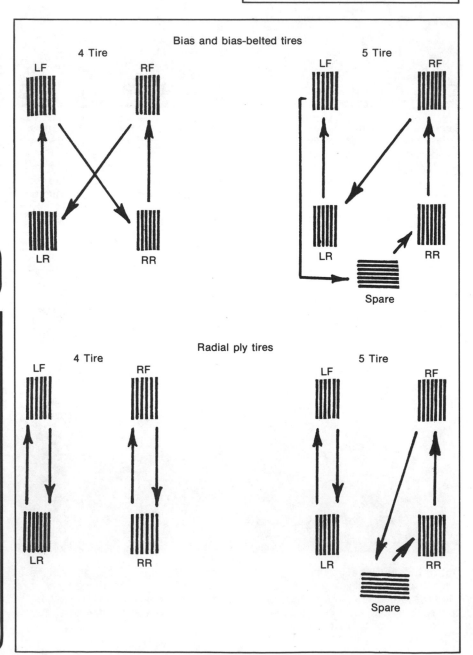

Removing and replacing wheels

1 Remove the wheel cover with a lug wrench or large screw driver.

2 Loosen all lug nuts or bolts one full turn only. *Caution: Check thread direction right or left as indicated with "R" or "L" on stud.* Jack up the car and support it on safety stands. See chapter 2.

3 Remove all lug nuts or bolts and put them in the wheel cover. Place the wheel cover on soft material to prevent scratching.

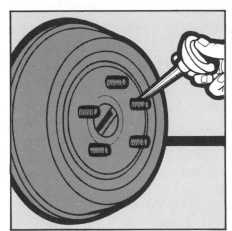

4 Before you install lug nuts or bolts put a little light oil on the studs. The tapered end of the nut must face toward the wheel.

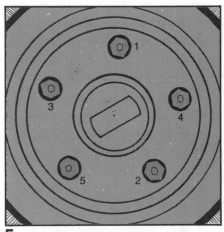

5 Using an alternating sequence, run the nuts firmly against the wheel. Lower the car just enough to keep the wheels from turning. Then tighten the nuts to specifications and lower the car all the way.

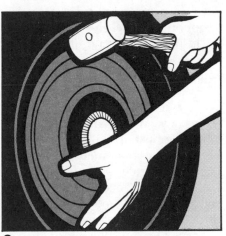

6 Replace the wheel cover using a rubber mallet. Reinflate the tire.

Repairing tubeless tires

Tubeless tires can only be repaired with the special equipment that a tire shop or service station has. While you should not attempt repairs yourself, you ought to make sure that whoever does the job does it right—from inside the tire out. Repairs made from outside the tire are very temporary and will shortly start leaking.

Wheel balancing

You cannot balance your wheels yourself, since expensive machinery is required. This job should be left to your local tire store or service station. But you should know that if a wheel assembly is out of balance, vibration and tire wear can result. For this reason, balancing is required whenever you mount tires on wheels or replace tires or wheels with new ones.

Changing Engine Oil and Oil Filter

Engine oil never wears out. But it does lose its ability to lubricate properly when it becomes contaminated with airborne dirt, metal particles from engine wear, and by-products of the combustion process.

Some of the by-products combine with the oil to form the tar-like deposit called sludge. The lead in ordinary gasoline is a major contributor to sludge, so the car that runs on lead-free gasoline produces less of it. Because this results in less contamination of the engine oil, the drain intervals on cars using lead-free gas can be extended somewhat.

As your car ages, it needs more frequent service. The engine that might need an oil and filter change at 6,000-mile intervals when it is young may require it at 4,000-mile intervals after 50,000 to 60,000 miles, because engine wear permits greater leakage of exhaust gases and other combustion products into the crankcase, contaminating the oil. The general rule is to change your oil and filter every 4,000 miles unless you use unleaded gas exclusively. If you do, then 6,000-mile intervals may be sufficient.

Whenever you change oil, or any of the other car fluids, you must find a safe way to dispose of the wastes. Never throw them down your toilet or into your cesspool. Because of ecological concerns, communities have developed a variety of laws governing this. In some cities, you may put the waste oil in any closed container in your garbage. In other areas, you must use a special safety container available from auto parts suppliers. Check with your sanitation department for the rules governing waste disposal in your area.

Car oil needs vary from four quarts to seven. The owner's manual and markings on the dipstick or on the engine decal will tell you how much oil your car requires.

Your owner's manual will also tell you the grade of oil you should use. This is a number designation indicating viscosity. If you do not have an owner's manual, the following information can serve as a guide.

Viscosity

The thickness of an oil, or its ability to flow, is called its viscosity. Viscosity also refers to its weight. The standard procedure, established by the Society of Automotive Engineers, is to number oils according to thickness—the higher the number, the thicker or heavier the oil. All numbers are preceded by the letters SAE, the abbreviation for the Society that sets the standards. If a number is followed by the letter W, the thickness was measured at 0°F. If no letter follows, it was done at 210°F.

Oil normally thins out as it is heated, but it is possible, by use of additives such as polymers, or because of the natural qualities of some oils, to retard the thinning out. Therefore, an oil with a viscosity of 10 at 0°F, a 10W oil, might also be able to pass the thickness test for a 30-, 40-, or even 50- or 60-weight oil at 210°F. This characteristic is called multi-viscosity and such an oil may be numbered 10W-30 or 10W-40.

Multi-viscosity is a highly desirable characteristic, because if the oil is relatively thin at low temperatures, it will flow easily and provide good lubrication when the engine is first started. It will also be easier to pump, and therefore will reduce or eliminate starting and cold-running difficulties caused by an oil that is too thick to pump readily. And by becoming relatively thick as the engine warms up, the oil can continue to provide good lubrication, whereas an ordinary 10-weight oil might be too thin. However, as the oil accumulates mileage, additives are used up, and the oil loses some of its ability to provide wide-viscosity-range performance.

Although most refiners put their best efforts into the manufacture of multi-viscosity oils, single viscosity oils—5W, 10W, 20, 30, 40, and 50—are also widely available. If you use single viscosity oil, it will be necessary to change your oil weight as seasonal temperatures change, making it less practical to purchase by the case.

Multi-viscosity oils cost more than single viscosity ones, but the same weight can be used year-round, and you can buy them by the case—the cheapest way.

Because the viscosity range, called the index, drops with mileage, a 10W-40 or greater range is a good starting point. If you change your oil very frequently, a 10W-30 is fine. In very cold climates, that is, rarely above 60°F and consistently below zero in winter, a 5W-30 or 5W-40 is the best choice.

Where the temperature variations are too great for one oil, buy two grades. If, however, you garage the car, you probably can get by with the 10W-40 year-round. Keeping the car indoors, even if the garage is unheated, will normally preclude starting difficulties caused by overly thick oil. Another possibility: if the temperatures are low during winter and the car is left outdoors, a coolant heater, an electric heater that plugs into a household outlet and keeps the coolant warm, can be installed. This not only will ease winter starting, but will enable you to turn on the car's passenger compartment heater immediately. There are some partly or wholly nonpetroleum oils, called synthetics, currently on the market. According to the manufacturers of these synthetic oils, a car can be driven up to 30,000 miles without an oil change. They also claim better gas mileage. But synthetic oils are more costly than petroleum oils.

Checking the oil level

The engine oil should be kept at the FULL mark on the dipstick, although it is safe to wait until the level is at the ADD mark to pour in a quart. An engine should not be run a quart low, and old wives' tales that the engine runs best that way are wrong. The oil should be checked when the car is on level ground and only after the engine has been shut off for at least a few minutes. This allows oil in various parts of the engine enough time to drain down to the crankcase.

Locate the dipstick. It is on one side of the engine or the other, possibly towards the front. The dipstick is a long metal rod one end of which is curled into a loop so you can insert a finger and pull it out of its tube. Use a rag to wipe off all the oil, then look at the end of the dipstick. You should be able to see the markings ADD and FULL. Insert the dipstick back into the tube, making sure you push it in as far as it will go. Now pull it straight out, keeping it in a vertical position, and read the oil level. If the oil is at the ADD mark, you need a quart. If it is on the FULL mark, your level is OK. Once in a while, when the car is very low on oil, you may not get a reading at all. In this case, put in a quart and take another reading. Continue to check the dipstick and add oil until the level is at FULL. *Caution: Do not overfill the engine with oil. This may cause the oil to foam while the engine is running, interfering with lubrication.*

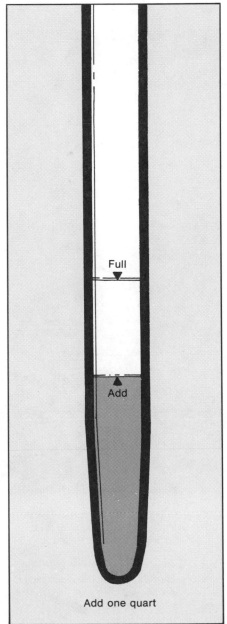

Full

Add

Add one quart

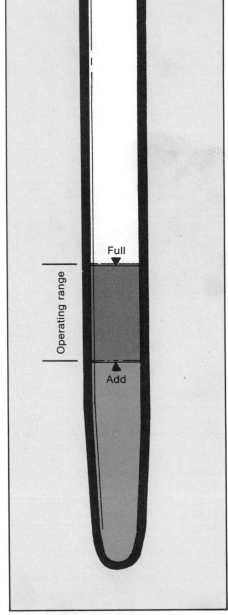

Operating range

Full

Add

Tools and equipment:

Oil.
Jack and safety stands, or ride-on ramps.
Large drain pan of at least six-quart capacity.
Droplight or flashlight.
Creeper.
Correct size box wrench or socket and handle for drain plug.
Hand cloth.
Funnel.
Can opener.
Goggles.
Fender covers.

Pro Shop
Fender covers

Fender covers are protective mats placed over the fender or grille. They're used whenever you are adding or draining oils or other fluids that can damage the finish of the car. While you can buy them, they're relatively expensive. Instead we suggest using an old shower curtain, blanket, or beach towel.

Changing the engine oil

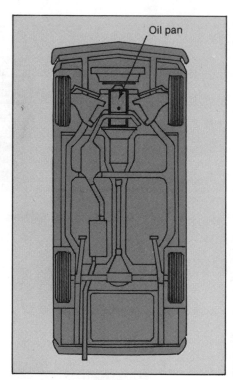

Oil pan

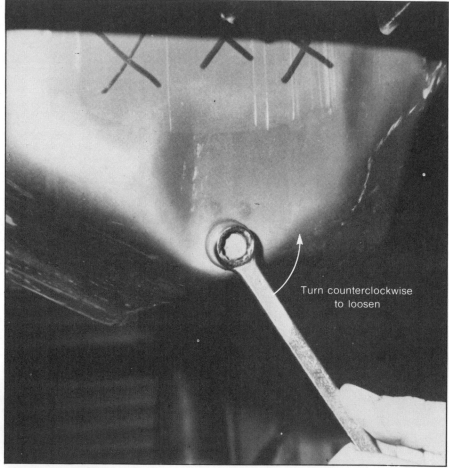

Turn counterclockwise to loosen

1 **Draining the oil.** Run the engine to allow the oil to reach operating temperature, permitting the oil to flow freely and carry out the contamination with it. Jack up and support the front of the car, and locate the oil drain plug on the oil pan. Place the proper size wrench on the plug. As you face the plug, turn the wrench counterclockwise just enough to loosen it. Place the drain pan in position under the plug and remove the plug by hand. *Caution: The oil is hot. To avoid burning your hand, remove the plug carefully and quickly.* Allow the oil to drain out completely. To do this it may be necessary to lower the car to the ground.

2 **Replacing the oil.** After the oil has stopped draining, clean the plug, and thread it back into the oil pan by hand. *Caution: Never use a wrench to start the plug. Also, if the plug had a washer, be sure to re-use it.* Tighten the drain plug securely and wipe with a cloth. Place the fender covers on the fenders. Add the specified amount of oil to the engine

slowly to avoid spilling. Remove the drain pan from under the car and dispose of the waste oil properly.
If you are not changing the oil filter, check the oil level before starting the engine, then start it up and visually check for oil leaks at the drain plug. Switch the engine off, and lower your car.

Changing the oil filter

To buy a new oil filter, you must know the year, make, and model of your car, and the cubic inch displacement (CI) of its engine. The CI is usually found on the air filter cover, the engine valve cover, or the inside of the front door panel. In addition, the owner's manual will state it.

Tools and equipment:

Oil filter.
Jack.
Safety stands.
Creeper.
Goggles.
Droplight or flashlight.
Can opener.
Oil filter wrench.
Oil pan.
Funnel.
One quart of oil.
Hand cloth.
Fender covers.

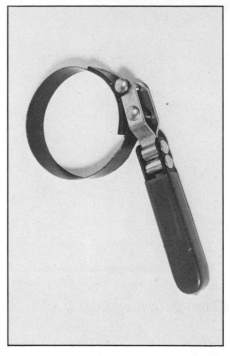

The strap-type filter wrench has a built-in handle so it requires proper positioning to allow the handle room to swing.

The filter wrench shown has a coil leaf spring which handles many different sizes of oil filters. Use an open-end box wrench or ratchet wrench with it.

Another oil filter wrench resembles a pair of pliers.

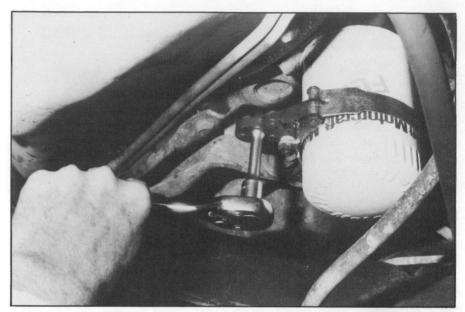

A strap-type filter wrench used with a ratchet and extension fits into hard-to-reach places.

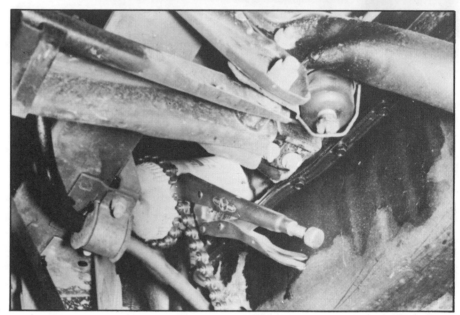

Chain vise pliers serve as a universal filter wrench, but are difficult to position in tight spaces.

1 **Removing the filter.** Locate the oil filter. If your car is a V-6 or V-8, it is probably mounted on the bottom of the engine, near the oil pan, and you will have to jack up and support the front of the car in order to get to it. On most four- or six-cylinder cars, it is on the side of the engine and accessible by reaching over the fender. Place the fender covers on the fenders, and put the oil drain pan in position below the filter. Using a suitable oil filter wrench, loosen the filter by turning it two turns counterclockwise. The oil from the filter will now drain into the pan. When the filter has stopped draining, remove it by hand. *Caution: Some oil will remain in the filter. Hold it in an upright position to prevent spillage.*

2 **Replacing the filter.** With the hand cloth, clean the filter mating surface on the engine. Coat the filter gasket with a thin film of clean engine oil. Thread the new filter onto the engine and hand tighten it. Do not use an oil filter wrench. Most filters have tightening instructions printed on their case or box.

Clean the filter and surrounding area with a hand cloth, and add one quart of engine oil. Before starting the engine, check the oil level. It may register slightly over full. Start the engine and check for leaks around the filter, then switch it off. Remove the drain pan and properly dispose of the waste oil and filter. Lower your car off the safety stands or ramps. Recheck the oil level and add oil if necessary.

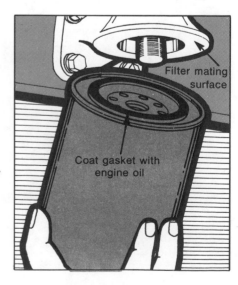

Filter mating surface

Coat gasket with engine oil

Chassis Lubrication

The owner's manual for your car gives the manufacturer's recommendations for frequency of lubrication. It is important to understand that these recommendations are based on the manufacturer's definition of "normal operating conditions." For many drivers, these normal conditions would be considered the ideal—moderate temperatures, light traffic, smooth roads, and trips long enough to allow the engine to warm up fully. If you encounter winter cold, summer heat, rain, snow, or traffic jams, you need to pay attention to the fine print indicating that more frequent service is necessary. Under severe operating conditions, as a general rule, follow the manufacturer's specifications for the first four years. Once a car is four years old or older, the following lubrication schedule suggests a good maintenance approach. Note that the figures are based on 1,000 miles per month of driving. If you drive less, lubricate on a time-equivalent basis.

The most effective long-term lubrication will be provided by a moly grease, a grease with a three to ten percent concentration of the lubricating compound molybdenum disulphide. This grease is required for all cars with long chassis lubrication intervals—25,000 miles and up. If you use a standard grease, 6,000-mile intervals are maximum.

Buy a water-resistant grease if the temperatures in your area are consistently below freezing during winter.

After some general tips on greasing your car, the detailed steps for each greasing procedure will be given. All of the underbody grease jobs require raising the car, so you will save time if you prepare to do these tasks in one series of operations. They include: greasing the front suspension, the steering linkage, and the universal joints; checking the lubricant levels in a standard transmission and in the differential; changing automatic transmission fluid; and repacking the front wheel bearings.

Grease jobs—general hints

The chart on locating grease fittings tells you how many fittings your car has and their general location.

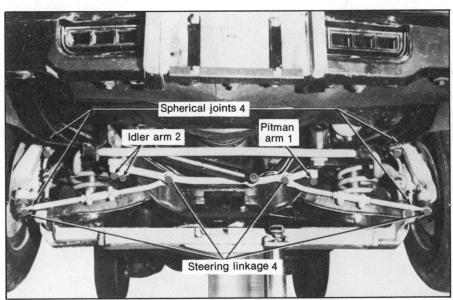

TYPICAL GENERAL MOTORS FRONT END

Finding the fittings. The first time you do a grease job, you will spend a lot of time looking for the fittings. Although the chart tells you how many fittings the car has, and in what basic area they're located, you will have to do the actual finding. As you locate a fitting, wipe it off with a clean cloth. This will help you spot it later and also prevent you from injecting dirt with the grease.

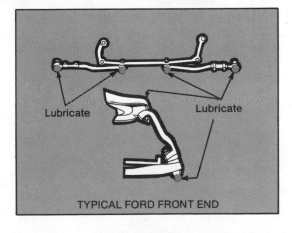

TYPICAL FORD FRONT END

Injecting the grease. A squeeze-handle type cartridge grease gun with a flexible injection tube will help you to get at hard-to-reach grease fittings. The injection tip of the grease gun should be a catch fit on the fitting nipple, which, once in place, will not slip off. Slight, straight-on pressure is all that is necessary for the gun tip to engage the fitting. Once that is done, pump the handle. On older cars (mid-1960's and before), it was a matter of watching the rubber grease seal on whatever the fitting was threaded. When the old grease came out, you stopped pumping. Today's tighter seals require somewhat more careful injection to prevent them from being damaged.

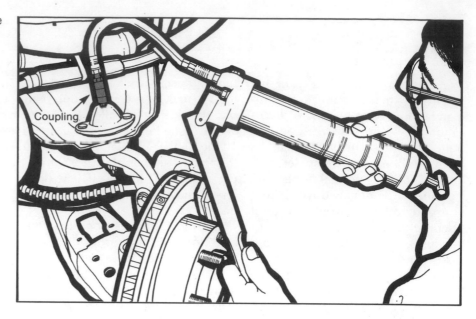

Coupling

Grease plugs. Some cars use grease plugs to prevent dirt and water from entering the steering parts, such as the ball joints and steering linkage. The plugs must be removed and replaced with grease fittings to make the next grease job faster.

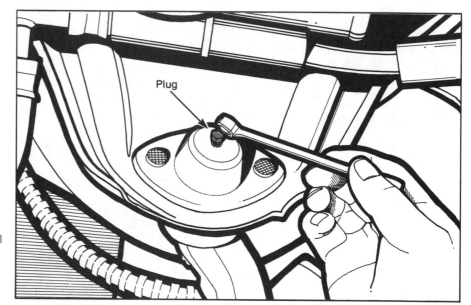

Plug

How to inject

American Motors and Ford: Pump slowly until the rubber boot can be felt or seen to swell slightly. Chrysler Corporation and General Motors: Pump slowly until the grease starts to flow from the bleed holes at the base of the seals, or until the seals start to swell. If the fitting fails to take grease, the lubricant will ooze out between the fitting and the tip of the gun. Do not keep pumping or you will have a mess. A bit of grease will seep out, but if the fitting is not taking grease, it should be replaced.

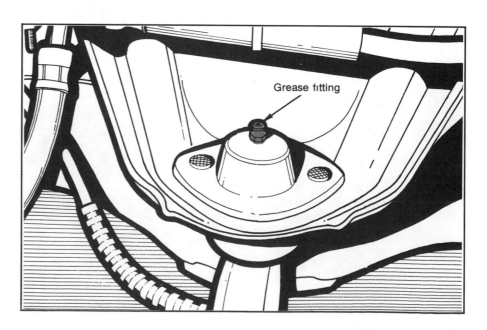

Grease fitting

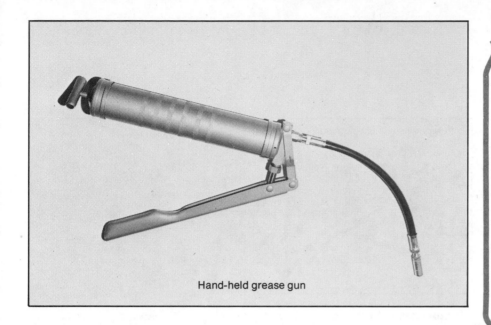
Hand-held grease gun

ECONOTIP

#3

Take a different route

The smoothest road surface gives the best gas mileage. If you have a choice of routes, take the one with the best roads. And stay away from unimproved gravel or dirt roads. Broken and patched asphalt roads extract a 15 percent fuel penalty. If you go on gravel roads, the penalty is 35 percent. If you regularly travel on any unimproved roads, try taking a longer route on smoother roads. Even though the distance is longer, you might get better mileage by staying off rough roads.

Lubrication schedule—for cars four years old and older

Activity	Special conditions	Frequency in miles
Change engine oil and filter	Using leaded gas	4,000
	Using unleaded gas only	6,000
Chassis lubrication		6,000
Change transmission oil and filter	No trailer	24,000
	Pulls trailer occasionally	12,000
	Pulls trailer regularly	6,000
Lubricate and adjust front wheel bearings		12,000
Lubricate body hinges		12,000
Change differential lubrication	No trailer	36,000
	Pulls trailer occasionally	24,000
	Pulls trailer regularly	12,000

Locating grease fittings

Car	Ball joints	Steering linkage	Universal joint	Clutch cross shaft
All Ford products	4	4	0	0
All Chrysler products	4	5	0	0
All American Motors	4	2	0	0
Buick	4	7	1(a)	0
Oldsmobile, except Toronado	4	7	1(a)	1(b) (d)
Olds Toronado	4	4	0	0
Pontiac	4	7	1(a)	1(b) (d)
1975-on Cadillac, except Eldorado	4	7	1(a)	0
1975-on Cadillac Eldorado	4	5	0	0
Chevrolet	4	7	1(a)	1(c) (d)
Volkswagen	2	2	0	0

Notes:
   (a): Flush fitting on rear (constant velocity) universal joint on full-size models except wagons.
   (b): Fitting or plug, used on all compacts and subcompacts, some intermediates. Replace plug with fitting.
   (c): Plug. Replace with fitting.
   (d): At 30,000 mile intervals, sooner only to eliminate binding in linkage.

Greasing the underbody

These tasks all require raising the whole car.

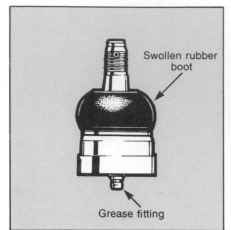

Swollen rubber boot

Grease fitting

1 Greasing the front suspension and steering linkage. The parts which require greasing are a series of joints like the one above. Locate the fittings and wipe them clean, or if grease plugs are used in place of fittings, remove them and install fittings. Snap the grease gun coupling onto the fitting, pump the gun and remove it. Grease the remaining fittings in the same way. When all the fittings have been greased, wipe away any excess. Be sure to check the chart on grease fittings for the number of spots you need to find.

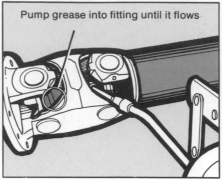

Pump grease into fitting until it flows

2 Lubricating the universal joints of the drive shaft. Place the transmission in neutral and release the parking brake, then turn the drive shaft slowly by hand to locate the grease fittings on the universal joints. After cleaning the fittings and attaching the tapered-tip tube adapter to the grease gun coupling, insert the tip of the tube onto the fittings, and pump the handle until grease starts to flow out of the joints. Remove the grease gun, clean any excess grease off the universal joints, set the parking brake, and put the transmission in "Park" position. Note: Check the chart—not all universal joints require greasing.

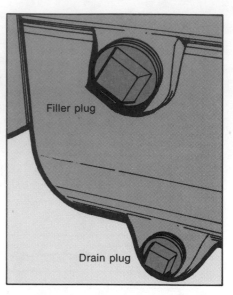

Filler plug

Drain plug

3 Checking the lubricant level in standard transmissions. Locate the filler plug on the side (left or right) of the transmission. With the proper-sized wrench, or a ratchet and extension square, remove the plug by turning it counterclockwise as you face it. *Caution: Do not remove the drain plug usually located on the bottom of the transmission.* The lubricant level in a standard transmission should be no lower than 1/2-inch below the filler hole. You can test it by inserting your finger into the filler hole and bending it at the first joint. You should feel the top of the lubricant. If the transmission requires lubricant, check the manufacturer's specifications for the correct one to use.

ECONOTIP

#4
Low viscosity oil gives better mileage

If a fleet of cars starts using a lower viscosity oil, such as switching from 40 weight to 30 weight, the fleet will use less gasoline. The same applies when switching from a single viscosity, such as 30 weight, to a multiple viscosity such as 10W-30. The gas mileage benefits from lower viscosity oil have been proved many times in fleet use. But will the use of lower viscosity oil in one car give better mileage? The answer is a definite yes, but the gain may be so small that you can't notice it over short periods of time. The car has to be run through several tanks of gas, or maybe several months of driving, to find out if the lower viscosity oil really helps. You must be careful, too, that you don't go lower in viscosity than the car manufacturer recommends. The lightweight oils do not have as much film strength, so there is a chance of damaging the bearings. This is particularly true on an older car, where the bearings are already worn. If you hear any knocking when running with lightweight oil, stop immediately and change to heavier oil.

Tools and equipment:

Jack.
Safety stands or drive-on ramps.
Droplight or flashlight.
Goggles.
Creeper.
Hand grease gun.
Tapered-tip tube adapter.
Hand cloth.
Combination wrenches and socket set.
Hand suction gun.
Fender covers.

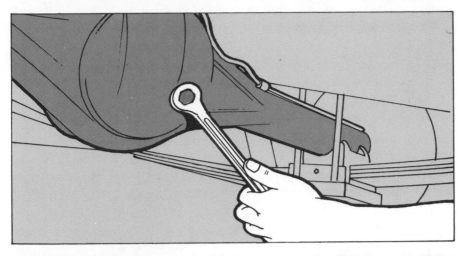

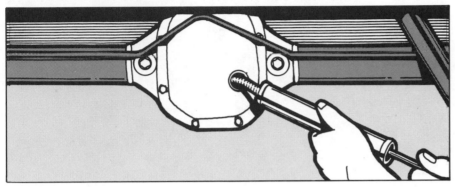

4 **Checking the differential fluid.** Located on the differential housing, right or left side, or on the rear cover, is a male or female filler plug. Using the correct-sized wrench, or a ratchet and extension square, remove the filler plug. Check the lubricant level of the differential in the same way you checked the transmission, judging it by the levels given in the chart on differential housing oil levels. If the level is low, check the manufacturer's specifications for the correct lubricant. Use the hand suction pump to fill the differential, then reinstall the filler plug securely, and clean the plug area.

Rear End Oil Level Chart
Differential housing oil levels

Manufacturer	Types	Oil levels
American Motors Corporation	All cars	Level with bottom of fill plug hole.
Chrysler Corporation	7½-inch axle (rear cover has nine bolts).	⅝-inch below bottom of fill plug hole.
	8¼-inch axle (rear cover has 10 bolts).	⅛-inch below bottom of fill plug hole.
	8¾-inch axle (rear cover is welded to housing).	Level with bottom of fill plug hole.
	9¼-inch axle (rear cover has 12 bolts).	⅜-inch below bottom of fill plug hole.
Ford Motor Company	All compacts, intermediates, and full-size cars.	Level with bottom of fill plug hole.
	Subcompacts (Mustang II, Pinto, Bobcat).	¼-inch below bottom of fill plug hole.
	Thunderbirds and Lincoln Continentals.	Loosen plug and back out slowly. If seepage occurs around the threads, level is correct and the plug should be turned back in to prevent oil loss. To fill or add oil to differential, jack up the appropriate end a bit more (front if fill plug hole is at the front of the housing, rear if the hole is at the rear of the housing). An additional four ounces should be sufficient.
General Motors Corporation	Chevrolet and Pontiac.	Level with bottom of fill plug hole.
	Buick and Oldsmobile, except Toronado.	Within ⅜-inch of fill plug hole.
	Toronado.	Level at oil level line stamped next to plug.
	Buick Apollo Wagon.	Within ¾-inch below bottom of fill plug.
	Cadillac (including Eldorado).	Within ½-inch of bottom of fill plug hole.
		Note: On Cadillac Eldorado and Oldsmobile Toronado, the final drive, which is bolted to the transmission case at the left front of the engine, is the equivalent of the rear axle on conventional rear-drive cars.
		The fill plug on these cars is on the left side of the final drive.

Changing the automatic transmission oil and filter

The automatic transmission drain plug was eliminated from the oil pan on American cars in the 1960's. If you have a newer car, therefore, you will have to remove the pan to change the oil. A few quarts of oil are drained when the pan is removed, perhaps a third of the total capacity. The fresh oil added will be sufficient to restore the performance of the fluid.

Tools and equipment:

Large oil drain pan.
Set of sockets.
³⁄₈ drive socket set.
Screwdriver.
Putty knife.
Scraper.
Hand cloth.
Droplight or flashlight.
Creeper.

Goggles.
Oil pan filter-gasket kit for your car.
Transmission oil for your car.
Non-hardening gasket sealer.
Torque wrench.
Funnel.
Can opener.
Fender covers.

1 The transmission oil pan. With the car on safety stands, locate the pan. It is a flat-bottom, sheet metal pan a foot or two to the rear of the engine and bolted to the transmission. Put a large drain pan of approximately three gallons capacity under the transmission oil pan. Using a socket wrench, remove all bolts holding the pan to the bottom of the transmission except those at the front, which should only be loosened. This will permit you to tilt the pan down slightly at the rear, so that the oil will drain out only at that location. Support the pan with one hand, so the weight of the oil does not cock the pan. If the pan sticks, free it up with a putty knife at the joint.

On some early-model cars, the transmission oil pan is equipped with a drain plug, and some models have a filler tube connected to the pan. Transmissions so equipped can be drained by removing the drain plug or the filler tube.

2 Removing and replacing the filter. When most of the oil has drained out, remove the front screws and lower the pan. Remove the oil filter or strainer assembly, which is sometimes attached with screws, other times pressed or snap-locked into the transmission. Replace the oil strainer or filter assembly with a new filter. Note: On General Motors Turbo Hydra-Matic transmissions, the filter has a long neck with an O-ring. Make sure the old O-ring comes out with the filter and position the new one at the bulge on the neck.

3 Scrape off the old gasket with a putty knife; then, using a screwdriver, clean gasket residue from the grooves in the pan and from the transmission's gasket surface.

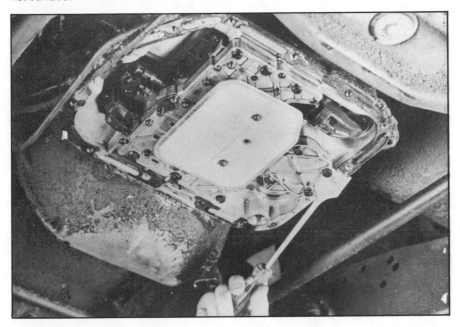

4 Replacing the gasket and pan. Clean the interior and exterior of the pan and the pan cap screws. Coat the pan's gasket surface with a film of non-hardening sealer, then place the gasket on it. Install the drain pan, threading in all cap screws hand tight, and then tightening them evenly with a wrench, working in a criss-cross fashion. To insure even tightening, use a torque wrench and work to specifications, typically ten foot-pounds on most transmissions.

5 Adding transmission fluid. After placing covers on the fenders, remove the transmission dipstick and install a funnel in the filler tube. Add two quarts of the type of automatic transmission fluid recommended in the manual for your car, then start the engine and check the fluid level with the transmission dipstick. Slowly add more fluid until the level is at the "ADD" mark on the dipstick. Allow the engine and transmission to reach operating temperature. While the engine is warming up, visually check the oil pan for leaks. When the engine and transmission are at normal operating temperature, check the fluid level and add fluid only if necessary to bring the level to the "FULL" mark on the dipstick. *Caution: Do not overfill the transmission with oil, since this may cause the oil to foam, damaging the transmission. Before lowering the car make certain the parking brake is set and the transmission is in "Park."*

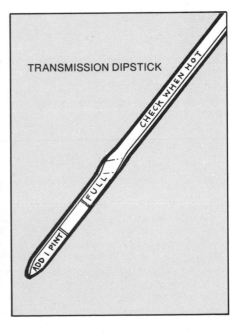

TRANSMISSION DIPSTICK

CHECK WHEN HOT

FULL

ADD 1 PINT

Repacking the front wheel bearings

This job is done while your car is still fully raised.

Tools and equipment:

Large screwdriver.
Lug wrench.
Diagonal pliers.
Water pump pliers.
Hammer.
Hand cloth.
⅛- by 2-inch or 3/16- by 2-inch cotter pin.
Grease seals for your model car.
Wheel bearing grease.
Front wheel grease seal installer.
Torque wrench.
Rubber mallet.

1 Removing the outer bearings. The outer wheel bearing can easily be reached for packing or replacement on wheels with either drum or disk brakes. Remove the two front wheel covers and the front wheel lug nuts or bolts, and store the lugs in the wheel covers. Remove the two front wheels. Grasp the dust cover with water pump pliers in a vertical position and pry it off using an up-and-down motion. Using diagonal pliers, remove the cotter pin and discard it. Using the water pump pliers again, loosen the hexagon nut by turning the pliers counterclockwise until the nut is almost at the end of the spindle. Grasp the brake drum by hand and pull it out toward you, then push the drum back in place. This will loosen the outer bearing from the brake drum hub. Completely remove the hexagon nut and tongue washer. Remove the bearing and place it on a clean surface.

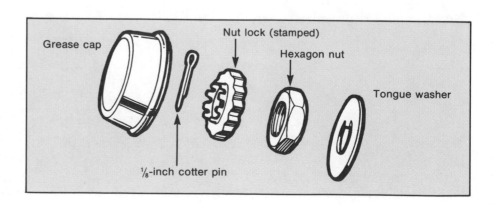

Grease cap   Nut lock (stamped)   Hexagon nut   Tongue washer   ⅛-inch cotter pin

2 Removing the inner bearings. To reach the inner wheel bearings on wheels with disk brakes, it is necessary first to remove the caliper so the rotor can be removed. From that point on, both types can be serviced or replaced following the same procedures.

If the wheel has drum brakes, securely grasp the brake drum with two hands and remove it by pulling it toward you. Place it on a clean surface with the lugs facing up. With a wood dowel, such as an old broomstick cut to about 12 inches long, and a hammer, remove the inner bearing. Put the dowel through the outer bearing opening in the drum and against the inner bearing. Striking the dowel with the hammer will release the inner bearing and the grease seal.

3 Cleaning the parts. Wipe clean both bearings, the inner hub of the brake drum, and the spindle. Hold the inner wheel bearing, the large one, in one hand, with the wider opening facing up.

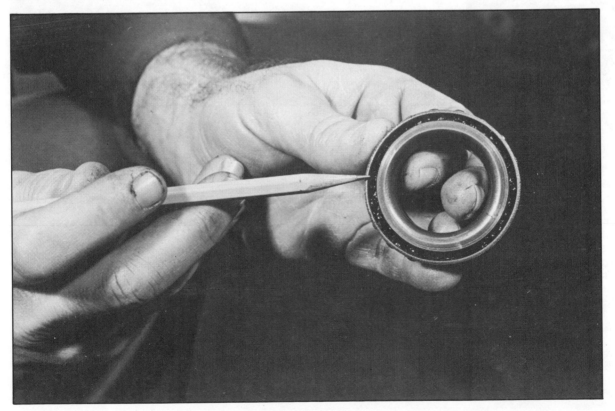

4 **Greasing the bearings.** Place a small amount of wheel bearing grease on the tips of the middle fingers of your other hand. Force the grease through the bearing until it oozes out of the opposite side. Repeat this operation until you have forced grease into the entire bearing by working your way around its circumference. Place the bearing on a clean surface, and repeat the above operation on the outer bearing, the smaller one. Install the inner bearing with the taper facing the inside of the drum.

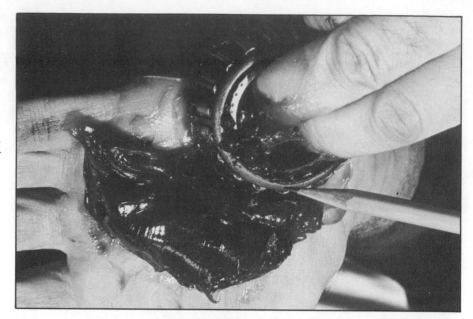

5 **Installing a new grease seal.** The grease seal can be installed in only one way; that is, by use of a front wheel grease seal installer. The wiper edge or lip of the seal must face the bearing. Apply a very small amount of grease to the lip. *Caution: Be sure the inside of the brake drum is free of any grease. Grease in this area will cause a braking problem.*

Grease-seal installer

6 **Replacing the bearings.** Carefully replace the brake drum onto the spindle, making sure it is fully seated against the back of the spindle. Then install the outer bearing, taper facing inward. Replace the tongue washer and hex nut, then seat the bearings by tightening with a torque wrench. Ball bearings should be seated at 25 foot pounds, then backed off and adjusted to 12 foot pounds. Tapered roller bearings should be seated at 15 foot-pounds, then backed off and adjusted to a loose fit, with .001- to .010-inch clearance.

Torque wrench

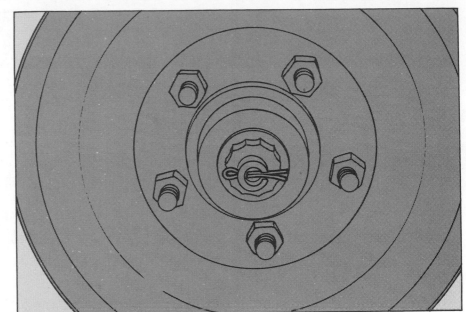

7 Replacing the cotter pin. If a stamped lock nut is used, replace the nut, aligning one opening with the cotter pin hole in the spindle. If a castellated nut is used, and the pin hole is covered, turn the nut counterclockwise until the nearest slot is in line with the hole in the spindle. Then the cotter pin may be installed.

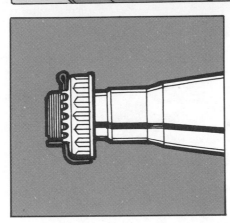

8 Securing the cotter pin. With diagonal pliers, spread the cotter pin ends that protrude down past the nut, pulling one end toward yourself. Cut that end even with the spindle. The second end must be pushed back towards the tongue washer, and cut so that it just touches the washer. Replace the dust cover using a rubber mallet, then replace the tire and wheel assembly. Lower the car.

Under hood and body lubrication

The following lubrications and checks are done with your car on the ground.

Tools and equipment:

Fender covers.
Goggles.
Droplight or flashlight.
Various size combination wrenches.
Common screwdriver.
Funnel.
Oil can.

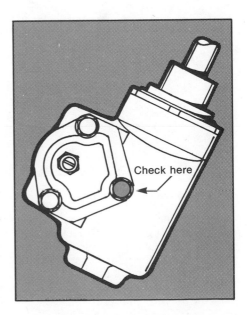

Check here

1 Oil check for conventional steering. On late-model cars the manual steering gearbox is lubed-for-life. However, if seals are leaking, the leak should be repaired and the gearbox filled. Place the fender covers over the fenders. Find the filler plug on top of the steering gearbox and remove it. The oil level should reach the bottom of the threads of the filler hole. If the level is low, refer to the manufacturer's specifications for the correct oil to be used. Fill to proper level and replace the plug.

2 **Oil check for power steering.**
Check the fluid level in the power steering pump only. If low, add enough to achieve the proper level.

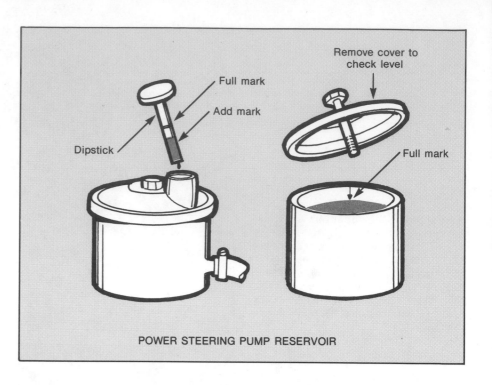

POWER STEERING PUMP RESERVOIR

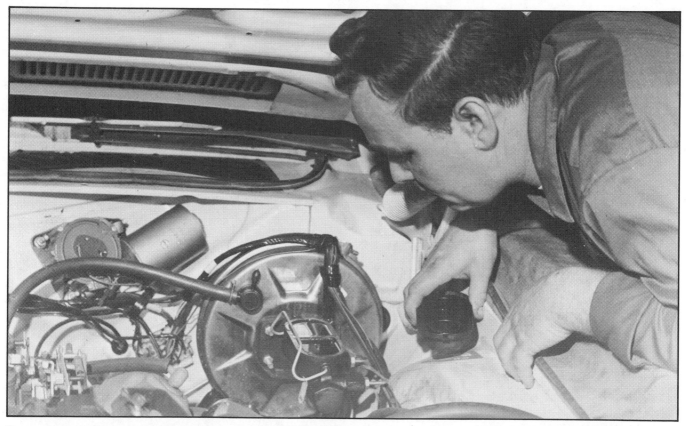

3 **Check the brake fluid** in the master cylinder by removing the cover or filler cap(s). The fluid level should be within ¼-inch of the top of the reservoir. When adding brake fluid, be certain that it meets the manufacturer's specifications. Replace the cover or cap. *Caution: Brake fluid spilled on the auto body will damage the paint.*

In addition to the tasks described above, do not ignore the following:
● Add window washer solvent to the appropriate container.
● Use a stick lubricant on door strikers.
● Lubricate the window channels with an aerosol silicone lube.
● Use a graphite lubricant for the door locks and speedometer cable.
● Grease the hood latch.

Adjusting Drive Belts

The modern car has a number of belt-driven components: the alternator, the water pump and fan, the power steering pump, the air conditioner compressor, and the air pump for the emission control system. Not all cars come equipped with all of the above. It depends on what options the auto has.

A drive belt must be adjusted to the correct tightness. If it's too loose or too tight, you will have problems. Some belts reveal incorrect adjustment by a loud squealing noise. If you hear such a noise coming from the engine compartment when you turn the steering wheel all the way to the right or left, look for a loose power steering belt. A similar noise heard when starting a cold engine or upon sudden acceleration may mean a loose drive belt.

ECONOTIP

#5
Timing the lights

There are many stretches of streets through cities that are wide and uncongested enough to invite higher than normal speeds. But often these streets have a traffic light every few blocks. Just about the time your car gets up to a good, fast cruising speed, you get caught by the next light. With a little practice this can be avoided, especially when you drive the same street regularly. By looking ahead and lowering your speed to reach the light after it has turned green, you will save a lot of gas. And you will arrive at your destination at the same time as the driver who speeds up and has to stop at every light.

Tools and equipment:

Belt tension gauge.
Fender covers.
Goggles.
Combination wrenches.
Socket wrenches (⅜ drive).
Pry bar.
Hand cloth.
Droplight or flashlight.

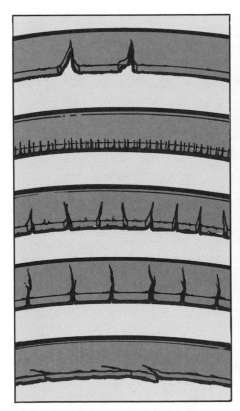

Inspect each belt for cracks, cuts, fraying, or severe glazing of the material.

To check drive belt tension, place the belt tension gauge halfway between the two pulleys of the belt you are adjusting. You will find instructions for the use of it on the gauge itself. The engine must be dead when checking the tension.

Adjusting drive belt tension. Drive belts are usually adjusted by moving the part which is driven by that particular belt. However, the water pump and fan belts are adjusted by moving the alternator. Locate and loosen the lock bolt or nut at least two turns on the part which is to be moved. This bolt or nut is usually found in a slotted bracket. Be extremely careful in positioning a pry bar where there is no special provision for leverage. When adjusting a power steering pump belt, for example, there may be a thick metal boss or ear against which the pry bar can lean. Never lean a bar against the pump reservoir.

When tightening an alternator belt, have a helper hold the alternator out if possible, unless there is a provision for the pry bar. If you must use a bar, do not lean it against the alternator fins.

The idler pulley. On some model cars, belt tension is adjusted by moving an idler pulley. Locate and loosen the pivot bolt or nut one turn on the part that is to be moved.

Tighten the belt to tension specification with the belt tension gauge in place. Hold the part in place when you reach the correct tension, and tighten the lock nut securely. Before tightening the pivot bolt, recheck the tension to be certain that it has not changed, then tighten the pivot bolt securely.

Checking the Battery and Battery Cables

Inspect the battery, cables, and surrounding area for signs of corrosion, loose or broken carriers, cracked or bulged cases, dirt and acid. The battery hold-down bolts should be properly tightened. Particular care should be taken to make sure that the top of the battery is kept clean of acid film and dirt, because they may disrupt current flow between the terminals and slowly discharge the battery.

For best results in cleaning a battery, first wash it with a diluted ammonia or soda solution to neutralize any acid present, and then flush off with clean water. But keep the vent plugs tight so that the neutralizing solution does not enter the cells. After cleaning, apply a coat of petrolatum to the battery hold-down bolts and cable clamps. The hold-down bolts should be kept tight enough to prevent the battery from shaking around in its carrier, but they should not be tightened to the point where the battery case will be placed under severe strain.

To insure good contact, the battery cables should be tight on the battery posts. If the battery posts or cable terminals are corroded, the cables should be removed and cleaned with a soda solution and a wire brush as described further on. *Caution: Remove the negative (−) battery cable first. This will prevent arcing at the terminal. Likewise, replace the positive (+) battery cable first.*

Tools and equipment:

Battery pliers.
Wire brush.
Soft brush.
Baking soda.
Combination wrenches.
Battery cable terminal puller.
Battery post cleaner.
Petroleum jelly.
Cable terminal spreader.
Fender covers.
Goggles.
Wipers.

Pro Shop

Jumper cable hookup

Jumper cables are one of the most frequently used of all automotive accessory tools. Yet it's amazing how many people hook them up wrong and damage vital electrical components such as the battery and alternator.

When hooking up battery jumper cables, always trace the negative battery cable from the battery to its ground. This is the only sure way to determine which is the negative and which is the positive battery terminal. A red cable doesn't always mean positive. Be sure before you hook up the jumpers.

Attach the clamp from the positive post of the good battery to the positive post of the dead battery. Attach the clamp from the negative post of the good battery to a good ground on the engine, away from the dead battery, so that sparks will not ignite battery gases.

If any sparking occurs, remove the booster cables and retrace your battery terminals to determine positive and negative sides.

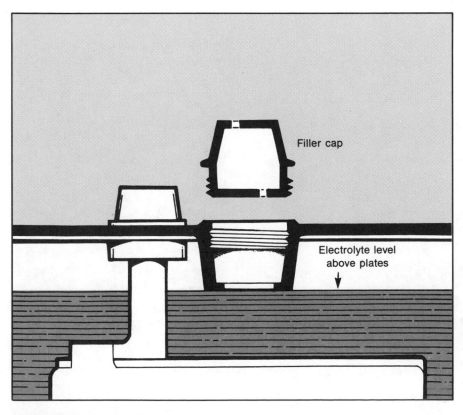

Filler cap

Electrolyte level above plates

Electrolyte level. Unless your battery is one of the new maintenance-free types, check the electrolyte fluid level. If it's too low, fill the battery cells with distilled or demineralized water only to the level of the split-ring located in the filler hole just above the plates.

Removing the battery cables

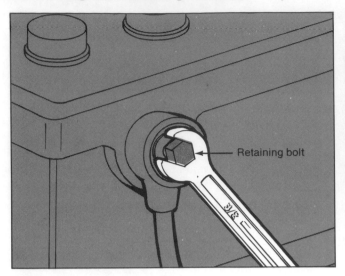

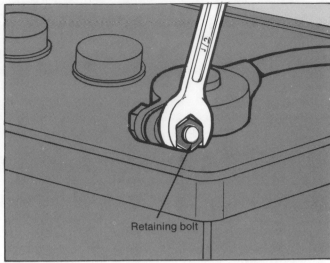

On side terminal batteries, loosen the retaining bolts using a $\frac{3}{8}$-inch wrench and disconnect the cable from the battery.

On all other types of batteries, loosen the cable retaining bolts using a $\frac{1}{2}$-inch or $\frac{9}{16}$-inch box wrench, then lift the cable off the battery posts.

Pro Shop

Side-mounted terminals

For best results, we suggest that you use a wire brush to clean the battery terminals. Remember to first remove the cable from the battery as described above.

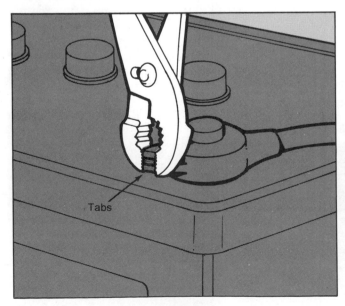

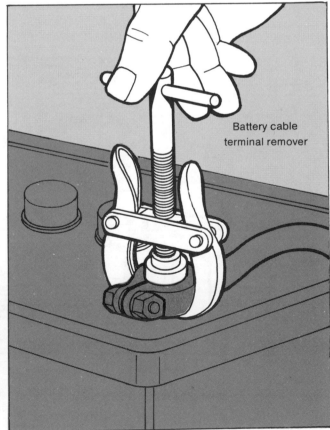

Using pliers, you can remove some cables by squeezing the tabs on the terminal and lifting the cable off the battery posts.

Use a terminal puller if the battery terminals are difficult to remove. Place the legs of the puller underneath the terminal and tighten the puller screw until the terminal is removed.

Cleaning the battery and cables

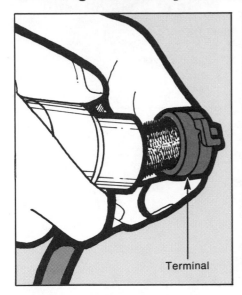

Terminal

Clean the cable terminals and battery posts using a terminal-and-post cleaning tool. Wash the battery top with a soft brush and a solution of water and baking soda. Cover the tops of the battery filler caps with a clean cloth to prevent any washing solution from entering the battery.

Clip-on emergency light

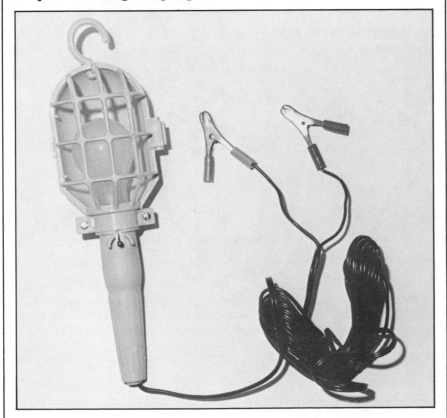

An emergency light that you can hook up to your car's battery might be just what you'll need some dark night. There is also a type, even more convenient when you have to work under the dash, that plugs into the cigarette lighter.

Reinstalling the cables

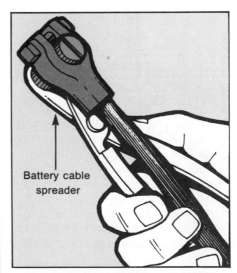

Battery cable spreader

To reinstall the cables on a side-terminal battery, place the cables on the battery and tighten the retaining screws, using a $\frac{3}{8}$-inch wrench. Remember to hook up the positive terminal first. Spread the battery cable terminals with the battery cable terminal spreader. Position the pliers as shown, and tighten the terminal bolts using a $\frac{1}{2}$-inch or $\frac{9}{16}$-inch box wrench. Coat the outside of the terminals with petroleum jelly to prevent corrosion. *Caution: Be very careful while working around the battery. Don't smoke. Avoid sparks and open flames. The electrolyte in the battery expells hydrogen gas, which is explosive. Be careful!*

Cooling System Service

Tools and equipment:

Antifreeze hydrometer.
Hand cloths.
Fender covers.
Droplight or flashlight.
Goggles.

Today's engines develop a tremendous amount of heat for the cooling system to dissipate, so this system should be given a quick inspection whenever you work under the hood.

Look for leaks around all hose connections, the water pump pulley, the radiator, and the thermostat housing. See Chapter 1. In addition, look for hose dry rot, cracks on the surface, or excessive swelling or hardening of the hoses. Also inspect the condition of the fan belts. Accumulations of bugs, leaves, and road film should be cleaned from the radiator fins, using a brush, household detergent, and a water hose. On cars with air conditioning, the finned condenser sits in front of the radiator, and its surface is the one that becomes blocked. Cleaning it is important because anything that blocks the flow of air through the condenser can cause overheating.

Antifreeze used in the cooling system year-round not only prevents winter freeze-ups, but also raises the boiling point of the water to prevent boiling over in summer.

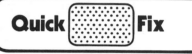

Quick 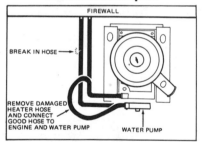 **Fix**

Heater hose repair

FIREWALL

BREAK IN HOSE →

REMOVE DAMAGED HEATER HOSE AND CONNECT GOOD HOSE TO ENGINE AND WATER PUMP

WATER PUMP

A damaged heater hose can put your car out of commission. This can be especially troublesome when you are on the road and away from any repair facility. A very easy method of temporarily correcting the problem and allowing you to safely drive the car to a repair facility is to bypass the heater completely.

Remove the damaged heater hose from both the heater core at the firewall and the water pump or engine, depending on which hose has broken. Then remove the undamaged hose from the heater core at the firewall and reroute the hose back into the engine. Thus, you'll have the one hose running from the engine to the water pump. You won't have a heater but you will be able to get to the nearest repair shop.

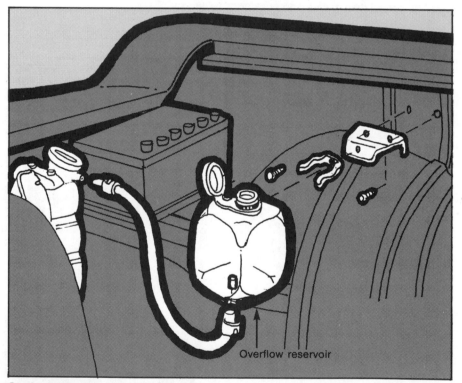

Overflow reservoir

Coolant recovery system. If your car is equipped with a coolant recovery system, do not remove the radiator cap. Coolant level is checked in the recovery overflow reservoir. If coolant level is not at manufacturer's specifications, use antifreeze to bring it to the proper level.

Pressure cap. If the radiator has a lever-type cap or a push-button type cap, release the pressure by lifting the lever or pushing the button down and then turning the cap counterclockwise. *Caution: The radiator cap should never be removed unless the pressure in the radiator is released.* Be sure to hold the cap with a hand cloth.

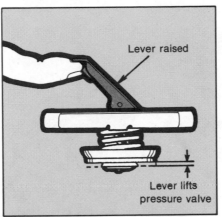

Lever raised

Lever lifts pressure valve

Push button

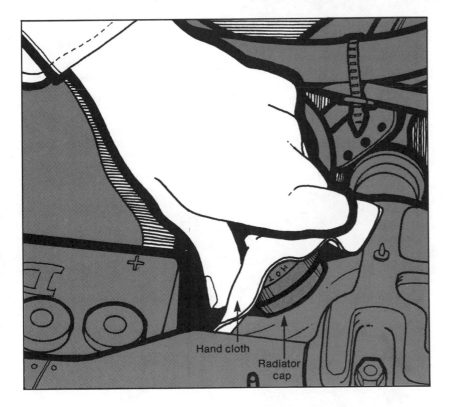

Hand cloth

Radiator cap

Quick Fix

Emergency radiator sealing

If your radiator develops a leak, it's best not to drive the car too far or engine damage will result from overheating. Try to get to a service station or repair shop. If one is not readily available, try to locate an automotive parts supply store where radiator sealant should be on sale. If this fails too, loosen the radiator cap to the first notch to relieve the pressure. This will reduce the leakage and may allow you to get to a repair place. There are any number of emergency concoctions that can be put in a radiator to stop leaks. Oatmeal, flaxseed, cornmeal, bran, and many other things that can be purchased at the grocery store have all been recommended over the years. They might work, but they might also plug up the heater, so beware.

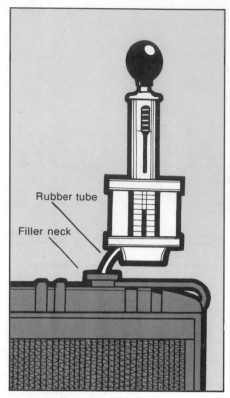

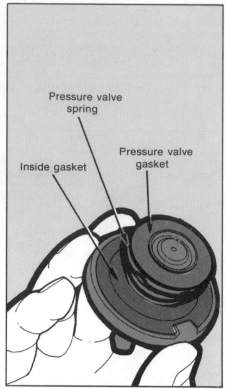

Pressure valve
spring

Pressure valve
gasket

Inside gasket

Rubber tube

Filler neck

Testing the antifreeze. Insert the rubber tube of the antifreeze hydrometer into the radiator neck and draw up a sample of coolant. There are several different types of hydrometers which work somewhat differently so follow the instructions for use printed on the tool. Add antifreeze only if the level is insufficient.

Before replacing the radiator cap, visually check the pressure valve gasket, inside gasket, and condition of pressure valve spring for rust or damage. Replace the cap securely.

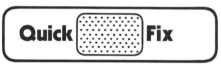

Damaged radiator

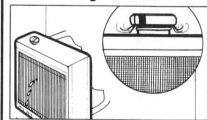

If your radiator develops minor leaks, there's always the possibility of engine damage due to overheating if the car is driven any length of time in a damaged condition. The overheating is caused by loss of coolant. The car can usually be safely driven to the nearest repair facility if the pressure cap on the radiator is not fully tightened. By not tightening the cap fully, the cooling system will not pressurize and the coolant will not be forced through the holes in the radiator.

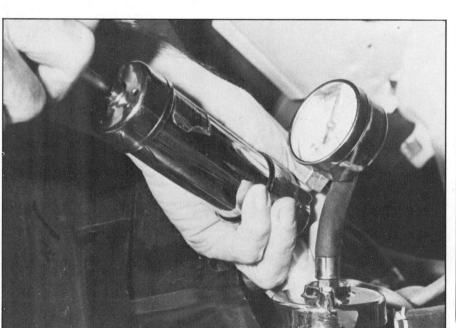

Use the radiator pressure tester to find out if there are leaks in the cooling system. If you can't afford to purchase this device, see if you can't find one at a tool rental shop.

CONTENTS

ENGINE TUNE-UP

An engine tune-up is a series of procedures that restore optimum engine performance, reduce exhaust emissions, increase fuel mileage, and prolong the useful life of the engine. It can save you a long walk home or an expensive tow job.

Since an engine tune-up is one of the most important elements of proper car care, it should be performed at regular intervals rather than after a failure occurs. If you are an average driver, every 10,000 miles is a good rule-of-thumb schedule for periodic engine tune-ups. If your car is used less frequently, 4,000–5,000 miles a year, then you must use a different schedule for tune-ups—one based on time rather than miles. In this case, a tune-up once a year will keep your car running at peak efficiency. If you put extremely high mileage on your car—40,000 or 50,000 miles a year—your tune-up schedule should be every 15,000 miles or so.

Different driving conditions will also call for different servicing schedules. For instance, excessive driving in dusty conditions will call for more frequent periodic service, as will excessive stop-and-go driving. Long trips and highway miles are easier on a car and will require less frequent tune-ups.

If one of the following warning signs is present, your engine probably needs a tune-up: 1. Engine performance is noticeably sluggish. 2. The engine consistently stalls. 3. The engine is hard to start. 4. The engine misfires. 5. Engine hesitation or surge is noticeable, especially in high gear at highway speeds.

Before beginning any tune-up, it is recommended that you carefully read through the instructions and study the diagrams in this chapter at least once and preferably twice to get an overview of what you will be doing and what you can expect next as you proceed from step to step. And since on most modern cars the emission control system is directly related to the engine tune-up, you should read the chapter on emission control before attempting to tune up your engine.

Also, be sure to read the paragraphs on parts and equipment before beginning. Have the right tools, equipment, and parts on hand before you begin. There is nothing more frustrating than beginning a job and then finding out that you do not have everything you need.

Engine tune-up steps

Before getting into any of the specific operations, it will be helpful for you to know all the steps involved in a complete basic engine tune-up. The following list is just that—a list. No explanatory steps are included here because each will be thoroughly described in detail on subsequent pages of this chapter, as indicated. Carry out the first eight steps in the order indicated. The order of the remaining operations may be varied.

Note: Before you begin any tune-up, you must determine whether your car's engine is equipped with a conventional or an electronic ignition system. The major difference is that the electronic ignition system does not include points or a condenser. Therefore, if your car has this system, you will exclude the steps for adjusting point gap, or dwell. All the other service procedures should be followed.

A basic engine tune-up consists of the following steps:

1. Remove the spark plugs.
2. Perform a compression test.
3. Service the spark plugs.
4. Replace the distributor cap and rotor.
5. Service the distributor.
6. Check the ignition wires with an ohmmeter.
7. Replace the ignition points and condenser.
8. Service the battery and battery cables (see Chapter 3 for detailed instructions).
9. Service the carburetor, choke, and linkages.
10. Replace the fuel filter.
11. Replace the air filter and crankcase filter.
12. Service the emission controls, manifold heat control valve, positive crankcase ventilation (PCV) valve, and exhaust gas recirculation (EGR) valve.
13. Check all the vacuum lines and hoses.

Safety precautions

Before starting the tune-up, be sure to observe the following precautions, both for your own safety and that of your vehicle:
1. Park your car on level ground.
2. Place the shift lever in the Park position on automatic transmission-equipped vehicles, or in Neutral for manual shift cars.
3. Apply the parking brake.
Caution: When doing a tune-up, never run your engine in an enclosed, poorly ventilated area, because of the danger of carbon monoxide fumes.

Tools and equipment:

1. Droplight.
2. Screwdriver set, 4-inch, 8-inch, and 12-inch.
3. Pliers.
4. Spark plug socket and ratchet, with $\frac{3}{8}$-inch drive and 1-inch, 3-inch, and 6-inch extensions.
5. Compression testing gauge.
6. Remote starter switch.
7. Feeler gauges—flat type for ignition point gap settings, wire type for spark plug gap.
8. Allen wrench set.
9. Distributor wrench or appropriate socket with long extension and swivel joint.
10. Ignition wrench.
11. Torque wrench.
12. Tach-dwell meter.
13. Ohmmeter and voltmeter.
14. Timing light.
15. Hand cloths.
16. Fender covers.
17. Breaker cam lube.
18. Combination wrenches.
19. Goggles.
20. Hand vacuum pump.
21. Length of $\frac{1}{4}$-inch hose.
22. 14-inch jumper wire with alligator clips.
23. Masking tape.
24. Spark plug wire remover.
25. Hand oil squirt can.
26. Wire hand brush.
27. Piece of chalk or scribe.

Parts you may need:

To make certain you get the right parts for your particular engine, consult your owner's manual, or the manufacturer's information plate or decal located under the hood or on the firewall. Your neighborhood auto parts supply store can also usually help you.

You will need the following parts to tune up your car:
1. Spark plugs.
2. Ignition breaker point assembly.
3. Condenser.
4. Fuel filter.
5. Air filter.
6. Positive crankcase ventilation (PCV) valve.
7. Crankcase filter (if required).
8. Distributor cap and rotor (if required).
9. Ignition wires (if worn).
10. Fuel vapor canister or canister filter (if worn).

Testing the Compression

An engine compression test enables you to determine the condition of the internal parts—the valves sealing, the piston rings sealing, and the compression chamber sealing. Unless engine compression readings are within the manufacturer's specifications, engine performance cannot be improved. If the fuel-and-air mixture is not compressed in the cylinder to the manufacturer's specification, the burning may not produce all the power the engine was designed to produce.

Before removing the spark plugs, check the battery voltage (see Chapter 7). Check the engine oil level to insure proper engine lubrication as shown in Chapter 3. Start the engine, allow it to reach normal operating temperature, and switch it off. Then remove the air cleaner assembly and identify the vacuum hoses which are attached to the air cleaner. Mark these with masking tape, using your own code, before disconnecting them.

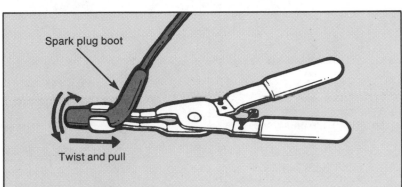
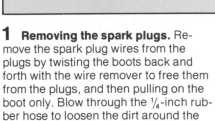

Spark plug boot

Twist and pull

1 Removing the spark plugs. Remove the spark plug wires from the plugs by twisting the boots back and forth with the wire remover to free them from the plugs, and then pulling on the boot only. Blow through the ¼-inch rubber hose to loosen the dirt around the base of the plugs, then take out all plugs.

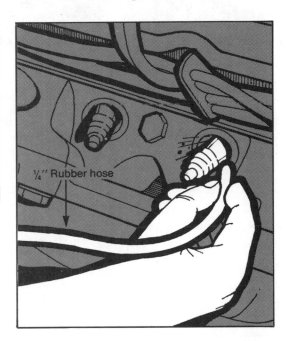

¼″ Rubber hose

ECONOTIP

#6
Will tampering give better mileage?

Tampering refers to changing the design of or adjustments on an engine. It includes removal of emission control devices, blocking of hoses, disconnecting wires or adjusting timing and mixture controls outside of factory specifications. Tampering is against federal law for any commercial auto repair establishment. It is not against the law for an individual car owner to tamper with his car, however.

The Environmental Protection Agency did a study of tampering and its effect on gas mileage. The study was done on a very small number of cars, but it showed that the average gas mileage after tampering was 3½ percent worse. However, one car showed a 9.9 percent improvement after tampering. All the cars were then taken to the EPA technicians for scientific tampering. The result was an average 7 percent improvement.

The answer about tampering is that an automotive engineer can do it and improve gas mileage. A repair shop can do it successfully only a small percentage of the time. So the chances that a do-it-yourselfer can improve mileage by tampering are not good. Instead, it will probably make the mileage worse.

Pro Shop

Spark plug holder

If the spark plugs are to be re-used, they should be stored in a safe place to prevent damage to the porcelain. We put them in an egg carton, a drilled block of wood, or push them into a piece of heavy cardboard.

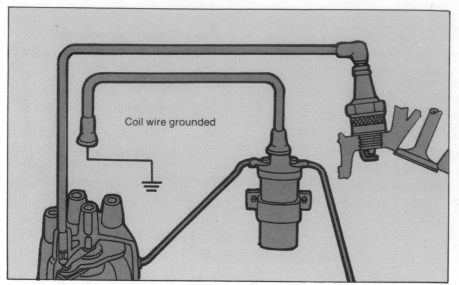

Coil wire grounded

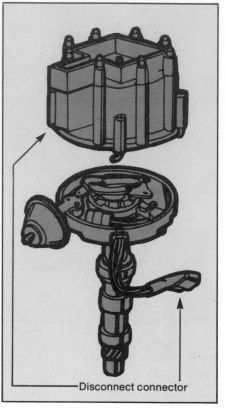

Disconnect connector

2 **Grounding the system.** Before you take out the spark plugs, remove the high voltage wire from the center of the distributor cap. Attach one end of the jumper wire to the metal terminal of the high voltage wire, and the other end to a convenient bolt or nut or metal engine part. This will ground the ignition system and prevent damage to it. Note: if your car is equpped with the General Motors HEI electronic ignition system, disconnect the electrical connector by pulling it out of the distributor cap. This will prevent the ignition system from operating. Open the carburetor throttle and choke plates.

3 **Disconnecting the primary distributor lead.** Disconnect the thin electrical wire connecting the distributor to the ignition coil from the negative post of the coil.

Pro Shop

Holding the throttle open

We suggest that you cut a piece of wood long enough to be wedged between the front seat and the gas pedal. This will hold the throttle plate open.

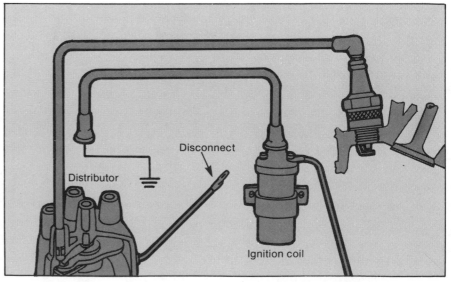

Distributor

Disconnect

Ignition coil

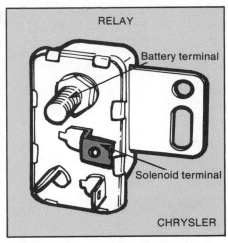

RELAY

Battery terminal

Solenoid terminal

CHRYSLER

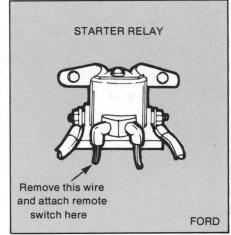

STARTER RELAY

Remove this wire
and attach remote
switch here

FORD

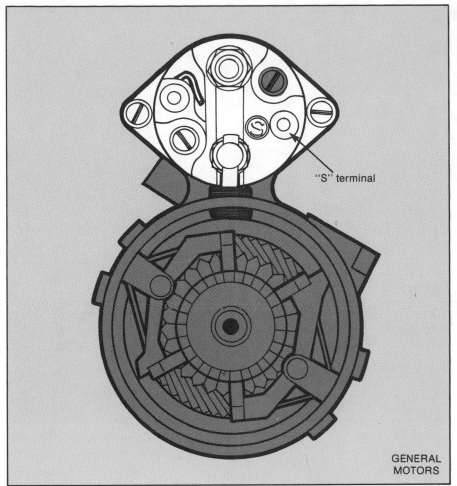

"S" terminal

GENERAL
MOTORS

4 **Connecting the remote control starter switch.** Connect the end terminal of the remote control starter switch to the positive terminal of the battery. Connect the second wire of the switch as follows: (a) On General Motors and American Motors cars, connect to the "S" terminal of the starter solenoid mounted on the starter. (b) On Chrysler Corporation cars, connect to the starter terminal on the relay mounted on the firewall or fender pan. (c) On Ford cars, disconnect the neutral safety switch wire at the starter relay, and connect the remote starter to this terminal.

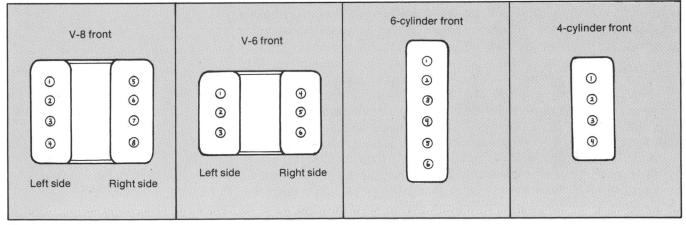

V-8 front

Left side   Right side

① ⑤
② ⑥
③ ⑦
④ ⑧

V-6 front

Left side   Right side

① ④
② ⑤
③ ⑥

6-cylinder front

①
②
③
④
⑤
⑥

4-cylinder front

①
②
③
④

5 **Taking the readings.** Have a pencil and pad for recorded compression readings. Draw a chart of the engine's cylinder sequence. Turn the ignition switch to the "on" position. *Caution: Failure to do this will result in a damaged grounding circuit on the switch.* Insert the compression gauge into one of the spark plug ports. With the help of an assistant, crank the engine with the ignition key until the needle on the compression gauge reaches its highest point, no less than four revolutions of the engine. Record the reading of this cylinder on your chart. Repeat this reading and recording for all of the cylinders.

Types of compression gauges. There are two types of compression gauges in general use, the more common push-in type, and the screw-in type. In most cases, the simpler push-in type works fine. But for difficult-to-reach spark plug port locations, a screw-in universal compression gauge should be used. It has a flexible hose and adapter which threads into the spark plug port. The screw-in type gauge allows you to take a reading without physically having to hold the gauge in place, which is not the case with the push-in type.

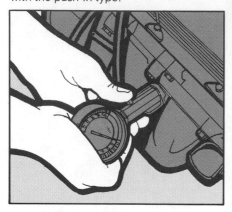

Interpreting the compression test

Compare your compression readings with the manufacturer's specifications in the back of this book. The readings should be within the tolerances allowed by each manufacturer. For example, Chrysler Corporation states that the variation in compression must be within 40 pounds per square inch (psi), and Ford says that the variation for all cylinders must be within 75%. Others indicate that the variation must not exceed 20 psi of the specifications. If the engine compression readings are uniform, and lower than the manufacturer's specifications but no lower than 100 psi for each cylinder, the engine is considered tuneable.

If the compression readings are low or uneven in any of the cylinders, add several squirts of engine oil through the spark plug openings of the affected cylinders and re-check the compression. If it im-

proves, the piston rings are probably worn. If the compression does not improve, the valves are probably sticking, seating poorly, or are burned. If the compression is low in two adjacent cylinders, the cylinder head gasket between these cylinders is probably damaged.

Excessive compression readings usually indicate a build-up of carbon deposits in the combustion chamber of the cylinder. If your engine shows low compression, less than 100 psi, uneven compression readings, or abnormally high compression readings, internal engine repair work is probably necessary and there is no point in proceeding with a tune-up.

When you have finished testing the compression, shut off the ignition switch and remove the block of wood holding the gas pedal open.

Spark Plugs and Wires

Spark plug cleaning and replacement

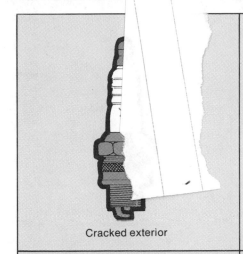

Cracked exterior

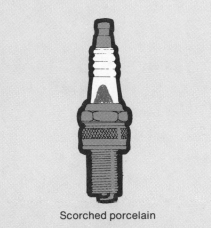

Scorched porcelain

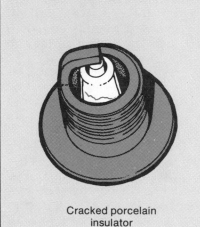

Cracked porcelain insulator

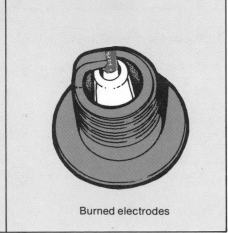

Burned electrodes

3 **Adjust the air gap.** Clean the electrode area with an emery cloth. If you use a wire hand brush or a grinder with a wire wheel, the metal bristles may come loose and if they get stuck in the plug they could short it. Wipe the porcelain with a clean rag. Adjust the air gap between the two electrodes by bending the side electrode with the spark plug adjusting tool. Insert the correct size wire feeler gauge according to the manufacturer's specifications—.030, .035, or .040 inch, for example. If you are installing new plugs, they must also be gapped.

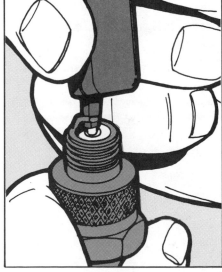

1 **Inspect the spark plugs** before cleaning, regapping, and reinstalling them. Look for:
- Cracked porcelain exterior.
- Cracked porcelain insulator.
- Scorched porcelain.
- Burned electrodes.

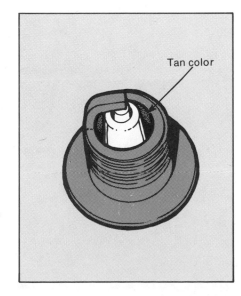

Tan color

2 **Check the color of the electrode end** of the plug. This area should be tan in color, like the color of a piece of medium-toasted bread. If the spark plugs are not tan, they should be discarded, and new ones purchased, according to the manufacturer's specifications.

ECONOTIP

#7
Missing plugs cost money

A driver who is sensitive to how his car runs can feel the uneven beat of a spark plug that is misfiring. It is probably easiest to feel at idle, but during acceleration and cruising it also can be very noticeable. The problem is that after the driver gets used to the missing, he ignores it. And this lowers mileage. One plug misfiring only half the time at 60 miles per hour can cost about 1.2 miles per gallon.

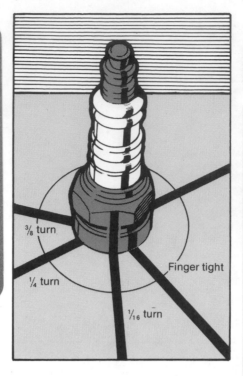

¾ turn

¼ turn

Finger tight

1/16 turn

4 **Replace the spark plugs.** Install the plugs by hand, being careful not to cross-thread them in their ports. If possible, tighten the spark plugs with a torque wrench. A good torque reading is 15 to 20 foot pounds. If you don't have a torque wrench, tighten the spark plug ¼ of a turn after it is seated in its port. A tapered spark plug is tightened 1/16 of a turn after it has been seated.

Servicing spark plug wires

Check spark plug wires for continuity, ability to conduct electricity, and resistance value—their opposition to the flow of electricity.

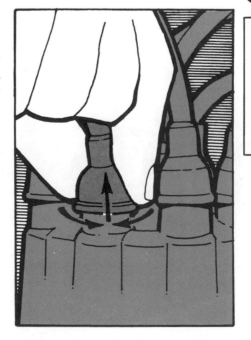

1 **Remove the spark plug wires** one at a time from the distributor cap by twisting and pulling the boots.

Pro Shop

Adapter for box wrench

No mechanic ever has enough special wrenches to handle every job that shows up. It's easy to make one or more adapters permitting two box wrenches to be used in combination on special jobs. The combination gives greater leverage and doubles the number of angles at which the box wrench can be used.

To make the adapter, use a short, heat-treated cap screw having the same head size as the box wrench opening. Install a flat washer on the cap screw and then a nut. Tighten the nut securely against the flat washer and head of the cap screw. Cut off the exposed threads and then rivet or weld the nut to the cap screw.

The head end of the adapter is placed in the end of one box wrench and a second box wrench is placed on the nut end. The flat washer keeps the adapter from falling through. Using two box wrenches doubles the leverage. With two 12-point box wrenches, 24 handle positions are available. It's a good idea to keep an assortment of sizes of cap screws and nuts already made up.

Arranging wires

Be sure the new wires are not resting on any moving parts or on any hot engine parts. If the wires were in a clip or a harness, put the new wires back in the same way.

2 **Check the condition of the distributor cap tower** for cracks or corrosion.

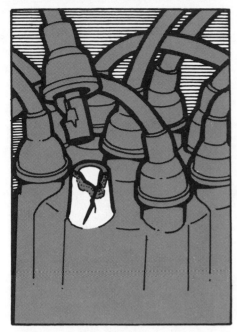

3 **Read the ohmmeter.** Following ohmmeter instructions, connect one lead from the ohmmeter to one end terminal of the wire, and the second lead of the ohmmeter to the other end terminal of the wire. Check the ohmmeter reading. A good rule of thumb is 1000 ohms per inch of wire. For example, a 12-inch wire should not exceed 12,000 ohms. Repeat this procedure with the remaining wires.

Check the spark plug wires for cracks, dry rot, oil-soaked or burned insulation, or corrosion on the terminals. Replace any wires that are not within an acceptable resistance reading or that show signs of wear, and match the new wire's length to that of the old one.

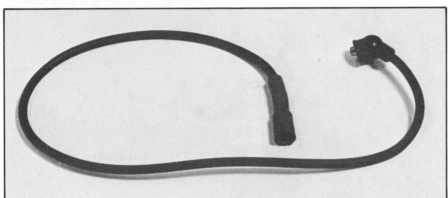

Pro Shop

Ohmmeter testing

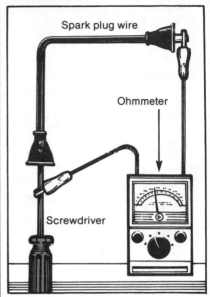

To make contact with the spark plug end of the wire, we insert a screwdriver through the boot and attach the wire to the ohmmeter lead.

Recommended installation torque

Spark plug	Cast iron heads		Aluminum heads	
Thread size	W/torque wrench	W/o torque wrench	W/torque wrench	W/o torque wrench
Gasket type		after seating		after seating
10mm	8–12 ft. lb.	¼ turn	8–12 ft. lb.	¼ turn
12mm	10–18 ft. lb.	¼ turn	10–18 ft. lb.	¼ turn
14mm	26–30 ft. lb.	¼ to ⅜ turn	18–22 ft. lb.	¼ turn
18mm	32–38 ft. lb.	¼ turn	28–34 ft. lb.	¼ turn
Tapered seat				
14mm	7–15 ft. lb.	1/16 turn (snug)	7–15 ft. lb.	1/16 turn (snug)
18mm	15–20 ft. lb.	1/16 turn (snug)	15–20 ft. lb.	1/16 turn (snug)

Distributor Cap and Rotor

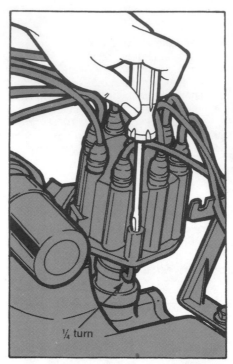

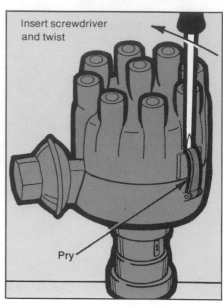

Insert screwdriver and twist

Pry

1 **Remove the distributor cap** with a screwdriver, leaving the spark plug wires connected to the cap. On General Motors and American Motors, V-6 and V-8 engines, the distributor cap is removed by pressing down on the spring-loaded cap screws and turning them ¼ turn in either direction. In order to remove the distributor cap on General Motors in-line 4- and 6-cylinder engines and on some American Motors engines, the two cap screws must be removed. All other manufacturers use two side clips attached to the distributor to hold the cap in place. Pry off the clips with a screwdriver and remove the cap.

¼ turn

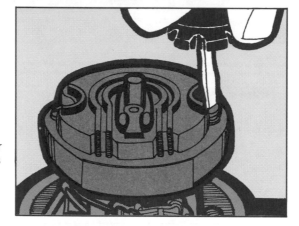

2 **Remove the rotor.** The rotor is either attached to the distributor by two screws or it is pressed in place.

3 **Install the new rotor.** The rotor on the General Motors V-8 engine has a round and a square aligning dowel protruding from the bottom. The press-on-

type rotor has a flat side or a key which aligns with the flat side or the keyway of the distributor shaft.

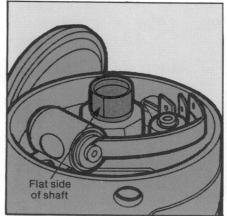

Flat side of shaft

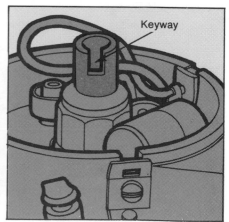

Keyway

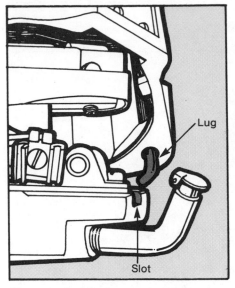

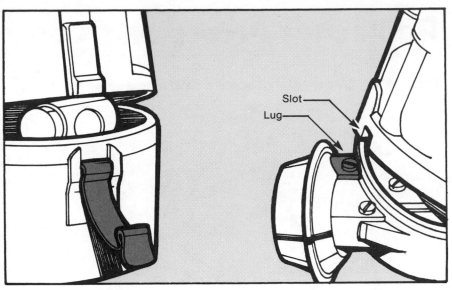

4 **Install the new distributor cap,** which is keyed to the body of the distributor, by locating lugs molded into the cap. These lugs match slots in the distributor body.

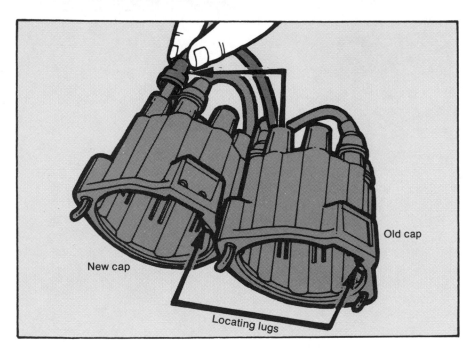

5 **Transfer the spark plug wires** from the old cap to the new one. First, align the old cap against the new one with the locating-lugs or slots. Identify a starting point, such as the first tower to the right of the screw or clamp. Then remove one wire at a time from the old cap and install it in the same tower of the new cap. Finally, insert the high-voltage coil wire into the center tower.

Pro Shop

Check out your work

At this point, replace the air cleaner and start the engine. If you have properly followed the above procedures for spark plugs and wires, distributor cap, and rotor replacement, the engine should start and run reasonably well. If it does not, the difficulty may be one of the following:
• An improperly installed distributor cap.
• One or more incorrectly attached spark plug wires.
• One or more spark plug wires installed in the wrong distributor cap tower.

Replacing Points and Condenser

Removing the ignition points and condenser

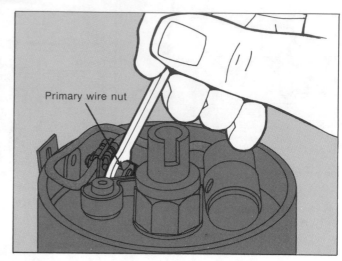

1 **Disconnect the ignition coil.** Make sure the ignition key is in the "off" position, then remove the air cleaner and the distributor cap and rotor. Disconnect the ignition coil primary wire which is attached to the ignition point spring with a screw. Note: Some General Motors distributor points do not use a screw to connect the wire to the spring. The point spring holds the wire in place. Remove it by exerting pressure on the spring and pulling up on the wire.

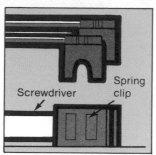

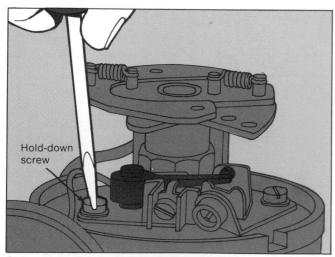

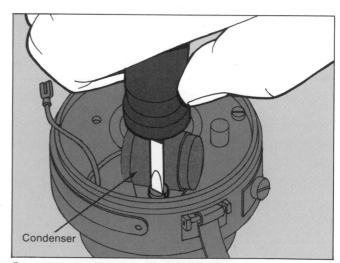

2 **Locate each ignition point screw.** Remove the screw, being careful not to drop it into the distributor body. Some distributors have a ground wire attached to one of the screws.

3 **Locate the condenser screw holding down the condenser.** Using a magnetic screwdriver, remove the screw, being careful not to drop it into the distributor body. Remove the points and condenser from the distributor.

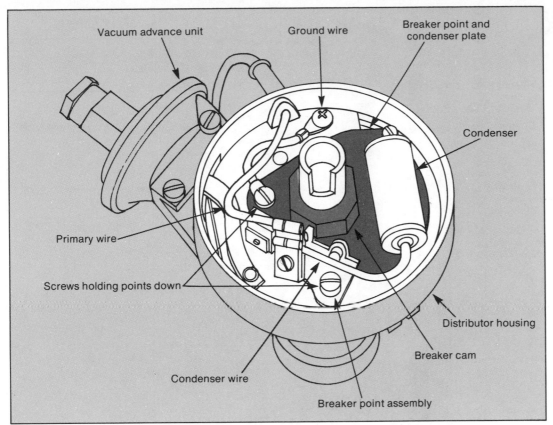

Vacuum advance unit

Ground wire

Breaker point and
condenser plate

Condenser

Primary wire

Screws holding points down

Distributor housing

Breaker cam

Condenser wire

Breaker point assembly

4 Clean and lubricate the breaker cam. Wipe the breaker cam and breaker plate clean with a cloth. The breaker cam must be lubricated with a special cam lubricant, available at your local auto parts store. Use only this type of lubricant, because other lubricants could interfere with the operation of the points. Use a very small amount of lube, about the size of a wooden match head, to coat the breaker cam. Install the new points and condenser by simply reversing the procedures for removal. If the distributor is equipped with a ground wire, be sure to attach it under the head of the screw. Do not place it between the breaker plate and the points.

Before installing a new ignition point set, make sure the points are in proper alignment with each other. This can be accomplished by carefully bending the point brace with needle-nose pliers.

Bend only the stationary point. Do not attempt to bend the movable point or its arm. Some stationary points are of such heavy metal that pliers will not bend them. A point bending tool is made for this purpose.

If the ignition breaker points are in proper alignment, thousands of extra miles can be added to their useful life.

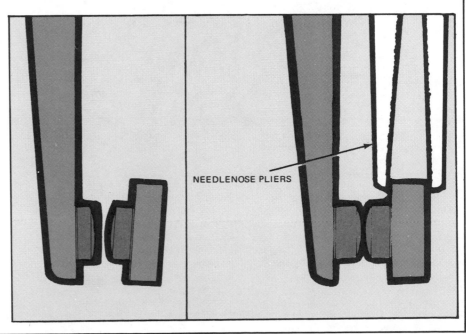

NEEDLENOSE PLIERS

Adjusting point gap with a feeler gauge

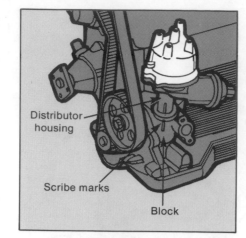

Distributor housing

Scribe marks

Block

Pro Shop

Magic touch

The drag on the feeler gauge should feel the same as it would if you pulled a piece of paper out of the center of this book when closed. Try it!

1 To insure correct realignment, mark a spot with chalk on the distributor body and mark the place it touches on the engine block.

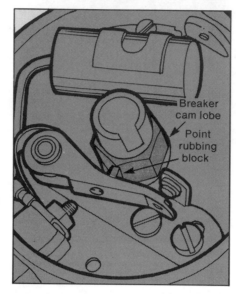

Breaker cam lobe

Point rubbing block

2 Aligning the breaker cam and rubbing block. Loosen the bolt holding down the distributor with the correct size wrench. Turn the distributor housing either to the right or left until the nearest lobe on the breaker cam is in direct contact with the point's rubbing block. This will allow you to use both hands to adjust the points.

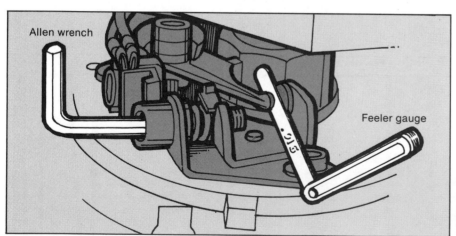

Allen wrench

Feeler gauge

3 Using a feeler gauge. Select the correct size flat feeler gauge according to the manufacturer's specifications, for example, .016. Wipe it clean. Loosen up the point lock screw just enough to permit point adjustment, then adjust the point opening by turning an Allen wrench or moving the points with a common screwdriver inserted in the slot. This operation will depend on the type of points used in your distributor. Insert the feeler gauge between the points, and adjust the point gap until the gauge has a slight drag when it is pulled out or pushed in between the points. Tighten the locking screw and recheck the adjustment. Loosen the distributor bolt and turn the distributor back to its original position by aligning the scribe marks. Install the distributor rotor and cap, and the air cleaner, then start the engine.

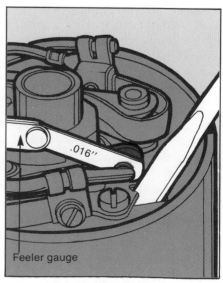

Feeler gauge

Adjusting ignition points

Using a tach-dwell meter is a more accurate method of adjusting the points than using a feeler gauge. Calibrate the dwell meter according to the manufacturer's instructions, and check specifications for the correct dwell for your car. Note: Your car should be in "Park" or "Neutral," with the parking brake set. Be sure the rotor is not installed.

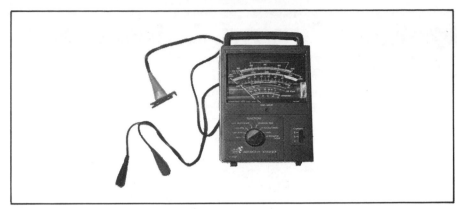

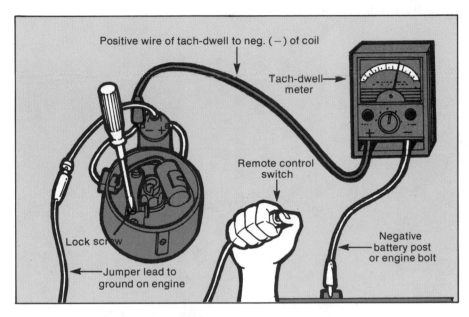

Positive wire of tach-dwell to neg. (−) of coil

Tach-dwell meter

Remote control switch

Lock screw

Jumper lead to ground on engine

Negative battery post or engine bolt

Connect the positive lead of the dwell meter to the negative terminal of the ignition coil on the distributor side. Connect the negative lead of the dwell meter to the negative post of the battery for a good engine ground, then connect the remote starter switch. Remove and ground the distributor high-voltage wire from the center tower of the distributor cap. Turn the ignition key on. Loosen the lock screw just enough to allow for adjustment.

Crank the engine with the remote starter switch. While the engine is cranking, observe the dwell meter and adjust the ignition points and dwell to the correct dwell reading with a screwdriver or Allen wrench. We recommend that this operation be done as quickly as possible to avoid overheating the starter motor or draining the battery voltage. Release the remote control switch, tighten the ignition point locking screw, and recheck

the dwell setting by cranking the engine once again. On some engines, the running dwell will be different from the cranking dwell. If necessary, adjust the cranking dwell to make the running dwell agree with specifications.

Pro Shop

External adjustment

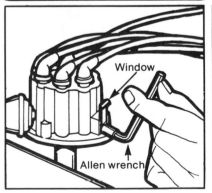

Window

Allen wrench

On General Motors V-8 engines, ignition points or dwell can be adjusted with the engine running, by turning the adjustment screw through a window with an Allen wrench.

Ignition Timing Adjustment

Ignition timing involves adjusting the precise firing of the spark plug in relation to the position of the piston, according to the manufacturer's specifications. The firing of the spark plug in the cylinder usually occurs just at the end of the compression stroke, or just at the beginning of the power stroke. See Chapter 1 for a description of the engine stroke cycle. Ignition timing is changed by slightly turning the entire distributor assembly clockwise or counterclockwise while the engine is running.

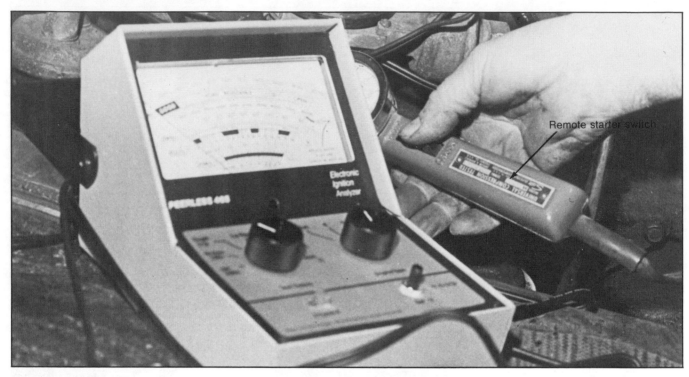

Remote starter switch

1 Connecting a tach-dwell meter. Install the distributor rotor and cap, then connect the high-voltage wire from the coil to the distributor. Connect a tach-dwell meter and a remote control starter switch as described in this chapter.

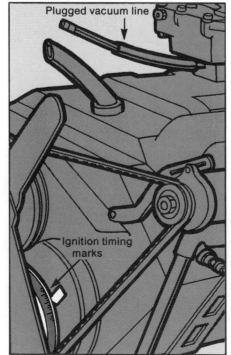

Plugged vacuum line

Ignition timing marks

2 Locating the timing marks. Crank the engine with the remote control starter switch to locate the ignition timing marks. These are usually stamped into the crankshaft pulley and onto the timing case cover at the front of the engine. Wipe them clean with a cloth.

Pro Shop

Lighten the timing marks

We use a piece of white chalk to lighten the stamped ignition timing marks. This will help you to see these marks clearly when the timing light hits them.

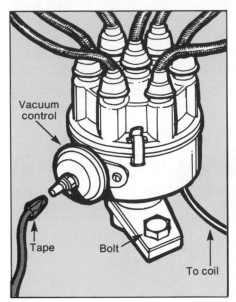

Vacuum control

Tape

Bolt

To coil

3 **Plugging the vacuum lines.** Disconnect and plug the end of the rubber vacuum line from the vacuum advance unit that is mounted on the side of the distributor. Also, plug all open vacuum lines or ports that were disconnected when the air cleaner was removed.

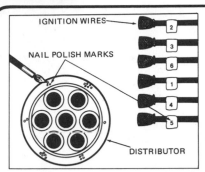

Pro Shop

Replacing distributor cap

IGNITION WIRES

NAIL POLISH MARKS

DISTRIBUTOR

2
3
6
1
4
5

If you have to replace the distributor cap, the best way to do it is to disconnect the cap from the distributor, then remove the wires one at a time from the old cap and insert them into the new one. Use a distributor attaching clip point or window in the distributor as a reference point.

Another good method of avoiding confusion when replacing a distributor cap is to use white nail polish to mark the cap and corresponding ignition wire. Put one dot for plug number one, two dots for plug number two, and so forth.

4 **Connecting the timing light.** Disconnect the remote control starter switch and reconnect any wires that you unhooked in order to use it. Connect the ignition timing light in the following way: Attach the positive lead, the red clip, of the timing light to the positive post of the battery. Attach the negative lead, the black clip, of the light to the negative battery post. Then attach the remaining lead of the timing light, the thicker wire, to the number one spark plug wire at the distributor cap tower. Check the manufacturer's specifications to locate this wire. Remove the wire at the distributor cap tower by twisting and pulling upward, being careful not to cause the cap to cock to one side. Now insert the spark plug wire adapter into the tower and connect the spark plug wire and timing light lead to the adapter.

Caution: Be sure that all the wires from the timing light are clear of all moving engine components and that the wires are not resting on hot areas, such as the exhaust manifolds.

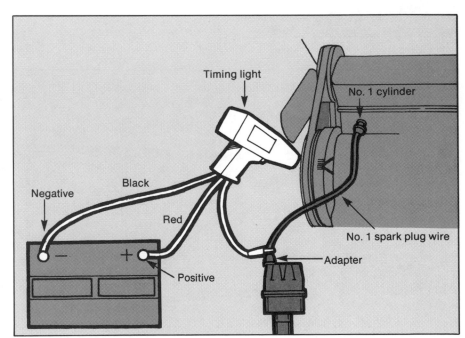

Timing light

No. 1 cylinder

Negative

Black

Red

No. 1 spark plug wire

Adapter

Positive

Timing marks

If your ignition system is electronic, please turn to the end of this chapter for testing and replacement procedures on the five systems used by American car manufacturers.

Pro Shop

Timing chain check

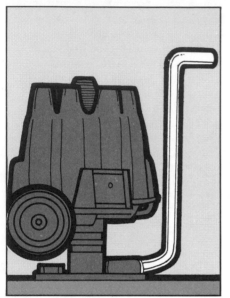

5 **Checking the timing.** Start your engine and allow it to reach normal operating temperature. After checking the manufacturer's specifications to find your correct timing degree, check the ignition timing by pointing the timing light at the timing marks. If the timing is not accurate, loosen the nut or bolt holding the distributor down and turn the entire distributor assembly clockwise or counterclockwise until the two timing marks are aligned. When the marks are aligned, tighten the nut or bolt securely, and recheck the ignition timing marks to make sure the timing has not changed.

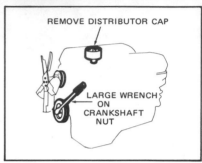

REMOVE DISTRIBUTOR CAP

LARGE WRENCH ON CRANKSHAFT NUT

A stretched timing chain can make an engine run poorly and lose power due to inaccurate valve timing. Usually, checking a timing chain for excessive stretch or wear is a time-consuming job which involves removal of the engine's front cover. There is another way, however, to check for excessive stretch without removing the cover.

Remove the distributor cap and turn the engine against the normal direction of rotation. This is done by using a large wrench on the crankshaft nut at the front of the engine. Turn until you can see movement in the distributor rotor. Stop turning and mark reference points on the front vibration damper and engine.

Now turn the engine again, but in the direction of normal rotation. Again, pay close attention to the distributor rotor. As soon as you notice rotor movement, stop turning. Now check your reference marks for the amount of engine travel before the rotor moved. Just measure the distance between the two marks. If the dimension is more than about two inches, your timing chain has excessive stretch and/or one of the timing gears is worn. In either case, replacement is in order.

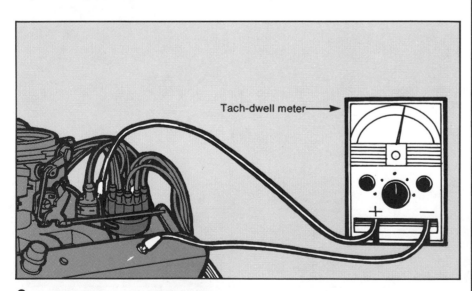

Tach-dwell meter →

6 **Finishing up.** Switch off the engine. Remove the ignition timing light and adapter, and replace the number one spark plug wire in the distributor cap tower. Remove the plug from the rubber vacuum hose which was disconnected from the vacuum advance unit and connect it back on the unit. Leave the tach-dwell meter connected and all vacuum lines plugged for the next job.

Adjusting the Carburetor

Precise adjustment of both the curb idle and the fuel-and-air mixture is essential to the performance of a car engine. Rough idling, poor gas mileage, engine stalling, dieseling (engine continues to run when ignition switch is turned off), and a highly polluting exhaust are results of incorrect carburetor adjustment.

On late-model carburetors, the screws which adjust the fuel-and-air mixture, located in the base of the carburetor, are set at the factory and sealed with plastic limiter caps to maintain the correct fuel-and-air mixture setting necessary to meet emission control specifications. The limiter caps should not be removed, disturbed, or tampered with. Only a qualified mechanic, using the proper equipment, should make any adjustments to these screws. If your carburetor is equipped with such caps, the only adjustment you can make is the curb idle RPM (revolutions per minute). For carburetors not equipped with limiter caps, adjustment of the fuel-and-air mixture screws will be explained and illustrated later in this chapter.

Adjusting the curb idle RPM. Start the engine and allow it to warm up to its normal operating temperature. Remember that the tach-dwell meter is still connected. When the engine has reached operating temperature, open and close the throttle quickly to allow the engine RPM to reduce down to a curb idle. Following the manufacturer's specifications for curb idle RPM, adjust the idle by turning the screw or solenoid, depending on which type of adjustment your carburetor has. At the same time, watch the tach-dwell meter readings. Replace the air cleaner and recheck the curb idle. If it is not correct, remove the air cleaner and readjust it. When it is correct, adjust the fuel-and-air mixture unless your car is equipped with plastic limiter caps. If it is, disconnect the tach-dwell meter, and check all vacuum lines for correct replacement.

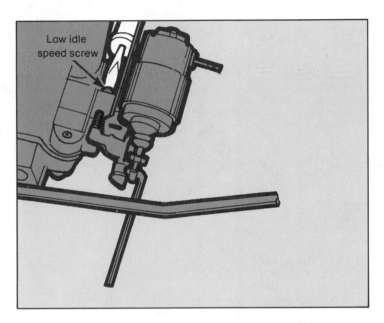

Low idle speed screw

Adjusting the fuel-and-air mixture screws

The following procedure is only for carburetors which are not equipped with plastic limiter caps.

Adjusting the fuel-and-air mixture using a tach-dwell meter. After adjusting the curb idle as described, locate the fuel-and-air mixture screw. Note: Some cars have more than one. Adjust the mixture by turning the screw with a screwdriver while observing the tach-dwell meter RPM readings. Continue to turn the screw in until the RPM starts to drop off. At this point, slowly turn the screw out until the highest RPM is just reached, then stop turning it. If your carburetor has two of these screws, repeat the above operation on the other one. When you have completed the fuel-and-air mixture adjustment, reset the curb idle adjustment if necessary. Remove the tach-dwell meter and replace all vacuum lines.

Fuel-and-air mixture screws
Turn in or turn out

Replacing Fuel and Air Filters

Replacing the fuel filter

There are several types of fuel filters. Check your owner's manual to determine which of the following your car has.

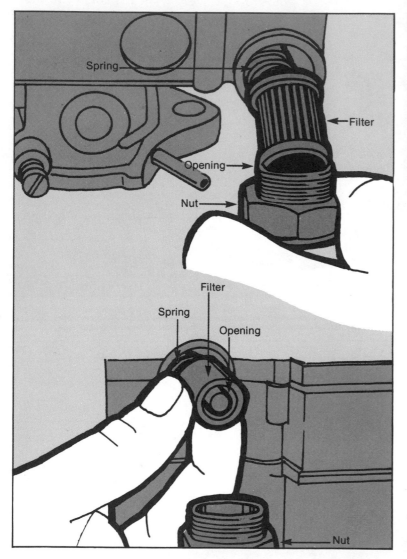

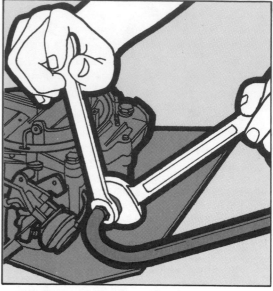

If the fuel filter is in the carburetor, place a clean cloth under the fuel inlet nut to absorb any spilled gasoline. Using two wrenches, loosen and remove the fuel line from the inlet nut. Remove the fuel nut and the filter. Install the new filter with the filter opening facing the fuel inlet port.

If the fuel filter is in the fuel pump, as on 1969–74 Cadillacs, first raise and support the front of the car. With two wrenches, loosen the fuel outlet line, the line that goes to the carburetor, to prevent twisting it. Remove the outlet nut, again with wrenches, and remove the old filter. *Caution: Use a flashlight, not a droplight, when working near gasoline.* Install the new filter with the open end of the filter seated inside the nut, then tighten the nut and fuel line.

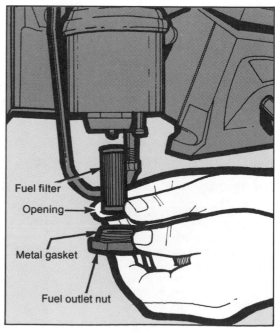

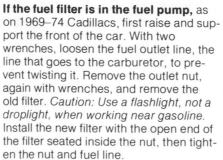

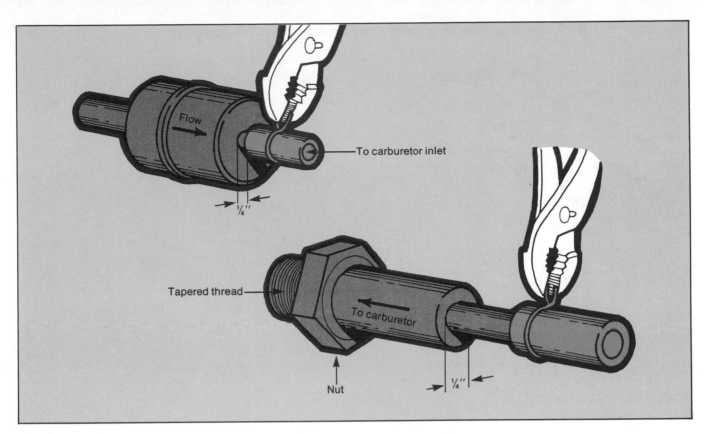

In-line fuel filter. Open the small wire clamps with pliers and slide them off the rubber hose. At the same time, twist and pull the filter from the hose. *Caution: Be sure to wipe up any spilled gasoline.* Install the new filter with new clamps and new rubber hoses. Be sure the printed arrow on the filter is pointed toward the carburetor inlet. Position the wire clamps about ¼-inch from the hose end.

In-line filter screwed into the carburetor. Slide the wire clamp off the rubber hose with pliers, then twist and pull the rubber hose off the filter. With the correct size wrench, unscrew the fuel filter from the carburetor. Install the new filter securely. *Caution: These filters have a tapered pipe thread. The nut part of the filter does not have to be seated against the carburetor.*

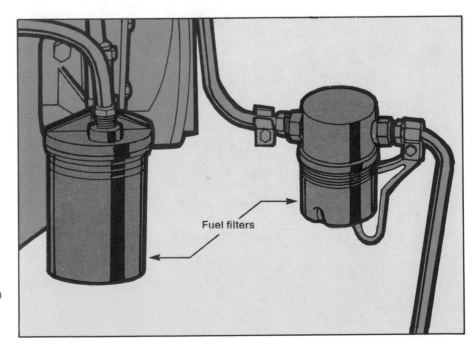

Removable canister-type filter. This type of fuel filter element resembles a small oil filter. Unscrew the canister by hand, and install a new one, then tighten it securely by hand only. After you have replaced the fuel filter, start the engine and check for gasoline leaks.

Checking and replacing air filter and crankcase filter elements

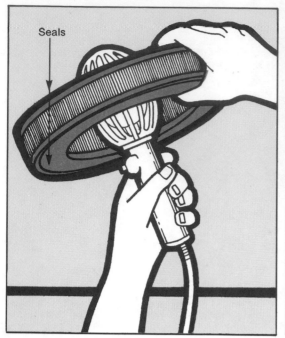

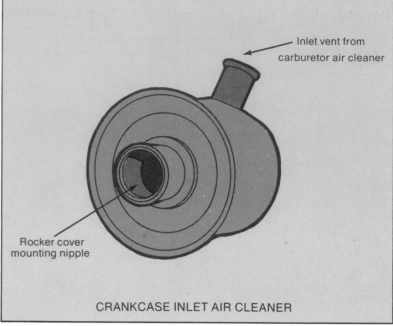

CRANKCASE INLET AIR CLEANER

1 **Remove the paper air filter element** and inspect the top and bottom rubber seals for cracks or deformities. Check for a clogged filter element by placing a droplight into its center, then rotating the element completely around the light. The light should be visible through the entire element; if not, you should replace it.

Chrysler Corporation vehicles use a crankcase filter that plugs into a grommet on the rocker cover. The filter should be washed in solvent and allowed to dry before replacing.

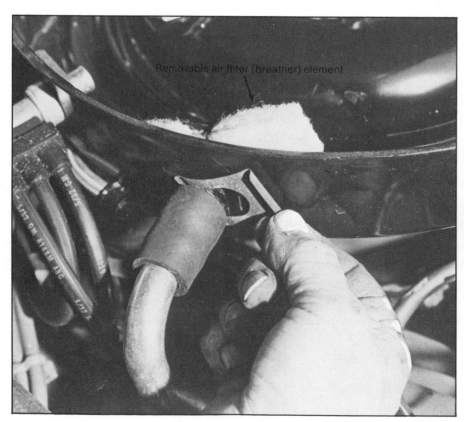

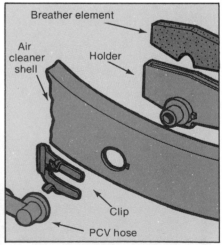

2 **Replace the crankcase filter** before installing the air filter element in the air cleaner housing.

Checking the Carburetor Choke

Certain basic carburetor choke and linkage checks should be included in every tune-up. First look at the linkage and choke vacuum for breakage or disconnected parts.

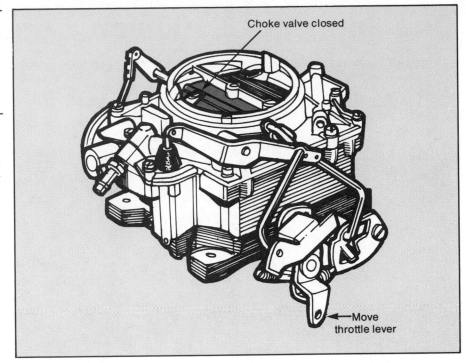
Choke valve closed

Move throttle lever

1 **While the engine is cold,** remove the air cleaner, open and close the throttle by moving the throttle lever attached to the linkage that leads to the accelerator. Observe the position of the choke valve. It should snap closed if it was open and remain closed.

2 **Start the engine,** and just as it starts, again observe the position of the choke valve. It should be open about one fourth of the distance between being fully closed and fully open.

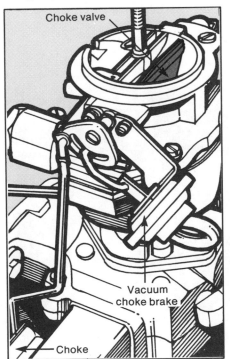
Choke valve

Vacuum choke brake

Choke

3 **With the engine at normal operating temperature,** the choke valve should be fully open. If the choke valve does not close when the engine is cold, the choke shaft or linkage is most likely gummed up or stuck. Using a choke spray cleaner, spray the area around the choke valve, choke shaft, and all linkages. After spraying, hold the throttle in the open position and operate the choke valve by hand several times. *Caution: Wipe up any spilled choke spray cleaner.*

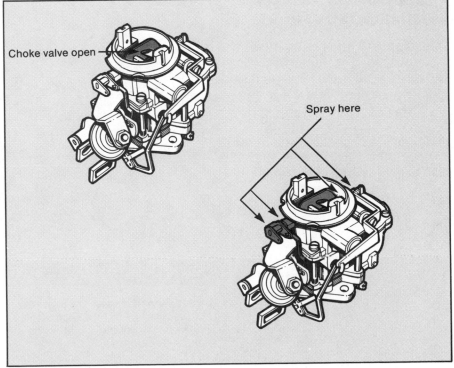
Choke valve open

Spray here

Checking the Emission Controls

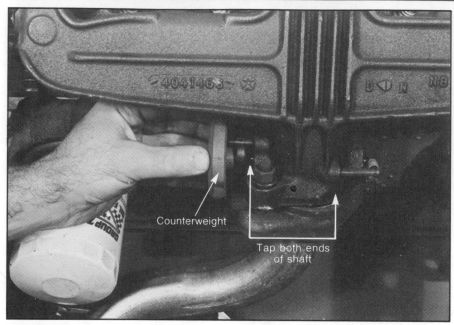

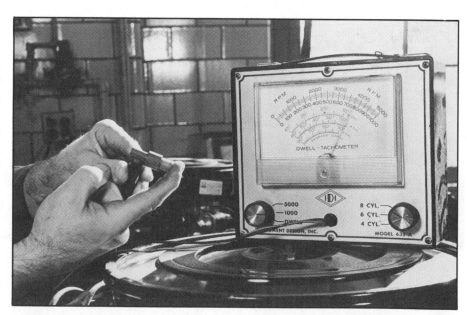

Check the manifold heat control valve for freedom of operation. To free the valve, tap the control valve shaft back and forth with a small hammer and rotate the counterweight. To prevent recurrence of the problem, apply a manifold heat control solvent to both ends of the shaft.

Vacuum-operated heat control valve. On some later-model cars, 1976 and up, the exhaust manifold heat control valve is vacuum-operated. To service this type of valve, the rod which is connected between the vacuum unit and the control valve must be disconnected to allow for freedom of movement.

The positive crankcase ventilation (PCV) valve

PCV valves have been required on cars since 1963. In California, cars of all years must have them. Manufacturers install the PCV valve in various locations. Some install it in one of the engine valve covers, on either the right or the left side of the engine. Others install it in the oil filler cap, in the intake manifold at the base of the carburetor, or in the valve lifter cover under the intake manifold.

Checking the PCV valve. Connect the tach-dwell meter. Start the engine and allow it to reach normal operating temperature. With the engine running at curb idle revolutions per minute, pull out the inlet end of the PCV valve and plug the opening of the valve with your finger. The engine should drop at least 40 RPM. If the RPM does not drop, the PCV valve is defective. Refer to the chapter on the emission control system for the necessary repairs.

The exhaust gas recirculating (EGR) valve

Since 1973, cars have been equipped with EGR valves. Manufacturers install the EGR valve in three different locations. Some put it on the intake manifold directly below the carburetor. Others install it on the intake manifold close to the carburetor, and on some in-line engines the EGR valve is mounted between the exhaust manifold and the intake manifold directly below the carburetor.

Checking the EGR valve. Start the engine and allow it to reach normal operating temperature. With the engine running at curb idle RPM, disconnect the vacuum hose that is attached to the EGR valve, and attach the hand vacuum pump hose to the valve. Operate the hand vacuum pump until the vacuum gauge reads at least four inches of mercury. At this point the engine should start to misfire. If there is no change in engine performance, the EGR valve is defective. Refer to the chapter on the emission control system for servicing it.

Checking the air pump injection system. Although all air injection system components are basically the same, manufacturers mount them in various locations. To test the air system, you must check the diverter valve, which is mounted either on the air pump, or in the air hose line between the air pump and the exhaust manifold. Start the engine and allow it to reach normal operating temperature. With the engine running at curb idle, place one hand over the vents of the diverter valve. Using the other hand, open and close the carburetor throttle to increase the RPM temporarily. At this point, if the air injection system is operating properly, you should feel and/or hear air escaping from the vents of the diverter valve for approximately four to five seconds. If you do not, the air system is not functioning properly. Refer to the chapter on the emission control system for repairs. *Caution: Be careful not to injure yourself on the hot exhaust manifold, the turning fan blades, the fan belts, the high voltage ignition wires, and all other turning pulleys.*

Checking the heated carburetor air system. With the air cleaner "cold," and properly mounted on the carburetor, and all vacuum hoses connected, start the engine. Observe the position of the air control valve door located in the air cleaner snorkel. The door should be closed at the opening of the snorkel, in the hot air position. As the engine operating temperature increases, the door in the snorkel should open fully to allow cold air to enter the air filter. If the control valve door does not operate this way, refer to the chapter on the emission control system for repairs.

Closed

Open

Troubleshooting flow chart: ignition system

Symptom	Probable cause	Remedy
A. Engine will not crank. For conventional or electronic systems.	1. Defective ignition switch.	1. Connect a jumper wire between the battery and the starter connections. If the solenoid clicks, the ignition switch is defective. Replace the switch to cure the problem.
	2. Loose or broken battery connections.	2. Clean cable terminals and tighten connections. Replace cables which are damaged.
	3. Defective neutral safety switch.	3. Replace defective neutral safety switch.
	4. If starter clicks, but engine will not crank.	4. Check for defective connections or defective starter motor. Repair or replace as necessary.
B. Engine cranks but will not start. Electronic ignition systems, 6, 7, 9, 10, 11, 12. Conventional ignition, all items.	5. Burned or pitted contact points.	5. Replace contact points and condenser.
	6. Corroded distributor cap towers or eroded terminals.	6. Replace distributor cap.
	7. Moisture in distributor cap or on spark plug wires.	7. Remove cap and dry out. Wipe spark plug cables dry with cloth.
	8. Defective condenser.	8. Replace condenser.
	9. Defective coil.	9. Pull center wire from the distributor cap and hold about $\frac{3}{8}$-inch from a good ground. Crank the engine. If there is no spark or if the spark is weak, the coil is defective. Before replacing the coil, check all the wiring of the primary circuit and correct as necessary.
	10. No fuel in gas tank.	10. Obtain fuel.
	11. Insufficient fuel supply at the carburetor.	11. Look into the carburetor and open the throttle. If fuel squirts into the carburetor throat, the fuel system is not at fault. If no fuel is evident, check the fuel pump pressure. If the fuel pump is OK, the trouble is in the carburetor.
	12. Extremely low compression.	12. Determine cause of low compression by performing a compression test.
C. Hard starting at all times. Electronic ignition systems, 14, 15, 16, 17, 18, 19. Conventional ignition, all items.	13. Weak spark.	13. Check condition of breaker points and all of the primary circuit wiring. Correct as necessary.
	14. Ignition coil.	14. See B-9 above.
	15. Spark plugs need adjustment or are fouled.	15. Clean and readjust the spark plug gaps.
	16. Defective spark plug cables.	16. Replace cables which are frayed or cracked.
	17. Low charge or defective battery.	17. Recharge or replace battery as necessary.
	18. Defective starter or solenoid.	18. Repair or replace starter or solenoid as necessary.
	19. Insufficient fuel supply.	19. Check for fuel delivery by looking down the carburetor throat and operating the throttle lever. If no fuel sprays into the carburetor throat, check the fuel pump pressure. If the fuel pump is OK, the trouble is in the carburetor.

Symptom	Probable cause	Remedy
D. Hard starting when cold. For conventional or electronic systems.	20. Poor compression. 21. Low battery charge or defective battery or cables. 22. Binding choke linkage. 23. Oil viscosity too high.	20. Take a compression test. 21. Recharge or replace the battery or cables. 22. Free up the choke linkage using a suitable choke cleaner. 23. Drain the oil and add the proper type and amount of oil.
E. Hard starting when hot. For conventional or electronic systems.	24. Insufficient spark intensity between spark and ground. 25. Choke stuck in closed position. 26. Defective starter motor or starter motor circuit. 27. Engine overheating.	24. If the spark cannot jump a $\frac{3}{8}$-inch gap, check the ignition system for defects and correct as necessary. 25. Free up choke using choke cleaner. 26. Check starter and circuit and repair or replace as necessary. 27. Check cooling system, and correct as necessary.
F. Engine stalls. For conventional or electronic systems.	28. Spark plugs fouled or incorrectly gapped. 29. Poor idle adjustment. 30. Breaker points dirty or corroded.	28. Clean and regap spark plugs. 29. Adjust idle. 30. Replace breaker points.
G. Engine runs but misses steadily at all speeds. For conventional or electronic systems.	31. One or more defective spark plugs. 32. Defective spark plug cables. 33. Defective distributor cap.	31. Connect a tachometer and check the RPM drop as each spark plug cable is disconnected. No RPM drop when a particular plug is disconnected indicates that that plug is defective. *Caution: Do not perform the above test on cars equipped with catalytic converters.* 32. Check the resistance of each cable. Replace cables which do not meet the specifications. 33. Inspect distributor cap for cracks, burned or eroded terminals, corrosion in the sockets, or carbon tracking. Replace the cap.
H. Engine runs but misses intermittently at all speeds. Electronic ignition 36, 37. Conventional ignition, all items.	34. Dirty or corroded breaker points. 35. Defective condenser. 36. Defective coil. 37. Worn insulation, broken strands, and loose or corroded terminals in the primary circuit.	34. Replace contact points. 35. Replace condenser. 36. Check coil. See B-9 above. 37. Check voltage drop across the primary resistance wire or ballast resistor with a voltmeter. Replace defective units if not within manufacturer's specifications.
I. Engine runs but misses at idle. Conventional ignition only.	38. Incorrect contact point setting. 39. Dirty or corroded breaker points. 40. Faulty coil or condenser.	38. Readjust gap and check with dwell meter. 39. Replace the contact points. 40. Check coil and replace condenser.
J. Engine runs but misses at high speeds. Both systems.	41. Spark plugs fouled or incorrectly gapped.	41. Clean and regap spark plugs as necessary.
K. Poor high speed performance. Electronic ignition, 42, 44. Conventional ignition, all items.	42. Ignition timing too late. 43. Defective contact points. 44. Spark plugs fouled, incorrectly gapped, or of an incorrect heat range for the specific engine. 45. Defective coil or condenser.	42. Reset timing to specifications. 43. Replace contact points and condenser. 44. Clean and regap spark plugs. If spark plugs are of an incorrect heat range, reinstall the correct spark plugs for the specific engine. 45. Test coil and replace condenser.
L. Excessive fuel consumption. Electronic ignition, 47, 48. Conventional ignition, all items.	46. Contact points dirty or incorrectly adjusted. 47. Ignition timing incorrectly adjusted. 48. Distributor advance mechanism malfunctioning.	46. Clean or replace as necessary and regap points to manufacturer's specifications. 47. Readjust ignition timing to manufacturer's specifications. 48. Have advance mechanism tested and repair or replace as necessary.
M. Poor acceleration. Electronic ignition, 49, 50. Conventional ignition, all items.	49. Ignition timing set too late. 50. Plugs fouled or incorrectly gapped. 51. Dirty contact points or incorrect adjustment.	49. Readjust ignition timing to manufacturer's specifications. 50. Clean and regap spark plugs to manufacturer's specifications. 51. Clean contact points as necessary and regap to manufacturer's specifications.

N. Engine knocks or pings. For conventional or electronic systems.	52. Timing incorrectly set.	52. Readjust timing to manufacturer's specifications.
	53. Spark plug heat range incorrect for specific application.	53. Install spark plugs of the correct heat range for the specific engine.
	54. Incorrect fuel octane rating.	54. Use correct octane rated gasoline.

Troubleshooting flow chart: fuel system

Symptom	Probable cause	Remedy
A. Hard starting under all conditions.	1. Insufficient fuel in carburetor.	1. Check fuel pump output by disconnecting line from carburetor and checking for fuel delivery when the engine is cranked. If there is no fuel delivery, check all the lines for obstructions. If all the fuel lines check out OK, replace the fuel pump.
B. Hard starting when cold.	2. Choke closes when the engine is hot.	2. Inspect for binding choke linkages and correct as necessary.
	3. Persistent vapor lock.	3. Wrap the fuel line between the fuel pump and carburetor with asbestos to minimize the heat transfer from the engine to the line.
	4. Carburetor flooding.	4. Check fuel pump for excessive pressure with a pressure gauge. If fuel pressure is excessive, replace the fuel pump. If fuel pump checks out OK, check the float level, needle, and seat in the carburetor. Correct or replace as necessary.
C. Engine stalls.	5. Idle speed set too low.	5. Reset idle speed to manufacturer's specifications.
	6. Idle fuel mixture too lean.	6. Reset idle mixture to manufacturer's specifications.
	7. Faulty choke operation.	7. Correct as necessary.
	8. Incorrect carburetor float setting.	8. Adjust carburetor float setting to manufacturer's specifications.
	9. Dirt or water in the fuel tank, fuel lines, pump, filter, or carburetor.	9. Clean out the fuel system.
	10. Clogged or restricted PCV valve.	10. Clean or replace the PCV valve as necessary.
	11. Dashpot (if used) incorrectly adjusted.	11. Check adjustment according to the manufacturer's specifications. Adjust as necessary.
	12. Carburetor linkage needs adjustment.	12. Clean carburetor linkage. Adjust as necessary.
	13. Carburetor accelerating pump stroke incorrectly set.	13. Check accelerating pump adjustment. Adjust as necessary according to manufacturer's specifications.
D. Engine misses erratically at all speeds.	14. Dirt or water in the fuel system.	14. Clean out the fuel system.
	15. Clogged fuel filter.	15. Replace the fuel filter.
	16. Carburetor float level set too high.	16. Readjust carburetor float level according to manufacturer's specifications.
E. Engine misses at idle only.	17. Idle mixture improperly adjusted.	17. Readjust idle mixture according to manufacturer's specifications.
	18. Restrictions in the idle fuel system of the carburetor.	18. Remove, disassemble, and clean out the carburetor.
F. Engine misses at high speed only.	19. Erratic fuel pump pressures.	19. Check fuel pump pressure and replace fuel pump if not within manufacturer's specifications.
	20. Carburetor power valve or passages clogged or damaged.	20. Disassemble carburetor and clean or replace components as necessary
	21. Restrictions in the fuel system.	21. Clean or correct as necessary.
G. Poor acceleration.	22. Throttle linkage incorrectly adjusted.	22. Readjust throttle linkages as necessary.
	23. Carburetor accelerating pump incorrectly adjusted.	23. Readjust carburetor accelerating pump to manufacturer's specifications.
	24. Incorrect carburetor float setting.	24. Readjust carburetor float setting according to manufacturer's specifications.
	25. Leaking power valve, gasket, or accelerating pump.	25. Repair or replace components as necessary.

What's Different About Diesels?

Many of the routine service procedures, tests, and common breakdown repairs on diesels are similar to those performed on cars with conventional gasoline engines. The different service procedures described in this chapter are still doable by a home mechanic.

The truck industry's experience with the diesel engine has been very good. Fuel mileage is superb, much routine maintenance (such as ignition) is eliminated and, while parts aren't inexpensive, their longevity almost makes up for their high price.

There are at least seven foreign and domestic car-makers with diesel-powered engines on the road in this country and more on the way. Although you will find something different on every one of these models, all diesels are different from gasoline engines in the design and/or function of the cylinder heads, combustion chambers, fuel distribution system, air-intake manifold, and method of ignition. This discussion will outline the service procedures for two significantly different types of diesels with a head-start on the US market: the Oldsmobile 350 V8 and the VW Rabbit.

The diesel engine requires little maintenance when compared with the gasoline engine, primarily because it doesn't have complicated ignition and carburetion systems as the gasoline engine has.

The intake stroke of the diesel is similar to the intake stroke of the gasoline engine, except that there is no carburetor to mix fuel with air and no throttle valve to restrict the amount of air entering the cylinder. Therefore, the cylinder fills with air only. When this air becomes compressed, its temperature rises above the ignition point of the fuel. As the piston nears the end of the compression stroke, fuel is injected into the combustion chamber by a fuel-injection system that meters, pressurizes, and distributes fuel to all cylinders. The fuel is ignited by the heat of the compressed air.

HOW THEY WORK

Since this type of ignition does not require an electrical-spark-ignition system, the diesel does not have a distributor, spark plug wires, spark plugs or high-voltage ignition. In very cold weather, tiny electrical heaters called glow plugs heat the precombustion chambers to assist in starting. They remain on a short time after the engine is started, then turn off when the air in the chamber reaches a high enough temperature to ignite the fuel when it is compressed.

Continued

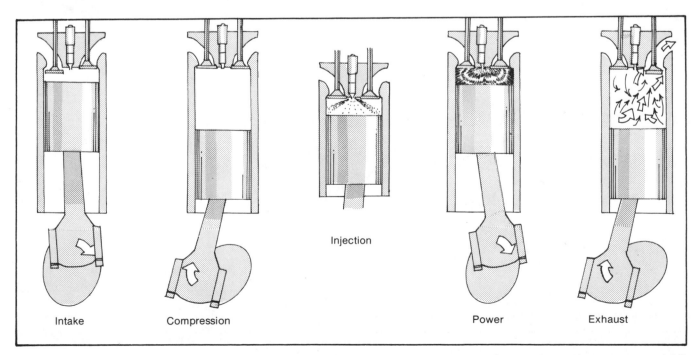

Intake   Compression   Injection   Power   Exhaust

SERVICING THE OLDSMOBILE 350 V8 DIESEL

The Oldsmobile diesel engine compares in size with the 350 V8 gasoline engine, which was the starting point in the engineering of the diesel version. However, the diesel's cylinder block, crankshaft, main bearings, rods, pistons, and pins are of heavier construction because of the higher compression ratio needed to ignite diesel fuel. Further, the Olds diesel does not have a catalytic converter or any emission control devices, except for a crankcase ventilation system.

Before attempting any Olds diesel engine maintenance service, read these two paragraphs:

1 Do not clean the engine until it has cooled to surrounding temperature. Spraying water or engine cleaning solvent on the diesel injection pump when it is warm or hot will damage the pump.

2 The Olds has many colored bolts, screws, etc. which are in metric measurement, but very close in dimension to fasteners in the current US system. So be careful when replacing the fasteners. Make sure the replacements have the

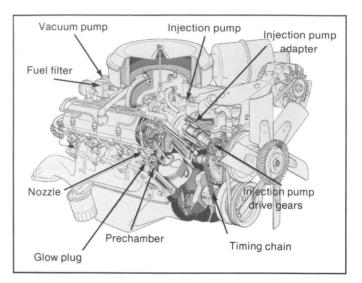

1 Overview of the Oldsmobile 350 V8 diesel engine. Note the two 12-volt batteries in parallel up front.

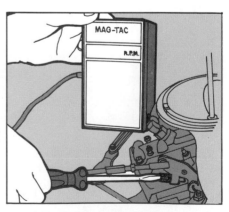

2 Remove the hold-down bolts of the air-intake muffler attached to the air cleaner.

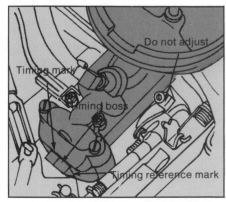

3 Air-intake manifold with air cleaner removed. Timing mark is on the injector, but the timing reference mark is on the engine.

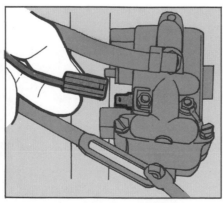

4 The power supply line must be disconnected from the diesel fuel heating unit prior to testing for continuity.

5 Adjust idle speed using the Mag-Tac, a pulse-actuated tachometer with digital readout. The unit is specially designed for diesel engines.

same measurements and strengths as those removed.

The fuel-injection pump is mounted on top of the diesel engine. This pump provides the required timing advance under all operating conditions. Timing advance is preset at the factory.

The fuel filter is located between the mechanical fuel pump and the injection pump. The diaphragm-type mechanical fuel pump is mounted on the right side of the engine and is driven by a cam on the crankshaft. There is also a fuel filter in the fuel tank.

There are two types of electrical glow plug systems used in Olds diesels—both operate off of two 12-volt batteries. One system has *two* relays on the firewall near the wiper motor that activate the *12-volt* glow plugs; the other has *one* relay box on the right fender filler panel that activates the *6-volt* glow plugs. Note: The two plugs are not interchangeable, so make sure you know which type your car takes. *Caution: The single relay box system supplies a pulsing current to the glow plugs. Do not bypass or apply*

electrical current to the relay because you will instantly damage the plugs.

To test the glow plugs, connect a positive voltmeter lead to the battery positive post and a negative voltmeter lead to the battery negative post. Now turn the ignition switch on. Note: The voltmeter should read battery voltage. You will have two to five minutes to perform this test before the ignition switch turns off automatically to prevent the batteries from running down if the ignition is accidentally left on. To reset the system, turn the ignition switch off and then on again. If the "wait" light comes on, proceed with the test. If it doesn't come on, it means the engine is too warm for glow plug operation and the thermistor must be disconnected before the test can be made. The thermistor is a heat-sensing device whose electrical resistance decreases as its temperature increases. If you are making the test with the thermistor disconnected, the voltmeter reading should drop off one or two volts below battery voltage. Replace any plugs that do not meet specs.

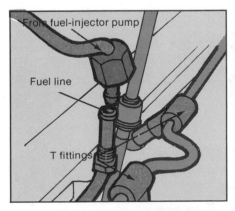

6 To replace the fuel filter, the fuel line must first be disconnected.

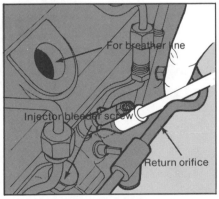

7 The power connector must be disconnected from the glow plug before the plug can be removed.

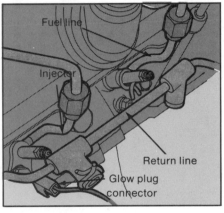

8 Each side of the engine has four fuel lines, four fuel injectors, four glow plugs, four plug connectors, and four fuel return T fittings.

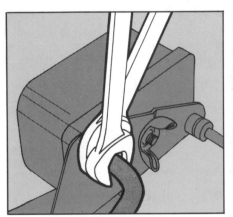

9 Remove the T fittings by pulling each one up a little at a time in sequence until they come off. Use two wrenches to uncouple the fuel line from the injector.

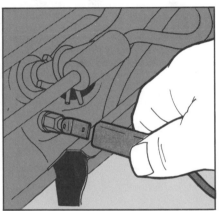

10 After the fuel line, return line, and glow plugs are disconnected, remove the injector retaining cap screw with a socket and extension ratchet.

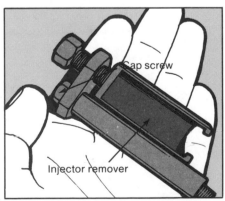

11 The special tool you will need to remove the fuel injector.

Continued

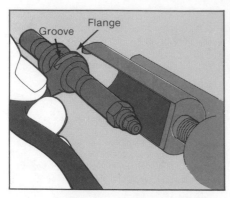

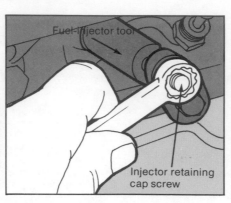

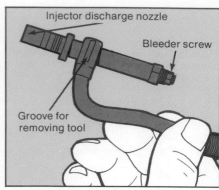

12 Install the injector removing tool so the flange of the tool enters the groove on the fuel injector. Lock the injector cap screw before beginning to pull out the injector.

13 Remove the injector from the engine with a $9/16$-inch closed-end wrench.

14 Identify different components of the injector nozzle assembly.

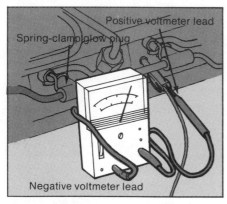

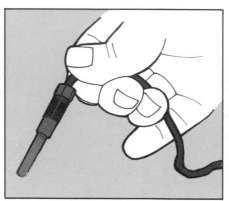

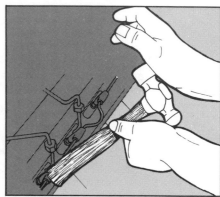

15 After attaching the voltmeter, turn the ignition key on and note the voltage reading.

16 With ignition switch on, connect the glow plug supply line to each plug and ground the plug. If it doesn't glow, check plug power circuit for continuity. If there's voltage, but no glow, replace the glow plug.

17 After all tests are completed, reassemble the system reversing the above procedures. A hammer handle will help you to seat the fuel return line.

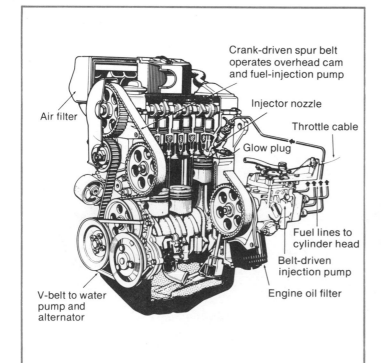

SERVICING THE VW RABBIT DIESEL

1 Engine rpm on the VW diesel is measured with a special vibration sensor to which a standard tachometer is connected.

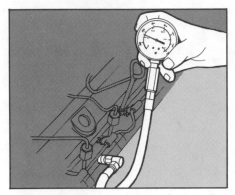

18 Remove a glow plug and install a special high-pressure compression tester in the plug hole.

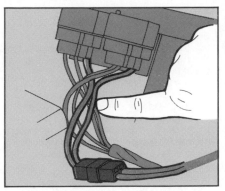

19 The finger points to the wires to be tested when checking a plug that does not glow.

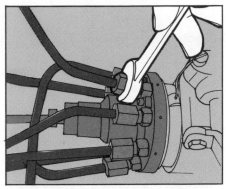

20 Remove the fuel injector line. The fuel injector has as many injector lines as there are cylinders in the engine. Note the similarity to the ignition wires in a conventional gasoline engine.

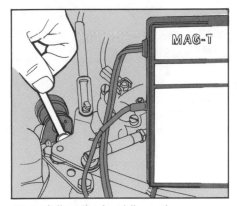

21 Adjust the fast idle on the solenoid with an open-end wrench. Use a Mag-Tac tachometer to monitor engine rpm.

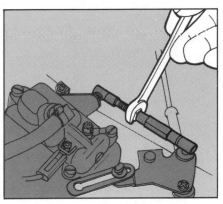

22 Make sure the throttle linkage is free and properly adjusted.

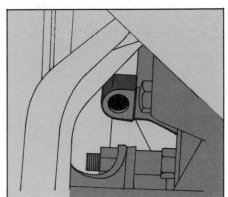

23 A magnetic pulse timing hole is designed to accept the Mag-Tac probe to measure engine speed.

The engine block, crankshaft, flywheel, and main bearings are straight out of the gasoline version. The cylinder head looks a lot like the one used on the VW gasoline engine, but it is modified to accommodate fuel injection directly into the cylinders.

The fuel-injection system is the major external difference between the VW diesel and the VW gasoline engine. The diesel has a mechanical pulley-and-belt system, and its injectors thread into tiny precombustion chambers leading directly to the main combustion chambers at the top of the cylinders.

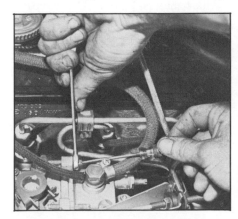

2 Engine idle is adjusted at the fuel-injection pump. Slacken the lock nut with a wrench and turn the screw to get the desired engine rpm.

3 The fuel shutoff solenoid automatically cuts off fuel to the engine. To service it, first remove the nut, then disconnect the wire.

Idle Speed

The first new procedure you face is setting the idle speed to specifications. This is new because there is no electrical ignition system to connect a tachometer to. VW's solution is a vibration sensor with a magnet in the base. Place it on the valve cover and connect its two lead wires to the car battery. Engine vibration and 12-volt battery current create an electrical pulse that will operate a standard tachometer (Fig. 1). To set idle-speed adjustment, loosen the lock nut and turn the

Continued

screw on the accelerator linkage at the fuel injection pump (Fig. 2).

There is no fast idle and no choke. For cold starts, you pull a dashboard knob, and linkage from the knob to the fuel injection pump operates an internal pump mechanism that advances the fuel injection on the crankshaft by 5°.

The VW diesel engine has a maximum speed of 5450 rpm which is controlled by a governor inside the fuel pump. Check the governed maximum speed by flooring the accelerator pedal. To adjust the governor, slacken the lock nut and turn the governor screw—it's next to the one for idle speed.

Fuel Flow Solenoid

To turn off the VW diesel, the fuel supply must be shut off. Fuel flow is controlled by a solenoid valve on the pump. When the solenoid is energized, the fuel passes into the injection circuits; when the key is turned off, the solenoid de-energizes and fuel flow stops. Whenever you work on the engine, particularly if it is cranked, it's standard procedure to disconnect the wire from the solenoid (Fig. 3).

The solenoid is a potential trouble point. If it fails to energize, the VW diesel engine won't start. If it doesn't disengage, the engine won't turn off. To check the solenoid, place your fingers on it. You should be able to feel it click when the key is turned on.

Fuel Injection Pump

The fuel injection pump on the VW diesel must time its fuel delivery to the injectors as precisely as ignition is timed on the gasoline engine. As engine speed increases, the injection system must spray fuel earlier. The advance system is built into the pump, just as spark advance is automatic in the distributor in the gasoline engine. But the basic pump timing must be correct.

Check the basic timing setting with a dial indicator inserted into the pump. First, turn the crankshaft pulley with a wrench, until the flywheel top dead center mark is lined up at the bell-housing opening (the same setup used for ignition timing on the gasoline engine) (Fig. 4). Next, insert the dial indicator until its rod

causes the dial needle to move a few millimeters. The rod is now bearing against the pump injection plunger, the part that pushes fuel under pressure up to the injectors.

Turn the crank backward until the dial needle stops moving, set the dial to zero, and turn the crank forward until the top dead center mark lines up again. The dial needle should have moved forward a specified distance, which is equal to the pump plunger stroke (0.83mm). If the reading is too great or too little, slacken the four mounting bolts on the pump and turn it one way or the other to get the exact reading on the dial (Fig. 5). The bolts pass through elongated holes to permit adjustment. This adjustment, plus engine speed and replacement of a defective shutoff solenoid, are the only jobs that can be done on the fuel pump. If the pump fails, it must be replaced.

To help extend fuel pump life, use No. 2 diesel fuel, which has better lubricating qualities than the lighter No. 1. Fuel is the pump's only source of lubrication, so this is important. A quality No. 2 is seasonally blended for cold weather, so startability should be tolerable. Only in extremely cold weather, with no other choice, should No. 1 fuel be used to ease starting.

Compression

The VW diesel develops much higher compression than a gasoline engine. The typical gas engine will run satisfactorily with cranking compression as low as 90 to 100 psi (pounds per square inch). The VW diesel should produce pressures in the 400 to 500 psi range in order to raise the air temperatures high enough to ignite diesel fuel.

A conventional compression gauge, with its 250 to 300 psi limit, won't do. VW supplies a model that not only reads to 600 psi, but includes a roll of paper and an automatic marking pen (in place of the standard indicator needle), to provide a permanent record of compression readings.

Since there is no spark plug hole on the diesel, the special diesel compression gauge is threaded into a fuel-injector hole. To get the VW injectors out, remove the fuel lines at the pump and at the injectors. Then take out the injectors with a ratchet and deep socket. When reinstalling the injectors, tighten them to specs with a torque wrench.

Next, withdraw the heat shields, which look like plug gaskets and sit over the injector holes, narrow-side down (Fig. 6). Thread the hose fitting into the injector hole and tighten with a wrench. Now you're set to crank the engine and take your readings.

4 The outer plug should be removed so the top dead center mark on the flywheel can be aligned with the pointer inside the bell housing.

5 Injection pump bolts are loosened with a curved wrench. Turn the pump to adjust the timing. The indicator checks the plunger stroke.

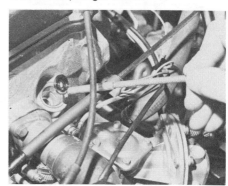

6 After the fuel injectors are removed, the heat shields are visible. Remove them with a magnet. Do not reuse the heat shields.

7 Drive belt replacement requires two simple tools. Here the camshaft is kept from turning with an L-shaped steel bar.

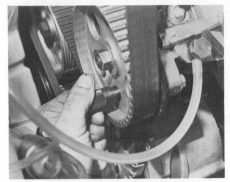

8 To change the drive belt, keep the injection pump pulley from turning with a simple locking plug.

9 This gauge measures belt tension. For adjustment, slacken the lock nut and turn the large hex nut on the idler pulley with a wrench.

10 In the VW system, the bus bar connects the glow plugs in a single circuit. Wire-brush the plugs' heating element tip as necessary.

11 A glow plug relay is a plug-in unit on the fuse box under the left side of the dash. It can be removed and replaced easily.

Drive Belt

The rubber drive belt on the VW diesel is reinforced with steel wire for longer life. If it breaks, serious engine damage could result, because there is very little clearance between the top of the piston and the closed valves when the piston is at the top of its stroke. If the belt snaps, the overhead camshaft stops and some valves are left open. The crank continues to rotate and when it brings the pistons up, they crash into the valves. This can also happen if the belt is loose and jumps a number of teeth on the pulley. There is no recommended replacement interval for the VW belt, but it is a good idea to pull the guard and check the belt periodically. If it is frayed or has stretched a bit, consider replacing it, although the belt can be retensioned.

You can change a drive belt with inexpensive but specialized tools. One holds the camshaft (Fig. 7); another locks the injection pump pulley (Fig. 8). Line up the flywheel timing marks so both tools can be inserted to prevent accidental turning of either pulley. Loosen the idler pulley lock nut, replace the belt, and tighten it. To measure tension accurately, a special gauge is used. The gauge, which measures belt deflection to the millimeter, is hooked onto the belt, the specified deflection is dialed in, and the idler pulley is tensioned with the wrench as shown (Fig. 9).

Valve Shims

The Rabbit engine—gasoline or diesel—has a shim-type valve clearance adjustment. The cam follower and valve must be pushed down to remove the old shim and install a replacement. Although this is normally a job for the dealer service department, which has a stock of replacement shims, note one problem area if you decide to do the job yourself: On the VW diesel, the limited clearance between the valve and the top of the piston means you can't push the valve down when the piston is at top dead center. Measure the clearance at this point, then rotate the crank 90° to bring the piston down. Now you can depress the cam follower and valve to replace the shim.

Glow Plugs

The VW diesel glow plugs are heated by battery current supplied by a key switch and a relay. The relay also turns off a dashboard indicator light when preheating is complete and the engine can be started. This second function is time-controlled according to engine temperature— the light may take anywhere from seconds to more than a minute to go off.

Failure of the glow plug circuit is a common cause of hard starting in cold weather. A simple check of the entire glow plug system begins with disconnecting the wire from the relay to the bus bar, which is the current supply bar connected to all the glow plugs. Then attach a test lamp to the wire and to a ground and have a helper turn the key to the glow position. The lamp should light. If it does not, listen for a click at the relay, which is a simple plug-in to the fuse box. If there is no click, the relay is probably bad (Fig. 10, 11).

Individual glow plugs can be tested by removing the bus bar, attaching a test lamp to the battery starter terminal, and touching the probe to each glow plug terminal. If the lamp lights, the plug is probably good. If the car has high mileage, remove each glow plug and inspect the heating element for carbon deposits. Wire-brush clean, if necessary.

Fuel System

As long as the diesel fuel is clean, the injectors should last indefinitely. The VW diesel manual calls for testing the injectors if the engine is misfiring and compression is normal. It takes an expensive pressure tester-pump device to pump fuel into the injector at operating pressure (1700 to 1850 psi), so you might consider giving this job to a pro. Since the price of an injector is less than two hours of a professional mechanic's labor charge, checking a suspect injector by substituting one you know is OK may be a cheaper way to make this test.

The VW diesel has a king-size spin-on fuel filter to protect the injectors and the pump. It should be changed every 15,000 miles. To replace the fuel filter, take it and the mounting adapter off the bracket, loosen the filter at the base with a wrench, then spin it off. Lube the new filter gasket with clean diesel fuel, then spin it on finger-tight and refit it to the bracket.

VW engine oil, which must be Service CC grade, should be changed at 7500-mile intervals. A good-quality gasoline oil may also qualify for CC, so check the markings on the can. Diesel oil blackens very quickly, sometimes in a few miles, so don't panic.

Testing Electronic Ignition Systems

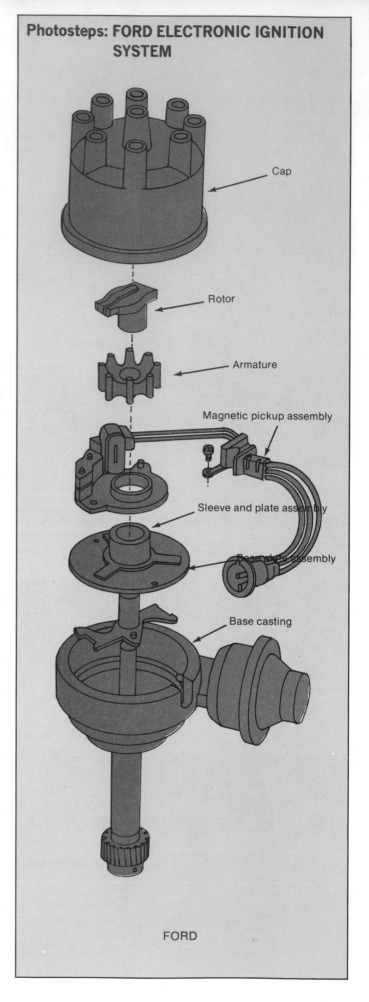

Cap

Rotor

Armature

Magnetic pickup assembly

Sleeve and plate assembly

Base plate assembly

Base casting

FORD

In an electronic ignition system, the points and condenser have been replaced by a non-mechanical triggering system, usually a reluctor and pickup assembly, installed where the breaker set would be in a conventional system. The primary voltage is no longer routed through a distributor, but through an electronic control unit where a switching transistor, activated by the reluctor and pickup, makes and breaks the primary circuit. Since there is no physical contact between the parts of the triggering system, only magnetic oscillations, parts do not wear out. The elimination of point wear has three advantages: greater output, increased reliability, and less service and maintenance.

Higher voltage output is necessary to fire the lean mixtures in today's low-compression, emission-controlled engines. When working on the electronic ignition system in your car, keep in mind that it is possible for your system to develop up to 47,000 volts. This higher voltage has a wearing effect on the secondary components that is only partially offset by the use of new materials. When problems develop in your ignition system, such as increased resistance from worn spark plugs, the high voltage supplied can burn holes in the distributor cap and rotor. In cases of electronic ignition-system failure, however, it's usually something other than the cap or rotor that's to blame. And you would be wise to carry spares of those parts most likely to fail in your car's electronic ignition system. As it happens, all these items lend themselves to replacement by a do-it-yourselfer. Now, what parts are we talking about?

If you're driving an American Motors car, the sensor assembly would be your best bet. It would be the most likely to fail and it's relatively inexpensive.

If your car is a Chrysler product, you should carry two items: a ballast resistor and a magnetic pickup. Make sure they fit your particular make and engine. For Ford Motor cars, carry a modulator stator for the model and year you're driving.

On General Motors cars, the pickup coil is most likely to fail, so be sure you have a spare when far from home.

And in every electronic ignition system, the spark plug cables can age before their time because of the high voltage and under-the-hood temperatures. So when you replace them, make sure you get the right ones, which are usually insulated with silicone.

The following pages present step-by-step photo sequences on service and testing procedures for the major electronic ignition systems found in today's cars.

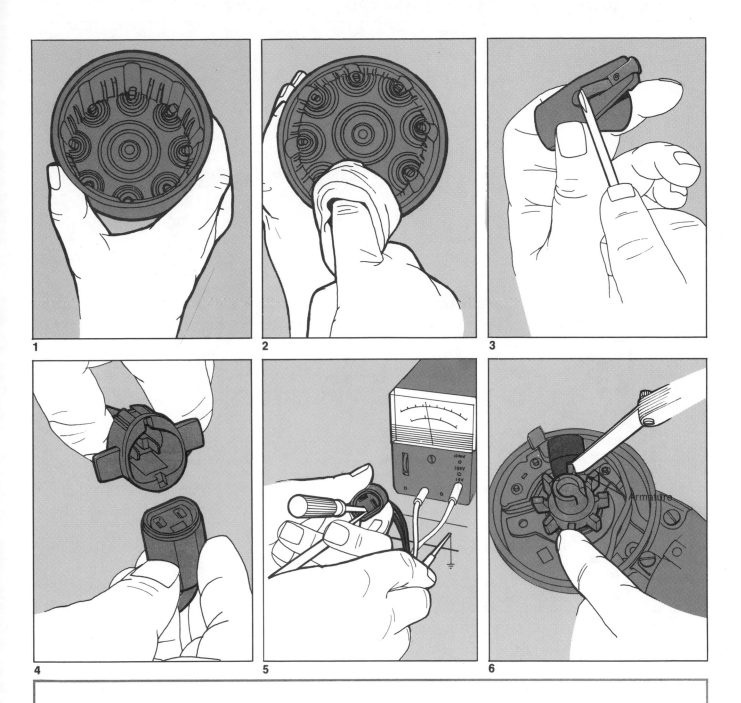

1 Remove the distributor cap and inspect the underside for arcing across the terminals, cracks on the side of the cap, and signs of rotor blade contact with the distributor spark plug terminals. Make sure the center carbon button is in good working order. It should move down when pressure is put on it and up when pressure is released. Replace the cap if necessary.

2 Wipe away any signs of contamination or moisture with a clean cloth.

3 Inspect the rotor blade and spring contact for wear, burns, and breaks. Replace the rotor if necessary.

4 Disconnect the triggering device from the distributor wire harness connector. Inspect both sides for corrosion, broken leads, and shorting. If the device shows any of these signs, replace the magnetic pickup assembly or the amplifier module, depending on which side of the 3-wire connector is defective.

5 Hold the female side of the connector facing you with the single terminal on top. With the ignition switch on, attach the positive voltmeter lead to the lower left terminal of the connector and the negative lead to a ground. The reading should meet specs. If it does not, replace the wiring harness and the amplifier module.

6 Make sure the armature is not making contact with the pickup coil. Use a feeler gauge to check for proper clearance.

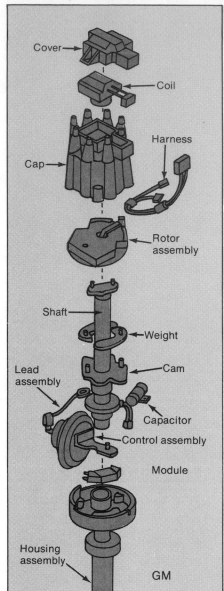

Cover

Coil

Cap

Harness

Rotor assembly

Shaft

Weight

Cam

Lead assembly

Capacitor

Control assembly

Module

Housing assembly

GM

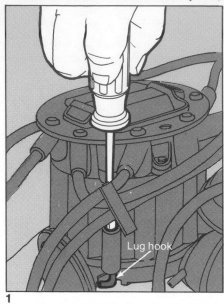

Lug hook

1

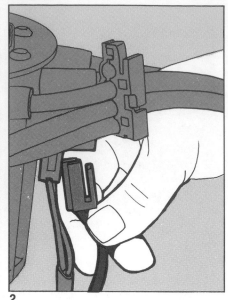

2

1 To inspect the HEI system, first remove the air-cleaner wing nut. Then remove the distributor cap by pressing down on the spring-loaded lug hook with a screwdriver and rotating the hook about one-half turn.

2 Remove the battery terminal from the connection on the distributor cap marked BAT. When removing the terminal, hold it by the plug, not by its wire.

3 Disengage the distributor harness from the coil assembly by inserting a screwdriver between the terminal and its lock and pushing down.

4 To remove the circular spark-plug-wire holder, insert a screwdriver between the holder and the ignition coil cover and then pry up. Carefully remove the holder and move it aside so you can inspect the distributor. Turn the distributor cap over and inspect the spark plug terminals for any heavy deposits and corrosion. Also, check for signs of rotor blade contact. If there are deposits or blade contact, replace the rotor and cap.

5 Remove the rotor and inspect its spring contact for tension and wear. Replace the rotor and cap if necessary.

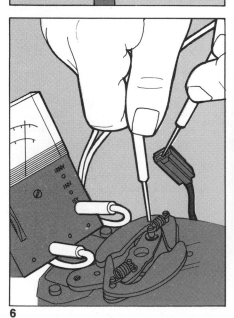

6

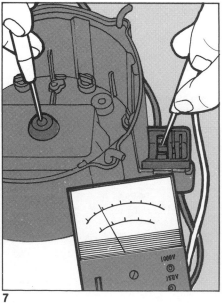

7

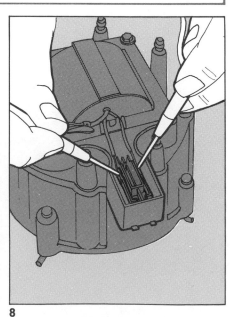

8

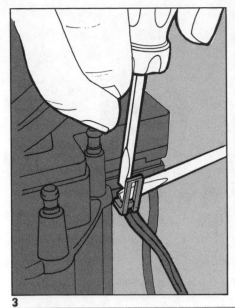

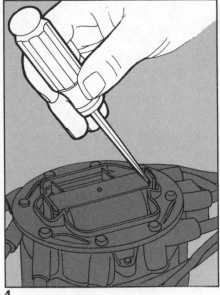

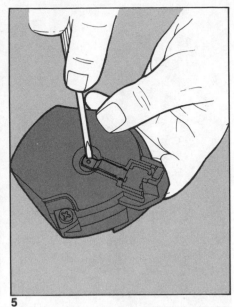

3

4

5

6 Touch the voltmeter negative lead to a ground and the positive lead to the white battery connector. Make sure the ignition switch is on. The voltmeter should read battery voltage. If it does not, check the ignition switch lead from the battery to the switch, and from the switch to the distributor battery terminal that connects to the coil. The voltmeter should read battery voltage.

7 To check the secondary resistance of the coil, touch one ohmmeter lead to the distributor high-tension terminal and the other lead to the coil wire. Make sure the ignition switch is off. The reading should be within specs. If it is not, replace the coil.

8 To check coil primary resistance, remove the three screws that attach the coil cover to the distributor cap and lift off the cover. Touch one lead of an ohmmeter to the battery terminal and the other lead to the coil wire. Make sure the ignition switch is off and the battery source is disconnected. The reading should meet specs. If it does not, replace the coil.

9 To test the distributor pickup coil, connect one lead of an ohmmeter to one connector terminal and the other lead to the second connector terminal. The reading should be within specs. If not, replace the pickup coil or see a professional mechanic. Inspect the connector wires for chafing, breaks or loose connections.

10 To replace the module, first unplug the two connectors, one on each side of it. Note that the module terminals are of different sizes to prevent improper installation. Now remove the two hold-down screws from the module and lift it out.

11 With a timing light, set the correct timing at the proper rpm. The vacuum line should be disconnected and plugged. Then adjust the idle speed to specs.

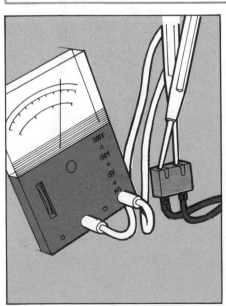

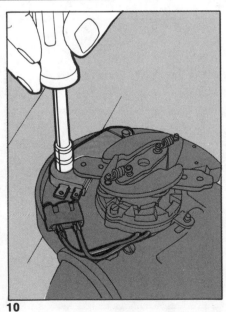

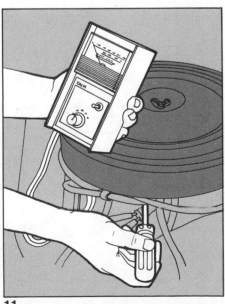

9

10

11

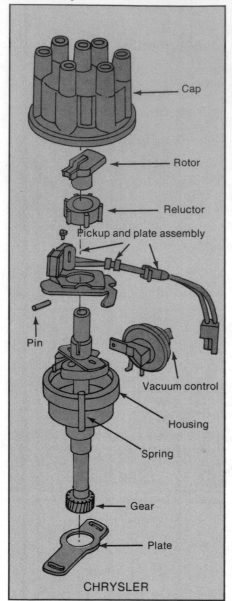

Cap

Rotor

Reluctor

Pickup and plate assembly

Pin

Vacuum control

Housing

Spring

Gear

Plate

CHRYSLER

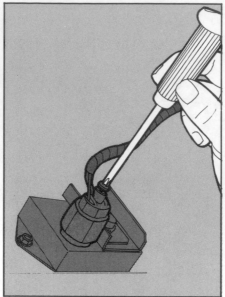

1

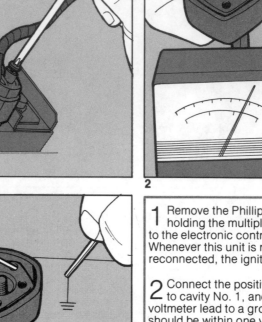

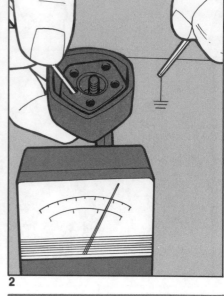

2

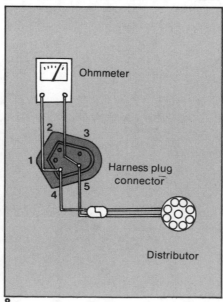

6

1 Remove the Phillips-head screw holding the multiple-wire connector to the electronic control unit. Note: Whenever this unit is removed or reconnected, the ignition must be off.

2 Connect the positive voltmeter lead to cavity No. 1, and the negative voltmeter lead to a ground. The reading should be within one volt of battery voltage with all accessories off and the ignition switch on.

3 If there is more than one-volt difference, test the circuit shown with a voltmeter at each connecting point until the problem is found.

4 With the ignition switch still on, touch cavity No. 2 with the positive voltmeter lead and ground the negative

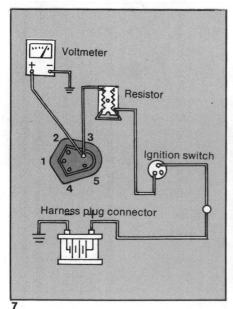

Voltmeter

Resistor

Ignition switch

Harness plug connector

2 3
1   5
  4

7

Ohmmeter

Harness plug connector

2 3
1   5
  4

Distributor

8

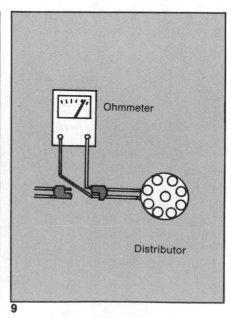

Ohmmeter

Distributor

9

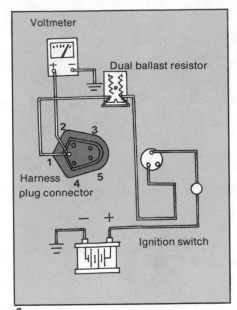

Voltmeter
Dual ballast resistor
Harness plug connector
Ignition switch

3

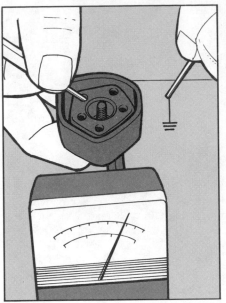

4

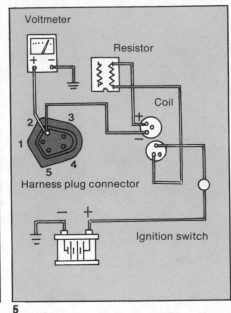

Voltmeter
Resistor
Coil
Harness plug connector
Ignition switch

5

lead. The reading should be within one volt of battery voltage.

5 If there is more than one-volt difference, repeat step 3 for the circuit shown.

6 Touch the positive voltmeter lead to cavity No. 3 and ground the negative lead. Again, the ignition switch must be on. The reading should be within one volt of battery voltage.

7 If the difference is more than one volt, repeat step 3 for the circuit illustrated.

8 To check the distributor pickup coil, turn off the ignition, and connect an ohmmeter between No. 4 and No. 5 cavities. The resistance should read

between 150 and 900 ohms. Note that the ignition switch must be off. Disconnect the dual lead connector if the reading is other than specified.

9 Now, with the ignition switch off, connect the ohmmeter leads to both terminals of the disconnected dual connector coming from the distributor. If the reading is not between 150 and 900 ohms, replace the pickup coil assembly in the distributor.

10 If the ohmmeter reading is within specs, check the wiring harness between the control unit and the dual lead connector with a volt/amp tester.

11 To check the electronic ground circuit, connect one ohmmeter lead to a good ground and the other lead to the control unit connector pin No. 5.

Make sure the ignition switch is off. The ohmmeter should show continuity (a full reading). If there is no continuity, loosen the control unit bolts and clean off any dirt around the bolts and the mounting area. Reinstall and tighten the bolts and retest. If there is still no continuity, replace the control unit. Reconnect the wiring harness at the control unit and distributor.

12 Check the air gap between the reluctor tooth and the pickup coil. To adjust the air gap, align one reluctor tooth with the pickup coil core. Loosen the pickup coil hold-down screw and place a .006-inch non-magnetic feeler gauge between the tooth and the core. Adjust the gap so contact is made between the tooth, feeler gauge, and core. Now tighten the hold-down screw.

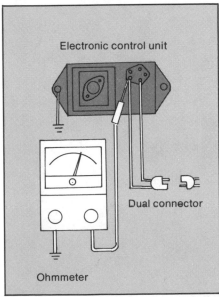

Electronic control unit
Dual connector
Ohmmeter

10

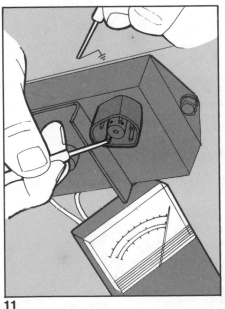

11

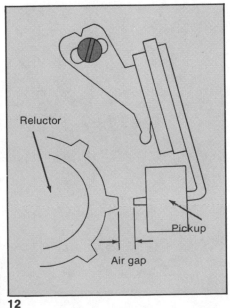

Reluctor
Pickup
Air gap

12

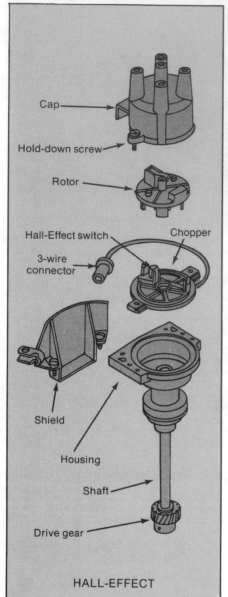

Cap

Hold-down screw

Rotor

Hall-Effect switch

3-wire connector

Chopper

Shield

Housing

Shaft

Drive gear

HALL-EFFECT

Distributor

Coil

1

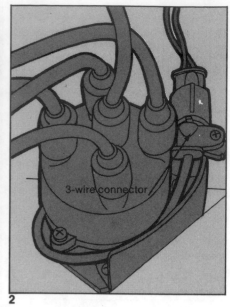

3-wire connector

2

6

1 Overview of the crowded Plymouth Horizon engine compartment showing a transverse engine. Note the distance between the ignition coil and the distributor.

2 A 3-wire connector is mounted on the side of the distributor.

3 Remove the coil high-tension wire from the distributor cap and put it aside for later testing.

4 To lift off the distributor cap, remove the two hold-down screws with a Phillips-head screwdriver.

5 After removing the distributor cap, lift out the rotor for inspection. Check for cracks, excessive burning of

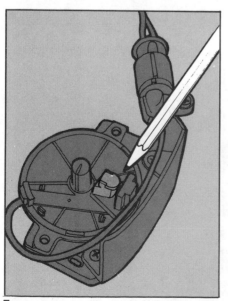

7

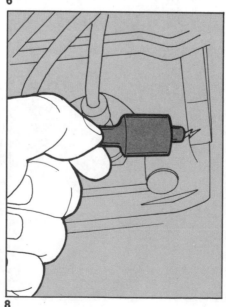

8

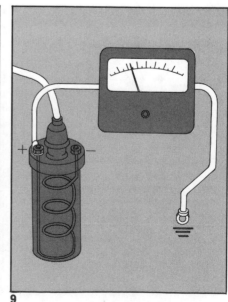

9

3

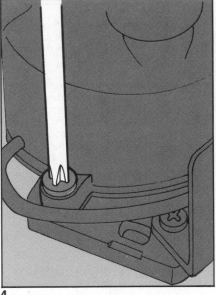

4

5

the blade tip, and proper tension of the spring terminal. *Caution: Silicone grease on the metal part of the rotor is normal. Do not wipe it off. Light scaling on the tip can be removed with a sharp knife. If scaling is excessive, replace the rotor.*

6 Inspect the underside of the rotor for carbon tracking. Check the chopper and make sure the leading and trailing edges of the four vanes are square. Replace the chopper if it is defective.

7 The pencil points to the Hall-Effect switch (sensor). As the chopper turns, current to the coil is turned off and a high-voltage spark is induced and routed to a spark plug.

8 Disconnect the wire from the negative terminal of the ignition coil. With the ignition switch on, connect one end of a jumper wire to the negative terminal of the coil. Now touch the other end momentarily to an engine ground while holding the coil high-tension wire you disconnected in step 3 one-quarter of an inch from a good engine ground. A spark should occur.

9 If there is no spark when performing step 8, with the ignition switch on check for voltage at the positive terminal of the coil. If the voltmeter reads at least nine volts, the coil is defective and should be replaced. If voltage is below nine volts, check the ballast resistor, wiring, and connections.

10 If a spark occurred in step 8, reconnect the negative coil wire to its terminal and disconnect the 3-wire distributor connector. Turn the ignition switch on and measure the voltage between pin B and a good ground. It should be the same as battery voltage.

11 If the voltmeter reading in step 9 was not battery voltage, turn the ignition switch off and disconnect the 10-wire harness connector (arrow) going to the spark control computer.

12 Check for continuity between pin B of the 3-wire connector and pin 3 of the 10-wire connector.

Continued

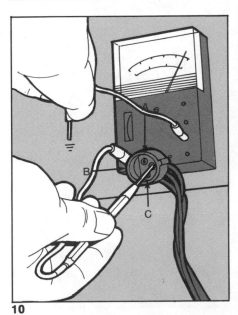

10

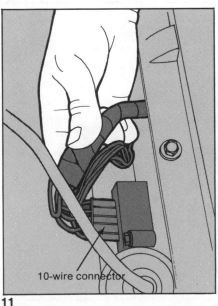

10-wire connector

11

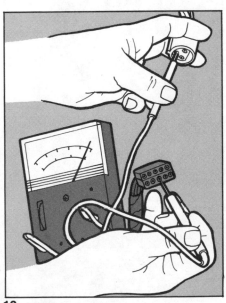

12

Hall-Effect, continued

13 If there is no continuity, turn the ignition switch on and measure the voltage between pin 2 and pin 10 of the disconnected 10-wire connector. The reading should be battery voltage. If it is not, the wiring and connections of pin 2 and pin 10 should be checked. If battery voltage is obtained, the spark control computer is defective and should be replaced.

14 With the ignition switch on and the 10-wire connector reconnected, hold the center wire of the coil one-quarter inch from a good ground. Pass a feeler gauge (metal) through the pickup coil gap. A spark should occur. If there is no spark, disconnect the 3-wire connector going to the distributor and momentarily touch 10A to pin C with a jumper wire or a paper clip. If a spark occurs, the pickup assembly is defective and must be replaced.

15 To replace the pickup assembly (switch plate), remove the two lock springs. The pencil points to one of them. Lift out the pickup assembly, then remove the two screws holding the shield to the distributor. Reverse these procedures to install the new pickup assembly.

16 To set the ignition timing, you can use either a magnetic pulse timing light at the probe hole or an induction-type timing light at the timing marks.

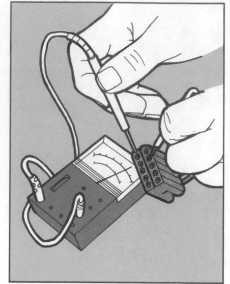

13

Photosteps: AMERICAN MOTORS (PRESTOLITE) ELECTRONIC IGNITION SYSTEM

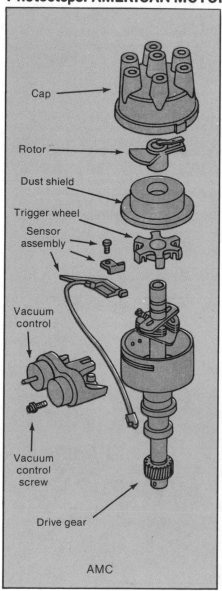

- Cap
- Rotor
- Dust shield
- Trigger wheel
- Sensor assembly
- Vacuum control
- Vacuum control screw
- Drive gear

AMC

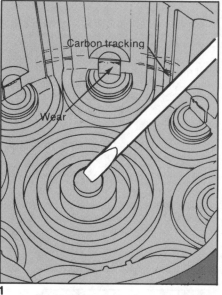

Carbon tracking

Wear

1

2

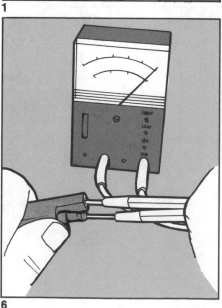

6

7

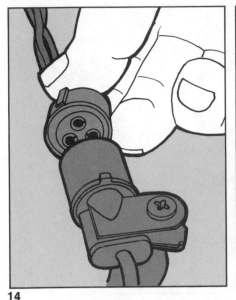

14

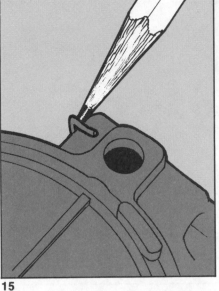

15

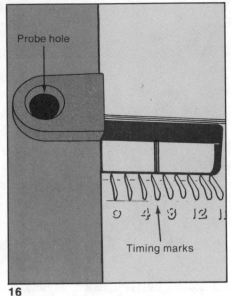

Probe hole

o 4 8 12 1.

Timing marks

16

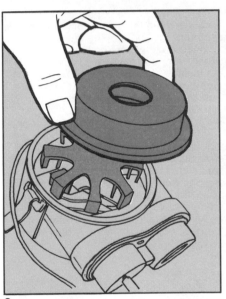

3

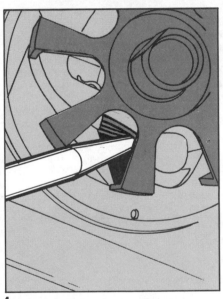

4

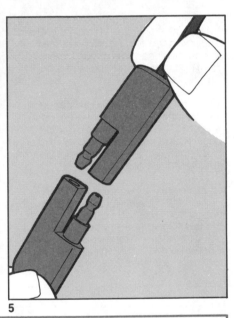

5

1 After removing the distributor cap, inspect the underside for wear or carbon tracking. Replace the cap if necessary. Inspect the carbon button in the center of the distributor cap. It should move down when pressure is put on it. When pressure is released, the button should move up due to spring action. If it does not, replace the cap.

2 Remove the rotor by lifting it off the distributor shaft. Inspect the rotor for worn blades and cracks, and replace it if necessary.

3 Remove the dust shield from the distributor to expose the vanes and trigger assembly for inspection.

4 The pen points to the small wires under the trigger wheel going to the sensor. Inspect these wires for chafing, breaks or shorting against the wheel. If the wires are damaged, the sensor unit must be replaced. A special tool, similar to a battery terminal puller, is necessary to remove the wheel.

5 Disconnect the dual-wire connector from the sensor. The connector is located on the side of the distributor.

6 To measure resistance in the sensor unit, use the distributor side of the disconnected dual-lead connector. Connect one ohmmeter lead to one terminal of the connector and the other

ohmmeter lead to the second terminal of the connector. Make sure the ignition switch is off. The reading should meet specs. If it does not, the sensor unit must be replaced. Wiggle the sensor wires while observing the ohmmeter reading. Any movement of the needle means trouble in that line, and you should replace the sensor unit.

7 To measure secondary resistance in the ignition coil, remove the coil wires. Touch one ohmmeter lead to the positive (primary) terminal of the coil and insert the other ohmmeter lead into the center (secondary) coil tower. The reading should meet specs. If it does not, replace the coil. **Continued**

Note: Prestolite is found in pre-1978 AMC cars. If you have a more recent model with electronic ignition, your **system will be either Ford or GM, depending on the model. Check the label on your distributor. If it says** **Motorcraft, you have a Ford system; Delco-Remy means GM. You will find these systems in the preceding pages.**

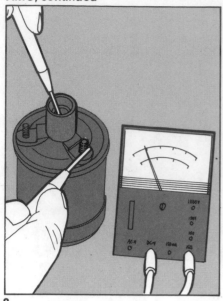

8

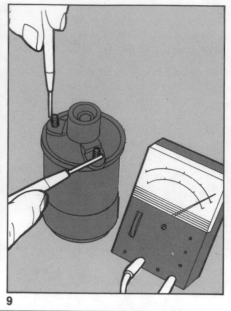

9

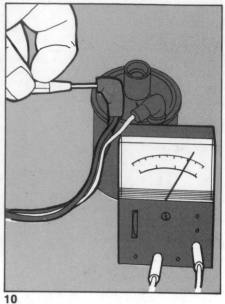

10

8 Now touch one ohmmeter lead to the negative (primary) terminal of the coil and insert the other ohmmeter lead into the center (secondary) coil tower. The reading should meet specs. If it does not, replace the coil.

9 To measure primary resistance in the ignition coil, remove the coil wires. Touch the ohmmeter leads to the positive and negative (primary) terminals of the coil. If the reading does not meet specs, replace the coil.

10 To test for voltage from the ignition switch to the coil, pull the positive coil lead off its terminal. Attach the positive voltmeter lead to the positive coil wire from the ignition switch.
Caution: To avoid a false reading, see that the positive voltmeter lead is not

touching any other terminals. Attach the negative voltmeter lead to a good ground. Make sure the ignition switch is on. If the reading is not within specs, check the ignition switch and wiring going to the battery at each connecting point until the problem is found.

11 To check continuity through the coil primary circuit, reconnect the positive coil lead (from the ignition switch) to the ignition coil. With the ignition switch on, disconnect the negative coil lead (distributor side) and touch a voltmeter positive lead to the negative coil terminal and a negative voltmeter lead to a ground. If the reading is not within specs, replace the coil.

12 To inspect the connections between the control unit and the distributor, disconnect the 4-wire connector (shown on the fender well). Inspect it for corrosion and broken terminals. If the connector on the control-unit side is defective, the unit must be replaced.

13 To check the 4-way connector on the distributor side, hold the connector facing you so the two male terminals are on the left and the two female terminals on the right. With the ignition switch off, touch one ohmmeter probe to the top female terminal and the other probe to the top male terminal. The reading should indicate continuity. If it does not, replace the 4-way connector.

11

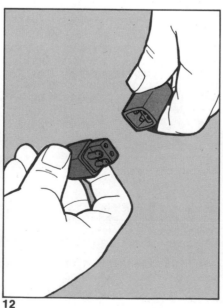

12

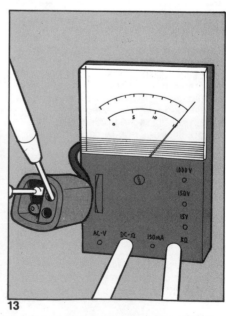

13

EMISSION CONTROL SYSTEM

Atmospheric pollution, or smog, is what results when any type of fossil fuel, gasoline, for example, burns and enters the atmosphere. One way these pollutants get up there is through incomplete combustion in your car engine.

When your car engine is running, the gasoline that serves as its fuel is not destroyed completely. The unburned portion, containing hydrocarbon compounds, reaches the atmosphere by way of the engine exhaust system. Hydrocarbons are also released as unburned fuel escapes into the crankcase during the compression stroke of the piston. A third source of hydrocarbon pollution is the carburetor. With the engine switched off, the fuel in the carburetor evaporates and enters the atmosphere through the air vent. A poorly-adjusted carburetor will also expel hydrocarbons; if the fuel-and-air mixture is set too lean, the fuel may be so diluted with air that the mixture will not ignite. The result is a misfire and further HC emission. And finally, hydrocarbons find their way into the atmosphere in the form of vapor escaping from the fuel tank.

Nitrogen oxide (NOx) emissions form as the engine operates. Air is mixed with fuel, then drawn into the engine, and ignited in the combustion chamber, where the temperature can exceed 4,500°. Above 2,500°F, nitrogen combines with oxygen and forms NOx, a colorless gas which combines further with oxygen when it enters the atmosphere, creating the compound nitrogen dioxide (NO_2). NO_2 chemically activates hydrocarbons in the presence of sunlight, adding to photochemical smog. As the sunlight interacts with the smog, a new pollutant is created, ozone (O_3). O_3 is an odorous gas which irritates the lung tissues and the eyes, affects the growth of some crops and plants, and causes deterioration of rubber products.

Carbon monoxide (CO), a by-product of combustion, is a poisonous gas having no color or odor. When inhaled, it takes the place of the oxygen in the bloodstream, and prolonged exposure to concentrated CO will cause death. Carbon monoxide chemically speeds the production of photochemical smog.

On most cars built since 1973, HC, NOx, and CO emissions are reduced by the installation of the following emission control devices: a charcoal canister controls the emission of HC from the fuel tank and the carburetor. A positive crankcase ventilating system (PCV) controls HC emissions from the engine's crankcase. An exhaust gas recirculation system (EGR) controls NOx from the engine's exhaust. Air injection reaction (AIR), thermostatic air cleaner, and catalytic converter systems control HC & CO in the engine exhaust.

CONTENTS

Charcoal Canister and Filter Replacement

The charcoal canister absorbs fuel vapor from the fuel tank and the carburetor when the engine is not running. When it is running, the fuel vapor in the canister is drawn through a vacuum hose into the intake manifold.

Tools and equipment:

Set of combination wrenches.
Screwdriver.
Droplight or flashlight.
Fender covers.
$\frac{3}{8}''$ drive socket set.
Masking tape.
Pliers.
Wire brush.
Wire gun-bore brush.
Scraper.
Torque wrench.
Goggles.
Hand vacuum pump.
Electric drill.
Set of twist drills.

Parts:

With the instructions given in this chapter, you may replace the following parts of the emission control system on your car if you need to:
Charcoal canister filter.
Charcoal canister.
Positive crankcase ventilating system (PCV) valve.
PCV hose.
Exhaust gas recirculation (EGR) valve.
Air pump.
Air pump belt.
Aspirator valve.
Vacuum motor.
Vacuum hose.

Fiberglass filter

Replacing the charcoal canister filter on American Motors, General Motors, and Chrysler cars. Open the hood and locate the charcoal canister, usually mounted on the inner fender pan close to the radiator in the engine compartment. Remove the canister from the holder or bracket and turn it upside down. Remove and discard the fiberglass filter, which resembles a large powder puff. Be careful not to tear the new filter when installing it. Replace the canister in the bracket or holder. Note: There is no filter on Ford cars.

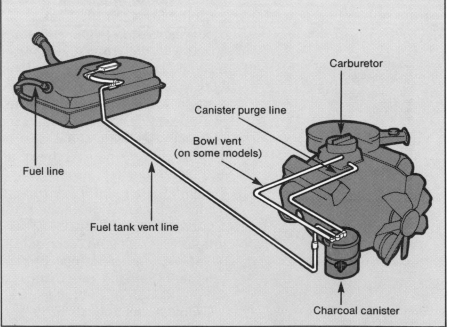

Carburetor

Canister purge line

Bowl vent (on some models)

Fuel line

Fuel tank vent line

Charcoal canister

Replacing the charcoal canister on all cars. Locate the canister in the engine compartment, and, using your own code, mark the vacuum hose lines with masking tape for correct reinstallation. Different cars use different vacuum line setups. Your car may have a fuel tank vent line, a purge line, and/or a carburetor vent line. After removing the lines, take the canister out of the holder or bracket and discard it. Replace the new canister in the holder or bracket and connect the hose lines. Note: on Ford products, the charcoal canister is mounted on the right side of the engine close to the oil pan.

Positive Crankcase Ventilation (PCV) Valve

State regulations

Some states require that all registered cars be equipped with emission control systems. Check your state laws for the requirements for your car. In addition, some states permit only licensed or qualified auto mechanics to test, service, and repair emission control systems. So, before attempting any testing, servicing, or repairing yourself, check your state laws.

The PCV system draws vapor, containing hydrocarbons, from the crankcase into the intake manifold. The PCV valve is a spring-loaded, vacuum-operated valve which regulates the flow of vapors to the intake manifold when the engine is running. In addition, it acts as a check valve when the engine is switched off or if a backfire should occur in the intake manifold. This action prevents igniting the vapors in the crankcase.

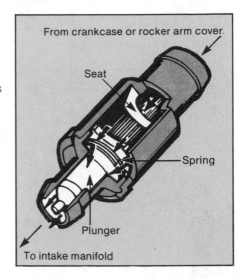

From crankcase or rocker arm cover.

Seat

Spring

Plunger

To intake manifold

Pro Shop

PCV valve paper check

We suggest that if you do not have a tach-dwell meter, remove the oil filler cap. While the engine is running at curb idle, place a piece of 8x10 paper over the oil filler opening. The paper should be sucked against the opening after the vacuum builds up.

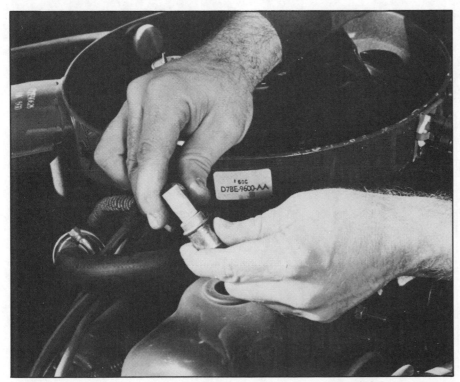

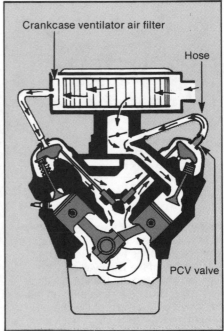

Crankcase ventilator air filter

Hose

PCV valve

Replacing the PCV valve and hose.
Remove the PCV valve by hand from the engine valve cover, filler cap, or the valve lifter cover located under the intake manifold. Remove the hose which runs from the PCV valve to the intake manifold and discard it. Install the new valve and hose.

Exhaust Gas Recirculating (EGR) System

The EGR system reduces NOx by introducing small amounts of exhaust gases into the intake manifold. These gases mix with and dilute the fuel-and-air mixture, thereby lowering the combustion temperature. The EGR valve is closed and does not receive vacuum at idle. Above idle, vacuum goes through the hose and opens the valve. If the valve opens at idle, it is stuck open or the vacuum hose is not connected properly.

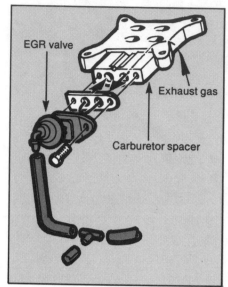

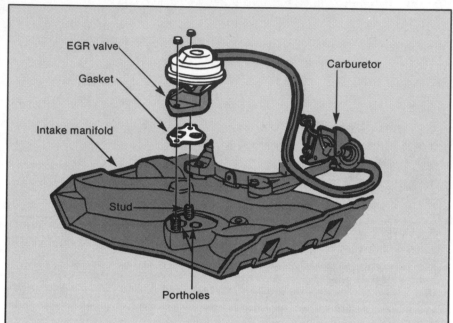

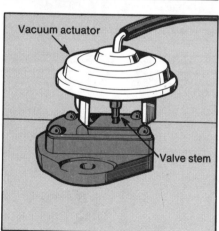

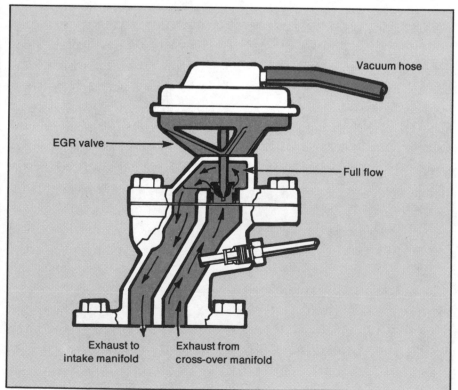

Replacing the EGR valve. Disconnect the vacuum hose from the diaphragm by hand. Remove the two mounting bolts which connect the EGR valve to the manifold and take out the valve. Clean the mating surface by scraping off the old gasket on the manifold with a scraper and a wire brush. Check and clean out the portholes in the intake manifold with a wire gun-bore brush or a small round wire brush, similar to a bottle brush. Install a new EGR valve and a new gasket. Tighten the holding bolts to manufacturer's torque specifications with a torque wrench, and connect the vacuum hose. Pictured are four types of EGR valves.

Air Injection Reaction (AIR) System

The air injection system reduces CO and HC in the exhaust of the engine. An engine-driven air pump brings fresh air into the exhaust system or exhaust manifold. The oxygen in the air helps ignite the unburned fuel in the exhaust gases, thus reducing HC and CO in the exhaust. On some late-model Chrysler products, to meet regulations in certain states, the manufacturer uses the vacuum which is created by the movement of the exhaust gases to draw fresh air into the exhaust manifold. An aspirator valve regulates fresh air flow without the need for an air pump. Some cars are clean enough without air injection and don't have it.

We recommend that you start the engine, then grasp the valve with your hand. You should feel a pulsating action in the valve. Disconnect the aspirator air hose from the aspirator. There should be no hot gases coming from the valve.

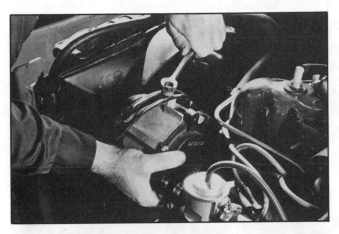

Replacing the air pump. Locate the air pump, which is mounted on the front of the engine and is driven by a belt. It looks like a small alternator. Free the adjusting arm bolt, and remove the drive belt, pump holding-bolts, and pump. Replace the pump and holding-bolts, replace the drive belt, and adjust the belt as described in Chapter 3. Start the engine and check the diverter valve with your hand as described in Chapter 4.

Replacing the diverter valve and hoses. Primarily on Ford cars, the diverter valve is connected in the air line with the hose connections between the air pump and the exhaust manifold. Loosen the four hose clamps that secure the hoses to the valve, the exhaust manifold tubing, and the air pump. Remove and discard the valve and hoses, and install new ones. Tighten the hose clamps securely. Start the engine and check the diverter valve again.

Replacing the aspirator valve on Chrysler products. Locate the aspirator valve, and remove the air hoses. Loosen and unscrew the valve from the aspirator tube, using two open-end wrenches, then screw the new valve into the tube and connect the hoses.

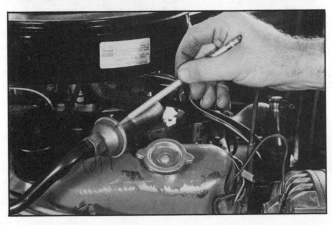

Carburetor-heated Air Systems

Pro Shop

Cutting new hoses to length

We've found it's easy to get the right fit if you simply use the old vacuum hoses as a guide to cut the new hoses to the correct length.

This system heats the air entering the carburetor when the engine is cold, and allows fresh air into the carburetor when the engine is at normal running temperature, thereby reducing HC and CO in the exhaust gases. The system is controlled by the engine vacuum and the ducted hot air from the exhaust manifold. When the engine is cold, a heat sensor, located in the air cleaner, controls engine vacuum to a diaphragm in the vacuum motor located on the top side of the snorkel tube. The vacuum motor operates a door in the snorkel which opens or closes the snorkel to heated air from the exhaust manifold or to cold air from the outside. Some manufacturers use a thermostat unit in place of the heat sensor and vacuum motor.

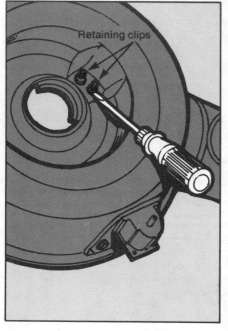

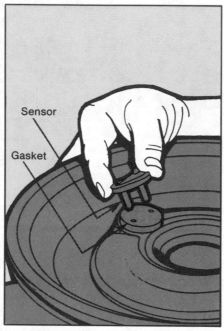

Replacing the carburetor-heated air system sensor. Remove the air cleaner, as shown in Chapter 4. Turn it upside down and remove the two retaining clips. Now turn it right side up and remove the sensor and gasket. Install the new gasket and sensor and secure them with the two new clips, then reinstall the air cleaner and attach all vacuum hoses.

Servicing the vacuum motor

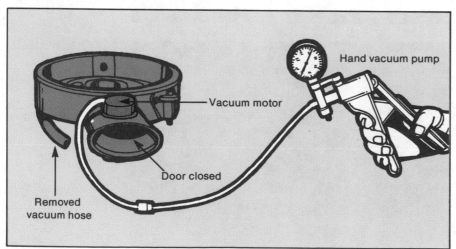

1 To check the vacuum motor, remove the vacuum hose which is attached to it. Connect a hand vacuum pump hose to the motor, and operate the pump until the vacuum gauge reads 20 inches of vacuum. The door in the snorkel should be closed to outside air. The vacuum gauge needle must not drop below ten inches of vacuum in five minutes.

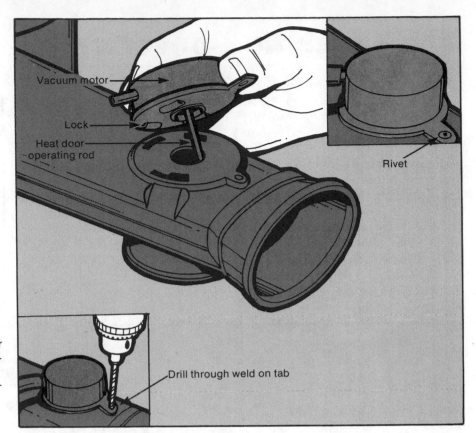

2 **To remove a defective vacuum motor,** drill out the two tack welds or rivets on the tabs which connect the motor to the snorkel. Unhook the heat door operating rod from the snorkel door and remove and discard the motor. Connect the new vacuum motor's heat door operating rod to the snorkel door and replace the motor; then secure the motor to the snorkel with the two sheet metal screws which come with it.

Vacuum motor

Lock

Heat door operating rod

Rivet

Drill through weld on tab

Replacing air cleaner vacuum hoses. Remove the air cleaner from the engine, turn it upside down, and to insure correct installation, replace one vacuum hose at a time. Replace the air cleaner.

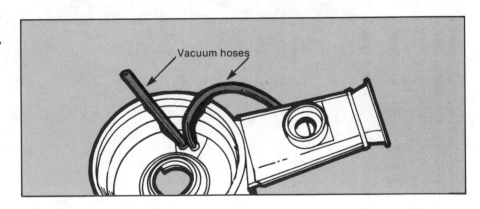

Vacuum hoses

Replacing the thermostat unit. Remove the air cleaner, the two sheet metal screws which hold the snorkel to the air cleaner assembly, and the snorkel. Loosen the thermostat or temperature sensor locking nut, and screw the thermostat in, clockwise, from the opening of the air cleaner side of the snorkel. Unhook the door operating rod and unscrew the thermostat from the snorkel. Install the new thermostat by screwing it into the snorkel with the locking nut attached, until the operating rod can be connected to the door. Connect the rod to the door and unscrew the thermostat until the door just closes to the outside air. Hold the thermostat and tighten the locking nut securely. Replace the snorkel onto the air cleaner and secure it with the two sheet metal screws. Replace the air cleaner on the engine.

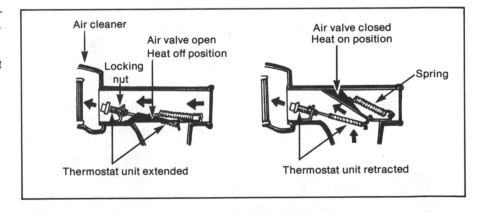

Air cleaner

Air valve open
Heat off position

Air valve closed
Heat on position

Locking nut

Spring

Thermostat unit extended

Thermostat unit retracted

The Catalytic Converter

The catalytic converter reduces HC and CO in the exhaust gases by means of a chemical reaction that takes place in a container resembling a small muffler, using either platinum or palladium as a catalyst. These substances add oxygen to the exhaust gases, thereby reducing HC and CO.

An exhaust gas analyzer should be used for a full check of a catalytic converter. However, physical damage—large dents, ruptures, punctures, or excessive heat discoloration of the converter and scorching of the auto underbody just above the converter—may indicate a defective unit. If you think your car's catalytic converter is defective, have it checked. A visual check can be misleading, however. For example, a poorly-tuned engine can cause the converter to overheat and discolor. Only an exhaust gas analyzer can determine if the converter is defective or if the engine is improperly functioning.

Pro Shop

Protect your catalytic converter

Some cases of damage to catalytic converters have been reported where the damage apparently has been caused by commercial carburetor cleaners that are sold in fluid or spray form. So if your car has a catalytic converter we suggest you do not use these cleaners unless the label OK's such use.

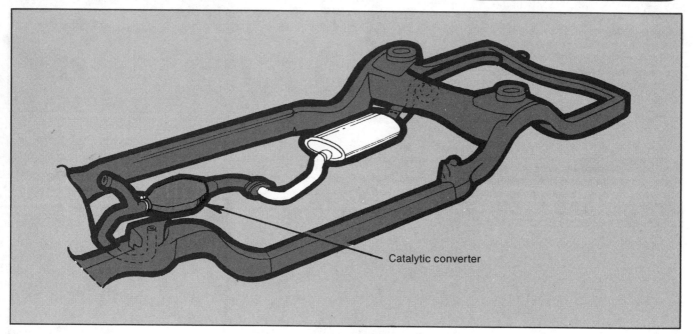

Catalytic converter

ECONOTIP

#8
Vehicle design and gas mileage

Of all the things car engineers can do to improve gas mileage, the biggest improvement comes from weight reduction. Generally speaking, a lightweight car is smaller than a heavier one. But it doesn't have to be a cramped fit for the driver and passengers. The designers have learned to make cars lighter and smaller, but still comfortable. Engine compartments have been reduced in size, and this makes more room in the passenger compartment.

When you buy a car, remember that no matter how good and careful a driver you are, a heavier car will not get as good mileage as a lighter car, if everything else is equal. There are some small car engines of older design which are not very efficient. In that case, a later model heavier car might get better mileage, because its engine is designed for mileage. But if you want to be a champion in the miles-per-gallon race, the lightest car with a modern engine will be a winner.

FUEL SYSTEM

The fuel system stores the fuel, delivers it to the carburetor, and mixes it with the proper amount of air to meet the varying speed and load conditions your car encounters. To accomplish these jobs, this system requires the following components: a storage tank, flexible and steel fuel lines, a pump, a filter, a carburetor, an air cleaner, and an intake manifold.

The fuel tank, the reservoir for the fuel system, is vented through either the charcoal canister or the gas cap. Most fuel tanks are designed with a pickup tube located just above the bottom of the tank, so that rust, dirt, or water which may collect at the bottom of the tank is not drawn into the fuel line, fuel pump, or carburetor.

The fuel lines are made up of steel tubing and neoprene sections. Usually the steel line runs along the chassis from the tank to the fuel pump and has flexible neoprene attachments to the fuel tank pickup at one end and to the fuel pump at the other. This arrangement allows for engine movement.

When the fuel system is in operation, the lines are subjected to both vacuum and pressure—vacuum from the tank to the pump and pressure from the pump to the carburetor. Over time, leaks in the form of air entering the system or fuel leaking out may result.

In most modern cars, the fuel pump is driven by the camshaft. The purpose of the pump is to draw the fuel from the tank and send it to the carburetor. In doing this, it must supply to the carburetor a constant quantity of fuel, at a prescribed pressure, to meet the engine's differing requirements. On some cars, certain Buick, Chevy, and Ford models, for example, there is an electrically-operated pump located in the fuel tank itself.

The carburetor is designed to mix the correct amount of fuel with air, by volume, to meet the full range of operating conditions from starting to full revolutions per minute (RPM). Gasoline is used as a fuel for the car engine because of its very high potential energy— three times that of dynamite. Composed of 15 percent hydrogen and 85 percent carbon, gasoline when mixed with air and atomized, forms a very highly combustible mixture capable of releasing huge amounts of heat energy.

In this chapter you will learn how to service and replace the fuel tank, fuel lines, the fuel pump, and the carburetor.

CONTENTS

Servicing the Fuel Tank

Before you attempt to remove the fuel tank, it must be empty. It is suggested that you drive your car until the gas gauge is at the "E," or empty, line, and then siphon out the remainder of the gas. *Caution: Do not use a droplight when you are working on any of the fuel system components. Spilled gasoline on a hot bulb can cause the bulb to* *explode and ignite the gasoline. Use a flashlight if it is necessary to illuminate the area where you are working. Never attempt to solder or weld a fuel tank or parts of the car near a fuel tank. Even when a tank is empty of fuel, it may contain enough gas to cause an explosion if the gas comes in contact with a flame or excessive heat.*

Removing and replacing the sending unit

Raise and support the front and rear of the car, then open the hood and disconnect the ground (usually negative) battery cable from its post.

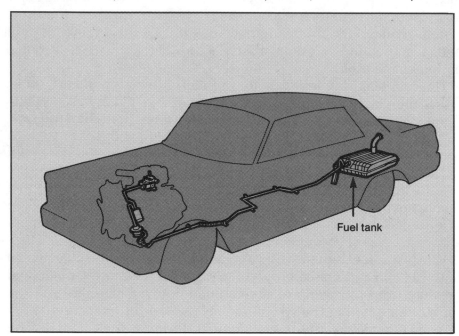

Fuel tank

Tools and equipment:

Floor jack.
Stands.
Flashlight.
Fender covers.
⅜" and ½" drive socket sets.
Common screwdrivers.
Pliers.
Masking tape.
A safety fuel can of five-gallon capacity.
Hand cloths.
Spray can of rust solvent (a penetrating oil).
Set of combination wrenches.
Siphon bulb and hose.
Creeper.
Goggles.
Lock ring removing tool.
Petroleum jelly.
Funnel.
Drain pan.
Fuel pump pressure gauge.
Sharp knife.
Class B type fire extinguisher.
Can of gasket sealer.
Scraper.
Note: a class B type fire extinguisher is one specifically designed to put out gasoline fires.

ECONOTIP

#9
Vapor control nozzles can spill gas

The new vapor control pump nozzles at gas stations will overflow the tank if not properly used. On the older nozzles, you could squeeze the handle a dozen times. Each time it would shut off when the gas backed up in the nozzle. Finally, the filler neck would be full and you could hang up the pump, knowing you had a really full tank.

This practice will cause some vapor control nozzles to overflow. Because of the vapor control, these new nozzles are not as sensitive to gas backup. They will shut the gas off the first time, and usually the second time. But if you continue to squeeze the handle, the gas will fill up the bellows and there will be a flood when you take the nozzle out of the filler neck.

Siphon hose

Fuel pump inlet

gas

Hose to fuel tank

1 **Disconnect the flexible fuel line** which runs from the fuel tank to the fuel pump and connect the siphon hose to the tank. Siphon the remainder of the gasoline from the tank into a clean five-gallon safety fuel can.

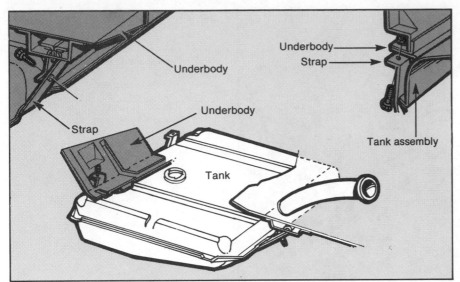

Underbody

Underbody
Strap

Underbody

Strap

Underbody

Tank

Tank assembly

2 **Locate the bolts holding the tank strap** and liberally spray them with a rust solvent or penetrating oil. While the bolts are soaking, find the vent lines connected to the fuel tank. Attach a piece of masking tape to each line, and, using your own code, mark them to insure correct reinstallation. Disconnect the vent lines and the plugged wire connected to the sending unit. This wire is usually mounted on the upper front or top section of the fuel tank.

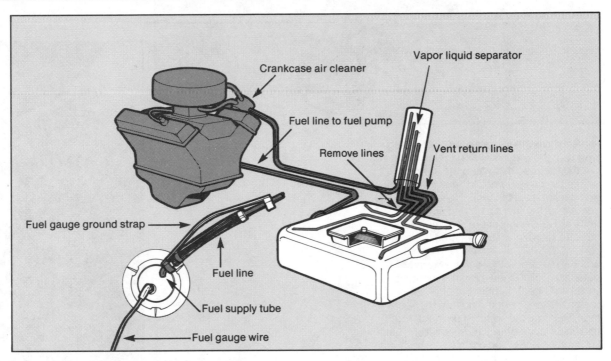

Crankcase air cleaner

Vapor liquid separator

Fuel line to fuel pump

Remove lines

Vent return lines

Fuel gauge ground strap

Fuel line

Fuel supply tube

Fuel gauge wire

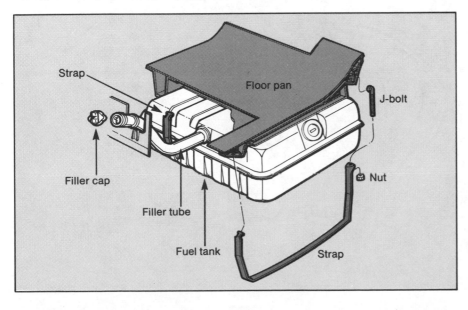

Strap

Floor pan

J-bolt

Filler cap

Nut

Filler tube

Fuel tank

Strap

3 **Loosen both bolts holding the fuel tank strap** until they are about two threads from the end. Holding the tank firmly against the underbody of the car with one hand, remove the two bolts and slowly lower the tank to the ground. Remove the filler cap and pour the remaining gasoline, if any, into the safety gas can.

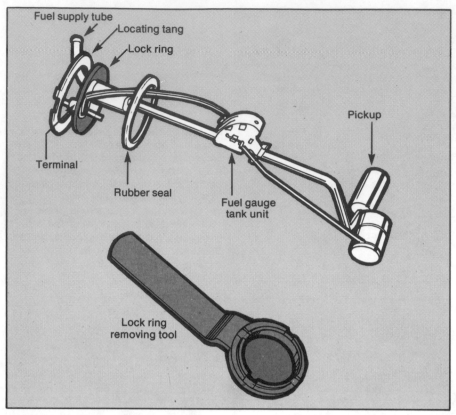

Fuel supply tube
Locating tang
Lock ring
Terminal
Rubber seal
Fuel gauge tank unit
Pickup
Lock ring removing tool

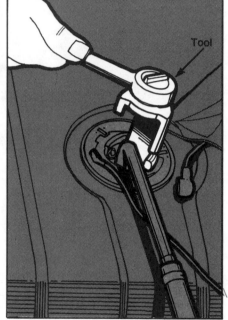

Tool

4 **Remove the sending unit retaining ring** with the ring removing tool or take out the screws which hold the sending unit to the tank. Remove the sending unit and gasket from the tank. Note: On some cars the fuel pump and sending units are one component, but the procedure for removal is the same as that described above. Lubricate the sending unit rubber seal with a small amount of petroleum jelly. Then align the locating tangs with the tank opening and install the gasket and sending unit on the fuel tank. Replace the sending unit lock ring or screws and tighten them securely. Lift the tank up under the car's underbody and hold it firmly with one hand while tightening the two tank strap bolts. Connect the vent lines, the fuel line, and the sending unit wires, and hook the fuel line back up to the fuel pump. Pour the siphoned gasoline back into the fuel tank, replace the filler cap, and lower the car. Connect the negative battery cable. Remember, your fuel level is very low, so gas up as soon as possible.

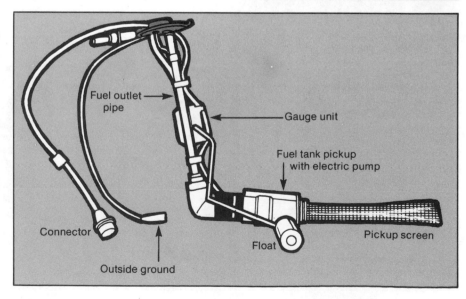

Fuel outlet pipe
Gauge unit
Fuel tank pickup with electric pump
Connector
Outside ground
Float
Pickup screen

Replacing Fuel Lines

A damaged fuel line must be replaced with one similar in construction to the original—a steel line must be replaced with a steel line, a neoprene line with a neoprene line. In some cases it may be necessary to jack up and support the entire car, or you may be able to gain access to the fuel lines by raising only the front or rear.

Replacing the flexible fuel line at the gas tank. Jack up and support the car. Remember to use a flashlight rather than a droplight. With the correct tool, remove the clamps which hold the flexible fuel line to the fuel tank sending unit and the steel fuel line. Place a drain pan under the line to catch any fuel spilled when you remove it. Now remove the flexible line by twisting and pulling it off of the fuel tank unit and the steel line. *Caution: Wipe up any spilled gasoline at once.* Install the new flexible line on the fuel tank unit and the steel line, then reinstall the clamps.

Pro Shop

Use the old to size the new

To insure a flexible fuel replacement line of the right length, lay the old line alongside the new one. Then with a sharp knife, cut the new line to the same length as the old one.

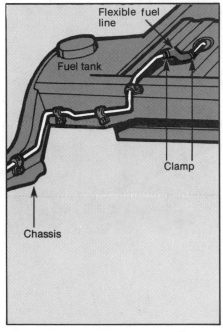

Flexible fuel line

Fuel tank

Clamp

Chassis

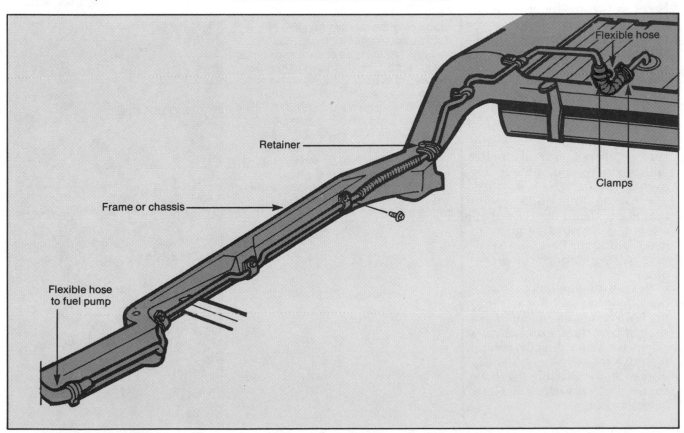

Flexible hose

Retainer

Clamps

Frame or chassis

Flexible hose to fuel pump

Replacing the fuel line between the fuel pump and the carburetor. Locate the fuel line between the fuel pump and the carburetor. Place a drain pan under the fuel pump outlet fitting. With the correct tool, remove the fuel line from the fuel pump outlet and the carburetor inlet fitting or nut. *Caution: Wipe up any spilled fuel.* Install the new fuel line. Connect the line at the fuel pump outlet and then at the carburetor inlet.

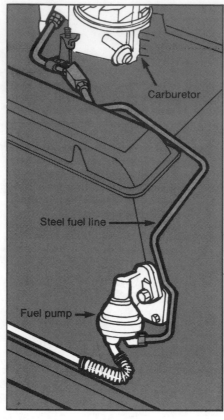

Carburetor

Steel fuel line

Fuel pump

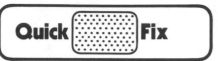

Securing cut hose connections

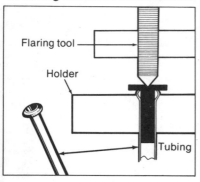

Flaring tool

Holder

Tubing

There are times when a fuel line is cut in two for the installation of an in-line filter. Other relatively low pressure lines to accessories and parts are also cut for various reasons. One problem is how to be sure the neoprene hoses installed on the cut ends of the tubing will stay in place when the car is back in service.

To make certain of a secure connection, put a partial double-lip flare on the end of the tubing over which the hose is installed. This can be done quickly, with the proper flaring tool, by starting out as if you were going to make a double flare, but stopping halfway through the procedure.

This provides an excellent sealing ridge that will not cut into the hose and holds tighter than a straight pipe does, expecially if a clamp is placed directly behind the ridge on the hose. It's cheap insurance to make sure that hose connections on fuel, oil, or water lines stay put.

Replacing the flexible fuel line at the fuel pump. The fuel pump is usually mounted on the front of the engine either on the right or left hand side. It may be necessary to raise and support the front of the car to do this job. Place a drain pan under the pump to catch any spilled fuel. With the correct tool, remove the clamps which hold the flexible line to the inlet fitting of the pump and the steel line. Remove the flexible line by twisting and pulling it away from the fuel pump inlet fitting and the steel fuel line. Install the new flexible line and the clamps.

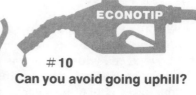

ECONOTIP

#10

Can you avoid going uphill?

Driving a car uphill, just like walking uphill, requires more energy. And the extra energy required depends on the steepness of the hill. On our interstate highways, the maximum grade is about 7 percent. That's not a particularly steep hill, but at 50 MPH you will get 55 percent less gas mileage, compared with a level road. On a 3 percent grade, the penalty is about 32 percent. If you are driving to the top of a mountain, there isn't anything you can do to avoid the hills. But be prepared for considerably less mileage on the trip.

Of course what goes up must come down. And downhill driving gives better mileage. But there will not be a sufficient improvement to offset the effects of climbing the hill.

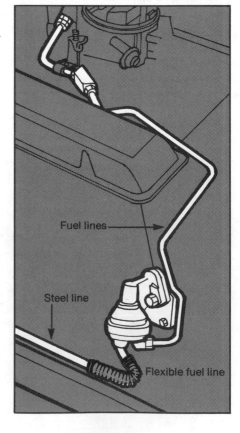

Fuel lines

Steel line

Flexible fuel line

Engine-driven Fuel Pumps

Testing the fuel pump for pressure

In testing the fuel pump for pressure, you must be very careful and take all precautions against fire. The engine will be running during the pressure test and the fuel line or lines will be connected to a gauge. Use only a flashlight, never a droplight, for lighting purposes.

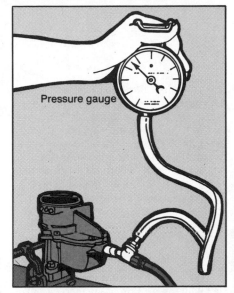

Pressure gauge

Pro Shop

Intake manifold vacuum leaks

SPREAD THIN LAYER OF OIL ON MATING SURFACES

An intake manifold vacuum leak will cause an engine to run rough and have a very rough idle no matter how finely the carburetor is adjusted. If you suspect an intake manifold vacuum leak, here's how to detect it.

Place some light engine oil around the surfaces where the intake manifold mates with the cylinder head. Start the engine. If the oil bubbles or the engine idle noticeably smooths out, there is indeed a vacuum leak at one of the intake manifold contact surfaces.

Retorque the intake manifold to the manufacturer's specifications. If the retorquing doesn't cure the problem, you'll have to replace the intake manifold gaskets.

Testing the fuel pump for pressure. Remove the air cleaner assembly. Then remove the fuel line which is connected to the carburetor inlet fitting or nut. *Caution: Wipe up any spilled fuel.* Connect the fuel pump pressure gauge to the fuel line according to the instructions accompanying the gauge. Be sure all the connections between the fuel line and the gauge are secure enough to prevent a fuel leak, and place a fire extinguisher in an accessible location very near to your work area. Have a helper start the engine for you and observe the pressure gauge. *Caution: If you see a fuel leak, have your helper switch off the engine at once.* Instruct your helper to switch off the engine as soon as the pressure gauge reaches its highest reading—five to six and a half pounds of pressure in about 15 to 20 seconds. Record the fuel pump pressure reading. For safety reasons, wrap a cloth around the fuel fittings at the fuel pump gauge and the fuel line connections. Then slowly open the fuel line connections, releasing the fuel pressure in the gauge. Remove the gauge, reconnect the fuel line to the carburetor, and wipe up any spilled fuel. Replace the air cleaner assembly. Check your fuel pump readings with the manufacturer's specifications in your owner's manual.

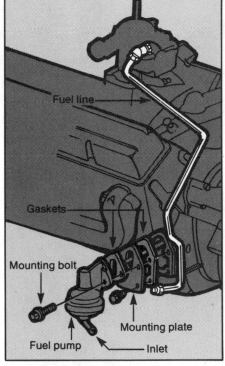

Fuel line

Gaskets

Mounting bolt

Fuel pump

Inlet

Mounting plate

Removing the fuel pump. Disconnect the ground battery cable from the battery post. Depending on the location of the fuel pump, you may have to jack up and support the front of the car. Place a drain pan under the pump to catch any fuel spilled from disconnected lines. With the proper tools, remove the fuel lines at the inlet and outlet fittings of the fuel pump. *Caution: Wipe up any spilled fuel.* Using the correct size socket-wrench setup, take out the bolts holding the fuel pump and remove the pump from the engine. With a scraper, remove all of the old gasket from the mounting area on the engine, then coat this area with gasket sealer. Also coat the replacement fuel pump mounting area with sealer. Now place the new fuel pump gasket on the freshly-coated fuel pump mounting surface, making sure the gasket is in alignment.

Replacing the fuel pump

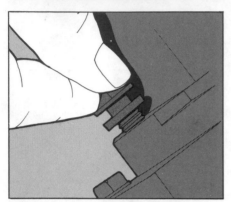

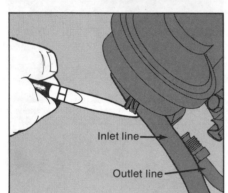

Rocker arm

1 **When installing the replacement fuel pump** on the engine, be sure the pump's rocker arm comes into full contact with the fuel pump lobe on the engine camshaft. You may have to insert the rocker arm at a slight downward angle, and apply inward pressure on the pump in order to get its mounting surface to mate with the engine mounting surface. This may take several attempts. *Caution: Be careful not to let the fuel pump gasket move out of alignment with the pump.*

2 **When the fuel pump is in full contact with the engine,** install the mounting bolts by hand, then securely tighten them.

3 **Reinstall the fuel pump inlet and outlet lines.** Reconnect the negative battery cable and start the engine to test the operation of the pump.

NOTE: Some engines use a pushrod between the pump and the camshaft. Make sure the pushrod is in the correct position when installing the pump.

Pro Shop

Chrysler Corporation engines

On some engines, Chryslers, for example, fuel pump installation is made easier by removing spark plug number one and bringing the piston in the number one cylinder to the top of its stroke. This procedure will position the fuel pump lobe on the engine camshaft to be off the rocker arm, and make it easy for you to push in on the fuel pump while you are installing the mounting bolts.

Inlet line →

Outlet line →

Outlet

Inlet

Replacing the Carburetor

Replacement carburetors may be either brand new or rebuilt. Cost is the major factor is deciding whether to buy a new carburetor or a rebuilt one. A new carburetor may cost more than twice as much as a rebuilt one. The decision rests with you.

Removing and reinstalling the carburetor. Disconnect the negative battery cable and remove the air filter assembly. If your carburetor has several vacuum lines attached to it, remove all the vacuum lines, using masking tape and your own code to mark them for reinstallation. Remove the throttle and choke linkages, and any other linkages which may be attached to the carburetor. You should mark each with masking tape and a code if there are several. Disconnect the fuel line at the carburetor. *Caution: Wipe up any spilled fuel.* With the correct socket wrench or combination wrench, remove bolts or nuts holding down the carburetor, and remove the carburetor from the engine, keeping it level. *Caution: The carburetor is full of fuel. Empty the fuel into the safety can.* Remove the old gasket from the intake manifold.

Remove the hand cloth carefully when you have finished scraping off all of the old gasket. Install the new carburetor and gasket according to the instructions on the carburetor box. Tighten the bolts or nuts securely, reconnect all the vacuum lines, the choke and throttle linkages, and any other linkages removed, then reconnect the fuel line. Replace the fuel-and-air filters with new ones. Reconnect the negative battery cable. Start the engine and check for fuel leaks. When the engine reaches operating temperature, adjust the carburetor curb idle and the mixture control screw or screws. *Caution: Never pour gasoline into the throat of the carburetor, commonly known as priming, in order to get the engine started. Before you crank the engine, attach the air cleaner assembly. Then allow the fuel pump to pump fuel to the carburetor by simply cranking the engine with the starter. Remember to stop after 30 to 40 seconds of continuous cranking. Permit the starter to cool off for three or four minutes and try again.*

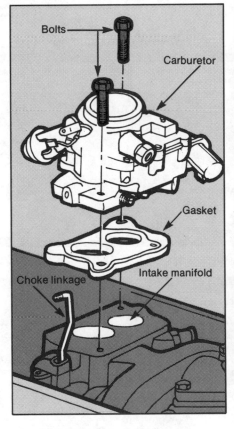

Bolts

Carburetor

Gasket

Choke linkage

Intake manifold

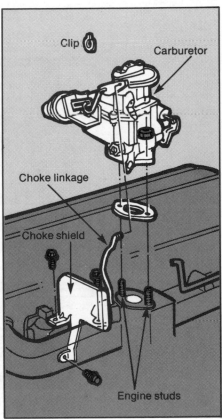

Clip

Carburetor

Choke linkage

Choke shield

Engine studs

Pro Shop

Plug up the holes in the intake manifold

If you must use a scraper to remove the old gasket, first plug up the openings in the intake manifold with a hand cloth. This will prevent any scrapings from falling into the manifold.

Troubleshooting Charts

In this chapter you learned how to repair some of the most common parts of the fuel system. The following Troubleshooting Charts were designed to help you locate and correct some typical fuel system problems. Also, for a slightly different treatment of some of these same conditions, see Troubleshooting Flow Chart: Fuel Systems at the end of Chapter 4. You will not be able to correct some of the problems named in these charts without special tools or testing equipment, or special knowledge or training. In such cases, you should have your fuel system repaired by a qualified mechanic.

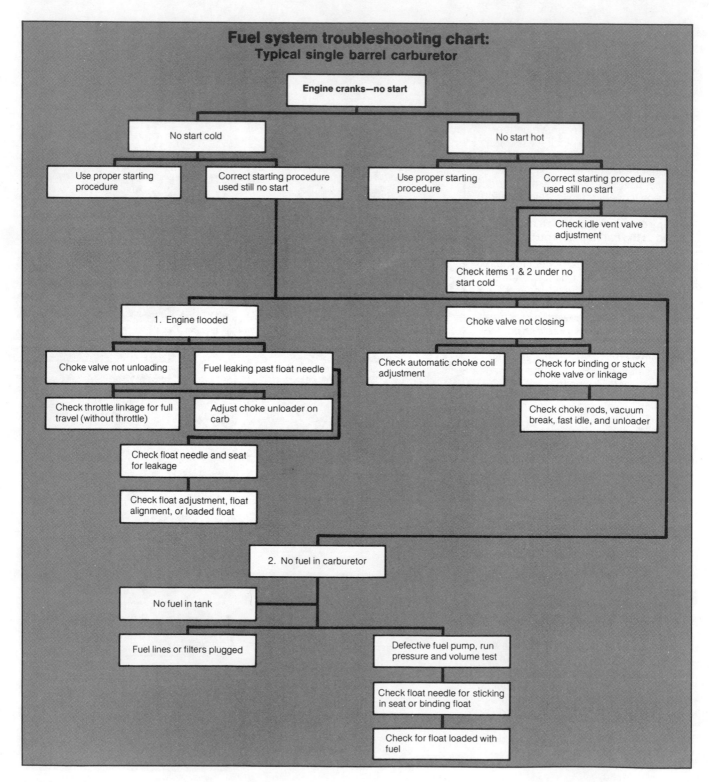

Fuel system troubleshooting chart:
Typical single barrel carburetor

Fuel system troubleshooting chart:
Typical single barrel carburetor

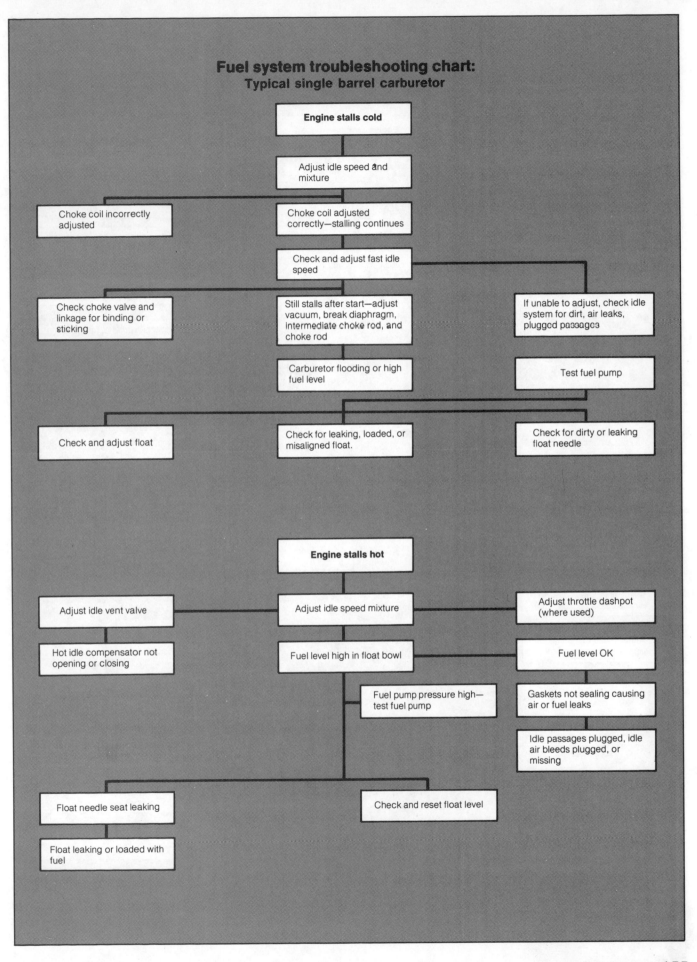

Engine stalls cold

Adjust idle speed and mixture

Choke coil incorrectly adjusted

Choke coil adjusted correctly—stalling continues

Check and adjust fast idle speed

Check choke valve and linkage for binding or sticking

Still stalls after start—adjust vacuum, break diaphragm, intermediate choke rod, and choke rod

If unable to adjust, check idle system for dirt, air leaks, plugged passages

Carburetor flooding or high fuel level

Test fuel pump

Check and adjust float

Check for leaking, loaded, or misaligned float.

Check for dirty or leaking float needle

Engine stalls hot

Adjust idle vent valve

Adjust idle speed mixture

Adjust throttle dashpot (where used)

Hot idle compensator not opening or closing

Fuel level high in float bowl

Fuel level OK

Fuel pump pressure high— test fuel pump

Gaskets not sealing causing air or fuel leaks

Idle passages plugged, idle air bleeds plugged, or missing

Float needle seat leaking

Check and reset float level

Float leaking or loaded with fuel

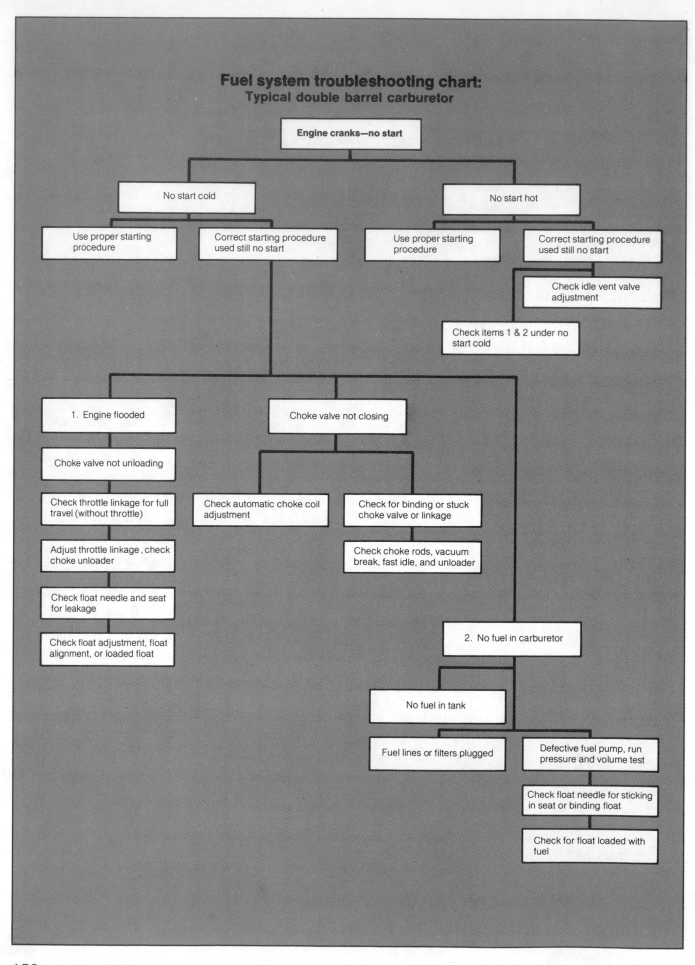

Fuel system troubleshooting chart:
Typical double barrel carburetor

Engine cranks—no start

No start cold

No start hot

Use proper starting procedure

Correct starting procedure used still no start

Use proper starting procedure

Correct starting procedure used still no start

Check idle vent valve adjustment

Check items 1 & 2 under no start cold

1. Engine flooded

Choke valve not closing

Choke valve not unloading

Check throttle linkage for full travel (without throttle)

Check automatic choke coil adjustment

Check for binding or stuck choke valve or linkage

Adjust throttle linkage , check choke unloader

Check choke rods, vacuum break, fast idle, and unloader

Check float needle and seat for leakage

Check float adjustment, float alignment, or loaded float

2. No fuel in carburetor

No fuel in tank

Fuel lines or filters plugged

Defective fuel pump, run pressure and volume test

Check float needle for sticking in seat or binding float

Check for float loaded with fuel

Fuel system troubleshooting chart:
Typical double barrel carburetor

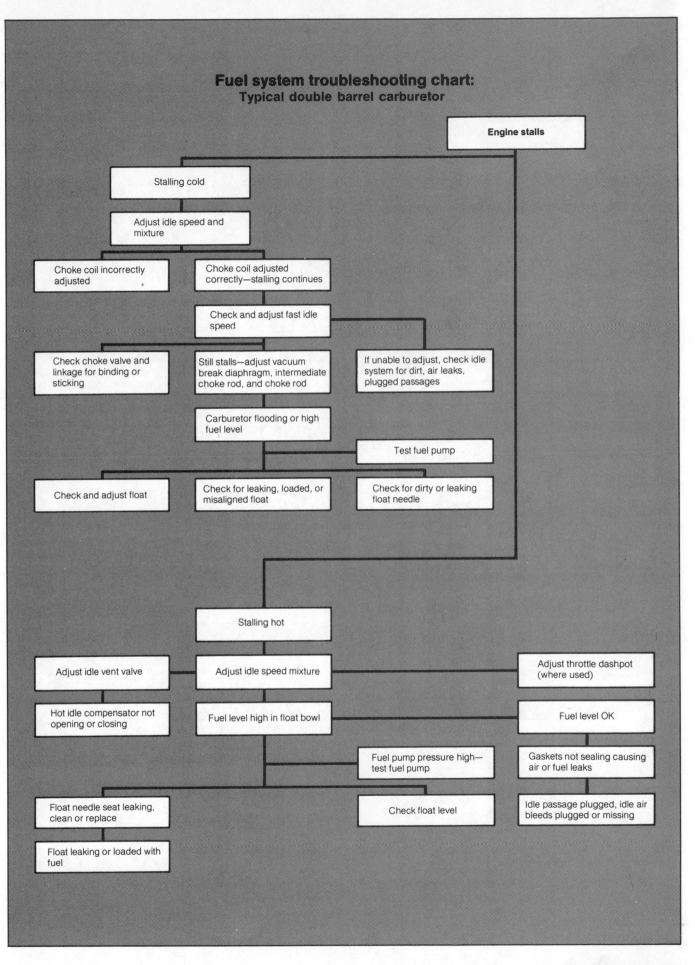

Engine stalls

Stalling cold

Adjust idle speed and mixture

Choke coil incorrectly adjusted

Choke coil adjusted correctly—stalling continues

Check and adjust fast idle speed

Check choke valve and linkage for binding or sticking

Still stalls—adjust vacuum break diaphragm, intermediate choke rod, and choke rod

If unable to adjust, check idle system for dirt, air leaks, plugged passages

Carburetor flooding or high fuel level

Test fuel pump

Check and adjust float

Check for leaking, loaded, or misaligned float

Check for dirty or leaking float needle

Stalling hot

Adjust idle vent valve

Adjust idle speed mixture

Adjust throttle dashpot (where used)

Hot idle compensator not opening or closing

Fuel level high in float bowl

Fuel level OK

Fuel pump pressure high—test fuel pump

Gaskets not sealing causing air or fuel leaks

Float needle seat leaking, clean or replace

Check float level

Idle passage plugged, idle air bleeds plugged or missing

Float leaking or loaded with fuel

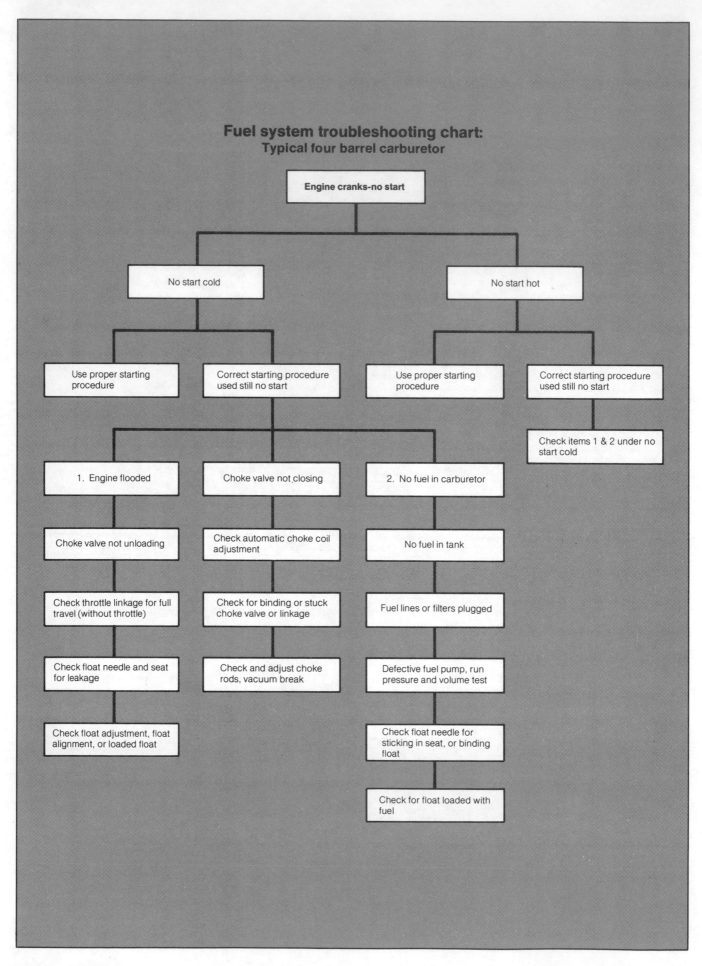

Fuel system troubleshooting chart:
Typical four barrel carburetor

Engine cranks-no start

No start cold

No start hot

Use proper starting procedure

Correct starting procedure used still no start

Use proper starting procedure

Correct starting procedure used still no start

Check items 1 & 2 under no start cold

1. Engine flooded

Choke valve not closing

2. No fuel in carburetor

Choke valve not unloading

Check automatic choke coil adjustment

No fuel in tank

Check throttle linkage for full travel (without throttle)

Check for binding or stuck choke valve or linkage

Fuel lines or filters plugged

Check float needle and seat for leakage

Check and adjust choke rods, vacuum break

Defective fuel pump, run pressure and volume test

Check float adjustment, float alignment, or loaded float

Check float needle for sticking in seat, or binding float

Check for float loaded with fuel

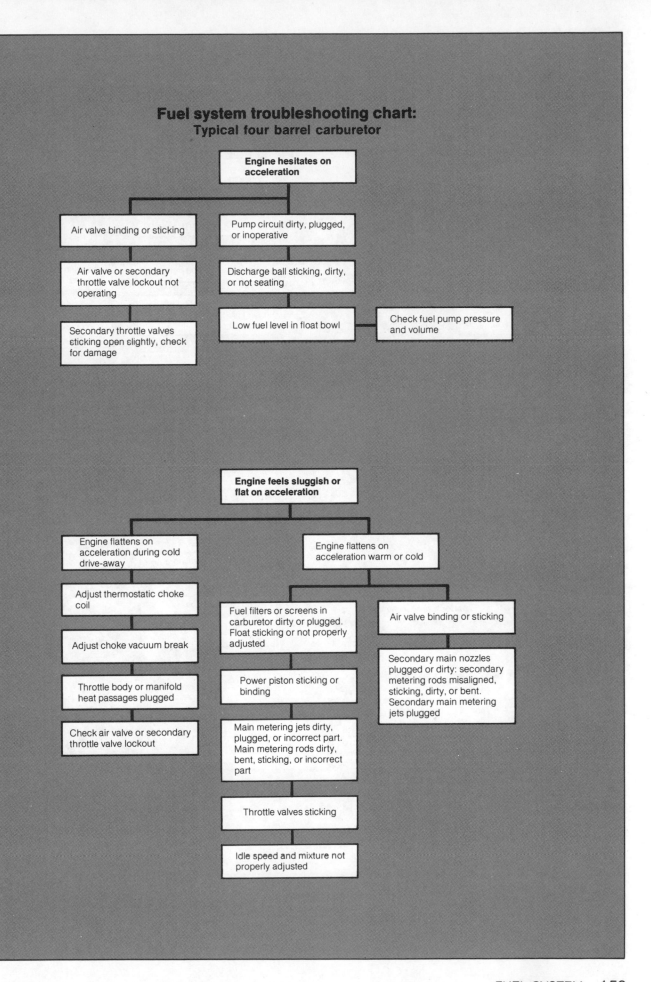

Fuel system troubleshooting chart:
Typical four barrel carburetor

Engine hesitates on acceleration

Air valve binding or sticking

Air valve or secondary throttle valve lockout not operating

Secondary throttle valves sticking open slightly, check for damage

Pump circuit dirty, plugged, or inoperative

Discharge ball sticking, dirty, or not seating

Low fuel level in float bowl

Check fuel pump pressure and volume

Engine feels sluggish or flat on acceleration

Engine flattens on acceleration during cold drive-away

Adjust thermostatic choke coil

Adjust choke vacuum break

Throttle body or manifold heat passages plugged

Check air valve or secondary throttle valve lockout

Engine flattens on acceleration warm or cold

Fuel filters or screens in carburetor dirty or plugged. Float sticking or not properly adjusted

Power piston sticking or binding

Main metering jets dirty, plugged, or incorrect part. Main metering rods dirty, bent, sticking, or incorrect part

Throttle valves sticking

Idle speed and mixture not properly adjusted

Air valve binding or sticking

Secondary main nozzles plugged or dirty: secondary metering rods misaligned, sticking, dirty, or bent. Secondary main metering jets plugged

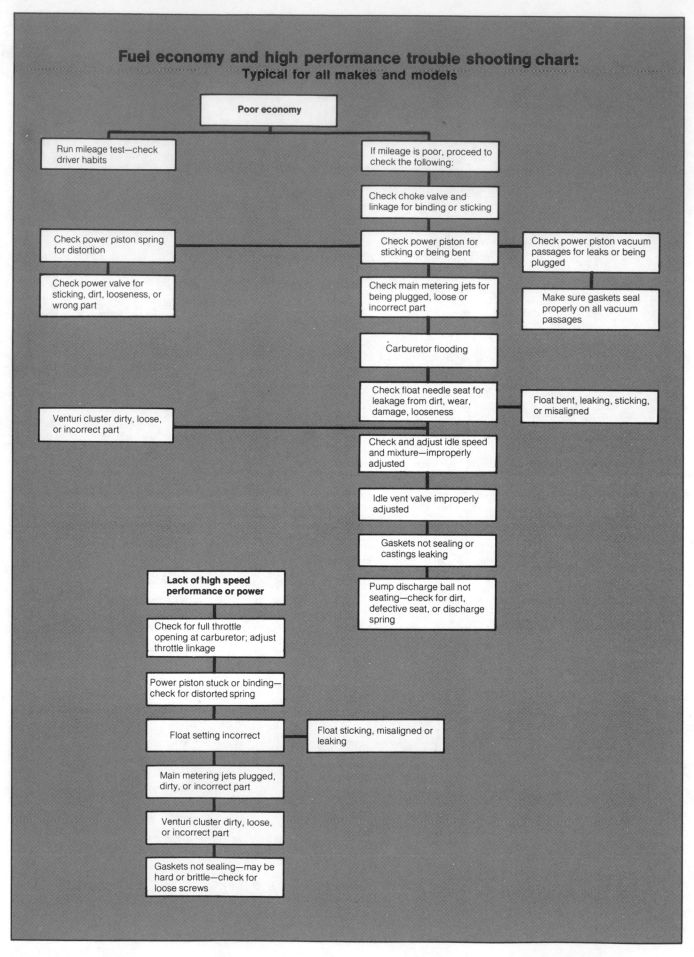

Fuel economy and high performance trouble shooting chart:
Typical for all makes and models

Poor economy

Run mileage test—check driver habits

If mileage is poor, proceed to check the following:

Check choke valve and linkage for binding or sticking

Check power piston spring for distortion

Check power piston for sticking or being bent

Check power piston vacuum passages for leaks or being plugged

Check power valve for sticking, dirt, looseness, or wrong part

Check main metering jets for being plugged, loose or incorrect part

Make sure gaskets seal properly on all vacuum passages

Carburetor flooding

Check float needle seat for leakage from dirt, wear, damage, looseness

Float bent, leaking, sticking, or misaligned

Venturi cluster dirty, loose, or incorrect part

Check and adjust idle speed and mixture—improperly adjusted

Idle vent valve improperly adjusted

Gaskets not sealing or castings leaking

Pump discharge ball not seating—check for dirt, defective seat, or discharge spring

Lack of high speed performance or power

Check for full throttle opening at carburetor; adjust throttle linkage

Power piston stuck or binding—check for distorted spring

Float setting incorrect

Float sticking, misaligned or leaking

Main metering jets plugged, dirty, or incorrect part

Venturi cluster dirty, loose, or incorrect part

Gaskets not sealing—may be hard or brittle—check for loose screws

CRANKING SYSTEM

The car's cranking system consists of a battery, battery cables, a starter motor, an ignition switch, a starter relay and/or a starter solenoid, and a neutral safety switch. The starter motor, sometimes referred to as the cranking motor, is a small but very powerful electric motor. It is designed to crank the engine of your car to start it. Here is the way the rest of the system's parts work.

When you turn on the ignition, the battery sends electrical energy to the cranking motor which then converts it to mechanical energy to crank the engine. The relay and/or solenoid, an electromagnetic switch, uses a small amount of battery current, five to ten amperes, in connecting the battery to the cranking motor, and allows a large amount of battery current, 150 to 250 amperes, to activate the cranking motor. Because of the very high amperage flow necessary to turn the cranking motor, even the tiniest resistance in the system can be critical. A cranking system that is operating correctly will crank the engine at approximately 180 to 250 revolutions per minute. Any resistance not only inhibits starting efficiency, but also lowers the voltage going to the primary circuit of the ignition system. Think of it in terms of the water main which supplies your neighborhood; any obstruction will lower the flow of water coming into your home.

Resistance is often caused by loose battery cable connections at either the battery, the relay, the starter motor, or the terminals; corroded connections at the battery post; poor ground; or a loose or defective cranking motor. There's one other possible cause of resistance: heat is created when the cranking motor is operated excessively, often because of a poorly-tuned ignition system that causes hard starting. The cranking motor gets hot because of the high amperage it needs to operate and its inability to dissipate the heat.

The cranking motor on American Motors, Chrysler Motors, and General Motors cars comes equipped with a dual purpose solenoid. It connects the battery to the starter electrically, and engages the starter drive gear to the engine flywheel gear mechanically. On some Ford products, the cranking motor gear is engaged not by a solenoid but by a fork which is operated by an electromagnetic switch located on the starter. This switch engages the starter gear and the flywheel gear and completes the circuit in the cranking motor.

All automatic and some standard transmissions incorporate a neutral safety switch, which prevents the engine from starting when the transmission is in gear. It is usually located on the steering post, close to the floorboard, or on the transmission. Most cars which are equipped with automatic transmissions cannot be push-started, that is, pushed by another car to get the engine going. Because of this situation, it is very important that all of the components of the cranking system be checked and serviced properly. In this chapter, you will learn how to check, charge, and replace the battery; replace the battery cables; and check and replace the cranking motor, the starter relay, and the solenoid.

CONTENTS

Servicing the Battery

Testing the battery

Hydrometer method. Some modern, maintenance-free batteries do not have caps. If yours is that type, see the voltmeter method which follows. Remove the battery vent filler caps, then insert the hydrometer rubber tube into one of the filler holes. Squeeze the bulb and release it slowly to draw in the electrolyte until the float begins to rise, then stop releasing the bulb. Do not remove the hydrometer from the battery. Holding the hydrometer in a vertical position, note the specific gravity reading of the float. When reading the float your eyes must be at the same level as the level of the electrolyte. After checking the specific gravity, squeeze the bulb to return the electrolyte back into the battery cell, and remove the hydrometer from the cell. Repeat the above operation in all remaining cells. Specific gravity readings must be within manufacturer's specifications. See the chart, Battery Testing with a Hydrometer. *Caution: Electrolyte consists of water and sulfuric acid. If the electrolyte is spilled on your hands or face, wash it off thoroughly with water to prevent acid burn. If it is spilled on your clothing, they must be washed at once or it will burn holes. Any electrolyte spilled on the battery, fender, or engine parts must be washed off with water to prevent damage. Rinse the hydrometer out with water when you have finished testing the battery.*

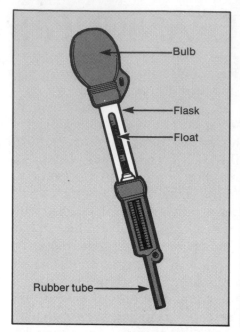

Bulb

Flask

Float

Rubber tube

Tools and equipment:
Combination wrenches.
Droplight or flashlight.
Goggles.
Fender covers.
Common screwdrivers.
$\frac{3}{8}$" or $\frac{1}{2}$" drive socket set.
Battery hydrometer.
Voltmeter.
Ammeter.
Battery charger.
Pliers.
Battery post cleaning tool.
Wire brush.
Floor jack.
Steel stands.
Creeper.
Hand cloths.
Remote control starter switch.
Jumper wire.
Battery strip.
Battery puller.
Masking tape.
Battery jumper cable.

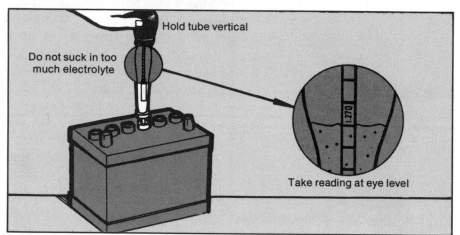

Hold tube vertical

Do not suck in too much electrolyte

1.270

Take reading at eye level

Troubleshooting flow chart: Battery testing with a hydrometer

Hydrometer test 80 degrees F	Condition of battery	Remedy
More than 1.300 specific gravity	Specific gravity too high	Adjust specific gravity with addition of distilled water.
1.250 to 1.295	Probably good	If variation among cells is less than 0.015 specific gravity, no correction is required. If greater than that amount, give high rate discharge test. If cells test OK, recharge and adjust specific gravity of cells.
1.225 to 1.250	Fair	Battery should be recharged. Check operation of voltage regulator. Also check electrical system for loose connections, shorts, grounds, and corroded terminals.
Less than 1.225	Poor	Recharge battery. Check voltage regulator, also electrical system for loose connections, shorts, grounds, and corroded terminals.
Cells show more than .025 variation in specific gravity	1. Short in low cell 2. Loss of electrolyte 3. Cracked cell partition	1. Replace battery. 2. Add distilled water to correct level, check charging rate of generator. 3. Replace battery.

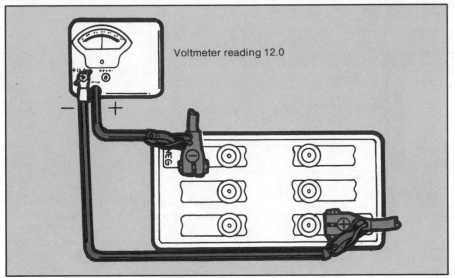

Voltmeter reading 12.0

Voltmeter method. Connect the voltmeter to the battery as follows: the red lead terminal (positive) goes to the positive post of the battery; the other lead (negative) goes to the negative post. If the voltmeter does not read at least 12.0 volts, the battery is not fully charged, and you should recharge it.

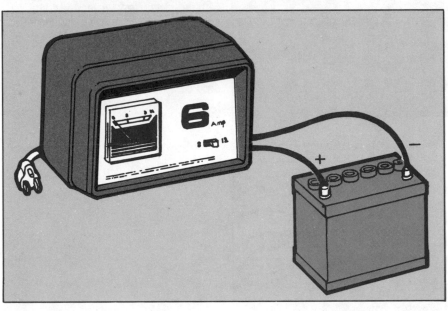

Using a battery charger. Disconnect both cables from their posts. Remove all filler caps, then check and correct the level of electrolyte in the battery. Connect the positive lead of the battery charger to the positive battery post, and the negative lead to the negative post. To operate the charger, refer to the instructions that come with it. The charg-ing rate should not exceed six amperes. When the battery is charged, disconnect the charger, install the vent caps, and connect the cables. *Caution: The area must be well-ventilated when charging a battery, because hydrogen gas is released from the cells. There should be no smoking and no open flames near the battery while it's being charged.*

Pro Shop

Recording specific gravity readings

Starting with the cell closest to the positive battery post, on a piece of paper draw and number the cells from one to six, then record the readings.

ECONOTIP

#11
Calculating mileage

The only way to get a true gas mileage figure is to fill the tank every time you get gas. The figure will be most accurate if you fill the tank to exactly the same level every time. This is easiest on older filler necks where you can see the fuel level. Newer necks with unleaded restrictors prevent seeing the level. The only thing you can do is wait until the automatic pump nozzle shuts off, then after a few seconds feed gas again until it shuts off once more.

After filling the tank, simply divide the number of gallons used into the miles driven since the last fillup. The result is miles per gallon. You should carry out the division far enough to get the answer in tenths of a gallon. If you have a pocket calculator, it will quickly do the figuring for you.

Battery load test using the cranking motor

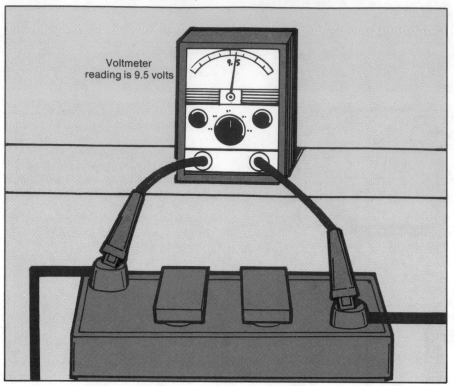

Voltmeter reading is 9.5 volts

Remove the air cleaner, unhook the high-voltage coil wire from the distributor cap center tower, and ground the wire. With the battery fully charged, connect the voltmeter to the battery. Connect a remote control starter switch to the solenoid or relay. Crank the engine with this switch for five seconds. Observe the voltage reading while the engine is cranking. The voltage should not drop below 9.5 volts. If it does, the battery may have a weak or defective cell and should be replaced. If it does not drop below 9.5 volts, disconnect the voltmeter and charge the battery with the charger.

Replacing the battery

Disconnect the negative battery cable from the battery, then disconnect the positive cable. Release or remove the mechanism holding the battery down, located either at its top or at its base. Note the position of the battery in the tray, that is, whether the positive or negative post faces the engine. Attach the battery strap to the post and lift out the battery. Lift batteries with side-mounted posts out by hand. Thoroughly clean the battery case and the mechanism holding it down. Attach the battery strap to the new battery and install it in the case, in the same position as the old one. Replace the mechanism holding down the battery and clean the cables. First connect the positive cable to the positive post, then connect the negative cable. See Chapter 3 for detailed instructions on battery maintenance.

Replacing battery cables

To replace battery cables, disconnect the negative cable from the post, then disconnect the positive cable. If the starter motor can be reached easily from the engine compartment, disconnect the cables from the starter, solenoid, and/or relay. On all V-type engines, the car must be raised and supported to gain access to the starter motor. Clean all connecting surfaces and install the new cables. Remember to install the positive cable before the negative. *Caution: Some cars have a positive ground system. On those cars, remove the positive cable first and replace it last to avoid injury from accidental ground.*

Pro Shop

Charging the battery

If you observe smoke coming from the battery cell(s), or see that the bubbling action of the electrolyte is much too vigorous, the charging rate may be too high. Lower it to about three or four amperes.

Replacing the Starter or Cranking Motor

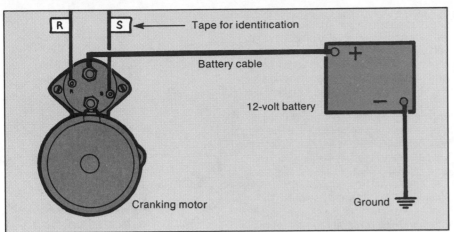

R S ← Tape for identification

Battery cable

12-volt battery

Cranking motor

Ground

1 **Disconnect the negative battery cable** from the post. Jack up and support the front of the car. Disconnect all wires attached to the starter. If your starter has more than one wire connected to it, attach a piece of masking tape to the wires, and, using your own code, mark them for correct reinstallation.

Quick 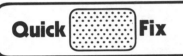 Fix

Battery corrosion

Because of the chemical processes involved in its operation, a storage battery tends to build up corrosion on its terminals. The corrosion can cause poor contact between the battery posts and cables and you won't be getting full power from the battery.

This can easily be avoided by purchasing inexpensive, chemically-treated felt washers. Install the washers over the posts and under the cable terminals. The washers are sold at regular automotive supply and parts stores and should prevent corrosion for about two years.

If there is a corrosive buildup on the battery mounting tray (in the form of a white, flaky material), it could be preventing the battery from putting out all the power it's capable of.

Remove the battery and wash off the mounting tray with hot water. Dry the tray and spray it with undercoat, which is available in aerosol cans at most auto supply houses. After the undercoat dries, replace the battery securely.

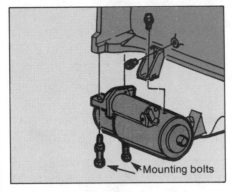

Mounting bolts

2 **Remove the starter support bracket,** if your car is equipped with one, and loosen the starter bolts, using the correct size socket wrench or box wrench. On some cars (mostly General Motors) loose shims are inserted between the starter motor and the engine to keep the starter motor level. Before you remove the bolts notice which shim goes under which bolt. Save the shims and put them back in the same spots when you install the new motor. Most rebuilt starter motors do not have new shims supplied with them.

3 **Remove the mounting bolts** and the starter, and install the replacement starter. First screw in all the holding bolts by hand, then tighten them evenly with the socket or box wrench. Tighten the bolts in turn *diagonally* across from each other to seat the motor evenly (for the same reason that you should tighten the wheel lugs in turn that are *opposite* each other, not *next* to each other around the wheel when you put a wheel back on your car).

4 **Connect the wires** to the starter and lower the car, then connect the negative battery cable to the post.

Pro Shop

Supporting the starter motor

The motor is heavy, so we suggest that when you are removing the last bolt, hold the motor against the engine with one hand and remove the bolt with the other. Reverse the procedure when you are replacing the starter.

Servicing the Neutral Safety Switch

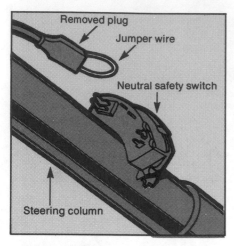

Testing the steering column-mounted neutral safety switch. On American Motors, General Motors, and Ford products that have the shift handle mounted on the steering post, the neutral safety switch is located on the steering post column inside the passenger compart-

ment close to the floorboard. Unplug the set of wires which are attached to the left side of the switch, the side facing the parking brake pedal. If the plug has two wires connected to it, hook up a jumper wire across the two contacts in the plug, then turn the ignition switch to the "start" position. If the starter cranks the engine, the neutral safety switch is defective and must be replaced. If the plug has four wires connected to it, attach the jumper wire to the two contacts on the left side of the plug, parking brake pedal side, then crank the engine with the ignition key to test the safety switch. *Caution: The jumper wire must only be used to test the neutral safety switch, never for any other purpose. With the jumper wire connected, the engine can be started in any gear causing the car to lunge forward or backward.*

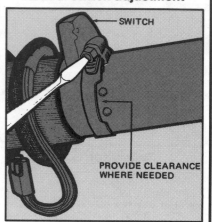

Neutral switch adjustment

If the attaching screws of the neutral safety switch for the automatic transmission shift lever become stripped, the screws will not hold the switch in proper adjustment. A worm-type hose clamp can be used to anchor the switch in its proper position.

First, grind a small strip off one side of the clamp to provide clearance for the projections on the jacket tube. Set the parking brake, put the shift lever in neutral, and remove the stripped screws from it.

Hold the selector lever firmly against the neutral stop, full left of the "Neutral" position, and install the clamp. Then check the switch operation. The engine should start with the selector lever in its normal "Neutral" position, but not when the lever is shifted to either drive or reverse. If the switch does not function correctly, it must be readjusted.

Testing the transmission-mounted neutral safety switch

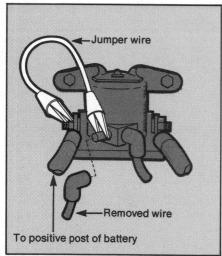

On Ford products, the starter relay is usually mounted on the inner fender pan close to the battery. Place the transmission in "Park" or "Neutral," and set the parking brake. Making sure that the ignition is in the "off" position, pull out the small wire attached to the small terminal closest to the positive post of the relay. Connect a jumper wire to the relay battery post, and touch the other end of the jumper wire to the terminal from which the small wire was removed. If the starter motor cranks the engine, the neutral safety switch is defective and must be replaced.

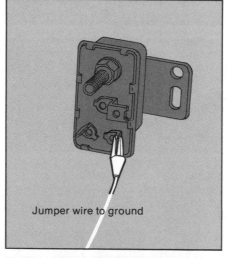

On Chrysler products, the starter relay is mounted on the fire wall or inner fender pan. Position the transmission in "Park" or "Neutral" and set the parking brake. If the starter will not operate when the switch is turned to "start," connect a jumper wire between the relay ground terminal and a good ground on the engine or body. Then turn the ignition switch to start. If the starter now cranks the engine, the neutral safety switch is either disconnected or defective.

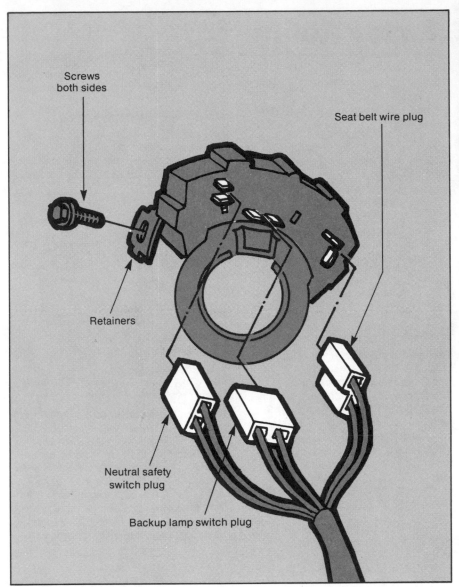

Screws both sides

Seat belt wire plug

Retainers

Neutral safety switch plug

Backup lamp switch plug

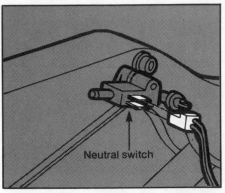

Neutral switch

Replacing the transmission-mounted neutral safety switch. Jack up and support the front of the car. If the neutral safety switch is screwed into the transmission case, place a drain pan directly below the switch to catch any oil that may drip when it is removed. Disconnect the wire(s) which is connected to the switch and remove and discard the switch. Install the new switch and connect the wire(s), then lower the car off the safety stands and replace any transmission fluid that may have been lost.

Replacing the steering column-mounted neutral safety switch. Unplug the wires that are plugged into the switch, and take out the two screws holding it to the column. Then remove and discard the switch. Install the new switch and plug the wires into it.

Pro Shop

Adjusting the switch

The starter should crank the engine when the transmission is in the "Park" position. If it does not, loosen the screws holding the neutral safety switch and slightly move the switch clockwise, towards the accelerator pedal. Tighten the screws and try the starter again.

Servicing the Starter Relay

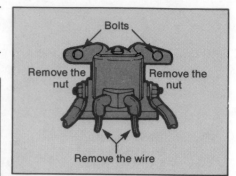

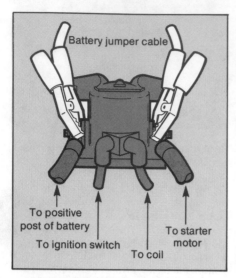

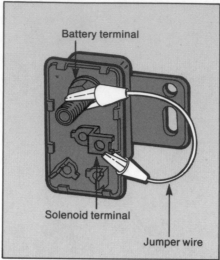

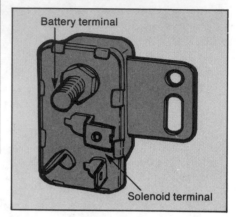

Testing the starter relay on Ford cars. Set the transmission in "Park" or "Neutral," and set the parking brake. First connect a battery jumper cable to the battery terminal of the relay—the terminal which is connected to the battery with a cable. Touch the other end of the jumper cable to the starter side of the solenoid. If the starter cranks the engine, the starter is OK. The cause of the no-crank condition must be in the relay or the wiring.

Testing the starter relay on Chrysler products. If the engine will not crank with the automatic transmission in "Park" or "Neutral," connect a jumper wire on the starter relay between the battery and solenoid terminals. If the engine cranks, the starter is okay. The trouble has to be in the relay, ignition switch or wiring. On manual transmission cars, a helper must depress the clutch pedal to close the clutch start switch while the test is being made.

Replacing the starter relay. Disconnect the negative battery cable from the post. Place masking tape on the wires which are connected to the relay, and, using your own code, mark the wires to insure correct reinstallation. Disconnect all wires from the relay and remove it. Then install the new relay and reconnect all the wires. Connect the negative battery cable to the post and test for cranking.

Replacing the Solenoid

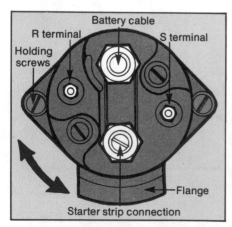

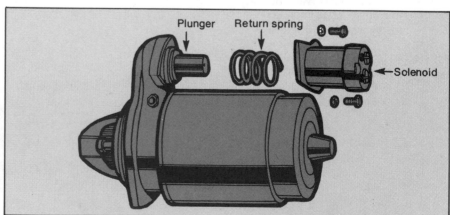

Disconnect the negative battery cable from the post, then jack up and support the front of the car. Remove the starter motor. Take out the nut or bolt that connects the starter motor strip to the solenoid. Press the solenoid inward, toward the starter, and twist it either right or left to release it from the starter. Now remove the solenoid, but do not remove the plunger return spring. Install the new solenoid by placing it against the return spring and pushing inward to the starter flange. Twisting the solenoid to either right or left until the bolt holes are aligned, attach the bolts and tighten them securely. Connect the starter strip to the solenoid with the bolt or nut and install the starter. Lower the car and connect the negative battery cable.

CHARGING CIRCUIT

The charging circuit supplies the proper amount of current for the car's lights, ignition system, radio, heater, and other electrical accessories. Also, it must maintain the battery in a charged state, and recharge it when necessary. This system has four basic components: The battery, the generator or alternator, the voltage regulator, and various cables and wires. The battery's functions are twofold. The previous chapter discussed its role as a supplier of electrical power for the starter motor and the ignition system while the engine is cranking. In addition, the battery must supply additional current for the car's electrical devices when the generator or alternator output cannot meet the electrical demand. On a cold, rainy night, for example, let's say your car is stopped at a traffic light. In this situation, the lights, heater, windshield wipers, ignition system, and radio all may be in operation. If the generator or alternator is not able to put out all the energy needed, the battery must make up the deficiency.

The generator or alternator is a mechanical device which converts mechanical energy into electrical energy. The mechanical energy comes from the engine via the fan belt. The electrical energy thus produced operates the car's electrical devices. The generator or alternator, when functioning properly, will meet all of the electrical requirements of the car at any speed. The principal difference between the generator and the alternator is the output at engine curb idle speed and slightly above. The alternator's output is higher, and this is the primary reason it has supplanted the generator in today's cars. On the other hand, one advantage the generator has over the alternator is that it does not need electricity to make electricity. The alternator does. In other words, the generator is "self-exciting," which means it is able to create electricity simply by turning about 600 revolutions per minute (RPM) with no electrical input.

When an alternator or generator is used, its electrical output must be controlled. If not, the enormous voltage generated would destroy the car's electrical devices. The voltage regulator is the control unit, regulating the generator or alternator output to a value preset by the manufacturer, which protects the battery and electrical accessories from high-voltage damage.

The car has either an ammeter or an indicator light on the dashboard indicating whether or not the charging system is operating trouble-free. Cables and wires are necessary to complete the circuits between the components. These must be kept in good condition. This means no loose or dirty connections, no exposed wires, and no frayed insulation.

In this chapter you will learn how to test and replace each component of the charging circuit. Although generators are something of a dying breed, there are still enough of them in use today to make discussion of them helpful.

CONTENTS

Servicing the Generator

To test the generator or alternator for output, you must have a new or fully-charged battery. Otherwise, the charging circuit cannot be tested accurately.

Tools and equipment:

Fender covers.
Droplight or flashlight.
Voltmeter.
Battery charger.
Battery hydrometer.
Distilled water.
Two jumper wires.
$\frac{3}{8}$" or $\frac{1}{2}$" drive socket set.
Set of combination wrenches.
Pliers.
Battery post cleaner.
$\frac{1}{4}$" drive socket set.
Belt tension gauge.
Tach-dwell meter.
Pen knife.
Small flat file.
Cotter pin.

Determining type

Determining type "A" or "B" generator circuit. Check the generator belt tension. Now, find out the type of generator you have, "A" or "B." As a rule, type "A" is used by American Motors, General Motors, and Chrysler, and type "B" is used by Ford. Remove the wire attached to the "F" terminal of the generator, and tape the end of the wire to prevent a short circuit. Connect the voltmeter positive lead to the generator "F" terminal and the negative lead to ground. Start the engine and operate it at a fast idle. If a voltmeter reading is indicated, the generator is an "A" type. If not, it's a "B." Switch off the engine, reconnect the wire to the "F" terminal, and remove the voltmeter.

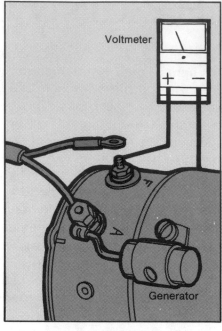

Testing type "A" generators for output. Locate the voltage regulator, either on the fire wall, the inner fender pan, or the radiator support. Disconnect the wire attached to the "F" terminal of the voltage regulator, and attach one end of a small jumper wire to the disconnected wire and the other end to the base of the voltage regulator which is grounded. Connect the voltmeter positive lead to the "BAT" terminal of the voltage regulator and the negative lead to a good ground. Start the engine and operate it at a fast idle. The voltmeter reading should be at least 15 to 16 volts. If it is not, the generator is defective.

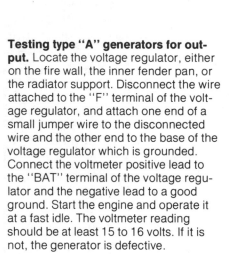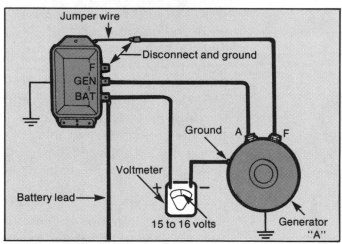

Testing type "B" generators for output. Disconnect the "F" and "A" wires at the generator, and tape the wire ends to prevent a short circuit. Connect a small jumper wire between the "F" and "A" terminals of the generator. Connect the positive lead of the voltmeter to the "BAT" terminal of the voltage regulator and the negative lead to ground. Start the engine and operate it at a fast idle. The voltmeter should read 15 to 16 volts. If not, the generator is defective.

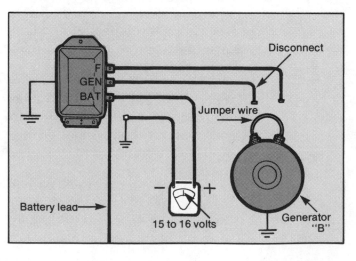

Removing and replacing

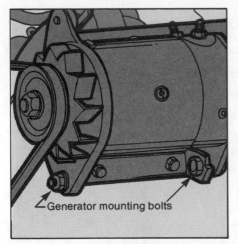

Generator mounting bolts

Removing the generator. Remove the negative battery cable, and with the correct size combination wrench, take off the wires attached to the generator terminals. With masking tape, use your own code to mark the wires for correct reinstallation. With a combination wrench, remove the adjusting nut and loosen the mounting nuts or bolts. Push the generator inward, toward the engine, to release the fan belt. Then remove the fan belt from the generator pulley. Remove the mounting bolts or nuts from the generator and remove the generator itself from its mounting.

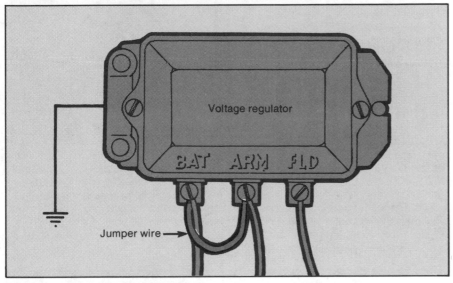

Voltage regulator

BAT   ARM   FLD

Jumper wire ⟶

Replacing the generator. Install the replacement generator and reconnect all wires to the generator terminals. Connect the fan belt and adjust the belt tension. Connect one lead of a jumper wire to the "BAT" terminal of the voltage regulator. Now simply touch the other end of the jumper wire to the "ARM" terminal of the voltage regulator. That's all you have to do to polarize any generator. Disconnect the jumper lead. *Caution: Type "A" generators are not interchangeable with type "B." You must replace the generator with one of the same type.*

Polarizing the generator

All generators must be polarized after they have been installed and before starting the engine. Polarizing electrically sets up the generator's magnetic field.

Pro Shop

Using an ammeter or indicator light

There's a way to test the output of the generator when a voltmeter is not available, through the use of an ammeter or indicator light. With an "A" type generator, disconnect the "F" wire at the voltage regulator and tape the end. With a jumper wire, connect the "F" terminal of the regulator to a good ground. When you start the engine, the ammeter or light should indicate a charge rate. On "B" type generators, connect the jumper wire ends to the "F" and "ARM" terminals of the regulator. When you start the engine, the ammeter should charge or the light should go out.

Servicing the Generator Voltage Regulator

Running charging circuit tests

Remember that the car's battery must be new or fully-charged before any accurate charging circuit tests can be run.

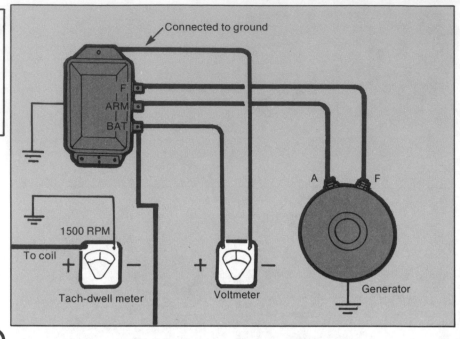

Connected to ground

F
ARM
BAT

1500 RPM
To coil
Tach-dwell meter

Voltmeter

A   F

Generator

Pro Shop

Clean for good contact

We use a small knife or small flat file to clean all wire ends before reconnecting them to the voltage regulator. This will insure a good electrical connection. While you're at it, also scrape clean the area where the voltage regulator is mounted.

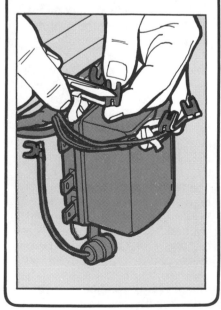

Testing the voltage regulator. Open the hood and test the generator for output. If it is OK then check the voltage regulator as follows: connect the positive lead of the voltmeter to the "BAT" terminal of the voltage regulator and the negative lead to a good ground. Con-nect a tach-dwell meter. Start the engine and adjust its speed to 1500 revolutions per minute (RPM's). The voltmeter reading should increase at least 0.5 volts, but not more than 2.0 volts above battery voltage. Lower or higher means a bad regulator.

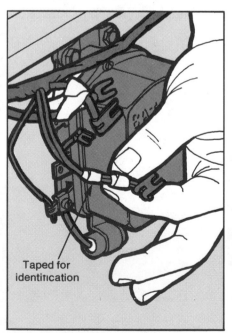

Taped for identification

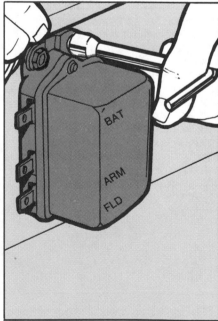

BAT

ARM

FLD

Replacing the voltage regulator. With masking tape and using your own code, identify all the wires which are attached to the voltage regulator. With the proper tools, first disconnect the negative battery cable and then the wires attached to the voltage regulator. Now remove the mounting bolts and the voltage regulator. Install the replacement voltage regulator, reconnect the wires to it, and reconnect the negative battery cable.

Servicing the Alternator

In a charging circuit which uses an alternator, the voltage regulator is either outside of the alternator or else it is part of the alternator itself. In this section, you will learn how to test each system starting with the external regulator.

Replacing the "F-R" plug

The "F-R" plug must be reconnected in the proper way. The shape of the plug fits the shape of the "F-R" opening of the alternator. At an auto salvage yard or parts supply store, purchase an "F-R" plug to use as an adapter. Cut the F wire approximately one inch from the insulation, and use this plug in place of a jumper wire to test your alternator. Completely remove the R wire from the "F-R" plug.

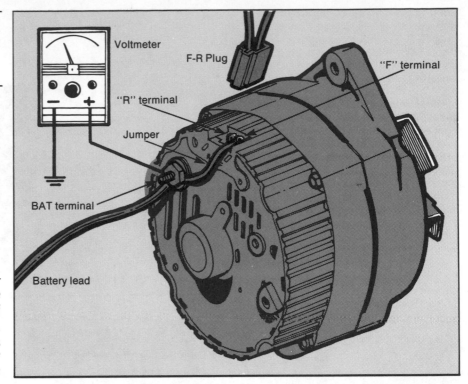

Testing the Delco-Remy alternator with external regulator. Check the fan belt for proper tension. Locate the alternator and disconnect the "F-R" plug at its upper rear by pulling the plug straight out. Connect the positive lead of the voltmeter to the "BAT" terminal of the alternator and the negative lead of the voltmeter to ground. Use a special jumper wire, with a single female terminal. Connect this terminal to the "F" terminal of the alternator and the other end of the lead to the "BAT." *Caution: A spark may occur when you connect the jumper lead to the "BAT" terminal.*

Start the engine and operate it at fast idle, then observe the voltmeter reading. A reading of 15 volts or higher indicates a good alternator. If the voltmeter reads only battery voltage, the alternator is not charging. *Caution: Do not operate the alternator under these conditions any longer than necessary to obtain a voltage reading, because the alternator is now running unregulated.* Switch off the engine, disconnect the voltmeter and the jumper wire, and reconnect the "F-R" plug.

Replacing the Delco-Remy alternator. If your test indicates that the alternator is not putting out sufficient electricity, replace it. Find a wrench of the correct size and disconnect the negative battery cable. Disconnect the "F-R" plug at the alternator and the "BAT" wire at the rear of the alternator. Using the correct size combination wrench, loosen the adjusting bolt and the holding bolt or bolts. Push the alternator towards the engine to free the fan belt from the alternator pulley, then remove the fan belt. Remove the alternator bolts and the alternator itself from the engine. Install the replacement alternator and adjust the fan belt tension. Reconnect all the wires, and reconnect the negative battery cable. Start the engine and test the alternator's electrical output as described previously. *Caution: Never polarize an alternator. To do so would severely damage its internal parts; and it is unnecessary.*

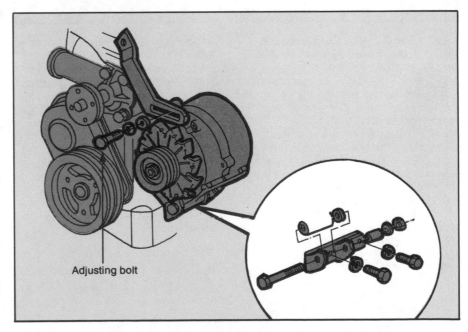

Adjusting bolt

Testing the Chrysler Corporation alternator, single-field type. Check the fan belt for correct tension, then connect the positive lead of the voltmeter to the battery terminal of the alternator and the negative lead to ground. Remove the wire plug which is connected to the "F" terminal of the alternator. Using a special jumper wire with a female terminal, connect this terminal to the "F" terminal and the other lead to the battery terminal of the alternator. *Caution: Sparking may occur at this point.* Now start the engine and operate it at a fast idle. Voltmeter readings must be at least 15 volts for the alternator to be putting out electricity. *Caution: Do not operate the alternator in this unregulated condition any longer than is necessary to obtain a voltmeter reading.* Switch off the engine, remove the jumper wire, reconnect the "F" wire plug, and remove the voltmeter.

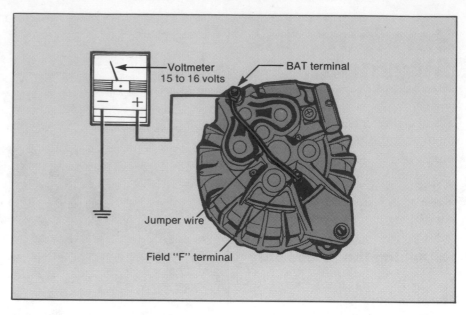

Voltmeter 15 to 16 volts — BAT terminal

Jumper wire

Field "F" terminal

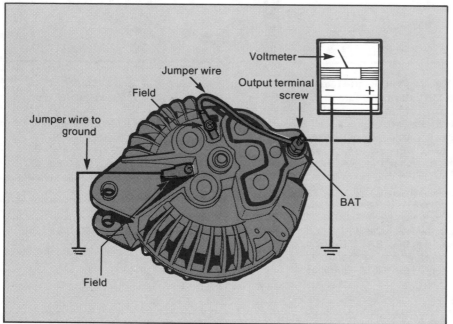

Voltmeter

Jumper wire

Field

Output terminal screw

Jumper wire to ground

BAT

Field

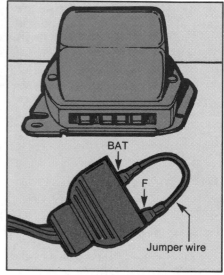

BAT

F

Jumper wire

Testing the Chrysler Corporation alternator, double-field type. A double-field type Chrysler alternator will have two "Field" ("F") terminal connections. Check the fan belt tension, then connect the voltmeter to the alternator as described above. Disconnect both "F" terminal wires at the rear of the alternator and connect the special jumper wire from one "F" terminal to ground. Carefully connect a second jumper wire from the "BAT" terminal of the alternator to the second "F" terminal of the alternator. *Caution: Be sure the second jumper wire touches only the "BAT" and "F" terminals to prevent a short circuit. Also, sparks may occur when you connect the second jumper wire.*

Start your engine and allow it to operate at a fast idle. Voltmeter readings should be 15 to 16 volts for a properly functioning alternator. Switch off the engine and disconnect the two jumper wires and the voltmeter. Reconnect the two "F" wires. *Caution: Do not allow the alternator to operate under these conditions any longer than is necessary to obtain a voltmeter reading, because the alternator is operating unregulated.* If the voltmeter indicates that your alternator is defective, remove and replace it in the same manner as described for the Delco-Remy alternator.

Testing the Ford-type alternator. Locate the regulator, which is usually found on the radiator support. Then release the wire harness plug from the regulator by loosening the clips on the side of the plug and prying it out with a screwdriver. Locate the "F" terminal and the "BAT" terminal of the plug. With a special jumper wire, a short wire with two male plug inserts which look like the terminals of the regulator, connect the "F" terminal with the "BAT" terminal of the plug. Connect the positive lead of the voltmeter to the positive post of the battery and the negative lead of the voltmeter to the negative post. Start the engine and operate it at a fast idle. Voltmeter readings should indicate 15 to 16 volts. If not, the alternator is defective.

Servicing the Alternator Voltage Regulator

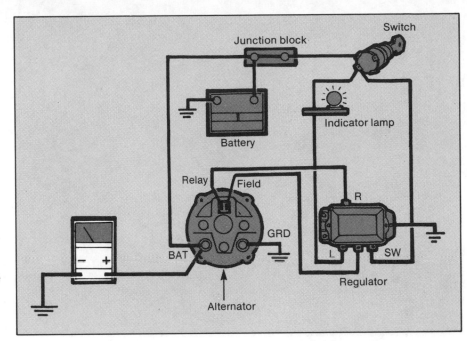

Testing the alternator voltage regulator. Connect the voltmeter to the alternator "BAT" terminal, and connect the tach-dwell meter. Start the engine and operate it at 1500 revolutions per minute (RPM). The voltmeter should indicate at least 14 volts. If it indicates battery voltage only, the voltage regulator is defective.

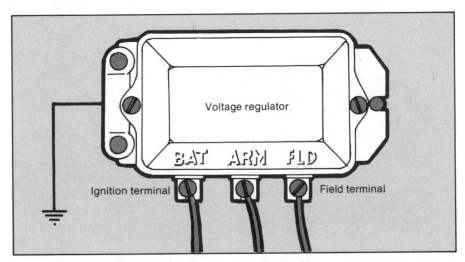

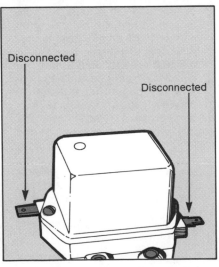

Replacing the external voltage regulator. When you have determined that the regulator is defective, replace it as follows: disconnect the wire plug attached to the regulator terminals. Some regulators have a locking clip that must be released before you take out the plug. With the correct socket set, remove the regulator screws or bolts. Then install the replacement regulator, tighten the screws or bolts securely, and reconnect the wire plug. Start your engine and test the regulator as described previously.

Alternators with internal voltage regulators

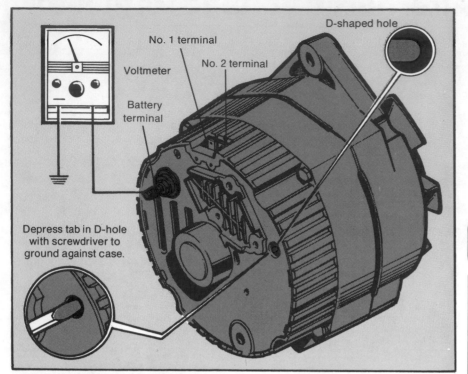

Voltmeter

No. 1 terminal

No. 2 terminal

Battery terminal

D-shaped hole

Depress tab in D-hole with screwdriver to ground against case.

Testing and replacing an alternator with an internal regulator. On alternators with internal regulators, the number one and number two plug terminals are parallel with the rear of the alternator. Check fan belt tension, then connect the positive voltmeter lead to the positive terminal of the battery. Connect the negative voltmeter lead to the negative post of the battery. Start the engine and allow it to operate at a fast idle. Insert a screwdriver or straightened cotter pin into the "D" shaped hole in the back of the alternator. If the voltmeter indicates 15 to 16 volts, the alternator is good, but the internal regulator is defective. Remove the cotter pin, switch off the engine, and disconnect the voltmeter. The alternator must be disassembled and the defective regulator replaced, and this should be done only by a qualified generator or alternator rebuilder. Remove the alternator and take it in for servicing.

ECONOTIP

 # 12
Shut it down or idle it?

Various tests have been carried out by car manufacturers and the federal government to find out whether idling or restarting uses more fuel. Especially with today's frequent gas lines, the right practice may save some fuel. Depending on the study conducted, you should not idle more than half a minute, or a full minute. If the engine idles longer than that, it will take less gas to restart it than to keep it running. It's clear from the studies that anything longer than a minute is wasteful. But your engine may be one of those that should not idle over half a minute. In the long run, you will probably save the most gas by turning the engine off the second you enter a line. That is much better than leaving the engine running in the hope the line will move quickly and ending up with a total idle time of five minutes.

Pro Shop

Booster cable safety light

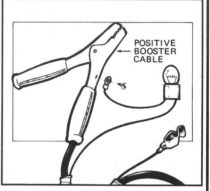

POSITIVE BOOSTER CABLE

Don't guess when connecting booster cables. It's easy to hook up a test safety light that can save you the cost of purchasing an alternator.

Use any 12-volt single contact socket and connect the hot lead to the metal part of the clamp on the positive booster cable. This can easily be done with a sheet metal screw.

Attach an alligator clip to a suitable length of wire and connect the other end of the wire to the ground side of the socket. Tape part of the wire to the cable to keep the wire from getting fouled up.

Before you hotshot a car, connect the alligator clip (negative) to any suitable ground on the car. Now touch the clamp on the positive booster cable to either battery terminal. When the bulb lights up, you have your positive post. Do not connect the negative booster cable until after the bulb has lit up and the positive cable has been connected.

COOLING SYSTEM

The cooling system keeps the engine at its most efficient operating temperature under all driving conditions. The burning of the fuel-and-air mixture may create temperatures of 4,500° in the cylinders during the combustion stroke. The cylinder heads, cylinder walls, pistons, and valves which absorb some of this heat must be cooled. If the heat becomes excessive, the lubricating oil film will break down, lose its lubricating properties, and destroy these components. However, if an engine runs too cool, its efficiency is reduced.

There are two types of cooling systems, air-cooled and liquid-cooled, but since the car engine generally uses the liquid-cooled system, that is the only one which will be discussed in this chapter.

The cooling system consists of a water pump used to circulate the coolant throughout the system, a fan, a radiator, water jackets, a thermostat, a radiator pressure cap, and various hoses.

The water pump is belt-driven by the crankshaft and circulates the coolant through the engine block and radiator. Mounted between the radiator and the block, the pump consists of a pump body, an impeller, a shaft and bearing, a fan pulley hub, and seals. The pump body, with an inlet and an outlet, houses the shaft, seals, and impeller. The impeller, mounted on a shaft, has curved vanes or blades which when turned throw the coolant outward by centrifugal force. The coolant is forced through the outlet of the pump body and into the cylinder block. The pump body inlet is connected by a hose to the bottom of the radiator, and water from the radiator is drawn through the inlet to replace the water forced through the outlet by the pump. The coolant used in the cooling system is a mixture of water and antifreeze. The amount of antifreeze required depends upon the capacity of the cooling system and local weather conditions.

Water jackets cast into the engine block and cylinder heads provide a path for the coolant to flow around the cylinder walls and through the cylinder heads to cool the engine.

The engine fan is mounted on the water pump shaft hub. There are several types of fans in use today—the standard fan, variable pitch blade fans, fluid-coupling fans, and thermostatically-controlled fans. Regardless of the design, the purpose of the fan is to provide a powerful draft of air through the radiator to cool the liquid. Some manufacturers use a shroud surrounding the fan to improve its ability to draw air through the radiator.

The radiator, designed to hold a large quantity of coolant in close contact with a large volume of air so that the heat of the coolant will be transferred into the air, consists of tubes, cooling fins, an upper tank, and a lower tank. In some cars, the lower radiator tank houses a transmission oil cooler to aid in cooling the transmission fluid.

The thermostat, mounted in a housing between the engine block and the radiator inlet or upper hose, controls the flow of water between the radiator and the block. When the engine is cold, the thermostat prevents flow to the radiator, allowing the coolant in the engine block to heat up more rapidly. As the engine heats up, the

CONTENTS

thermostat opens, allowing the coolant to flow to the radiator. The temperature at which the thermostat opens is predetermined by the engine manufacturer, for example, 160°, 180°, or 190°.

The radiator pressure cap is designed to make the cooling system more efficient. As the cap increases the pressure in the cooling system, the boiling point of the coolant is raised. For every one pound of pressure exerted by the cap, the boiling point of the coolant is increased approximately three degrees. That is, a 15-pound pressure cap will increase the boiling point of the coolant by 45°. The coolant can thus reach a higher temperature before boiling. This increase in temperature allows the engine to operate more efficiently.

The by pass hose is either a straight or curved hose connecting the cylinder head and the block or the intake manifold and the block. The hose allows water to circulate between the cylinder head and the block when the engine is cold and the thermostat closed. This by pass system allows the engine to heat up more rapidly and evenly, preventing hot spots in the block.

In this chapter you will learn how to inspect, test, and replace all these components of the cooling system.

Tools and equipment:

Fender covers.
Goggles.
Droplight.
Common screwdriver.
Wire brush.
Water pump pliers.
Common pliers.
$\frac{3}{8}$" and $\frac{1}{2}$" drive socket set.
Scribe.
Hand cloths.
Combination wrenches.
Flare nut wrenches.
Three-gallon drain pan.
Large funnel.
Scraper.

Garden hose.
Belt tension gauge.
Torque wrench.
Antifreeze hydrometer.
Cooling system pressure testing gauge.
Knife.

Parts you may need:

Thermostat housing gasket.
Thermostat.
Water pump.
Gasket sealer.
Heater hoses.
Radiator hoses.
Hose clamps.

Testing for Leaks

Leaks in the cooling system can very often be detected visually. As the engine heats up, the pressure in the system also builds up to approximately 15 psi (pounds per square inch), forcing the coolant out through a defective hose, a punctured or porous radiator tube, a porous expansion plug, or a worn water pump seal. In some cases, a defective part may not show signs of a leak unless additional pressure is exerted into the cooling system.

Installing the pressure testing gauge

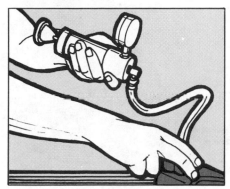

1 **With the engine cold,** remove the radiator cap, then start the engine and allow it to heat up to normal operating temperature. If necessary, add water to the cooling system, then switch the engine off. Install the pressure testing gauge on the radiator filler neck.

2 **Operate the pump** until the gauge needle reaches the pressure prescribed in the specifications for your engine. *Caution: Never exceed the prescribed pressure for your cooling system. This may damage it by rupturing the radiator or splitting the hoses.*

3 **With the pressure testing gauge** set at the prescribed pressure, look for leaks in the radiator hoses and connections, the heater hoses and connections, the thermostat housing gasket, the radiator tanks and core, and the water pump. If no leaks are detected, take a reading of the pressure gauge. It should maintain its reading for at least two minutes. If no visual leaks are detected but the pressure gauge needle drops slowly, there may be an internal leak caused by a cracked block, a cracked cylinder head, or a cracked water jacket. Have your car checked further by a mechanic.

Push hose to release pressure

4 **When the pressure test is completed,** release the pressure in the cooling system, referring to the operating instructions supplied with the pressure gauge. Then remove the gauge from the radiator.

Quick Fix

Straightening radiator fittings
You can't hammer much on a radiator inlet or outlet fitting to straighten it without running the risk of loosening soldered areas.

A quick and safe way to restore bent radiator pipes to their proper contour is first to install a worm gear-type hose clamp around the end of the pipe. Then take any suitable half-round object and, with one hand, hold it in place against the bent part of the pipe. Straddle the hose clamp and half-round piece with a pair of pliers or vise-grips and apply pressure. This will force the bent area of the pipe outward to conform to the contour of the hose clamp. And there's no risk of damage.

Testing the Radiator Pressure Cap

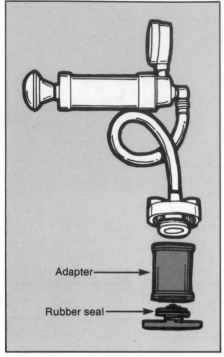

1 **Connect the radiator pressure cap adapter** to the gauge which is supplied with the test kit. Wet the cap's rubber seal with water and connect the cap to the adapter.

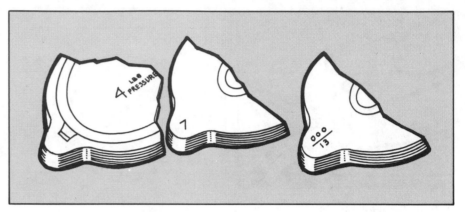

2 **Read the markings** on your pressure cap to find the specified number of pounds.

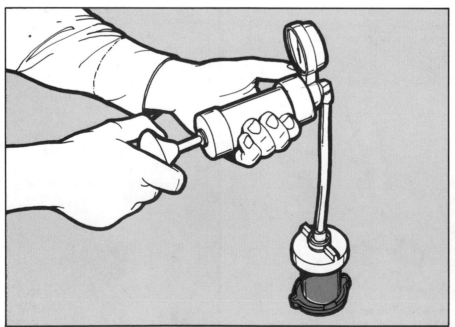

3 **Pump the test pump** until the gauge reads 15 psi (pounds per square inch).

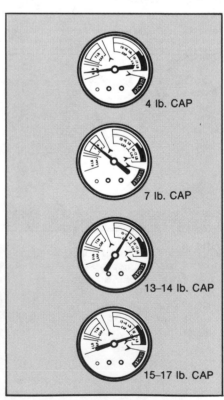

4 lb. CAP

7 lb. CAP

13–14 lb. CAP

15–17 lb. CAP

4 **This pressure reading** should hold for at least two minutes. If the pressure drops, the radiator cap is defective and you should replace it.

Servicing the Radiator and Heater Hoses

Removing hoses

Drain the cooling system as described on this page. If the coolant drained out was put in recently, it can be reused.

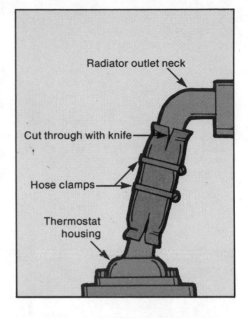

Loosen the upper radiator outlet hose clamps at the thermostat and radiator outlet hose connections, and slide the clamps toward the center of the hose. Using a knife, cut through the ends of the hose at both connections. Remove and discard the hose.

Draining and refilling the radiator

Carefully remove the radiator pressure cap, and place a clean pan under the radiator drain petcock or plug. If your car has a petcock, facing it, turn it counterclockwise. This will open it and allow the coolant to flow from the radiator into the drain pan. If your car's radiator is equipped with a drain plug, facing the plug, turn it counterclockwise to remove it. If your car is not equipped with either a petcock or a drain plug, place a pan below the lower radiator hose connection, and disconnect the hose from the radiator to drain the system. After the radiator is completely drained, close the petcock, install the drain plug securely, or reconnect the lower radiator hose.

First add the amount of antifreeze your car requires in your climate, then fill the radiator with water to just below the bottom of the filler neck. Start the engine with the radiator cap off, and allow it to reach normal operating temperature. Add more water if necessary and replace the radiator cap.

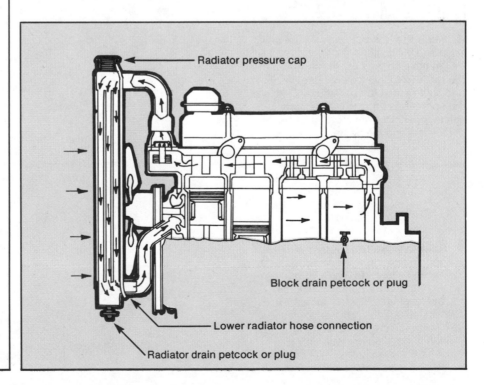

Replacing hoses

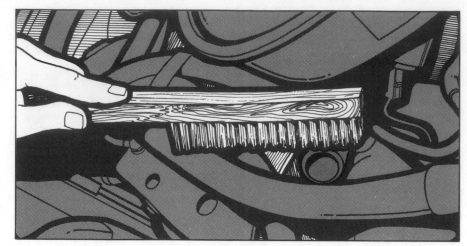

1 **Clean the radiator** and the thermostat outlet necks with a wire brush to insure a good seal for the hose, then apply a coating of gasket cement to the clean surface.

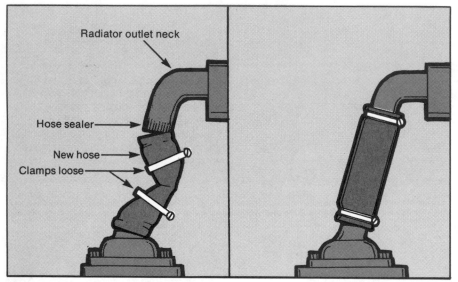

Radiator outlet neck

Hose sealer

New hose

Clamps loose

2 **Slide the hose clamps** on the new hose and install it. Position the clamps on the hose so they are in the center of the radiator or thermostat outlet neck, and tighten the clamps securely. Repeat the operations for removing and replacing the lower radiator hose, the bypass hose, and the heater hoses.

3 **Refill the cooling system** with the drained coolant or new coolant. Start the engine and allow it to reach normal operating temperature, then check the coolant level. If necessary, add antifreeze. Replace the radiator pressure cap. Allow the engine to run long enough to build up pressure in the system, at least three or four minutes, then check all hose connections for leaks.

Pro Shop

Hose removal

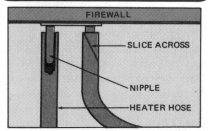

FIREWALL

SLICE ACROSS

NIPPLE

HEATER HOSE

After the heater and radiator hoses have been on a car for a long period of time, they tend to bond themselves to the connecting surfaces (nipples). This makes removal a real chore and can even damage the nipples if excessive force is used to remove the hoses.

One method for making hose removal easier is to slice a cut into the hose near its end. The cut will relieve the tension on the hose fabric and will make removal much easier.

Servicing the Thermostat

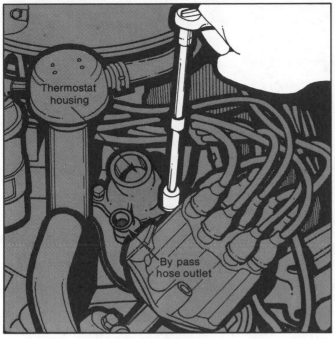

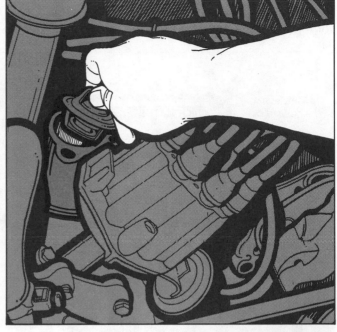

1 **Drain the radiator** and disconnect the upper radiator hose. If a coolant by-pass hose is attached to the thermostat housing, also disconnect it. Remove the bolts or nuts holding the thermostat housing to the engine, and lift out the housing. If it sticks, use a putty knife in the gasket joint to free it.

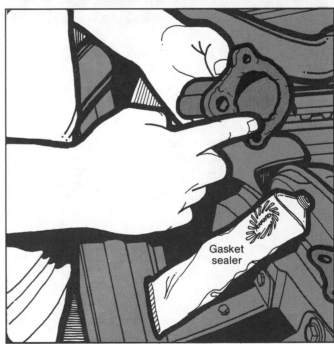

2 **Scrape the old gasket** from the housing and the engine with a putty knife. Do not use a screwdriver. After noting how the thermostat was installed, lift it out. Apply a thin film of non-hardening sealer to the thermostat housing, and put the new gasket in place.

3 **Install the new thermostat** by reinstalling the housing and bolts or nuts, then reconnecting the coolant hose or hoses. Run the engine, checking for leaks. If the housing leaks, stop the engine and remove the housing. Check the thermostat for correct alignment and the thermostat housing surface and gasket. Clean the surface again and replace the gasket. The thermostat mounting bolts must be tightened and torqued down to the manufacturer's specifications.

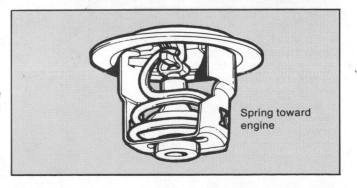

Servicing the Radiator

Although you will have to take your radiator to a professional mechanic for repairs or replacement, if you do the removing and replacing yourself, you will save a considerable amount of money.

Pro Shop

Checking automatic transmission fluid

Some of the transmission fluid may have been lost when the cooler lines were disconnected from the radiator. When the job is completed, check the transmission oil level and add fluid if necessary.

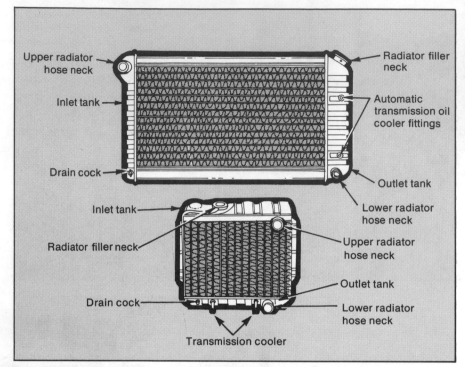

Upper radiator hose neck

Inlet tank

Drain cock

Inlet tank

Radiator filler neck

Drain cock

Transmission cooler

Radiator filler neck

Automatic transmission oil cooler fittings

Outlet tank

Lower radiator hose neck

Upper radiator hose neck

Outlet tank

Lower radiator hose neck

1 To remove the radiator, drain the cooling system, then remove the upper and lower radiator hoses. If the automatic transmission cooler lines are connected to the radiator tank, using the proper tools, loosen the connections at the tank and disconnect the lines. Note: Place a clean drain pan under the cooler line connection to catch any spilled oil. Locate the radiator supports, and with the proper size tool, remove the support bolts. If your car is equipped with a radiator shroud, remove the bolts which hold it and move it away from the radiator (toward the engine). Lift the radiator out of the engine compartment. *Caution: When lifting the radiator out, do not allow it to rub against any sharp objects, like the fan or hood latch.*

2 To install the repaired or new radiator in the engine compartment, replace the supporting bolts. Bolt the shroud in place and connect the transmission cooler lines, if necessary. Replace the upper and lower radiator hoses and fill the cooling system with coolant. Start the engine, allow it to reach normal operating temperature, then replace the radiator cap. Check for leaks, as described earlier in this chapter.

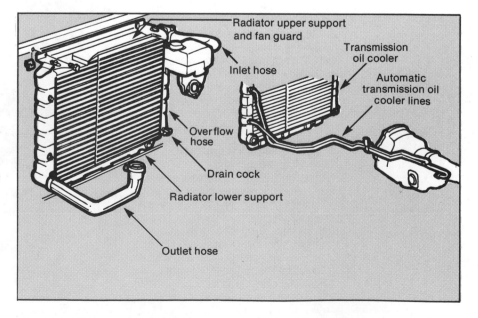

Radiator upper support and fan guard

Transmission oil cooler

Automatic transmission oil cooler lines

Inlet hose

Overflow hose

Drain cock

Radiator lower support

Outlet hose

Servicing the Water Pump

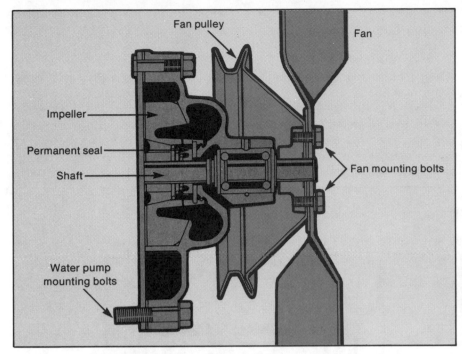

Fan pulley

Fan

Impeller

Permanent seal

Shaft

Fan mounting bolts

Water pump mounting bolts

1 Removing the water pump. Remove the radiator and shroud as described previously. Loosen and remove the drive belts mounted on the water pump pulley. If the front side of the fan is not marked, scribe a mark on the blade indicating the front for correct reinstallation. Remove the four fan mounting bolts and the fan and water pump pulley. Note: On some cars the fan is mounted with a spacer installed between the fan and the water pump hub. If your car has one, remove it. Apply a coating of gasket cement to the surface of the replacement water pump and place the new gasket on the pump. Place the pump, gasket side down, on a clean surface.

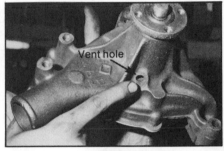

Vent hole

2 The position of the pump should be identical to that of the old pump which is still mounted on the engine. The water pump should always be installed with the vent hole at the bottom.

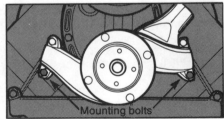

Mounting bolts

3 Water pump mounting bolts often differ in size and length, so to insure correct reinstallation, with the correct tool remove one bolt at a time and insert it in the corresponding hole of the replacement pump. Remove the old water pump and scrape off the old gasket from the engine block. Clean the surface thoroughly with a cloth and apply a coating of gasket cement to it.

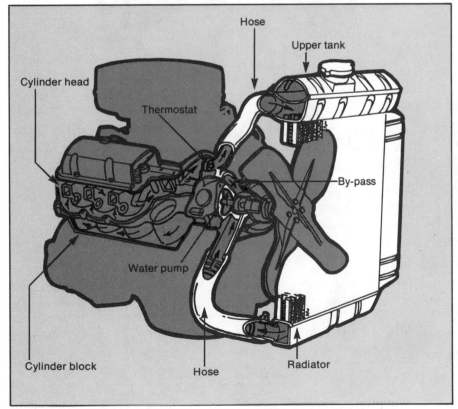

Hose

Upper tank

Cylinder head

Thermostat

By-pass

Water pump

Cylinder block

Hose

Radiator

4 Replacing the pump. Taking care not to drop or remove the bolts in the replacement pump, lift and position it against the engine. Start all bolts by hand only. Push the pump in toward the engine until it is properly seated against the block, and tighten the bolts evenly, checking the manufacturer's specifications for correct torque. Replace the water pump pulley, spacer, and fan, and tighten the bolts securely. Install the drive belts and adjust them using a belt tension gauge. Replace the radiator, hoses, and transmission cooler line.

Flushing the Radiator

With today's antifreezes, a radiator seldom becomes clogged with rust and other particles, unless maintenance has been poor. A more common occurence is for the radiator to be plugged by excessive corrosion at the inlet side of the tubes. In this case, the corrosion-sensitive solder joints virtually bloom with corrosive deposits and restrict the tubes. Thus, although the tubes themselves are clear, very little coolant can flow through them.

To test for a clogged radiator, warm up the engine. When it has reached normal operating temperature, switch it off and run your fingers over the radiator's finned surface. It should be hot at the inlet side and become gradually cooler as you reach the outlet side. On a down-flow radiator, run your hand across from top to bottom. On a cross-flow type, start at the inlet side and run your hand up and down, working across to the outlet side. If you feel cold spots, you have a clogged radiator. *Caution: If the plugging occurs in cold weather, the coolant may be frozen. Let the cooling system thaw out. Do not attempt to warm it by running the engine, or damage may result.*

Simple method for flushing the cooling system

Remove the radiator cap and open the drain cock, then remove the plug or disconnect the lower hose to drain the radiator. After it is empty, close the drain cock, and reinstall the plug or reconnect the hose. Top up the radiator with fresh water. Turn the heater control to "High" and start the engine. Place your hand on the radiator inlet tank to determine when the thermostat opens. You will feel the tank get hot when the thermostat permits water to flow through to the radiator. Five minutes after the thermostat opens, stop the engine, open the drain cock, remove the drain plug or disconnect the lower hose, and allow the radiator to drain completely.

The complete flushing procedure should be repeated as often as needed until the coolant draining from the radiator is clean. Tests have shown that if the radiator is flushed with this method three times, an average of 88 percent of the loose rust and old coolant is removed. If the job is done four times, about 94 percent is removed, and five times, approximately 97 percent.

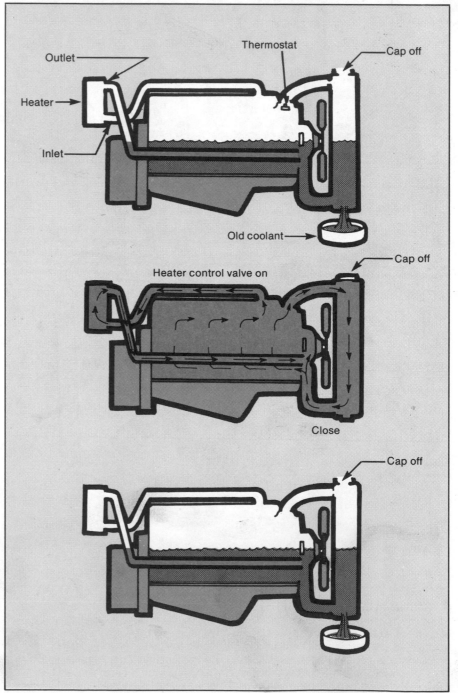

Reverse flushing of the radiator and block

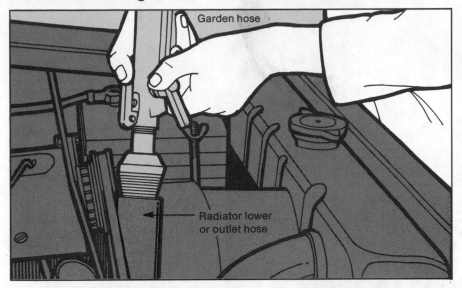

Garden hose

Radiator lower
or outlet hose

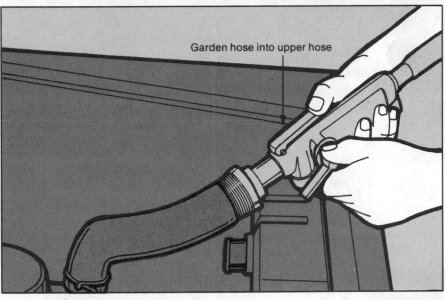

Garden hose into upper hose

Pro Shop

Coolant overflow can

A radiator overflow can is a very useful device that helps to reduce the overall engine coolant temperature by about ten degrees. A number of companies are selling overflow can kits and they're easily installed. The can itself is actually a plastic bottle.

Installation of an overflow can is relatively simple. Drill a hole to mount the can on an inner fender panel, reroute the radiator overflow tube into the can, and replace the standard radiator cap

with a nonremovable-type cap provided in the overflow can kit. The can must be installed at the same level as the top of the radiator so that overflow coolant will flow into the can by gravity.

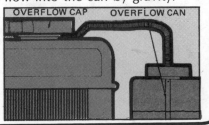

OVERFLOW CAP   OVERFLOW CAN

Reverse Flushing the Radiator

First, drain the cooling system by removing the radiator cap and opening the petcock. Remove the plug or disconnect the lower hose to drain the radiator. Disconnect the upper radiator hose from the thermostat housing and the lower hose from the water pump. Close the petcock and replace the pressure cap. Position the opening of the upper hose so it's pointing toward the ground, away from the engine. Insert a garden hose into the lower radiator hose opening and wrap a piece of cloth around the joint to seal it. Turn on the hose and allow water to flow into the lower section of the radiator, up through the radiator, and out through the upper radiator hose. Keep the water flowing until it is clear.

Reverse Flushing the Block

First, remove the thermostat and replace the thermostat housing gasket with a new one. Now's a good time to check the thermostat. Disconnect the upper radiator hose at the radiator, but leave it connected to the thermostat housing. Disconnect the lower radiator hose at the radiator, but leave it connected to the water pump. Position the hose so the opening faces the ground, away from the engine. Insert a garden hose in the opening of the upper hose. Allow the water to flow through the engine block and out of the water pump through the lower hose to the ground until the water runs clear. Replace the thermostat, housing, and the gasket, and connect the upper and lower hoses. Add the proper amount of antifreeze, then fill the radiator with fresh water. Start the engine and allow it to reach the normal operating temperature (at least 150° F). Now check the coolant level, top off with fresh water if necessary, install the pressure cap, and check for leaks.

COOLING SYSTEM—BASIC ELEMENTS IN WHITE

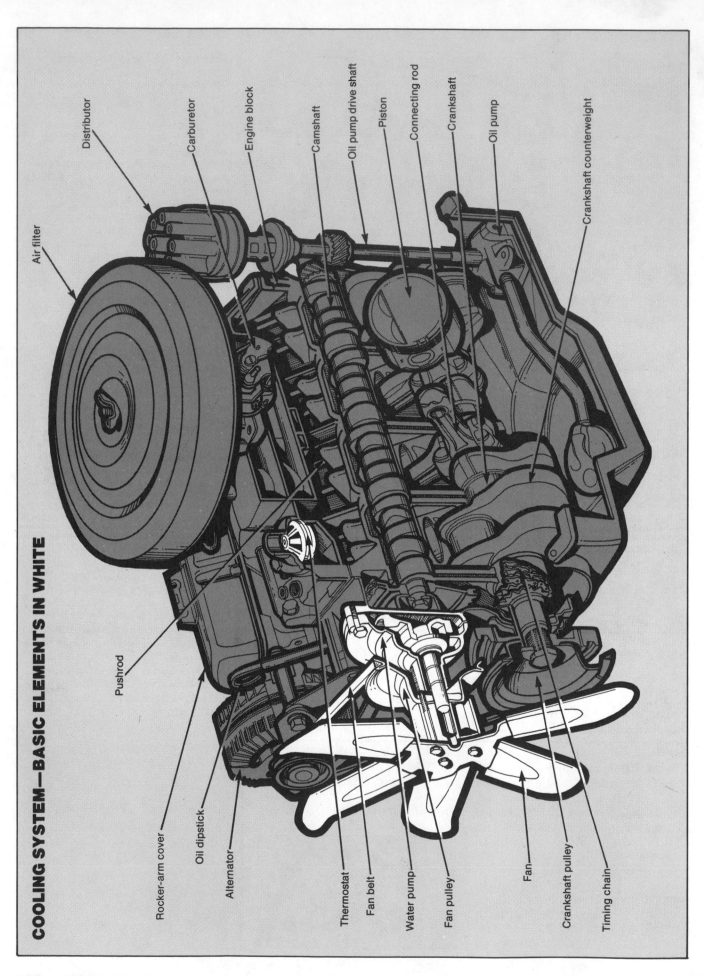

Air filter

Distributor

Carburetor

Engine block

Camshaft

Oil pump drive shaft

Piston

Connecting rod

Crankshaft

Oil pump

Crankshaft counterweight

Pushrod

Rocker-arm cover

Oil dipstick

Alternator

Thermostat

Fan belt

Water pump

Fan pulley

Fan

Crankshaft pulley

Timing chain

Troubleshooting flow chart: cooling system

Symptom	Probable cause	Remedy
A. Overheating due to cooling system malfunction.	1. Low water level.	1. Fill to proper level. See Note 1. Check system for leakage.
	2. Clogged radiator passages.	2. Clean with proper solution, reverse flushing, or by boiling out with chemicals. See Note 2.
	3. Thermostat stuck in closed position.	3. Replace thermostat if testing shows defect.
	4. Thermostat installed upside down.	4. Install correctly with sensing unit to block.
	5. Fan, water pump, and/or drive belt slipping.	5. Adjust or replace belt as necessary.
	6. Frozen coolant.	6. Thaw system. Then drain and replace with proper solution. See Note 3.
	7. Defective radiator pressure cap or cap seat.	7. Replace cap if defective.
	8. Clogged or kinked inlet or outlet water hoses.	8. Replace defective hose.
	9. Overflow tube blocked.	9. Open tube passage or replace.
	10. Defective temperature gauge.	10. Check with test gauge.
	11. Defective water pump.	11. Replace pump.
	12. Radiator fins clogged with foreign matter.	12. Clean fins of dirt and obstructions.
	13. Defective cylinder head gasket.	13. Replace head gasket.
	14. Fan too far from radiator.	14. Move closer with shims between pulley and fan. See Note 4.
	15. Fan with insufficient blade area or pitch.	15. Replace with large fan or one with more blades. Correct pitch by bending evenly.
	16. Defective water distribution tube (on some in-line engines).	16. Replace tube.
B. Overheating due to engine malfunction.	17. Improper ignition timing.	17. Adjust timing.
	18. Manifold heat control valve jammed open.	18. Free valve.
	19. Blown head gasket.	19. Replace head gasket.
	20. Incorrect valve timing.	20. Time valves properly.
	21. Exhaust system blocked.	21. Clean exhaust system.
C. Overheating due to other factors.	22. Slipping clutch.	22. Adjust or replace clutch.
	23. Dragging brakes.	23. Adjust or free brakes.
	24. Vehicle driven too long in lower gear.	24. Check driving habits or driving conditions.
	25. Surrounding temperatures too high.	25. Correct with larger radiator, or a fan with more blades, or increase idle speed.
D. Water loss through overflow.	26. Water level too high.	26. Allow settling as needed.
	27. Weak pressure valve in radiator cap.	27. Test cap pressure and replace if necessary.
	28. Defective thermostat.	28. Replace thermostat.
	29. Loose or defective fan belt.	29. Adjust or replace belt.
	30. Water pump failure.	30. Replace water pump.
	31. Slipping fan clutch.	31. Replace fan clutch.
	32. Clogged radiator.	32. Flush with two-step acid cleaner. If this does not work, remove radiator and have it professionally serviced.
	33. Collapsing or rotted radiator hose.	33. Replace hose.
	34. Poor air flow through radiator.	34. Clean foreign matter from front of radiator or AC condenser.
	35. Foaming coolant.	35. a. Worn-out or low-quality antifreeze should be replaced. b. Sources of air leaks into system should be found and corrected. c. Exhaust gas leakage source should be corrected.
	36. Violent coolant circulation.	36. Have loose or broken baffle in radiator repaired.
	37. Severe operating conditions.	37. Install overflow reservoir kit on cars not so equipped.
	38. Engine out of tune.	38. Tune engine.
	39. Brakes dragging.	39. Check brake self-adjusters and repair as necessary.

Cooling system continued

Symptom	Probable cause	Remedy
E. Overheating due to external leaks.	40. Check for leaks at hose connections, radiator, water pump, core plugs, thermostat housing, cylinder head.	40. When source of leak is found, replace part or tighten connection or mounting bolts as necessary.
	41. Water pump leaks through vent holes, corroded tubes.	41. Pressure test for leaks. Replace pump if required.
	42. Loose or rusted-through core hole (freeze-out) plug.	42. Replace plug.
	43. Defective gasket on cylinder head, thermostat housing, water pump.	43. Replace gasket. Torque evenly to specified pressure.
	44. Heater core leaks.	44. Repair or replace core.
	45. Leaks through engine accessory bolts or studs that pass into water jacket.	45. Remove bolts or studs. Replace after proper sealing. See Note 6.
	46. Loose or stripped threads on oil cooler fittings to radiator (automatic transmission).	46. Tighten, reseal, or replace fittings or radiator as required.
	47. Thermostat replaced cocked on seat.	47. Replace thermostat properly.
F. Overheating due to internal leaks.	48. Leaking automatic transmission oil cooler.	48. Replace cooler, flush out cooling sysem and replace hoses; transmission may need servicing.
	49. Loose cylinder head gasket.	49. Tighten or replace head gasket.
	50. Cracked engine block.	50. Replace block.
	51. Cracked cylinder head or engine block bore.	51. Replace head or engine.
	52. Oil cooler cracked inside radiator.	52. Repair or replace radiator.
G. Engine runs too cold.	53. Defective or missing thermostat.	53. Install proper thermostats.
	54. Coolant passes around thermostat. See 10 above.	54. Correct as necessary. See Note 7.
H. Fan belt fails to hold its adjustment.	55. Stretching of poor quality belt.	55. Replace with better belt.
	56. Failure to install double belt drives as matched pair.	56. Renew both belts in a two-belt drive system.
	57. Adjustment unit mounting not secure.	57. Tighten generator, alternator, or idler pulley support.
	58. Weak adjustment bracket bends.	58. Replace bracket.
	59. Bent pulley or pulleys.	59. Replace pulley.
	60. Belt improperly installed.	60. Belt should not touch center groove of pulley.
	61. Incorrect belt used. Adjustment set at limit.	61. Replace with correct belt.
	62. Pulleys out of line with each other. See 5, 39, 40–45 above.	62. Align pulleys by shims or by adjustment of belt-driven accessories.
I. Poor heater performance.	63. Defective thermostat.	63. Replace thermostat.
	64. Restricted hose.	64. Flush hose or reposition to eliminate kink.
	65. No thermostat.	65. Install thermostat.
	66. Clogged heater core.	66. Reverse flush heater core; if this does not help, have core professionally replaced.
	67. Defective heater control valve.	67. Replace control valve.

Note 1. Double-check all fittings after engine is hot. Allow work-out of air bubbles and time for thermostat to open. At this time, more coolant will be necessary. Thermostat will not usually open unless it is immersed in coolant.

Note 2. Reverse flushing means forcing hot water or water plus flushing solution through radiator and/or engine block in reverse direction to normal flow. Disconnect radiator hoses and remove the thermostat.

Note 3. Use caution with antifreeze protection gauge. Testing a mixture of several different antifreezes is not accurate. Allow a safe reserve of at least ten degrees.

Note 4. Where possible, provide a minimum of one inch clearance between the fan and the closest radiator projection.

Note 5. A rust mark, antifreeze stain, or repeated wet spot around hose connections, gasket lines, or the radiator seams or core often indicates leaks.

Note 6. All studs or bolts entering water chambers should be treated with a good sealer and secured.

Note 7. Some cars have extra height in their thermostat housings. It is important to replace the lock wire or flat locking ring that holds the thermostat up against its housing. Also make sure that the heavy rubberlike seal is in place to prevent coolant bypassing the thermostat to the radiator.

CONTENTS

EXHAUST SYSTEM

Your car's exhaust system has two functions. One is to carry away the poisonous, lethal gases from the passenger compartment, the other, to muffle the sound of the engine. If a leak develops anywhere in the system, fumes drifting upward through holes and crevices in the car's underbody and into the passenger compartment can make the people in the car sick. If a leak develops when you are on the road, drive with all the windows open until you can get it repaired.

Unfortunately, there is often little warning that your car's exhaust system is damaged. The first indication of danger may be the feeling of sickness caused by escaping carbon monoxide. If the muffler has developed a leak, you will hear a loud roaring noise, but the muffler is only one component of the exhaust system, and damage in the others can be silent. Periodic checks of the exhaust system, are, therefore, a must. By inspecting it every six months, you can spot weakened or damaged parts and loose connections, so that corrections can be made before problems develop.

The exhaust system starts at the exhaust manifold. From the engine compartment or from beneath the car, examine the joint connecting the exhaust pipe to the exhaust manifold. Start the engine, then watch and listen to the exhaust manifold/exhaust pipe joint. Now turn off the engine. From beneath the car, carefully examine every part of the exhaust system.

Most cars have a single exhaust system, but some with eight-cylinder engines have two. Both should be checked during an exhaust system examination. Continue your examination by tapping each part, except the catalytic converter, with a wrench. A sound part will emit a ringing noise, whereas one which has failed or is about to fail will produce a dull thud. The final test is to start the engine and visually examine the entire exhaust system.

Tools and equipment:

Combination wrenches.
3/8" and 1/2" drive ratchet set.
Muffler cutter.
Ball peen hammer.
Diagonal cutting pliers.
Cold chisel.
Goggles.
Fender covers.
Nut cracker.
Pipe cutter.
Hacksaw and extra blades.
Hand cloths.

Parts you may need:

Penetrating oil.
Muffler sealer.
Muffler.
Exhaust pipe.
Connecting pipes.
Tailpipe.
Hangers.
Clamps.

Hints and tips

● When parts are reassembled, there will be a number of common joints, such as the one between the tailpipe and the muffler. Before clamping these parts together, coat the joints with a sufficient amount of exhaust system joint sealer. The sealer, rather than the clamp, prevents leaks.

● If you remove the exhaust pipe from the exhaust manifold, check to see if there is a gasket. If so, discard it and replace it with a new one. Once the joint has been disassembled, the gasket loses its effectiveness.

● The most difficult part of the job may be separating the tailpipe from the muffler, because engine heat fuses the metal end connections together.

● If your check of the exhaust system indicates that repairs are necessary, the car should be raised and jack stands positioned at four places on the frame. Note: When working on the exhaust system, always wear goggles to protect your eyes.

● Before working on your exhaust system, make sure all the parts are cold. If the engine has been running, allow it to cool down for at least three hours.

● This job may involve loosening frozen fasteners. Saturate stubborn nuts and bolts with an ample amount of penetrating oil, and allow it to work for five to ten minutes. If you still cannot release the fastener, cut it away with a chisel.

American Motors Corporation

Models with six-cylinder engines without catalytic converters

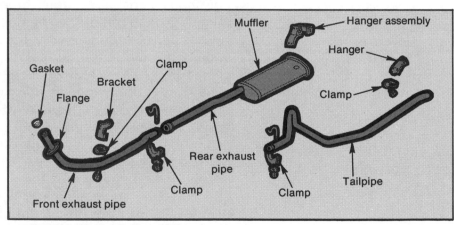

DISASSEMBLING THE SYSTEM

1 Unbolt the two bolts holding the front exhaust pipe flange to the exhaust manifold. Disconnect the front exhaust pipe from the one-piece rear exhaust pipe/muffler assembly by removing the screw holding the clamp at the front-to-rear exhaust pipe joint. The clamp is located near the pipe's midsection. Spread the clamp and slide the pipe out.

2 Disconnect the tailpipe from the muffler by removing the tailpipe-to-muffler clamp. Remove the tailpipe from the car by loosening and spreading the rear tailpipe clamp. Drop the rear exhaust pipe/muffler assembly by disconnecting it from its hangers. Examine all the brackets, hangers, and clamps, and remove and discard those which are damaged or badly corroded.

REINSTALLING THE SYSTEM

1 Install the brackets and hangers and set the front exhaust pipe into its clamp. Engage the clamp bolt and tighten it just enough to hold the pipe, but still allow it to be maneuvered. Make sure the seal between the front exhaust pipe and the exhaust manifold is in the correct position. Attach the front exhaust pipe to the exhaust manifold, then tighten the two front exhaust pipe-to-exhaust manifold flange bolts.

2 Slide the rear exhaust pipe/muffler assembly firmly onto the front exhaust pipe, and attach the muffler to its hanger assembly. Join the rear exhaust pipe and the front exhaust pipe, and tighten the clamp nut. Slide the tailpipe securely into the rear of the muffler and tighten the clamp bolts at each end of the tailpipe.

3 Go back over the entire system, making sure that each hanger and clamp bolt or nut is securely tightened. The exhaust system must be aligned so that there is no stress on parts and no part can bang against any area of the car.

Models with eight-cylinder engines and single exhaust systems

DISASSEMBLING THE SYSTEM

1 **Remove the bolts** holding the front exhaust pipe flange to the exhaust manifolds serving the cylinders on the left and right banks of the engine.

2 **Disconnect the front from the rear exhaust pipe** by removing the clamp at the joint, and remove the front pipe by taking out the clamp holding it at its midsection. Disconnect the rear exhaust pipe from the muffler by removing the clamp at the muffler/exhaust joint.

3 **Disconnect the tailpipe from the muffler** by removing the tailpipe-to-muffler clamp, and drop the tailpipe by removing the clamp holding it at its rear. Drop the muffler by disconnecting it from its hanger assembly.

4 **Examine** all the brackets, hangers, and clamps, and remove and discard those which are damaged.

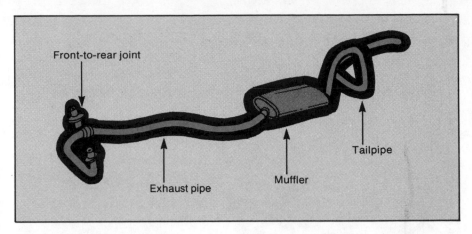

Front-to-rear joint

Exhaust pipe

Muffler

Tailpipe

REINSTALLING THE SYSTEM

1 **Install the brackets and hangers,** and set the front exhaust pipe into its clamp. Engage the clamp bolt and tighten it just enough to hold the pipe, but still permit maneuverability.

2 **Make sure the seals** between the front exhaust pipe and the exhaust manifolds serving the left and right banks of cylinders are in the correct position. Attach the front exhaust pipe to the left- and right-side exhaust manifolds.

3 **Tighten the front exhaust pipe-to-exhaust manifold flange bolts** on both the left and right sides. Slide the rear exhaust pipe firmly onto the front exhaust pipe, and attach and tighten the clamp at the joint formed by the two pipes. Slide the muffler onto the rear exhaust pipe, attach it to its hanger assembly, and tighten the clamp at the joint. Slide the tailpipe securely into the rear of the muffler, and position the tailpipe-to-muffler clamp around the joint and tighten the nut.

4 **Go back over the entire system,** making sure that each hanger and clamp bolt or nut is securely tightened. Be sure the exhaust system is aligned so there is no stress on the parts.

Models with eight-cylinder engines and dual exhaust systems

A dual exhaust system is really two individual systems, each of which is arranged exactly like a single system for each bank of cylinders. Therefore, treat each part of a dual exhaust system as a single system, and follow the instructions previously given for all models with eight-cylinder engines and single exhaust systems.

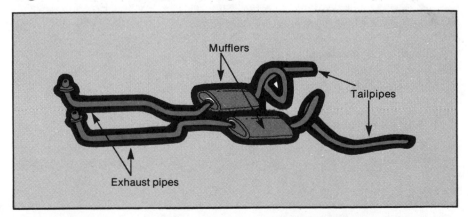

Mufflers

Tailpipes

Exhaust pipes

Chrysler Corporation

Valiant and Dart models with six-cylinder engines

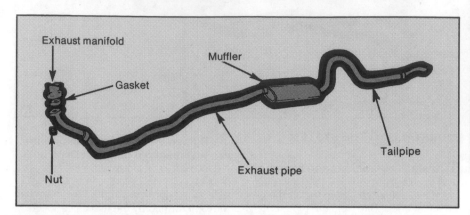

Exhaust manifold
Gasket
Muffler
Nut
Exhaust pipe
Tailpipe

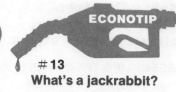

ECONOTIP

#13

What's a jackrabbit?

If you have ever watched a jack-rabbit start running, you know they get up to full speed almost instantly. Jackrabbits are built for fast starts, high speed, and quick turns. The modern passenger car is not. Trying to imitate a jackrabbit when starting from a dead stop can use 15 percent more gas. The best mileage comes from gradual acceleration.

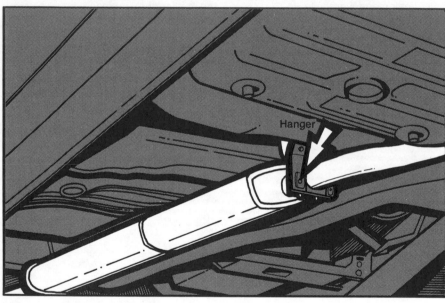

Hanger

Torquing

Torque the fasteners securely or to specification as follows:
1. Exhaust pipe-to-exhaust manifold nuts: 35 foot pounds.
2. Exhaust pipe U-bolt nuts: 95 inch pounds.
3. Muffler - to - tailpipe U-bolt nuts: 150 inch pounds.
4. Tailpipe support bolt: 200 inch pounds.

REINSTALLING THE SYSTEM

1 **Attach the exhaust pipe** to its U-bolt, and engage the U-bolt nuts loosely. *Caution: Support the muffler as you work at the exhaust pipe to keep it from falling and being damaged.*

2 **Install a new gasket** between the exhaust pipe flange and the exhaust manifold, then engage the two connecting nuts loosely.

3 **Install the small pipe extension** at the rear of the muffler through the hole in the U-bolt hanger assembly.

4 **Attach the small pipe extension** at the rear of the muffler to the tailpipe, and connect the tailpipe to the tailpipe support, engaging the bolt loosely. Install the U-bolt at the muffler/tailpipe joint, and engage the two U-bolt nuts loosely.

5 **Make sure the entire exhaust system** is properly aligned so there is no stress on any part and no part is in contact with the body, chassis, fuel or brake lines.

DISASSEMBLING THE SYSTEM

1 **Remove the two nuts** holding the exhaust pipe flange to the exhaust manifold, and discard the gasket between them. Remove the two nuts holding the U-bolt at the front of the exhaust pipe. Disconnect the muffler/exhaust pipe assembly, which is a one-piece unit.

2 **Examine the exhaust pipe U-bolt hanger assembly,** and remove and replace it if damaged.

3 **Remove the U-bolt** holding the muffler and tailpipe together. Slide the muffler forward so it disengages from the tailpipe, and lower the muffler/exhaust pipe assembly to the ground. Examine the muffler/tailpipe U-bolt hanger assembly, and replace it if damaged.

4 **Remove the bolt** holding the tailpipe support to the car's frame, then lower the tailpipe to the ground. Note: Some models have a resonator in the tailpipe. If one or the other is damaged, the entire unit must be replaced. Examine the tailpipe support. If it is damaged, remove and replace it.

Valiant and Dart models with eight-cylinder engines and single exhaust systems

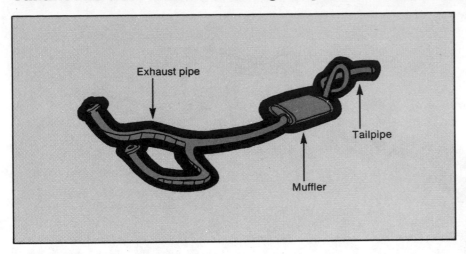

Exhaust pipe

Tailpipe

Muffler

Pro Shop

Rusted clamp and hanger nuts

Oddly enough, we've found that an easy way to break off rusted nuts is to tighten them instead of loosening them. And sometimes a badly-rusted clamp or hanger strap will snap off with surprising ease. Use a six-point socket for this operation. *Caution: Be careful not to cut your hands on the rusted metal parts.*

DISASSEMBLING THE SYSTEM

1 Remove the four nuts holding the exhaust crossover pipe to the exhaust manifolds serving the left and right banks of cylinders. Discard the gasket.

2 Remove the U-bolt and saddle holding the exhaust pipe and muffler at their common joint, then separate the two parts. At the exhaust pipe midsection, remove the two clamp screws attaching the clamp to the bracket held to the car's frame, releasing the exhaust pipe. Lower it to the ground.

3 At the rear of the muffler, remove the U-bolt holding the muffler and tailpipe together. Slide the muffler forward, away from the tailpipe, and lower the muffler to the ground.

4 Examine the muffler/tailpipe U-bolt hanger assembly, and remove and replace it if damaged. Remove the bolt holding the tailpipe support to the frame, then lower the pipe to the ground.

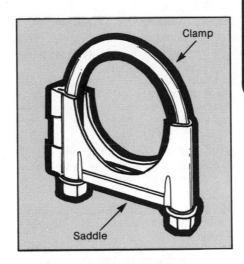

Clamp

Saddle

REINSTALLING THE SYSTEM

1 Attach the exhaust pipe at its midsection with the clamp, engaging the two clamp bolts loosely.

2 Install a new gasket on the left-side exhaust crossover pipe flange, and attach the flange loosely to the left side exhaust manifold. Install the gasket on the right side in the same way.

3 Slide the muffler and exhaust pipe together, attaching the U-bolt and saddle around the common joint. Attach U-bolt nuts and washers loosely. Connect the tailpipe to the muffler with the U-bolt, and again attach the nuts and washers loosely.

4 Then attach the rear of the tailpipe to the car frame by means of the tailpipe support, engaging the bolt loosely.

5 Make sure the exhaust system is properly aligned so that there is no stress on any part.

Torquing

Torque the fasteners securely or to specification as follows:
1. Exhaust pipe-to-exhaust manifold nuts: 24 foot pounds.
2. Exhaust pipe-muffler U-bolt nuts: 150 inch pounds.
3. Exhaust pipe midsection bolts: 200 inch pounds.
4. Muffler-tailpipe U-bolt nuts: 150 inch pounds.
5. Tailpipe support bolt: 180 inch pounds.

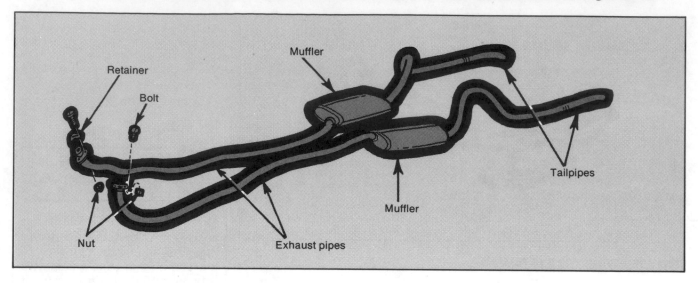

A dual exhaust system is really two identical, or almost identical, but individual systems in the same car. Each system is generally arranged to serve one cylinder bank of an eight-cylinder engine. The discussion below describes how to replace one of these systems. Be sure to repeat the procedure for both systems.

DISASSEMBLING THE SYSTEM

1 Remove the two nuts holding the exhaust pipe to the exhaust manifold, and discard the gasket. Support the exhaust pipe to keep it from falling and being damaged as you work on it.

2 Detach the nuts at the rear of the muffler which hold the U-bolt connecting the muffler and the tailpipe. Examine the muffler-tailpipe U-bolt hanger assembly, and remove and replace it if damaged. Remove the fasteners holding the muffler in its hanger, then lower the muffler/exhaust pipe to the ground. Loosen the rear of the tailpipe at the tailpipe support, and lower the pipe to the ground. *Caution: Some models have a resonator as an integral part of the tailpipe.*

REINSTALLING THE SYSTEM

1 Position the muffler/exhaust pipe assembly, and support the end of the exhaust pipe to prevent damage as you work on the muffler end. Attach the muffler hanger to the muffler, engaging the nut and washer loosely.

2 Install a new gasket on the exhaust pipe flange, then attach the flange loosely to the exhaust manifold.

3 Insert the small pipe extension at the rear of the muffler through the hole in the U-bolt hanger assembly.

4 Connect the tailpipe to the tailpipe support, engaging the bolt loosely. Securely attach the small pipe extension at the rear of the muffler to the tailpipe. Install the U-bolt at the muffler/tailpipe joint, engaging the two U-bolt nuts loosely. Make sure the entire exhaust system is properly aligned so there is no stress on any part.

Torquing

Torque the fasteners securely or to specification as follows:
1. Exhaust pipe-to-exhaust manifold nuts: 24 foot pounds.
2. Muffler-to-muffler hanger: 24 inch pounds.
3. Muffler - to - tailpipe U-bolt nuts: 150 inch pounds.
4. Tailpipe support bolt: 50 inch pounds.

Catalytic converters

Starting in 1975, most cars incorporated a part called a catalytic converter in the exhaust system, designed to combat air pollution. It should be checked visually for damage during an exhaust system examination. You can determine if your car has a catalytic converter by looking at the exhaust pipe between the engine and the muffler. The catalytic converter is shaped differently from the muffler and the resonator, and if your car has both a catalytic converter and a resonator, the resonator will be positioned in the tailpipe.

Fury, Satellite, Coronet, Charger, and Challenger models with six-cylinder engines

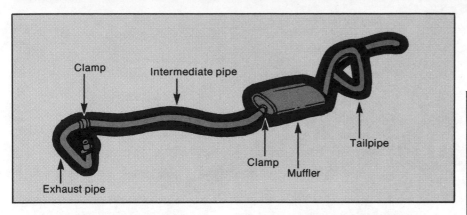

Clamp · Intermediate pipe · Tailpipe · Clamp · Muffler · Exhaust pipe

Torquing

Torque the fasteners securely or to specification as follows:
1. Front exhaust pipe-to-exhaust manifold nuts: 35 foot pounds.
2. Front exhaust pipe-to-rear exhaust pipe bolts: securely. *Caution: do not crush pipes.*
3. Rear exhaust pipe-to-muffler clamp nuts: 150 inch pounds.
4. Muffler-to-tailpipe clamp nuts: 150 inch pounds.
5. Tailpipe strap support bolt: securely.

DISASSEMBLING THE SYSTEM

1 **Unbolt the front exhaust pipe** from the rear exhaust pipe, and disconnect the front exhaust pipe flange from the exhaust manifold. Lower the front exhaust pipe to the ground.

2 **Remove the clamp** attaching the front of the rear exhaust pipe to the bracket. Support the pipe so it will not fall to the ground and get damaged.

3 **At the front of the muffler,** disengage the saddle clamp holding the rear exhaust pipe to the muffler. Pull the rear exhaust pipe forward, disengaging it from the muffler, and lower the pipe to the ground.

4 **At the rear of the muffler,** disengage the bolts securing the muffler to the tailpipe at the common hanger assembly. Then pull the muffler and tailpipe apart, and lower the muffler to the ground. Examine the common muffler/tailpipe hanger. If damaged, replace it.

5 **At the rear of the tailpipe,** unbolt the tailpipe support, releasing the tailpipe from its hanger. Lower the tailpipe to the ground, and examine the hanger. If it is damaged, replace it.

REINSTALLING THE SYSTEM

1 **Secure the rear exhaust pipe** in its bracket, then attach the clamp and engage the bolts loosely. Support the rear of the exhaust pipe, so it is not damaged as you continue working. Position the front exhaust pipe and attach it to the rear exhaust pipe, then bolt the two together loosely.

2 **Using a new gasket,** attach the front exhaust pipe flange to the exhaust manifold, engaging the bolts loosely.

3 **Insert the small pipe extension** on the rear of the muffler into its hanger assembly, and connect the front muffler assembly to the rear exhaust pipe. Place the saddle clamp around the rear exhaust pipe/muffler joint, and engage the bolts loosely.

4 **Connect the tailpipe** to the muffler, then clamp the joint together at the hanger assembly, engaging the bolts loosely. Connect the tailpipe support strap to the tailpipe support hanger, again attaching the bolt loosely. Make sure the exhaust system is properly aligned so there is no stress on any part. *Caution: Be sure that no exhaust part comes into direct contact with any section of the body, fuel tank, or brake lines.*

Fury, Satellite, Coronet, Charger, and Challenger models with eight-cylinder engines and single exhaust systems

The procedure for replacing exhaust systems in these cars is identical to the procedure in the same models with six-cylinder engines, with one exception. The front exhaust pipe is a crossover type, with two branches, one connected to the exhaust manifold serving the left bank of cylinders, and the other connected to the exhaust manifold serving the right bank.

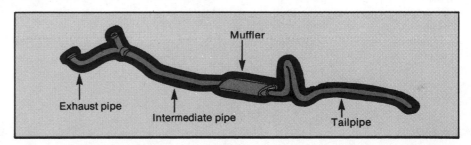

Muffler · Exhaust pipe · Intermediate pipe · Tailpipe

Fury, Satellite, Coronet, Charger, and Challenger models with eight-cylinder engines and dual exhaust systems

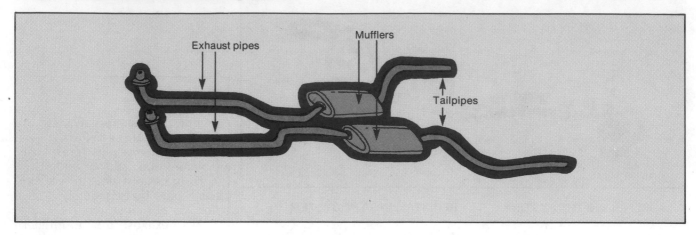

A dual exhaust system is two identical, or almost identical, but individual systems in the same car. Each system is usually arranged to serve one bank of cylinders in an eight-cylinder engine. The discussion below describes how to replace one of the two systems. Repeat the procedure for the other system.

DISASSEMBLING THE SYSTEM

1 **Remove the clamp** securing the front exhaust pipe to the rear exhaust pipe. It is located just to the rear of the front exhaust pipe neck. Unbolt the flange securing the front exhaust pipe to the exhaust manifold, and discard the gasket. Pull the front exhaust pipe loose and remove it.

2 **At the muffler,** unbolt the saddle clamp holding the rear exhaust pipe to the muffler, then release the bolt holding the bracket near the middle of the rear exhaust pipe, pulling the pipe loose. Then remove it from the car.

3 **Remove the clamp** at the rear of the muffler holding it to the tailpipe, and detach the bolt securing the muffler support strap to the frame. Disconnect the muffler and tailpipe, and remove the muffler. Examine the common muffler/tailpipe hanger. If it is damaged, replace it. Torque the attaching bolt to 200 inch pounds. Unbolt the tailpipe support strap, and remove the pipe.

REINSTALLING THE SYSTEM

1 **Position the exhaust pipe** and clamp it to the bracket, engaging the bolts loosely. Support the other end of the rear exhaust pipe to prevent damage to the pipe.

2 **Connect the front exhaust pipe** to the rear exhaust pipe, clamping them together loosely. Using a new gasket, loosely attach the front exhaust pipe flange to the exhaust manifold.

3 **At the muffler end of the rear exhaust pipe,** connect the pipe to the muffler, then loosely bolt the muffler support strap to the frame. Attach the saddle clamp to the joint formed by the muffler and the rear exhaust pipe, engaging the clamp fasteners loosely.

4 **Connect the tailpipe and muffler** at the support bracket, and attach the support clamp loosely. Attach the tailpipe support strap to its bracket, again engaging the bolt loosely. See that the exhaust system is properly aligned so there is no stress on any part.

Torquing

Torque the fasteners securely or to specification as follows:
1. Front exhaust pipe-to-exhaust manifold nuts: 24 foot pounds.
2. Front exhaust pipe-to-rear exhaust pipe clamp nuts: securely. *Caution: Do not crush pipes by overtightening the clamp.*
3. Rear exhaust pipe midsection clamp bolts: 95 inch pounds.
4. Rear exhaust pipe-to-muffler saddle clamp nuts: securely. *Caution: Do not crush pipes by overtightening the clamp.*
5. Front exhaust pipe-to-muffler clamp assembly nuts: 150 inch pounds.
6. Muffler support strap bolt: 200 inch pounds.

Ford Motor Company

Pinto, Mustang II, and Bobcat models with four-cylinder engines

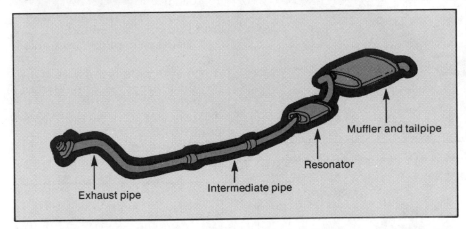

Exhaust pipe

Intermediate pipe

Resonator

Muffler and tailpipe

Torquing

Torque the fasteners securely or to specification as follows:
1. Exhaust pipe-to-exhaust manifold nuts: 25 to 35 foot pounds.
2. Exhaust pipe midsection nuts: 17 to 28 foot pounds.
3. Resonator-to-muffler support bracket nuts: 108 inch pounds.
4. Muffler hanger assembly bolts: 108 inch pounds.

DISASSEMBLING THE SYSTEM

1 Remove the fasteners from the hanger which attaches the midsection of the exhaust pipe to the pipe bracket, and support the pipe to keep it from falling and getting damaged.

2 Remove the nuts attaching the exhaust pipe to the resonator inlet pipe, and those attaching the exhaust pipe flange to the exhaust manifold. Release the exhaust pipe and remove it.

3 Support the assembly by attaching a piece of soft wire around the resonator inlet pipe and tying it to the chassis. At the front of the muffler, loosen and remove the hanger bolts securing the assembly to the car's underbody.

4 At the rear of the muffler, loosen and remove the bolts holding the muffler, and the rest of the assembly, to the hanger bracket, then release the assembly and lower it to the ground.

Replacement parts

Note: Instead of the two pieces which come with the original exhaust system for these models, replacement exhaust parts normally come as four separate pieces that are assembled with clamps. The four pieces are: an exhaust pipe, a resonator and intermediate pipe assembly, a resonator-to-muffler pipe, and a muffler-tailpipe assembly.

REINSTALLING THE SYSTEM

1 Loosely attach the midsection of the exhaust pipe to the hanger, and connect the exhaust pipe flange to the exhaust manifold.

2 Support the resonator inlet pipe to keep the resonator assembly from being damaged as you connect the pipe to the rear of the exhaust pipe. Seal and attach the clamp securely. *Caution: Do not crush pipes by overtightening the clamp.*

3 Suspend the resonator-to-muffler pipe from the hanger assembly, and attach the bolts loosely, then connect the resonator-to-muffler pipe to the rear of the resonator with a clamp. *Caution: Be sure no part comes in contact with the differential housing or the rear end.*

4 Secure the muffler-tailpipe assembly, and connect the rear of the muffler to the hanger assembly, attaching the bolts loosely. Connect the resonator-to-muffler pipe to the front of the muffler with a clamp. See that the exhaust system is properly aligned so there is no stress on any part and no part is in contact with the body, springs, shocks, or gas tank. This is to prevent the system from rattling.

Pro Shop

Original system

The resonator inlet pipe, resonator-to-muffler pipe, muffler, and tailpipe are all welded together in a single unit if the exhaust system is the car's original one. We suggest that you use a muffler cutter to cut the system at convenient points so that you may remove it easily.

Models with six-cylinder engines

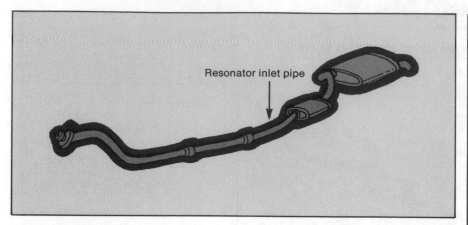

Resonator inlet pipe

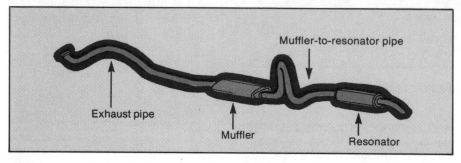

Muffler-to-resonator pipe

Exhaust pipe

Muffler

Resonator

Torquing

Torque the fasteners securely or to specification as follows:
1. Exhaust pipe-to-exhaust manifold nuts: 25 foot pounds.
2. Exhaust pipe midsection nuts: eight to 14 foot pounds.
3. Exhaust pipe-to-resonator inlet pipe flange: 20 to 30 foot pounds.
4. Resonator-to-resonator hanger bolts: 10–20 foot pounds.
5. Muffler-to-muffler bolts: eight to 14 foot pounds.

DISASSEMBLING THE SYSTEM

1 **Remove the fasteners** from the hanger which attaches the midsection of the exhaust pipe to the pipe bracket, and support the pipe to keep it from falling and getting damaged. Remove the nuts attaching the exhaust pipe to the resonator inlet pipe, and those attaching the exhaust pipe flange to the exhaust manifold. Remove the exhaust pipe.

2 **Support the assembly** by attaching a piece of soft wire around the resonator inlet pipe and tying it to the chassis. At the rear of the resonator, loosen and remove the two bolts holding the resonator to its hanger assembly.

3 **At the rear of the muffler,** loosen and remove the two bolts holding the muffler/tailpipe to its hanger assembly, then release the one-piece assembly, and lower it to the ground.

Replacement parts

Note: Instead of the two pieces which come with the original exhaust system, replacement exhaust parts normally come as four separate pieces that are assembled with clamps. The four pieces are: an exhaust pipe, a resonator and inlet pipe assembly, a resonator-to-muffler pipe, and a muffler-tailpipe assembly.

REINSTALLING THE SYSTEM

1 **Loosely attach the midsection of the exhaust pipe** to the hanger, then connect the exhaust pipe flange to the exhaust manifold, again attaching the nuts loosely.

2 **Support the resonator inlet pipe** to keep the resonator assembly from getting damaged as you connect the pipe to the rear of the exhaust pipe. Seal and attach the clamp loosely, then attach the resonator to its hanger, and secure these bolts loosely. *Caution: In securing clamps, tighten them sufficiently to hold the pipes steady, but do not overtighten and crush the pipes.*

3 **Connect the front of the resonator-to-muffler pipe** to the rear of the resonator, securing the joint with a clamp. Attach the muffler/tailpipe assembly to its hanger, and secure the bolts loosely. Connect the rear of the resonator-to-muffler pipe to the front of the muffler, securing the joint with a clamp.

4 **See that the exhaust system is properly aligned** so there is no stress at any point, and be sure no part of the system comes in contact with the body, chassis, shocks, rear end housing, fuel tank, or brake line.

Pro Shop

Cutting loose the old system

Sometimes the old exhaust system will not drop free of the body because of a large part which is in the way, such as the rear end or the transmission support. In these cases, we've found it's easy to cut the old system at certain points in order to make the parts smaller. Use a large cold chisel, a pipe cutter, a hacksaw, a muffler cutter, or a chain cutter.

Granada, Monarch, Comet, and Maverick models with eight-cylinder engines and single exhaust systems

The arrangement of the exhaust system in these cars is the same as that in models with six-cylinder engines. Therefore, most of the replacement instructions previously outlined apply, with the exception that a crossover-type exhaust pipe is used. One branch goes to the exhaust manifold on the left side of the engine, the other to the exhaust manifold on the right side.

All other models except Lincoln, Continental Mark III and Mark IV, and Thunderbird

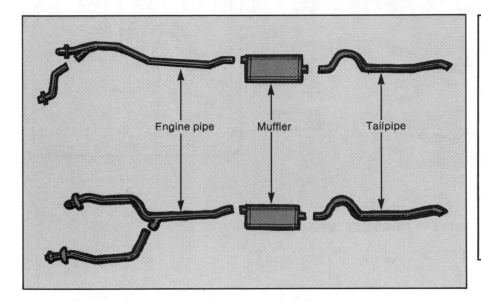

Engine pipe   Muffler   Tailpipe

Torquing

Torque the fasteners securely or to specification as follows:
1. Exhaust pipe branches-to-exhaust manifolds: 25 to 35 foot pounds.
2. Exhaust pipe-to-muffler clamp: 25 to 35 foot pounds.
3. Muffler - to - muffler hanger bolts: eight to 14 foot pounds.
4. Tailpipe-to-muffler clamp: 25 to 35 foot pounds.
5. Tailpipe support strap bolts: eight to 14 foot pounds.

DISASSEMBLING THE SYSTEM

1 **Loosen the clamp** and disconnect the exhaust pipe from the muffler. Support the pipe to keep it from falling and being damaged.

2 **Disconnect the exhaust pipe branches** from the exhaust manifolds on the left and right sides of the engine, then release the exhaust pipe and lower it to the ground.

3 **At the rear of the tailpipe,** loosen the tailpipe strap from the hanger, then loosen and release the muffler from the hanger. Note: On the original exhaust system, the muffler and tailpipe is one assembly. Move the tailpipe up and over so it clears the rear crossmember as you move the assembly toward the front of the car to remove it.

REINSTALLING THE SYSTEM

1 **Support the exhaust pipe** so you can attach it to the exhaust manifolds without damaging it. Note: The replacement muffler and tailpipe usually come as two separate pieces rather than as one assembly.

2 **Attach the exhaust pipe branches** to the left- and right-side exhaust manifolds, and secure the nuts loosely.

3 **Work the replacement tailpipe** over the rear crossmember, allowing it to rest on the crossmember. Connect the front of the muffler to the rear of the exhaust pipe, then attach the muffler to its hanger assembly, engaging the bolts loosely.

4 **Install the clamp** around the muffler-exhaust pipe joint, and connect the rear of the muffler to the front of the tailpipe. Install the clamp around the muffler-tailpipe joint.

5 **Attach the rear section** to its hanger, making sure the exhaust system is properly aligned so there is no stress at any point.

Continental Mark III and Mark IV, and Thunderbird

Pro Shop

One-piece resonator and tailpipe

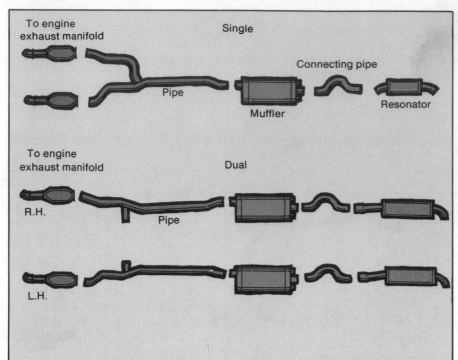

To engine exhaust manifold

Single

Connecting pipe

Pipe

Muffler

Resonator

To engine exhaust manifold

Dual

R.H.

Pipe

L.H.

Some models have a resonator as an integral part of the tailpipe, forming a one-piece unit. If one or the other is damaged, the entire unit must be replaced.

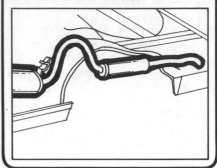

DISASSEMBLING THE SYSTEM

1 **Support the exhaust pipe** with a piece of soft wire so it does not fall and get damaged. Disconnect the branches of the crossover exhaust pipe and the left- and right-side exhaust manifolds.

2 **Disconnect the rear of the exhaust pipe** from the front of the muffler, then release the exhaust pipe and lower it to the ground.

3 **Support the rear** of the muffler-to-resonator pipe with a piece of soft wire so the assembly will not fall, then remove the bolts holding the resonator and the muffler to their hangers.

4 **To remove the assembly,** work the unit forward and up and over the cross-member.

REINSTALLING THE SYSTEM

1 **Begin reassembly** by supporting the exhaust pipe to prevent damage to it, then attach the branches of the exhaust pipe to the left and right exhaust manifolds, securing the bolts loosely.

2 **Work the tailpipe-resonator assembly** into position, allowing the pipe to rest on the crossmember as you attach the resonator to its hanger. Engage the bolts loosely.

3 **Connect the front of the muffler** with the rear of the exhaust pipe, and clamp them loosely. Then attach the rear of the muffler to its hanger assembly and loosely engage the bolts.

4 **Connect the rear** of the muffler with the front of the tailpipe and clamp, again loosely, making sure the exhaust system is properly aligned so there is no stress at any point.

Note: The original exhaust system in these models includes a crossover exhaust pipe, and a single assembly consisting of the muffler, muffler - to - resonator pipe, resonator, and tailpipe.

Torquing

Torque the fasteners securely or to specification as follows:
1. Exhaust pipe branches-to-exhaust manifolds: 25 to 35 foot pounds.
2. Exhaust pipe-to-muffler clamp: 25 to 35 foot pounds.
3. Tailpipe - to - muffler clamp: securely.
4. Muffler - to - hanger assembly bolts: eight to 14 foot pounds.
5. Resonator-to-hanger assembly bolts: eight to 14 foot pounds.

Models with eight-cylinder engines and dual exhaust systems

A dual exhaust system is really two identical single exhaust systems. Treat each in the same way as the single eight-cylinder systems described previously.

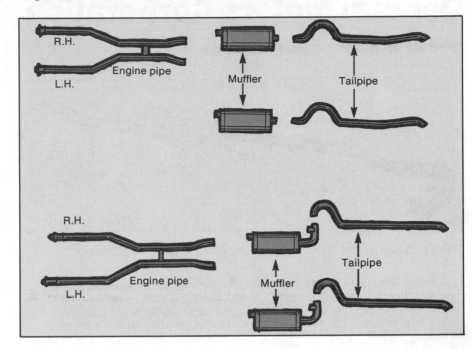

Jack stands for safety

Place jack stands under the chassis as shown here whenever you work under a car. Most jacks simply are not steady enough to be safe or may be let down accidentally. Jacks that come with most American cars are not only unsteady, but are designed to lift only 25% of the car's weight safely so they should not be used to raise the entire front or rear of a car at one time.

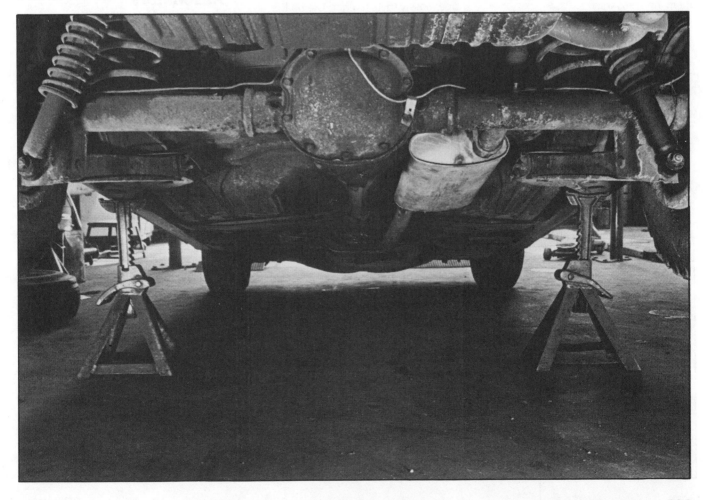

General Motors Corporation

Models with four-cylinder engines

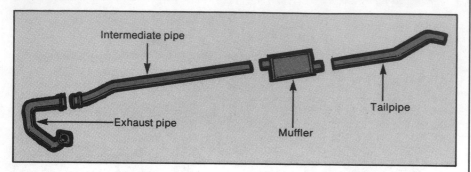

Intermediate pipe

Exhaust pipe

Muffler

Tailpipe

DISASSEMBLING THE SYSTEM

1 **Remove the exhaust pipe** at the exhaust manifold by loosening the nuts, then remove the nuts holding the exhaust pipe clamp to the muffler. Lower the exhaust pipe to the ground.

2 **Remove the tailpipe and muffler** from their hangers by loosening the bolts, then lower the muffler and tailpipe to the ground. Examine the tailpipe and muffler hangers for damage and replace them if necessary.

REINSTALLING THE SYSTEM

1 **Support the exhaust pipe** on the muffler hanger so the pipe will not fall as you work. Attach the exhaust pipe loosely to the exhaust manifold with the securing nuts, and connect the exhaust pipe to the muffler. Attach the muffler loosely to its hanger.

2 **Clamp the muffler** and the exhaust pipe together loosely, then connect the tailpipe and muffler, and attach the tailpipe loosely to its hanger. Clamp the muffler and exhaust pipe together, again engaging them loosely.

3 **See that the exhaust system is properly aligned** so there is no stress on any part, and make sure that no part comes in contact with the body, chassis, fuel tank, rear end, or brake lines.

Replacement parts

The original exhaust system in four-cylinder engine models consists of an exhaust pipe and a welded muffler/tailpipe assembly. Replacement parts usually consist of an exhaust pipe and an individual muffler and tailpipe. These parts are secured by clamps.

Clearances

General Motors recommends that exhaust system components have a clearance of at least ¾-inch from the floor pan. This will avoid possible overheating of the pan.

Resonators

Note: In some models, a resonator is an integral part of the tailpipe. In these models, if the tailpipe or resonator is damaged, the entire assembly must be replaced. In other models, the resonator and tailpipe are held together by a clamp so that the damaged component alone can be replaced. Still other models have tailpipes but not resonators. An examination of the tailpipe will quickly tell you the arrangement in your General Motors car.

What a torque wrench does

Simply put, a torque wrench tells you how much twisting pressure you are exerting on a nut or bolt.

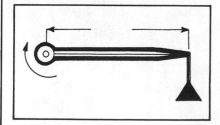

Too much force can strip threads or shear off a bolt; not enough, in this case, can allow the nut to loosen and vibrate off.

This diagram shows how pressure of one pound on the end of a wrench handle one foot long delivers one pound-foot (sometimes written "ft. lb.") of twist or torque. Simple torque wrenches have dials calibrated from 0–150 foot pounds and in inch pounds.

Torquing

Torque the fasteners securely or to specification as follows:
1. Exhaust pipe-to-exhaust manifold nuts: 15 foot pounds.
2. Exhaust pipe-to-muffler clamp: nine foot pounds.
3. Muffler-to-muffler hanger: 25 foot pounds.
4. Tailpipe-to-muffler clamp: nine foot pounds.
5. Tailpipe-to-tailpipe hanger: 25 foot pounds.

Models with six-cylinder engines

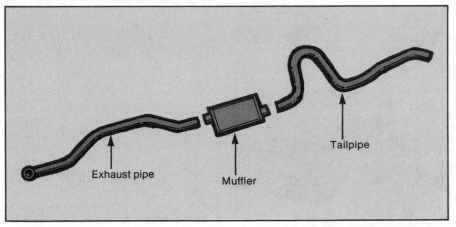

Exhaust pipe

Muffler

Tailpipe

Torquing

Torque the fasteners securely or to specification as follows:
1. Exhaust pipe-to-exhaust manifold nuts: 18 foot pounds.
2. Exhaust pipe-to-muffler pipe clamp: 15 foot pounds.
3. Tailpipe-to-resonator-to-muffler pipe clamp: 15 foot pounds.
4. Muffler hanger bolt: ten foot pounds.
5. Tailpipe-to-resonator clamp: 15 foot pounds.
6. Tailpipe hanger bolt: ten foot pounds.

DISASSEMBLING THE SYSTEM

1 **Unbolt the exhaust pipe** from the exhaust manifold, and support the pipe to keep it from falling as you work on the muffler. Detach the exhaust pipe-to-muffler clamp, then separate the pipe and muffler, and lower the exhaust pipe to the ground.

2 **Detach the tailpipe-to-muffler clamp** or resonator-to-muffler pipe clamp at the muffler, and separate the pipe from the muffler. Support the pipe to keep it from falling. Remove the muffler from its hanger assembly by loosening the bolt, and lower it to the ground.

3 **If the car has a detachable resonator,** loosen the tailpipe-to-resonator clamp at the rear of the resonator, then lower the resonator and the muffler-to-resonator pipe assembly to the ground. Examine the muffler and tailpipe hangers, and replace them if necessary.

REINSTALLING THE SYSTEM

1 **Position the exhaust pipe** and support it to keep it from being damaged. Attach the exhaust pipe to the exhaust manifold, engaging the bolts loosely.

2 **Connect the exhaust pipe** to the muffler, and secure the muffler to its hanger assembly, again engaging the bolts loosely. Place the clamp around the exhaust pipe/muffler joint and engage these nuts loosely.

3 **If the system is equipped with a resonator,** position the resonator and resonator-to-muffler pipe assembly. Support the pipe to keep it from being damaged. Connect the resonator-to-muffler pipe to the muffler, and clamp the joint, then connect the tailpipe to the resonator and clamp the joint. Attach the tailpipe to its hanger. Engage all these nuts and bolts loosely.

4 **If the system does not have a resonator,** connect the tailpipe to the muffler, clamping it loosely. Attach the tailpipe to its hanger, and engage the bolt loosely. See that the exhaust system is properly aligned so there is no stress on any part, and that all parts are free from contact with the body, chassis, rear end, shocks, brake lines, and fuel tank.

More work than it's worth?

Replacing individual components of an exhaust system can be a long, dirty, and very tiring job—frequently more work than it is worth. Rust freezes bolts and the intense heat tends to fuse parts together, especially the exhaust and tail pipes where they enter the muffler. (Professional muffler shops can cut through the pipes and fasteners with torches in a couple of minutes.) Before you tackle the job yourself of replacing one component, consider replacing all the com-

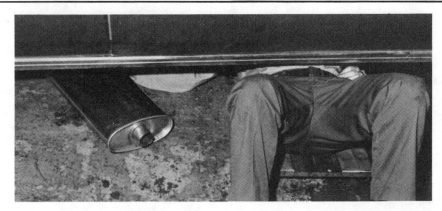

ponents at the same time, even if they don't all appear to need it yet. That way, you will have only to detach the old system from the car and re-attach the new one—not try to wrestle one old component free from another one.

Models with eight-cylinder engines and single exhaust systems

The exhaust pipe of a single exhaust system has two branches, one connecting to the exhaust manifold on the engine's right side, and the other to the exhaust manifold on the left. The same procedure is used to replace a single exhaust system in a General Motors car with an eight-cylinder engine as described above for a GM car with a six-cylinder engine, with one exception. When disassembling, and later reinstalling, the exhaust pipe, two connections must be handled, the one to the right manifold, and the one to the left.

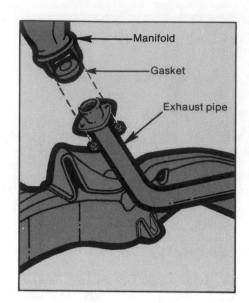

Manifold

Gasket

Exhaust pipe

Models with eight-cylinder engines and dual exhaust systems

The dual exhaust system is really two identical single exhaust systems. Each has an exhaust pipe, a muffler, and a tailpipe. One system serves the cylinders on the engine's left side, the other serves the right. To replace either side of the General Motors eight-cylinder dual exhaust system, follow the directions for the GM six-cylinder engine.

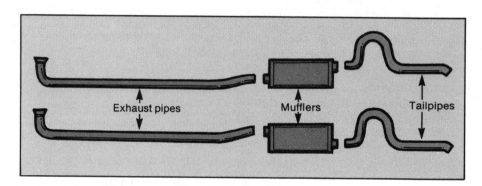

Exhaust pipes   Mufflers   Tailpipes

Troubleshooting flow chart: exhaust system

Symptom	Probable cause	Remedy
A. Leaking exhaust.	1. Leaks at pipe joints.	1. Reseal joints with exhaust system sealer. Tighten clamp bolts securely. If leaks persist, replace pipes.
	2. Rusted out pipes.	2. Replace.
	3. Damaged gasket at exhaust pipe-exhaust manifold joint.	3. Replace.
	4. Rusted out muffler.	4. Replace.
B. Exhaust noise.	5. Blown-out muffler or exhaust pipe.	5. Replace damaged part.
	6. Leak at exhaust pipe-exhaust manifold connection.	6. Replace damaged gasket and/or tighten loose bolts.
	7. Exhaust manifold cracked.	7. Replace.
	8. Leak between exhaust manifold and cylinder head.	8. Tighten manifold-to-cylinder head stud nuts or bolts to specification.
C. Engine hard to warm up or will not return to normal idle.	9. Heat control valve is frozen.	9. Most cars have this valve, which can be serviced by finding its counterweight beneath the exhaust manifold. If there is no counterweight, there is no valve. Free the valve by applying liberal quantities of manifold heat control valve solvent to the counterweight. If the valve does not free itself, replace it.

11

CONTENTS

BRAKE SYSTEM

The brake system is designed to retard the motion of the car by means of friction. Friction, the resistance between two moving bodies in contact, converts the car's momentum power (kinetic energy) into heat. The amount of pressure exerted by one moving body against the other will determine the amount of friction—the more pressure, the higher the friction; the less pressure, the lower the friction. In the car, this friction is created by the contact between the brake shoe lining and the brake drum surface.

Basically, brake linings are made up of asbestos fibers impregnated with special compounds to bind the fibers together. The most common type of brake lining in the modern car brake system is a molded lining composed of asbestos fibers ground up and pressed into shape. Manufacturers use various lining compounds for specific braking characteristics, such as brass linings added to the asbestos for heavy-duty braking.

In this chapter, you will learn how to detect a faulty power brake system and a faulty or leaking master cylinder or wheel cylinder and calipers, and how to check the condition of the brake shoes or brake friction pads.

Your car's brakes are its primary safety system. Every time you step on the brake pedal, you are calling on your car's brake system to perform a function that is potentially a life-or-death matter. Obviously, this is not the system to tamper with if you do not know what you are doing. If you want to test your basic mechanical ability, pick some other system of your car to begin with. For instance, if you try your own maintenance and repairs on the cooling system and make a mistake, you may have to take a long walk for help, but you will not endanger your safety.

While all the repair procedures given in this chapter should be within the ability of the novice mechanic, you should look over the entire chapter before beginning any brake service job. If you feel the procedures are too complex for you to handle, have your brake service work done by a professional mechanic.

You will not find any information in this chapter on how to service the hydraulic system of your brakes. There are too many places where a home mechanic can go wrong once he begins to disconnect the parts of this system.

The modern drum brake system

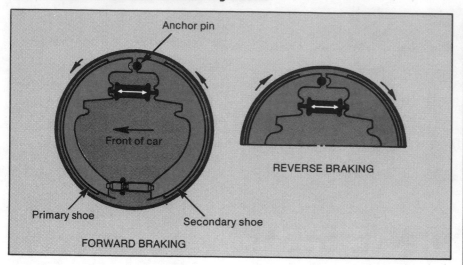

Anchor pin

Front of car

REVERSE BRAKING

Primary shoe

Secondary shoe

FORWARD BRAKING

Acceleration and braking

Tremendous force is necessary to stop a car in motion. In most cases, you will bring your car to a stop in a shorter distance and in less time than the distance and time it took you to gain traveling speed. As an example, a car with a 100-horsepower engine takes about 60 seconds to accelerate up to 60 miles per hour. This same car is expected to come to a stop when traveling at 60 miles per hour in less than six seconds. Brakes must accomplish the same amount of work done by the engine, but do it in one-tenth the time.

The modern drum brake system, with Bendix servo and self-energizing action, minimizes the amount of pedal pressure necessary to stop the car. This is accomplished by hooking a spring and adjusting screw between the heel of the primary brake shoe (the lower end of the forward shoe), to the toe of the secondary brake shoe (the lower end of the back shoe).

Since this system uses one spring to anchor both shoes at one end, it allows the other end of both shoes to move freely and simultaneously. When pressure is exerted on the foot brake pedal, fluid in the master cylinder, hydraulic lines, and wheel cylinder moves the pistons in the wheel cylinder outward. The pistons force the top ends of the brake shoes out against the drum. The forward (primary) shoe tends to lock to the revolving brake drum and tends to turn around with it. As the forward shoe tries to turn with the drum, it pushes the back (secondary) shoe against the drum. The secondary shoe tries to turn with the drum, but it is anchored at the top; so it jams into the drum, locks it, and stops the wheel from turning.

The modern disc brake system

The modern disc brake system uses a heavy disc in place of a drum, and brake friction pads in place of the brake shoes and linings. In place of the wheel cylinder, a caliper is bolted to the wheel spindle so that the friction pads on the caliper can sandwich the disc between them. When pressure is exerted on the brake pedal, the fluid in the caliper moves the pistons, which in turn force the friction pads against the disc, stopping the car.

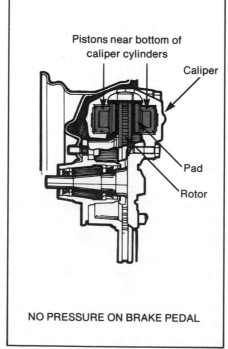

Pistons near bottom of caliper cylinders

Caliper

Pad

Rotor

NO PRESSURE ON BRAKE PEDAL

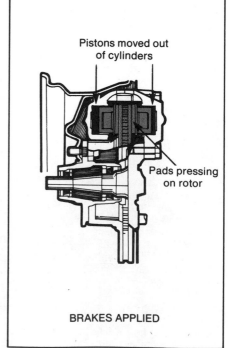

Pistons moved out of cylinders

Pads pressing on rotor

BRAKES APPLIED

General Maintenance

The drum brakes on all modern cars are equipped with automatic brake adjusters that maintain proper pedal height as the brakes wear. On most cars, these adjusters are activated when you put on the brakes while the car is moving backwards. So, if you have to push your brake pedal down more than a couple of inches before the brakes begin to take hold, find a safe area away from traffic and apply the brakes firmly several times while moving in reverse. If this fails to bring the pedal up to an acceptable height, remove the brake drums and inspect the adjusters to see if they are jammed or rusted.

Disc brakes are designed so they do not require periodic adjustment. As the linings slowly wear out and the brake pedal is applied, the piston in the caliper slowly moves out toward the rotor to compensate for brake pad wear. The area displaced directly behind the piston is slowly occupied by the brake fluid. For this reason, disc brakes require a greater amount of brake fluid.

You should adjust the parking brake when you have to move the foot pedal or handle a greater distance than usual to apply the brake.

Linings

At least once a year, more often if you do a lot of driving, or drive constantly in heavy stop-and-go city traffic, remove, or have your mechanic remove, the brake drums and inspect the linings. If they are permitted to wear excessively, the metal rivets securing the lining to the shoe, or the steel locking of the brake shoe itself, may grind grooves in the drum's braking surface. In such cases, the drum will have to be resurfaced or, if beyond specified tolerances, replaced.

Remove one of the front wheels and inspect the brake disc, caliper, and linings. See the detailed procedures provided later in this chapter, presented by make and model.

Do not get any oil or grease on the linings. If the pads are worn to within .030-inch of the surface of the steel shoe, replace both the front and/or rear sets of shoe and lining pad assemblies.

If the caliper is cracked or fluid leakage through the casting is evident, it must be replaced as a unit. While you have the wheel off to inspect the linings and pads, inspect all hydraulic brake lines. Look for leaks, cracks, lines that have become thin by rubbing against a suspension part, and any other signs of wear or deterioration. *Caution: Do not attempt to disconnect any hydraulic lines yourself. Take your car to a professional mechanic for this job. He is qualified to do it safely and correctly.*

As the linings eventually wear out and have to be replaced, remember that the rest of the brake system components have been in service just as long as the linings. At this time, it is very important to check the master cylinder, the wheel cylinders, the drums, and the shoe retaining and retracting springs. If these parts are not checked at this time, more than likely they will not be checked until the next overhaul, or until the brakes finally fail—when it will be too late.

Replacing the master cylinder, the wheel cylinders, and the internal components of drum brakes is best left to a professional mechanic. Repair and replacement procedures you can tackle are described on the following pages.

At the same time the brakes are relined, clean, inspect, and repack the wheel bearings with the proper lubricant. Adjust the wheel bearings to the manufacturer's specifications to prevent wheel wobble and unbalanced braking action. To be on the safe side, install new seals to prevent the wheel bearing grease from contaminating the new brake shoes. See Chapter 3.

Fluid level

Every time you change your engine oil, check the level of the brake fluid in the master cylinder. Checking the level is easy. Locate the master cylinder under the hood, then simply unlatch the cylinder cover, remove the top, and look at the fluid level. If it is low (more than ¼-inch below the top edge of the reservoir), add only the approved type heavy-duty brake fluid. Also, check for leaks around the hoses, lines, and at the wheels. If brake fluid has contaminated the linings, they must be replaced.

General hints

Before you begin work, jack up the car and support it on safety stands. Use fender covers to protect your car's body paint from damage caused by brake fluid. Be sure to wipe up any spilled fluid.

To prevent excess spillage, begin by removing at least two-thirds of the brake fluid from the larger compartment of the master cylinder. Use an ordinary kitchen baster with a tube and suction bulb. Discard the fluid. Do not reuse it.

To complete the job, after both front wheels have been serviced:
1. Fill the master cylinder and replace its cover. *Caution: Never pump the brake pedal with the cover of the master cylinder off. Fluid may squirt out of the cylinder and damage parts in the engine compartment or the body finish.*
2. If you have power brakes, start the engine.
3. Pump the brakes. They should feel hard and high. If not, recheck your work.
4. Turn off the engine.
5. Check for leaks.
6. Be sure the master cylinder fluid level is correct.
7. Lower the car.

Checking and Replacing Disc Brake Pads

Disc brake systems

Many different disc brake systems are used by car manufacturers. To find out what disc brake system is on your car, find the year and make on the list below.

When instructions for the makes and models listed here are not given in the following pages, they are essentially similar to those provided for other models listed.

Bendix opposed pistons
American Motors, 1969–70
Buick full-size cars, 1969
Dodge Coronet, 1969
Plymouth Belvedere, 1969

Bendix sliding caliper
American Motors, 1975 and later

Delco-Moraine opposed pistons
Camaro four-wheel disc option, 1969
Corvette, 1969 and later

Delco-Moraine single piston
Buick intermediate cars, 1969 and later
Buick full-size cars, 1970 and later
Buick Skyhawk, 1975 and later
Cadillac, 1969 and later
Checker Motors, 1969 and later
Chevrolet line (except Camaro four-wheel disc option and Corvette), 1969 and later
Eldorado, 1969 and later
Oldsmobile, 1969 and later
Pontiac, 1969 and later

Ford center abutment
Pinto, 1971–73

Ford sliding caliper
Comet, 1974 and later
Cougar, 1974 and later
Fairmont, 1978 and later
Ford full-size cars, 1973 and later
Granada, 1975 and later
Lincoln Continental, 1973 and later
Mark IV, 1972–76
Mark V, 1978–79
Mark VI, 1980 and later
Maverick, 1974 and later
Mercury, 1973 and later
Monarch, 1975 and later
Montego, 1972–76
Mustang II, 1974 and later
Pinto, 1974 and later
Torino, 1972–76
Thunderbird, 1972 and later
Versailles, 1978 and later
Zephyr, 1978 and later

Ford four-wheel disc brake
Continental, 1975 and later
Ford, 1976–78
Granada, 1975–78
Lincoln, 1975–78
Mark IV, 1975–76
Mark V, 1977–79
Mark VI
Mercury, 1975–78
Monarch, 1975–78

Thunderbird, 1975–76
Versailles, 1978 and later

Kelsey-Hayes opposed pistons
Dodge Dart, 1969–72
Plymouth Barracuda, 1969
Plymouth Valiant, 1969–72

Kelsey-Hayes floating caliper
American Motors, 1971–74
Chrysler, 1969–73
Chrysler Cordoba, 1975–76
Cougar, 1969–73
Charger SE, 1975–76
Coronet, 1975–76
Dodge Challenger and Coronet, 1970–74
Dodge Charger, 1969–74
Dodge Polara and Monaco, 1969–73
Fairlane, 1969–71
Falcon, 1969
Ford full-size cars, 1969–72
Imperial, 1970–73
Lincoln Continental, 1970–72
Mark III, 1969–71
Mercury, 1969–72
Montego, 1969–71
Mustang, 1969–73
Plymouth Barracuda, 1970–74
Plymouth Fury, 1969–73 and 1975–78
Plymouth Satellite, 1969–74
Thunderbird, 1970–71
Torino, 1969–71

Kelsey-Hayes sliding caliper
Chrysler (except Cordoba), 1974 and later
Dodge Aspen, 1976 and later
Dodge Dart 1973–76
Dodge Monaco, 1974–76
Dodge Royal, 1978 and later
Imperial, four-wheel disc brake, 1974–75
Plymouth Fury, 1974 and 1979 and later
Plymouth Gran Fury, 1976 and later
Plymouth Valiant, 1973–76
Volare, 1976 and later

Gypsy brake pads

The material of which brake pads are made must pass tests that measure, among other things, its ability to grip as it should when the brakes get hot. Brake pads made by large, name-brand manufacturers will show some markings stamped into the edges of the friction materials. But brake pads sold by so-called "gypsy" parts distributors usually do not carry these markings. Since they need not be tested, gypsy parts may not meet even the low standards set for friction materials by the Vehicle Equipment Safety Commission, which is funded by congress.

Tools and equipment:

Flat screwdrivers (6- and 12-").
Slip joint pliers.
Vise grip pliers.
Socket wrenches ($\frac{3}{8}$" and $\frac{1}{2}$" drive).
$\frac{3}{8}$" and $\frac{1}{2}$" drive ratchet handles.
Combination wrenches.
Allen wrenches.
Torque wrench (150 foot pound capacity).
Brake adjusting measuring tool.
Ball peen hammer.
C clamps (4- and 6-").
Drift pin punch.
Floor jack stands.
Goggles.
Droplight or flashlight.
Brake spring tool.
Spring removing tool.
Cape chisel.
Suction bulb.
Wire brush.
Four parts pans.
Wheel cylinder clamp.
Baling wire.
Sandpaper.
Brake adjusting spoon.
Front wheel seal installer.
Hand cloth.

Parts you may need:

Brake fluid.
Brake shoes.
Disc brake pads.
Brake lubricant.
Silicone spray can.
Wheel bearing grease seals.
Wheel bearing grease.
Lube plate lubricant.

Four wheel disc brakes

If your car is equipped with rear wheel disc brakes, because of the complexity of the system and the special tools and equipment required to replace them, you should take your car to a qualified auto brake specialist.

Bendix opposed pistons

1969 BUICK MODELS

1969 DODGE CORONET

1969 PLYMOUTH BELVEDERE

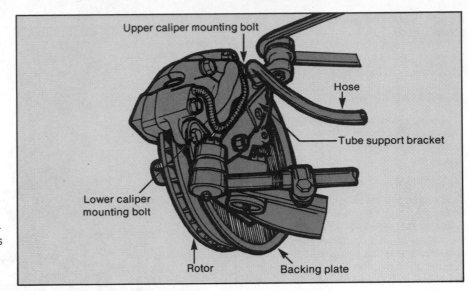

Upper caliper mounting bolt

Hose

Tube support bracket

Lower caliper mounting bolt

Rotor

Backing plate

1 **Remove the upper and loosen the lower caliper mounting bolts.** Then rotate the upper end of the caliper towards the rear. Drain two-thirds of the brake fluid from the master cylinder to prevent it from overflowing. Discard this fluid.

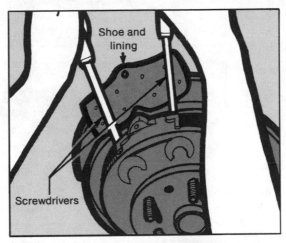

Shoe and lining

Screwdrivers

2 **Use a C clamp or two screwdrivers** to push the caliper pistons in until they are bottomed in the caliper bore. Remove the disc brake pads from the calipers by simply pulling the pads out. Then discard the pads. *Caution: Be sure no one steps on the brake pedal during this procedure. If depressed, the piston in the caliper may pop out, causing a hydraulic leak.*

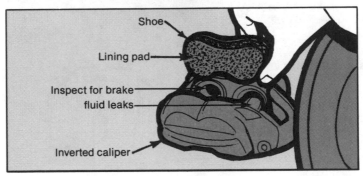

Shoe

Lining pad

Inspect for brake fluid leaks

Inverted caliper

3 **Clean any excess dirt and rust** from the caliper, using only a wire brush and a hand cloth. Then inspect the caliper for brake fluid leaks. If fluid is leaking from the caliper pistons, reassemble the old disc pads and the caliper, and take the car to a mechanic for repair.

4 **Visually inspect the rotor** for cracks or deep grooves. Clean the surface with a hand cloth. Remove the rotor if badly scarred or cracked and take it to a car parts store that services brakes for resurfacing or replacement.

5 **Insert the new disc pads** into the caliper with the metal side of the pads facing the pistons. Be sure the pads are well-seated into the caliper, then rotate the caliper back onto the rotor into its original position. Install the upper caliper mounting bolts, and torque the upper and lower bolts to 80 to 90 foot pounds.

6 **Repeat this procedure** on the opposite wheel, then complete the final check. Fill the master cylinder with a high-temperature brake fluid, replace the master cylinder cover, pump the brake pedal several times to fill the caliper, and finally, recheck the brake fluid level in the master cylinder and adjust it.

Bendix opposed pistons (continued)

1969–70 AMERICAN MOTORS MODELS

1   Using pliers and a hammer, remove the clip securing the flexible brake hose to the bracket located on the inner side of the spindle.

2   Loosen the caliper mounting bolts, then hold the lower edge of the caliper and remove the lower bolt. Shake the caliper until all the shims fall out, and keep these in a paper cup marked "Lower." Press in on the upper edge of the caliper to hold the shims on the upper mounting bolt, then remove this bolt and put these shims in a cup marked "Upper."

3   Support the caliper assembly on the frame or suspension using a length of wire hooked around it and attached to a suitable anchor point.

4   Using a pair of screwdrivers between the shoe and the pistons, press the pistons until they are bottomed in their cylinders; then remove the pad assembly from the calipers.

5   Inspect the disc brake caliper and the rotor as described previously for 1969 Buicks.

6   Insert new pads and plates in the caliper, locating the plates against the ends of the pistons. Be sure the plates are properly seated in the caliper, then spread the pads apart, and slide the caliper into position on the rotor. Install the caliper mounting bolts, making certain that the shims are installed in their original positions. Tighten the bolts to 80 to 90 foot pounds, and secure the hydraulic tube to the bracket with a clip.

Breaking in new brake pads

Drive with extra care for the first 1,000 miles after replacing your brake pads. Avoid sudden stops, harsh braking, or high speed driving that would overheat the rotors. Until the pads are properly seated, a careless driver can easily damage the pads and rotors.

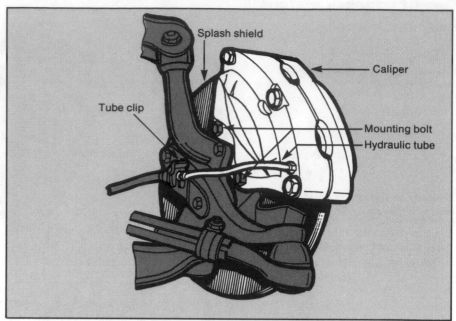

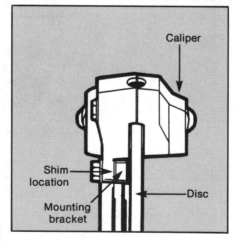

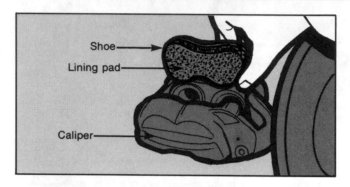

Pro Shop

Supporting the caliper

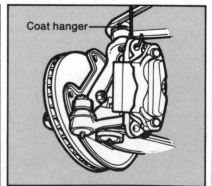

We've found that supporting the caliper by looping one end of a wire coat hanger around the upper control arm and the other end through the caliper mounting bolt hole works just fine.

Delco-Moraine opposed pistons

1 Remove the brake fluid from the master cylinder, and wedge two screwdrivers between the disc pad and the rotor. Compress the caliper pistons into the calipers on the inboard, then on the outboard side. Take out the inboard and outboard pads by pulling upwards.

2 Clean and inspect the caliper and rotor, then position the inboard and outboard pads one at a time. Install the retaining pin through the outboard caliper, the outboard shoe, the inboard shoe, and the inboard caliper. Insert a new $\frac{3}{32}$ x $\frac{5}{8}$-inch plated cotter pin through the retaining pin. On 1969–70 models with heavy-duty brakes, put in the two retaining pins.

3 Repeat the above procedure at each wheel where the pads are to be replaced. Then complete the final check: refill the master cylinder to the proper level, pump the brake pedal and test for leaks, and install the tire-and-wheel assembly.

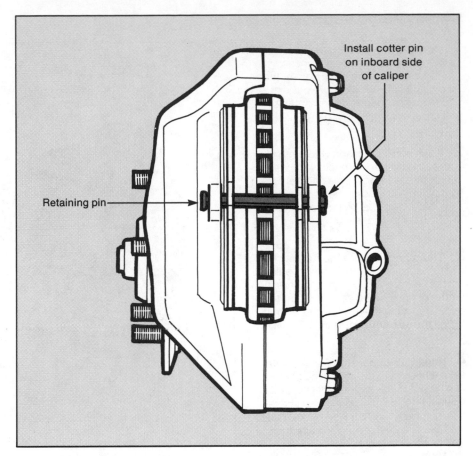

Install cotter pin on inboard side of caliper

Retaining pin

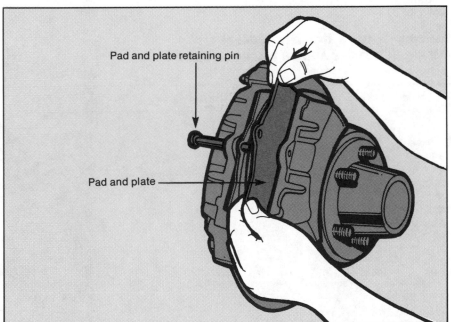

Pad and plate retaining pin

Pad and plate

Pro Shop

Using the retaining pin

If you don't use the retaining pin to hold the inboard plate and disc pad in place while installing the new outer disc pad and plate, we've found you'll never get it all reassembled.

Kelsey-Hayes opposed pistons

1 Remove the two cap screws located on the top of the caliper securing the pad retaining clip or clips to it, then take out the clips. Using two pairs of pliers, grasp the tabs on the outer ends of the pad and pull them out.

2 Push all the pistons back into their bores until bottomed to allow for installation of the new pads. This can be done by placing a flat-sided metal bar against the piston, and exerting a steady force until it is bottomed.

3 Clean and inspect the caliper and rotor, then slide the new pads into the caliper with the ears of the pads resting on the bridges of the caliper. Be sure the pads are facing toward the discs, then install the retainer clip(s) on the caliper.

4 Repeat the operation on the other front wheel, then complete the final check: pump the brake pedal several times until it is firm and the pads have been properly seated. Add brake fluid to the master cylinder, and replace the tire and wheel assembly.

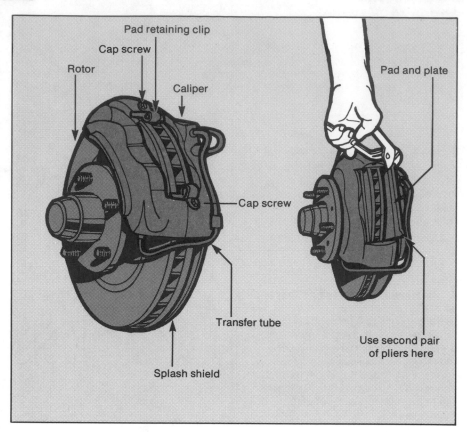

Kelsey-Hayes floating caliper
AMERICAN MOTORS AND CHRYSLER MODELS

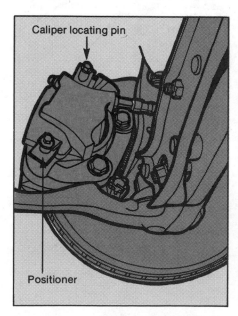

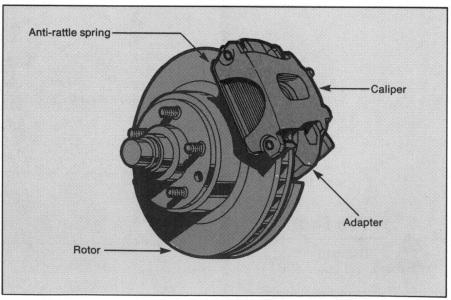

1 To prevent overflow, drain two thirds of the brake fluid from the master cylinder. With the correct size wrench, loosen and remove the caliper guide pins. On American Motors and 1969–72 Chrysler cars, take off the positioners and anti-rattle clips. Note their location for correct reinstallation.

2 Remove the caliper from the rotor and support it with a wire, then slide out the outboard and inboard brake pad assemblies from the caliper and adapter. Take out the inner and outer bushings from the caliper.

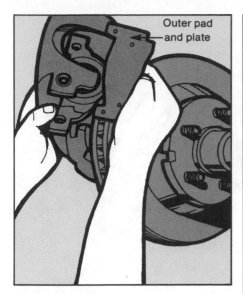

Outer pad
and plate

3 **Clean and inspect** the caliper and rotor. Install new inner and outer bushings, then slide the caliper down into position on the adapter and over the rotor. Align the guide pin holes of the adapter with the inner and outer brake pads. On American Motors and 1969–72 Chrysler models, locate the positioners over the guide pins with the open ends up facing the anti-rattle spring.

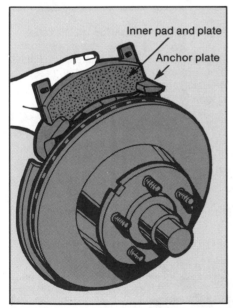

Inner pad and plate

Anchor plate

4 **Press in on the end** of the guide pin and thread the pin into the adapter, using extreme caution not to cross the threads. Torque the guide pins to 30 to 35 foot pounds, making sure that the tabs of the positioners are over the machined surfaces of the caliper.

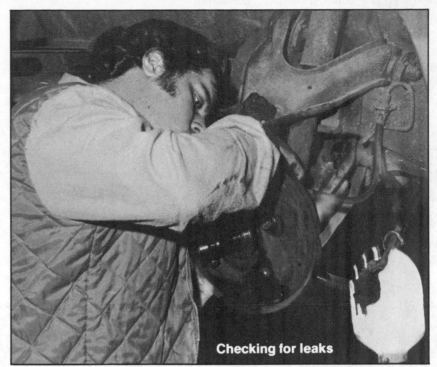

Checking for leaks

Note that on cars equipped with disc brakes, a slightly lower-than-normal brake fluid level does not necessarily mean there is a leak in the system. As disc brake linings wear, the piston moves outward to compensate for it, and brake fluid takes up the displaced area behind the piston. However, even if you have disc brakes, a low fluid level is a warning there may be a leak in the system, so always check for that possibility.

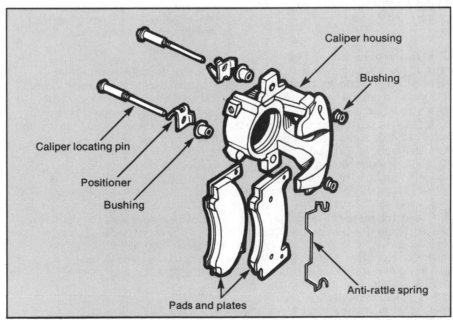

Caliper housing

Bushing

Caliper locating pin

Positioner

Bushing

Anti-rattle spring

Pads and plates

5 **Repeat these steps** on the other front wheel. Then complete the final check: refill the master cylinder, pump the brake pedal and test for leaks, and install the tire-and-wheel assembly.

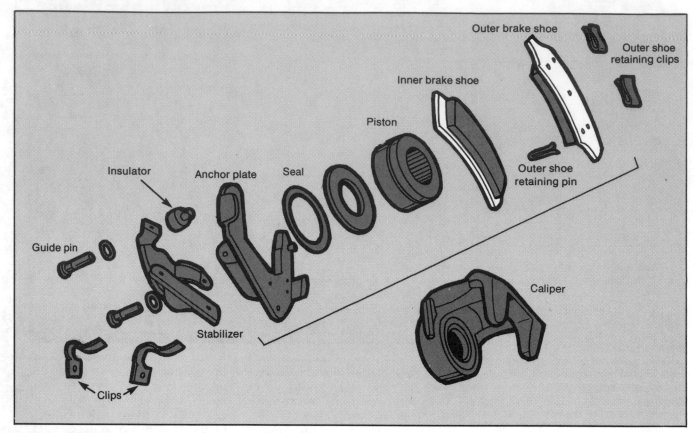

1 **To take out the caliper,** apply a steady inward pressure against the inner pad. Maintain the pressure until the piston has bottomed in the caliper bore, then remove the safety wire and the caliper bolts from the spindle, and lift the caliper from the rotor.

2 **Slide the outer two pad retaining clips** off the retaining pins, then remove the retaining pins and the pad from the stationary caliper. Slide the inner pad outward until it is free of the springs holding it in place, then take off the brake pad, the caliper locating pins, and the stabilizer bolts. Take out and discard the stabilizers, and remove the locating pin insulators from the anchor plate.

3 **Clean and inspect the caliper** and rotor and install the new caliper locating pin insulators in the anchor plate. Position the caliper onto the anchor plate, then insert new stabilizers and loosely insert the caliper locating pins. The pins should be free of oil, grease, and dirt. Note: If they are rusted or corroded, they should be replaced. Position the outer pad on the caliper and install the two retaining pins and clips.

4 **Install the inner brake pad** so the ears of the pad are on top of the anchor plate bosses and under the springs holding the pad down. Locate the pad assemblies so the caliper can be positioned over the rotor, and rotate a suitable size hammer handle between the pads to provide proper clearance.

5 **Install the caliper over the rotor,** then insert the caliper retaining bolts. First torque the upper bolt to 110 to 140 foot pounds, then the lower bolt to 90 to 120 foot pounds for full-size models and 55 to 75 foot pounds for intermediate models. Put in the safety wire and twist the ends at least five turns, pushing them against the spindle.

6 **Have a helper** apply moderate pressure on the brake pedal. Torque the stabilizer retaining screws to eight to 11 foot pounds, and the locating pins to 25 to 35 foot pounds.

7 **Repeat the operation** on the other front wheel. Fill the master cylinder to the correct level, and complete the final check: pump the brake pedal and test for leaks, and install the tire-and-wheel assembly.

Pro Shop

Releasing the caliper

Due to a ridge of rust that may have formed on the disc surface outside of the lining contact area, it may be necessary to force the piston back slightly into the caliper bore. We do this by forcing the shoe back with slip-joint pliers placed on a corner of the pad and caliper housing.

Kelsey-Hayes floating caliper (continued)

1970–72 FULL-SIZE FORDS

1 **Remove the clips** holding down the inner pad, then place a small screwdriver under the outer pad retaining clip tang, lift it away from the pin groove, and slide the clip from the pad retaining pin. Take out the outer pad retaining clip, the outer pad, the caliper locating pins, and the upper stabilizer-to-anchor plate bolt. Then remove the upper stabilizer to avoid interference with the brake hose.

2 **Lift the caliper assembly** from the anchor plate and remove the outer pad and retaining pins. Support the caliper from the upper control arm with a wire and take out the caliper locating pin insulators. Then remove the inner pad.

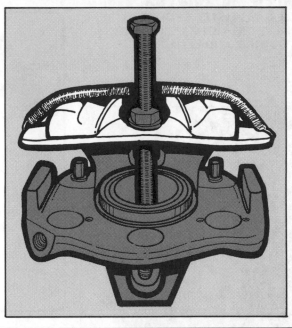

A piston retracting tool can be made from an old brake pad and a threaded rod as shown on page 222. Turn it one-half turn or less at a time and pause between turns to let the piston move inside the seal.

3 **Inspect and clean the rotor** and caliper. Install the inner brake pad in the anchor plate, the new caliper locating pin insulators, and the inner brake pad clips. Torque the retaining screws to six to ten foot pounds. Insert the piston pad retracting tool in the caliper with the brake pad lances positioned in the slots in the caliper outer legs, then retract the piston.

4 **Install the new outer brake pad and lining** assembly on the caliper and put on the retaining pins and clips. Repeat these steps on the other front wheel. Apply the brake pedal several times to seat the brake pads, then look for leaks. Refill the master cylinder to the correct level, and install the tire-and-wheel assembly.

1970–73 FORDS, INTERMEDIATE MODELS

1 **Remove the caliper** by taking out the safety wire and the two caliper assembly-to-spindle retaining bolts, then lift the caliper assembly from the rotor. Take out the inner brake pad clips and the locating pin insulators from the anchor plate, and the inboard pad.

2 **To remove the outer brake pad,** place a small screwdriver under the outer pad retaining clip tang, lift it away from the pin groove, and slide the clip from the brake pad retaining pin. Remove the outer pad retaining clip and the outer pad.

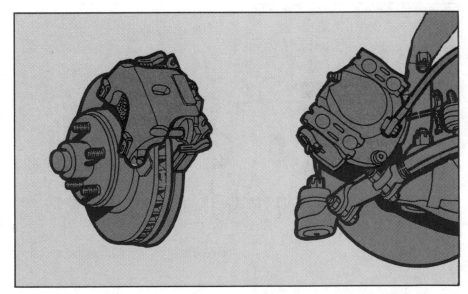

3 **Clean and inspect the caliper** and rotor, install the inner brake pad in the anchor plate, the new caliper locating pin insulators, and the inner brake pad clips. Torque the retaining screws to six to ten foot pounds. Insert the piston pad retracting tool in the caliper with the brake pad lances positioned in the slots in the caliper outer leg. Retract the piston.

4 **Install the new outer brake pad** and lining assembly on the caliper and the retaining pins and clips. Repeat these steps on the other front wheel, apply the brake pedal several times to seat the brake pads, check for leaks, and refill the master cylinder to the correct level. Then install the tire-and-wheel assembly.

Delco-Moraine single piston

ALL CARS LISTED EXCEPT ASTRE, CHEVETTE, MONZA, SKYHAWK, STARFIRE, AND VEGA

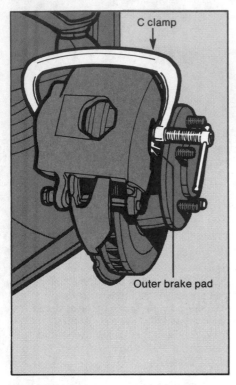

C clamp

Outer brake pad

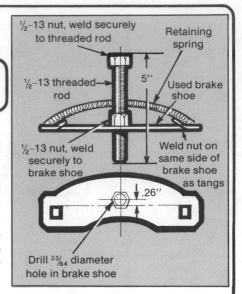

Pro Shop

Piston retracting tool

We've found you can make a piston retracting tool from a discarded outer brake pad and a threaded rod. When using such a tool, turn the threaded rod one-half turn at a time and pause to permit the piston to move into the seal. As the piston nears the bottom of its travel, reduce the time interval to insure proper bottoming.

½–13 nut, weld securely to threaded rod

Retaining spring

½–13 threaded rod

5″

Used brake shoe

½–13 nut, weld securely to brake shoe

Weld nut on same side of brake shoe as tangs

.26″

Drill ³³⁄₆₄ diameter hole in brake shoe

1 Place a C clamp against the outer brake pad and the back of the caliper to push the piston back into the caliper bore, then remove the two mounting bolts and lift the caliper from the rotor.

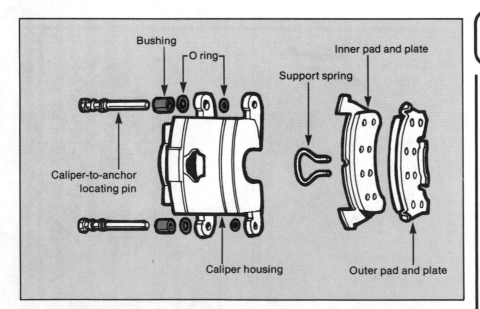

Bushing

O ring

Support spring

Inner pad and plate

Caliper-to-anchor locating pin

Caliper housing

Outer pad and plate

Pro Shop

Stop those squeaking disc brakes

Squeaks and squeals most often occur after the brake pedal has been applied and just before the car stops rolling, and they are caused by vibrations of the disc brake pad as it is forced against the rotor.

If not already supplied with the replacement pads, a thin piece of gasket material added to the back of the metal pad backing plate will help eliminate squeaks and squeals. You can also coat the pad back with an elastomeric multi-polymer compound. Spread this thick, blue, toothpaste-like material liberally over the back of the outboard pad and somewhat less generously over the back of the inboard pad. After ten minutes the material gets tacky (it never hardens) and the pad can be installed.

2 Take out the inboard pad, then dislodge the outboard pad and position the caliper on the front suspension so the brake hose will not be supporting the weight of the caliper. Remove the two bushings from the inboard ears of the caliper, and the four rubber O rings from the grooves in each of the caliper ears.

3 Clean and inspect the rotor and caliper. Lubricate the new bushings and rubber O rings, bushing grooves, and mounting bolt ends with silicone lubricant. Install the new bushings and O rings on the caliper ears. Position the bushings so the end toward the shoe is flush with the surface of the ear.

4 **Insert the pad support spring** into the piston cavity in the caliper, and position the inboard pad in the caliper so that the spring ends centrally contact the shoe edge, initially placing the shoe on an angle. Push the upper edge of the shoe down until the shoe is flat against the caliper. When properly seated, the spring ends should not extend past the shoe more than .1 inch.

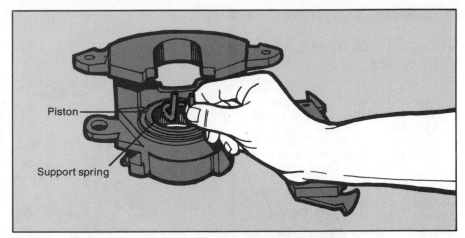

Piston

Support spring

5 **Position the outboard pad** in the caliper with the pad ears over the caliper ears and the tab at the bottom of the pad engaged with the caliper cutout. With the pads installed, lift the caliper and rest the bottom edge of the outboard lining on the outer edge of the brake disc to be sure there is no clearance between the outboard shoe tab and the caliper abutment. On 1969–72 models, using a ¼ x 1 x 2½-inch metal bar to bridge the caliper cutout, clamp the outboard shoe to the caliper with a C clamp. Bend both ears of the outboard shoe over the caliper until clearance between the shoe ear and the caliper measured at both the edge and side of the caliper is .005-inch or less. Remove the C clamp, install the caliper, and torque the mounting bolts to 30 to 40 foot pounds.

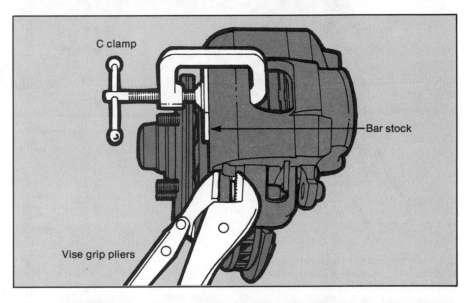

C clamp

Bar stock

Vise grip pliers

6 **On 1973–76 cars,** clinch the upper ears of the outboard shoe by positioning pliers with one jaw on top of the ear and one jaw in the notch on the bottom shoe opposite the ear. The ears are to be flat against the caliper housing with no radial clearance. If clearance exists, repeat the clinching procedure.

7 **Repeat the operation** on the other front wheel, and refill the master cylinder to the correct fluid level. Pump the brake pedal and test for leaks, then install the tire-and-wheel assembly.

8 **1980 Citation, Omega, Phoenix, and Skylark** have a caliper of a slightly different design. Repair procedures are basically the same.

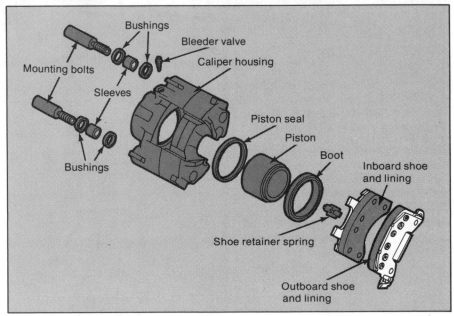

Bushings

Bleeder valve

Mounting bolts

Caliper housing

Sleeves

Piston seal

Piston

Boot

Inboard shoe and lining

Bushings

Shoe retainer spring

Outboard shoe and lining

Delco-Moraine single piston (continued)

**ASTRE, MONZA, SKYHAWK,
STARFIRE, AND VEGA**

1 **Remove the two mounting pin
stamped nuts** with a screwdriver and
slide out the pins. Then drain the fluid
from the master cylinder. Lift the caliper
assembly off the rotor and support it on
the suspension with a length of wire.

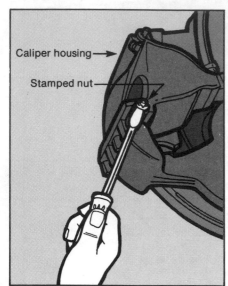

2 **Slide the inboard and outboard
pads** past the mounting sleeve openings
and remove the sleeves and bushing assemblies, then clean and inspect the
caliper and rotor.

3 **Install the new sleeves** with bushings on the caliper grooves. Note: The
shouldered end of the sleeve must be toward the outside. Put the inner pad on
the caliper and slide the pad ears over
the sleeve. Install the outer pads in the
same manner, then mount the caliper
onto the rotor.

4 **Install the mounting pins** from the
outside in and insert new stamped nuts.
These should be pressed on as far as
possible using a suitable size socket that
just seats on the outer edge of the nut.

5 **Repeat this procedure** on the other
front wheel, then refill the master cylinder to the correct level. Pump the brake
pedal, then install the tire-and-wheel assembly.

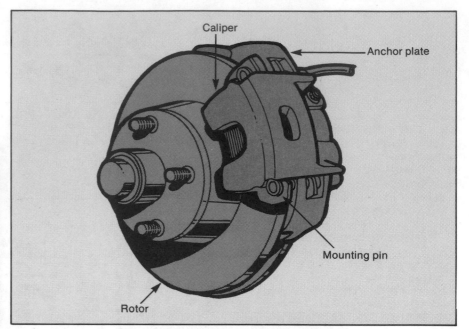

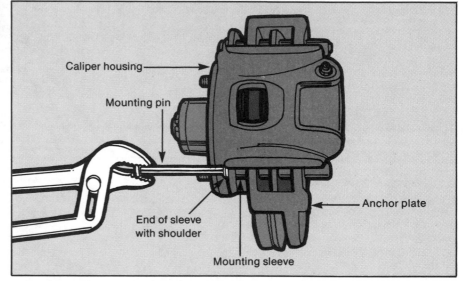

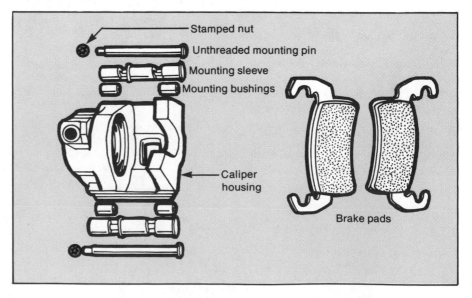

How to bleed the brakes

Caution: Bleeding the brakes is a difficult job and doing it incorrectly can result in loss of life and car. Before you attempt it, read over these instructions very carefully and make sure you understand them thoroughly. If you have any hesitations about your ability to do the job right, take your car to a mechanic for this repair.

If you loosen the wheel cylinders or any of the brake lines on your car for checking or maintenance, you must "bleed" the brake system. Bleeding eliminates any air bubbles which might be trapped in the brake lines where they can cause reduced braking force and a spongy pedal. The brake system is bled by opening a small valve. On drum brakes it is located on the back of each wheel backing plate like the one visible just above the finger pointing to the brake fluid hose in the photo. On disc brakes the bleed valve is located on the caliper where the hose enters it. When open, this valve allows brake fluid to escape, thus removing any air bubbles that may be in the system. *Caution: Brakes on the following cars must be power-bled by a mechanic: all Chrysler Corporation cars from 1969 onward, 1969 Lincolns, and 1970–72 Fords, Lincolns, and Mercurys.*

Before starting the job, make sure you have an adequate supply of brake fluid on hand, and a helper—bleeding the brakes is a two-man job. You open and close the valve at each wheel to let fluid and trapped air escape while your helper applies pressure to the brake pedal to force the fluid and air out of the system.

Hint: when you have finished bleeding the brakes, you will find the brake warning light on the dashboard lit. To turn it out on late-model cars, you just turn the ignition switch to the Acc or On position and apply the brakes once. But on older models, the light can only be turned off by centering the switch inside the metering valve housing, a very

tedious procedure. You can save yourself a lot of trouble by replacing the light switch with a small threaded stud (sold in auto parts stores) before bleeding the brakes.

Bleed the brakes in the sequence recommended by the manufacturer of your car (see diagram). If the master cylinder has a bleed valve, bleed it before doing any of the wheels. If your car has power brakes, start by pumping the pedal ten times, with the engine off, to use up any vacuum in the booster. If you have a 1974 or older American Motors car, unscrew the brake warning light switch from the metering valve before you begin. Replace it when you are finished bleeding the system.

Now jack up the car and support it on safety stands. If the bleed valve has a dust cap, remove it and clean off the valve. Most professional mechanics use a pressure bleeder, which provides air-free fluid to the top filler cap of the master cylinder, but you can use a length of clean vacuum hose instead, as long as you are very careful not to let the master cylinder reservoir run dry.

Attach the vacuum hose to one of the valves, holding the valve securely with a box wrench, then insert the other end of the hose into a jar partly filled with fresh brake fluid. With a wrench, open the valve three-quarters of a turn. Have your helper apply the brakes slowly but steadily. When the pedal reaches the floor, close the valve, then let the pedal slowly return to its normal position.

Repeat this procedure until air bubbles stop coming out of the hose. Check the reservoir every four to five pumps, refill it to within one-quarter inch of the top, and replace the cover. This prevents more air from entering the system through the reservoir while you are bleeding it. If the reservoir runs dry, air will enter the system and you will have to start the bleeding sequence all over again. Bleed each wheel in this way until the old fluid runs clear, then lower the car.

Before driving the car, start the engine and pump the brakes several times to make sure you have a firm pedal. Should the pedal feel spongy, there is still air in the system and you must repeat the above procedure.

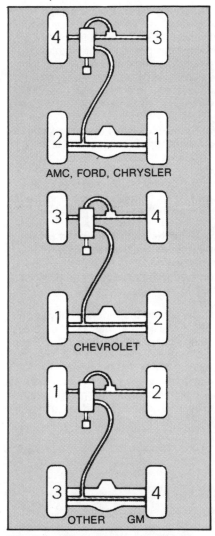

Bleed the brakes in the sequence recommended by the manufacturer of your car.

The bleeder valve is located just above the spot where the brake fluid hose enters the wheel backing plate.

Delco-Moraine single piston (continued)

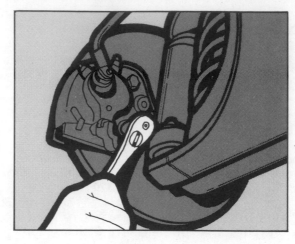

CHEVETTE

1 Install a seven-inch C clamp on the caliper with the solid end of the clamp on the caliper housing and the screw end on the metal portion of the outboard brake shoe. Remove two-thirds of the fluid from the master cylinder, and tighten the clamp until the piston bottoms in the caliper bore, then remove the clamp.

2 Take out the two steering knuckle-to-mounting bracket bolts. Note: Do not remove the socket head retaining bolts. Support the caliper when removing the second bolt to prevent the caliper from falling and rupturing the hydraulic brake hose.

3 Slide the caliper from the rotor, and remove the brake pads. If the brake pad retaining spring does not come off with the pads, remove it from the piston.

4 Clean and inspect the caliper and rotor. To install the pads, position the retaining spring on the inboard pad. Then place the single leg in the brake pad hole and snap the two outer legs over the notch in the brake pad. Position the caliper over the rotor, and align the mounting holes. Then install and torque the mounting bolts to 70 foot pounds.

ECONOTIP

 # 14

Slow down for better mileage

In traffic or town driving, your speed is limited by traffic conditions. But out on the highways, you can control your speed to affect fuel economy. Research by the federal government shows that a car getting 17.3 MPG at 70 MPH will get 19.7 MPG if the car slows to 60 MPH. At 50 there is another big jump, to 21.5 MPG. The 55 MPH speed limit may be annoying on long trips because of the extra time involved, but it will definitely save fuel if you stick to it.

Pro Shop

Start out slowly

After completing any work on your car's brake system, begin your road test cautiously, at low speed. Don't thoroughly road test your car until you have made sure you have full braking power.

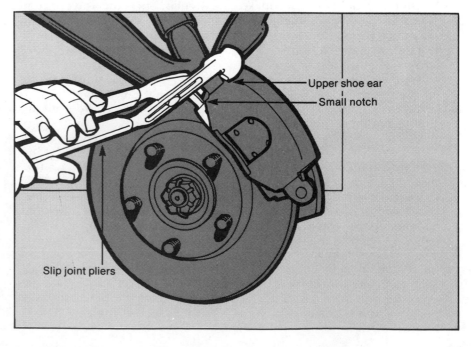

Upper shoe ear

Small notch

Slip joint pliers

5 Using a pair of slip-joint pliers, squeeze the outboard pad flanges to the caliper. Position one jaw of the pliers on the bottom edge of the pad, and place the other jaw on the flange. Squeeze the other brake pad flanges in the same manner. After squeezing, there should be zero to .005-inch between the pads and the caliper.

6 Repeat the operation on the other front wheel. Refill the master cylinder to the correct level, pump the brake pedal and test for leaks, and install the tire-and-wheel assembly.

Ford center abutment type

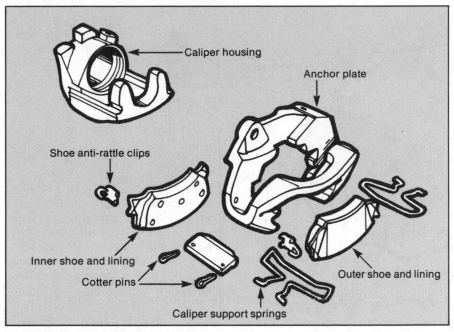

- Caliper housing
- Anchor plate
- Shoe anti-rattle clips
- Inner shoe and lining
- Cotter pins
- Caliper support springs
- Outer shoe and lining

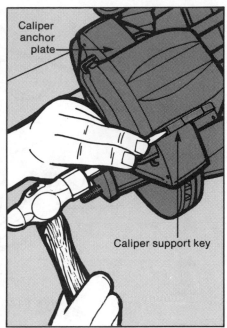

- Caliper anchor plate
- Caliper support key

1 **Remove the cotter pins** from the caliper support keys, and drain two-thirds of the brake fluid from the master cylinder. Using a drift and a light hammer, remove the caliper support key, taking care not to damage the key or the machined surfaces.

2 **Rotate the lower end** of the caliper housing toward the rear and upward, and separate the caliper from the anchor plate. It is not necessary to disconnect the hydraulic line for this operation.

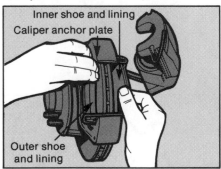

- Inner shoe and lining
- Caliper anchor plate
- Outer shoe and lining

3 **With the shoe and pad assemblies exposed,** tilt the upper edge of the pads away from the disc and take them out. They are identical and therefore can be interchanged.

4 **Inspect and clean the rotor** and caliper, and install the new shoe pad assemblies in the anchor plate by tilting the pad, then rotating them into the correct position, making sure the pad side is next to the rotor. Place a light coat of high-temperature grease on the anchor plate and caliper surfaces that will be contacting each other after the caliper is installed. Do not get grease on the brake pads or rotor.

5 **Place the caliper** in the anchor plate, making sure its top trailing edge is properly positioned and its support spring is under the projecting ledge. Insert a wide blade screwdriver or brake adjusting tool between the bottom leading edge of the caliper and the adjacent anchor plate surface. Pry downward so the caliper housing is pressed upward and inward toward the spindle. Install the caliper support key between the housing and the anchor plate. Make sure the key is properly positioned and the caliper support springs are still properly positioned. Center the support key so the cotter pin holes are on each side of the anchor plate and insert a new pin in each of the holes.

6 **Repeat this procedure** on the other front wheel. Refill the master cylinder to the correct level, pump the brake pedal and test for leaks, and install the tire-and-wheel assembly.

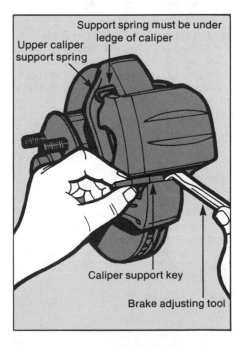

- Support spring must be under ledge of caliper
- Upper caliper support spring
- Caliper support key
- Brake adjusting tool

Ford sliding caliper

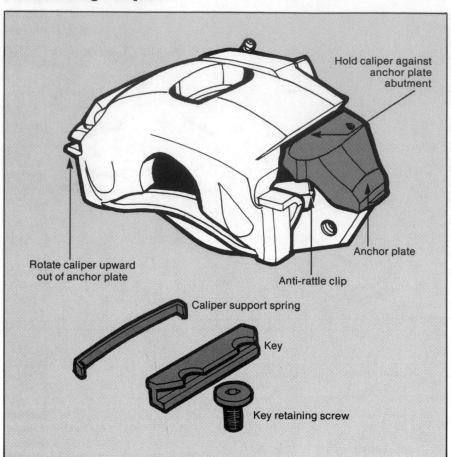

Hold caliper against anchor plate abutment

Anchor plate

Anti-rattle clip

Rotate caliper upward out of anchor plate

Caliper support spring

Key

Key retaining screw

Pro Shop

Handling brake fluid

Brake fluid is poisonous. It will damage paint, including the paint job on your car. If you drain the fluid from the system, dispose of the jars or cans you used for that purpose.

Brake fluid also deteriorates with time. Buy only one pint, keep it tightly capped, and discard it at the end of a year if it has been opened. It attracts moisture which, if introduced into the brake system, can cause corrosion and failure.

If the label on a can of brake fluid does not have this printed on it somewhere: "meets MVSS No. 116, DOT 4 specifications," it probably has been packaged by a distributor who has not tested it to be sure it meets minimum standards established by the US Department of Transportation.

1 **Remove the retaining screw** from the caliper retaining key, and drain two-thirds of the brake fluid from the master cylinder. Slide the caliper retaining key and support spring either inward or outward from the anchor plate. Use a hammer and drift, if necessary, to remove the key and the caliper support spring. Use caution to avoid damaging the key.

2 **Lift the caliper assembly** away from the anchor plate by pushing the caliper down against the anchor plate and rotating the upper end upward and out of the plate. Remove the inner pad from the plate. The inner pad of the brake pad anti-rattle clip may become displaced at this time. If so, reposition it on the anchor plate. Tap lightly on the outer pad to free it from the caliper.

3 **Clean and inspect the caliper** and rotor. To install new brake pads, use a four-inch C clamp and a wooden block 1¾ inches by one inch and about ¾-inch thick to seat the piston in the caliper to provide clearance for the caliper to fit over the new shoes. Or, you can use the old pad to seat the piston.

4 **Make sure the brake pad anti-rattle spring** is in place on the lower end of the inner brake pad with the loop of the clip toward the inside of the anchor plate. Position the inner pad on the anchor plate with the lining facing the rotor.

5 **Install the outer pad** with the lower flange ends against the caliper leg abutments and the upper flanges over the shoulders on the caliper legs. The upper flanges fit tightly against the shouldered, machined surfaces. If the same pads are to be reused, make sure they are reinstalled in their original positions. Remove the C clamp. The pistons will remain seated in the caliper bore.

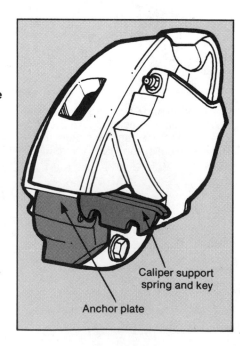

Caliper support spring and key

Anchor plate

6 **Position the caliper housing lower V-groove** on the anchor plate lower abutment surface. Pivot the caliper housing upward toward the rotor until the outer edge of the piston dust boot is about ½-inch from the upper edge of the inboard pad.

Position a piece of clean lightweight cardboard between the inboard pad and over the lower half of the piston dust boot. The cardboard prevents pinching the boot between the piston and the inboard pad during caliper installation. Rotate the caliper housing toward the rotor until a slight resistance is felt. Then pull the cardboard downward toward the rotor centerline while rotating the caliper over the rotor. Remove the cardboard and rotate the caliper completely over the rotor. Slide the caliper up against the anchor plate upper abutment surface and center the caliper over the upper anchor plate abutment.

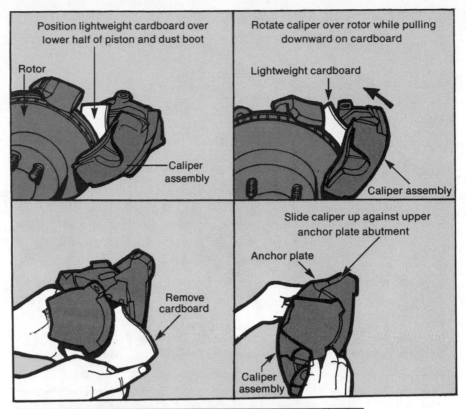

7 **Position the caliper support spring** and key in the key slot and slide them into the opening between the lower end of the caliper and the lower anchor plate abutment. Align the semi-circular slot in the key with the threaded hole in the anchor plate. Install the key retaining screw and torque to 12 to 16 foot pounds. Repeat these procedures on the other front wheel. Refill the master cylinder to the correct fluid level, pump the brake pedal and test for leaks, and install the tire-and-wheel assembly.

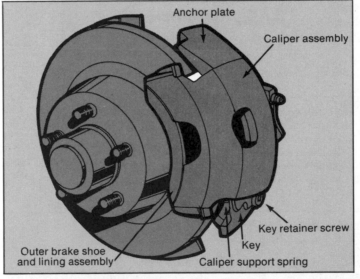

8 **Some models of Ford,** starting in 1978, use a pin slider mounting. Repair procedures are the same, except that the pins are unscrewed to remove the caliper.

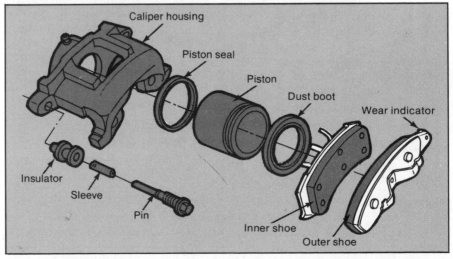

Kelsey-Hayes sliding caliper

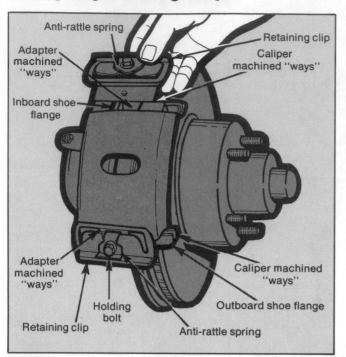

Anti-rattle spring
Adapter machined "ways"
Inboard shoe flange
Retaining clip
Caliper machined "ways"
Adapter machined "ways"
Holding bolt
Retaining clip
Outboard shoe flange
Anti-rattle spring

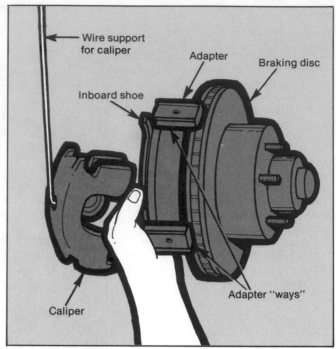

Wire support for caliper
Adapter
Braking disc
Inboard shoe
Adapter "ways"
Caliper

1 **Remove the caliper retaining clips** and the anti-rattle springs, and drain the fluid from the master cylinder. Slowly slide the caliper assembly out and away from the disc. Note: Using a length of wire, support the caliper on the front suspension to prevent it from falling and rupturing the hydraulic brake hose.

2 **Take out the outboard pad** by prying, using a screwdriver between the pad and the caliper fingers, since the flanges on the outboard pad retain the caliper firmly. Remove the inboard pad from the adapter. Using a screwdriver or C clamp, carefully push the piston back into the caliper bore until it is bottomed.

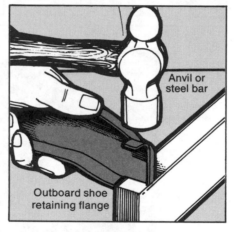

Anvil or steel bar
Outboard shoe retaining flange

3 **Clean and inspect the caliper** and rotor, and install the new outboard pad into the recess of the caliper. Note: There should be no free play between the brake pad flanges and the caliper fingers. If up-and-down movement of the shoe occurs, the pad must be removed and the flanges bent to provide a slight interference fit.

How to check brake fluid level

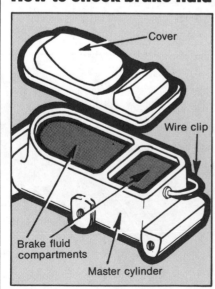

Cover
Wire clip
Brake fluid compartments
Master cylinder

If the level of the brake fluid in the master cylinder is too low, the brakes will not work. Warning signs are: unusually long play in the pedal before the brakes begin to take hold (or the pedal even sinks all the way to the floor), and/or, the pedal feels spongy rather than firm. The brake fluid level should be checked at least twice a year and before long trips. The fluid deteriorates chemically over time, so it should be replaced completely every couple of years.

This is the procedure for checking the fluid level in the master cylinder:
1. Park the car on level ground.

2. Locate the master cylinder at the rear of the engine compartment on the driver's side close to where the brake pedal comes through the fire wall.
3. You will need a screwdriver to pry open the spring clamp that holds the cover on. Wipe around the edge of the cover before you take it off so no dirt will fall into the fluid.

Lay the top aside in a place where it will stay clean, but not on a painted surface or within reach of children or pets.
4. The two chambers should be filled to within one-half inch of the top. Be sure the label on the brake fluid you use says "meets

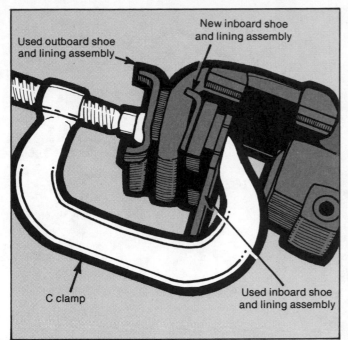

Used outboard shoe
and lining assembly

New inboard shoe
and lining assembly

C clamp

Used inboard shoe
and lining assembly

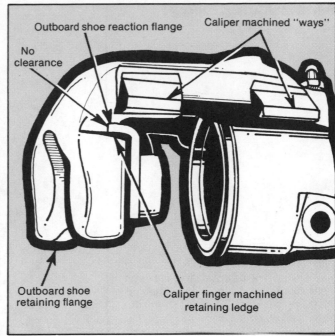

Outboard shoe reaction flange

Caliper machined "ways"

No
clearance

Outboard shoe
retaining flange

Caliper finger machined
retaining ledge

4 **Reinstall the pad** after any refitting, using light C clamp pressure if the pad cannot be finger-snapped into place. Position the inboard pad with the flanges inserted into the adapter "ways."

5 **Carefully slide the caliper assembly** into the adapter and over the disc, while aligning the caliper on the machined "ways" of the adapter. Note: Be sure the dust boot is not pulled out from its groove when the piston and boot slide over the inboard shoe. Install the anti-rattle springs and the retaining clips, and torque the retaining screws to 180 inch pounds. Note: The inboard shoe anti-rattle spring should be positioned on the top of the retainer spring plate. Repeat on the other front wheel.

6 **Refill the master cylinder** to the correct level, pump the brake pedal and test for leaks, and install the tire-and-wheel assembly.

MVSS No. 116, DOT 4 specifications." Don't buy more than a pint at a time, and store it as you would poisonous materials.

5. Replace the lid on the can of fluid very tightly, and discard any unused fluid left in the can after a year.

6. Put the top back on the master cylinder. If you allow any dirt to get in, you will have to drain and replace all of the fluid in the system.

7. Test the brakes with the engine running in neutral or park. If the pedal feels firm and normal, test the brakes with the car in motion.

Master cylinder brake fluid leaks

If your car is equipped with a manual brake system, and no power brake unit, locate the rubber master cylinder boot directly behind the brake pedal. With your fingers, lift the boot off the master cylinder and visually inspect for brake fluid leaks.

If your car is equipped with a power brake unit and your master cylinder fluid level is constantly low, and there are no visual signs of a leak in any part of the system, this could indicate the master cylinder is leaking into the power unit. In both cases, a mechanic or brake specialist should repair or replace the master cylinder.

Bendix sliding caliper

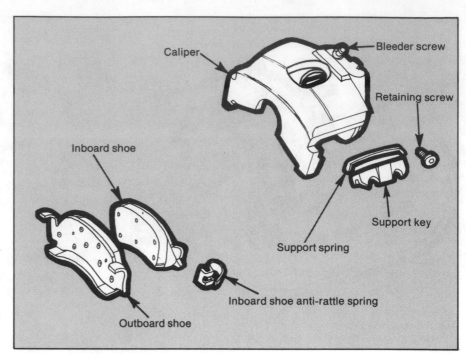

Caliper
Bleeder screw
Retaining screw
Inboard shoe
Support key
Support spring
Inboard shoe anti-rattle spring
Outboard shoe

1 Remove the fluid from the master cylinder. Bottom the piston in the caliper bore by inserting a screwdriver between the inboard pad and the piston. Then pry the piston back into the caliper bore. The piston can be bottomed in the caliper bore using a C clamp.

1/4 Inch hex or Allen wrench

2 Using a ¼-inch hex or Allen wrench, remove the support key retaining screw. Drive the caliper support key and spring from the anchor plate with a suitable drift and hammer. Lift the caliper off the anchor plate and rotor. Using a length of wire, support the caliper on the spring to prevent it from falling and rupturing the hydraulic brake hose. Do not allow the caliper to hang free. Remove the inboard brake pad from the anchor plate, then remove the anti-rattle spring from the brake pad, and the outboard pad from the caliper. It may be necessary to strike it gently with a hammer.

3 Clean and lubricate the abutment surfaces of the caliper and the anchor plate using molydisulphide grease. Clean and inspect the caliper and rotor, and attach the inboard brake pad anti-rattle spring to the brake pad rear flange, making sure the looped section of the clip is facing away from the rotor.

4 Insert the outboard brake pad into the caliper, making sure the brake pad flange is fully seated into the outboard arms of the caliper. It may be necessary to use a hammer to seat the pad.

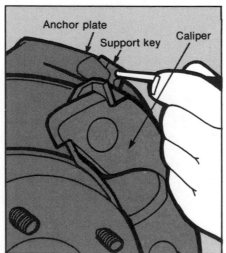

Anchor plate
Support key
Caliper

Stopping in time

You should leave sufficient space between your car and the car ahead of you so you can stop safely if he brakes suddenly.

On dry pavements under good driving conditions, stay back one car length (about 20 feet) for each ten miles per hour of speed. For instance, follow no closer than three car lengths (60 feet) at 30 miles per hour, and five car lengths (100 feet) at 50 miles per hour.

At higher speeds or in bad weather you should double these following distances. Selection of the proper following distance depends on your knowledge of your car's braking ability, and of changes in braking ability caused by rain, snow, ice, and road surface.

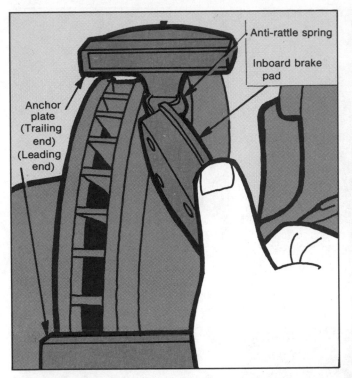

Anti-rattle spring

Inboard brake pad

Anchor plate (Trailing end) (Leading end)

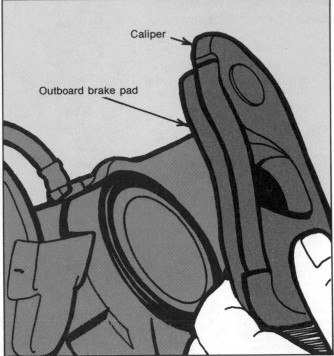

Caliper

Outboard brake pad

5 **Place the caliper assembly** over the rotor and position it on the anchor plate. Make sure that the dust boot is not torn or mispositioned by the inboard brake pad during reinstallation.

6 **Align the anchor** with the caliper plate abutment surfaces, then insert the support key and spring between the abutment surfaces at the trailing end of the caliper and the anchor plate. Using a hammer and brass drift, drive the support key and spring into position. Install and torque the support key retaining screw to 15 foot pounds. Repeat these steps on the other front wheel.

7 **Add brake fluid** to the master cylinder to bring the level to within ¼-inch from the top. Pump the brake pedal several times to seat the pads against the rotor, then replace the tire-and-wheel assembly.

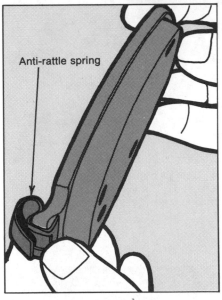

Anti-rattle spring

Brake failure

If your brake pedal suddenly sinks all the way to the floor, try pumping it to build up the pressure. If this does not work, use your parking brake. But apply it gently, holding the release lever so the brakes do not lock and cause a skid. If you can shift to a lower gear, the engine will slow you down. Or, you can turn off the engine, leaving the car in gear, and the engine will slow you down. But if you have power steering, you may lose it when you turn off the engine.

Photo Steps: replacing drum brake shoes

Most American cars are equipped with disc brakes on the front wheels and drum brakes on the rear. The following sequence of photographs shows the step-by-step procedure for replacing brake shoes. Although this sequence focuses on drum brakes with manual adjustment, the procedure for replacing self-adjusting drum brakes is very similar.

1 **Remove the rear wheel,** release the parking brake, and remove the brake drum from the car.

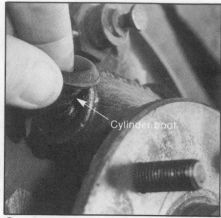

2 **Pull back the cylinder boots** to check for leaks, as discussed later in this chapter.

3 **Install a wheel cylinder clamp** on the cylinder.

4 **Using a cape chisel** and hammer, remove the C retainer to disconnect the parking brake lever from the secondary shoe.

5 **Using a brake spring tool,** remove both shoe retracting springs and the anchor plate.

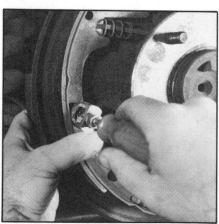

6 **Using a brake shoe tool** or pliers, take out the springs.

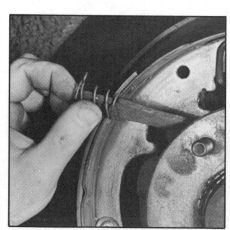

7 **Remove the strut bar** and springs. Then spread the shoes at the top and remove them.

8 **Crisscross the brake shoes** at the top to free the star adjuster and spring.

9 **Clean the brake backing plate** with a wire brush. Then lubricate the brake shoe contacts on the backing plate with a brake lubricant.

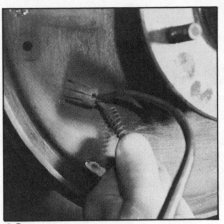

10 **Pull back the spring** on the parking brake cable and lubricate it with oil.

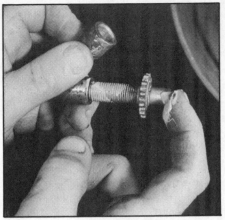

11 **Unscrew the star adjuster,** lubricate the threads and the pivot nut, and screw the adjuster in all the way.

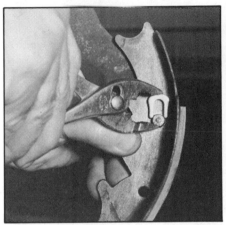

12 **Install the parking brake lever pin** on the brake shoe, then put on the C retainer. Bend the retainer around the pin with pliers.

13 **Install the star adjuster spring** to the bottom of both brake shoes and crisscross the shoes at the top to connect the star adjuster.

Actuating pin

14 **Spread the shoes** at the top and place them on the backing plate. Then put the actuating pins in the brake cylinder and position them on the brake shoes. Install the pins and springs with the spring tool.

15 **Slide the strut bar in place,** then install the anchor plate and the two brake shoe retracting springs.

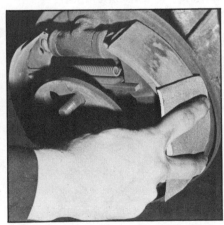

16 **Sand the lining lightly** to remove grease and oil stains.

Lug nuts

17 **Install the brake drum.** Invert two of the wheel lug nuts and put them on the axle studs to secure the drum while you are adjusting the brakes. Brake adjustment procedures are discussed later in this chapter.

Drum Brakes

The drum brake system used on today's American cars is the Bendix-type system, also known as the duo-servo brake system. It gets its name from the servo principle of brake action which was introduced in the late twenties. During a brake application, each shoe serves the other, and the motion of the car actually helps to apply the brakes. One of the main advantages of a duo-servo brake is that it is effective in either forward or reverse brake applications.

When the brakes are applied, the brake shoes are forced outward into the rotating drum. As the linings contact the drum, the primary shoe tends to move in the direction of drum rotation. The upper end of the primary shoe, the shoe closest to the front bumper, is pulled away from the anchor pin.

The force produced by the tendency to rotate with the drum is transmitted from the primary shoe through the adjusting screw to the secondary shoe, the shoe closest to the rear bumper. The result is that the secondary shoe is forced into tighter contact with the drum, and brake efficiency is greatly increased. During reverse braking, the upper end of the secondary shoe pulls away from the anchor pin and helps to apply the primary shoe.

Brake shoe linings

Two methods are used to attach the linings to the shoes. In the first, the lining is riveted to the shoes; in the second, the lining is bonded—cemented under high temperatures and pressures—to the shoes.

Replace drum brakes if:
● On riveted-type brakes, the surface of the lining is less than $\frac{1}{32}$ of an inch above the top of the rivet head.
● On bonded type-brakes, the thickness of the lining is less than $\frac{1}{16}$ of an inch.

The mounting of brake shoes is basically the same in both front and rear. On the rear, the parking brake system is added.

When relining the brake shoes, you should take the drums to your auto parts store or auto machine shop for inspection, measuring, and possible machining. Brake drums must be perfectly round and smooth, and must not exceed .060 inches over specification.

Using your own code, mark the drums for correct reinstallation: for example, "RF" on the right front drum and "RR" on the right rear.

Directions follow on how to replace the front and rear brake shoes for both self- and manual-adjusting systems. Before attempting to replace the brake shoes, check the wheel cylinders for brake fluid leaks. If there is any evidence of a leak, reassemble the brake drums and take the car to a mechanic or a brake specialist for repairs. Note: Jack up your car and support it on safety stands before starting to work on drum brakes.

Primary and secondary shoes

The difference between the primary and secondary shoe is the location and length of the lining. The secondary shoe normally has a full-length lining that is centered on the shoe. The primary shoe usually has a shorter length of lining that may be in a high, low, or centered position on the shoe. In addition, the brake shoes located in the front wheels are usually wider than those in the rear. Finally, the diameter of the brake shoes may be different. The front brake shoes, for example, may be ten inches in diameter and the rear nine.

Pro Shop

Brake spring installation

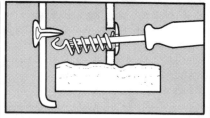

The spring holding down the brake shoes on some cars with drum brakes must be pulled or pushed to extend it so it can be connected to the retainer. This is easy to do with an old Phillips screwdriver.

When installing the spring, just slip it into place in the shoe. Hold the retainer in place with one hand and insert the screwdriver in the center of the spring with the other. The spring can easily be extended and moved as required with the screwdriver to speed installation. If preferred, the end of the screwdriver can be ground off and notched.

Replacing front wheel drum brake shoes on models with manual adjustment

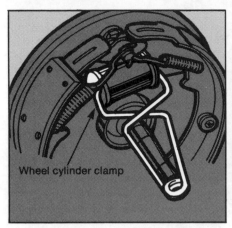

1 **Remove the front brake drums** as described in Chapter 3. Place the wheel cylinder clamp or some baling wire around the wheel cylinder to prevent the pistons from popping out.

2 **Using the brake spring tool,** remove both brake shoe return springs, then take out the anchor pin plate.

3 **Using the brake shoe tool,** push in on the spring tool while holding the pin with your other hand at the back of the backing plate. Then turn the tool a quarter of a turn to release the spring clip. Remove the springs from both shoes.

4 **Grasp both brake shoes** at the top with both hands, and spread them away from the anchor pin until they are free of the wheel cylinder. Pull the shoes toward you and crisscross them at the top to free the star adjustment. Then remove the star adjuster spring. Clean all parts with a non-flammable parts cleaning solvent. *Caution: Do not breathe in the brake dust. It is asbestos and is harmful to your health.*

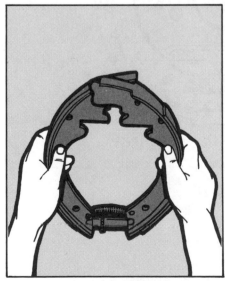

Pro Shop

Removing brake adjustment plugs

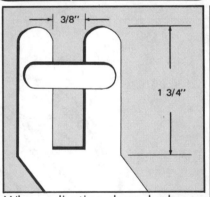

When adjusting drum brakes, a handy tool for removing the plugs from the brake adjustment slots in the backing plates can be made from a 1¾-inch length of ¼-inch scrap iron about one-inch wide. At one end, cut a slot ⅜-inch wide and about 1¾-inches deep to form a fork. Taper and bevel the ends of the fork. Then make a 30-degree bend in the tool at the base. This leaves a six-inch handle.

To use the tool, slide the tapered ends of the fork under the lips of the plug. The slot in the fork will span the projection on the plug. With the six-inch handle, and using the point of the bend as a fulcrum, the plug can easily be pried out of the slot in the backing plate.

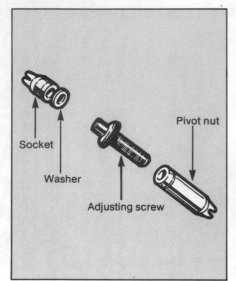

Socket

Washer

Adjusting screw

Pivot nut

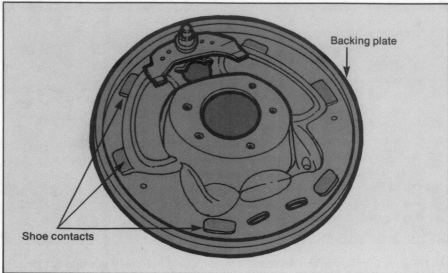

Backing plate

Shoe contacts

5 **Unscrew the star adjuster** and lubricate the threads with a thin coat of brake lube. Rethread the adjusting screw with the pivot nut, then place the washer on the screw. Put a small amount of brake lube on the pivot end of the adjuster and install the pivot on the adjusting screw.

6 **The backing plate.** Put a small amount of brake lube on the brake shoe contacts located on the brake backing plate. *Caution: Work with clean hands and don't get any grease on the brake lining.*

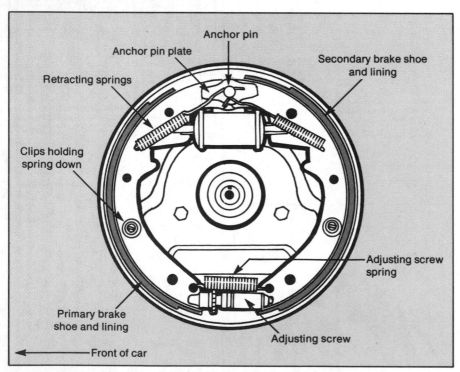

Anchor pin

Anchor pin plate

Retracting springs

Secondary brake shoe and lining

Clips holding spring down

Adjusting screw spring

Primary brake shoe and lining

Adjusting screw

← Front of car

7 **Position the replacement primary and secondary shoes** on a clean surface, directly below the brake backing plate, in the same manner as they will be installed on the plate. Attach the star adjuster spring to the primary and secondary brake shoes. Crisscross the top of the shoes and install the star adjuster, with the star wheel facing toward the front of the car. Return the shoes to their original position and install the brake shoes on the backing plate. Insert the brake shoe actuating cylinder pins, the springs holding the shoe down, and the clips on each shoe. Then position the brake anchor plate, and reinstall the primary and secondary brake retracting return springs. Finally, remove the cylinder clamp or wire. *Caution: Be careful when installing the brake shoe return springs. They may slip off the brake spring tool and hurt your hand.*

Recheck all of your work. Are the clips holding the spring down properly installed, the actuating pins set into the brake shoe web, and the anchor plate positioned properly? Using sandpaper, sand the lining lightly to remove any grease or oil stains, or dirt, that may have gotten on it. Repeat the above operation on the other front wheel. Clean and repack the front wheel bearings and install the two front wheel brake drums as described in Chapter 3.

Adjusting the brakes

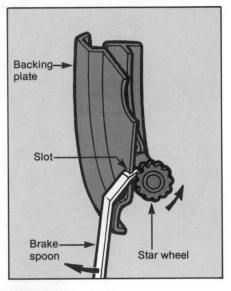

When the adjusting slot is in the backing plate, remove the dust cover from the brake adjusting slot located at the lower end of the brake backing plate. Insert the brake adjusting spoon into the slot until it comes into contact with the star wheel. Raising the handle of the spoon upward will turn the star wheel and expand the brake shoes against the drum. Rotate the drum and turn the star wheel with the spoon until the drum locks. Now, move the spoon in a downward motion turning the star wheel in the opposite direction until the drum rotates freely, without drag.

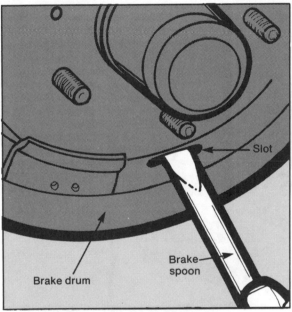

When the adjusting slot is in the brake drum flange, the adjustment is very similar to that described previously, except that the spoon is moved downward to lock the shoes to the drum and upward to loosen the brakes. When the brake adjustment is completed, pump the brake pedal several times, then keep firm pressure on it for about 15 seconds to test for leaks. Check the fluid level in the master cylinder, install the tire-and-wheel assembly, and install the rubber dust covers on the slot in the brake backing plate.

Replacing rear wheel drum brake shoes on models with manual adjustment

The procedure for removing and replacing the rear brake shoes is basically the same as that for the front. The main difference between the front and rear brake assemblies is that in the rear, the parking brake mechanism is attached to the secondary brake shoe and linked to the primary brake shoe.

Pro Shop
Emergency brake cable removal

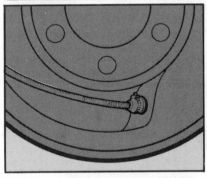

The emergency brake cable is a stickler to remove from the backing plate of the rear wheel on Ford and General Motors cars. The lock which secures the cable opens up like an umbrella when the cable is installed in the backing plate, and the lock must be retracted before the cable can be pulled out.

The job can be done easily by using a small worm gear-type hose clamp of the same size as that used for heater hoses. Slip the hose clamp over the lock, leaving a short gap between the clamp and the backing plate. After the fingers on the lock have been closed by tightening the screw on the clamp, the lock fingers can be started through the backing plate by pulling the cable. Then loosen the clamp and pull the cable out of the backing plate.

The parking brake

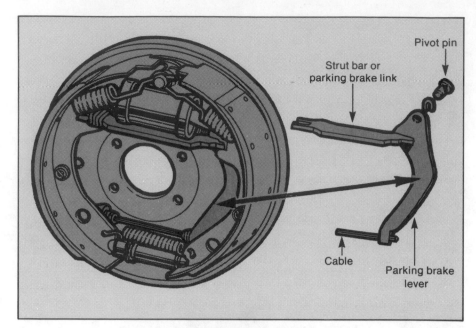

The parking brake mechanism consists of the following parts:
- A parking brake lever pinned to the top of the secondary shoe and connected to the parking brake cable at the bottom.
- A parking brake link or strut and spring connected between the parking brake lever and the primary brake shoe. When the parking brake is applied, the parking brake cable pulls the lever, which in turn pushes the strut bar or link against the primary shoe, spreading the brake shoes against the drum.

In removing and replacing the rear brake shoes and parking brake mechanism, do only one wheel at a time. Use the opposite wheel as a reference guide for the correct reinstallation of all brake parts. There are several methods used to pin the parking brake lever to the secondary shoe. The lever pin may be secured with a horseshoe retainer, a C lock, an E spring lock, a lock nut, or the lever may hook into a specially-designed slot in the secondary shoe.

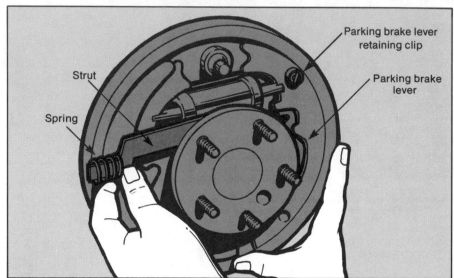

1 Be sure the parking brake is released, then remove the rear brake drum. You may need to put a small amount of penetrating oil on the rear axle studs and tap the drum flange with a hammer to loosen any rust which may have formed.

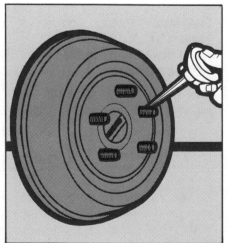

Check for brake fluid leaks, and if a leak is visible replace the drum and wheel and take the car to a qualified mechanic. If a grease leak is detected, refer to Chapter 13 for information on rear axle grease seal replacement.

If your car is equipped with a horseshoe or C retainer, take it out with a cape chisel and hammer. Place the chisel against the closed end of the horseshoe or C retainer and tap it out until the open end of the retainer spreads enough to allow you to remove it from the pin. Place a cylinder clamp or baling wire on the wheel cylinder. Remove the primary and secondary retracting springs and the two hold-down springs.

2 **Spread the brake shoes** at the top away from the anchor and remove the strut or link and spring. Remove the shoes and clean and lubricate the backing plate and the star wheel adjuster.

3 **Check the parking brake cable** for freeness by applying and releasing it. The cable should return to its normal position. If it is not free, it must be lubricated. To lubricate it, disconnect the opposite end of the cable from the front parking brake cable. Clean and lubricate the front part of the rear cable, then pull the lever and cable out of the backing plate and clean and lubricate the rear part. Pull the cable forward and connect it to the front cable, and attach the parking brake lever to the replacement secondary shoe. Install the horseshoe or C retainer clip on the pin and close it with pliers. Attach the star adjuster spring to both the primary and secondary shoes. Crisscross the top of the brake shoes and install the adjuster with the star wheel facing the front of the car.

Return the shoes to their original position and locate the brake shoes on the backing plate. Spread the shoes at the top and install the parking brake strut bar or link between the parking brake lever and the primary shoe. Insert the brake shoe actuating pins into the web of each shoe, then install the springs holding down the brake shoes and replace the clips on both shoes. Replace the primary and secondary brake shoe retracting springs, and remove the cylinder clamp or baling wire. Then clean the surface of the brake lining with sandpaper. Install the brake drum. To hold the drum in position while adjusting the rear brakes, invert two of the wheel lug nuts and put them on the axle studs. Adjust the rear brakes.

4 **Repeat these steps** on the opposite wheel. When both wheels are done remove the two lug nuts and install the tire-and-wheel assembly.

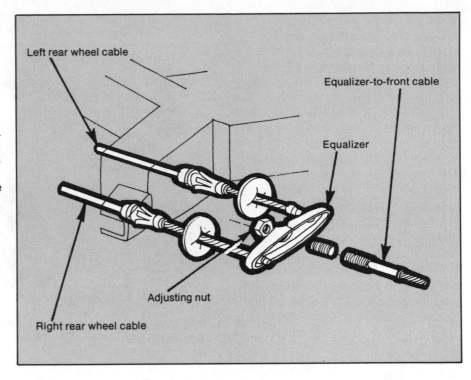

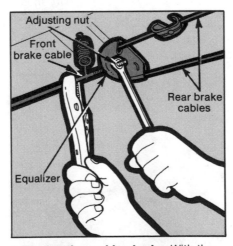

Adjusting the parking brake. With the parking brake lever released, turn the cable adjusting nut(s) clockwise until the rear wheels lock. Then loosen the adjusting nut(s) until both rear wheels turn freely. Check the master cylinder fluid level, and add fluid if necessary. Check the brake pedal for firmness.

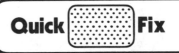

Emergency cable repair

Cables are not always immediately available when one breaks unexpectedly, such as during a rainstorm. In such cases a temporary repair can be made quickly to keep the car rolling.

Tie a knot in each end of the broken cable and slip the knots into a short length of ¼-inch copper tubing. Then crimp the ends of the tubing closed with a pair of pliers.

Replacing rear wheel drum brake shoes on models with self-adjusting brakes—Ford

The procedure for replacing the brake shoes on cars equipped with self-adjusting brakes is basically the same as for manual brakes, except for the self-adjusting mechanism and the initial brake adjustment procedure. You should familiarize yourself with the procedures in this chapter for removing and replacing the brake shoes on the manual adjusting-type brake system before attempting to replace the shoes on cars equipped with self-adjusting brakes.

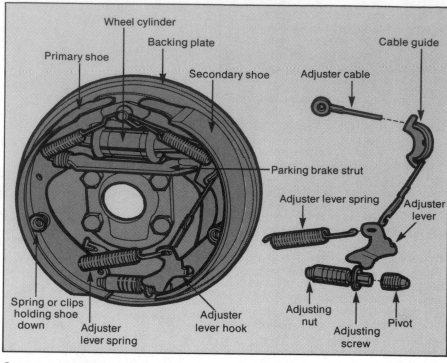

Primary shoe · Wheel cylinder · Backing plate · Secondary shoe · Cable guide · Adjuster cable · Parking brake strut · Adjuster lever spring · Adjuster lever · Spring or clips holding shoe down · Adjuster lever spring · Adjuster lever hook · Adjusting nut · Adjusting screw · Pivot

1 **Before removing the brake shoes,** be sure the parking brake is released. Take off the rear drum and install cylinder clamps or baling wire on the wheel cylinder. Then take out the horseshoe or C clip, using a cape chisel and hammer. Remove the automatic adjuster lever, the cable, the cable guide, and the anchor plate. Take out the springs holding the shoes down and the clips, the star adjuster, and the parking brake strut.

2 **To reassemble and adjust the brake shoes,** clean and lubricate the parts. Then attach the parking brake lever to the secondary brake shoe, and install the secondary and primary shoes on the backing plate with the springs and clips. Install the parking brake strut and spring between the parking brake lever and the primary shoe, making sure the brake shoe actuating pins are in place. Place the anchor plate and the loop of the cable on the anchor. Attach the primary retracting spring, position the cable guide on the secondary shoe web, and insert the short hook end of the secondary retracting spring into the hole

of the cable guide and the web. Attach the long hook end of the spring to the anchor pin, and position the cable on the cable guide.

Install the adjusting screw between the primary and secondary brake shoes with the star wheel to the rear, closer to the secondary shoe. Attach the short hook end of the adjuster spring to the primary shoe web and the other end to the adjuster lever, then connect the adjuster lever to the cable hook. By hand, grasp the adjuster lever, pull down and insert the lever hook into the brake shoe web.

Gauge · Drum · Set screw

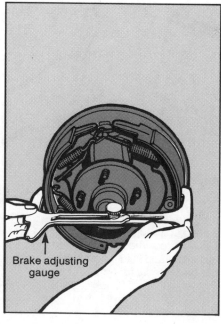

Brake adjusting gauge

3 **To adjust the brakes,** install and set the brake adjusting gauge to the inside diameter of the drum and tighten the set screw. Remove the gauge from the drum and position the other end of the gauge over the brake shoes, then turn the star wheel adjuster by hand to spread the shoes until the brake lining just contacts the gauge. Rotate the gauge around the lining to insure proper clearance, then repeat these steps on the opposite wheel. Sand the surface of the lining and install the drums. Adjust the parking brake. Note: The procedure for reinstalling the front brake shoes is the same as the rear, except for the parking brake mechanism.

Replacing rear wheel drum brake shoes on models with self-adjusting brakes— Chrysler

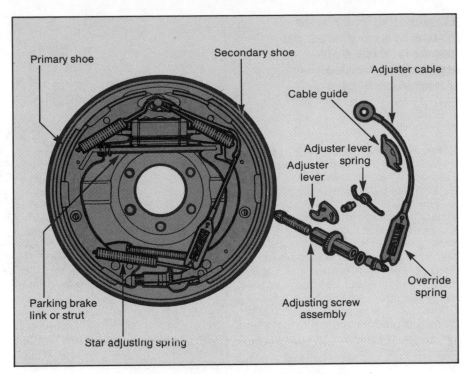

Primary shoe · Secondary shoe · Adjuster cable · Cable guide · Adjuster lever spring · Adjuster lever · Parking brake link or strut · Star adjusting spring · Adjusting screw assembly · Override spring

1 Before removing the brake shoes, be sure the parking brake is released. Take off the rear drum and install a cylinder clamp or baling wire on the wheel cylinder. Remove the horseshoe or C clip using the cape chisel and hammer, then remove the shoe retracting springs, the adjuster cable, the cable guide, and the anchor plate. Take off the springs and the clips holding down the brake shoes. Then remove the parking brake strut or link and spring, and the shoes, the star adjusting screw, and the adjusting screw spring assembly. Crisscross the shoes at the top and remove the star adjuster and spring.

2 To reassemble the brake shoes, clean and lubricate all parts. Drive or press a new adjuster lever pin in the small hole near the lower end of each secondary shoe web. Install the pins from the side of the shoe web facing outward when the shoes are on the car, making sure that the pins are fully seated. Pre-assemble the shoes, the star adjusting screw, and the adjusting spring prior to installing the shoes on the backing plate. Be sure that the override spring is installed with the open end of the hook facing outward toward your body. Put the parking brake lever on the secondary shoe, then assemble the shoes on the backing plate, securing them with the springs and clips.

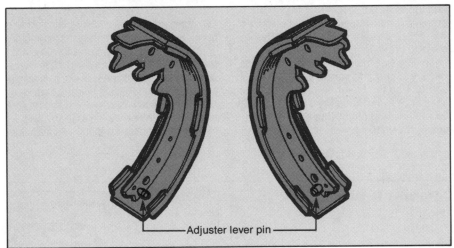

Adjuster lever pin

Install the spring on the parking brake strut, then position the strut between the parking brake lever and the primary shoe web. Locate the anchor plate and the loop of the adjuster cable on the anchor pin, then insert the primary shoe return spring. Position the cable guide on the secondary shoe web, then install the secondary shoe return spring, making sure that the actuating pins properly engage the shoe webs. Remove the wheel cylinder clamp.

Check the opposite wheel for correct reinstallation of all parts. Repeat the operation on the opposite wheel and install the drums. Sand the brake lining, then adjust the brake shoes and the parking brake. Note: The procedure for reinstalling the front wheel brake shoes is the same as the rear, except for the parking brake mechanism.

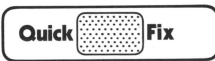
Quick Fix

Brake drum removal
When doing a brake job, it's often very difficult to remove the brake drums if they haven't been off the car for some time.

An effective remedy is to rap the brake drum with a five-pound hammer in the area between the studs. Be careful not to actually hit any of the studs. This should loosen the drums sufficiently so they can easily be pulled off by hand.

Replacing rear wheel drum brake shoes on models with self-adjusting brakes— American Motors

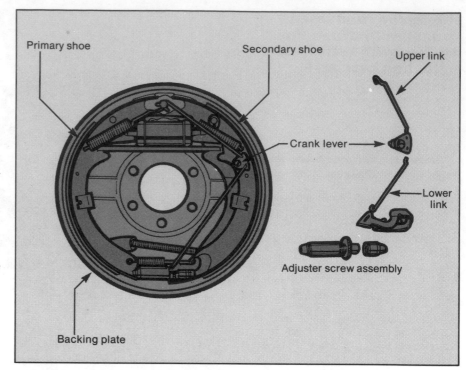

Primary shoe

Secondary shoe

Upper link

Crank lever

Lower link

Adjuster screw assembly

Backing plate

Before removing the brake shoes, make sure the parking brake is released. Take off the rear drum and install a cylinder clamp or baling wire on the wheel cylinder. Remove the horseshoe or C clip using the cape chisel and hammer. Remove the retracting springs, the upper and lower links, the anchor plate, both springs holding down the brake shoes, the parking brake strut or link, the shoes, the star adjusting screw, and the star adjusting screw spring assembly. Crisscross the shoes at the top and take off the star adjuster and the spring, then remove the crank lever from the secondary shoe web.

To reassemble the brake shoes, clean and lubricate all parts, then install the crank lever into the secondary shoe web with a self-threading screw. Attach the parking brake lever to the secondary shoe. Preassemble the primary and secondary shoes, the star adjuster, the spring, and the lower automatic adjuster links and lever. Place the shoe assembly on the backing plate. Position the strut link between the parking brake lever and

the primary shoe, then insert the actuating pins into the shoe webs. Install the two springs and the anchor plate, and replace the two brake shoe retracting springs. Attach the upper automatic adjuster link to the anchor plate. Check the opposite wheel for the correct reinstallation of all parts. Repeat this procedure on the opposite wheel. Adjust the brake shoes on both rear wheels, then sand the brake lining and install the drums.

Note: The procedure for reinstalling the front wheel brake shoes is the same as the rear, except for the parking brake mechanism.

Power brake check

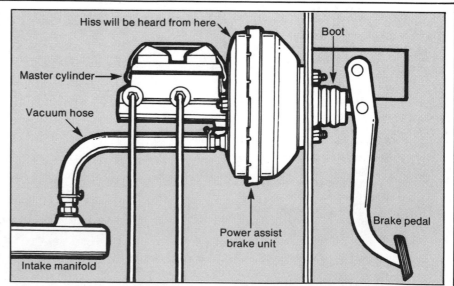

Hiss will be heard from here

Boot

Master cylinder

Vacuum hose

Power assist brake unit

Brake pedal

Intake manifold

With the engine ignition off, pump the brake pedal several times to bleed off the vacuum in the power unit. The pedal will become firm as you pump it. Apply heavy foot pressure on the pedal, and at the same time start the engine. If the power unit is operating properly, the brake pedal should sink slightly toward the floorboard.

A second check of the power unit may be done with a helper. Open the hood, and have your helper start the engine. Listen at the power unit under the hood

as your helper depresses the brake pedal and holds it down. If the power unit is operating properly, you should hear a momentary hiss coming from it. If the

unit continues to make a steady hissing sound, it is defective, and only a qualified mechanic or brake specialist should repair or replace it.

Replacing rear wheel drum brake shoes on models with self-adjusting brakes— General Motors

Before removing the brake shoes, make sure the parking brake is released. Take off the rear drum and install a cylinder clamp or baling wire on the cylinder. Remove the horseshoe or C clip using a cape chisel and hammer, then take off the shoe retracting springs and the adjuster link. Take off the anchor plate, the two springs and clips, the strut bar and spring, the self-adjusting lever, the bushing, the spring, and if necessary, the pawl on the adjuster lever. Remove the two shoes, then crisscross the shoes at the top and take off the star adjuster, the adjuster, and the adjuster spring.

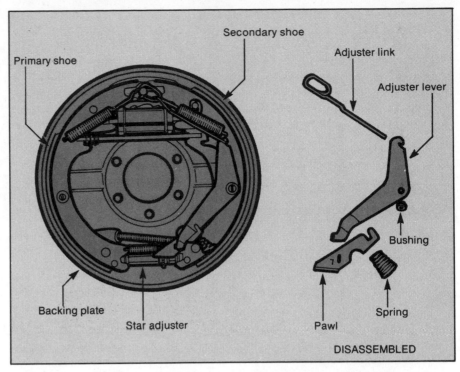

To assemble and adjust the brake shoes, clean and lubricate the parts. Attach the parking brake lever on the secondary shoe with the C clip. Reassemble the primary and secondary shoes with the star adjuster and the spring, and place the shoe assembly on the backing plate. Insert the strut or link and the spring between the parking brake lever and the primary shoe. Position the actuating pins in the shoe webbing. Install the spring holding down the primary shoe and clip, then put the adjuster lever, the bushing, and the spring and / or pawl on the secondary shoe. Attach the spring and clip holding down the secondary shoe. Then install the anchor plate, the adjuster link on the anchor pin, the adjuster lever, and the primary and secondary shoe retracting springs. Check the opposite wheel for correct reinstallation of all parts.

Repeat these steps on the other rear wheel. Lightly sand the brake lining to remove any grease, dirt, or oil, then adjust the brake shoes and install the drums. Adjust the parking brake. Note: The procedure for reinstalling the front wheel brake shoes is the same as the rear wheel brake shoes, except for the parking brake mechanism.

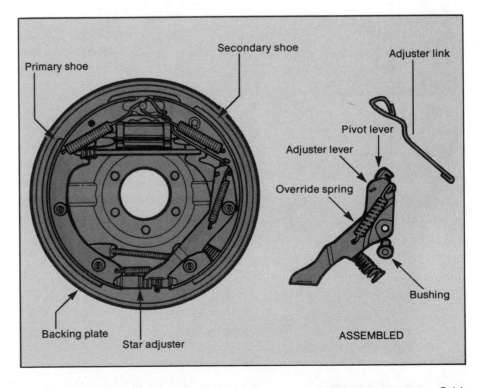

In this chapter you have learned the procedures for replacing disc brake pads and drum brake shoes, and for adjusting the brake shoes and parking brakes. If you have followed the step-by-step procedures as outlined for your car, you should have a safe and properly-operating brake system. Remember that cleanliness and accuracy are the most important ingredients when working on your car's brakes. Take your time replacing brake parts; don't rush through the job. Your life and the lives of others may be at stake.

The following brake troubleshooting charts will assist you in detecting various brake malfunctions, their causes and corrections.

Troubleshooting flow chart: drum brake system

Symptom	Probable cause	Remedy
Low pedal— Pedal may go to the floor.	1. Excessive clearance between drums and linings. 2. Automatic adjusters not working. 3. Bent or distorted brake shoes.	1. Adjust brakes. 2. Make several forward and reverse brake stops; if pedal does not come up, repair automatic adjusters. 3. Replace shoes and linings in axle sets.
Low pedal— On first application in morning only—OK rest of day.	1. Residual pressure check valves not holding pressure in lines.	1. Repair or replace master cylinder.
Springy or spongy pedal— Pedal has a soft, springy, or spongy feel when depressed.	1. Bent or distorted brake shoes. 2. Shoes not centered in drum. 3. Cracked or thin drums.	1. Replace shoes and linings in axle sets. 2. Adjust anchor pins (if car has adjustable anchor pins). 3. Replace drums in axle sets.
Hard pedal— Excessive pedal pressure is required to stop car.	1. Poor quality brake linings and brake fade. 2. Grease or brake fluid-soaked linings. 3. Glazed linings. 4. Damaged or distorted shoes. 5. Scored, barrel-shaped, or bell-mouthed drums.	1. Replace with approved shoes and linings in axle sets. 2. Repair grease seal or wheel cylinder, as necessary, and replace shoes and linings in axle sets. 3. Sand lining surface or replace shoes and linings in axle sets. 4. Replace shoes and linings in axle sets. 5. Refinish or replace drums in axle sets.
Grabby brakes— Severe reaction to pedal pressure.	1. Incorrect or distorted shoes. 2. Incorrect linings or linings loose on shoes. 3. Grease or brake fluid on linings. 4. Shoes not centered in drums. 5. Loose or distorted brake backing plate. 6. Scored, hard spotted, or out-of-round drums.	1. Replace with correct shoes and linings in axle sets. 2. Replace with correct shoes and linings in axle sets. 3. Repair grease seal or wheel cylinder, as necessary, and replace shoes and linings in axle sets. 4. Adjust anchor pins (if car has adjustable anchor pins). 5. Tighten or replace backing plate. 6. Refinish or replace drums in axle sets.
Car pulls to one side.	1. Incorrect or distorted shoes. 2. Incorrect linings or linings loose on shoes. 3. Grease or brake fluid on linings. 4. Shoes not centered in drums. 5. Loose or distorted brake backing plate. 6. Scored, hard spotted, or out-of-round drums, or different-sized drums on same axle. 7. Water on linings. 8. Sticking wheel cylinder piston.	1. Replace with correct shoes and linings in axle sets. 2. Replace with correct shoes and linings in axle sets. 3. Repair grease seal or wheel cylinder, as necessary, and replace shoes and linings in axle sets. 4. Adjust anchor pins (if car has adjustable anchor pins). 5. Tighten or replace backing plate. 6. Refinish or replace drums in axle sets. 7. Apply brakes a few times to dry linings. 8. Repair or replace wheel cylinder.
Pulsating brake pedal.	1. Out-of-round drums. 2. Bent rear axle.	1. Refinish or replace drums in axle sets. 2. Replace axle.

Drum brakes, continued:

Symptom	Probable cause	Remedy
Noise and chatter— Squealing, clicking, or scraping sound upon brake application.	1. Bent, damaged, or incorrect shoes. 2. Worn-out linings (shoes rubbing drum). 3. Foreign material imbedded in linings. 4. Broken shoe return springs, shoe hold-down pins, or springs holding shoes down. 5. Rough, grooved, or dry shoe ledges or pads on backing plate. 6. Cracked or threaded drums (lathe marks).	1. Replace with correct shoes and linings in axle sets. 2. Replace shoes and linings in axle sets. 3. Replace shoes and linings in axle sets. 4. Replace defective parts. 5. Smooth shoe ledges and pads, and apply high temperature lubricant. 6. Replace drums in axle sets.
Decreasing brake pedal travel.	1. Weak or broken shoe return springs. 2. Sticking wheel cylinder piston.	1. Replace return springs. 2. Repair or replace wheel cylinder.
Rear brakes drag.	1. Frozen parking brake cables 2. Improper brake shoe adjustment.	1. Free up and lubricate cables, or replace. 2. Adjust shoes and repair automatic adjusters, if necessary.
One brake drags.	1. Weak or broken shoe return springs. 2. Improper brake shoe adjustment. 3. Sticking wheel cylinder pistons. 4. Swollen wheel cylinder cups. 5. Bent or distorted brake shoe.	1. Replace return springs. 2. Adjust shoes and repair automatic adjuster, if necessary. 3. Repair or replace wheel cylinders. 4. Repair or replace wheel cylinder, flush hydraulic system, and fill with approved fluid. 5. Replace shoes and linings in axle sets.

Troubleshooting flow chart: disc brake system

Symptom	Probable cause	Remedy
Low pedal— Pedal may go to floor on first application; is OK on subsequent applications.	1. Pad and plate knockback caused by loose wheel bearings or faulty front suspension.	1. Adjust or tighten parts, or replace faulty parts, as necessary.
Hard pedal— Excessive pedal pressure required to stop vehicle.	1. Grease or brake fluid-soaked pads.	1. Repair grease seal or caliper, as necessary, and replace pads and plates in axle sets.
Grabby brakes— Severe reaction to pedal pressure.	1. Incorrect pads, or pads loose on plate. 2. Grease or brake fluid on pads. 3. Loose caliper or caliper mounting bracket.	1. Replace with correct pads and plates in axle sets. 2. Repair grease seal or caliper, as necessary, and replace pads and plates in axle sets. 3. Tighten to specifications.
Car pulls to one side.	1. Incorrect or loose pads. 2. Grease or brake fluid on pads. 3. Loose caliper or caliper mounting bracket. 4. Caliper piston sticking.	1. Replace with correct pads and plates in axle sets. 2. Repair grease seal or caliper, as necessary, and replace pads and plates in axle sets. 3. Tighten to specifications. 4. Repair or replace caliper.
Pulsating brake pedal.	1. Excessive variation in rotor thickness. 2. Excessive lateral runout in rotor.	1. Refinish or replace rotor. 2. Refinish or replace rotor.
Noise and chatter— Squealing, clicking, or scraping noise upon brake application.	1. Bent, damaged, or incorrect pads and plates. 2. Worn-out pads (plates rubbing rotor). 3. Foreign material imbedded in pad.	1. Replace with correct pads and plates in axle sets. 2. Replace pads and plates in axle sets. 3. Replace pads and plates in axle sets.
One front brake has excessive drag.	1. Sticking caliper piston. 2. Swollen caliper piston seal.	1. Repair or replace caliper. 2. Repair caliper, flush hydraulic system, and fill with approved fluid.

Troubleshooting flow chart: drum or disc brakes

Symptom	Probable cause	Remedy
Low pedal— Pedal may go to the floor under steady pressure.	1. Leak in hydraulic system.	1. Check master cylinder, wheel cylinders, calipers, tubes, and hoses for leakage—repair or replace faulty parts.
	2. Air in hydraulic system.	2. Bleed hydraulic system.
	3. Poor quality brake fluid (low boiling point).	3. Drain hydraulic system and fill with approved brake fluid.
	4. Low brake fluid level.	4. Fill master cylinder and bleed hydraulic system.
	5. Weak brake hoses that expand under pressure.	5. Replace defective hoses.
	6. Improperly adjusted manual master cylinder push rod.	6. Adjust push rod (if car has adjustable push rod).
	**7. Improperly adjusted power brake hydraulic push rod.	7. Adjust push rod.
Springy or spongy pedal— Pedal has a soft, springy, or spongy feel when depressed.	1. Poor quality brake fluid (low boiling point).	1. Drain hydraulic system and fill with approved brake fluid.
	2. Weak brake hoses that expand under pressure.	2. Replace defective hoses.
	3. Air in hydraulic system.	3. Bleed hydraulic system.
Hard pedal— Excessive pedal pressure is required to stop car.	1. Clogged master cylinder tubes or hoses.	1. Replace tubes or hoses, as necessary.
	2. Frozen master cylinder piston(s).	2. Repair or replace master cylinder.
	**3. Low engine vacuum supply to power brake.	3. Tune or repair engine to obtain correct vacuum.
	**4. Loose or leaking vacuum hose to power brake.	4. Tighten clamps or replace hose, as required.
	**5. Defective power brake vacuum check valve.	5. Replace check valve.
	**6. Faulty power brake.	6. Replace power section of power brake.
Grabby brakes— Severe reaction to pedal pressure.	1. Rough or corroded master cylinder bore.	1. Repair or replace master cylinder.
	2. Binding brake pedal linkage.	2. Free up and lubricate.
	**3. Faulty power brake.	3. Replace power section of power brake.
Car pulls to one side.	1. Faulty suspension parts.	1. Repair suspension system.
Pulsating brake pedal.	1. Worn or damaged front wheel bearings.	1. Replace bearings.
Decreasing brake pedal travel.	1. Plugged master cylinder compensating port(s).	1. Repair or replace master cylinder.
	2. Swollen master cylinder cups.	2. Repair or replace master cylinder, flush hydraulic system, and fill with approved brake fluid.
All brakes drag— But brake adjustment is correct.	1. Binding brake pedal.	1. Free up and lubricate.
	2. Soft or swollen rubber parts caused by incorrect or contaminated brake fluid.	2. Replace all rubber parts, flush hydraulic system, and fill with approved brake fluid.
	3. Plugged master cylinder compensating port(s).	3. Repair or replace master cylinder.
One brake drags.	1. Loose or worn front wheel bearings.	1. Adjust to specifications or replace.
	2. Defective brake hose or hydraulic tube (preventing return of brake fluid).	2. Replace defective hose or tube, as necessary.

** Cars equipped with power brakes..

CONTENTS

FRONT END AND STEERING

The front suspension system must allow the wheels to move up and down. At the same time, it must allow the wheels to pivot from side to side so that the car can be steered. One of the first front suspension systems used on cars was the conventional front axle suspension, the I beam. This system is still used on heavy-duty trucks.

Modern American cars have ball joint independent front suspension. This system consists of an upper and lower control arm allowing the up-and-down movement of the car. The inner ends of these arms are attached to pivots mounted to the frame. The outer ends are connected to the steering knuckle and the spindle support with ball joints. There are three variations of this system. One uses a coil spring mounted between the lower control arm and the frame; another uses a coil spring mounted between the upper control arm and the frame; and a third, used on Chrysler Corporation cars, Toronados and Eldorados, has a torsion bar connected to the frame at one end and the lower control arm at the other.

The independent twin I beam suspension system is used on Ford truck F-100, F-250, and F-350 series. One end of each twin I beam is attached to the frame with a pivot, and the outer ends of the beams are attached to the spindle. Coil springs support the weight of the vehicle in this system, and a radius arm prevents the outer ends of the beams from moving forward or backward. Twin I beam suspension was designed to provide the strength needed to carry the load of trucks and the flexibility to provide a smoother ride.

In this chapter you will learn how to replace shock absorbers, tie-rod ends, stabilizer links, and the power steering pump and hoses.

Tools and equipment:

Floor jack.
Safety stands.
Goggles.
Fender covers.
⅜" and ½" drive socket sets.
Combination wrenches.
Ball peen hammers.
Common screwdrivers.
Droplight or flashlight.
Block of wood.
Single piston hydraulic jack.
Hand cloths.
Torque wrench.
Wire brush.
Sharp pen knife.
2 x 4 block of wood.
3-foot bar or pipe.
Drain pan.
Set of flare nut wrenches.
Belt tension gauge.

Parts you may need:

Spray can of penetrating oil.
Shock absorbers.
Tie-rod ends.
Cotter pins.
Power steering hoses.
Power steering fluid.

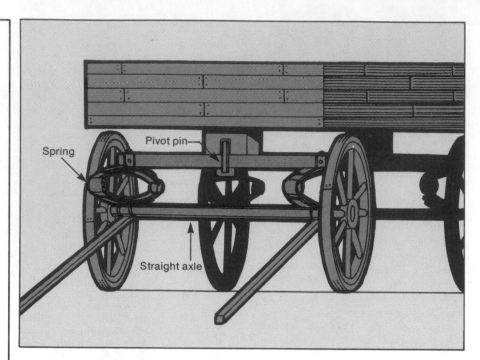

The front suspension of the horse-drawn wagon was simply a straight axle. To turn the wagon, the entire axle and supporting springs had to be swiveled at the center. Although the wagon could carry heavy loads, it was very difficult to steer, and the ride was rough.

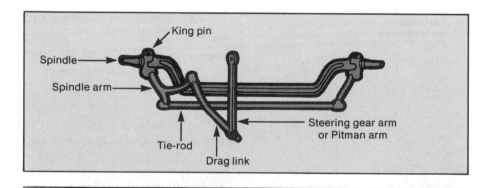

The I Beam, one of the first front suspension systems used on cars, is still used today on heavy-duty trucks.

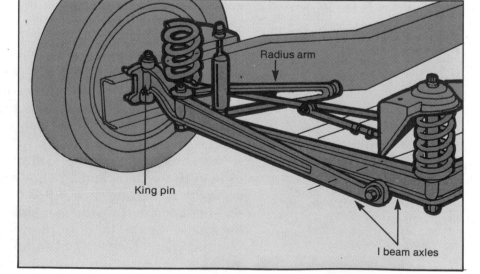

The independent twin I beam suspension system was designed to carry the load of trucks and yet have the flexibility to provide a smoother ride than the single I beam.

Function of Shock Absorbers

Why shock absorbers are needed

The term shock absorber is actually a misnomer. A shock absorber does not absorb shocks at all. Your car's springs actually perform that function. However, if a spring were left unimpeded, it would continue to oscillate after hitting a bump. Since the springs support the frame, and the body is attached to the frame, the whole car would bob up and down until internal friction in the spring itself caused it to stop oscillating. This would not only be uncomfortable, but unsafe. A car in such an unstable condition would be extremely difficult to control and maneuver.

Early automobile designers recognized the need to damp out these oscillations by controlling spring movement. Because a modern-day shock absorber actually does this job—it damps out oscillations—you may also hear it referred to as a damper, or just a shock, for short.

If your car seems unstable on the road, you should test your shock absorbers. Indications of instability include feeling road shocks, bobbing up-and-down of the car for a long period after hitting a bump, or a general lack of control in handling. Also, any clunking sounds from beneath the car when it hits a bump or makes a turn should lead you to suspect weak or worn shock absorbers.

Shock failure—the hidden hazard

Shocks don't go bad all at once. Unlike a tire that goes flat, leaving no doubt something is wrong, shock absorbers lose their ability to maintain vehicle stability over a period of time. Deterioration is gradual.

Because failure occurs slowly, drivers are seldom aware of the differences in handling weakened shock absorbers cause. Since a potentially dangerous situation can develop without your being aware of it, you should take a few minutes every six months to test the shock absorbers in your car.

Before outlining the testing procedure, it is first necessary to understand how shock absorbers work and what can go wrong with them.

How shock absorbers work

A shock absorber can be described as a telescopic, double-acting, hydraulic component. The term telescopic indicates that a shock absorber assembly consists of two cylinders. One, the upper assembly, overrides the other, the lower, in the same way one tube of a telescope rides over the other tube. Double-acting refers to a shock absorber's ability to damp out movement in two directions.

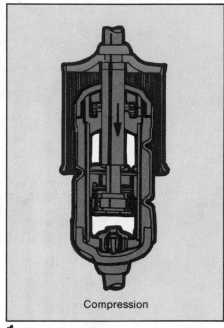

Compression

1 On compression, when the wheels and the rest of the car are pushed together, the two cylinders are pushed together.

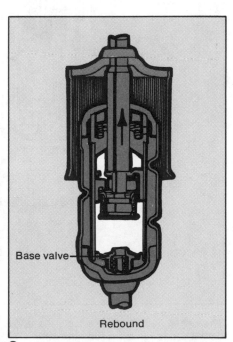

Base valve

Rebound

2 On rebound, when the wheels and the rest of the car return to their normal riding position, the two cylinders are extended from compression to the pressure-off position.

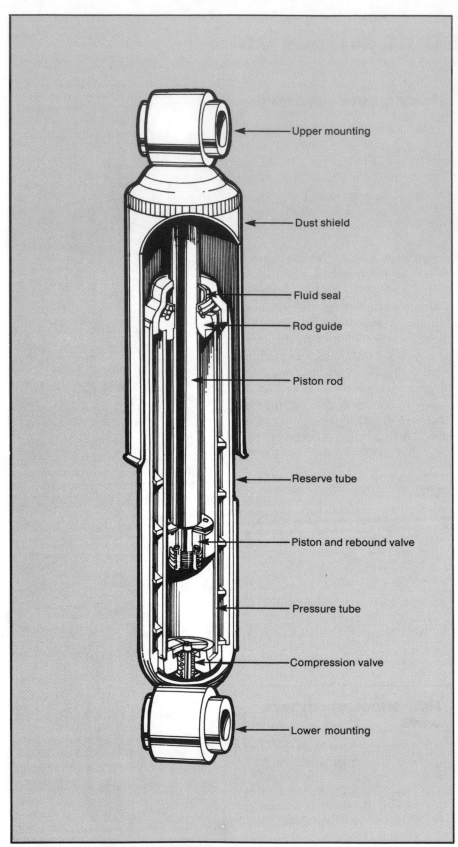

Upper mounting

Dust shield

Fluid seal

Rod guide

Piston rod

Reserve tube

Piston and rebound valve

Pressure tube

Compression valve

Lower mounting

The upper cylinder of a shock absorber contains a long piston rod, and serves primarily as a dust cover in which the lower cylinder rests. The piston rod extends down through the upper cylinder into the lower one and ends in a piston assembly.

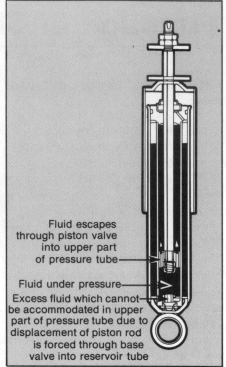

Fluid escapes through piston valve into upper part of pressure tube

Fluid under pressure

Excess fluid which cannot be accommodated in upper part of pressure tube due to displacement of piston rod is forced through base valve into reservoir tube

The main shock absorbing component inside the lower cylinder is a measured amount of hydraulic fluid which does the job of controlling movement.

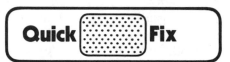

Quick Fix

Elongated shock bolt hole

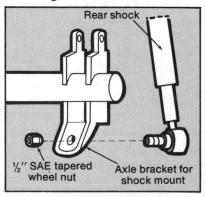

Rear shock

½″ SAE tapered wheel nut

Axle bracket for shock mount

When the shock bolt going through the lower bracket loosens on most GM cars, it quickly elongates the hole. One cure is to weld a suitable flat washer to the outside of the bracket. To really complete the job, however, use a tapered wheel nut, which holds nicely. If the loose nut is caught before the elongation becomes severe, the tapered wheel nut alone will take up the slack in the hole.

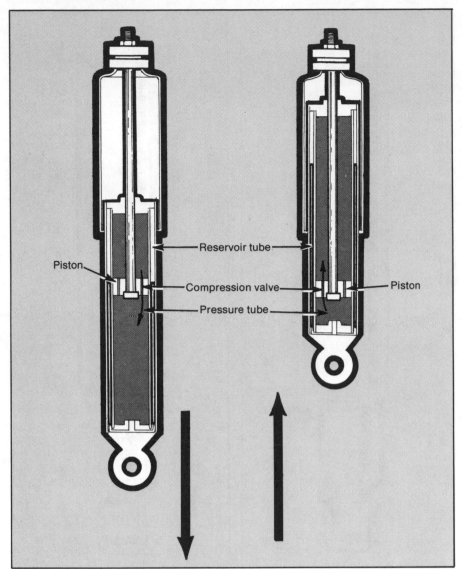

Piston

Reservoir tube

Compression valve

Pressure tube

Piston

All shock absorbers work the same way. They are firmly attached to an upper and lower support. The upper support is a stationary part, such as the wheel housing, which prevents the upper cylinder from moving. The lower support is a component of the car's suspension system which is also attached to a spring, such as the lower control arm. Thus, any impact received by the spring will be damped by the shock.

As the wheels hit bumps, the lower cylinder section of a shock absorber moves with the wheel and is telescoped into the upper cylinder section. As the two cylinders compress, the piston plunges into the thick hydraulic fluid, forcing it through various small orifices. The fluid slows and controls movement. Following impact, shock absorbers extend themselves. The lower cylinder slides from the upper, the piston retracts, and the fluid that was displaced returns to the lower cylinder for storage.

Failure of shock absorbers

There is no way to predict the life expectancy of shock absorbers. And don't be misled into believing that so-called heavy-duty shocks will outlast standard-duty units. The terms heavy-duty and standard-duty do not refer to the length of service shocks provide, but rather to the type of service they are intended to perform. Of course, standard-duty shock absorbers used under heavy-duty conditions will fail much sooner than if they had been used as intended.

Shock absorber life depends primarily on the roads over which you drive. Shocks can provide safe, adequate service for as long as 50,000 miles, or they can fail in as little as 5,000 miles. Shock absorber manufacturers generally advise car owners to replace their shocks at 20,000 to 30,000 miles. This advice is intended for people who do not inspect their shocks periodically. The only way to guard against premature replacement, be sure of adequate performance, and protect yourself against the hazards of driving with weak shocks, is to inspect them every six months. A shock absorber cannot be repaired. Except for a loose mounting bolt, which may be tightened, when shocks fail, they must be replaced.

Shock absorbers fail in three ways:

1. The seal cover which is supposed to keep hydraulic fluid inside the lower cylinder deteriorates and hydraulic fluid is lost.
2. The parts mounting the shock firmly at the top and bottom cylinders, more often at the bottom, wear excessively and loosen. This causes the shock to wobble. A shock absorber that has side-play cannot provide strong damping action. Furthermore, a loose shock absorber causes instability.
3. Internal parts, such as the piston and various springs, wear excessively. This reduces shock damping capability. Of the three types of damage, this is the one which takes the longest to occur.

Choosing New Shocks

Once you know you need new shock absorbers, the next task is to choose the right type of replacement shock, among the many different types and brands available.

Go to an auto parts supply house and you will see standard, heavy-duty, radial-tuned, racing and competition, overload, air, and spring shocks. To help you make an intelligent choice, some of the more common types of shock absorbers are described here.

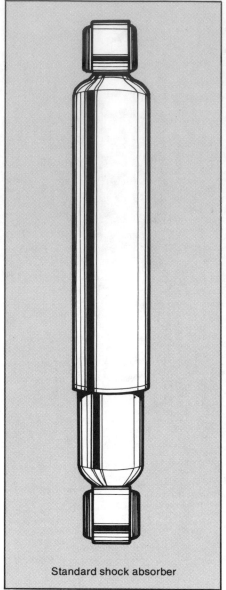

Standard shock absorber

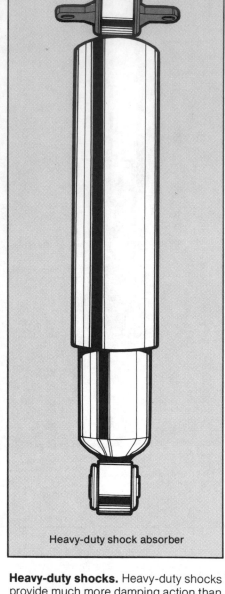

Heavy-duty shock absorber

Competition and racing shocks

These shocks are used for just what their name implies. In most cases, they are designed to give maximum control at a sacrifice in ride comfort. They are generally not suitable for street use, and you should not install them unless you actually plan to race. If you do, seek advice on various types and usages from someone familiar with the type of racing you are planning on doing.

Standard-duty shocks. Most original equipment shock absorbers are standard-duty with a one-inch diameter body. They provide adequate service for cars driven primarily on smooth roads and not carrying full loads of cargo and/or passengers. Standard-duty shocks do not have the capacity to control the kind of violent or abnormal vehicle movement that might occur on extremely rough roads or with full loads, but in normal use, they provide a soft ride. That is, they do not damp out a great deal of movement, but they spread out the movement over a longer period of time.

Heavy-duty shocks. Heavy-duty shocks provide much more damping action than standard-duty. They will make your car ride more firmly, with less rocking and up-and-down movement, and will make control easier when carrying heavy loads. Although your car will feel more responsive and more stable with heavy-duty shocks, do not install them if you do not like a firmer ride.

Heavy-duty shocks come in two grades. The best units usually have a 1½-inch or 1⅜-inch valve body, and the added capacity gives the shock more control capacity. They also cost the most.

Heavy-duty shocks which have the same one-inch valve body as the standard-duty are less effective. They get their added control from internal valving modifications which cause the hydraulic fluid to flow more slowly, thereby inducing more damping action as the piston moves through it.

Overloading a Car

Shock absorbers ordinarily do not support anything. The springs do all the supporting. When a heavy load is in the trunk, the rear of the car may sag. In extreme conditions, when the passenger compartment is also full, the whole car can sag below the original design height.

This sagging can be very dangerous. If the rear end sags, your headlight aim will be off, possibly blinding oncoming drivers. And the chance of striking a foreign object is increased. This may not only damage the car, but it can cause you to lose control. A car with a heavy load is unstable because the suspension components are not working effectively.

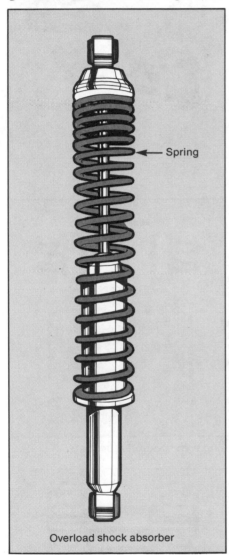

Overload shock absorber

Overload shocks are heavy-duty shock absorbers with auxiliary springs wound around the body. The shock functions in the usual way, but the auxiliary coil spring helps support heavy loads and reduces the tendency for the car to sag. Overload shocks can keep a car level even with a heavy load. They are available for most cars for both the front and rear. The only disadvantages are a slightly harsher ride and a higher sitting car when not fully loaded.

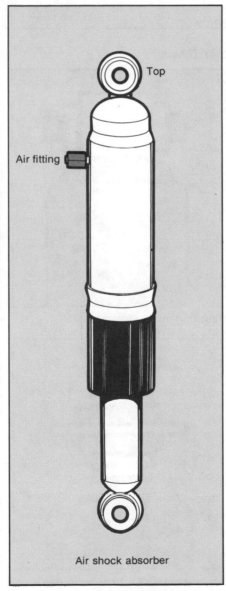

Air shock absorber

The air shock, located in the rear of a car, is used only for very heavy loads, such as towing a trailer. They are installed the same way as ordinary rear shock absorbers or overload shocks, but they have an air line connecting each shock to a common tee where the lines join together and converge into a single one. The air line ends at an air valve which projects through an easy-to-reach access area, such as the trunk floor, the rear panel, or the rear bumper. Air is added to or bled from air shocks, depending upon the load, by means of an air valve. Adding or bleeding air is done in the same way you would add or bleed air from a tire.

When you know you are going to haul a heavy load, you use a service station air hose to inflate the air shocks to the rating suggested by the manufacturer for the weight of your particular load. When no support is needed, air is bled from the shocks by pushing in on the air valve core. However, most manufacturers recommend that a minimum of 20 psi (pounds per square inch) of air pressure be maintained at all times.

In effect then, you have air doing the same job as the auxiliary spring on the overload shock. However, you do not have the disadvantages of overload shocks when the car is not loaded. *Caution: If you plan to have air shocks installed in your car for the first time, make sure the air lines are positioned away from parts that get hot, such as exhaust system components. The lines are generally made of plastic which can be damaged by heat. Also, keep the air valve covered with a tire valve cap to prevent dirt from entering the system.*

The automatic load leveler system is an optional piece of equipment now offered by car manufacturers for their more expensive models. Some of the highest-priced luxury cars, including the Eldorado, Seville, Imperial, and Lincoln, have automatic load leveling systems added as standard equipment.

This system consists of two air shock absorbers in the rear served by an air compressor. As the car is loaded, the compressor, operated by the engine, automatically feeds air through a pressure-regulating valve to the shock absorbers. When the load is relieved, the shocks automatically empty themselves of air. *Caution: You should not attempt to replace or otherwise service an automatic load leveler system. The setup is complicated and requires special training and tools. However, you can replace the front shock absorber of a car equipped with automatic load levelers.*

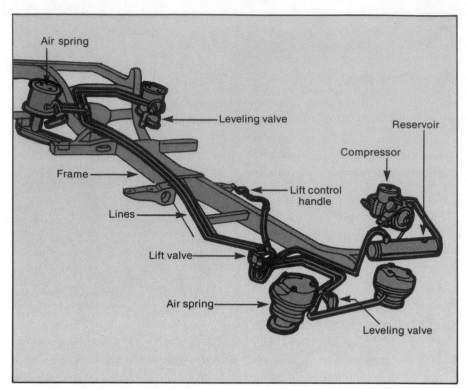

Types of shock absorber mountings

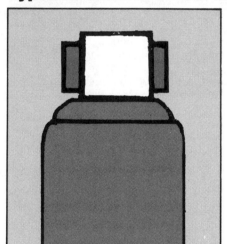

Ring with rubber bushing

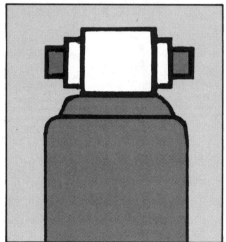

Ring with metal sleeve insert

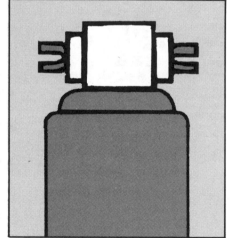

Ring with two-bolt crossbar

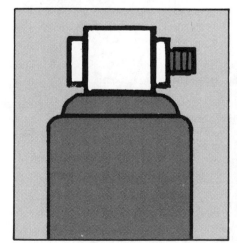

Ring with right-angle stud

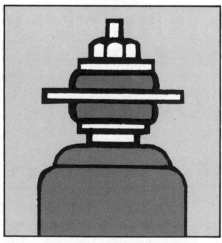

Stud mount with rubber bushings

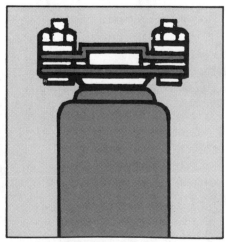

Two-bolt plate

Testing Shock Absorbers

Testing shocks for wear

You do not need any tools to test your shocks. Park the car on level pavement, then turn off the engine. If your car has an automatic transmission, set it in "Park." If it has a manual transmission, set it in gear. Set the parking brake firmly. Then, standing at any corner of the car, place your hands on the bumper or fender and press down with as much force as you can muster. When the corner reaches its maximum downward point, let up. Keep doing this until the car is rocking up and down.

While the car is rocking on a downward stroke, when the corner has been pushed to its maximum point, quickly remove your hands from the bumper or fender. If the car's body comes up one time and settles level, the shock absorber in that corner is probably OK. If the body bounces up and down again—that is, if it keeps bouncing instead of settling level and in a smooth manner—the shock absorber in that corner is weak. Perform this test at each of your car's other three corners.

Testing shocks for leaks

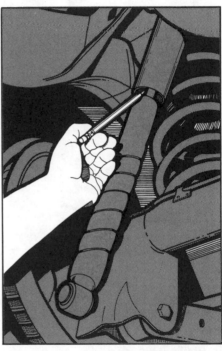

Jack up and support the car. Then visually check the lower section of the shock for fluid leaks. If a leak is detected, the shock must be replaced.

Checking for loose shock bushings

Bushing location

With the rear of the car jacked up and supported, grasp the shock absorber with your hand and twist it from side-to-side while checking the bushings for excessive movement. If the bushings are worn, replace the shock.

Replacing Front Shock Absorbers

Shock absorbers differ from manufacturer to manufacturer and from model to model, so no single set of instructions on replacement can be given. To replace your shocks, find the directions for the make, model, and year of your particular car in the pages which follow.

American Motors, 1968–69

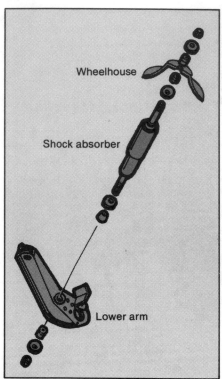

1 **Lift the hood** and disconnect the single top mounting nut, washer, and grommet on the shock absorber stem, which projects through the wheelhouse. This is called a bayonet-type stem.

2 **Beneath the car,** disconnect the single bottom mounting nut, washer, and grommet holding the shock to the lower control arm. Reach up and compress the shock absorber, then remove it from its position in the lower control arm.

3 **Work the new shock** into position inside the lower control arm, and reach up and extend the shock so it reaches its mounting position in the wheelhouse and in the lower control arm.

4 **Attach the shock absorber** to the lower control arm, tightening the nut securely. Position the shock on the top of the wheelhouse, again tightening the nut securely.

5 **Repeat these steps** on the other front wheel.

American Motors, 1970 on, except Pacer

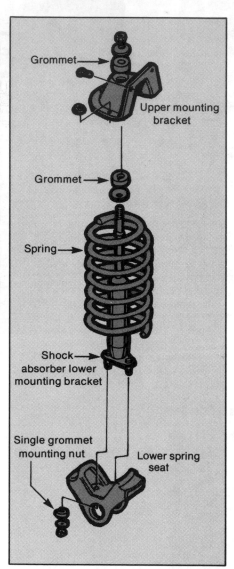

1 **From beneath the car,** remove the two nuts, washers, and grommets holding the bottom shock absorber mounting bracket to the lower spring seat.

2 **Lift the hood,** and you will see the top mounting of the shock protruding through an upper mounting bracket on the wheelhouse. Remove the retaining nut and bolt from this bracket. Lift the shock absorber, still attached to the bracket, out through the top of the wheelhouse.

3 **Remove the grommets** from the two lower mounting studs. Take out the shock absorber upper retaining nut, grommet, and washer and separate it from the upper mounting bracket. Discard the shock and all hardware except the upper mounting bracket.

4 **Insert the stem** of the new shock through the hole in the upper mounting bracket, then attach the grommet, washer, and retaining nut. Tighten the nut to eight foot pounds. Extend the shock absorber to its full rebound position, and place the two grommets on the lower mounting studs.

5 **Lower the shock absorber** down through the wheelhouse so it extends through the coil spring.

6 **Beneath the car,** maneuver the lower mounting so the attaching studs fall into the holes in the lower spring seat. Install the two grommets, washers, and nuts in the seat. Tighten the lower shock mounting nuts securely.

7 **In the engine compartment,** install the retaining nut and bolt on the upper mounting bracket, and tighten the bracket retaining nut and bolt securely.

8 **Repeat these steps** on the other front wheel.

American Motors, Pacer model

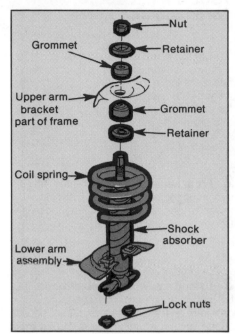

1 **Jack up and support the car,** then disconnect the shock absorber at the upper mounting on the frame. Take out the two lock nuts at the lower control arm, and remove the shock down through the spring and arm.

2 **Install the new shock** with one grommet and one retainer on the shaft going up into the lower control arm and spring. Make sure the upper mounting stud comes through the mounting hole, then attach the rubber grommet and one retainer and nut, and the lower mounting lock nuts, tightening all nuts securely.

3 **Repeat these steps** on the other front wheel then lower the car.

Pro Shop

Loosening the shock nuts

Before you attempt to remove the nuts or bolts anchoring the shock absorber to the frame or control arm, spray a generous amoung of penetrating oil on them and allow it to soak in. This should loosen rusted and stubborn nuts or bolts.

General Motors, Buick, 1968 on, Cadillac, 1977 on, except Eldorado

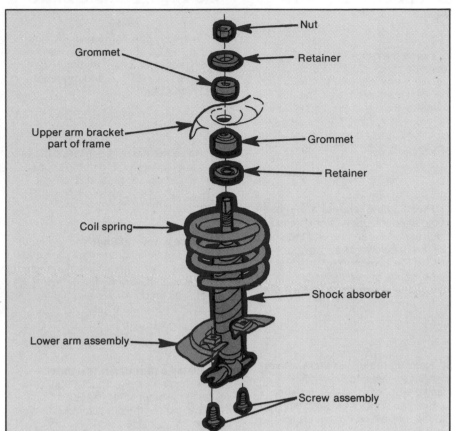

1 **Lift the hood** and open the covers to the shock absorber upper mounting nut access holes in the wheelhousing. Then, using a short extension on a ratchet, remove the shock's upper mounting nut, retainer, and grommet.

2 **Get beneath the car** and remove the two mounting bolts from the shock absorber, then lower it out through the lower control arm.

3 **Extend the new shock** to its full length, and place a grommet retainer and grommet, in that order, on the upper shock stem.

4 **Maneuver the shock** up through the lower control arm and coil spring until the upper stem extends through the hole in the wheelhouse. Extend the two mounting bolts through the two lower mounting holes, and screw them into their respective nuts on the lower control arm. Tighten the lower mounting bolts securely. In the engine compartment, attach the grommet, positioner, and nut on the shock stem and tighten the nut securely.

5 **Repeat these operations** on the other front wheel.

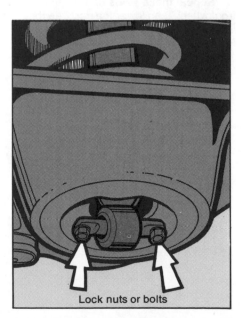

Lock nuts or bolts

General Motors, Chevrolet, 1968 on, except Chevette and Vega

1   Raise the car, then from below, grasp the shock's upper stem with an open-end wrench to keep it from turning. The stem is squared to permit this. Remove the upper stem retaining nut, and the two bolts holding the shock's lower pivot to the lower control arm. Pull the shock out through the hole in the arm.

2   Place a new retainer and rubber grommet on the upper stem of the new shock absorber, and extend the shock fully. From below, guide the shock up through the lower control arm and coil spring, so the upper stem passes through the mounting hole in the upper control arm frame.

3   Holding the upper stem with an open-end wrench to keep it from turning, install the upper grommet, retainer, and nut over the shock's upper stem. Tighten the upper retaining nut securely.

4   Insert the retainers which attach the shock's lower pivot to the lower control arm, and tighten the lower mounting retainer securely.

5   Repeat these steps on the other front wheel, then lower the car. See the illustration accompanying the directions for the Buick, 1968 on, and Cadillac, 1977 on, except Eldorado.

General Motors, Chevrolet Chevette and Vega, Pontiac Astre

1   In the engine compartment, tightly hold the shock absorber upper stem extending from the wheelhousing and remove the nut, retainer, and grommet from both sides.

2   Raise the car, then unscrew the two bolts from the lower end of the shock, remove the old shock, and discard it.

3   Place a new retainer and grommet on the upper stem of the new shock, and extend the shock and install the upper stem through the spring tower. Insert the lower bolts on both sides and tighten securely, then lower the car.

4   Install a new upper grommet, retainer, and nut on the shock stem, and, holding the stem firmly to keep it from turning, tighten the nut securely. Be sure to tighten both sides.

5   Repeat these steps on the other front wheel. See the illustration accompanying the directions for the Buick, 1968 on, and Cadillac, 1977 on, except Eldorado.

General Motors, Oldsmobile and Pontiac, 1968 on, except Toronado and Astre

1   Lift the hood and open the covers to the shock absorber upper mounting nut access holes in the wheelhousing. Using a short extension on a ratchet, remove the shock upper mounting nut, retainer, and grommet.

2   From beneath the car, remove the two mounting bolts from each shock, lower the shock through the lower control arm, and discard it.

3   Extend a new shock absorber to its full length, and place a retainer and grommet on the upper stem. Move the shock up through the lower control arm and coil spring until the upper stem engages the hole in the wheelhousing.

4   Screw the two mounting bolts into the two lower mounting holes and engage them with their respective nuts. This attaches the shock's lower end to the lower control arm. Tighten the lower mounting bolts securely.

5   Back in the engine compartment, place the grommet, retainer, and nut on the shock absorber stem, and tighten the nut securely.

6   Repeat these steps on the other front wheel. See the illustration accompanying the directions for the Buick, 1968 on, and Cadillac, 1977 on, except Eldorado.

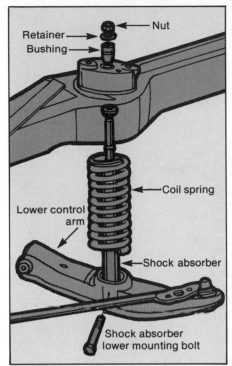

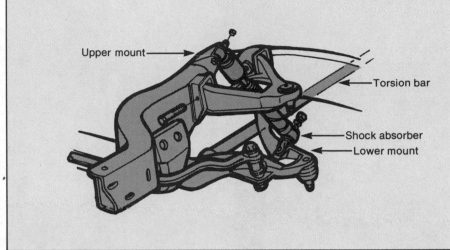

General Motors, Cadillac, 1968 on, except Eldorado

1 **Raise the hood** and remove the covers on the access holes to the shock's top mountings in the wheelhousings. Then grasp the shock's upper stem with a wrench to keep it from turning. It is squared at the top to permit this. With another wrench, remove the upper retaining nut and the retainer at the frame spring tower.

2 **Beneath the car,** remove the bolt, nut, and lock washer which attach the lower end of the shock to the lower suspension arm, and remove the shock through the bottom of the arm.

3 **Install a retainer** in the new shock's upper stem, and extend the shock fully. Insert it up into the coil spring, guiding the upper stem through the grommet in the wheelhouse.

4 **Place the lower end of the shock** into position in the lower suspension arm. Install the bolt, lock washer, and nut, then tighten the shock's lower mounting bolt securely.

5 **Install the retainer** and nut on the shock's upper stem, and, holding the stem with a wrench so it will not turn, tighten the upper nut securely.

6 **Repeat these steps** on the other front wheel.

General Motors, Cadillac, 1968 on, Eldorado

1 **With the car on the ground,** reach up and disconnect the shock absorber at its upper mount, then disconnect it at its lower mount. Compress the shock from the top down, and work the lower mount free from the mounting bolts. If necessary, insert a screwdriver under the mount's inner sleeve to detach the bolt. Guide the shock down and toward the rear of the car to get it free, moving it past front wheel drive components.

2 **Compress the new shock absorber** and guide it up through the opening in the upper control arm. Position the unit on the lower attaching stud, if necessary using a screwdriver inserted inside the mount inner sleeve to get the stud through the bushing.

3 **Pull the shock** to its full extension from the top, extending it into the frame attaching bracket. Have a helper press down on the fender to compress the suspension, which will facilitate installation.

4 **Line up the shock upper mounting holes** in the shock and frame attaching bracket. Install the upper attaching bolt and nut, and the lock washer and lower attaching nut, and tighten all securely.

5 **Repeat these steps** on the other front wheel.

General Motors, Oldsmobile Toronado, 1968–78

1 **Raise the car,** then reach up and remove the upper attaching nut with a wrench and the upper attaching bolt with a socket. Do the same to the lower attaching bolt and nut. Carefully maneuver the old shock absorber from the car and discard it.

2 **Extend the new shock** and work it up into position so the upper eye engages the holes in the mounting bracket. Insert a bolt and secure it finger tight with its nut, then do the same at the shock's lower mounting. Tighten both upper and lower mounting nuts securely.

3 **Repeat these steps** on the other front wheel. See the illustration accompanying the directions for the Cadillac, 1968–78 Eldorado.

Chrysler, 1968 on

On Chrysler cars, either one of the illustrated shocks may be used. The directions to follow indicate the models on which they most frequently appear. Before beginning work, identify the system on your particular car and proceed accordingly.

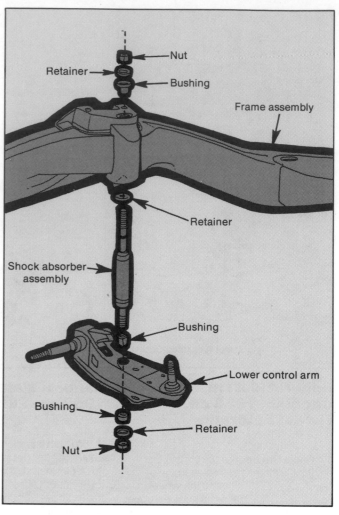

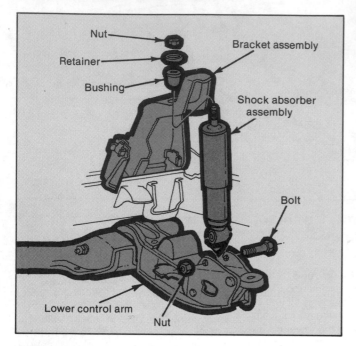

1 Raise the car, and remove the wheel-and-tire assemblies as described in Chapter 3. Reach in under the fender and loosen the upper shock absorber nut and retainer, leaving the upper stem of the shock free.

If you are working on a Valiant, Dart, Fury, Coronet, Barracuda, Challenger, Cordoba, or Charger, remove the shock's lower attachment bolt from the side of the lower control arm by grasping both bolt and nut with wrenches and exerting opposing force on the tools. This frees the eye of the shock.

If you are working on a Gran Fury, Monaco, Chrysler Imperial, Aspen, or Volare, remove the nut, retainer, and bushing from the bottom of the lower control arm. This leaves the lower stem of the shock free.

2 Push upward on the shock, compressing it. Then pull the unit out by releasing it from its top mounting bushing. If the rubber bushing in the upper mounting bracket looks worn, dried out, or cracked, pry the inner sleeve from inside the bushing with a screwdriver. Then pry out the bushing.

3 Remove the inner sleeve from a new bushing, and soak it in warm water to make it pliable. Work the bushing into the upper mounting bracket hole with a twisting motion, then tap it in place with a hammer. Carefully tap the inner steel sleeve into the bushing hole.

4 Compress the new shock, and insert its upper stem into the upper mounting bushing. Then install the upper retainer and upper nut. The retainer's concave side must be in contact with the rubber bushing. Lower the car to the ground and tighten the shock's upper nut securely.

On the Gran Fury, Monaco, Chrysler Imperial, Aspen, and Volare, install the bushing way up on the lower stem of the shock absorber. Extend the shock so the lower stem protrudes through the hole in the lower control arm, and attach the bushing, retainer, and nut. Tighten the nut securely. The car must be on the ground for this operation.

On the Valiant, Dart, Fury, Coronet, Cordoba, Charger, Barracuda, and Challenger, extend the shock and align the unit's lower eye with the holes in the lower control arm. Insert the bolt and attach the nut. Tighten the nut securely. The car must be on the ground for this operation.

Ford, models having coil springs positioned on the lower control arm: all full-size 1968 on Ford and Mercury models—Thunderbird, Lincoln, Mark III, Mark IV, Pinto, Mustang, Bobcat, and Elite, 1972 on Torino, 1972 on Montego, 1974 on Cougar

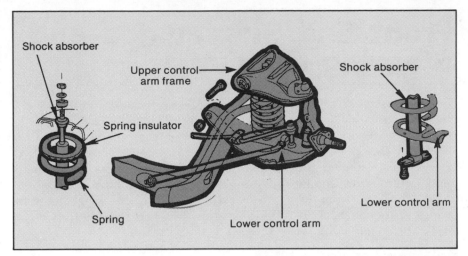

1 **Reach up and remove the upper mounting nut,** washer, and bushing. Compress the shock absorber and remove the washer and bushing from the upper stem.

2 **Raise the car,** then remove the shock absorber from its lower mounting on the lower control arm by disconnecting the two thread-cutting bolts attaching the shock bracket which extend through the eye of the shock to the control arm. Let the shock slide down through and out the coil spring and the opening in the lower control arm.

3 **Place a new bushing** and washer on the new shock absorber's upper stem, and extend the new shock. Work it up through the control arm and coil spring. Engage the shock's upper stem in the mounting hole in the upper mounting seat. Install the two thread-cutting bolts through the holes in the shock's lower bracket and into the holes in the lower control arm. Tighten the two lower bolts securely, then lower the car to the ground.

4 **Reach up and place a new bushing** and washer on the shock's top stem mounting nut securely.

5 **Repeat these steps** on the other front wheel.

Ford, models having coil springs positioned on the upper control arms: Maverick, Comet, Granada, Monarch, Falcon, Fairlane, 1968–73 Cougar, 1968–71 Montego, 1968–71 Torino

1 **Lift the hood** and remove the shock absorber's upper mounting bracket-to-spring tower attaching nut.

2 **Raise the car,** and locate and remove the two nuts holding the two shock retaining bolts to the upper control arm along with their washers and insulators.

3 **Beneath the hood again,** remove the shock absorber and bracket, which are attached to one another, from the spring tower. Disconnect the shock from the bracket. Discard the shock and keep the bracket.

4 **Position the new shock** and bracket together, tightening the shock-to-bracket bolts securely. Then install insulators on the shock's lower attaching studs.

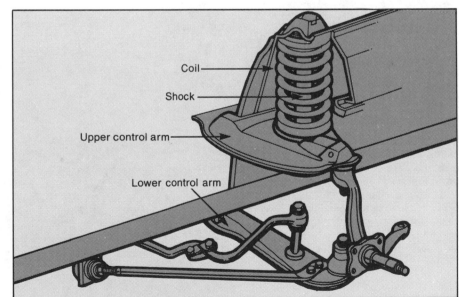

5 **Maneuver the shock** down through the spring tower, making sure the shock's lower mounting studs fall into the holes in the pivot plate. Screw on the two nuts on the shock's lower studs, tightening them securely. Install the three shock upper mounting bracket-to-spring tower attaching nuts, then tighten the nuts securely.

6 **Lower the car,** and repeat the operation on the other front wheel.

Front End Suspension and Steering Checks

For the various jobs which follow, the front of your car should be jacked up and supported by safety stands. In this position, the front wheels are suspended and the ball joints, control arms, and tie-rods are under tension from the front springs or torsion bars. In order to check these parts for wear there must be no tension on them. There are special procedures to relieve the tension on these parts so you may check for wear on either of the two different types of front end suspension. You should have a helper assist you when checking the front suspension and steering for wear.

Relieving tension on the front suspension

Cars with coil springs mounted between the frame and the lower control arm and cars equipped with torsion bars. Place a floor jack or single piston hydraulic floor jack under the lower control arm as close to the ball joint as possible. Raise the arm until the frame is about to lift off the safety stand, then stop. Now check the front suspension for wear.

MacPherson struts

These are frequently used on foreign cars but only recently have begun to replace standard shock absorbers on American models. This type of suspension system can be identified by looking for a very heavy and thick tube-shaped strut attached to the wheel assembly at the base and slanting upward away from the wheel. A coil spring is visible around the outside of the strut at the top, and an A-shaped arm runs horizontally from the base of the strut so its two legs attach to the frame.

The shock absorber is inside the tubular strut. You cannot replace it without taking part of the suspension system apart. That job should be left to someone who has professional experience with this new type of suspension.

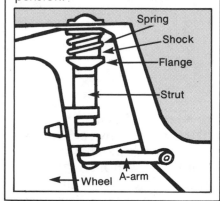

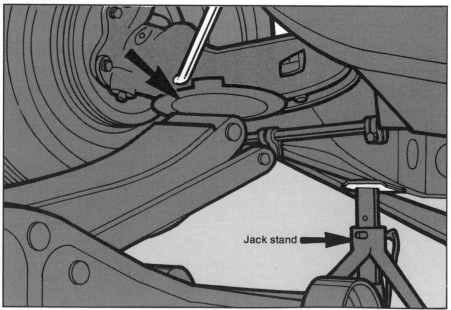

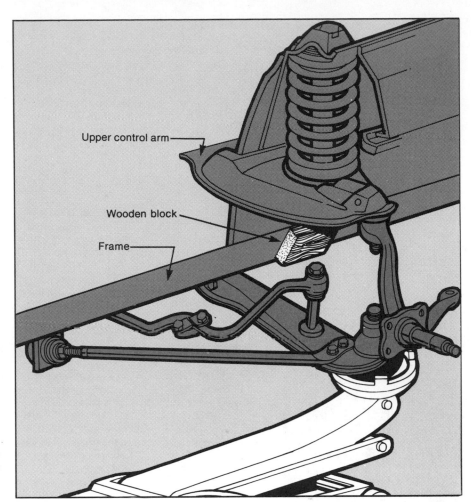

Upper control arm

Wooden block

Frame

Cars with coil springs mounted between the frame and the upper control arm. Jack up the lower control arm as described previously. Place a block of wood, a 2 x 4 will do, between the upper control arm and the frame. Slowly release the jack from the lower control arm, making sure neither the block of wood nor the upper control arm moves. Now the front suspension is ready for inspection. *Caution: Remember to remove the block of wood after you have completed your inspection of the front end.*

Checking the upper and lower control arm bushings for wear

Forward Backward

1 **With the front end jacked up** and supported under the lower control arm as described previously, have a helper sit in the car and firmly apply the foot brake. This will lock the front wheels. With both hands, grasp one front tire at its front and rear. Now, attempt to rotate it forward and backward. You must apply vigorous force for this operation. While attempting to rotate the tire, watch the upper and lower control arms for excessive side-to-side movement.

2 **Repeat these steps** on the other front wheel. If excessive wear is present, you should take your car to a qualified mechanic who has the special tools, equipment, and training to replace the control arm bushings.

ECONOTIP

#15

Weight—an enemy of good mileage

The next time you open your trunk, see how much excess weight you are carrying. That 100-pound sack of fertilizer you just never got around to removing can cost you two-tenths of a mile per gallon. If you carry as much as 500 pounds of unnecessary weight, the penalty is one mile per gallon. So if you're not using the excess baggage regularly, clean out the trunk and watch your mileage improve.

Checking the upper ball joint for wear

1 **With the front end jacked up** and supported under the lower control arm as described previously, grasp the bottom of one front tire with your left hand. With your right hand grasp the top, then pull out at the bottom while simultaneously pushing in at the top. Have your helper watch the play in the upper ball joint.

2 **Check the manufacturer's** specifications for allowable ball joint play and wear. Repeat the procedure on the other front wheel. If there is excessive wear, you should take your car to a qualified mechanic or front end specialist who will replace the defective ball joint, since this requires special tools and skills.

Checking the lower ball joint for wear

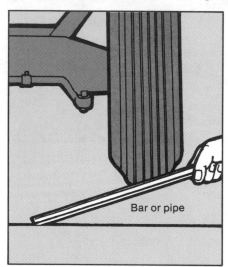

Bar or pipe

1 **With the front end jacked up** and supported under the lower control arm as described previously, place a bar or pipe directly under the center of the tire. Wedge it against the ground, and lift it. Have a helper look at the lower ball joint for wear. You may have to pick up and release the bar several times to get a good visual check.

2 **Check the manufacturer's specifications** for allowable play and wear for your car. Repeat the operation on the other front wheel. If you find the ball joint has excessive play and wear, take your car to a qualified mechanic or front end specialist for repairs. He has the tools and skills to do the job.

Checking for wear in the steering linkage

Side-to-side

1 **Refer to Chapter 1** for a description of the steering linkage components. With the front end jacked up and supported under the lower control arm as described previously, grasp one tire at the front and rear as you did when you checked the upper control arm. Now, vigorously shake the tire from right to left. Have your helper check all parts of the steering linkage for excessive wear.

2 **Repeat the procedure** on the opposite front tire. Check the tie-rod ends, the intermediate arm (known as the center link), and the idler arm. There should be no play or sign of wear in any of these parts. The idler arm must not move up and down, although it may move horizontally with the other linkages.

Pro Shop
Ball joint removal

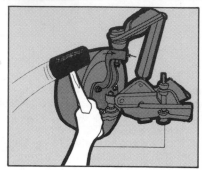

Most mechanics use a ball joint fork to remove the ball joints from the front suspension. There is a way to loosen or break ball joints from the steering knuckle without the special tool.

Jack up the car and support it properly by the body, not by the frame. This will put tension on the ball joint. Remove the cotter pin and back off the attaching nut about three-quarters of the way. Do **not** remove the nut completely. Use a five-pound hammer and give both sides of the steering knuckle a good shot. The ball joint should jar loose and break out of the steering knuckle.

Now put a jack stand under the lower control arm and release the weight off the suspension components. Since there is no load on the attaching nut, its removal is now easy and safe. Be sure all tension is released from the control arm before attempting to remove the attaching nut.

Before installing the new ball joint, check the fit of the tapered stud in the hole. If the hole is worn, the part must be replaced.

Replacing Steering Linkage Parts

Replacing tie-rod ends

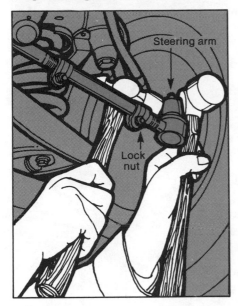

1 **Jack up and support** the front of the car. Locate the tie-rod end and count the number of threads exposed between it and the sleeve. Record this number for correct reinstallation of the new tie-rod end. Spray the sleeve lock nut and bolt, the tie-rod threads, and the tie-rod castellated lock nut with penetrating oil. Loosen the tie-rod sleeve lock nut, remove the cotter pin from the castellated nut, and loosen the nut four to five turns but do not remove it yet. Hold a heavy ball peen hammer against the back side of the steering arm, directly behind the area where the tie-rod end fits into the arm. With a second ball peen hammer, strike the steering arm with a sharp, heavy blow. This should release the tie-rod end from it. Several attempts may be required to free the tie-rod end. When free, remove the castellated nut, and unscrew the tie-rod end from the sleeve.

2 **Install the new tie-rod end** into the sleeve, screwing the end in until only the original number of counted threads remain exposed. Insert the tie-rod end into the steering arm, then install the castellated nut and torque to specifications. Put in the new cotter pin. If the cotter pin access hole in the tie-rod end does not line up, tighten the nut just until the hole is exposed. Tighten the tie-rod end sleeve lock nut to specifications.

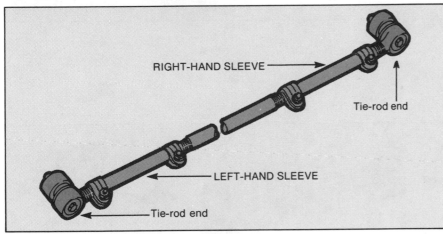

3 **Repeat the operation** on any other worn tie-rod ends. When your work is finished, you must have your front wheels checked for alignment, especially for toe-in. This must be done by an auto mechanic or a front end specialist with wheel alignment equipment. *Caution: Tie-rod ends have either left-hand or right-hand threads.*

Replacing front sway bar links

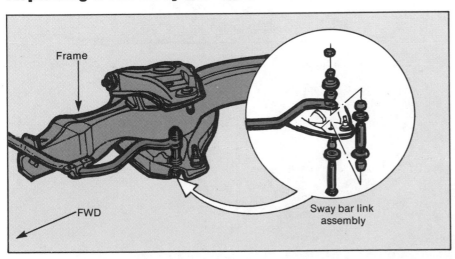

1 **Jack up and support** the front of your car. Support the lower control arm as described in the beginning of this chapter. Spray the sway bar link assembly nut with penetrating oil, then, with the correct size box wrenches, remove the link assembly. Some assemblies may have a lock nut or pal lock nut.

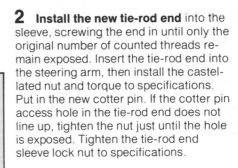

2 **Install the new sway bar link assembly** using the other side of the car as a guide for reinstallation. Torque the sway bar link nut to specifications.

3 **Repeat these steps** on the other side of the front end.

Replacing the center or drag link

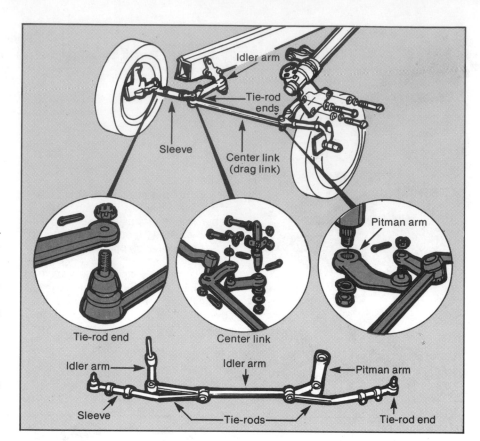

1 Jack up and support the front of your car. Locate the center link, and remove the cotter pins from all the castellated nuts, the tie-rod ends, the idler arm, and the Pitman arm, which are attached to the center link. Loosen all the castellated nuts, then using two ball peen hammers, loosen the ball studs as described previously in the discussion on replacing tie-rod ends. Remove the castellated nuts and the center link.

2 Install the new center link and the castellated nuts, and torque the nuts to specifications. Remember to have your front wheels checked for alignment.

Replacing the idler arm

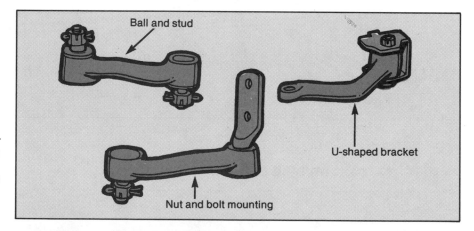

1 Jack up and support the front of your car. Locate the idler arm, which is on the right-hand side of the car attached to the frame. Remove the tie-rod type ball stud from the center link as described in the discussion in this chapter on replacing tie-rod ends. There are several different ways in which the idler arm is attached to the frame. Some cars use a ball and stud. Other mountings are in a U-shaped bracket, and some are mounted with nuts and bolts. Remove the idler arm as a complete unit.

2 Install the new idler arm on the frame, then torque the stud nut to specifications. If the idler arm is attached to the frame with bolts, these should be torqued to the manufacturer's specifications. Insert the cotter pin as described in the discussion on replacing tie-rod ends. *Caution: If your car is equipped with the type of idler arm which has a bushing mounted in both the center link and the frame support, do not attempt to replace it. This type must be replaced by a qualified mechanic or front end specialist.*

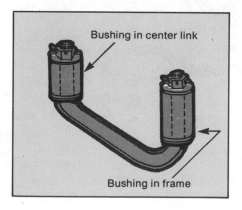

Replacing Power Steering Parts

Replacing hoses on the integral-type power steering system

The integral-type power steering system has two hoses connected between the pump and the steering gear, the pressure hose, which is usually thicker and has metal tubes at each end, and the return hose.

1 **Open the hood** and locate the power steering pump, then place a small drain pan directly under it, where the hose connects.

2 **With the proper size flare nut wrench,** loosen and remove the pressure hose fitting from the pump. At this point, fluid will drain out of the pump and into the drain pan. Using the correct size flare nut wrench, remove the other end of the pressure hose from the steering gear assembly. *Caution: Wipe up any spilled power steering fluid.*

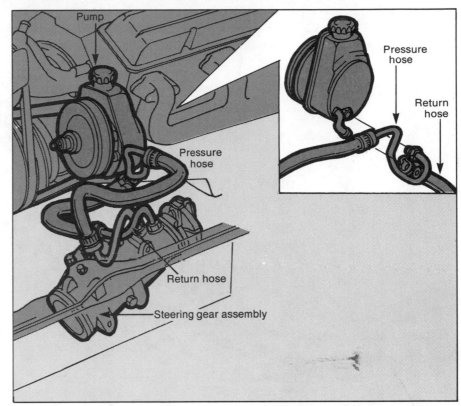

Pump

Pressure hose

Pressure hose

Return hose

Return hose

Steering gear assembly

3 **Install the new pressure hose,** starting the fittings by hand and tightening them securely. *Caution: Be sure the hose does not come into contact with any engine, frame, or moving parts. The hose must be installed in its original position.* Replace the return hose by removing the fitting at the pump side.

4 **Remove the fitting** at the steering gear assembly with the correct size flare nut wrench, and tighten the new return hose connections securely. *Caution: Again be sure the hose is in its original position and not in contact with any engine, frame, or moving parts. Wipe up any spilled power steering fluid.*

5 **Remove the power steering pump cover** and fill the pump with the manufacturer's recommended fluid, then replace the cover. Start the engine and turn the steering wheel to a full left-hand turn and then a full right-hand turn. Return the steering wheel to the straight-ahead position, and switch off the engine. Check and refill the fluid level in the power steering pump, then replace the cover. Start the engine and repeat the above turning operation. This will bleed air from the system. When the engine has reached operating temperature, switch it off and recheck the fluid level. Check all connections for leaks.

Basic steering systems

The two basic steering systems, Pitman and rack-and-pinion, can both be power-assisted. The fluid level should be checked every few weeks. The power system pump has a dipstick permanently attached to the underside of the cap. The pump is usually mounted on the driver's side of the engine compartment near the radiator and is driven by a V-belt. Check the type of fluid for your car in your owner's manual.

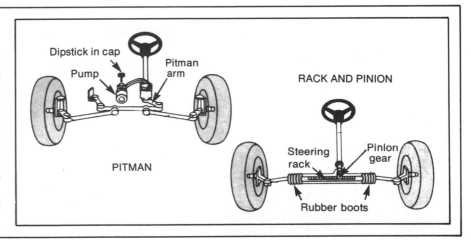

Dipstick in cap

Pump

Pitman arm

RACK AND PINION

Steering rack

Pinion gear

PITMAN

Rubber boots

Replacing hoses on the linkage-type power steering system

In contrast to the integral-type system, on the linkage-type power steering system it may be necessary to replace four hoses. Two hoses, one pressure and one return, are connected between the power steering pump and the valve assembly. The other two hoses are connected between the valve assembly and the booster cylinder, which is attached to the center link and the frame.

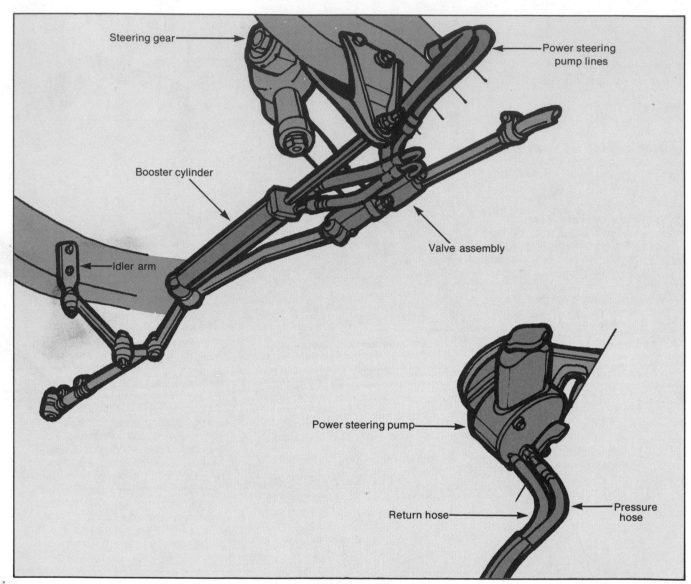

Steering gear

Power steering pump lines

Booster cylinder

Idler arm

Valve assembly

Power steering pump

Return hose

Pressure hose

1 **Jack up and support** the front end of the car, then open the hood and locate the power steering pump. Place a small drain pan directly under the valve assembly where the hoses are connected. With the correct size flare nut wrench, loosen and remove the pressure hose fitting. Allow the fluid from the hose to drain into the pan. Now, remove the other end of the pressure hose from the pump. Note the routing of the hose for correct reinstallation.

2 **Install the new pressure hose** at the valve assembly, starting the fitting by hand and tightening it securely. Route the pressure hose correctly to the pump, and install the hose fitting by hand, tightening it securely. Repeat the above operation for replacing the return hose from the pump to the valve assembly.

3 **Before you attempt** to remove the two hoses connecting the valve assembly and the booster cylinder, you must code both to insure correct reinstallation. If possible, replace one hose at a time. *Caution: Incorrect installation of these two hoses will cause the steering wheel to turn sharply, by itself, to the right or left, when the engine is started.* With the correct size flare nut wrench, remove and replace the hoses, then tighten the fittings securely. To fill the pump and bleed the system, follow the procedure described previously for the integral-type system. Lower the car to the ground.

Replacing the power steering pump

There are many different methods for mounting the power steering pump on the engine. Before you attempt to remove and replace the pump, you should code the bolts, nuts, brackets, and hoses for correct reinstallation.

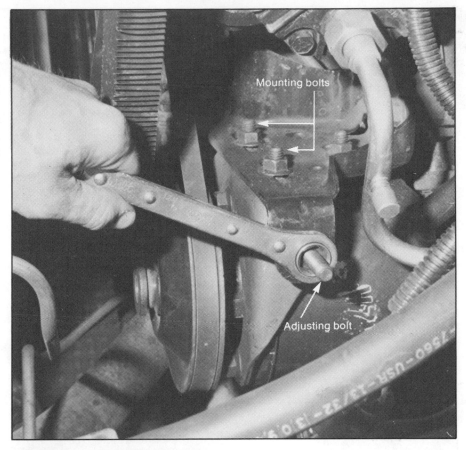

1 **Open the hood** and disconnect the battery ground cable. Locate the power steering pump, and loosen the adjusting nuts or bolts and the nuts or bolts holding it in place. Push the pump body toward the engine to free the belt from the pulley.

2 **Follow the procedure** described previously and remove the hoses from the pump, then remove all the nuts, bolts, and brackets holding down the power steering pump mounting. Remove the pump.

3 **Loosely install** the replacement pump with its nuts or bolts and all brackets. Install the fan belt and adjust the tension as described in Chapter 3. Tighten all the nuts or bolts securely, install the two hoses attached to the pump, and reconnect the battery ground cable. Fill and bleed the system as described in this chapter.

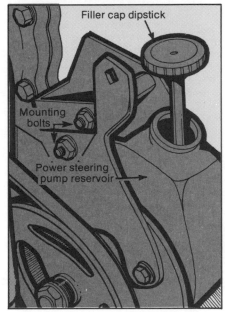

In this chapter you have learned how to repair or replace certain components of the car's front suspension and steering system. The power steering system, like the brake system, is important for safety. Do not rush the repair work. Take your time, keep the work area clean, be sure of correct hose routing, and double-check your finished work.

The following Troubleshooting flow chart: front suspension and Steering, will help you to diagnose many problems you may have with this system in your car.

Troubleshooting flow chart: front end suspension and steering

Symptom	Probable cause	Remedy
A. Noise from front end.	1. Loose or worn front wheel bearings. 2. Worn shock absorbers. 3. Loose steering gear. 4. Worn control arm bushings. 5. Worn strut bushings.	1. Adjust, if possible, or replace. 2. Replace. 3. Tighten or replace worn parts. 4. Replace worn parts. 5. Replace worn parts.
B. Too much steering play.	6. Loose or worn front wheel bearings. 7. Loose or worn steering shaft coupling. 8. Loose steering gear-to-chassis mounting. 9. Worn tie-rod ends. 10. Worn idler arm. 11. Incorrect steering gear adjustment.	6. Adjust, if possible, or replace. 7. Tighten or replace worn parts. 8. Tighten or replace worn parts. 9. Replace. 10. Replace. 11. Adjust to specifications.
C. Front wheel shimmy.	12. Loose or worn front wheel bearings. 13. Wheels or tires out of balance. 14. Tires out of round or uneven tire wear. 15. Worn tie-rod ends. 16. Worn strut bushings. 17. Incorrect front wheel alignment, particularly caster. 18. Worn shock absorbers.	12. Adjust, if possible, or replace. 13. Balance wheels and tires. 14. Replace worn tires. Determine cause of uneven wear and correct front end alignment. 15. Replace. 16. Replace. 17. Align front end. 18. Replace.
D. Instability or wander.	19. Low or uneven tire pressure. 20. Loose wheel bearings. 21. Broken or weak rear spring. 22. Bad shock absorber. 23. Worn idler arm. 24. Improper steering gear adjustment. 25. Loose or worn strut bushings. 26. Incorrect front wheel alignment.	19. Inflate tires to proper pressure. 20. Adjust. 21. Replace. 22. Replace. 23. Replace. 24. Adjust to specification. 25. Replace. 26. Align front end.
E. Hard steering.	27. Low or uneven tire pressure. 28. Loose, worn, or glazed power steering drive belt. 29. Low power steering fluid level. 30. Inoperative power steering system. 31. Ball joints require lubrication. 32. Steering gear low on lubricant. 33. Steering gear not adjusted properly. 34. Incorrect front wheel alignment.	27. Inflate tires to proper pressure. 28. Adjust or replace. 29. Add fluid. 30. Find faulty component and correct. 31. Lubricate. 32. Add lubricant. 33. Adjust steering gear to specification. 34. Align front end.
F. Car pulls to one side when not braking.	35. Low or uneven tire pressure. 36. Broken or weak rear spring. 37. Power steering control valve not adjusted properly. 38. Worn strut bushings. 39. Incorrect front wheel alignment, particularly camber.	35. Inflate tires to proper pressure. 36. Replace. 37. Adjust to specification. 38. Replace worn parts. 39. Align front end.

13

REAR END AND AXLES

The rear end suspension allows the rear wheels to move up and over bumps and down and out of road depressions. The rear axle powers the rear wheels, unless, of course, the car has front wheel drive. The rear end consists of a differential assembly, a differential housing, two axles and axle housings, two coil or leaf springs, control arms, a sway bar, and shock absorbers. There are two general types of rear suspension systems used on cars today, coil spring and leaf spring.

Coil springs are made from a spring steel rod heated and shaped into a coil. This rod is then tempered to the proper tension for flexibility and strength. On cars equipped with coil springs, other components—control arms and bushings, a sway bar, a track bar, and shock absorbers—hold the rear end housing in place. The control arms are located between the rear axle housing and the front of the car. They permit upward and downward movement of the rear axle housing and prevent side or backward and/or forward movement. The control arm bushings prevent metal-to-metal contact between the arm and the frame and the rear axle housing. They act as a bearing surface and also absorb road shock.

The sway bar, also known as the track or stabilizer bar, is connected on one end to the right or left side of the rear axle housing, and on the other to the frame. This bar keeps the body of the car from swaying from side-to-side.

Rear leaf springs may be multi- or single-leaf. Multi-leaf springs are composed of a number of graduated lengths of flat spring steel plates placed one on top of the other and secured with a center bolt. Some are equipped with side clips to prevent the individual leaves from shifting. Spring manufacturers may use inserts made of various materials, such as rubber pads, to allow for slippage between the leaves and to act as a lubricant.

The longest leaf, the main leaf, is rolled on both ends to form spring eyes through which the spring is mounted on the frame. The front end eye of the spring is attached to the frame with bushings and a bolt assembly. The rear end eye is attached with a shackle assembly allowing the spring to flex and change length when the rear wheels move up and down. The center of the spring is mounted on the rear axle housing with two U bolts.

The shock absorbers are mounted to the rear axle housing on one end and to the frame on the other. They restrain spring oscillation. Full details on how shock absorbers work were given in the previous chapter. The two rear axles are splined into the differential assembly and held in place with either a flange cap bolted to the outside ends of the axle housing, where the brake backing plate is also mounted, or with a C-type axle lock inside the differential assembly. The rear axle supports the weight of the rear of the car, through the rear axle bearing, and delivers turning power to the rear wheels. The differential assembly was described in Chapter 1.

In this chapter you will learn how to remove and replace the rear shock absorbers, the rear coil springs, the rear axles and bearings, and the rear axle seals.

CONTENTS

Tools and equipment:

Floor jack.
Safety stands.
Fender covers.
⅜" and ½" drive socket set.
Combination wrenches.
Wire brush.
Hammer.
Droplight or flashlight.
Torque wrench.
Slide hammer puller.
Axle seal installing tool.
Drain pan.
Scraper.
Hand pump.
Wipers.
Goggles.
Rubber mallet.
Seal puller.
Creeper.

Parts you may need:

Spray can of penetrating oil.
Shock absorbers.
Lube plate lubricant.
Rear end gears.
New rear axle housing cover
   gasket.
Wheel bearing grease.
Gasket cement.

Caution: Rear shock absorbers lie near the brake lines. Be very careful not to strike the lines with tools during reinstallation or they may be damaged.

Collapsed springs

Coil springs are mounted between the frame and the axle housing. Rubber insulators between a spring and its contact point prevent metal-to-metal contact. Signs of rubbing between individual coils indicate the coils have made contact, and suggest a collapsed spring. Another indication of a weak or collapsed coil spring is a sagging, tail-dragging ride. Still another is bottoming, a loud, heavy, thumping sound when going over bumps or road dips with a normal passenger load.

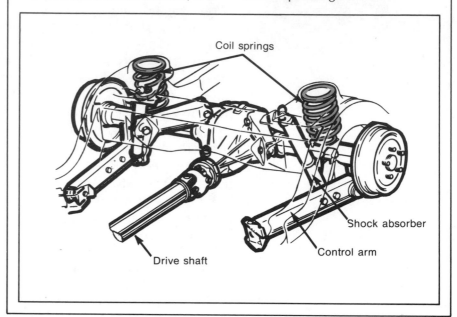

Single-leaf and double-leaf springs

The single-leaf spring is a one-piece semielliptical spring which is long and wide. It is used on lighter cars and is mounted and functions in the same way as the multi-leaf spring.

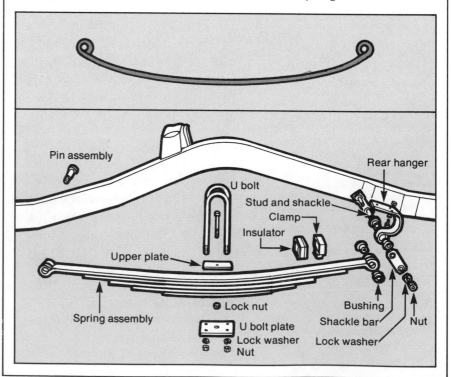

Replacing Rear Shock Absorbers

The rear of your car must be jacked up and supported by the rear axle housing for this job. To make it easier to replace the rear shock absorbers, remove the rear tire-and-wheel assembly first. Although this is not always necessary, in many cases the shocks will be more accessible. Do not remove the brake drum. Find instructions for your make and model car in the following pages.

American Motors, 1968 on

1 **Remove the lower mounting nut,** washer, and grommet. Take off the two bolts holding the upper shock absorber, and remove the shock and bracket. Take out the upper mounting nut and grommet holding the upper bracket to the shock absorber. Discard the shock and hardware, but keep the bracket.

2 **Place a new retainer and grommet** on the new shock absorber's stem, then position the upper mounting bracket on it. Install the grommet, retainer, and nut, and tighten the nut to eight foot pounds. Locate the shock absorber so the upper mounting bracket lines up with the mounting holes. Compress the shock, and insert the bolts through the upper mounting bracket holes and tighten them securely.

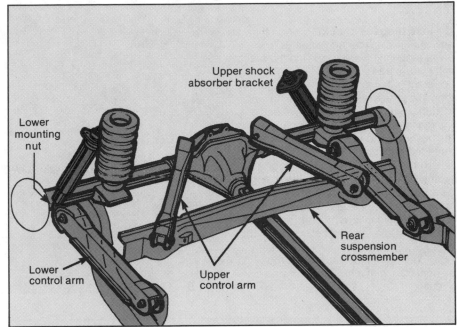

On cars with leaf springs—Hornet, Gremlin, Rambler—slide a new retainer and grommet onto the lower mounting stem. Extend the new shock so this stem extends through the hole in the spring plate. Install the grommet, retainer, and nut, and tighten the lower mounting nut securely.

On cars with coil springs—Matador, Ambassador—extend the new shock absorber after the upper mounting bracket has been attached so the lower cylinder lines up with the axle tube. Attach the bolts and retainers, and tighten the lower mounting bolts securely.

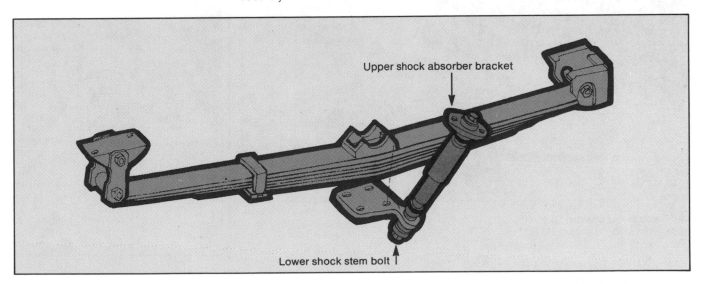

3 **Repeat these steps** on the other rear shock absorber. Lower the car and test the shock absorber as described in Chapter 12.

General Motors, Buick, 1968 on

1 Removing the shock. Get under the car and disconnect the single bolt, lock washer, and nut from the lower end of the shock. Now, working through the wheelhousing, reach in behind the brake drum and disconnect the two bolts, washers, and nuts from the shock's upper mounting.

2 Installing the shock. Position the new shock absorber so the holes in the unit's mounting plate align with the holes in the car's frame bracket. Attach the upper mounting hardware finger tight, then align the lower shock bushing with the hole in the bracket that is welded to the rear axle tube. Insert the bolt through the bushing, and place a washer on the threaded end. Slide the bolt through the hole in the bracket, then insert a lock washer and tighten the nut with your fingers. Torque the upper mounting nut securely. The shock's stud must not be allowed to rotate when the bolts are being tightened. Hold it with a box or open-end wrench. Tighten the lower nut securely. Again keep the shock stud from rotating by holding it with a box or open-end wrench.

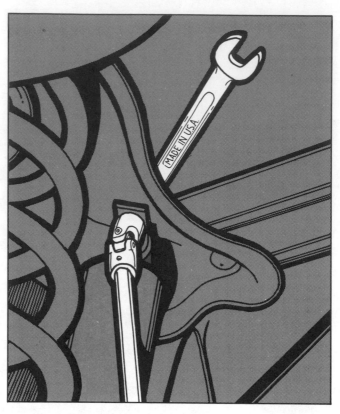

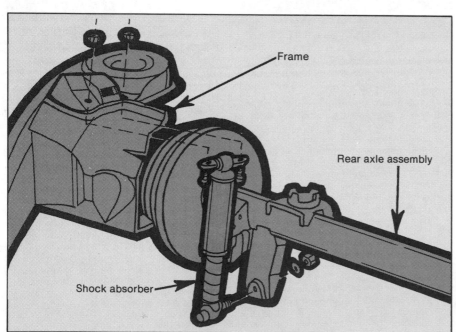

Frame

Rear axle assembly

Shock absorber

3 Repeat the operation on the other side, then lower the car and test the shock absorber action as described in Chapter 12.

Pro Shop

Soaking bolts or nuts

We spray the shock absorber mounting bolts or nuts liberally with penetrating oil, then let the oil soak in and lubricate the rusted threads.

General Motors, Cadillac, 1968 on, all models except Eldorado and Seville

1 **Take a 12-point,** ½-inch box-end wrench and bend it to a 45° angle one-inch back from the center of the box-end diameter. With this wrench, grasp the shock absorber mounting nuts at the rear frame kickup. Remove the upper retaining bolts and nuts, and unbolt the shock at its lower mounting, holding the stem next to the grommet so it does not turn. Remove the retaining nut, then take the shock off its mounts. Work the upper mounting of the new shock absorber onto the frame kickup.

2 **Install the upper retaining nuts** and bolts. Using the homemade wrench described previously, grasp the upper mounting nuts and tighten the bolts to 12 foot pounds. Guide the shock's lower stud into its mounting bracket, and install the retaining nut. Tighten the nut securely.

3 **Repeat these steps** on the other side, then lower the car and test the shock absorbers as described in Chapter 12. See the illustrations for the Buick, 1968 on.

General Motors, Cadillac, 1968 on, Eldorado, and Seville

If you have one of these models, you should leave the testing and installation of the rear shock absorbers to a qualified Cadillac service technician. The rear shock absorbers in the Eldorado are not standard units. The 1968–70 models had two shocks for each rear wheel—one vertical and one horizontal. Models since 1971 and Seville have automatic level control systems.

General Motors, Chevrolet, 1968 on, Monte Carlo, and Chevelle

1 **Reach up and disconnect** the upper shock absorber mounting by removing the two retaining bolts. If the car is a station wagon, reach in between the tire and the frame and put a wrench on the nuts located between them. Reaching with an extension, detach the upper mounting bolts as you turn the bolts and the nuts in opposing directions. Remove the old shock absorber.

2 **Work the new shock absorber** into position and install the two upper mounting bolts finger tight. Position the lower attaching stud in the axle bracket and attach the lock washer and nut with your fingers. Tighten the upper attaching bolts securely. Hold the lower attaching stud with a wrench and tighten the nut securely.

3 **Repeat these steps** on the other side, then lower the car and test the shock absorbers as described in Chapter 12. See the illustrations for the Buick, 1968 on.

General Motors, Chevrolet Chevette, Vega, and Pontiac Astre

1 **Reach up and unscrew** the two upper attaching bolts, then remove the attaching bolt from the shock's lower end. Take out the shock and discard it.

2 **Extend the new shock** and position its lower end in the lower bracket, and its upper end so the two holes in its eye bracket line up with the two holes in the upper mounting bracket. Install the upper retaining bolts and tighten them securely. Attach the lower shock retaining bolt and nut and tighten securely.

3 **Repeat the operation** on the other side, then lower the car and test the shock absorbers as described in Chapter 12. See the illustrations for the Buick, 1968 on.

General Motors, Pontiac, Oldsmobile, 1968 on, all models except Firebird, Ventura, and Safari wagons

1 **Disconnect the lock washer** and nut from the shock absorber's stud. Working through the wheelhousing, reach in behind the brake drum and disconnect the two bolts, washers, and nuts from the shock's upper mounting.

2 **Position the new shock** so the holes in its mounting bracket align with the holes in the frame. Attach the upper mounting hardware finger tight, then set the shock's lower end so the holes line up with the holes in the mounting bracket. Tighten the mounting nuts securely.

3 **Repeat the operation** on the other side, then lower the car and test the shock absorbers as described in Chapter 12. See the illustrations for the Buick, 1968 on.

General Motors, Pontiac Firebird, Ventura, and Safari wagons

1 **Remove the shock's single lower mounting bolt** from its eye, loosening the shock from its lower anchor plate. Reach up and withdraw the two bolts holding the shock to the upper mounting bracket, then remove the old shock and discard it.

2 **Extend the new shock absorber** and maneuver it into position, then loosely install the two upper attaching bolts. Square the shock's eye with the mounting holes in the lower anchor plate and install the bolt and nut. The nut must be to the rear. Tighten the lower mounting nut securely, then reach up and tighten the upper bolt securely.

3 **Repeat these steps** on the other side, then lower the car. Test the shock absorbers as described in Chapter 12.

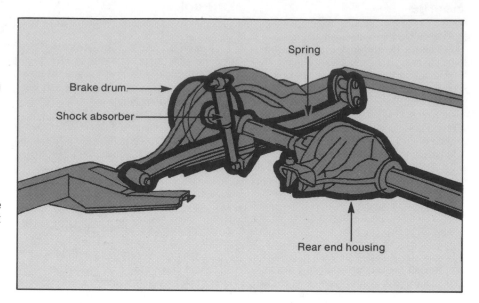

Spring

Brake drum

Shock absorber

Rear end housing

General Motors, Chevrolet Nova, 1968 on

1 **Remove the lower mounting bolt** from the shock absorber eye, and withdraw the two bolts from the upper mounting bracket, then remove the shock absorber.

2 **Extend the new shock** and position it in place. Install the two upper attaching bolts finger tight. Insert the shock eye into the lower mounting bracket and install the bolt and nut. *Caution: The lower mounting bolt must be to the rear.* Tighten the lower mounting bracket nut and the two upper mounting bolts securely.

3 **Repeat these steps** on the other side, then lower the car, and test the shock absorbers as described in Chapter 12.

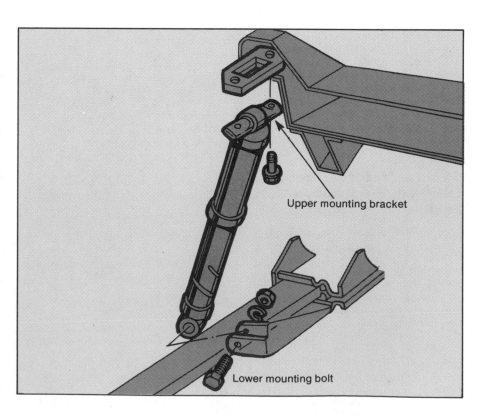

Upper mounting bracket

Lower mounting bolt

General Motors, Chevrolet Camaro, 1968 on

1 **Remove the shock absorber's lower nut,** retainer, and grommet, so the unit can be loosened from its position on the bracket welded to the leaf spring. Reach up and take out the two upper attaching bolts from the bracket attached to the frame.

2 **Insert a new retainer** and grommet on the new shock's lower stem. Extend the shock absorber so the holes in the unit's mounting bracket, which is inserted through the upper eye, are aligned with the holes in the upper mounting bracket on the frame. Screw the upper retaining bolts finger tight. Place the lower stem into the mounting hole in the bracket welded to the spring. Tighten the upper and lower mounting bolts securely.

3 **Repeat these steps** on the other side, then lower the car and test the shocks as described in Chapter 12.

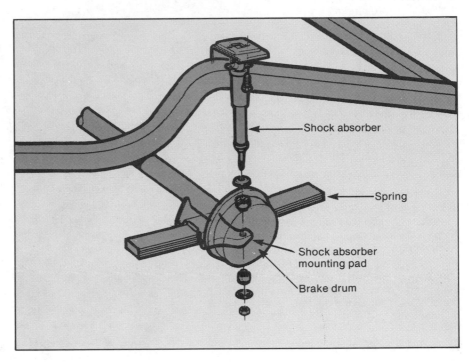

Shock absorber

Spring

Shock absorber mounting pad

Brake drum

General Motors, Chevrolet Corvette, 1968 on

1 **Hold the upper mounting stud** with a wrench while disconnecting the upper mounting bolt. When it is loose, slip the bolt out of the frame bracket. Remove the shock absorber's lower mounting nut and lock washer, then slide the shock upper eye out of the frame bracket and pull the lower eye and grommets off the strut rod mounting shaft.

2 **Install the new shock absorber** by sliding the upper mounting eye into the frame mounting bracket. Attach the bolt, lock washer, and nut finger tight. Place a grommet on the strut rod mounting shaft, and install the shock's lower eye on the shaft. Attach the inboard grommet, washer, and nut on the shaft. *Caution: Install the washer with the curve pointing inward, away from the grommet.* Tighten the upper mounting bolt and the lower mounting nut securely.

3 **Repeat these steps** on the other side, then lower the car and test the shock absorbers as described in Chapter 12.

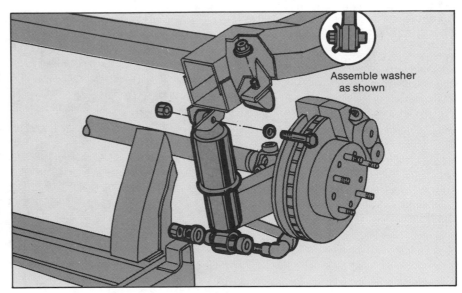

Assemble washer as shown

Chrysler

1 **Remove the nut** and retainer holding the shock absorber's lower mounting to the spring plate mounting stud, and slide the lower end of the shock from the stud.

If you have a Dart or Valiant, loosen and remove the nut retainer from the upper shock mounting stud, then slide the shock off it. Slip a new retainer on the stud, and position the shock's upper mounting on the stud, followed by another retainer and nut. Tighten the nut finger tight.

With all other models, remove the upper mounting bolt and nut from the frame crossmember and take out the shock absorber. The mounting nut on the Barracuda and Challenger is reached from inside the luggage compartment. Align the shock upper eye with the mounting hole in the frame crossmember and slip on the bolt, then attach the nut and tighten it finger tight.

2 **Slip a new retainer** on the stud of the lower shock absorber mounting plate, extend the shock, and slip the lower eye onto the stud. Insert the retainer and nut, tightening the nut finger tight. Tighten the upper and lower nuts securely.

3 **Repeat these steps** on the other side, then remove the supports and lower the car to the ground. Now test the shock absorbers as described in Chapter 12.

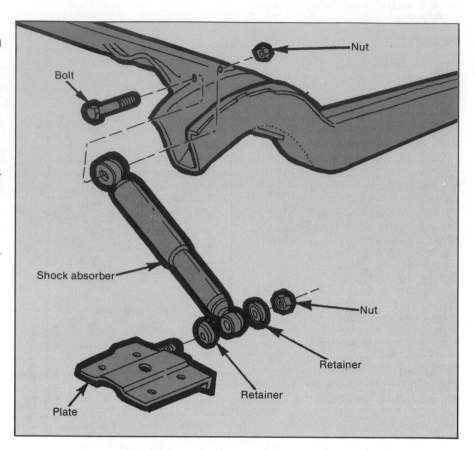

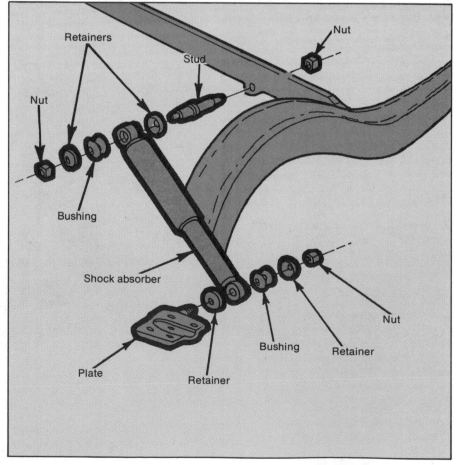

Ford: Maverick, Comet, Granada, Monarch, Falcon, 1968–70 Fairlane, 1968–73 Cougar, 1968–71 Montego, and 1968–71 Torino

1 Remove the nut, washer, and grommet from the lower shock absorber stem where it intercepts the plate welded to the spring. Compress the shock and remove the grommet and washer from the stem. Take off the nut from the shock's upper mounting bolt, and then remove the shock. *Caution: The upper mounting nut for all models except 1971–73 Comets, Mavericks, and convertibles is reached from inside the luggage compartment. The upper mounting nut for 1971–73 Comets and Mavericks is reached from below. The upper mounting nut for convertibles is reached by removing the rear seat and opening the access covers.*

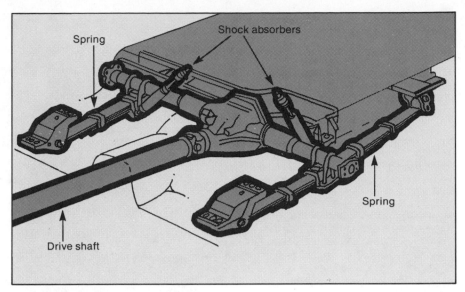

2 Insert the stud in the upper eye of the new shock through the hole in the mounting bracket and attach the nut finger tight. Work the shock into the lower end of the plate which is welded to the spring. Attach the grommet, washer, and nut to the lower stem. Tighten the nut securely, then tighten the shock's upper mounting nut securely.

3 Repeat these steps on the other side, then lower the car. Test the shock absorbers as described in Chapter 12.

After jacking up the rear of your car and supporting the rear axle housing on jack stands, rock the car gently from side to side to make sure that it cannot be knocked off the stands should someone lean against the car or climb into it. Only after this safety check should you begin working on the rear shock absorbers.

Ford Pinto and Bobcat station wagons

1 Remove the nut, washer, and bushing from the shock absorber's lower stem. Compress the shock so the stem is pulled from its seat in the spring plate, then remove the washer and bushing from the stem. Reach up and detach the two nuts holding the shock's upper end to the studs on the crossmember, and remove the shock.

2 Place a washer and bushing on the new shock absorber's lower stem, then install the new shock so the holes in its upper mounting brace, which extends through the eye, intercept the studs protruding from the crossmember. Attach the two upper nuts and tighten them securely. Push the shock's lower stem through the spring plate, then install the bushing, washer, and nut. Tighten the nut securely.

3 Repeat these steps on the other side, then lower the car and test the shock absorbers as described in Chapter 12. See the illustrations for the Ford models described previously.

Ford Mustang, Pinto, and Bobcat sedans

1 **Disconnect the bolt** and nut from the shock absorber's lower end at the point where it connects to the spring plate. Reach up and remove the three bolts holding the shock's mounting bracket to the frame, then compress the shock and remove the unit. Unscrew the shock from the mounting bracket and discard the shock, retaining the bracket.

2 **Insert a washer and bushing** on the shock's upper stem and connect the stem through the mounting bracket. Secure the shock with the bushing, washer, and nut, tightening the nut to 14 to 26 foot pounds. Now get beneath the car and attach the mounting bracket to the underbody with the three bolts, tightening them securely. Install the lower end of the shock absorber to the spring plate with the bushing, washer, bolt, and nut. Tighten the lower mounting bolt securely.

3 **Repeat these steps** on the other side, then lower the car and test the shock absorbers as described in Chapter 12.

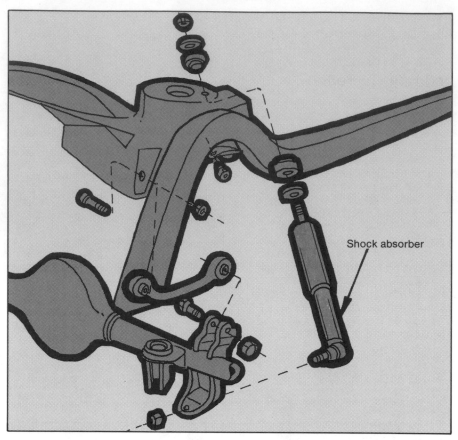

Shock absorber

Pro Shop

Cleaning the new threads

Before installing a new shock absorber, use a wire brush to remove all the paint from the threads, then apply a small coat of light oil to the threads. This will allow you to install the bolts or nuts easily.

Full-size Ford and Mercury models:
1968 on Thunderbird, Lincoln, Mark III, Mark IV, Elite, 1974 on, Cougar, 1972 on, Montego, and 1972 on Torino

1 **Reach up near the wheelhousing** to the upper side of the spring's upper seat and remove the nut, washer, and insulator from the shock absorber's upper stem. Compress the shock from the top down, so the upper stem clears the hole in the spring seat. Remove the shock's inner insulator and washer from the upper stem.

2 **At the shock's lower mounting,** remove the attaching nut from the shock's lower stud, and knock the stud from the shock mounting bracket on the axle housing. Then discard the shock.

3 **Place an inner washer** and inner insulator on the new shock's upper stem. Maneuver the new shock so the upper stem engages the hole in the spring seat. Hold the shock steady and install the outer insulator, washer, and nut on the upper stem, then tighten the nut securely. Extend the shock and put its lower mounting bolt through the hole in the mounting bracket on the axle housing. Install the nut, tightening it securely.

4 **Repeat these steps** on the other side and lower the car. Test the shock absorbers as described in Chapter 12. See the illustration for the Ford Mustang, Pinto, and Bobcat sedans.

Servicing Rear Axles

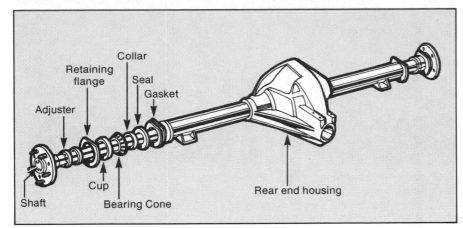

Collar
Retaining flange
Seal
Gasket
Adjuster
Cup
Shaft
Bearing Cone
Rear end housing

Chrysler Corporation cars with adjustable rear axle bearings must be taken to a qualified auto mechanic for any rear axle repair work. The end play of the axle bearing must be adjusted after the replacement of parts using special tools and instruments. You can identify the adjustable-type rear axle bearing by removing the right rear tire-and-wheel assembly and the brake drum. Look behind the axle flange for a claw-type lock which fits into a spanner adjuster collar. This lock is located on the bolt holding the forward lower brake backing plate.

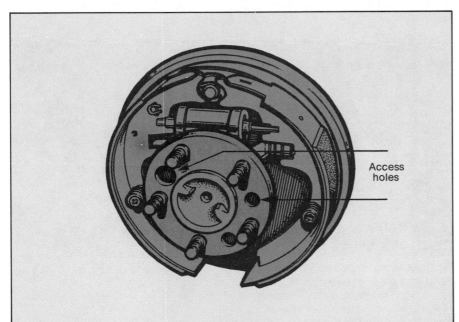

Access holes

B-O-type axle. There are two methods of securing the rear axles to the differential assembly. In one method the axle is held in place with a flange secured to the brake backing plate and the rear axle housing by four bolts and nuts. On this type the bearing is pressed and locked to the axle just at the brake backing plate of the differential housing. To see if your car has this kind of axle, remove the tire assembly and the brake drum. Then look at the axle flange for an access hole. If there is one, you have the B-O type axle.

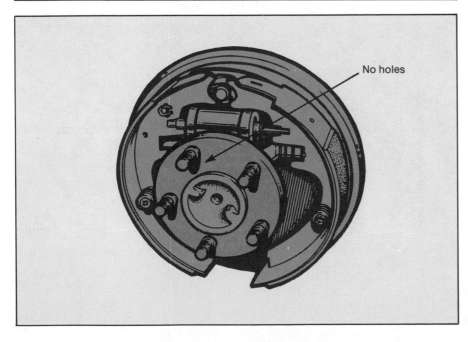

No holes

The C-type axle lock. The other method of securing the rear axle uses a C-type axle lock. The axle bearing fits into the rear end housing at the brake backing plate.

Photo Steps: replacing rear axles

The following sequence of photographs shows the step-by-step procedure for removing an axle from a car which uses a C-type axle lock to hold the rear axles in place. The C-type lock is discussed later in this chapter.

1 **Place a drain pan** under the differential housing and, using the correct size socket wrench, remove two or three lower bolts and one upper bolt to allow the rear end grease to spill out of the housing.

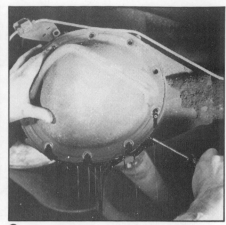

2 **Remove the remaining bolts** and the cover. If the cover is stuck to the housing, use a screwdriver to pry it free.

3 **Use a scraper** to remove the old gasket from both the cover and the axle housing.

4 **Turning the drive shaft** with one hand, rotate the rear end slowly until the lock bolt pin is just at the bottom of the rear end housing. Now loosen the lock bolt with a box or Allen wrench.

5 **Remove the lock pin.**

6 **Slide the pinion shaft pin out** just until it clears the end of the axle. Do not remove the pin.

7 **Have a helper push in on the axle flange** until the C lock is exposed.

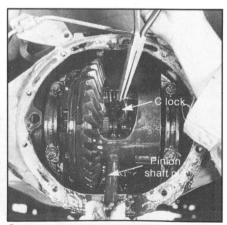

8 **Using long-nose pliers,** remove the C lock from the axle.

9 **Have a helper pull the axle out** and remove it. Then push the pinion shaft pin back into place and loosely install the lock pin.

10 **Using a slide hammer seal-removing tool,** take out the axle bearing and/or seal.

Pro Shop

Reinstalling a thrust washer

Should the pinion gear thrust washer move out of place, it can be reinstalled after the axle is replaced. Using the pinion shaft pin as an alignment tool, push the pin up into the pinion gear but not through it. Then slide the thrust washer between the gear and the case and push up on the pin simultaneously.

11 **Using a seal-installing tool** and a hammer, install the new seal in the axle housing. Now have your helper install the axle. Once again, remove the lock pin, slide the pinion shaft out far enough to allow the axle to slide into place, and install the C lock on the axle. With the C lock in place, have your helper pull out on the axle until it sets in place. Again slide the pinion shaft pin into the case and tighten the lock bolt securely.

12 **Coat the differential housing** cover with gasket cement.

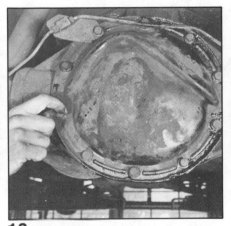

13 **Install a new gasket** on the differential cover, and put the cover on the housing. First start all cover bolts by hand, then tighten them using the tightening sequence described later in this chapter.

14 **Fill the differential assembly** with rear end grease as described in Chapter 3.

Replacing the B-O type axle bearing and seal

On this type axle, the bearing and seal are usually one unit, although some cars do have a separate seal. If so, it should be replaced whenever the bearing is replaced.

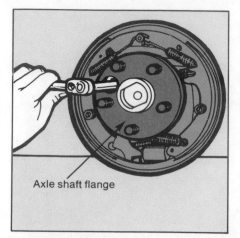

Axle shaft flange

1 Removing the flange-type axle.
Jack up and support the rear of the car, and remove the tire assembly as described in Chapter 3. Take off the brake drum as illustrated in Chapter 11. Using the correct size socket and ratchet extension, loosen and remove the four bolts or nuts holding the axle flange. Then attach the slide hammer puller to the flange and remove the axle.

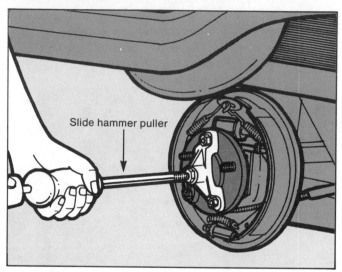

Slide hammer puller

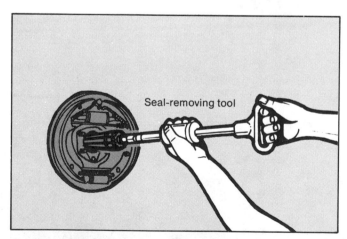

Seal-removing tool

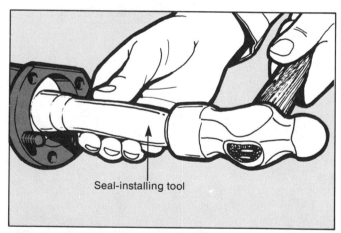

Seal-installing tool

2 Use a seal-removing tool to remove the axle grease seal if your car has one.

Take the axle to an auto mechanic who will remove the old bearing and retainer and press on the new ones. If your car has an inner seal, lubricate its rubber surface with lube plate. Coat the other edge of the seal with gasket cement.

3 Install the seal with a seal-installing tool. Coat the outside edge of the new bearing with lube plate for easier installation. Position the axle. It may be necessary to rotate it by hand to line up the splines with the differential assembly. Once the axle starts to slide into the housing, you may need to tip it and use a heavy rubber mallet to fully seat it. Do not use a hammer, which might damage the flange. Install the four bolts holding the axle and torque them to 35 foot pounds. Install the brake drum and the tire assembly, and lower the car.

Replacing the C-type axle lock bearing and seal

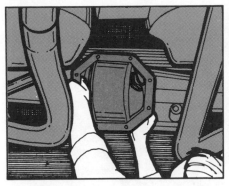

1 **Removing the cover.** Jack up and support the rear of the car. Take off the rear tire-and-wheel assembly according to the directions in Chapter 3. Remove the brake drum, following the instructions in Chapter 11. Place a drain pan under the differential housing, and, using the correct size socket wrench, remove the two lower and upper bolts. At this point rear end grease will spill out of the housing into the pan. Take off the remaining bolts and the cover. If the cover is stuck to the housing, use a screwdriver to pry it free. With a scraper, remove the old gasket from both the cover and the rear axle housing.

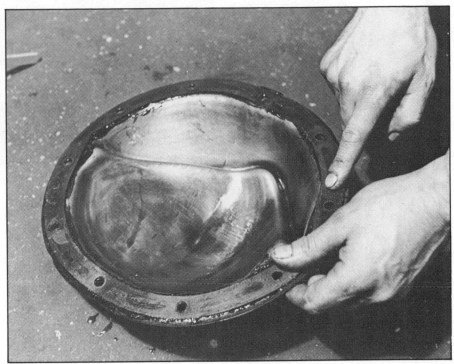

Pro Shop

Use of brake drum

If you do not have a slide hammer puller, invert the brake drum and position it on the axle flange. Then install the lug nut inverted, yes inverted, until the stud is just even with the end of the lug. With both hands, grab the brake drum and use it as a slide hammer to remove the axle.

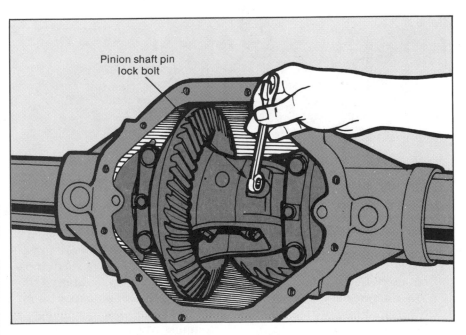

Pinion shaft pin
lock bolt

2 **Removing the pinion shaft bolt.**
Grab the drive shaft with one hand and turn it until the pinion shaft lock bolt is exposed. Using the proper size box wrench, remove the bolt.

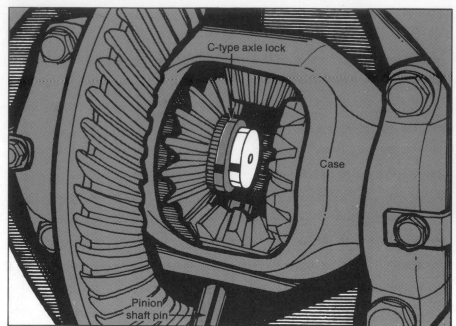

C-type axle lock

Case

Pinion shaft pin

3 **Removing the C-type axle lock.**
Rotate the rear end very slowly until the lock bolt pin is just at the bottom of the rear axle housing. Slide the pinion shaft pin out until it just clears the axle. *Caution: Do not remove or release the pin.* Have a helper push in on the axle flange and take out the C-type axle lock from the end of the axle.

Axle shaft

Full-time 4-wheel drive

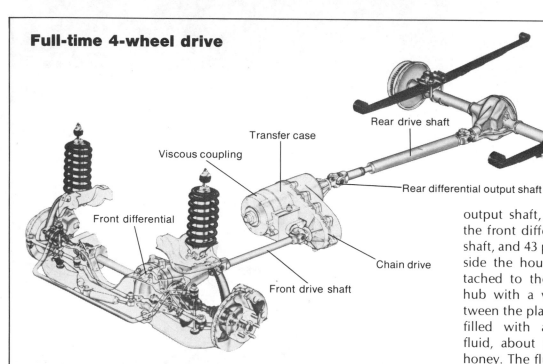

Transfer case

Viscous coupling

Front differential

Rear drive shaft

Rear differential output shaft

Chain drive

Front drive shaft

American Motors' Eagle passenger car has full-time 4-wheel drive. The 4-wheel drive is always engaged. In fact, there isn't any shift lever to engage or disengage it. The transfer case mounted behind the transmission is a new design, using a limited, slip differential and chain drive. A viscous coupling limits the slip between the front and rear drive shafts. The device will permit differential action if the

relative motion is slow and gentle, as in normal turns. If the differential action becomes too fast, the viscous coupling restricts the relative motion. In vehicle use on slippery-road and/or rough-terrain conditions, the coupling prevents power from going to the axle, which has a spinning wheel.

The viscous coupling consists of an aluminum housing attached to the rear differential

output shaft, a hub attached to the front differential, the output shaft, and 43 plates contained inside the housing alternately attached to the housing and the hub with a very small gap between the plates. The coupling is filled with a viscous silicone fluid, about the consistency of honey. The fluid is sealed within the coupling assembly, preventing any mixing of the fluid with the 10W-30 engine oil used in the transfer case.

The transfer of power to the front drive shaft is through a silent chain. It is similar in design to the chain used with timing sprockets, but is considerably wider, at $1\frac{3}{4}$-inches. Other than the transfer case, the Eagle 4-wheel drive is similar to 4-wheel drives used on AMC Jeeps.

Pinion shaft pin

Pinion shaft pin lock bolt

4 **Keep the parts in place.** Instruct your helper to pull out the axle, then push the pinion shaft pin back into place, and loosely install the lock bolt to keep all the differential parts in place.

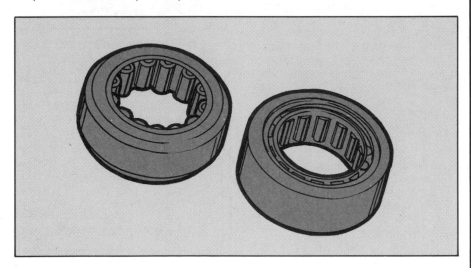

5 **Removing the bearings.** With the seal-removing tool, take out the axle seal, then remove the axle bearing by hand. Install the new bearing and lubricate it with fiber grease. Coat the rubber part of the new seal with lube plate and install it.

Pro Shop

Adapter for box wrench

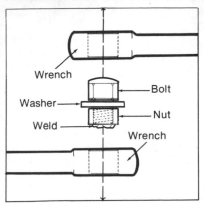

Wrench

Bolt

Washer

Nut

Weld

Wrench

No mechanic ever has enough special wrenches to handle every job that shows up. It's easy to make one or more adapters permitting two box wrenches to be used in combination on special jobs. The combination gives greater leverage and doubles the number of angles at which the box wrench can be used.

To make the adapter, use a short, heat-treated cap screw having the same head size as the box wrench opening. Install a flat washer on the cap screw and then a nut. Tighten the nut securely against the flat washer and head of the cap screw. Cut off the exposed threads and then rivet or weld the nut to the cap screw.

The head end of the adapter is placed in the end of one box wrench and a second box wrench is placed on the nut end. The flat washer keeps the adapter from falling through. Using two box wrenches doubles the leverage. With two 12-point box wrenches, 24 handle positions are available. It's a good idea to keep an assortment of sizes of cap screws and nuts already made up.

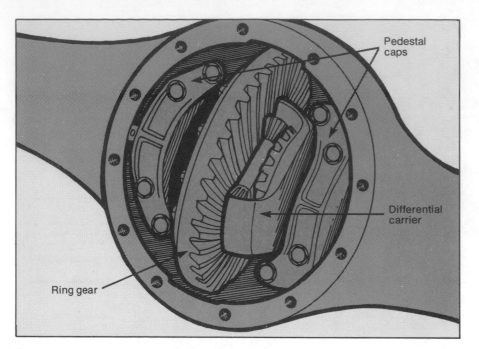

Pedestal caps

Differential carrier

Ring gear

6 Reinstalling the C-type axle lock. Install the axle as described previously for the B-O type bearing and seal. Take out the pinion shaft pin lock bolt and slide the pin out just as you did before to remove the C-type axle lock. Do not remove the pin from the case. Have your helper push the axle as far out as possible. Install the C-type axle lock on the slot at the end of the axle, then have your helper pull back on the axle to seal the C lock. Push the pin back up into the case and attach the lock bolt, then torque the bolt to 12 to 15 foot pounds. *Caution: Wipe up any spilled rear axle grease that may have gotten on the* *brake backing plate or the brake parts.* Coat the differential housing and cover it with gasket cement, then install the gasket and cover on the differential housing. Attach each cover bolt by hand. Then, using the following tightening sequence, tighten them: start at the 12 o'clock position, then move to the 6 o'clock, the 9 o'clock, the 3 o'clock, 10 o'clock, 5 o'clock, 11 o'clock, and so on. Torque the bolts to seven to ten foot pounds.

Fill the differential assembly with rear end grease as described in Chapter 3. Replace the brake drum and the tire-and-wheel-assembly, then lower the car.

Pro Shop

Limited slip rear end

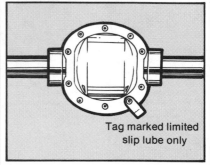

Tag marked limited slip lube only

Cars equipped with limited slip (non-slip) differential assemblies require a special rear end lubricant. To see if your car is equipped with this type of rear end, look for a small metal tag attached to one of the rear end cover bolts. If there is no tag on the cover bolt and you are still not certain as to the type of rear end in your car, use the following check: with the rear of the car jacked up and supported on safety stands, the parking brake released, and the transmission in "Neutral," rotate one rear wheel by hand. If you have a limited slip rear end, both rear wheels will rotate in the same direction. If you have a conventional rear end, the other wheel will rotate in the opposite direction.

ECONOTIP

#16
Gear ratios on new cars

Changing rear-axle ratios to get better gas mileage certainly works. But the cost of the gear change is high and will take a lot of driving to pay off. So it isn't practical. But if you are buying a new car, selecting the right rear-axle ratio can make a lot of difference in the gas mileage you will get. When selecting a ratio, the higher the number, the faster the engine will turn, and the worse the gas mileage. For example, a 6-cylinder automatic transmission engine with a 2.71 rear axle will get two percent less mileage if a 2.94 ratio is used. Go to a 3.21 ratio, and the loss is seven percent. On a V-8 with an automatic transmission and a 2.45 ratio, the loss is six percent when going to a 2.71 ratio. Use a 2.94 ratio and the loss is 11 percent. It jumps to a whopping 17 percent when using a 3.21 ratio. All of these figures are for highway driving. The difference is much less in city driving, because the lower ratio helps only during steady cruising.

DRIVE SHAFT

Rear-driven cars with front-mounted engines have a drive or propeller shaft running from the transmission to the differential on the rear axle. On modern cars, it is a hollow shaft connected at both ends by a universal joint. Some drive shafts are in two pieces with a third universal joint between them for additional support. Universals are double-hinged joints with two U-shaped yokes fastened at right angles to a cross-shaped member called a cross shaft or spider. The yokes pivot on the arms of the cross and allow power to be carried through two shafts that are at an angle to each other.

The angle between the drive shaft and the transmission output shaft changes because the rear wheels move up and down with each bump in the road, causing the end of the drive shaft connected to the differential to move up and down also. The transmission at the other end, meanwhile, is more or less rigidly connected to the frame. The universal simply allows the drive shaft to keep on turning while the angle changes.

There are two types of universal joints used on today's cars. The conventional type, and the constant velocity or CV type. Larger, more expensive cars such as the Buick, Cadillac, and Lincoln are usually equipped with the CV joint. The disadvantage of the conventional universal joint is a slight vibration set up in the drive shaft each time the rear end of the car moves up and down. To eliminate this vibration, the CV joint has two single joints connected by a steel link or yoke, kept in relative position by a special centering ball and socket. This arrangement usually eliminates drive shaft vibrations while going over a bump or road dip.

While you may replace a drive shaft, you should not rebuild a CV joint. Complete replacement of the entire drive shaft unit with a new one is necessary because the CV joint drive shaft requires special balancing.

In this chapter you will learn how to remove a complete drive shaft assembly, replace the conventional-type universal joint, and install a drive shaft. If the universal joints and drive shaft on your car are enclosed in a torque tube, you should take it to a mechanic for any repairs. Special tools and equipment along with specific adjustments are required when servicing or repairing a torque tube assembly.

CONTENTS

Replacing the Drive Shaft

One-piece drive shaft

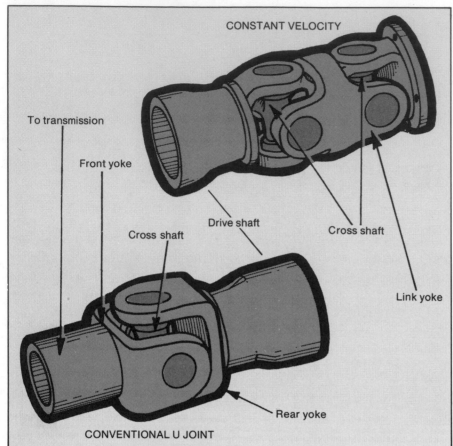

CONSTANT VELOCITY

To transmission

Front yoke

Cross shaft

Drive shaft

Cross shaft

Link yoke

Rear yoke

CONVENTIONAL U JOINT

1 **Jack up and support** the car, both front and rear. Place a drain pan under the extension housing of the transmission. With the correct size box wrench, remove the nuts or bolts holding the rear universal joint to the differential yoke. Slide the drive shaft toward the transmission, then lower the drive shaft and pull it out of the transmission extension housing. *Caution: Do not allow the slip yoke, the part of the drive shaft going to the transmission, to fall to the ground when you remove the shaft. This may damage the yoke.*

Tools and equipment:

Floor jack.
Safety stands.
Goggles.
Creeper.
Droplight.
Hammer.
3/8" drive socket set.
Flashlight.
Scribe.
Wire brush.
Screwdrivers.
Bench vise.
9/16" and one-inch sockets.
Brass or soft metal drift pin.
Box wrenches.
Drain pan.
Hand cloths.
Needle nose and common pliers.
Cutting pliers.
Hand grease gun.

Parts you may need:

Lube plate.
Universal joints.
Transmission fluid.

Pro Shop

Checking for clutch slippage

On cars with manual transmissions, an easy way to check for clutch slippage is to lock the parking brake tightly, put the shift lever in high gear, release the clutch suddenly in one quick motion, and feed about one-quarter throttle.

If the engine stalls immediately, the clutch is OK. If the engine doesn't stall immediately, the clutch is slipping.

Before trying this, be sure your parking brake is in good condition and there is no one in front of the car.

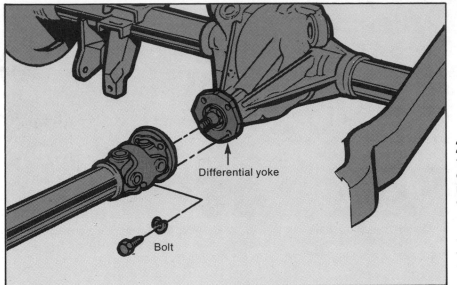

Differential yoke

Bolt

2 **Apply a light coat** of lube plate to the replacement slip yoke surface, and carefully slide the replacement slip yoke into the transmission extension housing, engaging the transmission output shaft. Line up the rear universal mounting bolt holes with the holes on the differential yoke, install the bolts and nuts, and tighten all nuts securely. Check the transmission fluid level as described in Chapter 3. Lower the car.

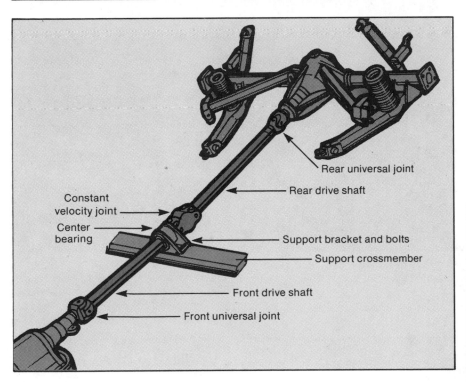

Rear universal joint

Rear drive shaft

Constant velocity joint

Center bearing

Support bracket and bolts

Support crossmember

Front drive shaft

Front universal joint

Drive shaft with a center bearing

1 **The procedure for removing** and replacing this type of drive shaft is the same as that described for the one-piece shaft except that the center bearing bolts must be removed first. Locate the center bearing bolts, usually positioned halfway along the drive shaft. With the correct size wrench, remove the bolts. Some models use shims between the support bracket and the crossmember. Code them for correct reinstallation.

2 **Install the replacement drive shaft** as described previously, putting the center bearing bolts in last. If your car came equipped with shims, locate them between the crossmember and the bracket support. Position the bolts and tighten them securely. *Caution: Do not attempt to rebuild this type of drive shaft on your own. Any slight error can result in excessive vibration which may damage the transmission and / or rear end.*

ECONOTIP

#17

How much difference in time?

The 55 MPH speed limit saves gas, but it takes longer to get where you are going. How much longer was answered a few years ago by Buick Division of General Motors. They ran several cars from San Diego, California, to Washington, DC. One group of cars ran at 50 MPH, while the other group ran at 70. This was before the 55 MPH limit was enacted. The 50 MPH group took 14 hours longer to cross the country than the 70 MPH group. But they used 22.9 percent less gasoline than the faster cars. It was not reported how much more the slower group spent on motel bills and meals during the extra time they were on the road. Since the savings of gas amounted to about one tankfull, it probably did not equal the extra spent for meals and gas. 55 MPH saves gas, wear on the car, and maybe your life, but it obviously increases the cost of a long trip.

Photo Steps: replacing universal joints

Power from the engine and transmission is delivered to the rear differential and axles by the drive shaft. The universal joints at both ends of the drive shaft allow power to be transmitted from the engine to the rear wheels. When the universal joints are worn, they will cause noise and/or vibration in the drive shaft. The following sequence of photographs shows the step-by-step procedure for replacing universal joints.

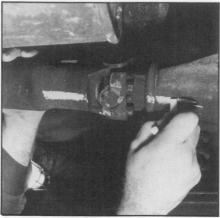

1 **Using a piece of chalk** or a scribe, mark a line on the drive shaft and the differential housing to insure correct reinstallation.

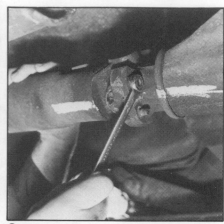

2 **With the correct size box wrench,** loosen and remove the four U bolt lock nuts.

3 **Remove the two U bolts.**

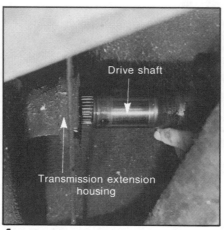

Drive shaft

Transmission extension housing

4 **Slide the drive shaft** out of the transmission extension housing.

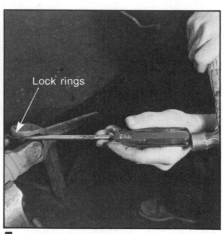

Lock rings

5 **Clamp the drive shaft** in the vise and remove the lock rings from the four bearings. Some original joints have plastic filler instead of lock rings.

1″ socket

9/16″ socket

6 **Open your vise** to allow the width of the drive shaft, plus the length of a one-inch socket and a 9/16″ socket, to fit between its jaws. Placing the 9/16″ socket on one bearing and the one-inch socket over the opposite bearing, tighten the vise. The 9/16″ socket will push the opposite bearing and cross shaft into the one inch socket. This action will shear the plastic locks, if used.

7 **Loosen the vise,** and remove the sockets and the extruding bearing.

8 **Reverse the procedure** and remove the opposite bearing. Repeat these steps to remove the remaining bearings and cross bar from the yoke.

9 **Install the replacement cross shaft** on the drive shaft.

Cross shaft

10 **Place the end of the drive shaft** and one bearing in the jaws of the vise and tighten until the bearing is pressed flush into the end of the shaft.

Bearing

11 **Install the opposite bearing** and press it in with the vise.

12 **Install the two lock rings** that come with the replacement joint.

13 **Using a hand grease gun,** pump grease into the bearing.

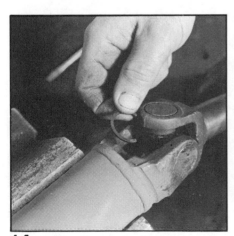

14 **Repeat the same operation** to install the yoke, then put on the lock rings.

15 **Install the drive shaft,** align the scribe marks, and tighten the lock nuts on the U bolts with a box wrench.

Replacing Universal Joints

The rear universal joint

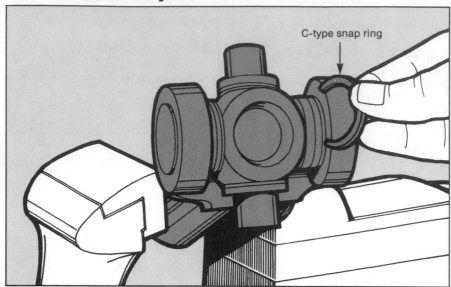

C-type snap ring

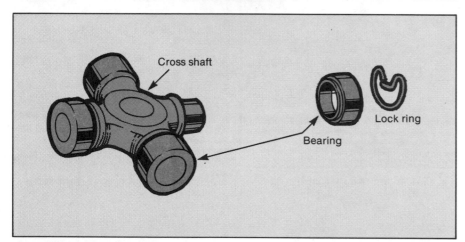

Cross shaft

Bearing

Lock ring

1 **Remove the drive shaft** as described previously in this chapter.

2 **Removing the ring.** The bearings are secured to the drive shaft yoke with a snap ring or lock ring. The snap ring may be located in a groove at the base of the bearing. The lock ring may be found at the top of the bearing in a groove in the drive shaft yoke. Remove the ring with the correct tools. Note: Some late-model cars use an injected nylon retainer on the universal joint bearings. When service is necessary, pressing the bearings out will shear the nylon retainer. Replace the retainer with the conventional snap ring.

Pro Shop

Mark for accuracy

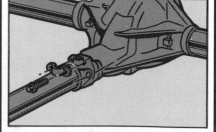

To ensure correct reinstallation, take a sharp pointed tool and scribe a mark on the drive shaft yoke and companion flange or the rear end housing.

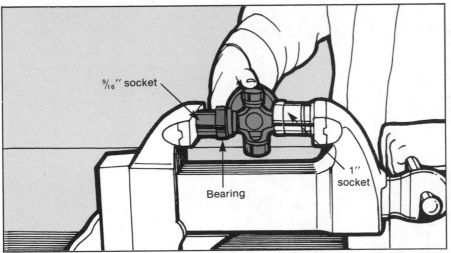

3 **To remove the bearing** in the drive shaft yoke, open your bench vise wide enough to allow the entire bearing, the length of a one-inch socket and a $\frac{9}{16}''$ socket, to fit between the jaws. Place the $\frac{9}{16}''$ socket on the bearing, then put the one-inch socket on the drive shaft yoke opposite the $\frac{9}{16}''$ socket. By tightening the vise, the $\frac{9}{16}''$ socket will push the bearing and cross shaft out into the one-inch socket. Remove the drive shaft and sockets from the vise. If the bearing is not free of the yoke, use a hammer and tap the bearing out.

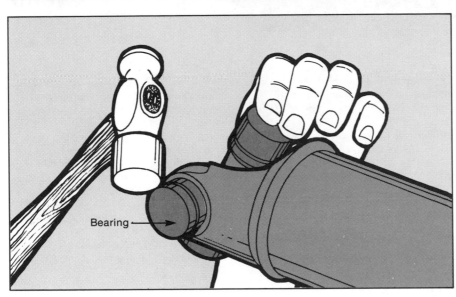

4 **Place the cross shaft** across the vise jaws, then with a brass or soft drift pin and hammer, remove the other bearing. Remove the cross shaft, and clean the drive shaft yoke with a wire brush. Apply a thin coat of lube plate to the inside of the yoke where the bearings are installed.

Removing the bearings

You will need a vise to remove the bearings in the drive shaft yoke. If you are going out to buy a vise for this job, remember— the bigger and heavier the better, within reason. A 12- to 40-pound vise with $3\frac{1}{2}$- to 5-inch jaws is a good choice. Look for a vise with a box frame to guide the moving jaw and cover the jack screw that closes it. Keeping filings off the threads and out of the nut makes it much easier to turn the handle.

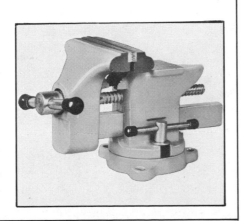

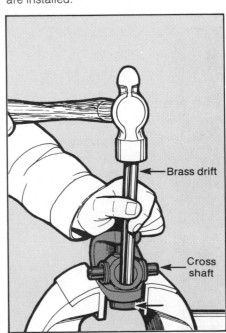

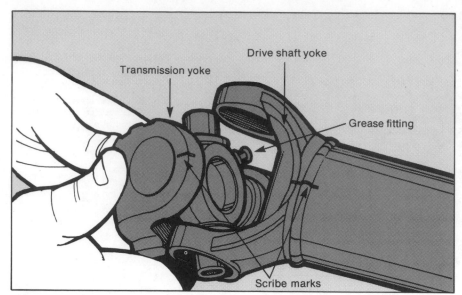

Transmission yoke

Drive shaft yoke

Grease fitting

Scribe marks

5 **Installing the new cross shaft.** Remove all the bearings from the new cross shaft, and position it in the yoke with its grease fitting facing the drive shaft. Extend the cross shaft out of one of the bearing holes in the yoke.

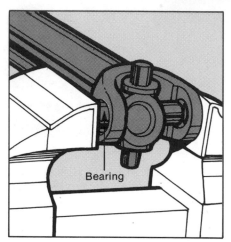

Bearing

6 **Reinstalling the joint.** Put one new bearing on the cross shaft and guide it into the yoke. Be sure the cross shaft and bearing are not cocked to one side. Holding the cross shaft firmly with one hand, gently tap the bearing into the yoke until it is started. Using the vise as a clamp, press the bearing completely into the yoke. *Caution: Press the bearing into the yoke only far enough so it is flush with the yoke. This will prevent squeezing or destroying the yoke.*

Place the $9/16''$ socket on the newly-installed bearing and the one-inch socket on the opposite side of the yoke. Put this assembly into the vise and press the bearing in until the cross shaft extends out about $1/8$ of an inch beyond the opposite side of the yoke. Remove the drive shaft from the vise, and locate the new bearing on the extended cross shaft. Put the drive shaft back into the vise, and, as before, press the second bearing until it is flush with the yoke, then install the new snap ring lock on the first bearing or in the yoke. Place the $9/16''$ socket on the second bearing and press it in until the snap ring can be installed. Reinstall the drive shaft as described in this chapter.

The front universal joint

The procedure for removing the front universal joint is the same as described previously for the rear universal joint, with the exception that you must press the new bearings into the transmission yoke as well as into the drive shaft yoke. Before removing the front joint, scribe alignment marks on the drive shaft and transmission yokes.

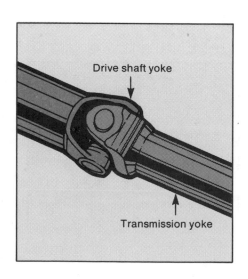

Drive shaft yoke

Transmission yoke

AIR CONDITIONING

Air conditioning was used on a few passenger buses as far back as 1938. Then in 1940 Packard introduced the first air-conditioned car. It is now the most popular accessory on all cars manufactured in the United States. In 1962 only 11 percent of American cars were factory-equipped with air conditioners. The percentage of new-model, factory-equipped air-conditioned cars rose each year to 80 percent in 1970 and today accounts for over 90%.

As described in Chapter 1, air conditioning removes heat from the passenger compartment and delivers it into the atmosphere. Air conditioning simultaneously cleans, cools, circulates, and removes moisture from the air within the passenger compartment. Air conditioning and refrigeration are basically the same process. Considerable training and practice are required to service the components of an air-conditioning system. When one part needs to be serviced or replaced, the system must be drained of refrigerant. Then, after the part is reinstalled, the system must be cleaned, dried, and a vacuum created. This is accomplished with an evacuator or a vacuum pump. Finally, the system is charged with a refrigerant, R-12.

Training in air conditioning and in the use of special equipment, particularly the manifold gauge set, is needed to accurately diagnose some malfunctions in the system and to recharge it. However, in this chapter you will learn how to diagnose some of the malfunctions not requiring the use of a manifold gauge set, and, when necessary, how to add refrigerant to the system. A small amount of refrigerant seepage may occur when the air conditioning is not used for long periods of time, such as in winter. This refrigerant can be replaced without evacuating the system by using a one-pound can of refrigerant, R-12, and a special air-conditioning service hose and can adapter. Before doing any work on this system, you should check the air-conditioning compressor belt for tension, as described in Chapter 3.

CONTENTS

Charging the System

Before attempting to charge the system, read the discussion in Chapter 1 on air-conditioning. Familiarize yourself with all the components of the system so you will understand how to check and charge it, and add refrigerant to it.

Tools and equipment:

Fender covers.
Goggles.
New one-inch paint brush.
Refrigerant charging hose and
    can tap and valve kit.
Hand cloths.
Droplight or flashlight.
Hot water and pail.
Screwdriver.
Open end wrenches.
Jumper wire.
Parts:

One can of R-12 refrigerant.
Soap-and-water solution.

Locating the sight glass

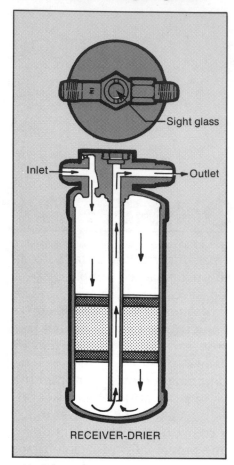

Sight glass

Inlet — Outlet

RECEIVER-DRIER

The quickest way to determine if your air-conditioning system is low on refrigerant is to check the system through the sight glass usually located on the outlet side of the receiver-drier. Some sight glasses have a protective cover made of cardboard or stiff paper. Remove the cover if there is one on your system. On some cars, the sight glass is not mounted on the receiver-drier, but on the line between the condenser and the expansion valve.

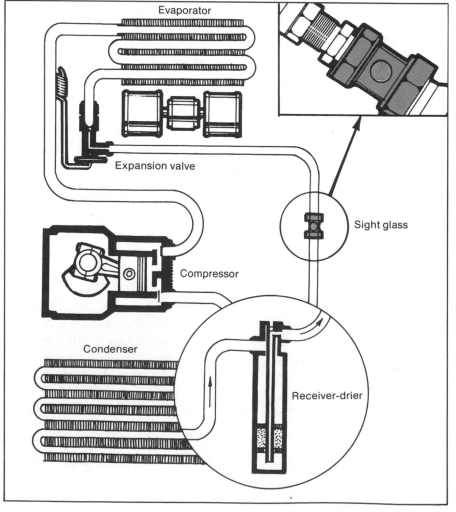

Evaporator

Expansion valve

Sight glass

Compressor

Condenser

Receiver-drier

Bypassing a damaged heater core

Your heater core may be damaged if you notice fogginess, dampness, or actual leakage of engine coolant into the passenger compartment. These signs are most noticeable when the heater is on. A quick-fix so you can use the car while the heater core is being repaired is to place a six-inch piece of ⅝-inch-diameter tubing into both heater hoses after disconnecting them from the heater core at the firewall. This will bypass the heater system entirely.

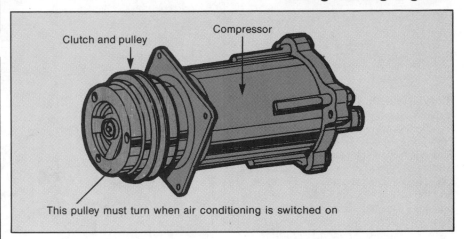

This pulley must turn when air conditioning is switched on

1 Checking the clutch. Start the engine with the parking brake applied and the transmission in "Park." Set the air-conditioning controls to maximum cooling and high fan levels. Open the hood, and make sure the entire compressor clutch assembly is being turned by the air-conditioning belt. Have a helper switch the air-conditioner control off and on while you observe the clutch assembly engaging and disengaging. If the clutch is not engaging, you cannot check the system at this time. Trouble-shooting this problem will be covered later in this chapter.

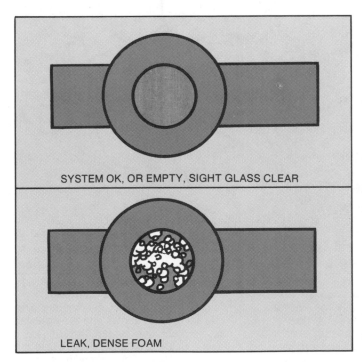

SYSTEM OK, OR EMPTY, SIGHT GLASS CLEAR

LEAK, DENSE FOAM

2 Looking into the sight glass, nothing should be visible—it should appear empty. If it does, and cold air is circulating in the passenger compartment, the system is sufficiently charged. If the sight glass is clear but there is no cold air circulating in the passenger compartment, the system may be empty. Take your car to an auto mechanic or air-conditioning specialist for further checking and servicing. If the sight glass shows bubbles that look like moving water bubbles, the system needs to be charged with refrigerant.

Adding refrigerant

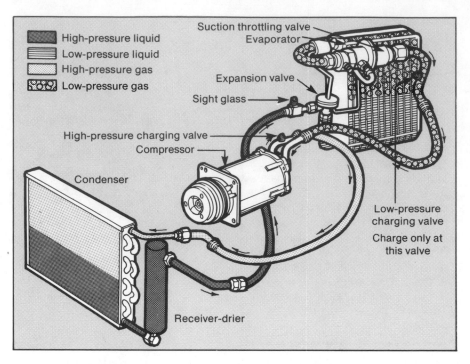

High-pressure liquid
Low-pressure liquid
High-pressure gas
Low-pressure gas

Suction throttling valve
Evaporator
Expansion valve
Sight glass
High-pressure charging valve
Compressor
Condenser
Low-pressure charging valve
Charge only at this valve
Receiver-drier

1 **Removing the low-side Schrader valve.** Place fender covers over the front fenders. Wearing eye goggles for protection, locate the low-side charging Schrader valve. It looks like a tire valve with its cover removed, and is usually located in the line between the evaporator and the compressor directly on the compressor, or on the suction throttle valve. Remove the valve's acorn cap cover. *Caution: There is a second Schrader valve located in the line between the compressor and the condenser. This is the high-pressure charging valve, and you should not work on it. It should only be serviced by a mechanic using a manifold hand set.*

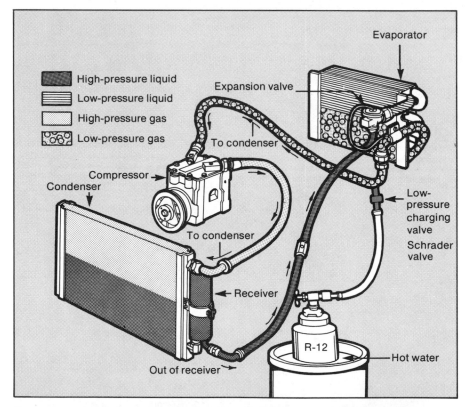

High-pressure liquid
Low-pressure liquid
High-pressure gas
Low-pressure gas

Evaporator
Expansion valve
To condenser
Compressor
Condenser
To condenser
Low-pressure charging valve
Schrader valve
Receiver
R-12
Hot water
Out of receiver

2 **Install the refrigerant can tap and hose** on the can according to the instructions accompanying the tap and hose kit. Connect the hose to the low-side Schrader valve finger tight, then loosen the hose connection at the can tap slowly until a small amount of refrigerant escapes from the connection. This will purge the hose, removing all air and moisture from it. Then tighten the connection finger tight again. Open the valve on the can tap. At this point the refrigerant should start to flow into the system.

3 **Have your helper operate the engine** at a fast idle while you place the R-12 can upright in a pail of hot water. The water will raise the temperature of the refrigerant, increasing the pressure and permitting it to flow into the system easily. *Caution: Do not invert the refrigerant can. If you do, liquid refrigerant, instead of a gas refrigerant, will enter the system and damage the compressor.*

4 **While the system is charging,** watch the sight glass. Continue charging until the bubbles vanish and the sight glass is clear, then turn off the can tap valve. Have your helper run the engine at normal idling speed. Allow the engine and the system to operate for a few minutes to stabilize it, then recheck the sight glass. With the engine still idling, place a hand cloth around the hose connection at the Schrader valve and very quickly remove the hose fitting. Replace the acorn nut cover.

Checking for Leaks

Most leaks occur at the fittings where connections are made between various parts of the air-conditioning system. Leaks may also occur in the condenser or the evaporator. The simplest way to check for leaks is with a solution of soapy water. You may have used this method to check for gas leaks in your home.

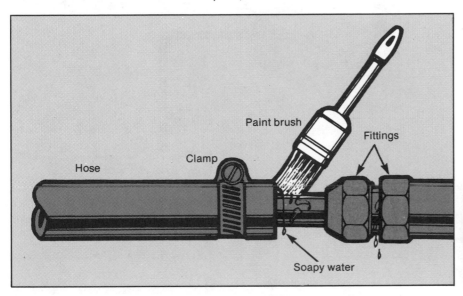

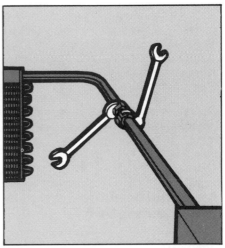

Testing for leaks with a soapy water solution. A quick way to determine if a fitting is leaking is to look for an oily, dark, dirty film around it. Using a new paint brush soaked with soapy water, brush a generous amount of the solution on the fitting and look for bubbles. Check all fittings and connections. The system does not need to be working when making this test. If a leak is detected tighten the fittings securely using two wrenches or a screwdriver.

Leak detectors—but not for you

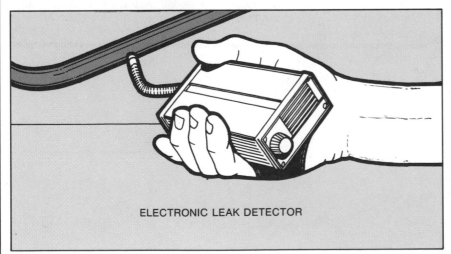

ELECTRONIC LEAK DETECTOR

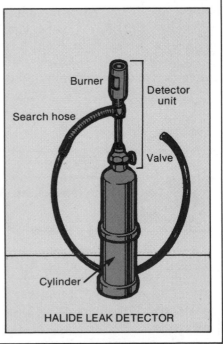

HALIDE LEAK DETECTOR

Stay away from electronic and Halide leak detectors. The first is too expensive and overly sensitive—it is really designed for the professional air-conditioning mechanic. The second uses an open flame to test for leaks. It could set fire to the engine or ignite the refrigerant, generating deadly phosgene gas.

Checking the Clutch

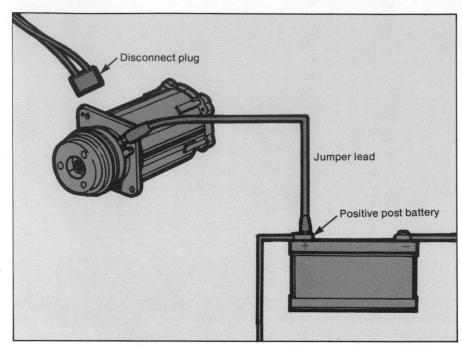

Disconnect plug

Jumper lead

Positive post battery

Open the hood and locate the compressor, then find the wire plug attached to the compressor clutch and remove it. Connect one end of a jumper wire to the positive post of the battery. If the compressor has two terminals, connect a second jumper between one of the compressor terminals and ground. Touching the battery wire to the other terminal (or the single terminal) should make the clutch engage. If not, the clutch is defective and must be repaired by an air conditioning specialist. NOTE: Some clutches will only click the first time the wire is connected. The click indicates that the clutch is working.

Air conditioning Troubleshooting

Remember, a condenser clogged with paper, leaves, bugs, and dirt will impede an air conditioner's functioning. Clean the condenser with a brush or vacuum cleaner as you do your car's radiator exterior.

The following is a Troubleshooting flow chart for your system. Some of the repairs and replacements listed must be done by an auto mechanic or air-conditioning specialist.

ECONOTIP

#18
Turn off that air conditioner

An air conditioner puts an extra load on the engine. Power that would be used to move the car is used to operate the air conditioning compressor. The result is reduced mileage. Air conditioners have the greatest effect on mileage in stop-and-go, hot weather driving. This, of course, is when you need the air conditioner the most. But if you can leave it off and suffer through the heat, you may avoid the 20 percent reduced mileage you'll get with it on. Not all cars will be that badly affected, but an average mileage reduction with the air conditioning on is 9 percent.

Pro Shop

Testing refrigerant

Is the refrigerant entering the system? If it is, the can of R-12 should feel very cold to the touch. Remove the can from the water and test it, remembering not to invert it.

Troubleshooting flow chart: air conditioning

Symptom	Probable cause	Remedy
A. System produces no cooling.	**Electrical** 1. Blown fuse. 2. Disconnected or broken wire. 3. Disconnected or broken ground wire. 4. Clutch coil disconnected or burned out. 5. Switch contacts in thermostat (if used) burned excessively, or sensing element defective. 6. Blower motor burned out or disconnected.	1. Replace fuse. 2. Repair or replace. 3. Repair or replace. 4. Repair or replace. 5. Replace. 6. Repair or replace.
	Mechanical 1. Loose or broken drive belt. 2. Compressor completely or partially frozen. 3. Compressor reed valves inoperative. 4. Expansion valve stuck open.	1. Replace belt. 2. Replace or rebuild. 3. Replace or rebuild. 4. Replace. Also replace receiver-drier.
	Refrigeration 1. Broken refrigeration line. 2. Fusable plug blown (if used). 3. Leak in system. 4. Compressor shaft seal leaking. 5. Clogged screen or screens in receiver-dehydrator or expansion valve.	1. Replace line. 2. Replace link. 3. Correct leak or repair. 4. Reseal or rebuild compressor. 5. Replace both units.
B. Insufficient cooling.	**Electrical** 1. Blower motor operates sluggishly.	1. Check, replace if necessary.
	Mechanical 1. Compressor clutch slipping. 2. Obstructed blower discharge passage. 3. Clogged air intake filter. 4. Outside air vents open. 5. Insufficient air circulation over condenser coils; fins clogged with dirt, leaves, or insects. 6. Evaporator clogged. 7. Evaporator regulator defective or improperly adjusted. See Note 1.	1. Replace clutch. 2. Clear passage. 3. Clean out vents. 4. Check and close vents. 5. Clean out parts with brush or vacuum cleaner. 6. Replace evaporator. 7. Adjust or replace.
	Refrigeration 1. Insufficient refrigerant in system. 2. Clogged screen in expansion valve. 3. Expansion valve thermal bulb has lost its charge. 4. Clogged screen in receiver. 5. Excessive moisture in system. 6. Air in system. 7. Thermostat defective or improperly adjusted (if used).	1. Charge system. 2. Remove and replace. Also replace receiver-drier. 3. Replace bulb. 4. Replace unit. 5. Replace receiver-drier and evacuate system. 6. Same as 5. 7. Adjust or replace.

Troubleshooting flow chart, continued:

Symptom	Probable cause	Remedy
C. System cools intermittently.	Electrical 1. Defective circuit breaker, blower switch, or blower motor. 2. Partially open, improper ground, or loose connection in compressor clutch coil.	1. Check for short circuit, replace unit if necessary. 2. Repair circuit or replace unit.
	Mechanical 1. Compressor clutch slipping.	1. Replace clutch assembly.
	Refrigeration 1. Unit icing up; may be caused by excessive moisture in system, incorrect super-heat adjustment in expansion valve, or thermostat adjusted too low (if used). 2. Thermostat defective (if used).	1. Check suction throttle valve pressure, EPR valve pressure, and thermostat capillary tube bulb on tailpipe. 2. Replace thermostat.

Note 1: The evaporator regulator includes the suction throttling valve (STV) used on Ford cars, the Pilot-Operated Absolute (POA) valve used on General Motors cars, and the Chrysler Evaporator Pressure Regulator (EPR) or Evaporator Temperature Regulator (ETR) valve. When any of these devices is used in a system, it can be assumed that the system contains no thermostat control.

CONTENTS

VISION AND SIGNALING

Being able to see the road ahead is a prerequisite for safe vehicle operation. This means that your lights and windshield wipers must operate effectively. And, of course, other drivers depend on your lights to tell them where you are and which way you are going.

In inclement weather, your driving vision is impaired. Here is where your windshield wipers become one of the most important safety devices on your car. Lighting, too, is doubly important. In bad weather, lights are frequently used during daylight hours as a safety device. This does not increase your own vision as much as it makes your car easier for other motorists to see.

Most problems in a car's lighting system—which is part of the electrical system—are caused by burned-out bulbs, fuses, or flasher units. Actual short circuits are much less frequent. This is a happy state of affairs for you, the novice mechanic, because bulb, fuse, headlight, and flasher replacement jobs are well within your capability. Instructions for these jobs follow in the pages ahead. When it comes to aligning headlights, you should take your car to a professional mechanic. He has the special tools and the expertise needed to handle such jobs. In this chapter you will also learn how to change wiper blades and wiper arm assemblies.

Windshield Wiper Service

General check

Your car's windshield wipers are powered by a small electric motor. To protect the windshield and give you maximum vision in rain, sleet, or snow, make sure the rubber blades are not cracked, brittle, or pulled loose from the blade retainer. Replacement blades are inexpensive and easy to install. The investment is small. The benefit is great—unobstructed vision through a clear windshield.

You can test wiper unit arm tension by pulling them about an inch away from the windshield and then releasing them. They should snap back against the glass. If they do not, the tension may not be sufficient to effectively wipe the glass clean. If the tension cannot be adjusted, you should replace the unit. Merely changing the blades will not solve the problem.

Most cars now have windshield washers. To clean a dry windshield while you are driving, first spray it with washer fluid, then turn on the wipers. This protects the glass against scratches. If temperatures drop below freezing in your area, be sure to put protective solvent in the washer container. It is available wherever auto products are sold.

The procedure for replacing wiper blades varies by make and model of car. Find the instructions for your particular car in the following pages, which are organized by make and model.

Tools and equipment:

Windshield wipers

Wiper arm removal tool.
Small flat screwdriver.
12-inch screwdriver.
$\frac{3}{32}$-inch drill or pin.

Electrical system

#2 Philips screwdriver.
Flat screwdriver.
Fuse puller.

Ford Motor Company

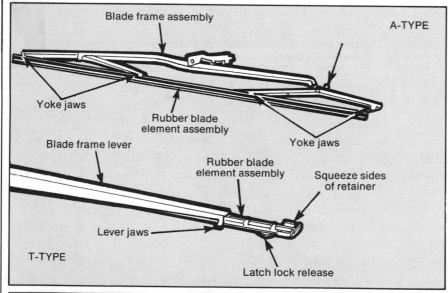

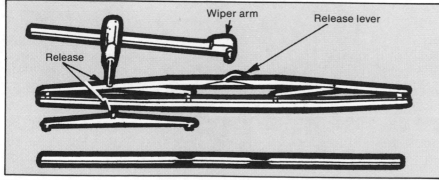

WIPER BLADES

All Ford Motor Company cars
These models use Trico and Anco blades, which come in two types, the bayonet type and the side-saddle pin type.
To remove a bayonet-type Trico blade:
1. Press down on the arm to unlock the top stud.
2. Then depress the tab on the saddle and pull the blade from the arm.

To remove a bayonet-type Anco blade:
1. Press inward on the tab on the saddle.
2. Pull the blade from the arm.
To reinstall the Trico- or Anco-type blade, slip it onto the wiper arm and push in until the latch engages the arm. Make sure the blade is properly engaged by attempting to pull it out.
To remove a side-saddle pin-type Trico or Anco blade:
1. Insert an appropriate tool such as a small screwdriver into the spring release opening of the blade saddle.

Ford Motor Company

2. Depress the spring clip with the tool and pull the blade off the wiper arm.

To reinstall the blade, slip it onto the wiper arm and push in until the latch engages the arm. Make sure the blade is properly engaged by attempting to pull it out.

WIPER BLADE ELEMENT

1969 on Thunderbird, Ford full-size, and Mercury full-size, 1969–72 Lincoln Continental except 1972 Mark IV, 1970–71 Fairlane, Torino, and Montego, 1971–73 Cougar and Mustang

To remove the rubber element on a Trico blade, squeeze the latch lock release and pull the element out of the lever jaws.

To remove the rubber element on an Anco-type blade, depress the latch pin and slide the element out of the yoke jaws.

To reinstall the element on either type blade, insert it through the yoke or lever jaws until the latch pin or lock engages it. Make sure the element is engaged underneath all the claws of the blade.

WIPER ARMS

1. Swing the arm and blade assembly away from the windshield to release the spring-loaded attaching clip in the arm from the pivot shaft.
2. Insert a $3/32$-inch pin through the pin hole to hold the wiper arm in the release position. Do not remove the pin until after the wiper arm has been reinstalled.
3. Remove the arm by rocking it off the shaft. Do not pry it off using a screwdriver.
4. Before reinstalling the arm, make sure the pivot shaft is in the park position. To reinstall the arm, position it on the shaft and push it into place. Remove the $3/32$-inch pin to lock it on the shaft.

Note: The 1970 Cougar, Falcon, and Mustang, and the 1970 on

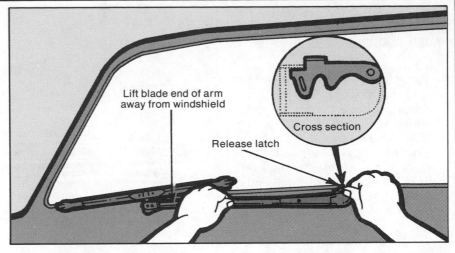

Lift blade end of arm away from windshield

Cross section

Release latch

Comet, Granada, Maverick, and Monarch models do not have a hole in the wiper arm and blade assembly to install a pin. On these models:

1. Swing the arm and blade assembly from the windshield, releasing the spring-loaded retaining clip from the shaft.
2. Remove the arm and blade assembly from the shaft by rocking it off. Do not attempt to pry it off with a screwdriver.
3. Before reinstalling the arm and blade assembly, make sure the pivot shaft is in the park position.
4. To reinstall the assembly, hold it in the swung-out position and push it onto the pivot shaft. The arm will automatically lock onto the shaft.

1972 on Montego, Torino, and Continental Mark IV, 1974 on Lincoln Continental

1. On 1973 on Lincoln Continental and 1974 on Mark IV models, disconnect the windshield washer hose from the wiper arm.
2. On all the above models, swing the wiper arm and blade assembly away from the windshield and move the side latch away from the pivot shaft. This will unlock the arm and hold the assembly away from the windshield.
3. Remove the assembly by rocking it off the shaft. Do not try to pry the arm off the shaft with a screwdriver.
4. Before reinstalling the arm and blade assembly, make

sure the pivot shaft is in the park position.
5. To reinstall the assembly, position it on the pivot shaft. Then, while holding the arm slightly outward, slide the latch toward the shaft and carefully swing the arm onto the windshield.
6. On 1973 on Lincoln Continental and 1974 on Mark IV models, reconnect the windshield washer hose to the wiper arm.

Mustang II and Pinto

1. Swing the arm and blade assembly away from the windshield. Then, while holding the assembly in the swung-out position, pull the arm off the pivot shaft using an appropriate tool.
2. To reinstall the assembly, hold it in the swung-out position and push the arm onto the pivot shaft. Then slowly swing the arm onto the windshield.

Chrysler Corporation

WIPER BLADES

1. Turn the wiper switch to "On" and move the blades and arms to a convenient location on the windshield by turning the ignition switch "On" and "Off" several times.
2. Lift the wiper blade off the glass, then depress the release lever on the center bridge and remove the blade from the wiper arm.
3. Using a screwdriver, depress the release button or lever on the end of the bridge. Then pull the blade through the end of the bridge.
4. To reinstall the blade, push the end opposite the one with the release latch into the bridge until the latch engages the bridge. If the wiper blade

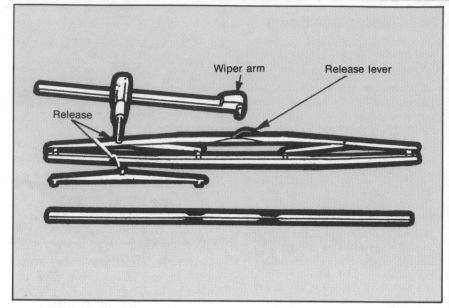

Wiper arm   Release lever   Release

is properly installed, all four bridge claws should be engaged and properly positioned on it.

5. Check the release latch for complete engagement with the bridge after the blade is installed.

WIPER ARMS

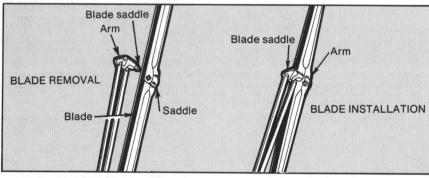

Blade saddle   Arm   BLADE REMOVAL   Blade   Saddle   Blade saddle   Arm   BLADE INSTALLATION

Caution: Using a screwdriver or other tool to pry the arm off may distort it. Special tools are available for removing wiper arms. Also, do not push or bend the spring clip at the base of the arm in an attempt to release it. The clip is self-releasing.

1. Place the wiper motor in the park position.
2. On cars with non-concealed wiper arms, position the special tool on the wiper arm assembly and lift off the arm by gently rocking the tool and arm unit.
3. To reinstall the arm on cars with non-concealed wiper arms, position the special tool in the same manner as before, then squeeze the tool and the

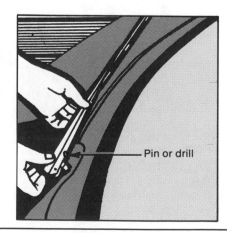

Pin or drill

wiper arm together, and install the arm on the pivot shaft. Make sure the arm and blade will return to the park position when the wiper switch is turned off.

4. On 1971 on models with concealed wipers, lift the hood to gain access to them. Then lift the arm, pull out the latch, and using a rocking motion, remove the arm from the pivot shaft.

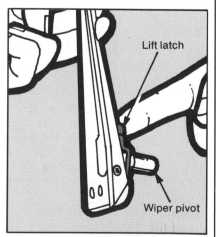

Lift latch   Wiper pivot

5. To reinstall the wiper arm on 1971 on models with concealed wipers, pull the release latch outward and rock the arm onto the pivot shaft. If the arm is properly installed, it should just barely contact the stops at the bottom of the windshield.

General Motors Corporation

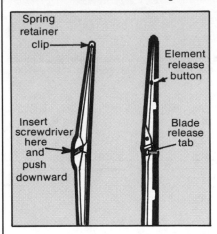

Spring retainer clip

Element release button

Insert screwdriver here and push downward

Blade release tab

WIPER BLADES

All models except Cadillac

1. Wiper blade assemblies are held in place by two methods: On the press-type release tab, depress the tab and slide the blade off the wiper arm pin. On the coil spring retainer, insert a screwdriver on the top of the spring and push it downward, then slide the blade assembly off the arm.
2. Wiper blades are held in their assemblies in two ways, a press-type release button or a spring-type retainer clip. To remove the blade element, either push the button or squeeze the clip, and slide the element off the blade.
3. To reinstall, reverse the above procedure. When the wiper element is properly installed, the release button or retaining clip should be at the end of the blade assembly nearest the wiper transmission.

WIPER ARMS

With rectangular motor:

1. Put the wiper motor in the park position. Note: Special tools are available for removing wiper arms. Using a screwdriver or other tool to pry them off may damage them. Using the appropriate tool, remove the arm by prying up to disengage it from the shaft.
2. Before reinstalling the arm, make sure the shaft is still in the park position. Then rotate the shaft the required distance and direction so the blades rest in the proper park position.

With round motor:

1. Put the wiper motor in the park position, then raise the hood to gain access to the wiper arms.
2. On all intermediate models, remove the wiper arm by rocking it off the pivot shaft.
3. On the left arm assembly, slide the articulating arm lock clip away from the pivot pin and lift the arm off the pin.
4. On full-size models, lift the wiper arm and slide the latch clip out from underneath it.
5. Remove the arm assembly by rocking it off the pivot pin.
6. To reinstall the right arm assembly, align the keyway in the wiper arm with the slot in the pivot shaft and push the assembly onto the shaft.

7. To reinstall the left arm assembly, place the articulating arm over the pin and slide the lock clip toward the pin until it locks in place. Reinstall the left wiper arm in the same way you did the right.

1971 on Cadillac

1. Raise the hood to gain access to the wiper arms. Lift the arm and slide the latch clip out from under it.
2. Release the wiper arm and remove it from the pivot shaft by rocking it off.
3. On the left arm assembly, slide the articulating arm lock clip away from the pin and lift the arm off the pin.

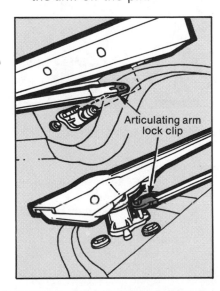

Articulating arm lock clip

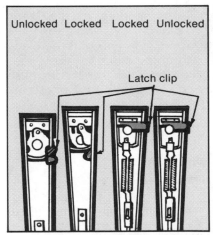

Unlocked   Locked   Locked   Unlocked

Latch clip

4. To reinstall the left wiper arm, place the articulating arm over the pin and slide the lock clip toward the pin until it locks in place. Reinstall the wiper arm on the pivot shaft, aligning the keyway in the arm with the slot in the shaft.
5. Lift the wiper arm outward and slide the latch clips under it. Carefully return the wiper arm and blade assembly to the windshield.

American Motors Corporation

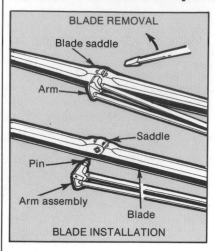

BLADE REMOVAL

Blade saddle

Arm

Saddle

Pin

Arm assembly

Blade

BLADE INSTALLATION

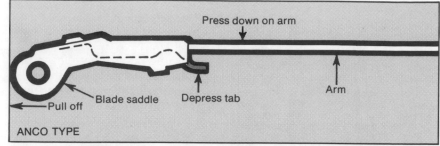

Press down on arm

Blade saddle

Pull off

Depress tab

Arm

ANCO TYPE

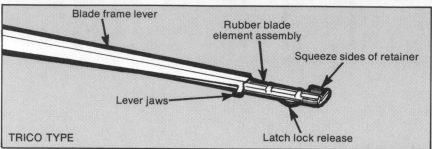

Blade frame lever

Rubber blade element assembly

Squeeze sides of retainer

Lever jaws

Latch lock release

TRICO TYPE

WIPER BLADES

1974 on Matador X

1. Insert a suitable tool or small screwdriver into the spring release opening of the blade saddle, then depress the spring clip and pull the blade from the arm.
2. To reinstall the blade, push the saddle onto the pin so the spring clip engages it. Make sure the blade is securely attached to the arm.

WIPER ARMS

1974 on Matador X

1. Raise the arm from the windshield and move the release latch away from the pivot shaft, then disconnect the washer hose.
2. On the driver's side, disengage the auxiliary arm from the pivot pin, and remove the wiper arm from the pivot shaft.
3. To reinstall the wiper arm, on the driver's side only, position the auxiliary arm over the pivot pin. Holding the auxiliary arm down, push the main arm head over the pivot shaft. Make sure the shaft is in the park position and the blade is positioned against the stop.
4. Hold the main arm end on the pivot shaft while raising the blade end of the wiper arm, then push the release latch into the lock under the shaft.
5. Lower the blade onto the windshield. If the two do not touch, the slide latch is not

1969 on, except Matador X

1. Press down on the arm to unlatch the top stud, then depress the tab on the saddle and pull out the blade.
2. To reinstall the blade, slide the saddle over the end of the wiper arm until the locking stud snaps into place, making

completely engaged. Now attach the washer hose.

1969 on, except Matador X

1. Lift the arm against the spring tension. Then, using a screwdriver, slide the cap away from the serrated shaft. Note: The arms are stamped L or R to indicate left- or right-side installation on the car.

sure the blade is securely attached to the arm.
3. To remove the blade element, squeeze the latch lock and pull it out.
4. To reinstall the element, insert it through each of the lever jaws, making sure that it is engaged in all of them.

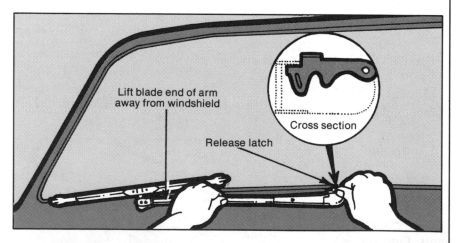

Lift blade end of arm away from windshield

Cross section

Release latch

2. Run the wiper motor for a few cycles, then turn it off to position the pivot shafts in the park position before installing the wiper arms.
3. Reinstall the arms and blades on the pivot shafts with the tips of the blades to the right side of the car.

Light System Service

All cars are equipped with a variety of lights, each of which performs a specific function. The major lights you'll find on your car include headlights (possibly two sets, one for low beams and one for high), and parking, backup, tail, brake, and side marker lights. In addition, some cars have auxiliary lighting for interiors, dash gauges, and trunk and underhood compartments.

Rear stop lights and rear turn signals are always red, except for a few models which have amber rear turn signals. Front turn signal lights are amber, and emergency flasher and side marker lights are amber in the front and red in the rear.

Most states require all lights to be fully operative and of the proper color, so you and other drivers can communicate intended changes of direction and other planned maneuvers in plenty of time to avoid accidents.

Once you begin working on your car's lighting system, you will find that the headlights are of the sealed-beam type. That is, you can't remove the bulb alone. You must remove and replace the entire unit including the lens and reflector. All other lights on a car use a separate bulb, so if one burns out, just the bulb need be replaced, not the whole assembly.

Lighting checkout

You can check all your car lights in less than a minute with a helper outside the car. Turn on the headlights. On dim (low beam), two of the four sealed-beam lights should shine down and to the right. On high beam, the two other headlights should flash on and light the road at a greater distance. If your car has only two headlights, both should shine with the dimmer switch in either the low or high beam position.

Turn the ignition switch to the accessory position and put the turn signal indicator-arm down. The appropriate light on the dashboard should light up and click on and off. If it stays on, either the front or rear indicator bulb on that side is burned out or the connection is bad. Repeat to check the other directional signal.

Flip on the emergency flasher light switch located on the steering column or the dashboard. Have your helper check the front flashers first. Then in the rear of the car he can check four sets of lights—the flashers, the driving lights, and the stop lights—as you push down on the brake pedal, and the backup lights as you reverse gear.

Headlights drain more electricity from the battery than the other lights, so make sure they are turned off when the engine is not running. And start the car before turning them on.

The emergency flasher lights should be turned on whenever you stop on the side of the road, so other drivers know your car is stopped. Flashers use very little electrical current and operate with the ignition key turned off.

Headlight aim

Testing headlights for direction and illumination is part of the regular safety inspection in 32 states and the District of Columbia. But, required or not, it's equally important that you have your lights tested in a service facility at least once a year.

Make sure your headlights are adjusted with the normal load you usually carry in the trunk and in the passenger compartment. Extra weight in the trunk pushes down the rear of the car and raises the headlight beams. Adjusting headlights under this condition, but then driving most of the time with the trunk empty, beams the lights too low.

Before making a trip, have your headlights adjusted to the load you will be carrying.

Disassembling headlights

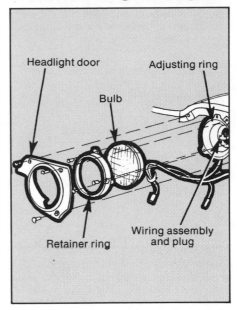

Headlight door

Adjusting ring

Bulb

Retainer ring

Wiring assembly and plug

1 **If your car is equipped with concealed headlights,** open the headlight doors by turning the headlights on. Refer to your owner's manual on how to keep the doors open while the headlights are not working.

2 **Remove the headlight trim retaining screws** and the trim. On some cars with concealed headlights, the headlight door has to be removed.

3 **Remove the retaining ring.** Three slotted tabs are placed 120° apart around some rings. To remove these, loosen the three retaining screws. Then turn the ring counterclockwise until the enlarged portion of the slots comes under the screw heads.

Some rings have unslotted tabs. In this case, remove the screws and the ring.

Still another type of ring is held by a hook on one side and a spring on the other. To remove these, unhook the spring from the ring using a pair of needle-nose pliers and disengage the ring from the hook. *Caution: When removing the retaining ring, be careful not to let the bulb slip out.*

4 **Pull the headlight forward** and unhook the electrical connector.

Reinstalling headlights

1 Attach the wiring connector to the new bulb. On two-headlight systems, make sure you install a Number 2 light. Four-headlight systems take a Number 2 light on the outboard side and a Number 1 light on the inboard side.

2 Place the light in position, then align the tabs on the light with the slots in the adjusting ring.

3 Reinstall the retaining ring. If it has slotted tabs, position it with the enlarged portion of the slotted holes over the retaining screw heads, then turn the screws clockwise and tighten them.

If the retaining ring does not have slotted holes in the tabs, position it on the adjusting ring and install the screws.

If the retaining ring is held by a spring and hook, use needle-nose pliers to engage one side of the ring on the hook and the other side on the spring.

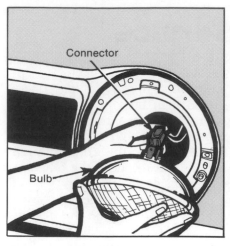

Connector

Bulb

4 Check the headlights on both high and low beam to make sure they are operating properly.

5 Reinstall the headlight trim and retaining screws. If removed, reinstall the headlight door.

6 Have the headlight adjustment checked.

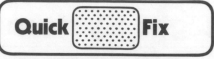

Quick Fix

Headlight spring installation

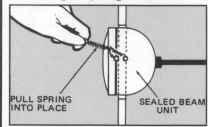

PULL SPRING INTO PLACE

SEALED BEAM UNIT

A spring is attached to the retaining ring of the sealed beam headlight unit on most cars. It's easy to unhook this spring from the retaining ring when a sealed beam unit is removed. Getting the spring hooked up again when the parts are reassembled is not so easy.

A simple way to do the job is to use a discarded brake shoe return spring. The type with two long hooks extending from a single coil spring in the center is fine for the job. Using one of the hooks as a handle, you can reach right in with the other hook and pull the spring into place.

Replacing dome light bulbs

1 If the dome light does not have retaining screws around it, squeeze the lens and snap it out. If it has screws, remove them and take the lens out.

If the bulb is long and cylindrical and resembles a fuse, insert a screwdriver under its end and pry it out of the clips. To reinstall a new bulb, position it on the clips and press it into place.

If the bulb is long and cylindrical and the ends are flat, push on the prong toward the bulb and lift it out. To install a new bulb, position and insert it.

2 To remove conventional bulbs, depress the bulb in the socket and rotate it counterclockwise, pulling it from its socket. Inspect the pins at the base of the bulb. If they are not the same distance from the bottom of the base, they must be aligned in the proper slots in the socket. Reinstall the bulb in the socket and rotate it clockwise. If it will not rotate, the pins are in the wrong slots. Remove the bulb, rotate it one-half a turn, then reinstall it and the lens.

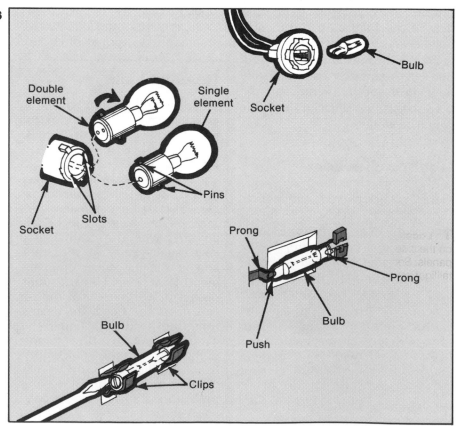

Double element

Single element

Bulb

Socket

Socket

Slots

Pins

Prong

Prong

Push

Bulb

Bulb

Clips

Replacing stop, turn signal, parking, and backup light bulbs

1 Locate the bulbs. They are usually installed in the trunk lid, front or rear bumper, front grille, or on the body of the car. If the lens of the malfunctioning bulb has retaining screws which are visible from the outside of the car, the bulb can be reached by removing the screws and the lens. If no screws are visible, reach in through the trunk or engine compartment and remove the bulb by twisting it counterclockwise or rocking it.

2 To install a new bulb, align the pins on the base with the proper slot in the socket. The locating pins on the base of bulbs with double filaments are staggered to prevent incorrect installation. Insert the bulb into the socket and turn it clockwise to lock it in place. If the bulb does not turn, it is incorrectly aligned. Remove the bulb, turn it one-half a turn, and reinstall it.

3 If necessary, reinstall the lens and retaining screws.

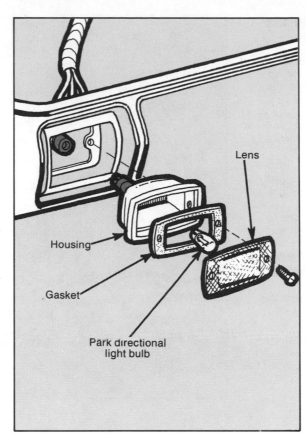

Lens

Housing

Gasket

Park directional light bulb

Replacing side marker lights

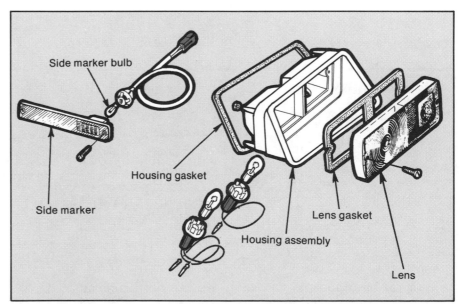

Side marker bulb

Side marker

Housing gasket

Lens gasket

Housing assembly

Lens

1 Locate the lights. They are installed on the side of the fenders and quarter panels. Some cars use a wrap-around taillight assembly which doubles as the side marker lights. If the side marker lens has retaining screws visible from the outside of the car, remove the screws and the lens and take out the bulb. If not, access to the bulb will be through the trunk or engine compartment or behind the fender through the wheel opening. Two types of bulbs are used. The first is removed by rotating it counterclockwise and pulling it straight out, the second by just pulling it out.

2 Install the new bulb. If the bulb was removed by rotating and pulling it out, reinstall it by aligning the pins on its base with the slots in the socket. Then rotate it clockwise to lock it in place. If the bulb was removed by pulling it straight out, reinstall it by pushing straight in.

3 If the lens was removed to get the bulb out, reinstall the lens and its retaining screws.

4 If the bulb was removed through the trunk or engine compartment or through the wheel opening, install it by aligning the tabs on the socket with the slots in the housing. Then either twist the socket or rotate it into place.

Replacing license plate lights

1 Remove the housing retaining screws and work the housing out from behind the bumper.

2 Remove the lens retaining screws, the lens, and the gasket. Then take out the bulb. Two types of bulbs are used. The first is removed by rotating it counterclockwise and pulling it straight out, the second by just pulling it straight out.

3 Install the new bulb. If it was removed by rotating and pulling it out, reinstall it by aligning the pins on its base with the slots in the socket. Then insert the bulb into the socket and twist it clockwise to lock it in place. If the bulb was removed by pulling it straight out, reinstall it by pushing it straight in.

4 Reinstall the gasket, the lens, and the retaining screws.

5 Work the housing back into place and install the retaining screws.

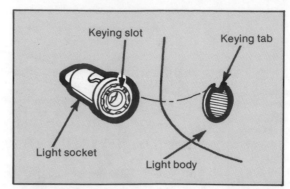

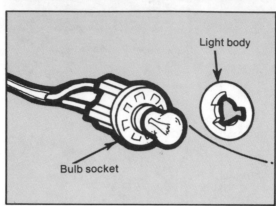

Flasher units

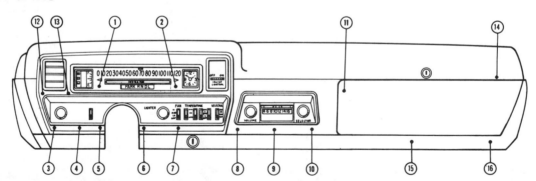

Your car has two little tin can-shaped or box-shaped units that go click-click. One is for the blinking turn-signal lights (TSF), and the other for the hazard warning (HWF) lights that blink on all four corners of the car. If the flashers do not work and you do not hear any clicks when you turn them on, the units may have to be replaced. They are located behind the dashboard in different places for different makes, models, and years of manufacture.

On the chart opposite, find the horizontal row with the make and model of your car in the left column. Find the year in the row across the top and run down that column. The box where they meet will show a bold number.

Look for that number on the diagram of a typical dashboard on this page. You will find your car's signal unit behind the dashboard at, or close to, that spot.

If you find a small circled number in the chart, it refers you to the corresponding number in the special notes.

Flasher Unit Locations

Car	1975 TSF	1975 HWF	1976 TSF	1976 HWF	1977 TSF	1977 HWF	1978 TSF	1978 HWF	1979 TSF	1979 HWF	1980 TSF	1980 HWF
American Motors	3	[9]	3	[9]	3	[9]	3	[3]	3	3	3	3
Astre & Vega	5	3	5	3	5	3	—	—	—	—	—	—
Buick, Century & Regal	3	3	4	3	4	3	3	3	3	3	3	3
Buick Apollo & Skylark	10	3	10	3	10	3	10	3	10	3	6	15
Cadillac Exc. Seville	[2]	3	[2]	3	3[11]	3	3[11]	3	3	3	3	3
Cadillac Seville	—	—	4	3	4	3	4	3	4	3	3	3
Camaro	8	3	4	3	4	3	4	3	4	3	4	3
Capri & Mustang	7	7	7	7	7	7	7	7	4	4	4	4
Chevelle, Malibu & Monte Carlo	4	3	4	3	4	3	3	3	3	3	3	3
Chevette	—	—	13	3	13	3	13	3	13	3	13	3
Chevrolet	6	3	7	3	3	3	3	3	3	3	3	3
Chevrolet Citation	—	—	—	—	—	—	—	—	—	—	6	15
Chevrolet Nova	10	3	10	3	10	3	10	3	10	3	—	—
Chrysler, Imperial & LeBaron	5	5	5	3	5[13]	3	5[13]	3	7[13]	6[13]	7[13]	6[13]
Comet & Maverick	4	3	4	3	4	3	—	—	—	—	—	—
Cordoba & Mirada	3	6	13	[5]	13	[5]	14	4	9	3	5	5
Corvette	16	3	16	3	16	3	16	3	3	3	3	3
Cougar & LTD II	5	5	3	3	4	4	4	4	4	4	—	—
Dart & Valiant	4	5	5	5	—	—	—	—	—	—	—	—
Dodge & Plymouth Full Size	5	5	5	5	5	3	5	3	7	6	7	6
Dodge & Plymouth Intermed.	13	[5]	[10]	4[7]	[12]	3[13]	[12]	3	[1]	3	3	3
Dodge Omni & Plymouth Horizon	—	—	—	—	—	—	3	3	3	3	3	3
Firebird & LeMans	3	3	3	3	4	3	3[8]	3	3[8]	3	3[8]	3
Ford & Mercury Full Size	3	4	3	4	3	3	3	3	3	3	3	3
Ford Fairmont & Mercury Zephyr	—	—	—	—	—	—	14	11	14	11	14	11
Ford Pinto & Mercury Bobcat	11	11	11	11	11	11	11	11	6	6	—	—
Granada, Monarch & Versailles	8	4	10	4	6	4	10	4	8	5	—	—
Grand Am & Grand Prix	3	3	3	3	3	3	3	3	3	3	3	3
Lincoln	11[6]	3	10[6]	3	10[6]	3	10[6]	3	3[4]	3	—	—
Montego, Torino & Elite	3	3	3	3	—	—	—	—	—	—	—	—
Monza, Skyhawk, Starfire & Sunbird	5	3	12	12	12	12	12[14]	4	12[14]	4	12	4
Oldsmobile	4	3	4	3	3	3	3	3	3	3	3	3
Oldsmobile Cutlass	4	3	4	3	4	3	3	3	3	3	3	3
Olds. Omega	10	3	10	3	10	3	10	3	10	3	6	15
Oldsmobile Toronado	4	3	4	3	4	3	4	3	3	3	3	3
Pontiac	3	3	3	5	3	3	3	3	3	3	3	3
Pont. Phoenix & Ventura	10	3	10	3	10	3	10	3	10	3	6	15
Thunderbird	3	3	3	3	4	4	4	4	3	3	—	—

TSF: Turn Signal Flasher.   HWF: Hazard Warning Flasher.

[1]—Location 9 on Magnum. Location 3 on Aspen, Diplomat & Volaré.
[2]—On the underside of steering column lower cover.
[3]—Location 3 on Concord & Gremlin. Location 4 on Matador. Location 5 on Pacer.
[4]—Location 10 on Mark V.
[5]—On right side of brake pedal support.
[6]—Location 3 on Mark IV & V.
[7]—On right side of brake pedal support on Charger, Coronet & Fury models.
[8]—Location 4 on Firebird.
[9]—Location 6 on Gremlin & Hornet. Location 4 on Matador. Location 5 on Pacer.
[10]—Location 3 on Aspen & Volaré. Location 13 on Charger, Coronet & Fury.
[11]—On underside of steering column cover on Eldorado models.
[12]—Location 3 on Aspen, Diplomat & Volaré. Location 13 on Charger, Fury, Magnum & Monaco.
[13]—On right side of brake pedal support on Charger, Fury & Monaco.
[14]—Location 5 on Monza "S" Coupe, Sunbird Coupe & all Sta. Wag.
[15]—Location 3 on LeBaron.

Replacing fuses

1 Locate the fuse panels. They are usually attached to the fire wall on the driver's side, underneath the instrument panel, or in the glove box.

2 Make sure the ignition is off.

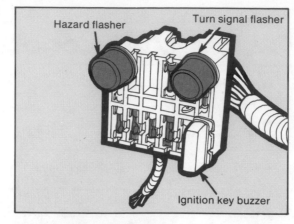

3 Remove the fuse with a fuse puller if you have one. If not, it can be pried out using half a clothespin. Use firm, steady pressure to remove it without breaking it.

4 Position the new fuse against the retaining clips, then press both ends of the fuse inward against the clips until the fuse snaps into place.

5 Check the operation of the circuit for which the fuse was replaced. If the fuse burns, there is a short in the circuit and a mechanic should repair it.

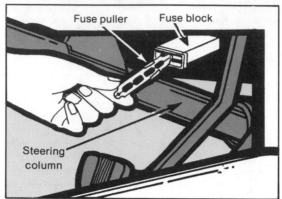

Tooting the horn

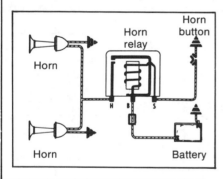

Every car has one or more horns. They are usually mounted behind the grille in the engine compartment. The horn circuit consists of a horn ring at the steering wheel, which completes the relay circuit by grounding the relay when the ring is depressed or squeezed, a horn relay, an electromagnetic switch electrically connecting the horn or horns to the battery, a fuse or circuit breaker to protect the circuit, and the horn or horns themselves. Inside the horn is a metal diaphragm which vibrates when electricity passes through it.

On the opposite page you will find a Troubleshooting Flow Chart to assist you in diagnosing horn problems.

Tips on electrical service

- If you suspect an electrical problem, first check the fuse box for a blown or defective fuse, except with headlights, which have circuit breakers.
- Remember: You could have a bad fuse without a visible separation of the fuse filament.
- To quickly check the condition of a bulb, hold it up to the light and tap it with your finger. If the filament itself or loose shreds shake around inside, replace the bulb.

- Caution: Be very careful when changing fuses. They break easily and the glass particles can cut you. Also be careful when inserting a light bulb into its socket.
- When inserting a bulb into its socket, make sure there is a good contact between the bulb itself and the contact strip in the socket.
- If the bulb goes on and off when lightly shaken, you are getting a poor contact be-

tween the bulb and the socket. Take out and reinsert the bulb to get a better contact.
- All parking and side marker lights have a sealing rubber gasket behind the lens. When replacing bulbs behind these lenses, be careful not to rip the gasket. If you should rip it, replace it. Otherwise, the whole assembly can fill up with water and short out the bulb.

Replacing turn signal and hazard warning flashers

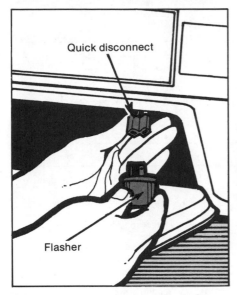

Quick disconnect

Flasher

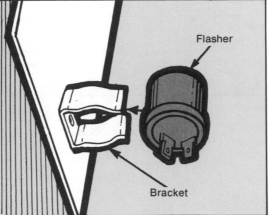

Flasher

Bracket

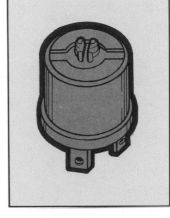

1 Locate the flashers. They are mounted in several different ways. They may be plugged into the fuse panel; they may be of the tab-and-slot type, where the end of the flasher has a slot which engages a tab underneath the instrument panel; they may be retained on a bracket; or they may be taped to an existing wiring harness.

2 Remove the flasher.

If it is mounted on the fuse panel, pull it straight out.

If it is of the tab-and-slot type, disengage it by pulling it off the tab and disconnecting the wiring connector.

If the flasher is retained by a clip, pull it from the clip and disconnect the wiring connector.

If it is taped to an existing harness, pull it from the connector and leave the connector attached to the wiring harness.

3 Install the new flasher. If it is mounted on the fuse panel, align the

prongs on the flasher with the slots in the panel and push it into place.

If it is of the tab-and-slot type, connect it to the wiring connector and engage the slot on the flasher with the tab.

If the flasher was retained by a clip, connect it to the wiring connector and snap it onto the clip.

If it is taped to the wiring harness, reconnect it to the connector.

Troubleshooting flow chart: horns

Symptom	Probable cause	Remedy
Horns inoperative.	1. Loose connection in circuit. 2. Defective horn switch. 3. Defective horn relay. 4. Defects within horn.	1. Check and tighten connections. Be sure to check ground straps. 2. Replace defective parts. 3. Replace relay. 4. Replace horn.
Horns have poor tone.	1. Low available voltage at horn, or defects within horn.	1. Check battery and charging circuit. Although horn should blow at any voltage above 7.0, a weak or poor tone may occur at operating voltages below 11.0. If horn has weak or poor tone at operating voltages of 11.0 or higher, remove horn and replace it.
Horns operate intermittently.	1. Loose or intermittent connections in horn relay or horn circuit. 2. Defective horn switch. 3. Defective relay. 4. Defects within horn.	1. Check and tighten connections. 2. Replace switch. 3. Replace relay. 4. Replace horn.
Horns blow constantly.	1. Sticking horn relay. 2. Horn relay energized by grounded or shorted wiring. 3. Horn button grounded by sticking closed.	1. Replace relay. 2. Check and adjust wiring. 3. Adjust or replace damaged parts.

Troubleshooting flow chart: headlights

Symptom	Probable cause	Remedy
One headlight inoperative or intermittent.	1. Loose connection. 2. Defective sealed beam.	1. Secure connections to sealed beam, including ground. 2. Replace sealed beam.
One or more headlights dim.	1. Open ground connection at headlight. 2. Ground wire mislocated in headlight connector (Number 2 sealed beam).	1. Repair ground wire connection between sealed beam and body ground. 2. Relocate ground wire in connector.
One or more headlights have short life.	1. Voltage regulator maladjusted.	1. Readjust regulator to specifications.
All headlights inoperative or intermittent.	1. Loose connection. 2. Defective dimmer switch. 3. Open wiring—light switch to dimmer switch. 4. Open wiring—light switch to battery. 5. Shorted ground circuit. 6. Defective light switch.	1. Check and secure connections at dimmer switch and light switch. 2. Check voltage at dimmer switch with test light. If test light bulb goes on only at switch "Hot" wire terminal, replace dimmer switch. 3. Check wiring with test light. If bulb goes on at light switch wire terminal, but not at dimmer switch, repair open wire. 4. Check "Hot" wire terminal at light switch with test light. If light does not go on, repair open wire circuit to battery (possible open fusible link). 5. If, after a few minutes of operation, headlights flicker on and off, and/or a thumping noise can be heard from the light switch (circuit breaker opening and closing), repair short to ground in circuit between light switch and headlights. After repairing short, check for headlight flickering after one minute of operation. If flickering still occurs, the circuit breaker has been damaged and light switch must be replaced. 6. Check switch, replace if necessary.
Upper or lower beam will not light or intermittent.	1. Open connection or defective dimmer switch. 2. Short circuit to ground.	1. Check dimmer switch terminals with test light. If bulb lights at all wire terminals, repair open wiring between dimmer switch and headlights. If bulb will not light at one of these terminals, replace dimmer switch. 2. Follow remedy above for all headlights inoperative or intermittent.

Troubleshooting flow chart: side marker lights

Symptom	Probable cause	Remedy
One light inoperative.	1. Turn signal bulb burned out (front light). 2. Side marker bulb burned out. 3. Loose connection or open wiring.	1. Switch turn signals on. If signal bulb does not light, replace it. 2. Replace bulb. 3. Using test light, check "Hot" wire terminal at bulb socket. If test light goes on, repair open ground circuit. If light does not go on, repair open "Hot" wire circuit.
Front or rear lights inoperative.	1. Loose connection or open ground connection. 2. Multiple bulbs burned out.	1. If associated tail or parking lights do not operate, secure all connectors in "Hot" wire circuit. If tail and parking lights operate, repair open ground connections. 2. Replace bulbs.

Side marker lights, continued:

Symptom	Probable cause	Remedy
All lights inoperative.	1. Blown fuse.	1. If parking and taillights do not operate, replace blown fuse. If new fuse blows, check for short to ground between fuse panel and lights.
	2. Loose connection.	2. Secure connector to light switch.
	3. Open wiring.	3. Check taillight fuse with test light. If test light goes on, repair open wiring between fuse and light switch. If not, repair open wiring between fuse and battery (possible open fusible link).
	4. Defective light switch.	4. Check light switch, replace if necessary.

Troubleshooting flow chart: tail, parking, and license plate lights

Symptom	Probable cause	Remedy
One side inoperative.	1. Bulb burned out.	1. Replace bulb.
	2. Open ground connection at bulb socket or ground wire terminal.	2. Jump bulb base socket connection to ground. If light goes on, repair open ground circuit.
Both sides inoperative.	1. Taillight fuse has blown.	1. Replace fuse. If new fuse blows, repair short to ground in "Hot" wire circuit between fuse panel through light switch to lights.
	2. Loose connection.	2. Secure connector at light switch.
	3. Open wiring.	3. Using test light, check circuit on both sides of fuse. If neither light goes on, repair open circuit between fuse panel and battery (possible open fusible link). If test light goes on at light switch terminal, repair open wiring between light switch and lights.
	4. Multiple bulbs burned out.	4. If test light goes on at light socket "Hot" wire terminal, replace bulbs.
	5. Defective light switch.	5. Check light switch, replace if necessary.

Troubleshooting flow chart: turn signal and hazard warning lights

Symptom	Probable cause	Remedy
Turn signals inoperative on one side.	1. Bulb(s) burned out (flasher cannot be heard).	1. Turn hazard warning system on. If one or more bulbs are inoperative, replace them.
	2. Open wiring or ground connection.	2. Turn hazard warning system on. If one or more bulbs are inoperative, use test light and check circuit at light socket. If test light goes on, repair open ground connection. If not, repair open wiring between bulb socket and turn signal switch.
	3. Defective bulb or turn signal switch.	3. Turn hazard warning system on. If all front and rear lights operate, check for defective bulb. If bulbs are OK, replace turn signal switch.
	4. Short to ground (flasher can be heard, no bulbs operate).	4. Locate and repair short to ground by disconnecting front and rear circuits separately.
Turn signals inoperative on both sides.	1. Blown turn signal fuse.	1. Turn hazard warning system on. If all lights operate, replace blown fuse. If new fuse blows, repair short to ground between fuse and lights.
	2. Defective flasher.	2. If turn signal fuse is OK and hazard warning system will operate lights, replace flasher.
	3. Loose connection.	3. Secure steering column connector.

Turn signal and hazard warning lights, continued:

Symptom	Probable cause	Remedy
Hazard warning lights inoperative.	1. Blown fuse.	1. Switch turn signals on. If lights operate, replace fuse if blown. If new fuse blows, repair short to ground (could be in stoplight circuit).
	2. Defective hazard warning flasher.	2. If fuse is OK, switch turn signals on. If lights operate, replace defective flasher.
	3. Open wiring or defective turn signal switch.	3. Using a test light, check hazard switch feed wire in turn signal steering column connector. If light does not operate on either side of connector, repair open circuit between flasher and connector. If light goes on only on feed side of connector, clean connector contacts. If light operates on both sides of connector, replace defective switch assembly.

Troubleshooting flow chart: stoplights

Symptom	Probable cause	Remedy
One bulb inoperative.	1. Bulb burned out.	1. Replace bulb.
One side inoperative.	1. Loose connection, open wiring, or defective bulb.	1. Turn on directional signal. If light does not operate, check bulbs. If bulbs are OK, secure all connections. If light still does not operate, use test light and check for open wiring.
	2. Defective directional signal switch or cancelling cam.	2. If light will operate by turning directional signal on, switch is not centering properly during cancelling operation. Replace defective cancelling cam or directional signal switch.
All lights inoperative.	1. Blown fuse.	1. Replace fuse. If new fuse blows, repair short to ground in circuit between fuse and lights.
	2. Stop switch maladjusted or defective.	2. Check stop switch. Adjust or replace if required.
Lights will not turn off.	1. Stop switch maladjusted or defective.	1. Readjust switch. If switch still malfunctions, replace it.

Troubleshooting flow chart: backup lights

Symptom	Probable cause	Remedy
One light inoperative or intermittent.	1. Loose or burned out bulb. 2. Loose connection. 3. Open ground connections.	1. Secure or replace bulb. 2. Tighten connectors. 3. Repair bulb ground circuit.
Both lights inoperative or intermittent.	1. Neutral start or backup light switch maladjusted. 2. Loose connection or open circuit.	1. Readjust switch. 2. Secure all connectors. If OK, check continuity of circuit from fuse to lights with test light. If light does not operate on either side of fuse, correct open circuit from battery to fuse.
	3. Blown fuse.	3. Replace fuse. If new fuse blows, repair short to ground in circuit from fuse through neutral start switch to backup lights.
	4. Defective neutral start or backup light switch.	4. Check switch, replace if necessary.
	5. Defective ignition switch.	5. If test light operates at ignition switch battery terminal but not at output terminal, replace ignition switch.
Lights will not turn off.	1. Neutral start or backup switch maladjusted. 2. Defective neutral start or backup light switch.	1. Readjust switch. 2. Check switch, replace if necessary.

TIRES

The original equipment tires that came with your car are comparable to the 100-level or "first line" tires of the five major manufacturers. Second line and third line tires are of lower quality but produced by the same manufacturers. Premium tires are "top of the line" and the most expensive on the market.

If you were satisfied with the performance of your original equipment tires, you should specify 100-level when the time comes to replace them. If your car is used only for short hops—to the shopping center and other local trips—a second line tire may serve your purpose. If you do not expect to keep the car much longer and its current use is limited to very short trips, a third line tire will probably do.

Retreads are another possibility for a car used only for local trips and with a short life expectancy. However, you must know the reputation of the retreader before buying them. Good retreads are good but bad ones are really bad.

Price is a fairly good indicator of new tire quality. But what if you find yourself choosing between two tires that look alike, except one costs twice as much as the other? The cheaper tire may have a lower grade of fabric and a narrower, shallower tread that will wear rapidly on the road. In that case, the costlier tire would be the better bargain. Your best bet in choosing tires is to know the dealer.

Section 203 of the National Traffic and Motor Vehicle Safety Act, passed by Congress in 1966, provided for the establishment of a uniform quality grading system for car tires. The aim was to make it easier for the consumer to select the best tires for his car. In 1974, the National Highway Traffic Safety Administration (part of the Department of Transportation) proposed a set of standards which include ratings for tread wear, traction, and temperature resistance.

These ratings show as moulded or printed symbols on the side of the tire. The symbol for tread wear is a number. One number indicates the tire wears at the standard rate set by the NHTSA. A lower or higher number shows the tire will wear, say, twice or half as fast. The symbol for traction is a capital letter, A, B or C. The symbol for resistance to temperature and the ability to dissipate heat is a lower case letter ranging from a through c.

CONTENTS

Construction fundamentals

A normal tire has four parts—the tread, the sidewall, the bead which holds the tire securely to the metal wheel rim, and fabric plies. The character of the fabric plies, which give the tire its skeletal structure, determines the tire's strength, stability, and resistance to bruises, fatigue, and heat. The plies vary in number and material. Without them, a rubber tire would be little more than a soft rubber balloon. The latest developments in tire design have been in the areas of tread width and ply construction.

Bias-ply tires were the most common type until a few years ago. They are still used frequently, mainly because of their low cost. But, as tire fabricating has advanced technologically, other construction methods have become more popular because they offer better performance.

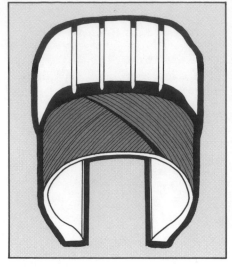

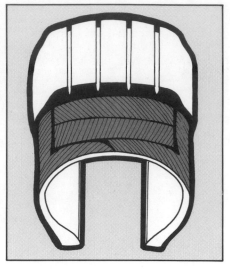

In bias-ply construction, the fabric cords or plies are molded to the carcass of the tire in a crisscrossed pattern much like a herringbone tweed. The angle these cords make with each other determines certain characteristics of the tire—high speed stability, ride harshness, and handling. Generally speaking, the lower the cord angle, the better the high speed stability, but also the harsher the ride. Usually, cord angles are about 35 degrees from the centerline of the tire, giving strength to both sidewall and tread. Alternate plies extend in opposite directions. These layers of cord can be made of one of several materials—rayon, nylon, or polyester.

Bias-ply tires come in either 2-ply, 4-ply, 6-ply, or 8-ply. Most 2-ply tires now use very strong, heavy plies and have the equivalent strength of four normal plies. These tires are designated as 2-ply/4-ply rating. The same up-grading can hold true for a 4-ply tire; it may carry an 8-ply rating. This construction provides flexibility and two-directional strength in both tread and sidewall areas. It is a very serviceable construction and one that has been a standard in the tire-making industry for many years.

The bias-belted tire has gained wide acceptance both as original equipment and as a replacement tire. It offers the car owner high mileage and great resistance to road hazards, plus excellent traction. Basically, the bias-belted is an improvement upon the bias-ply. It is constructed with two or four plies of a strong inner fabric to which rubber sidewalls and tread are bonded. However, before the tread is applied, belts which encircle the circumference of the tire are added.

A tire with bias-belted construction keeps its tread firmly on the road, greatly reducing tread squirm, a major cause of tire wear. The belts make the tire much more resistant to punctures, cuts, and bruises. A bias-belted tire can be made of several combinations of materials. Plies and belts of rayon, nylon, polyester, fiberglass, and steel are common. But it is the construction principle, the combination of body plies and belts, more than the materials, which gives the bias-belted tire its many advantages.

Though more expensive than the conventional tire, the bias-belted provides greater value for the motorist. For an investment of approximately 25 percent more, he can expect to gain up to 40 percent more mileage compared with a regular bias tire.

When do you need new tires?

You should carefully inspect your tires at least once a month. Certainly you should never go more than 5,000 miles without checking them.

If a tire is smooth, get a new one. If the tire is worn unevenly, it indicates a mechanical malfunction somewhere. The tire probably should be replaced and the condition that caused the damage should be corrected. Uneven wear can indicate several things wrong—misalignment, the most common reason for fast wear; worn shock absorbers; a worn, loose front end; wheels out-of-balance; or a combination of these.

Tire Sizes

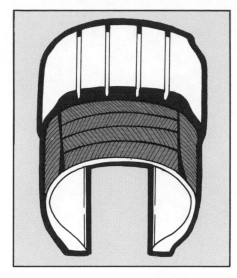

The radial-ply tire provides the best combination of wear, handling, and overall performance. A radial tire has a body made of cords which run straight up and over in hoop fashion from rim-edge to rim-edge. To provide puncture resistance, long life, and tread stability, two or more very stable and strong belts are run around the tire's circumference under the tread. The belts encircle the tire to add support to the body and to help hold the tread grooves open for effective traction. The belts also enable the elements of the tread pattern to resist the normal tendency to squeeze closed during road contact, effectively prolonging tread life. This combination results in a tire with extremely flexible sidewalls and a strong, stable tread area. The tire deflects more than bias or belted tires and therefore has a soft or under-inflated look.

Radial tires are produced with various combinations of rayon, polyester, steel cord, or other new fibers in plies and belts. Because the manufacturing process for a radial tire is more complicated, it costs more than other tire types, but the difference in purchase price will be made up through greater tread wear. Tread mileage for radial tires is frequently guaranteed for 40,000 miles. *Caution: Because the radial has a quicker steering response, radials should not be mixed with other types of tires.*

For long, sustained, high-speed runs on the open road, the radial tire has no equal. It runs cooler, handles well, and is quiet. In tests, engineers have found that most radials deliver from 40 to 100 percent more tire mileage than other kinds of tires, and their lower rolling resistance helps you get slightly better gas mileage. So, they may be worth the higher initial cost. One drawback: if your car is not engineered for radials and a slightly harder ride at lower speeds bothers you, then you'd better check into other types.

The profile ratio of a tire is the relation of it's cross-section height, from tread to bead, compared to its cross-section width, from sidewall to sidewall. A 70-series tire, for example, has a profile ratio of 70, that is, the height of the tire is 70 percent of the width.

For many years, a profile ratio of approximately 83 was considered standard or conventional for most bias-ply passenger car tires. With the advent of bias-belted and radial-ply constructions, lower profile tires with ratios of 78, 70, and even 60 have become popular. Today, most new cars are equipped with 70- or 78-series tires.

Both tire construction and profile ratio can have a pronounced influence on the handling and performance characteristics of a car. In selecting new tires, therefore, it is advisable first to check the manufacturer's specifications in the owner's manual.

Prior to 1967, common tire size designations consisted of numbers, such as 7.75-14 or 9.50-15. In numerical designations, the first number (7.75) refers to the approximate cross-section width in inches of an inflated tire, and the second number (14) is the rim diameter. Tires with numerical size designations have an 83 profile ratio and are all but obsolete except on second line economy tires.

With the advent of wider profile ratios in 1967, a new series of size designations using letters and numbers went into effect. Tires from 78-series through 50-series use the letters A through N to identify size, with A being the smallest tire and N the largest. The letter is followed by a number to indicate the tire's approximate height-to-width ratio, followed by the rim diameter. For instance, on an F78-14 tire, the number 78 means that the tire is 78 percent as high as it is wide. The number 14 indicates that it fits a 14-inch rim. Radial tire manufacturers

use several size designations. One uses a combination of metric and inch designations. In the case of a 195 R 14 size, for example, the number 195 refers to the approximate cross-section width in millimeters. R means radial and 14 is the rim diameter in inches. Radials of the 78, 70, 60, and 50-series use the same size designations as their bias-ply or bias-belted equivalents with the addition of the letter R.

Even this letter designation system is not universally accepted. Some companies are using a metric system to designate a 70-series tire. So you might see a tire marked 185 70-13. This identifies a 70-series tire that is equivalent to the old 185 metric size.

Other tire markings

You might see a tire marked GR70VR-15. This tire fits on a 15-inch rim and it is a 70-series radial, size G. The V is a speed designation. There are three letters used to indicate at what maximum speed a tire is safe. A tire marked S is good for up to 113 miles per hour; a tire marked H is good to 130; and a tire marked V is safe to 165 miles per hour. These designations are given after a tire is operated at that speed for 24 hours under a full load.

Reading the Tire

By reading the sidewalls of a tire, you can learn its size, design, and construction specifications.

F78-14 (replaces 7.75-14). This indicates a current size marking together with its equivalent bias tire size designation.

Load range B. The letter B indicates a 4-ply rating. As letters progress in the alphabet, load range increases. For example, D would be the same as a former 8-ply rating.

Maximum load 1500 lbs. @ 32 psi (pounds per square inch) maximum pressure. This indicates the tire's load limit and maximum cold inflation. For normal operation, follow pressure recommendations in the owner's manual or on the instruction sticker in the car.

4 plies under tread (2xxxx cord) + (2 xxxx cord) sidewall 2 plies xxxx cord. This indicates tire ply composition which depends upon the materials used.

DOT xxxx xx xxxx. The letters DOT certify compliance with Department of Transportation tire safety standards. Adjacent to this symbol is a tire identification number, the first two characters of which identify the tire manufacturer. The remaining characters identify size, type, and date of manufacture. When buying new tires, be sure the seller records your name, address, and tire identification numbers as required by federal law.

Tubeless. The tire must be marked either tubeless or tube-type. If a radial tire, the word radial must also be carried.

Tire saving tips

- Break in a new tire gradually. Don't go over 50 miles per hour for the first 50 miles the tire is on the car.
- Check the air pressure regularly when tires are cold; that is, before starting out. Maintain the specified pressure found in the owner's manual.
- When traveling overloaded, or prior to a long trip, inflate your tires properly. This usually means increasing the air pressure. See your owner's manual.
- Drive with anticipation. Avoid jamming on the brakes at traffic lights and intersections. Eliminate jackrabbit starts. Corner at posted speeds. Drive around chuckholes and curbs.
- Check your tires before, during, and after a long trip.
- Do not bleed your tires during a long trip, even if the air pressure increases somewhat.
- Inspect the tires frequently for irregular wear patterns that could signify bad shocks, misalignment, or out-of-balance tires. Keep in mind that most tires are worn out due to defective front end steering parts.
- Check the valve stem and dust cap if the tire is losing air.
- Be sure your spare tire is properly inflated at all times and ready to roll if and when you need it.
- Consolidate your shopping trips around town to make maximum use of your car when it is out. Don't make several trips when one would do.

Read any good tire sidewalls lately?

P metric tires were introduced into the marketplace during 1977 and are now furnished as original equipment on a number of cars.

Alpha-numeric tire size designations have been in widespread use in the US for some time.

The P series metric tire size designations are set up as explained in the following example:

P 205/75R14

P identifies passenger car tire

205 is the width in millimeters (one millimeter = .04 inch)

75 is the height-to-width ratio

R identifies radial construction (B if bias-belted or D if diagonal or bias)

14 is the rim diameter in inches

While these tires are designed in terms of kilograms (kg) for load and kilopascals (kPa) for inflation, tire sidewall labeling will also show loads in pounds and inflation in psi.

There are several important considerations when replacing one of the above types with the other. The most important of these are: load and inflation, dimensions, and construction type.

A replacement tire must have an adequate capacity to carry the maximum load for which the car was designed. Consult the vehicle tire information placard to find the recommended original equipment tire size(s) and recommended inflation pressures, from which you can find the corresponding tire load. The placard is usually located on the driver's doorpost or on the glove box door. Select a replacement tire size which has a load-carrying capacity equal to or greater than the original tire size at the highest similar inflation pressure.

You may use a replacement tire with slightly less load capacity (at the pressure referred to above for the original tire) by adjusting its inflation pressure to obtain the necessary load capacity.

The load capacity of the replacement tire at the new adjusted inflation pressure must always equal or exceed the load capacity of the original equipment tire at its recommended inflation pressure.

ECONOTIP

#19

Tires and mileage

The next time your car needs tires, consider buying radials. They have considerably less rolling resistance than bias ply tires. You can actually feel this if you ever have occasion to push a car a few feet by hand. The bias ply tires make it difficult or almost impossible to get the car moving. Radials make even the heaviest car easy to push. The usual improvement in mileage is about three percent. The only disadvantage to radials is their somewhat harsher ride. The shock of hitting tar strips or pavement ridges is not absorbed by a radial tire. But this is a small penalty to pay for the better mileage.

Bad weather driving

- Stopping on a wet road can take up to four times the normal distance it takes on a dry road. Stopping on glare ice takes ten times the normal distance.
- Test traction on different road surfaces and in bad weather by occasional light braking.
- Keep tires properly inflated. To avoid swerving when braking, front tire pressures must be kept equal.
- Do not tailgate.
- Slow down on slippery roads. When braking, pump to avoid locking wheels, which can cause skids.
- If a skid starts, take your foot off the gas, keep off the brakes, and steer in the direction of the skid. When the car has straightened out, pump the brakes gently to slow down.
- Winter note: since cold weather reduces tire pressure approximately one pound per square inch for every 10 degree drop in temperature, tires should be checked more frequently during winter months to make sure pressures are at the levels recommended by your car owner's manual.
- Light rain or drizzle, especially after a dry spell, produces a thin, greasy film on the road surface which is almost as slippery as ice. Be on your guard against other skid hazards, including wet leaves or mud, or sand, dirt, and gravel on dry roads.
- Rain water on the pavement reduces traction, and as the water accumulates on the road surface, tires begin to hydroplane as speed increases, particularly over 40 miles per hour. This can lead to loss of traction and control of the vehicle.
- Snow, slush, and ice are twice as hazardous in the freezing range, around 32 degrees, as at 0 degrees. Snow tires or studded tires are recommended for such conditions. Studded tires double the traction of regular tires on glare ice.

Tire Cord Materials

Cords may be made of rayon, nylon, or polyester. The choice depends upon the use you expect the tires to have. Rayon was used for years and years before the nylon revolution in the early '60's. Rayon is a good cord material for tires that are subjected to normal use; that is, low to moderate speed in urban areas on paved roads. Rayon will deliver good performance under these conditions but does not have the inherent strength needed to cope with high-speed, long-mileage runs for extended periods or abusive use on rough, unpaved, or semi-paved roads. However, since rayon is the least expensive of all the cord materials, rayon tires will generally cost less than comparable nylon or polyester tires.

Lately, rayon has made a comeback as a cord material because some companies have developed a special kind of rayon with much greater tensile strength. Tire cord made of high tensile rayon is less expensive than nylon cord and almost as strong and tough. Rayon has also been used recently as a belting material in both bias-belted and radial-ply tires. Some companies have recently introduced rayon-cord tires with rayon belts under the tread and also rayon cord tires with fiberglass belts. Both types are considerable improvements over rayon non-belted tires and good buys for a motorist who wants the added strength and stability of a belted tire but does not want to pay premium prices.

Nylon is still the strongest, toughest tire cord material made. It is stronger, pound-for-pound, than steel. Because it is elastic, it can take a terrific amount of abuse without coming apart—an ideal material for tire cord. Almost all high performance and high speed tires are made of nylon cord. Nylon has only one disadvantage. When a nylon-tire equipped car is parked for any length of time, the nylon cord material cools and takes a "set." It actually flattens out at the point where the tire touches the ground. The next time the car is driven, the flat spot in the tire will remain until the nylon heats and expands. Under normal conditions, this takes only a block or two even in very cold weather. However, many people object to the thump caused by this slight flat spot on the cold nylon tire.

Introduced in 1962, polyester is relatively new to the tire business. Polyester cord tires were not marketed in earnest until around 1968, but when all the American car manufacturers announced that their 1970 models would be equipped with polyester cord tires as standard equipment, polyester became as important as nylon or rayon. Actually, polyester cord combines many of the best qualities of nylon and rayon but without the disadvantages. A polyester cord tire runs as smoothly as a rayon tire but is much tougher. It is almost as tough as a nylon tire, but gives a much smoother ride and does not develop a flat spot even after standing for several weeks.

Fiberglass, as a reinforcing material for rubber, is also a relatively new development. In 1966, layers of fiberglass were first laid under the tread of a conventional bias-ply tire, and the fiberglass-belted bias-ply tire was born.

A few years ago, when bias-belted tires were standard equipment on about 98 percent of all new cars, fiberglass accounted for a considerable share of the belted tire market. Today, with more and more companies going to steel-belted radials as standard equipment, fiberglass usage has dropped off somewhat. It is still very popular as a replacement tire, and some new cars have fiberglass bias-belted tires as original equipment.

Recently, all-fiberglass radial tires with fiberglass used for both cord and belting have been introduced and, since fiberglass is less expensive than steel, they cost less. Steel-belted radials are today's most highly-advertised and highest-priced tires. Steel is much tougher than either rayon or fiberglass as a belt material, but it gives a slightly rougher ride because the steel belt does not give under impact as does a rayon or fiberglass belt. Whether you pay the extra price for steel belts will depend upon the car you drive, the way you drive it, and the loads you carry.

Basic tire buying rules

● Never choose a smaller size than those which came with the car. Tires should always be replaced with the same size designation, or approved options, as recommended by the car or tire manufacturer.
● For best all-round car-handling performance, tires of the same size or construction should be used on all four wheel positions unless designed for special service to improve performance, winter-type tires for example.
● When radial tires are used with bias-ply or bias-belted constructions on the same vehicle, the radials must always be placed on the rear axle.

● If you are buying only two replacement tires of the same size and construction as those on the car, they should be put on the rear wheels for better traction, handling, and extra protection against flats. A single new tire should be paired on the rear axle with the tire having the most tread depth of the other three.

TOOLS

18

CONTENTS

Whole encyclopedias have been written about the tools of various trades, car repair included. This chapter covers hand tools, power tools, bench tools, special tools, mechanical gauges, electrical test equipment, and scopes. Some items are things you must have to do a certain repair on your car. Others help you to work faster, but are not strictly necessary.

Before getting into specifics, consider what you do as a home mechanic that is different from what a pro does. You are trading your time and effort to avoid the high cash outlay required for most minor and some major car maintenance and repair jobs. The pro is making a living by working on cars, trading his time for your money. He works 50 weeks a year. Speed on the job, whether he has to beat a flat rate schedule or just get the work out, is his stock in trade. Thus, if there is a special tool that will save him ten minutes doing a job and the job comes up roughly once a week, that tool saves him 500 minutes a year—about $8\frac{1}{2}$ hours.

You, on the other hand, will be doing the job once a year or perhaps only once every other year. If there is a way to get the job done—and done right—without that special tool, you can do without it. Otherwise, you will become a tool collector rather than a money-saving home mechanic.

The pro cannot afford anything less than the best because he will be using his tools all day, every day, and better tools mean faster work and more profit. But if you are working on your car purely to save money and avoid the trouble of getting it serviced, then you want the least expensive tool that will effectively do the job. The problem is to know how good is good enough for your purposes. As a rule of thumb, you will find the very cheapest tool is almost always so inadequate that buying it is a waste of money. And the very best is so super-adequate for your purposes that buying it is also a waste of money. So your best bet is the moderately priced tool.

Wrenches

Open-end wrenches

The open-end wrench is the simplest type. It has one or two C-shaped ends with flat sides that fit over a hex-head bolt. By pulling on the handle of the wrench, you can turn the bolt. When you apply force to the handle of the wrench to turn a tight bolt, the flat sides of the open-end wrench bear on two corners of the bolt. This tends to round off those corners, and to spread the parallel sides of the wrench opening. If the bolt is a tight one, you may round it off so much that you cannot get it out at all. The better the wrench, the more closely it will fit the bolt. So a good open-end wrench really works better than a cheaper one, and it is often lighter as well. The least expensive open-end wrenches are made from stamped sheet steel. They bend easily, and round off nuts and bolts. Do not buy them.

Better open-end wrenches are made from steel forgings shaped to fit your hand as well as a specific size hex-head nut or bolt. Some pretty good ones are left just as they were forged, with the exception of the openings that are machined to size. These are the least expensive of this type and will serve you well. For very little extra, you can buy chrome-plated wrenches which look a lot better, will not rust, and are easier to wipe clean. They are also a lot nicer to use. Most home mechanics and many professionals use them. Slightly better finish and tougher steels drive the price up fast, making the best wrenches several times as costly as the ordinary ones. Handle some and examine them before deciding what will do the job to your satisfaction.

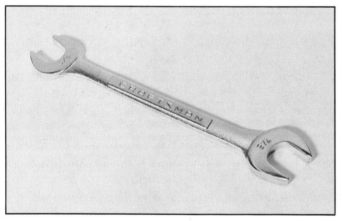

A wrench is the first tool you think of when you consider automotive tools. Ever since the first car was bolted together some time in the last century, bolts have been holding cars and most of their parts together. To turn a bolt, you use a wrench. Since the bolts holding your car together are hidden in various inaccessible places, it takes a great variety of wrenches to turn all of them.

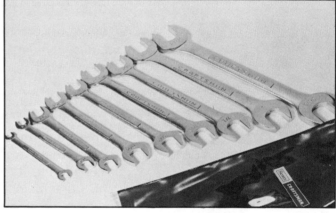

Most wrenches come in sets of six to 12 units, but you can buy them individually. It will usually pay to buy a standard set of open-end wrenches. Sooner or later, you will come across fasteners of most common sizes. Besides, each wrench in a set costs less than when bought separately.

Inches vs. metric

If you have an American car—with a couple of notable exceptions—it will have standard US SAE, Society of Automotive Engineers, fasteners. These are measured in inches across the flats of the hexagonal head. A ⁹⁄₁₆-inch open-end wrench will be about .005-inch larger than ⁹⁄₁₆-inch between the sides of its opening to fit a ⁹⁄₁₆-inch hex-head.

But the metric system is coming. By about the mid-1980's, you will need metric wrenches to work on any car from any country. Now you need them for European and Japanese cars plus the engine on the Ford Pinto and just about everything on the Chevrolet Chevette. General Motors is designing all new components according to the metric system, so more and more metric tools will be required. The other car makers will not be far behind.

Box wrenches

The next most common type of wrench is a box wrench. Like the open-end, it is made from a steel bar, but the opening forms a ring rather than a letter C. The inside of the ring is shaped in the form of a six-sided or 12-sided figure to fit over a hexagonal nut or bolt. The box or ring will not spread the way the jaws of an open-end wrench will, and the sides grip all six corners of the nut. So, with a box wrench, you can apply a lot more torque to a tight nut or bolt without the risk of slipping off it or rounding off the corners. The disadvantage is that you have to lift the box opening off the nut every time you reposition the wrench for another swing. This is slower than slipping an open-end wrench over the nut.

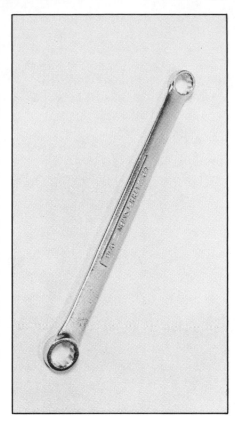

Six-point openings let you twist harder, but the more common 12-pointers fit on the fastener in more positions—an advantage when working in tight quarters. For larger nuts, 12-point box wrenches work fine, but for really tiny ones, six-point wrenches sometimes work better.

Adjustable wrenches

These descendants of the now nearly forgotten monkey wrench are often necessary when you cannot carry a complete set of fixed-opening wrenches with you, or for turning nuts and bolts of odd sizes which you encounter so rarely it does not seem worth getting a special wrench to fit them. When using an adjustable wrench, set it to fit the fastener tightly, then pull on the handle on the same side as the stronger fixed jaw to loosen a tight bolt.

Adjustable wrenches are weaker than those with fixed openings. Check an adjustable wrench carefully before you use it. Make sure the jaws are parallel when you look at the end and the side of the wrench, that they are not wobbly, and that there are no cracks, particularly in the narrow web area where the movable jaw fits into the body of the tool. The adjustment screw should turn smoothly throughout the full range of openings. Some of the latest adjustable wrenches have a locking feature which clamps the jaws a bit tighter on the bolt you are turning and locks them there. These are expensive, but they are the best type of adjustable open-end wrench for the amateur mechanic since they are less apt to round off nuts and bolt heads.

Socket sets

The socket wrench and handle set, after a combination box and open-end wrench set, is usually the second type to be acquired by most home mechanics.

A socket wrench is simply a steel cylinder shaped to fit over a bolt and to turn it when it is twisted by a ratcheting handle. The square end of the handle fits into a square hole in the socket. There are a great variety of extensions and handles that snap into sockets to turn them.

$\frac{3}{8}$-inch square drive sockets and extensions will be adequate for most automotive work. Professional mechanics often prefer the more rugged $\frac{1}{2}$-inch square drive size, but these are heavier as well as stronger than $\frac{3}{8}$-inch. Handle a set of each size before you buy. You can get $\frac{1}{4}$-inch square drive sockets and handles for alternator, gener-

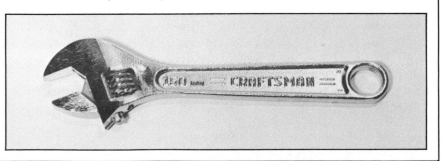

ator, or starter motor work.

Buy your sockets by the set. They come in neat metal trays to keep them in order and to prevent loss when not in use.

Good quality sockets are available from almost all auto parts and supply sources. Prices vary greatly between top quality professional tools which are sold through distributors and cheaper versions. Take the time to examine an example of each of these, and you will see the difference immediately. The top quality socket is much smaller and lighter than the cheaper version designed to fit the same size bolt. It is smoothly contoured and chrome-plated. The cheap socket will have much thicker walls to keep it from breaking. The reason for this disparity is the quality of the steel used to produce each socket. Soft, low-carbon steel in the cheaper socket must be thicker even though it is less strong than the chrome vana-dium of the top-line socket. To a professional mechanic who works with his wrenches all day, the lighter weight counts for a lot. Further, the thinner walls of the good sockets help them fit in tight places where thicker ones will not. As with all your other tool purchases, the middle price level brings a big increment in quality over the lowest price and yet the sockets still cost little more than half as much as the most expensive you can get.

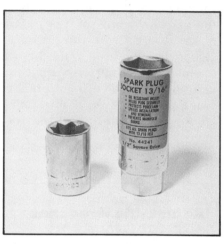

Socket openings take the same form as those in box wrenches. They come in 4-, 6-, 8-, and 12-point styles for square and hex-head fasteners. Some of the best have flutes machined or swaged into the angles between the flats so they will not round off the corners of the hex, just like the newer and better box wrench openings. These are worth getting in preference to straight-cut sockets.

Sockets come in standard depths for most nuts, and deep sockets are made for removing spark plugs and nuts that have a lot of bolt sticking out from them. Standard sockets will do almost everything you need with the exception of spark plug work. For this, get a 13/16-inch spark plug socket. It fits most standard plugs. Late-model cars use a 5/8-inch spark plug socket. Check what size plugs your car has, and then get the right socket to handle them, 13/16 or 5/8.

Ratchets, handles, and extensions

Having decided on your sockets, give a bit more thought to the ratchets and handles you will use to turn them. Again, quality varies greatly and directly with price, but in this case, price is really less of an object because you will require only one ratchet handle to turn your many sockets. Since you hold the handle in your hands, you should select it carefully to make sure it feels right.

Your first ratchet handle will probably be a straight handle with a ratchet that can be set for "ON" or "OFF" to tighten or loosen nuts and bolts. The general finish should be smooth and the length relatively short. Given a choice of two handle lengths, pick the shorter one.

You also get a choice of the number of teeth in the ratchet. The finest teeth enable you to work in tighter spaces because it takes less handle swing-arc to reach the next tooth to get a new bite. Bigger teeth—fewer clicks per turn—are more rugged but may not give you a small enough swing. Since your wrenches will not be used all day, every day, the convenience factor of finer teeth usually outweighs the strength advantage of bigger ones. But do not abuse your ratchet by using it to break loose really tight bolts or nuts.

Ratchets sometimes come with a locking button designed to retain the socket or extension and to pop it off when you need to change. These can be more trouble than simply pulling off the socket over its spring-loaded ball retainer. Try handles using both systems and then pick the one that works the best for you.

Handles take many forms, and prices vary for ¼- and ¾-inch straight ratchet designs. You will be looking at the ⅜- and ½-inch ratchets to start with. If you are on a tight budget, the ⅜-inch size is cheaper as well as lighter and works for most jobs.

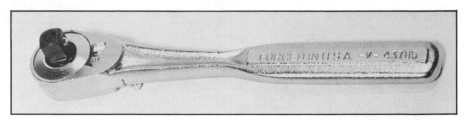

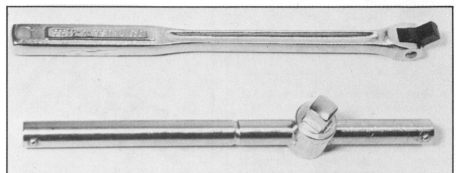

Breaker bars. After, or perhaps even before, you get a ratchet handle, you should buy a breaker bar. This, or a slide-bar handle, turns sockets like a ratchet without the ratchet feature. While not so convenient, use it to break loose tight fasteners and avoid the wear and strain on your ratchet. Breaker bar handles are longer than standard ratchet handles, making it a bit easier to turn a tight bolt. The same strictures about not increasing leverage with a pipe or hammering on the handle apply to ratchets and breaker bars as well as to box or open-end wrenches.

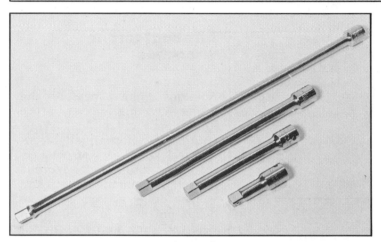

Extensions are simple steel rods with a square drive socket on one end and a drive square on the other. They come in various lengths. Get them all, including at least one long one. A typical set of extensions includes 3-, 6-, 10-, and 20-inchers. Here is a place to save money by buying the middle quality level. As with sockets, the very top line extensions are a bit smoother, but there are other tools you can get for the price differential that you need more.

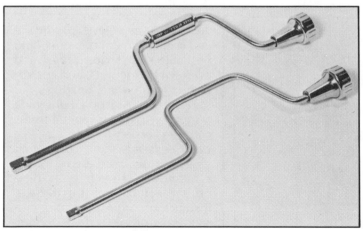

Speed handles look like an old fashioned brace but with a square drive end rather than a chuck to hold a wood boring bit. Use them to spin loosened nuts or bolts on or off. Again, the rule about getting one that really feels good applies because it is a tool you will use often. They are especially useful for cranking on wheel lugs or nuts where there are a number of easy-to-reach fasteners to turn.

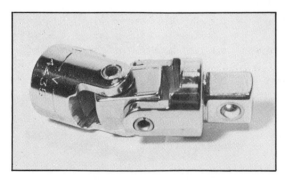

Adapters let you use ⅜-square-drive handles and extensions to turn ¼- or ½-inch sockets. If you have both ⅜- and ½-inch sockets, by all means get an adapter rather than a complete set of handles and extensions. Adapters go both ways. So if you have ⅜-inch sockets and a ½-inch drive torque wrench, get both.

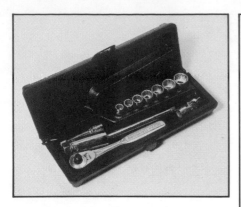

The least expensive way to buy socket wrenches is in sets, which cost about 25 percent less than the components purchased separately. A good set to start with is a ³⁄₈'' square drive, standard measure, with the following 13 pieces in it: seven 12-point standard sockets (³⁄₈-, ⁷⁄₁₆-, ¹⁄₂-, ⁹⁄₁₆-, ⁵⁄₈-, ¹¹⁄₁₆-, and ³⁄₄-inch); one six-point deep socket for spark plugs; a reversible ratchet handle; a universal joint; two extension bars (three- and six-inches); and a storage case. In addition, you might want the following items: a ten-inch breaker bar; a speed handle; and a U joint.

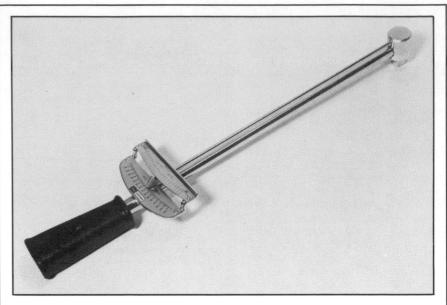

All about torque wrenches

A torque wrench measures the torque—twisting force—you use to tighten a nut or bolt. While you may develop a pretty accurate feel with years of practice, there is no substitute for a torque wrench on a number of jobs you will be doing as you get more deeply involved in working on your car. They are necessary for replacing cylinder heads, covers on transmissions, connecting rod and main bearing caps, intake and exhaust manifold nuts, and desirable for spark plugs and even wheel lug nuts, and for adjusting front wheel bearings.

The reason for bolt tightening torque is that uneven tightness can warp expensive castings, like cylinder heads, and cause their gaskets to leak. Excessive torque can twist or stretch bolts right off, shear studs, and strip threads. Insufficient torque can cause elusive leaks of oil, water, vacuum, combustion gases, fuel, and hydraulic fluids in the various systems of the car.

Torque is measured in pounds-feet (lbs. ft.), often incorrectly called foot pounds, which is a measure of energy. In the car repair field, almost everyone says foot pounds, so this book uses the term foot pounds, even though it is technically incorrect.

One foot pound is a weight of one pound at the end of a lever one foot long. For smaller fasteners and screws, torque is also measured in inch pounds (in. lbs.). One inch pound is the amount of torque applied by a one-pound weight on a one-inch lever.

Torque wrenches come both plain and fancy. The fancier types are easier and quicker to use, but do not offer you any increment in accuracy worth their cost. The torque range you need to cover is zero to 150 foot pounds. The plain deflecting beam wrench is the one for you. Most of these have ¹⁄₂-inch drive squares that plug right into your sockets and extensions. If you standardize on ³⁄₈-inch square drive, get a ¹⁄₂- to ³⁄₈-inch adapter. And, if you want to treat yourself, also get a ¹⁄₂-inch square drive ratchet that turns your torque wrench into a ratchet handle. Remember, though, just because you have an extra long ratchet handle in the form of your torque wrench, do not use it for a breaker bar. Your torque wrench is a precision measuring instrument, and you don't want to reduce its accuracy by bending it.

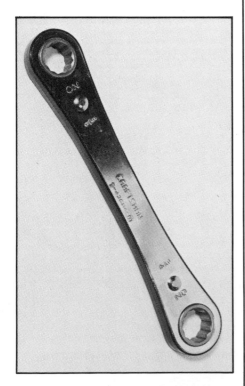

Other ratcheting wrenches include box wrenches, which are a little bulkier than straight box wrenches so their drive heads can ratchet inside the end of each wrench. They are not expensive, and are primarily tools to speed your work.

Specialized wrenches

Ignition wrenches come in both open-end and box types. They are very small wrenches for turning the small nuts used in mechanical distributors and, mostly on older cars, for securing the primary wires to the coil. When considering specialized wrenches like these, it's a good idea to hold off buying them until you really need them.

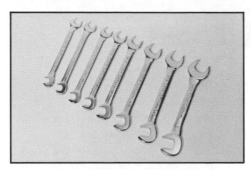

Flare-nut wrench. A flare-nut wrench is a sort of cross between the box wrench and an open-ender. It offers some of the best features of each type and was designed specifically for tightening brass nuts connecting metal tubing used in fuel, hydraulic, and other fluid lines. Flare-nut·wrenches are specialized tools of particular value to the professional mechanic who will use them often. You may not use them enough to justify their relatively high cost. If you use it carefully, the right size open-end wrench usually does the job.

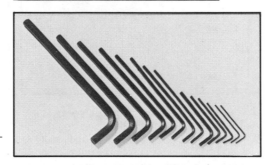

Allen wrenches. An Allen wrench has become more and more necessary for automotive work. This is an L-shaped hexagonal bar that fits in a hexagon-shaped hole in the end of the fastener. An internal hex is stronger than an external one, and these wrenches can be used with more force in tighter places than other types.

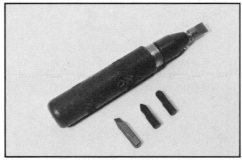

The hand impact wrench is a specialized hand tool specifically designed to replace the pro's power tool. This is a hand-held driver for high strength sockets that can be set either to tighten or loosen.

A tappet wrench is an open-end wrench with a longer-than-standard handle and a much thinner cross section. It is used for adjusting the valve tappets on L-head engines which have two hardened steel nuts locked together to set the valve clearance. Since working space is limited and engine heat makes these nuts extremely tight, tappet wrenches are made of the toughest steel to stand the strain and are therefore expensive. Usually, you use two of the same size at one time. If you need to adjust the valves on your engine, ordinary wrenches simply will not do the job.

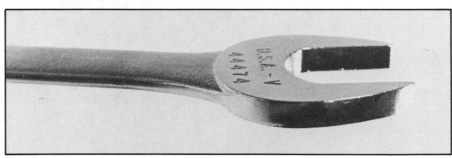

Some box or open-end wrenches have handles bent like pretzels to reach specific nuts on certain cars. Starter bolts and distributor locking bolts that are buried in the machinery may require one of these special wrenches.

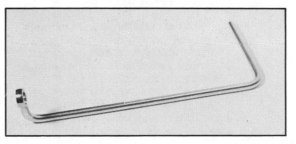

General Hand Tools

Screwdrivers

Screwdrivers are, without a doubt, the most abused tools you have. Good ones should be kept for work on screws, so you need some of the best you can afford and a couple of cheap ones you can be careless with. The latter can also be ground to fit special screws if you have to turn odd sizes on your car.

Fancy screwdrivers include offset or ratchet head models, special starters for different types of screws that hold the screw while you start it in its threads, magnetic screwdrivers with interchangeable tips of different sizes, test light screwdrivers with built-in electrical system test lamps, and flashlight screwdrivers which shine a light on screws in dark corners.

All of these have their uses but they are tools to acquire as you require them—unless your ambition is to become a tool collector. There is nothing wrong with tool collecting, but first ask yourself if you can afford it—in storage space as well as money.

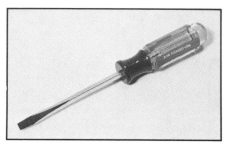

Standard screwdrivers for slotted screws come in a variety of sizes. You need at least three—small, medium, and large. An extra-large screwdriver with a long shank can be very useful for lining up parts and dealing with big screws. Short or knobby screwdrivers help you to work in tight places such as under the dashboard.

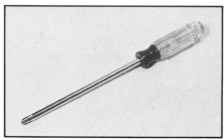

Most cars also use Phillips screws. These have cross slots in their heads and come in four sizes: #0, #1, #2, and #3. You can probably get by with a size #2 in the beginning, but you will need the others eventually.

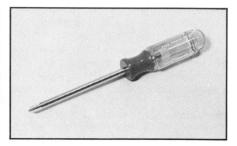

Reed Prince tips look a lot like Phillips, but are much more sharply pointed and do not interchange. Like other specialized tools, either you need them or you don't. Buy as required. The same goes for clutch or butterfly screwdrivers. If you have the fasteners and need to turn them, get the right tool. Many newer cars use these screws.

Pliers

High quality is most noticeable and important in pliers, even more than in screwdrivers. The stresses developed can be great and cheap pliers simply cannot stand up to them. Cheap pliers are awkward. They slip, spread their jaws, do not work smoothly, break, and are both dangerous and unpleasant to use. It is far better to get a few good ones than to have lots of poor ones.

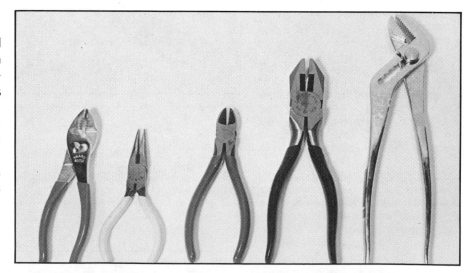

You need at least three pairs of pliers for general use: regular slip-joint steel pliers about six- to eight-inches long, long nose pliers about six inches long, and diagonal wire cutting pliers also about six inches long. Next on your list should come a set of linesman's pliers eight inches or longer, and then mechanic's pliers with a number of openings up to two inches and handles about ten inches long. The better quality of this latter type have arc-shaped grooves to control the size of adjustments rather than indentations along a slot. They are strong enough to justify their added cost and weight, though the others will do for starters and cost about half as much.

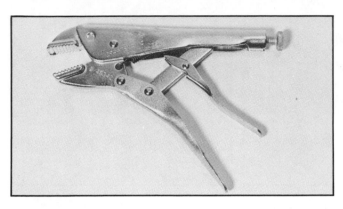

Locking jaw pliers take many forms, and should be included in your tool collection early in the game. A typical toolbox will have 8-, 6-, and 4-inch long locking pliers. You will find them very useful for holding parts together while inserting fasteners, holding bolts when you cannot keep a wrench from falling off the opposite end from the one you are trying to turn, unscrewing studs, and many other jobs. They come with slightly curved or straight jaws. Either style is useful but you probably do not need both of them.

Hammers

The basic hammer for auto mechanics is the ball peen with one flat striking surface and one rounded end for setting rivets. Get a good one with an 8-, 12- or 16-ounce head. The best ones have drop-forged, heat-treated heads, and fiberglass handles. Get a 12-ounce ball peen. You can get cheaper ones, but the handles often break or the heads fly off. The metal in the head can chip, throwing off dangerous chunks of steel. The basic rule when working with a machinist's hammer is never to hit a hardened surface with it, such as another hammer head, a hardened steel rod, an anvil, or a car part. That is what causes chipping or splitting.

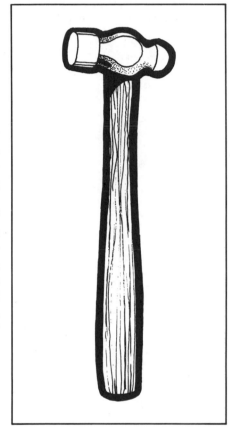

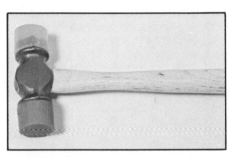

A plastic tip mallet works well where less force is needed or for tapping a carburetor body to jar dirt loose from the float valve, for example.

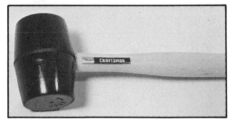

A rubber mallet is needed for replacing snap-on hubcaps and similar jobs where you do not want to bend or mar relatively light metal. This is one instance where the cheaper version does just about as well as the more expensive tool.

Cutters and pullers

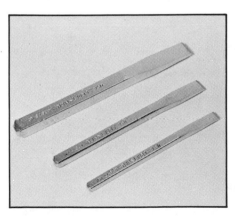

A cold chisel is a steel bar with a hardened cutting edge for shearing steel. They come in various sizes, and a set can prove useful. You can use them for cutting off rusted-on bolt heads, removing exhaust system parts, and similar jobs where there is no chance of saving the fastener and it must be removed.

A drift is a round steel punch with a flat tip used for driving pins into or out of assemblies. If it has a point on the end, it is a center punch used for marking metal before drilling a hole in it so the drill bit will not walk around the hole but will start off right. Drifts or large-size center punches can be useful for lining up sheet metal parts when bolting them together.

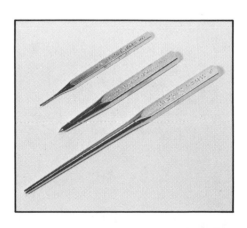

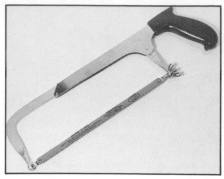

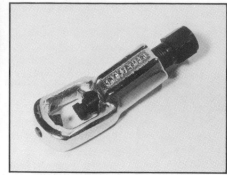

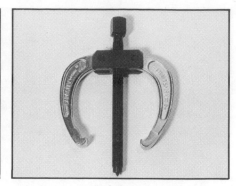

Hacksaws. The hacksaw is simply a U-shaped frame with a handle. The blade is stretched across the open side of the U and tightened with a wing nut. Install the blade so it cuts as you push the saw away from you. You need only a general-purpose metal cutting blade. Since you will not use it often, save money by buying an expensive blade instead of a low price one.

A nut splitter is another metal cutting tool. It fits over a rusted-on nut and has a screw jack you can tighten with a wrench to force a chisel blade into the nut. This will crack it—making it possible to remove it without damaging the bolt or stud. Then you can replace the ruined nut with a new one.

Pullers. Pullers come in all sizes for separating stuck or press-fitted parts. The cost depends on the size. There are small ones for lifting battery post clamps and large ones for removing flywheels. Wheel pullers are usually used to remove rear brake drums on live-axle vehicles. Most pullers can be rented from tool rental shops.

Files. You will need only a couple of files. Start out with an ignition point file, which is small, finely cut, and designed to file ignition points—but you will not be using it for that. You can use it for smoothing a sharp edge on a piece of metal or repairing a screw.

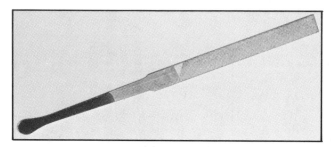

Lubrication tools

One of the jobs you can start with is lubrication. This can call for a bunch of specialized tools right at the beginning, but fortunately they are relatively inexpensive. You will need a wrench to turn the drain plug on your car's oil pan. This may be a standard hex which a box, socket, or open-end wrench can turn. Or it may be an indented square. Special drain plug wrenches are available. Sometimes you can use a ½-inch square drive extension without a socket for this job. But more often, you need the special tool.

For a drain pan, you can buy a cheap plastic dishpan or make one out of a 10-quart square oil can. This has the advantage of being shallower. You might not have to jack up the car, but be sure to fold over the cut edges of the pan so you do not cut yourself when fishing for the oil drain plug, which often falls in with the drained oil.

To change the oil filter, you need a wrench to unscrew a spin-on filter. Most consist of a metal band with a handle that grips the filter to turn it.

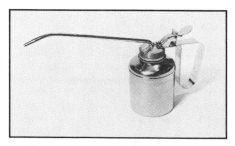

For general lubing you will need an oil can. Get one with a pump lever, since these are the most convenient for working on a car. Also get a pump-action sprayer to dispense penetrating oil. If you object to aerosols, a spritz pump on a plastic bottle does the job almost as well without Freon emissions and at lower cost.

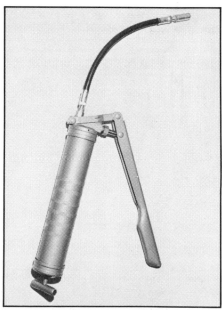

For chassis greasing, you need a hand-operated grease gun and lots of secondhand paper towels. The gun should take grease cartridges because they are much easier to handle than bulk grease and have a long lever to develop the pressure required to force grease into fittings. If your car does not have them, you will also need fittings. Lube points are making a comeback on new cars, so you will be seeing more of them.

Wiring tools

Sooner or later, you will be making some repairs to your car's electrical system. This calls for simple circuit testing—see the electrical instruments section later in this chapter—and working with wires. You will need wire cutters, an insulation stripper, and a means of splicing various sizes of electric wiring.

The two types of spark plug wires

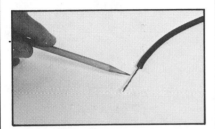

Steel core

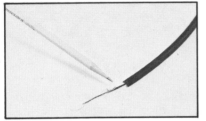

Carbon core

ECONOTIP

#20

Averaging mileage on separate trips

If you use three tanks of gas and get 20.0 miles per gallon, 10 MPG, and 11.1 MPG on each tankfull, don't expect to add those three figures and divide by three for the average. If you do add the three averages together and divide by three, the answer is 13.7. Let's say you drove 200 miles on each tankfull and used 10 gallons, 20 gallons, and 18 gallons, for a total of 48 gallons in the 600 miles. 600 divided by 48 equals 12.5 MPG, not 13.7. A practical use of this is to find your gas mileage for the entire year. To do it correctly, add up the total miles driven for the year and divide by the total gallons of gas used.

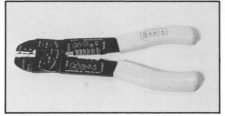

One very good wire stripper is the one that comes as a part of solderless connector pliers. But there are other simpler and fancier strippers. Most have sharp edges like wire cutters and round nicks of different sizes so the blades cut the insulation without cutting the wire. These work well. A yank on the wire after cutting the insulation pops off the end to be stripped. Some have built-in end-poppers, great if you have a lot of wire to strip, and some are combination crimper-strippers. You can also use a pocket knife to strip wires.

Solderless terminals. Once the wire is cut to length and stripped, you will splice or attach it to something. Solderless terminals do this neatly but expensively. These are copper—often cadmium plated—sleeves that fit over the wire and are crimped in place with a special crimper that looks like a blunt-jawed pair of pliers. Terminals come with or without insulation sleeves and cost very little. They also come in a great variety of push connectors, rings, forks, and other designs for snapping or screwing to electrical accessories.

Miscellaneous equipment

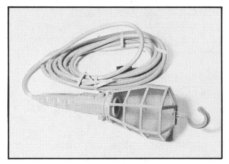

Lighting. You will also need good lighting. If possible, set up shop in a well-ventilated area where you also have electricity. Then try to pick up some used fluorescent light fixtures or, if not possible, buy a couple of new ones. A double-tube four-foot light over the bench will make a big difference in the quality of any work you do. For working directly on the car, you will need either a standard droplight or one of the newer fluorescent tube droplights. The fluorescent costs quite a bit more than the couple of bucks you will spend on a cheap one, but it is both easier and safer to work with.

Fire extinguishers. Fire is a distinct possibility whenever you work on a car, since gasoline can spill when you change a fuel filter or do other carburetor or fuel system work. Therefore, get a good CO_2 or Purple K fire extinguisher designed for oil or electrical fires. Make sure it is charged and keep it handy. With an extinguisher at hand, a small fire can be snuffed out before it causes real damage or danger.

Creepers. Everyone has seen a professional mechanic roll under a raised car on a creeper. It does make his job easier and speeds his work.

Power Tools

While there are three basic power tools home mechanics may need, high cost means you will probably have only a portable electric drill. The other two—a saber saw and a power wrench—while useful, probably cost more than they will be worth to you. The saw might be a good investment because you can also use it for general home repairs. But the wrench is expensive and therefore beyond the means of most people.

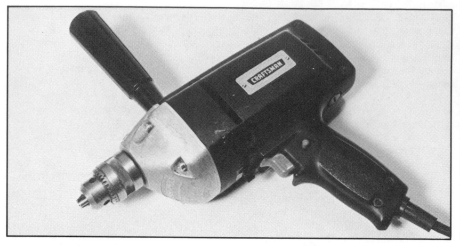

There are two drill options—¼-inch and ⅜-inch. The ¼-inch drill runs faster—usually 2250 revolutions per minute—but the greater power and capacity of the slower-turning ⅜-inch drill make it worth the few dollars extra that it costs. A reversing model with variable speeds is worth its price to you because it can also be used as a nut runner or power screwdriver once the fasteners are loose.

A drill stand is the most useful attachment you can get for your electric drill. This is a simple sheet metal frame to hold the drill horizontally on your workbench. Snap or clamp the drill into the stand, then insert a small grinding wheel in the chuck and put on your safety glasses. Working slowly and carefully, you can do most of the metal grinding jobs—like cold chisel sharpening—that

a bigger and better grinder could do, but at a fraction of the cost of a grinder.

A grinder is a versatile and useful bench power tool. Set it up with one general purpose wheel and a wire wheel on the other end. While a light-duty grinder may give you the bare capability you require, you could probably do as well with a drill stand at less cost. The next move up is at least a 5- or 6-inch wheel, and the 7-inch size is pretty standard, but expensive. As with electric drills, look for at least medium-duty service ratings. Easy-to-remove end covers help when you want to change a wheel. Built-in lights are useful but add considerably to the cost.

What to wear

No matter how neat you are, car work is often dirty work. The black grease you will be getting on your clothes can defy the efforts of the most powerful washing machine. So, get yourself some coveralls or other heavy denim work clothes and keep them for car work. You will save quite a bit of money by not ruining the clothes you use when doing yard work or other jobs around the house or apartment.

While you are out getting clothes, get a pair of comfortable work boots—preferably with reinforced steel toes. If you have ever dropped a hammer or a heavy car part on your foot, you will agree that the modest investment is well worth it to avoid smashed or bruised toes.

Gauges and Test Equipment

Gauges

Gauges come in two basic types—mechanical and electrical. You will need both. Time was when a set of feelers or even a thin dime—a real silver dime at that—would do for setting point gaps, but now you need a dwell meter as well, if you have distributor points in your car.

You still need feeler gauges for much automotive work. These are inexpensive flat strips of steel graduated in thickness which you slide between two parts—distributor points, for instance—to check the clearance between them. Even though you will use relatively few leaves on the gauge set, they are so cheap that it pays to have a complete one.

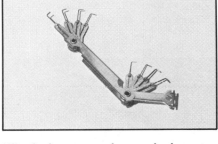

Flat feeler gauges. Flat feelers come in straight thicknesses and in go-no-go sets. On straight gauges each blade is of a given thickness—say .012-inch—throughout its length. A go-no-go set has the tip of each leaf ground to the nominal size of the blade, but the body of the blade behind the tip is about .001-inch thicker. To use go-no-go blades you insert the feeler in the gap—the clearance measured between the rocker arm and the valve stem, for instance—and then try to insert the thicker part of the blade. If it goes in, you readjust the clearance until only the thinner section fits.

Wire feeler gauges for spark plug gaps. You cannot use a flat feeler gauge to gap spark plugs because the electrodes tend to become misshapened in a way that would give you an inaccurate reading. You need a wire feeler gauge set for plug gaps. These are inexpensive too. They come as sets of wires and small flat blades, L-shaped wires in a

metal frame, or U-shaped loops on a flat metal disc.

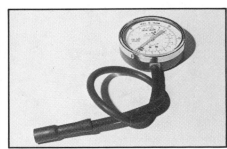

Compression gauges. Most home mechanics can use a simple type of compression gauge. It has a dial that reads from 0 to 300 psi (pounds per square inch). You insert it in a spark plug hole and crank the engine to check the compression developed in each cylinder. This test is a vital part of engine tune-up, because without proper compression none of your work can pay off in better mileage and performance.

The simplest compression testers have a short, angled spout with a rubber cone on the end which you press into the spark plug hole and hold in place with your hand while a helper cranks the engine with the starter. If you cannot reach your spark plug holes—as is the case on many V-8 engines and some others—you need a compression gauge with a flexible hose that screws into the plug opening. Compression testers come with complete instructions.

Vacuum gauges look a lot like compression gauges. They measure intake manifold vacuum with the engine running. Some models also measure fuel pump output pressure. Like compression testers, they come with complete instructions. Properly used, vacuum gauge readings can tell you a lot about your engine's health and efficiency.

Tire gauges. There are two types—the pencil type that has a calibrated rod to indicate pressure, and the dial type that reads like a compression gauge. Dial gauges are more expensive than the pencil type. Both types are accurate, but the dial gauge is easier to read. Get one with a range of five- to 35-psi (pounds per square inch) because that is the range you need for passenger car tires. Also, the markings are further apart than on the more common five- to 55-pound models.

Belt tension gauges are considered necessary by professional mechanics. They are used to test the slack in fan belts and other drive belts.

Radiator pressure testers. This tool is designed to help you find a leak in your cooling system, and it will also test the condition of your radiator pressure cap. The cost may be too high, for most home mechanics, but radiator pressure testers can be rented from a tool rental shop.

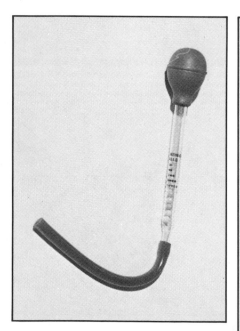

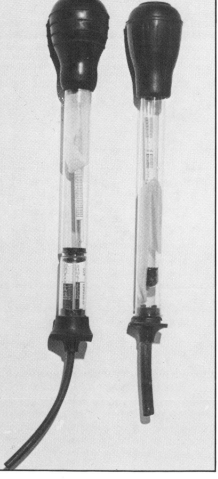

You need two hydrometers, one to test your antifreeze concentration, the other for the battery. Both testers come in two types. One uses a glass float in a glass flask to measure the specific gravity of the liquid under test. The other has four or five tiny plastic balls in a similar but much smaller syringe. Each ball is made of material of a different specific gravity, and you test the fluid by the number of balls which float or sink.

Coolant testers with simple floats or plastic balls cost very little. Fancy models with thermometers built in to allow for coolant expansion when hot are more expensive. The plastic balls expand or contract at the same rate as the coolant to give accurate readings. Whatever the type, an antifreeze tester measures the ethylene glycol concentration in the coolant to tell you whether or not your car is safe from freezing at low temperatures. It will not tell you the anti-corrosion protection left in your coolant.

Until recently, electrical testers were not necessary, but more sophisticated cars now require them. The kinds of car tuning you do will determine the testers you need. If you limit your ambitions to basic tune-up—replacing spark plugs, points, and condenser; setting ignition timing; replacing oil, air, and fuel filters; and cleaning and tightening electrical connections, then you can get by with a lot less equipment than you would need for serious troubleshooting or major engine modifications.

The basic engine tune-up calls for the compression and vacuum gauges already discussed, plus a power timing light and a combination tachometer and dwell meter, usually called a tach-dwell meter.

The tach-dwell meter is used for setting ignition point gap on cars that still have points and for adjusting carburetor idling speed. Most cars made in the past four years in the US have electronic ignition systems which have no points.

Dwell is the time the points are closed measured in degrees of distributor cam rotation. Timing is the point where the spark plug of the number one cylinder fires, measured in degrees of crankshaft rotation. While the dwell should remain fairly constant at different engine speeds, timing is greatly affected by engine speed and must be checked at the recommended engine revolutions per minute— usually idling.

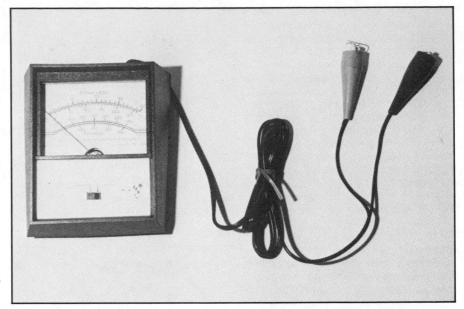

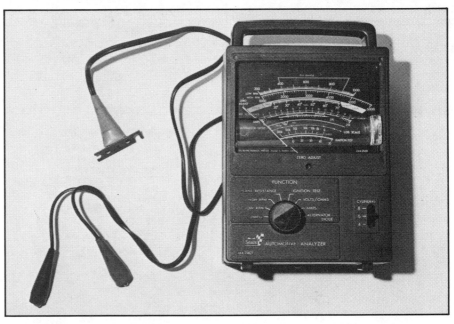

Tach-dwell meters vary considerably in price. The more expensive ones are incorporated into fancy multi-meter test systems. They also come with a built-in timing light. To use a tach-dwell meter, you must set the instrument for the number of cylinders in your engine. Some only read for sixes or V-8's, in which case you must double the readings in your head for fours. Then connect two alligator clips to the engine wiring—the positive lead to the primary circuit (the small wire) from the coil to the distributor, and the other to ground.

Tach-dwell and multiple-test meters come as small hand-held meters that can be hard to read or as substantial instruments you rest on a workbench or fender. The larger ones are easier to work with.

If you do electronic kit building, you can save a bit of money by assembling a complete multi-tester from a mail-order electronic kit company.

Timing lights come with neon or stroboscopic tubes. You want a strobe, or power timing light as it is sometimes called, because the much brighter light makes it much easier to see the timing marks. Since you must work near the whirling fan blades while using an electronic device that is connected to a high voltage spark plug wire, the strobe helps you stay far enough away to keep out of trouble. To use a power timing light, connect its power clips to the battery posts and T-adapter between the number one spark plug and its lead. Some timing lights have the adapter built into the input lead, while others use a sepa-

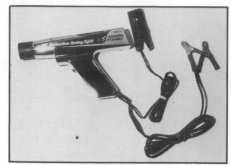

rate adapter and have an alligator clip you attach to it. The built-in type is handier if you are working on a car with a conventional ignition wiring harness.

Battery chargers. Prices vary considerably depending on whether you are considering a small trickle charger or a pro model. You can get a four-amp model with automatic shutoff that will be completely adequate for your needs at a reasonable cost. As with other electrical gear, battery chargers come with instructions and hookup is simple.

Storing tools

Once you start collecting car repair tools, you will need a place to keep them. In the beginning, a simple tool box or maybe even a .50 caliber surplus ammo box will hold everything. But you will soon outgrow it. If you have a more or less permanent shop in a secure area, a pegboard is the answer. You can arrange your wrenches, sockets, handles, hammers, pliers, screwdrivers, and any other tools on it in such a way that each one has a place. You will be able to find tools quickly and not spend half of your working time looking in the bottom of a dark box for a missing tool.

Mechanic's tool chests. These are about the best and most secure way to keep your tools, but also the most expensive. For a really large tool collection, you may need to make a considerable dollar investment. Considering the value of the tools, this investment makes sense, but the cost may be prohibitive.

More realistically, you can get a two-drawer tool box with a top compartment at a much lower cost. This should hold most of the things that will not go on the pegboard, and it is reasonably transportable.

Instruments you should know about but don't need to buy

These two test instruments you probably do not need to own.

Oscilloscopes

The oscilloscope looks like a small television screen which produces trace patterns showing what is happening to the voltage passing through your car's ignition system. In theory, you can take one look at the pattern and tell immediately what is wrong. In practice, it takes a pretty well-trained eye to spot troubles quickly. What is more, there are very few things you can spot on a scope that you cannot also identify by examining the parts or using a much cheaper electrical multi-tester.

Oscilloscopes—even the ones intended for enthusiastic home mechanics—do not come cheap. A kit to build a simple oscilloscope was available several years ago. But the current model with a 12-inch screen for pros combines a lot more functions and costs a lot more.

Exhaust gas analysers

An exhaust gas analyzer is necessary to check emissions on modern smog-controlled cars. Good, professional infrared instruments can cost in the thousands. Cheaper ones are not quite so far out of reach, but there are many other tools you need more. And, there is a very good chance that new laws requiring still more stringent smog control on future cars will make any instrument you buy obsolete.

Automotive Parts

Buying Tips

Car parts come from a number of sources. Many parts can be purchased at your local service station, or from a new car dealer. But some parts, such as cylinder heads and fenders, you can only get new from a new car dealer, or used from a wrecker. When a car is new, you may want to get factory OEM—Original Equipment Manufacturer—parts to be certain you keep your warranty in force, even if the particular repair is not something that can be done under warranty.

Jobbers

Auto parts jobbers supply many of the parts bought by local service stations and the smaller professional repair shops. They have two prices for everything—a mechanic's price and a retail price. Since perhaps 30 percent of their business is now cash-over-the-counter from do-it-yourself mechanics, they will most likely grant you the mechanic's price once you become known to them.

Parts jobbers are a good source of parts and tools because you are dealing with professionals. They know a lot more about their business—and yours—than a clerk in an auto department or a discount store does, and they will usually help you get good quality parts to do the job.

The prices, with the discount, will be about average. They run a bit higher than those charged by department stores, discount houses, and mail-order auto specialty houses, but they are lower than prices at new car dealers and service stations.

In addition to parts, most of the best jobber shops also run machine shops. They can completely rebuild an engine, turn a brake drum, rebuild a cylinder head, boil out a cylinder block, turn down a crank-shaft, fit bearings, assemble press-fitted parts—in short they handle all the jobs the smaller shops farm out. By farming out your work to them directly, you save the commission on the deal which would be collected by the garage or service shop as part of their repair fee. And if there is some specialized machine work you require, the jobber shop knows where to get it done.

Auto specialty stores

Speed shops or custom car shops can be a good source of special parts or specialized machine shop services. On some things their prices will be on a par with, or cheaper than, your local jobbers. They specialize in hot rod work, and if that is your major interest, they are the place to go with your business.

Department and discount stores

Auto specialty stores are another source of parts and tools. Their prices are generally lower. But quality will also be lower. They are better for dress-up or trim items than for hard parts like wheel bearings or ignition points.

Auto departments in department or discount stores offer about the lowest prices for most parts and tools you will find anywhere. The quality of branded, known merchandise is okay and, especially when bought on sale, you can get many things at true bargain prices. The best things to buy here are sealed cans of antifreeze, motor oil by the case (but watch out for brand names that look familiar but are a little different from the known brand), and fast-moving parts that require frequent replacement such as oil filters, air filters, and ignition parts. Brand name spark plugs can also be an excellent deal.

Local auto departments of the big mail-order houses offer the lure of one-stop auto supply shopping and usually have good quality parts at prices very little higher than the super discounters. These are also good places to look for tools on sale. You may be able to get a wrench set at half the price a parts jobber would charge.

Mail order

Mail order opens the shelves of some of the largest auto parts suppliers to you at very reasonable prices. Even considering that you must pay postage on top of the catalog prices, you can do very well at a mail-order house. The only drawback in dealing with one is the wait while your order is being filled. Between one and three weeks for delivery to your door is par for the course, with most orders arriving in under two weeks. If you know ahead of time what equipment or parts you need for a specific job, mail order is a good way to go. The catalogs often list parts you will not find on a jobber's shelves or even in a mail-order store's local auto department.

New or rebuilt?

At all of these parts stores, you have a choice of buying new or rebuilt parts. It is usually better to buy some items new, such as brake shoes, heater motors, water pumps, clutch pressure plates, and voltage regulators. A lot depends on the quality of the rebuilding shop. Some remanufacturers, as they like to call themselves, produce parts that are definitely better than new. Check both the price and the guarantee that comes with the parts. The higher the price and the better the guarantee, then probably the higher the quality of the component. Super low prices on rebuilt parts usually indicate poorer quality workmanship that will show up in shorter life and more early failures than the higher-priced remanufactured items.

Wrecking yards

Auto wrecking yards can be a superior source for a number of the parts you will be needing—particularly if yours is an older-model car. Most of the better yards are tied in with others across the country by teletype, so there is an excellent chance they can get something for you that would be hard to come by through other sources.

With respect to mechanical parts, wreckers are a good source for engines, transmissions, complete rear axle assemblies, wheels, tires, batteries, starters, and generators or alternators. Most of these parts will come with a guarantee stating that you can exchange them for another if they do not work. Engines will be guaranteed not to have cracked blocks or to burn excessive amounts of oil, for example.

If your car is old it may make little economic sense to put a new or rebuilt engine in it. But an engine from a low-mileage wreck could extend the usefulness of the car for another couple of years at half the cost of a rebuilt engine. In other words, if your car has a life expectancy, when repaired, of another 25,000 miles, why give it a 50,000-mile engine?

Body parts, especially doors, fenders, hoods, deck lids, seats, trim, light fixtures, and steering wheels, are better than new ones when bought used. Better than new ones? If you buy a new door, you get just that, the door, in prime and without any other parts. You have to remove the latches, hinges, chrome trim, window mechanism, inside trim panel, and weather stripping, from your bent or rusted-out door and install them on the new one. Then you have to paint it to match your car. A used door can be checked for dents and rust, and, with a little bit of luck, you may be able to find one already painted the right color to match your car. The price will be about half to two-thirds that of a new door. And putting it in your car will be a lot less work than installing a new one.

Parts that are usually not worth getting from wrecking yards include voltage regulators, windshield wiper motors, carburetors, and similar parts that may have been weather-damaged from outside storage, and which will cost negligibly less than rebuilt parts. As a general rule of thumb, used parts should cost about half as much as new ones.

Deals: good and bad

Replacement glass, particularly windshields, is probably the worst deal at a wrecking yard. The price is hardly less than new glass because of the labor required to remove it. Glass is scarce in the wrecking yard because so much is broken before the cars even arrive. Rear axles are a good deal. The demand for them is low because they rarely break. Yet the supply is good because they often survive in good condition when the rest of the car does not.

Now, you are in business. You know where to get the tools and parts required to do any repair or maintenance job you might care to tackle, and how to do it in a businesslike and safe manner.

Every job you undertake will teach you something about your car and yourself. And as you become more experienced, you will learn how to do your own maintenance as well or better than the pros can do it for you, and at far less cost.

19

CONTENTS

EXTERIOR MAINTENANCE

If you have ever shopped a used car lot, you know that dealers try to get their cars as clean and shiny and new looking as possible both inside and out. For any car with monetary value, they will shampoo the interior, give it a good vacuuming, and polish the chrome on the dashboard and on window and door handles. Outside, dealers will compound, polish, and wax, touch up paint nicks and scratches, and fill in dents. They will remove all the rust they can from the bumpers, and, in general, try to make the car look like new.

What does all this tell you? It says that a clean car brings more money in resale. But it also suggests that there is a practical limit to how much you should spend to renew and maintain a car. To the dealer, that limit depends on the particular model and on how much its value can be improved. If you are just sharpening up your car for the satisfaction that comes from keeping it looking new, you must decide how much time, money, and effort should go into it.

If you buy a new car, or a used one spruced up by the dealer, it is easier to start regular body and interior maintenance right away. The key is to make it a routine procedure and keep on top of it. That way, you will spend less time than the owner who lets it go for months, then tries to catch up in one fell swoop.

Exterior Maintenance

Regular washing

The first step in body maintenance is regular washing. Depending on where you live and where you drive, regular washing may be needed once a week or only once every three weeks. The latter suggests a car housed in the country where the air is clean, and used only for shopping and church. Most cars need a good washing once a week.

You can simply run your car through an automatic car wash to keep it clean, but if you have ever stopped to wipe off the water that did not quite dry under the blower, you know even the best auto laundry can leave water spots. The worst merely rearranges the surface dirt.

However, if the exterior is really filthy, it pays to go to an automatic car wash first if you can, or get a wash at a service station which has a hand-operated hot water pressure washer. Some car owners schedule one or the other at least once a month because either method loosens the dirt in hard-to-get-at places like rocker panels, valence panels, and wheels.

Ideally, set aside some time on a particular day each week to wash your car, and have all the necessary equipment ready.

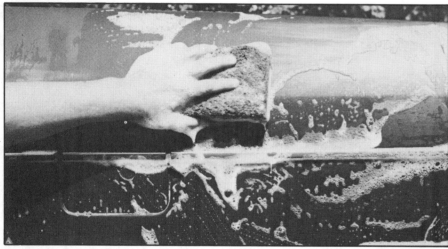

1 Set the hose nozzle to give maximum pressure and work from the bottom of the car to the top. Take a sponge from your pail of wash suds and, using a circular motion, apply suds to one portion of the lower part of the car at a time, rubbing out problem spots where necessary. Don't knock yourself out pressing down too hard. Use a good medium pressure and let the detergent do some of the work. After sudsing, hose off the surface.

2 Now do another section of the car adjoining the cleaned portion and hose that off. As you complete a section, wipe it down with your chamois or rag. It's a good idea to switch sponges frequently. Don't worry too much about the windows because you will be doing them over with window cleaner after the wash job. Leave the wheels for the very last.

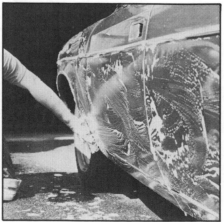

Pro Shop

Waxing inside or out?

While some wax manufacturers say their products can be used in sunlight, most prescribe shade. We've found that most products work best if you do your waxing inside your garage.

3 **After you have done the hood,** trunk, and fender tops, proceed to the roof and greenhouse of the car. The greenhouse is that part, including the windows, above the hood and trunk lid. Follow the same procedure, sudsing, hosing off, and wiping down with a chamois.

4 **Hose the wheels** with maximum jet at close range. Then suds them with a brush, remembering to loosen the dirt that accumulates around the wheel rim. Grease and tar on the wheel is usually very thick and must be attacked with a special solvent or a household cleaner.

Caution: Read the label carefully before you use a detergent on tire whitewalls. Some detergents, especially those containing alcohol, can damage the rubber.

Now hose off the wheels again, and wipe them with a rag rather than the chamois, to save the chamois for future use.

5 **Black rubber dressing** should be applied to blackwall tires with a paint brush. This improves the tire's looks and helps preserve the rubber.

6 **Clean the windows** after you have finished washing and drying the rest of the car. Use any one of the many available household window cleaners, or take a bucket and add a bit of ammonia to some water. Starting with the inside windows, apply window cleaner liberally.

7 **Wipe off the cleaner** with a clean rag. Then wash the outside windows in the same way.

Hints and tips

- Pay attention to how sunny it is while you are washing your car, and to how much body surface you can work on at one time given the outside temperature. No matter what the directions on the detergent say, if you are working in full sunlight, do a little less surface at a time.

- If you find problem spots like bird droppings, dead insects, and leaves you can get a small sponge with a roughened side to clean off these areas during the cleaning/hosing cycle. Make sure, however, that the rough side does not scratch the windows or the paint. You can also use a small brush, like those made for applying shoe polish.

- On fenders and lower door areas, you may encounter little black specks or even lumps of road tar. These spots should respond to your sponge or brush. If they do not, get a special product at an auto supply store for removing tar, or try a household foam cleaner. But read the directions on the product to make sure it is not harmful to painted surfaces. Whatever you use, hose it off just as you do the suds.

Compounding

Sometimes even the complete washing described previously will not get the car exterior really clean. The surface may have been neglected so badly that the paint is dulled. And if the car is old, there may be incipient rust areas on the body. You can spot them if there is a little cluster of what looks like bumps under the paint.

These problems suggest that you may need a special pre-wax cleaner or even a compound. How do you decide what your car needs? For the regularly-maintained car, a pre-wax cleaner—which usually contains some compound—is sufficient. But if the paint is severely discolored or, with yellow, white, or pastel-colored cars, the exterior still looks dirty even after washing, then you must use compound.

Most chemical companies with an automotive car care line offer a pre-wax cleaner, a polish, and a compound among their products. The first two come in aerosol can, liquid, or paste form. Compound is always in paste form.

In case you are not familiar with these products, a pre-wax cleaner combines wax with a mild abrasive (a minute amount of compound) to actually scrape away mild surface scratches and lay down a wax coating for shine. A polish lays down a coating of wax to protect the paint

finish and make it lustrous. Compound is simply an abrasive. If rubbed in enough, it will take off scratched layers of paint and bring the finish down to an underlayer which is not scratched and weathered. Rubbed in too much, compound can actually take all the paint off.

To use compound, take a clean, soft rag, dip it in clean water, fold it into a small piece, then put a very small amount of compound on it. Rub in small circles, using only enough pressure to do the job.

Rub only until the hand-sized area is clean and shiny, and work from the top of the area down. Rinse and turn the cloth after each area is cleaned, and keep a new supply of cloth handy.

Waxing

A well-maintained car only needs a wax job every three months even in the most pollution-ridden or salt-laden atmosphere.

There are literally hundreds of waxes on the market, and they are made of a wide variety of ingredients. But all contain carnauba wax, which has been used to make cars shine for many years.

How to wax your car

If you use one of the many conventional paste waxes, or one of the liquid creams, here is a general step-by-step procedure for waxing your car:
1. Thoroughly wash and dry the car. If you try waxing over a body surface that is less than 100 percent clean, you are simply waxing in dirt even if there is a cleaning agent already in the wax.
2. If no applicator is furnished with the wax, use clean, lint-free rags, or a superstrength household cleaning cloth as long as it is not abrasive. Fold the cloth or rag to a hand-size rectangle.
3. Apply the wax to the cloth or rag. Do not pour it directly on the finish. Starting from the uppermost painted surface on your car, apply the wax evenly using circular motions with medium hand pressure.
4. Different manufacturers recommend doing various size sections at one time up to doing the whole car at once, but a quarter of a roof is a practical-size area to begin with. Follow the directions exactly for when you should wipe off, otherwise you will wipe all your protection right off. All carnauba wax finishes take time to harden and are actually still hardening 24 to 72 hours after a wax job is done.
5. To bring the sheen up, wipe lightly with a new clean cloth or buff the surface with a sheepskin buffing attachment on your power drill.

Pro Shop

When to wash and wax touch-ups

Let most touch-up jobs dry about a week before washing the area with cold water and applying a coat of wax. For larger paint jobs, like a major portion of a door or a quarter panel, give it a fortnight.

Compounding metal

Compound can also be used on chrome bumpers and most metal work to remove the film of grime dulling the metal. *Caution: Do not put compound on any rubber part of your car. Like most car cleaners, it contains petroleum, which ages the rubber and causes it to crack.* If, after compounding, your car finish is still dull, or if scratches or cracks are still visible on the paint surface, you need a new paint job.

Ford Motor Company's 1980 Keyless Entry System

Keyless entry permits entry to the car simply by pushing buttons on the outside of the driver's door. All the doors can also be unlocked or locked, and the deck lid can be released. In addition, all the doors are automatically locked when the transmission is shifted into gear.

The only visual part of the system is a row of five buttons on the outside of the driver's door below the window. These buttons are in addition to the keyhole, which can be used if desired. Each button is identified with two digits. The first button has 1 and 2. The second button has 3 and 4, and so on. The last button has the numbers 9 and zero. The buttons are connected to a minicomputer located inside the trunk under the package tray. The electric power door locks and the power deck lid release are also connected to the minicomputer.

To enter the car, the driver punches in a five-digit code. This unlocks the driver's door. If he also wants to unlock the other doors, he must push the second button with-

in five seconds after unlocking the driver's door. He can also unlock and release the deck lid if he pushes the third button within five seconds after unlocking the driver's door.

When leaving the car, all the doors can be locked by pushing the fourth and fifth buttons at the same time. It is not necessary to enter any code before locking the doors. If it is too dark to see the buttons, the driver pushes the first button before doing anything. This will turn on the interior lights and light up the individual lights around the buttons and the door locks. A timer turns off the lights after 30 seconds.

It uses codes

Two codes are used in the system. One is a permanent factory code that cannot be erased. The car owner can also make up his own code and enter it in the minicomputer. The personal code allows the owner to select a code that is easy to remember, such as

his birthday.

All codes are five digits long. Because the five buttons have two digits each, this means that with some codes a button may be pushed twice, or not at all. To enter an owner's code, the five-digit factory code is first entered. The owner then has five seconds to enter his own five-digit code by pressing the buttons. After that, the door can be opened with either the permanent code or the owner's code. The owner's code can be changed by first entering the factory permanent code and then entering the new code within five seconds.

To automatically lock all doors, four conditions must be met simultaneously. All the doors must be closed and the driver's seat occupied. The ignition switch must be in the running position and the transmission must be shifted into or pass through the reverse position. There is no automatic unlocking. To unlock and get out, the doors are unlocked either manually or by the inside electric door lock button.

CONVERSION TABLE

INCH FRACTIONS AND DECIMALS TO METRIC EQUIVALENTS

Inches (Fractions)	Inches (Decimals)	m m	Inches (Fractions)	Inches (Decimals)	m m	Inches (Fractions)	Inches (Decimals)	m m
—	.0004	.01	—	.4331	11	31/32	.96875	24.606
—	.004	.10	7/16	.4375	11.113	—	.9843	25
—	.01	.25	29/64	.4531	11.509	1	1.000	25.4
1/64	.0156	.397	15/32	.46875	11.906	—	1.0236	26
—	.0197	.50	—	.4724	12	1-1/32	1.0312	26.194
—	.0295	.75	31/64	.48437	12.303	1-1/16	1.062	26.988
1/32	.03125	.794	—	.492	12.5	—	1.063	27
—	.0394	1	1/2	.500	12.700	1-3/32	1.094	27.781
3/64	.0469	1.191	—	.5118	13	—	1.1024	28
—	.059	1.5	33/64	.5156	13.097	1-1/8	1.125	28.575
1/16	.0625	1.588	17/32	.53125	13.494	—	1.1417	29
5/64	.0781	1.984	35/64	.54687	13.891	1-5/32	1.156	29.369
—	.0787	2	—	.5512	14	—	1.1811	30
3/32	.094	2.381	9/16	.5625	14.288	1-3/16	1.1875	30.163
—	.0984	2.5	—	.571	14.5	1-7/32	1.219	30.956
7/64	.1093	2.776	37/64	.57812	14.684	—	1.2205	31
—	.1181	3	—	.5906	15	1-1/4	1.250	31.750
1/8	.1250	3.175	19/32	.59375	15.081	—	1.2598	32
—	.1378	3.5	39/64	.60937	15.478	1-9/32	1.281	32.544
9/64	.1406	3.572	5/8	.6250	15.875	—	1.2992	33
5/32	.15625	3.969	—	.6299	16	1-5/16	1.312	33.338
—	.1575	4	41/64	.6406	16.272	—	1.3386	34
11/64	.17187	4.366	—	.6496	16.5	1-11/32	1.344	34.131
—	.177	4.5	21/32	.65625	16.669	1-3/8	1.375	34.925
3/16	.1875	4.763	—	.6693	17	—	1.3779	35
—	.1969	5	43/64	.67187	17.066	1-13/32	1.406	35.719
13/64	.2031	5.159	11/16	.6875	17.463	—	1.4173	36
—	.2165	5.5	45/64	.7031	17.859	1-7/16	1.438	36.513
7/32	.21875	5.556	—	.7087	18	—	1.4567	37
15/64	.23437	5.953	23/32	.71875	18.5	1-15/32	1.469	37.306
—	.2362	6	—	.7283	18.256	—	1.4961	38
1/4	.2500	6.350	47/64	.73437	18.653	1-1/2	1.500	38.100
—	.2559	6.5	—	.7480	19	1-17/32	1.531	38.894
17/64	.2656	6.747	3/4	.7500	19.050	—	1.5354	39
—	.2756	7	49/64	.7656	19.447	1-9/16	1.562	39.688
9/32	.28125	7.144	25/32	.78125	19.844	—	1.5748	40
—	.2953	7.5	—	.7874	20	1-19/32	1.594	40.481
19/64	.29687	7.541	51/64	.79687	20.241	—	1.6142	41
5/16	.3125	7.938	13/16	.8125	20.638	1-5/8	1.625	41.275
—	.3150	8	—	.8268	21	—	1.6535	42
21/64	.3281	8.334	53/64	.8281	21.034	1-21/32	1.6562	42.069
—	.335	8.5	27/32	.84375	21.431	1-11/16	1.6875	42.863
11/32	.34375	8.731	55/64	.85937	21.828	—	1.6929	43
—	.3543	9	—	.8662	22	1-23/32	1.719	43.656
23/64	.35937	9.128	7/8	.8750	22.225	—	1.7323	44
—	.374	9.5	57/64	.8906	22.622	1-3/4	1.750	44.450
3/8	.3750	9.525	—	.9055	23	—	1.7717	45
25/64	.3906	9.922	29/32	.90625	23.019	1-25/32	1.781	45.244
—	.3937	10	59/64	.92187	23.416	—	1.8110	46
13/32	.4062	10.319	15/16	.9375	23.813	1-13/16	1.8125	46.038
—	.413	10.5	—	.9449	24	1-27/32	1.844	46.831
27/64	.42187	10.716	61/64	.9531	24.209	—	1.8504	47

INCH FRACTIONS AND DECIMALS TO METRIC EQUIVALENTS/continued

Inches		m m	Inches		m m	Inches		m m
Fractions	Decimals		Fractions	Decimals		Fractions	Decimals	
1-7/8	1.875	47.625	—	3.0709	78	—	4.7244	120
—	1.8898	48	—	3.1102	79	4-3/4	4.750	120.650
1-29/32	1.9062	48.419	3-1/8	3.125	79.375	4-7/8	4.875	123.825
—	1.9291	49	—	3.1496	80	—	4.9212	125
1-15/16	1.9375	49.213	3-3/16	3.1875	80.963	5	5.000	127
—	1.9685	50	—	3.1890	81	—	5.1181	130
1-31/32	1.969	50.006	—	3.2283	82	5-1/4	5.250	133.350
2	2.000	50.800	3-1/4	3.250	82.550	5-1/2	5.500	139.700
—	2.0079	51	—	3.2677	83	—	5.5118	140
—	2.0472	52	—	3.3071	84	5-3/4	5.750	146.050
2-1/16	2.062	52.388	3-5/16	3.312	84.1377	—	5.9055	150
—	2.0866	53	—	3.3464	85	6	6.000	152.400
2-1/8	2.125	53.975	3-3/8	3.375	85.725	6-1/4	6.250	158.750
—	2.126	54	—	3.3858	86	—	6.2992	160
—	2.165	55	—	3.4252	87	6-1/2	6.500	165.100
2-3/16	2.1875	55.563	3-7/16	3.438	87.313	—	6.6929	170
—	2.2047	56	—	3.4646	88	6-3/4	6.750	171.450
—	2.244	57	3-1/2	3.500	88.900	7	7.000	177.800
2-1/4	2.250	57.150	—	3.5039	89	—	7.0866	180
—	2.2835	58	—	3.5433	90	—	7.4803	190
2-5/16	2.312	58.738	3-9/16	3.562	90.4877	7-1/2	7.500	190.500
—	2.3228	59	—	3.5827	91	—	7.8740	200
—	2.3622	60	—	3.622	92	8	8.000	203.200
2-3/8	2.375	60.325	3-5/8	3.625	92.075	—	8.2677	210
—	2.4016	61	—	3.6614	93	8-1/2	8.500	215.900
2-7/16	2.438	61.913	3-11/16	3.6875	93.663	—	8.6614	220
—	2.4409	62	—	3.7008	94	9	9.000	228.600
—	2.4803	63	—	3.7401	95	—	9.0551	230
2-1/2	2.500	63.500	3-3/4	3.750	95.250	—	9.4488	240
—	2.5197	64	—	3.7795	96	9-1/2	9.500	241.300
—	2.559	65	3-13/16	3.8125	96.838	—	9.8425	250
2-9/16	2.562	65.088	—	3.8189	97	10	10.000	254.000
—	2.5984	66	—	3.8583	98	—	10.2362	260
2-5/8	2.625	66.675	3-7/8	3.875	98.425	—	10.6299	270
—	2.638	67	—	3.8976	99	11	11.000	279.400
—	2.6772	68	—	3.9370	100	—	11.0236	280
2-11/16	2.6875	68.263	3-15/16	3.9375	100.013	—	11.4173	290
—	2.7165	69	—	3.9764	101	—	11.8110	300
2-3/4	2.750	69.850	4	4.000	101.600	12	12.000	304.800
—	2.7559	70	4-1/16	4.062	103.188	13	13.000	330.200
—	2.7953	71	4-1/8	4.125	104.775	—	13.7795	350
2-13/16	2.8125	71.438	—	4.1338	105	14	14.000	355.600
—	2.8346	72	4-3/16	4.1875	106.363	15	15.000	381
—	2.8740	73	4-1/4	4.250	107.950	—	15.7480	400
2-7/8	2.875	73.025	4-5/16	4.312	109.538	16	16.000	406.400
—	2.9134	74	—	4.3307	110	17	17.000	431.800
2-15/16	2.9375	74.613	4-3/8	4.375	111.125	—	17.7165	450
—	2.9527	75	4-7/16	4.438	112.713	18	18.000	457.200
—	2.9921	76	4-1/2	4.500	114.300	19	19.000	482.600
3	3.000	76.200	—	4.5275	115	—	19.6850	500
—	3.0315	77	4-9/16	4.562	115.888	20	20.000	508
3-1/16	3.062	77.788	4-5/8	4.625	117.475	21	21.000	533.400

APPENDIX

Specifications

This section provides manufacturers' specifications for engines, cooling systems and tune-up procedures used in domestic automobiles manufactured between 1975 and 1980. On this page you will find a list of the specifications included in the service section for each make and model. The page number on which those specifications begin is given below next to the make of the car. Occasionally you will find a footnote that refers you to the service section for another make. That means the same engine is also used in that make and you must turn to that section.

Manufacturer's Recommended Service Schedules start on page 454.

Data included in this section

General engine specifications
- Engine identification
- Carburetor
- Bore and stroke
- Piston displacement in cubic inches
- Compression ratio
- Horsepower
- Torque
- Normal oil pressure

Cooling system and capacity
- Cooling system capacity
- Radiator cap pressure
- Thermostat opening temperature
- Fuel tank capacity
- Engine oil refill capacity
- Transmission oil capacity
- Rear axle oil capacity

Tune-up specifications
- Spark plug type
- Spark plug gap
- Ignition point gap
- Dwell angle
- Firing order
- Initial ignition timing
- Idle speed
- Air fuel ratio

Contents by make and model

SERIAL NUMBER LOCATION:

1975–80: Plate is attached to top of instrument panel, on driver's side.

ENGINE IDENTIFICATION

4-121 (1977–79): The engine code is located on a machined flange at the left rear of the cylinder block adjacent to the oil dipstick. The letter "G" denotes the 4-121 engine.

6-232 & 6-258 (1975–80): The engine code is located on a pad between number two and three cylinders. The letter "A" denotes the 258 engine with one barrel carburetor. The letter "C" denotes the 258 engine with two barrel carburetor. The letter "E" denotes the 232 engine.

V8-304, & 360 (1975–79): The engine code is located on a tag attached to the right bank rocker cover. The letter "H" denotes the 304 engine. The letter "N" denotes the 360 engine with 2 barrel carburetor while the letter "P" denotes the 360 engine with 4 barrel carburetor.

GENERAL ENGINE SPECIFICATIONS

Year	Engine	Carburetor	Bore and Stroke	Piston Displacement, Cubic Inches	Compression Ratio	Maximum Brake H.P. @ R.P.M.	Maximum Torque Lbs. Ft. @ R.P.M.	Normal Oil Pressure Pounds
1975	90 Horsepower② 6-232	1 Barrel	3.75 × 3.50	232	8.0	90 @ 3050	163 @ 2200	37–75
	95 Horsepower② 6-258	1 Barrel	3.75 × 3.90	258	8.0	95 @ 3050	179 @ 2100	37–75
	120 Horsepower② V8-304	2 Barrel	3.75 × 3.44	304	8.4	120 @ 3200	220 @ 2000	37–75
	140 Horsepower② V8-360	2 Barrel	4.08 × 3.44	360	8.25	140 @ 3300	251 @ 1600	37–75
	180 Horsepower② V8-360	4 Barrel	4.08 × 3.44	360	8.25	180 @ 3600	280 @ 2800	37–75
1976	90 Horsepower② 6-232	1 Barrel	3.75 × 3.50	232	8.0	90 @ 3050	170 @ 2000	37–75
	95 Horsepower② 6-258③	1 Barrel	3.75 × 3.90	258	8.0	95 @ 3050	180 @ 2100	37–75
	95 Horsepower② 6-258④	1 Barrel	3.75 × 3.90	258	8.0	95 @ 3050	180 @ 2000	37–75
	120 Horsepower② 6-258	2 Barrel	3.75 × 3.90	258	8.0	120 @ 3400	200 @ 2000	37–75
	120 Horsepower② V8-304③	2 Barrel	3.75 × 3.44	304	8.4	120 @ 3200	220 @ 2200	37–75
	120 Horsepower② V8-304④	2 Barrel	3.75 × 3.44	304	8.4	120 @ 3200	220 @ 2000	37–75
	140 Horsepower② V8-360	2 Barrel	4.08 × 3.44	360	8.25	140 @ 3200	260 @ 1600	37–75
	180 Horsepower② V8-360	4 Barrel	4.08 × 3.44	360	8.25	180 @ 3600	280 @ 2800	37–75
1977	80 Horsepower② 4-121	2 Barrel	3.41 × 3.32	121	8.1	80 @ 5000	105 @ 2800	28½
	90 Horsepower② 6-232	1 Barrel	3.75 × 3.50	232	8.0	90 @ 3050	163 @ 2200	37–75
	95 Horsepower② 6-258	1 Barrel	3.75 × 3.90	258	8.0	95 @ 3050	179 @ 2100	37–75
	120 Horsepower② 6-258	2 Barrel	3.75 × 3.90	258	8.0	120 @ 3600	200 @ 2000	37–75
	120 Horsepower② V8-304	2 Barrel	3.75 × 3.44	304	8.4	120 @ 3200	220 @ 2000	37–75
	140 Horsepower② V8-360	2 Barrel	4.08 × 3.44	360	8.25	140 @ 3300	251 @ 1600	37–75
1978	80 Horsepower② 4-121	2 Barrel	3.41 × 3.32	121	8.2	80 @ 5000	105 @ 2800	28.5
	90 Horsepower② 6-232	1 Barrel	3.75 × 3.50	232	8.0	90 @ 3400	168 @ 1600	37–75
	100 Horsepower② 6-258	1 Barrel	3.75 × 3.90	258	8.0	100 @ 3400	200 @ 1600	37–75
	120 Horsepower② 6-258	2 Barrel	3.75 × 3.90	258	8.0	120 @ 3600	201 @ 1800	37–75
	130 Horsepower② V8-304	2 Barrel	3.75 × 3.44	304	8.4	130 @ 3200	238 @ 2000	37–75
	140 Horsepower② V8-360	2 Barrel	4.08 × 3.44	360	8.25	140 @ 3350	278 @ 2000	37–75
1979	80 Horsepower② 4-121	2 Barrel	3.41 × 3.32	121	8.1	80 @ 5000	105 @ 2800	28.5
	90 Horsepower② 6-232	1 Barrel	3.75 × 3.50	232	8.0	90 @ 3400	168 @ 1600	13–75
	100 Horsepower② 6-258	1 Barrel	3.75 × 3.90	258	8.0	100 @ 3400	200 @ 1600	13–75
	110 Horsepower② 6-258	2 Barrel	3.75 × 3.90	258	8.3	110 @ 3200	210 @ 1800	13–75
	125 Horsepower② V8-304	2 Barrel	3.75 × 3.44	304	8.4	125 @ 3200	220 @ 2400	13–75
1980	Horsepower⑥ 4-151⑤	2 Barrel	4.0 × 3.0	151	8.2	⑥	⑥	36–41
	Horsepower⑥ 6-258	2 Barrel	3.75 × 3.90	258	8.3	⑥	⑥	13–75

①—Police
②—Ratings are net (as installed in the vehicle).
③—Except Matador.
④—Matador.
⑤—GM-built engine.
⑥—Not available

TUNE UP SPECIFICATIONS

The following specifications are published from the latest information available. This data should be used only in the absence of a decal affixed in the engine compartment.

★ When using a timing light, disconnect vacuum hose or tube at distributor and plug opening in hose or tube so idle speed will not be affected.

● When checking compression, lowest cylinder must be within 80 percent of highest.

▲ Before removing wires from distributor cap, determine location of the No. 1 wire in cap, as distributor position may have been altered from that shown at the end of this chart.

Year & Engine	Spark Plug		Ignition Timing BTDC ① ★				Curb Idle Speed ②		Fast Idle Speed		Fuel Pump Pressure
	Type	Gap	Firing Order Fig. ▲	Man. Trans.	Auto. Trans.	Mark Fig.	Man. Trans.	Auto. Trans.	Man. Trans.	Auto. Trans.	
1975											
6-232	N12Y	.035	A	5°	5°	E	600	③	1600④	1600④	4–5
6-258	N12Y	.035	A	3°⑤	3°⑥	E	600⑦	③	1600④	1600④	4–5
V8-304	N12Y	.035	B	5°	5°	C	750	700D	1600④	1600④	5–6½
V8-360	N12Y	.035	B	—	5°	C	—	700D	—	1600④	5–6½
1976											
6-232	N12Y	.035	A	5°	5°	E	850	③	1600④	1600④	4–5
6-258 1 Barrel	N12Y	.035	A	6°	8°	E	850	③	1600④	1600④	4–5
6-258 2 Barrel	N12Y	.035	B	6°	8°	C	600	700D	1600④	1600④	4–5
V8-304	N12Y	.035	B	5°	⑧	C	750	700D	1600④	1600④	5–6½
V8-360	N12Y	.035	B	—	⑧	C	—	700D	—	1600④	5–6½
1977											
4-121⑨	N8L	.035	F	12°	⑩	G	900	800D	1600⑪	1600⑪	4–6
6-232 Exc. Calif.	N12Y	.035	A	⑫	10°	E	600	550D	1500④	1600④	4–5
6-232 Calif.	N12Y	.035	A	10°	10°	E	850	700D	1500④	1600④	4–5
6-258 1 Barrel Exc. Calif.⑬	N12Y	.035	A	6°	⑭	E	600	550D	1500④	1600④	4–5
6-258 1 Barrel Calif.	N12Y	.035	A	—	8°	E	—	700D	—	1600④	4–5
6-258 1 Barrel High Alt.	N12Y	.035	A	10°⑮	10°⑯	E	600	550D	1500④	1600④	4–5
6-258 2 Barrel	N12Y	.035	A	6°	8°	E	600	⑰	1500④	1600④	4–5
V8-304 Exc. Calif.	RN12Y	.035	B	—	10°	C	—	600D	—	1600④	5–6½
V8-304 Calif.	RN12Y	.035	B	—	5°	C	—	700D	—	1800④	5–6½
V8-360 Exc. Calif. & High Alt.	RN12Y	.035	B	—	10°	C	—	600D	—	1600④	5–6½
V8-360 Calif.	RN12Y	.035	B	—	5°	C	—	700D	—	1600④	5–6½
V8-360 High Alt.	RN12Y	.035	B	—	10°	C	—	700D	—	1800④	5–6½
1978											
4-121⑨	N8L	.035	F	12°	⑩	G	900	800D	1600⑪	1600⑪	4–6

Continued

TUNE UP SPECIFICATIONS—Continued

Year & Engine	Spark Plug Type	Gap	Ignition Timing BTDC① ★ Firing Order Fig. ▲	Man. Trans.	Auto. Trans.	Mark Fig.	Curb Idle Speed② Man. Trans.	Auto. Trans.	Fast Idle Speed Man. Trans.	Auto. Trans.	Fuel Pump Pressure
6-232	N13L	.035	H	8°	10°	E	600	550D	1500④	1600④	4–5
6-258 1 Barrel	N13L	.035	H	6°	8°	E	850	700D	1500④	1600④	4–5
6-258 2 Barrel	N13L⑱	.035	H	6°	8°	E	600	600D	1500④	1600④	4–5
V8-304 Exc. Calif. & High Alt.	N12Y	.035	I	—	10°	D	—	600D	—	1600④	5–6½
V8-304 Calif.	N12Y	.035	I	—	5°	D	—	700D	—	—	5–6½
V8-304 High Alt.	N12Y	.035	I	—	10°	D	—	700D	—	1600④	5–6½
V8-360 Exc. Calif. & High Alt.	N12Y	.035	I	—	10°	D	—	600D	—	1600④	5–6½
V8-360 Calif.	N12Y	.035	I	—	10°	D	—	650D	—	1800④	5–6½
V8-360 High Alt.	N12Y	.035	I	—	10°⑲	D	—	700D	—	1800④	5–6½
1979											
4-121 Exc. Calif.⑨	N8L	.035	F	⑳	12°	G	㉑	800D	1800⑪	1800⑪	4–6
4-121 Callf.⑨	N8L	.035	F	—	8°	G	—	800D	—	1800⑪	4–6
6-232	N13L	.035	H	8°	10°㉒	E	600	550D	1500④	1600④	4–5
6-258 1 Barrel	N13L	.035	H	—	8°	E	—	700D	—	—	4–5
6-258 2 Barrel	N13L	.035	H	4°	8°	E	700	600D	1500④	1600④	4–5
V8-304	N12Y	.035	I	5°	8°	D	800	600D	1500④	1600④	5–6½
1980											
4-151 Exc. Calif.	R44TSX㉓	.060	J	10°	12°	K	900	700D	2400㉔	2600㉔	6½–8
4-151 Calif.	R44TSX㉓	.060	J	12°	10°	K	㉕	㉖	2400㉔	2600㉔	6½–8
6-258 Exc. Eagle	N14LY㉗	.035	H	6°	㉘	E	700	600D	1700④	1850④	4–5
6-258 Eagle Exc. Calif.	N13L㉗	.035	H	—	10°	E	—	600D	—	1850④	4–5
6-258 Eagle Calif.	N13L㉗	.035	H	—	8°	E	—	600D	—	1850④	4–5

① —BTDC—Before top dead center.

② —Idle speed on man. trans. vehicles is adjusted in Neutral & on auto. trans. equipped vehicles is adjusted in Drive unless otherwise specified. When two idle speeds are listed, the higher speed is with the A/C or idle solenoid energized.

③ —Except Calif., 550D RPM; California, 700D RPM.

④ —With stop screw on 2nd step of fast idle cam, TCS & EGR disconnected.

⑤ —Except distributor No. 3227331; distributor No. 3227331, 6 BTDC.

⑥ —Except distributor No. 3227331; distributor No. 3227331, 8 BTDC.

⑦ —Set Matador sta. wag. with distributor No. 3227331 at 850 RPM.

⑧ —Except Calif., 10° BTDC; California, 5° BTDC.

⑨ —Point gap, .018″; dwell angle, 44–50°.

⑩ —Except Calif., 12° BTDC; California, 8° BTDC.

⑪ —With stop screw on low step of fast idle cam against shoulder of high step & EGR disconnected.

⑫ —Except high altitude, 8° BTDC; high altitude, 10° BTDC.

⑬ —Except high altitude.

⑭ —Except Matador, 8° BTDC; Matador, 6° BTDC.

⑮ —When operating at altitudes below 4000 ft., set to 6° BTDC.

⑯ —When operating at altitudes below 4000 ft., set to 8° BTDC.

⑰ —Except Calif., 600D RPM; California, 700D RPM.

⑱ —On models with auto. trans. & 2.53 rear axle ratio, use N12Y.

⑲ —When operating at altitudes below 4000 ft., set to 5° BTDC.

⑳ —Except emission control label code EH, 12° BTDC; emission control label code EH, 16° BTDC.

㉑ —Except emission control label code EH, 900 RPM; emission control label code EH; 1000 RPM.

㉒ —On models with 2.37 rear axle ratio, set at 12° BTDC.

㉓ —AC.

㉔ —With fast idle screw on highest step of fast idle cam.

㉕ —A/C switch off or solenoid disconnected, 900 RPM.

㉖ —A/C switch on or solenoid connected, 1250 RPM.

㉗ —Champion.

㉘ —Concord & Spirit, 10° BTDC; Pacer, 8° BTDC.

Continued

AMERICAN MOTORS

TUNE UP NOTES—Continued

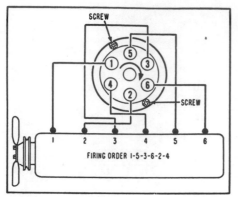

Fig. A

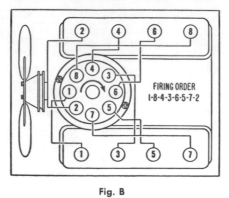

Fig. B

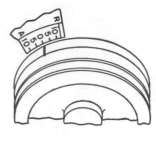

Fig. C

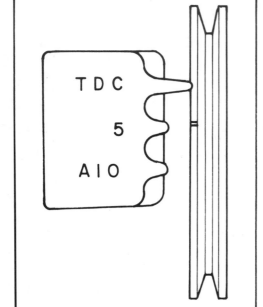

Fig. D

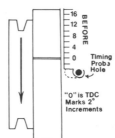

Fig. E

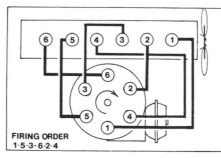

Fig. F

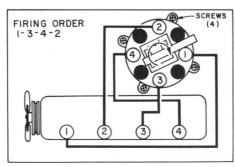

Fig. H

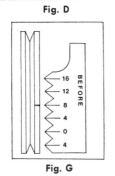

Fig. G

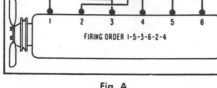

Fig. J

Fig. I

Fig. K

COOLING SYSTEM & CAPACITY DATA

Year	Model or Engine	Cooling Capacity, Qts.		Radiator Cap Relief Pressure, Lbs.		Thermo. Opening Temp. [1]	Fuel Tank Gals.	Engine Oil Refill Qts. [2]	Transmission Oil			Rear Axle Oil Pints
		Less A/C	With A/C	With A/C	No A/C				3 Speed Pints	4 Speed Pints	Auto. Trans. Qts. [3]	
1975	6-232, 258	(18)	(6)	15	15	195	(9)	4	3½(19)	—	8½	(7)
	Gremlin, Hornet V8-304	16	16	15	15	195	(9)	4	3½	—	8½	(7)
	Matador (20) V8-304	16½	16½	15	15	195	(9)	4	3½	—	8½	(7)
	Matador (21) V8-304	18½(17)	18½(17)	15	15	195	24½	4	3½	—	8½	(7)
	Matador (20) V8-360	15½	15½	15	15	195	(9)	4	3½	—	9½	(7)
	Matador (21) V8-360	17½(17)	17½(17)	15	15	195	24½	4	3½	—	9½	(7)
1976	6-232, 258	(22)	(23)	15	15	195	(24)	4	(15)	—	8½	(7)
	V8-304 Gremlin, Hornet	16	16	15	15	195	(24)	4	3½	—	9½	4
	V8-304 Matador (20)	16½(17)	16½(17)	15	15	195	(24)	4	3½	—	9½	4
	V8-304 Matador (21)	18½	18½	15	15	195	24½	4	3½	—	9½	4
	V8-360 Matador (20)	15½(17)	15½(17)	15	15	195	(24)	4	—	—	9½	4
	V8-360 Matador (21)	17½	17½	15	15	195	24½	4	—	—	9½	4
1977	4-121 Gremlin	6½	6½	14	14	189	15	4	—	2.4	7.1	3
	6-232, 258 Gremlin	11	14	15	15	195	21	4	3½	3½	8½	3
	6-232, 258 Hornet	11	11½	15	15	195	22	4	3½	3½	8½	3
	6-232, 258 Matador	(11)	(11)	15	15	195	(12)	4	—	—	8½	4
	6-232, 258 Pacer	14	14	15	15	195	22	4	3½	3½	8½	3
	V8-304 Hornet	16	16	15	15	195	22	4	3½	3½	8½	4
	V8-304 Matador	(14)	(14)	15	15	195	(12)	4	—	—	8½	4
	V8-360 Matador	(14)	(14)	15	15	195	(12)	4	—	—	9½	4
1978	4-121 Gremlin	6½	6½	14	14	190	(4)	3½(5)	—	2.4	7.1	3
	6-232, 258 Gremlin	11	14	14	14	195	(13)	4	3	3.3	8.5	3
	6-232, 258 Concord & AMX	11	14	14	14	195	(13)	4	3	3.3	8.5	3
	6-232, 258 Matador	(11)	(11)	14	14	195	(16)	4	—	—	8.5	4
	6-232, 258 Pacer	14	14	14	14	195	20	4	3	3.3	8.5	3
	V8-304 Concord & AMX	18	18	14	14	195	22	4	3	—	8.5	4
	V8-304 Pacer	18	18	14	14	195	20	4	—	—	8.5	4
	V8-360 Matador	(8)	(8)	14	14	195	(16)	4	—	—	8.2	4
1979	4-121 AMX, Spirit	6½	6½	14	14	190	21	3½(5)	3	2.4	7.1	3
	4-121 Concord	6½	6½	14	14	190	22	3½(5)	3	2.4	7.1	3
	6-232, 258 AMX, Spirit	11	14	14	14	195	21	4	3	3.3	8.5	3
	6-232, 258 Condord	11	14	14	14	195	22	4	3	3.3	8.5	3
	6-232, 258 Pacer	14	14	14	14	195	21	4	3	3.3	8.5	3
	V8-304 AMX & Spirit	18	18	14	14	195	21	4	—	3.3	8.5	3
	V8-304 Concord	18	18	14	14	195	22	4	—	3.3	8.5	3
	V8-304 Pacer	18	18	14	14	195	21	4	—	3.3	8.5	3
1980	4-151 Spirit & Concord	6.5	6.5	14	14	195	13(25)	3(5)	—	3.3	4(26)	3
	6-258 Spirit, AMX & Concord	11	14	14	14	195	21(25)	4	—	3.3	4(26)	3
	6-258 Pacer	14	14	14	14	195	21	4	—	3.3	4(26)	3
	6-258 Eagle	11	14	14	14	195	22	4	—	—	4(26)(27)	3(28)

(1)—With permanent type anti-freeze.
(2)—Add one quart with filter change.
(3)—Approximate. Make final check with dip-stick.
(4)—With man. trans., 13 gals.; with auto. trans., 15 gals.
(5)—Add ½ qt. with filter change.
(7)—7 9/16" axle, 3 pints. 8⅞" axle, 4 pints.
(8)—Coupe 17½ qts.; Sedan & Sta. Wag., 15½ qts.(17)
(9)—Gremlin, 21 gals.; Hornet, early 17 gals.; late 22 gals.; Matador exc. wagon, 24½ gals.; wagon, 21 gals.; Pacer, 22 gals.
(11)—Coupe, 13½ qts.; sedan & wagon 11½ qts.
(12)—Except wagon, 24½ gals.; wagon, 21 gals.

(13)—Gremlin, 21 gals.; Concord, 22 gals.
(14)—Sedan & wagon: V8-304 16½ qts. V8-360 15½ qts. Add 2 quarts with coolant recovery system; Coupe models: V8-304 18½ qts., V8-360 17½ qts.
(15)—Except Pacer, Matador & overdrive, 2½ pt.; Pacer & Matador, 3½ pts.; all models with overdrive, 4 pts.
(16)—Except Sta. wag., 25 gals.; sta. wag., 21 gals.
(17)—Add two quarts with coolant recovery system.
(18)—Exc. Pacer, 11 qts.; Pacer, 10½ qts.
(19)—With overdrive exc. Pacer, add 1 pt.; Pacer with overdrive, add ½ pt.
(20)—Sedan & wagon.

(21)—2 dr. coupe.
(22)—Exc. Pacer, 11 qts.; Pacer, 14 qts.
(23)—Exc. Pacer & Matador 2 dr. coupe, 11½ qts.; Pacer, 14 qts.; Matador 2 dr. coupe, 13½ qts.
(24)—Gremlin, 21 gals.; Hornet, 22 gals.; Matador exc. wagon, 24½ gals.; Wagon, 21 gals.; Pacer, 22 gals.
(25)—Concord, 22 gal.
(26)—Drain and Refill.
(27)—Transfer Case, 3.0 qts.
(28)—Front Axle, 2.5 pts.

BUICK—Exc. Skyhawk & 1980 Skylark

ENGINE IDENTIFICATION

Buick engines are stamped with two different sets of numbers. One is the engine production code which identifies the engine and its approximate production date. The other is the engine serial number which is the same number that is found on the vehicle identification plate. To identify an engine, look for the production code prefix letters, then refer to the following table for its identification.

Buick built engines have the distributor located at the front of the engine. On 1976–79 models, the engine production code is located on the right front of block. On 1975 models, the fifth digit in the VIN denotes the engine code.

On Chevrolet built 6-250 engines, the code is stamped on the cylinder block next to the distributor. Chevrolet built V8 engines have the distributor located at rear of engine with clockwise rotor rotation; the code is stamped on the engine case pad located below the cylinder head on the right hand side of the engine.

Oldsmobile built engines have the distributor located at the rear of the engine with counter-clockwise rotor rotation and right side mounted fuel pump. The engine production code is located on the oil filler tube on 1975–early 1978 engines or the left side valve cover on late 1978–79 engines.

Pontiac built V8 engines, have the distributor located at the rear of the engine with counter-clockwise rotor rotation and left side mounted fuel pump. The engine production code is located on the right front of the cylinder block.

ENGINE CODES

Engine	Code Prefix
1975 V6-231	C
6-250⑤	D
V8-260④	F
V8-350 2 Bar. Carb.	H
V8-350 4 Bar. Carb.	J
V8-400③	S
V8-455	T
1976 V6-231 Man. Trans.①	FA
V6-231 Auto. Trans.①	FB, FC
V6-231 Auto. Trans.①	FD, FE
V6-231 Auto. Trans.②	FF, FG
V6-231 Auto. Trans.①	FP, FR
V8-260 Man. Trans.① ④	QA, QD
V8-260 Auto. Trans.① ④	QB, QC
V8-260 Auto. Trans.② ④	TE, TJ
V8-350 2 Bar. Carb.①	PA, PB
V8-350 2 Bar. Carb.①	PC, PD
V8-350 4 Bar. Carb.①	PE, PF
V8-350 4 Bar. Carb.②	PK, PL
V8-350 4 Bar. Carb.②	PM, PN
V8-350 4 Bar. Carb.②	PR, PS
V8-350 4 Bar. Carb.①	PT, PU
V8-455 Auto. Trans.①	SA
V8-455 Auto. Trans.②	SB
1977 V6-231	RA, RB
V6-231	SG, SI, SJ, SK, SL
V6-231	SM, SN, ST, SU
V8-301③	YF, YJ, YW, YX
V8-305⑤	CPA, CPY
V8-350 2 Bar. Carb.	FA, FB, FK
V8-350 4 Bar. Carb.	FC, FD, FG
V8-350 4 Bar. Carb.	FH, FL
V8-350④	QK, QL
V8-350④	QP, QQ, Q2, Q3, Q6, Q7
V8-350④	Q8, Q9, TK, TL, TN
V8-350④	TO, TQ, TX, TY
V8-350⑤	CKM, CKR
V8-403④	UA, UB, U2, U3
V8-403④	VA, VB, VJ, VK
1978 V6-196	PA, PB
V6-231 2 Bar. Carb.⑥	
	EA, EG, OH, OK
V6-231 2 Bar. Carb.⑥	
	EG, EI, EJ, EK, EL
V6-231 2 Bar. Carb.⑦	EO, OL
V6-231 4 Bar. Carb.⑦	EP, ER, ES
V8-301③	XA, XC
V8-305 2 Bar. Carb.⑤	
	CEK, CPZ, CRU, CRX
V8-305 2 Bar. Carb.⑤	
	CRY, CRZ, CTM, CTR
V8-305 2 Bar. Carb.⑤	
	CTW, CTX, C3P
V8-350 4 Bar. Carb.	MA, MB
V8-350 4 Bar. Carb.④	Q2, Q3, TO
V8-350 4 Bar. Carb.④	TP, TQ, TS
V8-350 4 Bar. Carb.⑤	
	CHM, CKM, CMC
V8-403④	UA, UB, U2
V8-403④	U3, VA, VB
1979 V6-196 2 Bar. Carb.①	
	FA, FB, FE, FG, FH
V6-231 2 Bar. Carb.⑥	
	RA, RJ, RB, RW, NJ, RC, RG, NL, RX, RY
V6-231 4 Bar. Carb.⑦	
	RR, RU, RV, RO, RS, RP, RT
V6-231 2 Bar. Carb.②	RM, RN
V8-301 2 Bar. Carb.① ③	XP, XR
V8-301 4 Bar. Carb.① ③	PXL, PXN
V8-305 2 Bar. Carb.⑤	DNJ
V8-305 4 Bar. Carb.⑤	DNX, DNY, DTA
V8-350 4 Bar. Carb.④	DRJ, DRY
V8-350 4 Bar. Carb.④	VA, UZ, U9, VK
V8-350 4 Bar. Carb.①	SA, SB
V8-403 4 Bar. Carb.④	
	QB, Q3, TB, GB, G3
1980 V6-231 4 Bar. Carb.⑦	ED, EE, EH, EJ
V6-231 2 Bar. Carb.⑥	
	EA, EB, EC, EF, EG, EM
V6-231 4 Bar. Carb.⑦	EV, EXY
V6-252 4 Bar. Carb.	MF
V8-301 4 Bar. Carb.③	XS, XU, XT, XW
V8-301 4 Bar. Carb.③	
	XU, XX, XW, X3, X7
V8-350 4 Bar. Carb.④	AF
V8-350 4 Bar. Carb.	MA, MB, MJ, ML
V8-350 4 Bar. Carb.④	AS, AT

①—Except California
②—California
③—Pontiac built engine.
④—Oldsmobile built engine.
⑤—Chevrolet built engine.
⑥—Except turbocharged engine.
⑦—Turbocharged engine.

GENERAL ENGINE SPECIFICATIONS

Year	Engine	Carburetor	Bore and Stroke	Piston Displacement, Cubic Inches	Compression Ratio	Maximum Brake H.P. @ R.P.M.	Maximum Torque Lbs. Ft. @ R.P.M.	Normal Oil Pressure Pounds
1975	105 Horsepower② 6-250①	1 Barrel	3.875 × 3.53	250	8.25	105 @ 3800	185 @ 1200	40
	110 Horsepower② V6-231	2 Barrel	3.80 × 3.40	231	8.0	110 @ 4000	175 @ 2000	37
	110 Horsepower② V8-260⑤	2 Barrel	3.50 × 3.385	260	8.0	110 @ 3400	205 @ 1600	35
	145 Horsepower② V8-350	2 Barrel	3.80 × 3.85	350	8.0	145 @ 3200	270 @ 2000	37
	165 Horsepower② V8-350	4 Barrel	3.80 × 3.85	350	8.0	165 @ 3800	260 @ 2200	37
	190 Horsepower② V8-400⑥	4 Barrel	4.12 × 3.75	400	7.6	190 @ 3400	350 @ 2400	55–60
	205 Horsepower② V8-455	4 Barrel	4.3125 × 3.90	455	7.9	205 @ 3800	345 @ 2000	40
1976	110 Horsepower② V6-231	2 Barrel	3.80 × 3.40	231	8.0	110 @ 4000	175 @ 2000	37
	110 Horsepower② V8-260⑤	2 Barrel	3.50 × 3.385	260	8.5	110 @ 3400	210 @ 1600	—
	145 Horsepower② V8-350⑦	2 Barrel	3.80 × 3.85	350	8.0	145 @ 3200	270 @ 2000	37
	160 Horsepower② V8-350⑧	4 Barrel	3.80 × 3.85	350	8.0	160 @ 3800	260 @ 2200	37
	165 Horsepower② V8-350	4 Barrel	3.80 × 3.85	350	8.0	165 @ 3800	260 @ 2200	37
	Horsepower② V8-455	4 Barrel	4.3125 × 3.90	455	7.9	—	—	40

Continued

GENERAL ENGINE SPECIFICATIONS—Continued

Year	Engine	Carburetor	Bore and Stroke	Piston Displacement, Cubic Inches	Compression Ratio	Maximum Brake H.P. @ R.P.M.	Maximum Torque Lbs. Ft. @ R.P.M.	Normal Oil Pressure Pounds
1977	105 Horsepower[2] ... V6-231	2 Barrel	3.80 × 3.40	231	8.0	105 @ 3200	185 @ 2000	37
	135 Horsepower[2] ... V8-301[6]	2 Barrel	4.00 × 3.00	301	8.2	135 @ 4000	250 @ 1600	38-42
	145 Horsepower[2] ... V8-305[1]	2 Barrel	3.736 × 3.48	305	8.5	145 @ 3800	245 @ 2400	32-40
	140 Horsepower[2] ... V8-350	2 Barrel	3.80 × 3.85	350	8.1	140 @ 3200	280 @ 1400	37
	155 Horsepower[2] ... V8-350	4 Barrel	3.80 × 3.85	350	8.0	155 @ 3400	275 @ 1800	37
	170 Horsepower[2] ... V8-350	4 Barrel	3.80 × 3.85	350	8.0	170 @ 3800	275 @ 2400	37
	170 Horsepower[2] ... V8-350[1]	4 Barrel	4.00 × 3.48	350	8.5	170 @ 3800	270 @ 2400	32-40
	170 Horsepower[2] ... V8-350[5]	4 Barrel	4.057 × 3.385	350	8.5	170 @ 3800	275 @ 2400	30-45
	185 Horsepower[2] ... V8-403[5]	4 Barrel	4.351 × 3.385	403	8.5	185 @ 3600	315 @ 2400	30-45
1978	90 Horsepower[2] ... V6-196	2 Barrel	3.50 × 3.40	196	8.0	90 @ 3600	165 @ 2000	37
	105 Horsepower[2] ... V6-231	2 Barrel	3.80 × 3.40	231	8.0	105 @ 3400	185 @ 2000	37
	150 Horsepower[2] ... V6-231[9]	2 Barrel	3.80 × 3.40	231	8.0	150 @ 3200	245 @ 2400	37
	165 Horsepower[2] ... V6-231[9]	4 Barrel	3.80 × 3.40	231	8.0	165 @ 4000	265 @ 2800	37
	135 Horsepower[2] ... V8-301[6]	2 Barrel	4.00 × 3.00	301	8.2	135 @ 4000	245 @ 2000	30-40
	145 Horsepower[2] ... V8-305[1]	2 Barrel	4.736 × 3.48	305	8.5	145 @ 3800	245 @ 2400	30-40
	155 Horsepower[2] ... V8-350	4 Barrel	3.80 × 3.85	350	8.0	155 @ 3400	275 @ 1800	37
	170 Horsepower[2] ... V8-350[5]	4 Barrel	4.057 × 3.385	350	8.0	170 @ 3800	275 @ 2000	30-45
	170 Horsepower[2] ... V8-350[1]	4 Barrel	4.00 × 3.48	350	8.5	170 @ 3800	270 @ 2400	32-40
	185 Horsepower[2] ... V8-403[5]	4 Barrel	4.351 × 3.385	403	8.0	185 @ 3600	320 @ 2200	30-45
1979	105 Horsepower[2] ... V6-196	2 Barrel	3.50 × 3.40	196	8.0	105 @ 3800	160 @ 2000	37
	115 Horsepower[2] ... V6-231	2 Barrel	3.80 × 3.40	231	8.0	115 @ 3800	190 @ 2000	37
	170 Horsepower[2][11] ... V6-231[9]	4 Barrel	3.80 × 3.40	231	8.0	170 @ 4000	265 @ 2400	37
	175 Horsepower[2][10] ... V6-231[3][9]	4 Barrel	3.80 × 3.40	231	8.0	175 @ 4000	275 @ 2600	37
	185 Horsepower[2] ... V6-231[9][4]	4 Barrel	3.80 × 3.40	231	8.0	185 @ 4000	280 @ 2400	37
	140 Horsepower[2] ... V8-301[6]	2 Barrel	4.00 × 3.00	301	8.2	140 @ 3600	235 @ 2000	35-40
	150 Horsepower[2] ... V8-301[6]	4 Barrel	4.00 × 3.00	301	8.2	150 @ 4000	240 @ 2000	35-40
	130 Horsepower[2] ... V8-305[1]	2 Barrel	3.736 × 3.48	305	8.5	130 @ 3200	245 @ 2000	32-40
	160 Horsepower[2] ... V8-305[1]	4 Barrel	3.736 × 3.48	305	8.5	160 @ 4000	235 @ 2400	32-40
	155 Horsepower[2] ... V8-350	4 Barrel	3.80 × 3.85	350	8.0	155 @ 3400	280 @ 1800	34
	160 Horsepower[2] ... V8-350[1]	4 Barrel	4.00 × 3.48	350	8.5	160 @ 3800	260 @ 2400	32-40
	170 Horsepower[2] ... V8-350[4]	4 Barrel	4.057 × 3.385	350	8.0	170 @ 3800	275 @ 2000	30-45
	185 Horsepower[2] ... V8-403[5]	4 Barrel	4.351 × 3.385	403	8.0	185 @ 3600	320 @ 2000	30-45
1980	110 Horsepower[2] ... V6-231	2 Barrel	3.80 × 3.40	231	8.0	110 @ 3800	190 @ 1600	37
	170 Horsepower[2] ... V6-231[9]	4 Barrel	3.80 × 3.40	231	8.0	170 @ 4000	265 @ 2400	37
	125 Horsepower[2] ... V6-252	4 Barrel	3.97 × 3.40	252	8.0	125 @ 4000	205 @ 2000	37
	150 Horsepower[2] ... V8-301[6]	4 Barrel	4.00 × 3.00	301	8.2	150 @ 4000	240 @ 2000	35-40
	155 Horsepower[2] ... V8-305[1]	4 Barrel	3.736 × 3.48	305	8.5	155 @ 4000	230 @ 2400	32-40
	155 Horsepower[2] ... V8-350	4 Barrel	3.80 × 3.85	350	8.0	155 @ 4000	280 @ 1600	34
	160 Horsepower[2] ... V8-350[4][5]	4 Barrel	4.057 × 3.385	350	8.0	160 @ 3600	270 @ 1600	30-45
	105 Horsepower[2] ... V8-350[5][12]	—	4.057 × 3.385	350	22.5	105 @ 3200	205 @ 1600	30-45

[1]—Chevrolet-built engine.
[2]—Net Rating—As installed in vehicle.
[3]—Dual exhaust.
[4]—Riviera.
[5]—Oldsmobile-built engine.
[6]—Pontiac-built engine.
[7]—Except California.
[8]—California.
[9]—Turbocharged engine.
[10]—Century.
[11]—Regal and LeSabre with single exhaust.
[12]—Diesel.

TUNE UP SPECIFICATIONS

The following specifications are published from the latest information available. This data should be used only in the absence of a decal affixed in the engine compartment.

★ When using a timing light, disconnect vacuum hose or tube at distributor and plug opening in tube or hose so idle speed will not be affected.

● When checking compression, lowest cylinder must be within 80 percent of highest.

▲ Before removing wires from distributor cap, determine location of the No. 1 wire in cap, as distributor position may have been altered from that shown at the end of this chart.

Year & Engine	Spark Plug Type	Gap	Firing Order Fig. ▲	Ignition Timing BTDC① ★ Man. Trans.	Auto. Trans.	Mark Fig.	Curb Idle Speed② Man. Trans.	Auto. Trans.	Fast Idle Speed Man Trans.	Auto. Trans.	Fuel Pump Pressure
1975											
6-250 Exc. Calif.③	R46TX	.060	I	10°	10°	D	425/850	425/550D④	1800⑤	1700⑤	3½-4½
6-250 Calif.③	R46TX	.060	I	—	10°	D	—	425/600D	—	1700⑤	3½-4½
V6-231	R44SX	.060	J	12°	12°	K	600/800	500/700D	—	—	3 Min.
V8-260 Exc. Calif.⑥	R46SX	.080	L	—	18°⑦	M	—	550/650D	—	900⑧	5½-6½
V8-260 Calif.⑥	R46SX	.080	L	—	14°⑦	M	—	600/650D④	—	900⑧	5½-6½
V8-350	R45TSX	.060	H	—	12°	F	—	600D	—	1800⑨	3 Min.
V8-400⑩	R45TSX	.060	N	—	16°	C	—	650D	—	1800⑨	5½-6½
V8-455	R45TSX	.060	H	—	12°	F	—	600D	—	1800⑨	4½ Min.
1976											
V6-231	R44SX	.060	J	12°	12°	K⑪	600/800	600D	—	—	3 Min.
V8-260 Exc. Calif.⑥	R46SX	.080	L	—	18°⑦	M	—	550/650D	—	900⑧	5½-6½
V8-260 Calif.⑥	R46SX	.080	L	—	14°⑦	M	—	600/650D④	—	900⑧	5½-6½
V8-350	R45TSX	.060	H	—	12°	F	—	600D	—	1800⑨	3 Min.
V8-455	R45TSX	.060	H	—	12°	F	—	600D	—	1800⑨	4½ Min.
1977											
V6-231⑫	R46TS	.040	O	12°	12°	P⑬	⑭	600D	—	—	3 Min.
V6-231⑮	R46TSX	.060	A	—	15°	B⑬	—	600/670D	—	—	3 Min.
V8-301⑩	R46TSX	.060	N	—	12°	G	—	550/650D	—	1700⑯	7-8½
V8-305③	R45TS	.045	E	—	8°	D	—	500/650D	—	—	7½-9
V8-350 2 Barrel⑰	R46TS	.040	H	—	12°	P⑬	—	600D	—	—	3 Min.
V8-350 4 Barrel⑰	R46TS	.040	H	—	12°	P⑬	—	550D	—	1800⑧	3 Min.
V8-350 4 Barrel③⑱	R45TS	.045	E	—	8°	D	—	⑲	—	1600⑳	7½-9
V8-350 4 Barrel Exc. Calif.⑥㉑㉒	R46SZ	.060	L	—	20°⑦	M	—	550/650D④	—	900㉓	5½-6½
V8-350 4 Barrel Calif.⑥㉑	R46SZ	.060	L	—	㉔	M	—	550/650D④	—	1000㉓	5½-6½
V8-350 4 Barrel High Alt.⑥㉑	R46SZ	.060	L	—	20°⑦	M	—	600/650D④	—	1000㉓	5½-6½
V8-403 Exc. Calif. & High Alt.	R46SZ	.060	L	—	24°⑦	M	—	550/650D④	—	900㉓	5½-6½
V8-403 Calif. & High Alt.	R46SZ	.060	L	—	20°⑦	M	—	④㉕	—	1000㉓	5½-6½
1978											
V6-196	R46TSX	.060	A	15°	15°	B⑬	600/800	600D	—	—	3 Min.
V6-231㉖	R46TSX	.060	A	15°	15°	B⑬	600/800	600/670D	—	—	3 Min.
V6-231㉗	R44TSX	.060	A	—	15°	B⑬	—	650D	—	—	5
V8-301⑩	R46TSX	.060	N	—	12°	G	—	550/650D	—	2200	7-8½
V8-305 2 Barrel Exc. Calif.③㉒	R45TS	.045	E	—	4°	D	—	500/600D	—	—	7½-9
V8-305 2 Barrel Calif.③	R45TS	.045	E	—	6°	D	—	600/700D	—	—	7½-9

Continued

TUNE UP SPECIFICATIONS—Continued

Year & Engine	Spark Plug Type	Gap	Firing Order Fig. ▲	Ignition Timing BTDC ①★ Man. Trans.	Auto. Trans.	Mark Fig.	Curb Idle Speed ② Man. Trans.	Auto. Trans.	Fast Idle Speed Man Trans.	Auto. Trans.	Fuel Pump Pressure
V8-305 2 Barrel High Alt.③	R45TS	.045	E	—	8°	D	—	600/700D	—	—	7½–9
V8-305 4 Barrel③	R45TS	.045	E	—	4°	D	—	500/600D	—	—	7½–9
V8-350⑰	R46TSX	.060	H	—	15°	B⑬	—	550D	—	1550	3 Min.
V8-350③⑱	R45TS	.045	E	—	8°	D	—	㉘	—	1600	7½–9
V8-350⑥㉑	R46SZ	.060	L	—	20°⑦	M	—	㉙	—	1000	5½–6½
V8-403 Exc. Calif. & High Alt.	R46SZ	.060	L	—	20°⑦	M	—	550/650D	—	900	5½–6½
V8-403 Calif. & High Alt.	R46SZ	.060	L	—	20°⑦	M	—	㉙	—	1000	5½–6½
1979											
V6-196	㉚	.060	A	15°	15°	B⑬	600/800	550/670D	2200	2200	3 Min.
V6-231 Exc. Calif.㉒㉖	㉚	.060	A	15°	15°	B⑬	600/800	550/670D	2200	2200	3 Min.
V6-231 Calif.㉖	㉚	.060	A	15°	15°	B⑬	600/800	㉛	2200	2200	3 Min.
V6-231 High Alt.㉖	㉚	.060	A	—	15°	B⑬	—	600D	—	2200	3 Min.
V6-231㉗	R44TSX	.060	A	—	15°	B⑬	—	㉜	—	2500	5
V8-301 2 Barrel⑩	R46TSX	.060	N	—	12°	G	—	500/650D	—	2000	7–8½
V8-301 4 Barrel⑩	R45TSX	.060	N	—	12°	G	—	500/650D	—	2200	7–8½
V8-305 2 Barrel③	R45TS	.045	E	—	4°	D	—	㉝	—	1600	7½–9
V8-305 4 Barrel Calif.③	R45TS	.045	E	—	4°	D	—	500/600D	—	1600	7½–9
V8-305 4 Barrel High Alt.③	R45TS	.045	E	—	8°	D	—	600/650D	—	1750	7½–9
V8-350⑰	㉚	.060	H	—	15°	B⑬	—	550D	—	1500	3 Min.
V8-350 Calif.③⑱	R45TS	.045	E	—	8°	D	—	500/600D	—	1600	7½–9
V8-350 High Alt.③⑱	R45TS	.045	E	—	8°	D	—	600/650D	—	1750	7½–9
V8-350 Exc. Calif.⑥㉑	R46SZ	.060	L	—	20°⑦	M	—	㉙	—	900	5½–6½
V8-350 Calif.⑥㉑	R46SZ	.060	L	—	20°⑦	M	—	500/600D	—	1000	5½–6½
V8-403 Exc. Calif & High Alt.	R46SZ	.060	L	—	20°⑦	M	—	550/650D	—	900	5½–6½
V8-403 Calif.	R46SZ	.060	L	—	20°⑦	M	—	500/600D	—	1000	5½–6½
V8-403 High Alt.	R46SZ	.060	L	—	20°⑦	M	—	600/700D	—	1000	5½–6½
1980											
V6-231 Exc. Calif.㉒㉖	R45TSX	.060	A	15°	15°	B⑬	600/800	㉞	2000	2000	3 Min.
V6-231 Exc. Calif.㉒㉗	R45TS	.040	A	—	15°	B⑬	—	㉜	—	2200	5 Min.
V6-231 Calif.㉖	R45TSX	.060	A	—	15°	B⑬	—	㉟	—	2200	3 Min.
V6-231 Calif.㉗	R45TS	.040	A	—	15°	B⑬	—	㉜	—	㊱	5 Min.
V6-252 Exc. Calif.	R45TSX	.060	A	—	15°	B⑬	—	㊲	—	2000	3 Min.
V6-265 Exc. Calif.	R45TSX	.060	N	—	10°	G	—	㊳	—	2200	7–8.5
V8-301 Exc. Calif.⑩	R45TSX	.060	N	—	12°	G	—	㊴	—	2500	7–8.5
V8-305③	R45TS	.035	E	—	4°	D	—	㊳	—	2200	7.5–9
V8-350 Exc. Calif.⑰	R45TSX	.060	H	—	15°	B⑬	—	㉞	—	1850	3 Min.
V8-350 Calif.⑥㉑㊵	R46SX	.080	L	—	18°	M	—	650D	—	700D	5.5–6.5
V8-350 Exc. Calif.⑥㉑㊶	R46SX	.080	L	—	18°	M	—	650D	—	700D	5.5–6.5
V8-350 Calif.⑥㉑㊶	R46SX	.080	L	—	16°	M	—	650D	—	700D	5.5–6.5
V8-350⑥㊷	—	—		7°㊸	—	—	—	600D	—	700D	—

BUICK—Exc. Skyhawk & 1980 Skylark

TUNE UP NOTES

①—BTDC—Before top dead center.
②—Idle speed on man. trans. vehicles is adjusted in Neutral & on auto. trans. equipped vehicles is adjusted in Drive unless otherwise specified. Where two idle speeds are listed, the higher speed is with the A/C or idle solenoid energized.
③—Chevrolet-built engine.
④—With A/C on & Compressor clutch wires disconnected.
⑤—On high step of fast idle cam with vacuum hose to EGR & distributor vacuum advance disconnected & plugged & A/C off.
⑥—Oldsmobile-built engine.
⑦—At 1100 RPM.
⑧—On low step of fast idle cam with vacuum hose to EGR disconnected & plugged & A/C off.
⑨—On high step of fast idle cam with vacuum hose to EGR disconnected & plugged & A/C off.
⑩—Pontiac-built engine.
⑪—These engines use two different harmonic balancers. The harmonic balancer used on late engines has two timing marks. The mark measuring 1/16 in. is used when setting timing with a hand held timing light. The mark measuring 1/8 in. is used when setting timing with magnetic timing equipment.

⑫—Except Even-Fire engine.
⑬—The harmonic balancer on these engines has two timing marks. The timing mark measuring 1/16 in. is used when setting timing with a hand held timing light. The mark measuring 1/8 in. is used when setting timing with magnetic timing equipment.
⑭—Except Calif., 500/800 RPM; California, 600/800 RPM.
⑮—Even fire engine.
⑯—On 2nd step against high step of fast idle cam.
⑰—Distributor located at front of engine.
⑱—Distributor located at rear of engine, clockwise rotor rotation.
⑲—Except high altitude, 500/650D RPM; high alititude, 600/650D RPM.
⑳—On high step of fast idle cam.
㉑—Distributor located at rear of engine, counter clockwise rotor rotation.
㉒—Except high altitude.
㉓—On low step of fast idle cam with vacuum hose to EGR disconnected & plugged & A/C off.
㉔—Except sta. wag. 18 BTDC at 1100 RPM; sta. wag., 20 BTDC at 1100 RPM.
㉕—Except high altitude, 550/650D RPM; high altitude, 600/650D RPM.
㉖—Except turbo charged engine.

㉗—Turbo charged engine.
㉘—Except high altitude, 500/600D RPM; high altitude, 600/650D RPM.
㉙—Except high altitude, 550/650D RPM; high altitude, 600/700 D RPM.
㉚—R45TSX or R46TSX.
㉛—Models less idle solenoid, 600D RPM; models with idle solenoid, 580/670D RPM.
㉜—Except Riviera, 650D RPM; Riviera, 600/650D RPM.
㉝—Less A/C, 500/600D RPM; with A/C, 550/650D RPM.
㉞—With idle solenoid—550/670D. Without idle solenoid—550D.
㉟—With idle solenoid—550/620D. Without idle solenoid—550D.
㊱—Riviera—2500. Exc. Riviera—2200.
㊲—With idle solenoid—550/680D. Without idle solenoid—550D.
㊳—With idle solenoid—500/650D. Without idle solenoid—550D.
㊴—With idle solenoid—500/650D. Without idle solenoid—500D.
㊵—Except Riviera.
㊶—Riviera.
㊷—Diesel.
㊸—Injection timing at 800 RPM.

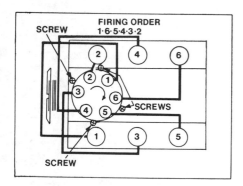

Fig. A

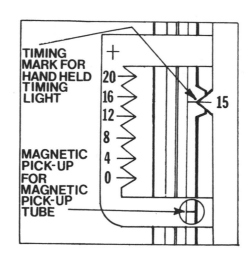

Fig. B

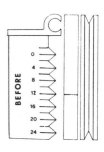

Fig. C

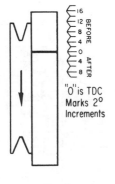

Fig. D

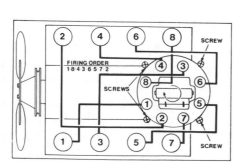

Fig. E

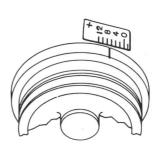

Fig. F

Fig. G

Continued

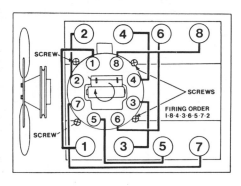

Fig. H

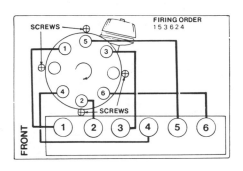

Fig. I

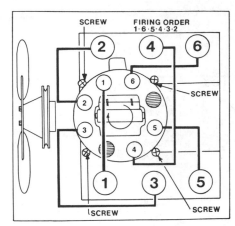

Fig. J

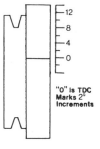

"0" Is TDC
Marks 2°
Increments

Fig. K

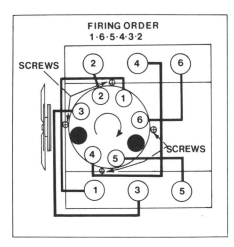

Fig. L

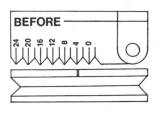

Fig. M

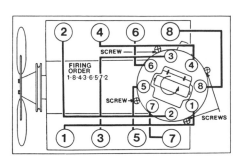

Fig. N

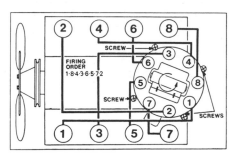

Fig. O

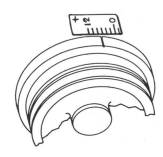

Fig. P

BUICK—Exc. Skyhawk & 1980 Skylark

COOLING SYSTEM & CAPACITY DATA

Year	Model or Engine	Cooling Capacity, Qts. Less A/C	Cooling Capacity, Qts. With A/C	Radiator Cap Relief Pressure, Lbs.	Thermo. Opening Temp.	Fuel Tank Gals.	Engine Oil Refill Qts. ①	Transmission Oil 3 Speed Pints	Transmission Oil 4 Speed Pints	Transmission Oil Auto. Trans. Qts. ②	Rear Axle Oil Pints
1975	6-250	16.3	16.4	15	190	21	4	3½	—	⑮	4.25
	V6-231⑦	16.5	16.6	15	190	21	4	3½	—	⑮	4.25
	V6-231⑪	15.3	15.3	15	190	22	4	3½	—	⑮	4.25
	V8-260⑦	22.4	22.9	—	195	21	4	3½	—	⑮	4.25
	V8-350⑦	17.9	18.6	15	190	21	4	—	—	⑮	4.25
	V8-350⑪	16.9	17.2	15	190	22	4	3½	—	⑮	⑳
	V8-350⑩	16.9	17.2	15	190	26	4	—	—	⑮	4.25
	V8-400	23.6⑧	⑨	15	190	26③	4	—	—	—	⑳
	V8-455	19.6	20⑤	15	190	26③	4	—	—	⑯	⑳
1976	V6-231⑦	16.6	16.7	15	195	21	4	3½	—	⑮	4.25
	V6-231⑩	15.5	15.4	15	195	26③	4	—	—	⑮	4¼
	V6-231⑪	15.5	15.4	15	195	22	4	3½	—	⑮	4.25
	V8-260⑦	22.4	22.9	15	195	21	4	3½	—	⑮	4.25
	V8-350⑦	17.9	18.5	15	195	21	4	—	—	⑮	4.25
	V8-350⑪	16.9	17.2⑫	15	195	22	4	—	—	⑮	4.25
	V8-350⑩	16.9	17.2⑫	15	195	26③	4	—	—	⑮	4.25
	V8-350④	16.9	17.2⑫	15	195	26	4	—	—	⑮	5½
	V8-455	19.7	20㉑	15	195	26③	4	—	—	⑯	5.5
1977	V6-231⑦	12.7	12.8	15	⑰	21	4	3½	—	⑮	3.5
	V6-231⑪	12.8	12.7	15	⑰	22	4	3½	—	⑮	4¼
	V6-231⑩	12.7	12.7	15	⑰	21	4	—	—	⑮	4¼
	V8-301⑦	18.6	19.2	15	195	21	4	—	—	⑮	3.5
	V8-301⑩	18.2㉒	18.1㉒	15	195	21	4	—	—	⑮	4¼
	V8-305⑦	17	18	15	195	21	4	—	—	⑮	3.5
	V8-350⑪㉓	14.3㉔	14.9㉔	15	195	22	4	—	—	⑮	4¼
	V8-350⑥⑩㉓	14.2㉕	14.1㉕	15	195	㉖	4	—	—	⑮	㉗
	V8-350⑦⑱㉘	15.6	15.6	15	195	21	4	—	—	⑮	3.5
	V8-350⑪⑱㉘	15.3㉙	15.9㉙	15	195	22	4	—	—	⑮	4¼
	V8-350⑥⑩㉘	14.6㉚	14.5㉚	15	195	㉖	4	—	—	⑮	㉗
	V8-350⑦㉘	17	18	15	195	21	4	—	—	⑮	3.5
	V8-350⑪㉘	14.8	15.4	15	195	22	4	—	—	⑮	4¼
	V8-403⑪	16.4㉛	17㉛	15	195	22	4	—	—	⑮	4¼
	V8-403⑥⑩	15.7㉜	15.6㉜	15	195	㉖	4	—	—	⑮	㉗
1978	V6-196	13.1	13.2	15	195	17.5	4	3½	—	⑮	4¼
	V6-231⑦	13.6	13.7	15	195	21	4	3½	—	⑮	4¼
	V6-231⑪	13.1	13.2	15	195	17.5	4	—	3½	⑮	4¼
	V6-231⑩	12.9	12.9	15	195	21	4	—	—	⑮	4¼
	V8-301	20.9⑤	20.9⑤	15	195	21	4	—	—	⑮	4¼
	V8-305⑦	15.9㉝	16.3㉝	15	195	21	4	3½	—	⑮	4¼
	V8-305⑪	19.2㉞	18.9㉞	15	195	17.5	4	—	—	⑮	4¼
	V8-305⑩	16.6	16.7	15	195	21	4	—	—	⑮	4¼
	V8-350⑦	16.1	16.9	15	195	21	4	—	—	⑮	4¼
	V8-350⑪	19.2㉞	18.9㉞	15	195	17.5	4	—	—	⑮	4¼
	V8-350⑥⑩㉓	14.1㉟	14.1㉟	15	195	⑲	4	—	—	⑮	4¼
	V8-350⑥⑩⑱	14.6㉚	14.5㉚	15	195	⑲	4	—	—	⑮	4¼
	V8-350⑥⑩㉘	16.6㊱	16.7㊱	15	195	⑲	4	—	—	⑮	4¼
	V8-403	15.7	16.6	15	195	⑲	4	—	—	—	4¼

Continued

COOLING SYSTEM & CAPACITY DATA—Continued

Year	Model or Engine	Cooling Capacity, Qts.		Radiator Cap Relief Pressure, Lbs.	Thermo. Opening Temp.	Fuel Tank Gals.	Engine Oil Refill Qts. (1)	Transmission Oil			Rear Axle Oil Pints
		Less A/C	With A/C					3 Speed Pints	4 Speed Pints	Auto. Trans. Qts. (2)	
1979	V6-196, 231 (11)	13.5	13.5	15	195	18.1	4	3.5	3.5	(15)(41)	(38)
	V6-231 (10)(14)	12.9	12.9	15	195	25.3	4	—	—	(15)	(38)
	V6-231 (7)	13.8	13.9	15	195	21	4	3.5	—	(15)	(38)
	V6-231 Turbo (11)(37)	13.7(43)	13.8(43)	15	195	18.1	4	—	—	(15)(41)	(38)
	V6-231 Turbo (13)(37)	—	14(4)	15	195	20	4	—	—	(9)	3.2
	V8-301 (11)	20.3(27)	21(27)	15	195	18.1	4	3.5	3.5	(15)(41)	(38)
	V8-301 (10)(14)	21(5)	21(5)	15	195	21(3)(42)	4	—	—	(15)	(38)
	V8-305 (7)	15.9(33)	16.3(33)	15	195	21	4	3.5	—	(15)	(38)
	V8-305 (11)	17.6(36)	17.6(36)	15	195	18.1	4	3.5	3.5	(15)(41)	(38)
	V8-350 (11)	17.6(36)	18.1	15	195	18.1	4	3.5	3.5	(15)(41)	(38)
	V8-350 (7)	16.1(33)	16.9	15	195	21	4	3.5	—	(15)	(38)
	V8-350 (39)(10)(14)	14.1(25)	14.1(25)	15	195	21(3)(42)	4	—	—	(15)	(38)
	V8-350 (40)(10)(14)	14.6(20)	14.5(30)	15	195	21(3)(42)	4	—	—	(15)	(38)
	V8-350 (40)(13)	—	14.9(30)	15	195	20	4	—	—	(9)	3.2
	V8-403 (40)(10)(14)	15.7(32)	16.6	15	195	21(3)(42)	4	—	—	(15)	(38)
1980	V6-231 (11)(44)	13.4	13.4	15	195	18	4	3.5	3.5	(63)	(38)
	V6-231 (11)(45)	(46)	(47)	15	195	18	4	3.5	3.5	(63)	(38)
	V6-231 (44)(48)	13	13	15	195	(49)	4	—	—	(63)	(38)
	V6-231 (45)(48)	(50)	(50)	15	195	(49)	4,	—	—	(63)	(38)
	V6-231 (13)	—	(51)	15	195	(20)	4	—	—	(9)	3.2(62)
	V6-252 (14)	13.0	13.0	15	195	25	4	—	—	(9)	4.25
	V8-265 (11)	19.2(64)	19.2(64)	15	195	18.1	4(65)	—	—	(66)	(38)
	V8-301 (11)	(53)	(54)	15	195	18	4	—	—	(63)	(38)
	V8-301 (48)	18.9	18.9	15	195	(49)	4	—	—	(63)	(38)
	V8-305 (11)	(55)	(55)	15	195	18	4	—	—	(63)	(38)
	V8-350 (39)(48)	(56)	(57)	15	195	(49)	4	—	—	(63)	(38)
	V8-350 (40)(48)	14.5	(58)	15	195	(49)	4	—	—	(63)	(38)
	V8-350 (48)(59)	18.3	18	15	195	27	4	—	—	(63)	(38)
	V8-350 (13)	—	(60)	15	195	(52)	4	—	—	(5)	3.2(62)

(1)—Add one quart with filter change.
(2)—Approximate. Make final check with dipstick.
(3)—Estate Wagon 22 gallons.
(4)—With heavy duty cooling system, 14.5 qts.
(5)—With heavy duty cooling system, 21.6 qts.
(6)—Estate Wagon, Electra & Riviera.
(7)—Apollo & Skylark.
(8)—With heavy duty cooling system, 25.6 qts.
(9)—Total 12 qts. Oil pan only 5 qts.
(10)—LeSabre.
(11)—Intermediates.
(12)—With heavy duty cooling system, 18.7 qts.
(13)—Riviera.
(14)—Electra.
(15)—Total 10 qts.; pan only 3 qts.
(16)—Total 11½ qts. Oil pan only 3½ qts.
(17)—Exc. Calif., 195°; Calif., 180°.
(18)—Oil filler tube located on engine front cover.
(19)—LeSabre, 21; Estate Wagon, 22.5; Electra, Riviera, 25.3.
(20)—Exc. wagon, 4¼ pts.; wagon, 5.4 pts.
(21)—With heavy duty cooling system, 21.5 qts.
(22)—With heavy duty cooling system, 19.1 qts.
(23)—Distributor at front of engine.
(24)—With heavy duty cooling system, 16.4 qts.
(25)—With heavy duty cooling system, 15 qts.
(26)—LeSabre 21 gal.; Electra & Riviera, 24.5 gal.; Estate wagon, 22 gal.
(27)—With heavy duty cooling system, 20.8 qts.

(28)—Distributor at rear of engine.
(29)—With heavy duty cooling system, 17.4 qts.
(30)—With heavy duty cooling system, 15.4 qts.
(31)—With heavy duty cooling system, 18.5 qts.
(32)—With heavy duty cooling system, 16.6 qts.
(33)—With heavy duty cooling system, 16.9 qts.
(34)—With heavy duty cooling system, 19.6 qts.
(35)—With heavy duty cooling system, 14.9 qts.
(36)—With heavy duty cooling system, 18.0 qts.
(37)—4 Barrel Carb.
(38)—7½ inch axle, 3.5 pts.; 8½ inch axle, 4.25 pts.; 8¾ inch axle, 5.4 pts.
(39)—Buick built engine.
(40)—Oldsmobile built engine.
(41)—THM 200—total 9.5 qts.; 3.5 qts. oil pan only.
(42)—Electra, 25.3 gal.
(43)—With heavy duty cooling system, 14.1 qts.
(44)—Exc. Turbocharged engine.
(45)—Turbocharged engine.
(46)—Except heavy duty cooling; 13.7. With heavy duty cooling; 14.
(47)—Except heavy duty cooling; 13.8. With heavy duty cooling; 14.1.
(48)—Electra & LeSabre.
(49)—Station wagon; 22. Except Station wagon; 25. All with diesel engine; 27.
(50)—Except heavy duty cooling; 13.4. With heavy duty cooling; 13.8.
(51)—Except heavy duty cooling; 13.6. With heavy duty cooling; 14.7.

(52)—Except diesel; 20. With diesel; 23.
(53)—Except heavy duty cooling; 20.3. With heavy duty cooling; 20.8.
(54)—Except heavy duty cooling; 21. With heavy duty cooling; 20.8.
(55)—Except heavy duty cooling; 17.6. With heavy duty cooling; 18.1.
(56)—Except heavy duty cooling; 14.3. With heavy duty cooling; 14.8.
(57)—Except heavy duty cooling; 14.2. With heavy duty cooling; 14.7.
(58)—Except heavy duty cooling; 14.5. With heavy duty cooling; 15.2.
(59)—Diesel engine.
(60)—Except heavy duty cooling; 14.9. With heavy duty cooling; 15.6.
(61)—Except diesel engine; 20. With diesel engine; 23.
(62)—Final drive, pints.
(63)—THM 200, total capacity 9½ qts.; oil pan 3½ qts. THM 250C, total capacity 10½ qts.; oil pan 3 qts. THM 350, total capacity, 10 qts.; oil pan 3 qts.
(64)—With heavy duty cooling system, 19.7 qts.
(65)—With or without filter change.
(66)—T.H.M. 200 & 200C, refill 3½ qts., after overhaul 9½ qts.; T.H.M. 250C, refill 4 qts., after overhaul 10¾ qts.; T.H.M. 350 & 350C, refill 2¾ qts., after overhaul, 10¼ qts.

CADILLAC

SERIAL NUMBER LOCATION:

On top of instrument panel, left front.

ENGINE NUMBER LOCATION:

On all engines except V8-350, engine unit number is located on cylinder block behind left cylinder head. V.I.N. derivative is located on cylinder block behind intake manifold.

On 1976-80 V8-350, engine identification number is located on left hand side of cylinder block at front below cylinder head. On 1979-80 V8-350, engine code label is located on top of left hand valve cover and engine unit number label is located on top of right hand valve cover.

GENERAL ENGINE SPECIFICATIONS

Year	Engine	Carburetor	Bore and Stroke	Piston Displacement, Cubic Inches	Compression Ratio	Maximum Brake H.P. @ R.P.M.	Maximum Torque Lbs. Ft. @ R.P.M.	Normal Oil Pressure Pounds
1975–76	190 Horsepower① V8-500	4 Barrel	4.300 × 4.304	500	8.5	190 @ 3600	360 @ 2000	35 Min.
1976	180 Horsepower① V8-350	Fuel Inj.	4.057 × 3.385	350	8.5	180 @ 4400	275 @ 2000	30–35
	215 Horsepower① V8-500	Fuel Inj.	4.300 × 4.304	500	8.5	215 @ 3600	400 @ 2000	35 Min.
1977	180 Horsepower① V8-350	Fuel Inj.	4.057 × 3.385	350	8.5	180 @ 4400	275 @ 2000	30–45
	180 Horsepower① V8-425	4 Barrel	4.082 × 4.060	425	8.2	180 @ 4000	320 @ 2000	35 Min.
	195 Horsepower① V8-425	Fuel Inj.	4.082 × 4.060	425	8.2	195 @ 3800	320 @ 2400	35 Min.
1978	120 Horsepower① V8-350②	Fuel Inj.	4.057 × 3.385	350	22.5	120 @ 3600	220 @ 1600	30–45
	170 Horsepower① V8-350	Fuel Inj.	4.057 × 3.385	350	8.0	170 @ 4280	270 @ 2000	30–45
	180 Horsepower① V8-425	4 Barrel	4.082 × 4.060	425	8.2	180 @ 4000	320 @ 2000	35 Min.
	180 Horsepower① V8-425	Fuel Inj.	4.082 × 4.060	425	8.2	180 @ 4000	320 @ 2000	35 Min.
1979	125 Horsepower① V8-350②	Fuel Inj.	4.057 × 3.385	350	22.5	125 @ 3600	225 @ 1600	30–45
	170 Horsepower① V8-350	Fuel Inj.	4.057 × 3.385	350	8.0	170 @ 4200	270 @ 2000	30–45
	180 Horsepower① V8-425	4 Barrel	4.082 × 4.060	425	8.2	180 @ 4000	320 @ 2000	35 Min.
	195 Horsepower① V8-425	Fuel Inj.	4.082 × 4.060	425	8.2	195 @ 3800	320 @ 2400	35 Min.
1980	105 Horsepower① V8-350②	Fuel Inj.	4.057 × 3.385	350	22.5	105 @ 3200	205 @ 1600	30–35
	160 Horsepower① V8-350	Fuel Inj.	4.057 × 3.385	350	8.0	160 @ 4400	265 @ 1600	30–35
	145 Horsepower① V8-368	Fuel Inj.	3.800 × 4.060	368	8.2	145 @ 3600	270 @ 2000	40–48
	150 Horsepower① V8-368	4 Barrel	3.800 × 4.060	368	8.2	150 @ 3800	265 @ 1600	40–48

①—Net rating—as installed in the vehicle.   ②—Oldsmobile-built engine.

TUNE UP SPECIFICATIONS

The following specifications are published from the latest information available. This data should be used only in the absence of a decal affixed in the engine compartment.

★ When using a timing light, disconnect vacuum hose or tube at distributor and plug opening in hose or tube so idle speed will not be affected.

● When checking compression, lowest cylinder must be within 80 percent of highest.

▲ Before removing wires from distributor cap, determine location of No. 1 wire in cap, as distributor position may have been altered from that shown at the end of this chart.

Year & Engine	Spark Plug		Ignition Timing BTDC★				Curb Idle Speed①		Fast Idle Speed③		Fuel Pump Pressure
	Type	Gap	Firing Order Fig. ▲	Std. Trans.	Auto. Trans.	Mark Fig.	Std. Trans.	Auto. Trans.②	Std. Trans.	Auto. Trans.	
1975											
V8-500 Exc. E.F.I.	R45NSX	.060	C	—	6°	D	—	600D	—	1225④	5¼-6½
V8-500 E.F.I.	R45NSX	.060	C	—	12°	D	—	600D	—	—	—
1976											
V8-350 Exc. Calif.	R47SX	.060	B	—	10°	A	—	600D	—	—	—
V8-350 Calif.	R47SX	.060	B	—	6°	A	—	600D	—	—	—
V8-500 Exc. E.F.I.	R45NSX	.060	C	—	6°	D	—	600D	—	1400④	5¼-6½
V8-500 E.F.I.	R45NSX	.060	C	—	12°	D	—	600D	—	—	—

Continued

TUNE UP SPECIFICATIONS—Continued

Year & Engine	Spark Plug Type	Gap	Ignition Timing BTDC★ Firing Order Fig. ▲	Std. Trans.	Auto. Trans.	Mark Fig.	Curb Idle Speed① Std. Trans.	Auto Trans.②	Fast Idle Speed③ Std. Trans.	Auto. Trans.	Fuel Pump Pressure
1977											
V8-350 Exc. Calif.	R47SX	.060	B	—	10°	A	—	600D	—	—	—
V8-350 Calif.	R47SX	.060	B	—	8°	A	—	600D	—	—	—
V8-425 Exc. Calif. & E.F.I.	R45NSX	.060	C	—	18°⑤	E	—	⑥	—	1400⑦	5¼-6½
V8-425 Calif. Exc. E.F.I.	R45NSX	.060	C	—	18°⑤	E	—	⑥	—	1500⑦	5¼-6½
V8-425 E.F.I.	R45NSX	.060	C	—	18°⑤	E	—	650D	—	—	—
1978											
V8-350 E.F.I. Exc. Calif.	R47SX	.060	B	—	10°	A	—	650D	—	—	—
V8-350 E.F.I. Calif.	R47SX	.060	B	—	8°	A	—	650D	—	—	—
V8-350 Diesel⑧	—	—	—	—	⑧	—	—	650D	—	—	—
V8-425 Exc. E.F.I.	R45NSX	.060	C	—	⑨	E	—	600D	—	⑦⑩	—
V8-425 E.F.I.	R45NSX	.060	C	—	18°⑪	E	—	600D	—	—	—
1979											
V8-350 E.F.I.	R47SX	.060	B	—	10°	A	—	600D	—	—	—
V8-350 Diesel⑧	—	—	—	—	⑧	—	—	650D	—	—	—
V8-425 Exc. E.F.I.	R45NSX	.060	C	—	23°⑪	E	—	550/650D	—	⑦⑫	—
V8-425 E.F.I.	R45NSX	.060	C	—	18°⑤	E	—	650D	—	—	—
1980											
V8-350 E.F.I.	R47SX	.060	B	—	10°	A	—	600D	—	—	—
V8-350 Diesel⑧	—	—	—	—	7°⑮	—	—	575/650D	—	—	—
V8-368 4 Barrel Exc. Calif.	R45NSX	.060	C	—	10°⑭	E	—	500/650D	—	1450	5¼-6½
V8-368 4 Barrel Calif.	R45NSX	.060	C	—	10°⑭	E	—	575/650D	—	1350	5¼-6½
V8-368 D.E.F.I.	R45NSX	.060	C	—	10°⑬	E	—	550D	—	—	10

① —Where two idle speeds are listed, the higher speed is with idle solenoid energized. Curb idle speed is adjusted with A/C off, while solenoid idle speed is adjusted with A/C on.

② —D: Drive.

③ —With transmission in Park position & parking brake fully applied.

④ —With cam follower on highest step of fast idle cam.

⑤ —At 1400 RPM.

⑥ —Except Eldorado, 600/675D RPM; Eldorado, 600D RPM.

⑦ —With cam follower on 2nd step of fast idle cam, distributor vacuum hose & EGR vacuum hose disconnected & plugged & A/C off.

⑧ —Oldsmobile-built engine.

⑨ —Except Eldorado, except high altitude, 21° BTDC at 1600 RPM; high altitude, 23° BTDC at 1600 RPM. Eldorado, except Calif. & high altitude, 21° BTDC at 1600 RPM; California, 18° BTDC at 1600 RPM; high altitude, 23° BTDC at 1600 RPM.

⑩ —Except carburetor No. 17058230, 1500 RPM; carburetor No. 17058230, 1400 RPM.

⑪ —At 1600 RPM.

⑫ —Except carburetor No. 17059230, 1500 RPM; carburetor No. 1705923, 1000 RPM.

⑬ —Engine wiring harness test lead, green connector, must be grounded.

⑭ —At 800 RPM.

⑮ —Injection timing at 800 RPM.

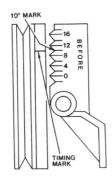

Fig. A

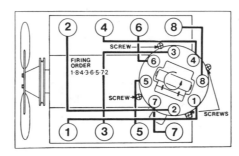

Fig. B

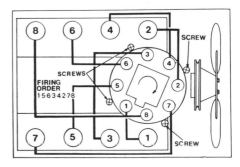

Fig. C

Continued

TUNE UP NOTES—Continued

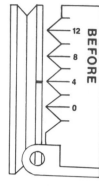

Fig. D

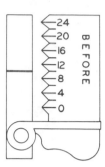

Fig. E

COOLING SYSTEM & CAPACITY DATA

Year	Model or Engine	Cooling Capacity, Qts.		Radiator Cap Relief Pressure, Lbs.	Thermo. Opening Temp. ①	Fuel Tank Gals.	Engine Oil Refill Qts. ②	Transmission Oil			Rear Axle Oil Pints
		Less A/C	With A/C					3 Speed Pints	4 Speed Pints	Auto. Trans. Qts. ③	
1975	Eldorado	23	23	15	180	27½	5	—	—	⑥	4⑧
	Series 75	25.8	25.8	15	180	27½	4	—	—	⑤	5
	Others	23	23	15	180	27½	4	—	—	⑤	5
1976	Eldorado	23	23	15	180	27½	5	—	—	⑦	4④⑧
	Series 75	25.8	25.8	15	180	27½	4	—	—	⑤	4④
	Seville	18.9	18.9	15	180	21	4	—	—	⑤	4¼
	Others	23	23	15	180	27½	4	—	—	⑤	4④
1977	Eldorado	—	25.8	15	195	27½	5	—	—	⑥	4
	Seville	—	17.25	15	195	21	④	—	—	⑤	4¼
	Others	—	20.8	15	195	24½	4	—	—	⑤	4¼
1978	Eldorado	—	24.3	15	195	27½	5	—	—	⑥	4⑧
	Seville Exc. Diesel	—	17.25	15	180	21	4	—	—	⑤	4¼
	Seville Diesel	—	18.9	15	195	21	7⑭	—	—	⑪	4¼
	Others	—	19.8	15	195	24	4	—	—	⑤	4¼
1979	Eldorado Exc.Diesel	—	14.75⑨	15	180	19.6⑬	4	—	—	⑩	3⅕⑧
	Eldorado Diesel	—	18.5	15	195	19.6	7⑭	—	—	⑩	3⅕⑧
	Seville Exc. Diesel	—	17.25	15	180	21	4	—	—	⑫	4¼
	Seville Diesel	—	20	15	195	21	7⑭	—	—	⑪	4¼
	Others Exc. Diesel	—	20.8	15	195	25	4	—	—	⑫	4¼
	Others Diesel	—	23.8	15	195	27	7⑭	—	—	⑪	4¼
1980	Eldorado V8-350 E.F.I.	—	15.2	15	180	20.6	4	—	—	⑩	3⅕⑧
	Eldorado V8-368 D.E.F.I.	—	22.4	15	195	20.6	5	—	—	⑩	3⅕⑧
	Eldorado Diesel	—	18.4	15	195	23	7⑭	—	—	⑩	3⅕⑧
	Seville V8-350 E.F.I.	—	15.2	15	180	20.6	4	—	—	⑩	3⅕⑧
	Seville V8-368 D.E.F.I.	—	22.4	15	195	20.6	5	—	—	⑩	3⅕⑧
	Seville Diesel	—	18.4	15	195	23	7⑭	—	—	⑩	3⅕⑧
	Others Exc. Diesels	—	21.4	15	195	25	4	—	—	4⑮	4¼
	Others Diesel	—	23.7	15	195	27	7⑭	—	—	⑪	4¼

①—For permanent anti-freeze.
②—Add one quart with filter change.
③—Approximate. Make final check with dip-stick.
④—Exc. 3.15 rear axle ratio 3.15 rear axle ratio, 5 pts.
⑤—Oil pan 4 qts. Total capacity 12½ qts.
⑥—Oil pan 5 qts. Total capacity 13 qts.
⑦—Oil pan 5¾ qts. Total capacity 13½ qts.
⑧—Front drive axle.
⑨—Heavy duty cooling system, 15½ qts.
⑩—Oil pan 5 qts. Total capacity 12 qts.
⑪—Oil pan 3 qts. Total capacity 9 qts.
⑫—Oil pan 4½ qts. Total capacity 12½ qts.
⑬—Early models, 19.6 gals.; late models, 18.1 gals.
⑭—Includes filter. Recommended diesel engine oil—1978, use oil designated SE/CD; 1979–80, use oil designated SE/CC.
⑮—Oil pan only.

SERIAL NUMBER LOCATION

Plate on left front door pillar or top of left side instrument panel

ENGINE NUMBER LOCATION

4 & 6 CYL.: Pad at front righthand side of cylinder block at rear of distributor

V8 ENGINES: Pad at front righthand side of cylinder block

ENGINE IDENTIFICATION CODE

Engines are identified in the following table by the code letter or letters immediately following the engine serial number.

CAMARO

CODE			CODE			CODE		
CCD	6-250	1977	CHT	8-350	1976	DKB	6-250	1979
CCF	6-250	1977	CHU	8-350	1976	DKD	6-250	1979
CCW	6-250	1977	CML	8-350	1976	DNF	8-305	1979
CJL	6-250	1975	CPA	8-305	1976	DNH	8-305	1979
CJM	6-250	1975	CPB	8-305	1976	DNK	8-305	1979
CJR	6-250	1975	CPJ	8-305	1976	DRC	8-350	1979
CJT	6-250	1975	C2K	8-305	1977	DRD	8-350	1979
CJU	6-250	1975	C2L	8-305	1977	DRF	8-350	1979
CJF	6-250	1975	C8Y	6-250	1977	DRH	8-350	1979
CJY	6-250	1975	9M	8-350	1976	DRL	8-350	1979
CJZ	6-250	1975	9W	8-305	1976	DRY	8-350	1979
CKH	6-250	1977	CCC	6-250	1977	DTM	8-305	1979
CKM	8-350	1977	CCH	6-250	1978	DTR	8-305	1979
CKR	8-350	1977	CCJ	6-250	1978	C8B	8-305	1979
CKS	8-350	1977	CCK	6-250	1978	C8C	8-350	1979
CMU	8-350	1975	C3Y	6-250	1978	CRA	V6-229	1980
CRC	8-350	1975	CTH	8-305	1978	CRC	V6-229	1980
CMF	8-350	1975	CTJ	8-305	1978	OM	V6-231①	1980
CMH	8-350	1975	CTK	8-305	1978	ON	V6-231①	1980
CRX	8-350	1975	C3N	8-305	1978	C8X	8-267	1980
CHW	8-350	1975	CHF	8-350	1978	CPD	8-267	1980
CHS	8-350	1975	CHJ	8-350	1978	D9B	8-305	1980
CHT	8-350	1975	CHL	8-350	1978	CEJ	8-305	1980
CPA	8-305	1977	CHR	8-350	1978	CEL	8-305	1980
CPC	8-305	1977	CHS	8-350	1978	CEM	8-305	1980
CPY	8-305	1977	CHT	8-350	1978	CET	8-305	1980
CCC	6-250	1976	CHU	8-350	1978	CML	8-305	1980
CCD	6-250	1976	C3T	8-350	1978	CHA	8-350	1980
CCF	6-250	1976	DKA	6-250	1979	CEU	8-350	1980

CHEVROLET

CODE			CODE			CODE		
CCC	6-250	1977	CUB	8-350	1977	CHF	8-350	1978
CCF	6-250	1977	CUC	8-350	1977	CHH	8-350	1978
CCR	6-250	1977	CUD	8-350	1977	CHJ	8-350	1978
CCS	6-250	1977	CXX	8-454	1975	CHK	8-350	1978
CKA	8-350	1977	CXY	8-454	1975	CHL	8-350	1978
CKB	8-350	1977	CHS	8-350	1976	CHM	8-350	1978
CKC	8-350	1977	CMJ	8-350	1976	CNT	8-350	1978
CLL	8-350	1977	CMM	8-350	1976	DCA	6-250	1979
CMJ	8-350	1975	CSF	8-400	1976	DCB	6-250	1979
CMM	8-350	1977	CTL	8-400	1976	DCC	6-250	1979
CRU	8-350	1975	CXX	8-454	1976	DCD	6-250	1979
CRW	8-350	1975	CCA	6-250	1977	DKB	6-250	1979
CRY	8-350	1975	CJA	6-250	1977	DKC	6-250	1979
CSA	8-400	1975	CJB	6-250	1977	DKD	6-250	1979
CPM	8-305	1977	CJF	6-250	1977	DKF	6-250	1979
CPR	8-305	1977	CCH	6-250	1978	DNL	8-305	1979
CTL	8-400	1975	CCK	6-250	1978	DNM	8-305	1979
CTM	8-400	1975	CCL	6-250	1978	DNR	8-305	1979
CTU	8-400	1975	CCM	6-250	1978	DRA	8-350	1979
CTW	8-400	1975	CEJ	8-305	1978	DRB	8-350	1979
CTY	8-400	1975	CEK	8-305	1978	DRH	8-350	1979
CTZ	8-400	1975	CTL	8-305	1978	DRJ	8-350	1979

Continued

ENGINE IDENTIFICATION CODE—Continued
CHEVROLET—Continued

CODE				CODE				CODE			
DRK	8-350		1979	DUB	8-350		1979	CEH	8-305		1980
DRL	8-350		1979	DUC	8-350		1979	CMH	8-305		1980
DRY	8-350		1979	DUD	8-350		1979	CMJ	8-305		1980
DRZ	8-350		1979	CLC	V6-229		1980	CMR	8-305		1980
DTC	8-305		1979	ES	V6-231①		1980	CMS	8-305		1980
DTD	8-305		1979	ET	V6-231①		1980	CMT	8-305		1980
DTY	V8-305		1979	CPC	8-267		1980	CHC	8-350		1980
DTZ	V8-305		1979	CPH	8-267		1980	VBS	8-350 Diesel②		1980
DXA	V8-305		1979	CED	8-305		1980	VBT	8-350 Diesel②		1980

CHEVELLE, MALIBU & MONTE CARLO

CODE				CODE				CODE			
CCC	6-250		1977	9R	8-350		1976	DNU	8-305		1979
CCD	6-250		1977	9W	8-305		1976	DNW	8-305		1979
CCF	6-250		1977	EA	6-231①		1978	DNX	8-305		1979
CJL	6-250		1975	OH	6-231①		1978	DNY	8-305		1979
CLM	6-250		1975	OK	6-231①		1978	DRX	8-350		1979
CJR	6-250		1975	CWA	6-250		1978	DTA	8-305		1979
CJT	6-250		1975	CWB	6-250		1978	DTB	8-305		1979
CJU	6-250		1975	CWC	6-250		1978	DTF	8-305		1979
CJF	6-250		1975	CWD	6-250		1978	DTH	8-305		1979
CJZ	6-250		1975	CER	8-305		1978	DTJ	8-305		1979
CKH	8-350		1977	CPZ	8-305		1978	DTS	8-305		1979
CKJ	8-350		1977	CRU	8-305		1978	DTU	8-305		1979
CKK	8-350		1977	CRW	8-305		1978	DTW	8-305		1979
CKM	8-350		1977	CRX	8-305		1978	DTX	8-305		1979
CKR	8-350		1977	CRY	8-305		1978	DUF	8-350		1979
CMF	8-350		1975	CRZ	8-305		1978	DUH	8-350		1979
CMH	8-350		1975	CMA	8-350		1978	DUJ	8-350		1979
CMJ	8-350		1975	CMB	8-350		1978	CLA	V6-229		1980
CMU	8-350		1975	CMC	8-350		1978	CLB	V6-229		1980
CPY	8-305		1977	CMD	8-350		1978	CRC	V6-229		1980
CRT	8-350		1975	NJ	V6-231①		1979	ED	V6-231①		1980
CRU	8-350		1975	RA	V6-231①		1979	EF	V6-231①		1980
CRX	8-350		1975	RB	V6-231①		1979	EG	V6-231①		1980
CSM	8-400		1975	RJ	V6-231①		1979	EH	V6-231①		1980
CTL	8-400		1975	RM	V6-231①		1979	OP	V6-231①		1980
CTU	8-400		1975	SJ	V6-231①		1979	OR	V6-231①		1980
CTX	8-400		1975	SO	V6-231①		1979	CPA	8-267		1980
CXW	8-454		1975	DHA	V6-200		1979	CPB	8-267		1980
CCC	6-250		1976	DHB	V6-200		1979	CEA	8-305		1980
CCD	6-250		1976	DHC	V6-200		1979	CEC	8-305		1980
CCF	6-250		1976	DMA	8-267		1979	CER	8-305		1980
CPB	8-305		1976	DMB	8-267		1979	CMC	8-305		1980
CMH	8-350		1976	DMC	8-267		1979	CMD	8-305		1980
CMJ	8-350		1976	DMD	8-267		1979	CMF	8-305		1980
CMM	8-350		1976	DMF	8-267		1979	CMM	8-305		1980
CSB	8-400		1976	DMH	8-267		1979	CHB	8-350		1980
CSF	8-400		1976	DNS	8-305		1979				
CSX	8-400		1976	DNT	8-305		1979				

CHEVY NOVA

CODE				CODE				CODE			
CCD	6-250		1977	CJZ	6-250		1975	C2K	8-305		1977
CCF	6-250		1977	CKH	8-350		1977	C2L	8-305		1977
CCS	6-250		1975	CKM	8-350		1977	C8Y	6-250		1977
CCT	6-250		1975	CKR	8-350		1977	9M	8-350		1976
CCT	6-250		1977	CKS	8-350		1977	9W	8-305		1976
CCU	6-250		1977	CMF	8-350		1975	CRX	8-350		1975
CCU	6-250		1975	CMH	8-350		1975	CZF	8-262		1975
CCW	6-250		1975	CMU	8-350		1975	CZH	8-262		1975
CCW	6-250		1977	CPA	8-305		1977	CZJ	8-262		1975
CGC	8-262		1975	CPC	8-305		1977	CZK	8-262		1975
CGD	8-262		1975	CPY	8-305		1977	CZL	8-262		1975
CGF	8-262		1975	CRC	8-305		1975	CZM	8-262		1975
CGH	8-262		1975	CCB	6-250		1976	CZY	8-262		1975
CHW	8-350		1975	CCC	6-250		1976	CZZ	8-262		1975
CJF	6-250		1975	CCD	6-250		1976	CCH	6-250		1978
CJL	6-250		1975	CCF	6-250		1976	CCK	6-250		1978
CJM	6-250		1975	CHT	8-350		1976	CCJ	6-250		1978
CJR	6-250		1975	CHU	8-350		1976	C2D	6-250		1978
CJS	6-250		1975	CML	8-350		1976	CTH	8-305		1978

Continued

ENGINE IDENTIFICATION CODE—Continued
CHEVY NOVA—Continued

CODE				CODE				CODE			
CJT	6-250		1975	CPA	8-305		1976	CTJ	8-305		1978
CJU	6-250		1975	CPB	8-305		1976	CTK	8-305		1978
CJW	6-250		1975	CPJ	8-305		1976	C2K	8-305		1978
CJX	6-250		1975	C2D	6-250		1977	CHJ	8-350		1978
CHL	8-350		1978	RY	V6-231		1979	DNJ	8-305		1979
NG	V6-231		1979	SL	V6-231		1979	DNK	8-305		1979
NL	V6-231		1979	SR	V6-231		1979	DRJ	8-350		1979
NO	V6-231		1979	DKA	6-250		1979	DRY	8-350		1979
RF	V6-231		1979	DKB	6-250		1979	DTM	8-305		1979
RX	V6-231		1979	DKD	6-250		1979	C8D	8-305		1979
				DNF	8-305		1979				

CORVETTE

CODE				CODE				CODE			
CHA	8-350		1975	CLS	8-350		1976	ZAA	8-350		1979
CHB	8-350		1975	CHC	8-350		1976	ZAB	8-350		1979
CHC	8-350		1975	CKC	8-350		1976	ZAC	8-350		1979
CHR	8-350		1975	CKW	8-350		1976	ZAD	8-350		1979
CHU	8-350		1975	CKX	8-350		1976	ZAF	8-350		1979
CHZ	8-350		1975	CHD	8-350		1977	ZBA	8-350		1979
CKZ	8-350		1977	CKD	8-350		1977	ZBB	8-350		1979
CLA	8-350		1977	CHW	8-350		1978	ZCA	8-305		1980
CLB	8-350		1977	CLM	8-350		1978	ZAK	8-350		1980
CLC	8-350		1977	CLR	8-350		1978	ZBC	8-350		1980
CLD	8-350		1977	CLS	8-350		1978	ZAM	8-350		1980
CLF	8-350		1977	CMR	8-350		1978	ZBD	8-350		1980
CLH	8-350		1977	CMS	8-350		1978				

①—Buick built engine. ②—Oldsmobile built engine.

GENERAL ENGINE SPECIFICATIONS

Year	Engine	Carburetor	Bore and Stroke	Piston Displacement, Cubic Inches	Compression Ratio	Maximum Brake H.P. @ R.P.M.	Maximum Torque Lbs. Ft. @ R.P.M.	Normal Oil Pressure Pounds
1975	105 Horsepower①........6-250	1 Barrel	3.875 × 3.53	250	8.25	105 @ 3800	185 @ 1200	36—41
	110 Horsepower①........V8-262	2 Barrel	3.671 × 3.10	262	8.5	110 @ 3600	200 @ 2000	32—40
	145 Horsepower①........V8-350	2 Barrel	4.00 × 3.48	350	8.5	145 @ 3800	250 @ 2200	32—40
	155 Horsepower①........V8-350	4 Barrel	4.00 × 3.48	350	8.5	155 @ 3800	250 @ 2400	32—40
	165 Horsepower①........V8-350	4 Barrel	4.00 × 3.48	350	8.5	165 @ 3800	255 @ 2400	32—40
	205 Horsepower①........V8-350	4 Barrel	4.00 × 3.48	350	9.0	205 @ 4800	255 @ 3600	32—40
	175 Horsepower①........V8-400	4 Barrel	4.125 × 3.75	400	8.5	175 @ 3600	305 @ 2000	42—46
	215 Horsepower①........V8-454	4 Barrel	4.251 × 4.00	454	8.15	215 @ 4000	350 @ 2400	42—46
1976	105 Horsepower①........6-250	1 Barrel	3.875 × 3.53	250	8.25	105 @ 3800	185 @ 1200	36—41
	140 Horsepower①........V8-305	2 Barrel	3.736 × 3.48	305	8.5	140 @ 3800	245 @ 2000	32—40
	145 Horsepower①........V8-350	2 Barrel	4.00 × 3.48	350	8.5	145 @ 3800	250 @ 2200	32—40
	165 Horsepower①........V8-350	4 Barrel	4.00 × 3.48	350	8.5	165 @ 3800	260 @ 2400	32—40
	185 Horsepower①........V8-350	4 Barrel	4.00 × 3.48	350	8.5	185 @ 4000	275 @ 2400	32—40
	195 Horsepower①........V8-350	4 Barrel	4.00 × 3.48	350	8.5	195 @ 4400	275 @ 2800	32—40
	210 Horsepower①........V8-350	4 Barrel	4.00 × 3.48	350	9.0	210 @ 5200	255 @ 3600	32—40
	270 Horsepower①........V8-350	4 Barrel	4.00 × 3.48	350	8.5	270 @ 4400	380 @ 2800	32—40
	175 Horsepower①........V8-400	4 Barrel	4.125 × 3.75	400	8.5	175 @ 3600	305 @ 2000	32—40
	235 Horsepower①........V8-454	4 Barrel	4.251 × 4.00	454	8.5	235 @ 4000	360 @ 2800	42—46
1977	110 Horsepower①........6-250	1 Barrel	3.875 × 3.53	250	8.25	110 @ 3800	195 @ 1600	36—41
	145 Horsepower①........V8-305	2 Barrel	3.736 × 3.48	305	8.5	145 @ 3800	245 @ 2400	32—40
	170 Horsepower①........V8-350	4 Barrel	4.00 × 3.48	350	8.5	170 @ 3800	270 @ 2400	32—40
	180 Horsepower①........V8-350	4 Barrel	4.00 × 3.48	350	8.5	180 @ 4000	270 @ 2400	32—40
	210 Horsepower①........V8-350	4 Barrel	4.00 × 3.48	350	9.0	210 @ 5200	255 @ 3600	32—40

Continued

GENERAL ENGINE SPECIFICATIONS—Continued

Year	Engine	Carburetor	Bore and Stroke	Piston Displacement, Cubic Inches	Compression Ratio	Maximum Brake H.P. @ R.P.M.	Maximum Torque Lbs. Ft. @ R.P.M.	Normal Oil Pressure Pounds
1978	95 Horsepower① V6-200	2 Barrel	3.50 × 3.48	200	8.2	95 @ 3800	160 @ 2000	34–39
	103 Horsepower①② V6-231	2 Barrel	3.80 × 3.40	231	8.0	103 @ 3800	180 @ 2000	37
	90 Horsepower① 6-250	1 Barrel	3.875 × 3.53	250	8.2	90 @ 3600	180 @ 1600	36–41
	110 Horsepower① 6-250	1 Barrel	3.875 × 3.53	250	8.2	110 @ 3800	195 @ 1600	36–41
	135 Horsepower① V8-305	2 Barrel	3.736 × 3.48	305	8.5	135 @ 3800	240 @ 2000	45
	145 Horsepower① V8-305	2 Barrel	3.736 × 3.48	305	8.5	145 @ 3800	245 @ 2000	45
	160 Horsepower① V8-350	4 Barrel	4.00 × 3.48	350	8.2	160 @ 3800	260 @ 2400	32–40
	170 Horsepower① V8-350	4 Barrel	4.00 × 3.48	350	8.2	170 @ 3800	270 @ 2400	32–40
	175 Horsepower① V8-350	4 Barrel	4.00 × 3.48	350	8.2	175 @ 3800	265 @ 2400	32–40
	185 Horsepower① V8-350	4 Barrel	4.00 × 3.48	350	8.2	185 @ 4000	280 @ 2400	32–40
1979	95 Horsepower① V6-200	2 Barrel	3.50 × 3.48	200	8.2	95 @ 3800	160 @ 2000	45
	115 Horsepower①② V6-231	2 Barrel	3.80 × 3.40	231	8.0	115 @ 3800	190 @ 2000	37
	90 Horsepower① 6-250	1 Barrel	3.876 × 3.53	250	8.1	90 @ 3600	175 @ 1600	40
	115 Horsepower① 6-250	1 Barrel	3.876 × 3.53	250	8.0	115 @ 3800	200 @ 1600	40
	125 Horsepower① V8-267	2 Barrel	3.50 × 3.48	267	8.2	125 @ 3800	215 @ 2400	45
	125 Horsepower① V8-305	2 Barrel	3.736 × 3.48	305	8.4	125 @ 3200	235 @ 2000	45
	130 Horsepower① V8-305	2 Barrel	3.736 × 3.48	305	8.4	130 @ 3200	245 @ 2000	45
	155 Horsepower① V8-305	4 Barrel	3.736 × 3.48	305	8.4	155 @ 4000	225 @ 2400	45
	160 Horsepower① V8-305	4 Barrel	3.736 × 3.48	305	8.4	160 @ 4000	235 @ 2000	45
	165 Horsepower① V8-350	4 Barrel	4.00 × 3.48	350	8.2	165 @ 3800	260 @ 2400	45
	170 Horsepower① V8-350	4 Barrel	4.00 × 3.48	350	8.2	170 @ 4000	265 @ 2400	45
	170 Horsepower① V8-350	4 Barrel	4.00 × 3.48	350	8.2	170 @ 3800	270 @ 2400	45
	175 Horsepower① V8-350	4 Barrel	4.00 × 3.48	350	8.2	175 @ 4000	270 @ 2400	45
	195 Horsepower① V8-350	4 Barrel	4.00 × 3.48	350	8.9	195 @ 4000	280 @ 2400	45
	195 Horsepower① V8-350	4 Barrel	4.00 × 3.48	350	8.2	195 @ 4000	285 @ 3200	45
	225 Horsepower① V8-350	4 Barrel	4.00 × 3.48	350	8.9	225 @ 5200	270 @ 3600	45
1980	115 Horsepower① V6-229	2 Barrel	3.74 × 3.48	229	8.6	115 @ 4000	175 @ 2000	45
	110 Horsepower①② V6-231	2 Barrel	3.80 × 3.40	231	8.0	110 @ 3800	190 @ 1600	45
	170 Horsepower①②③ ... V6-231	4 Barrel	3.80 × 3.40	231	8.0	170 @ 4000	265 @ 2400	37
	120 Horsepower① V8-267	2 Barrel	3.50 × 3.48	267	8.3	120 @ 3000	215 @ 2000	45
	170 Horsepower①⑥⑦ ... V8-301	4 Barrel	4.00 × 3.00	301	8.2	170 @ 4400	240 @ 2200	55–60
	155 Horsepower① V8-305	4 Barrel	3.74 × 3.48	305	8.5	155 @ 4000	230 @ 2400	45
	155 Horsepower① V8-305	4 Barrel	3.74 × 3.48	305	8.2	155 @ 4000	240 @ 2600	45
	190 Horsepower① V8-350	4 Barrel	4.00 × 3.48	350	9.0	190 @ 4200	280 @ 2400	45
	105 Horsepower①④ ... V8-350⑤	—	4.057 × 3.385	350	22.5	105 @ 3200	205 @ 1600	30–45

①—Ratings are net—As installed in the vehicle.
②—Buick-built engine.
③—Turbocharged.
④—Oldsmobile-built engine.
⑤—Diesel.
⑥—Pontiac-built engine.
⑦—E/C (electronic control) engine.

TUNE UP SPECIFICATIONS

The following specifications are published from the latest information available. This data should be used only in the absence of a decal affixed in the engine compartment.

★ When using a timing light, disconnect vacuum hose or tube at distributor and plug opening in hose or tube so idle speed will not be affected.

● When checking compression, lowest cylinder must be within 80 percent of highest.

▲ Before removing wires from distributor cap, determine location of the No. 1 wire in cap, as distributor position may have been altered from that shown at the end of this chart.

Year & Engine	Spark Plug		Ignition Timing BTDC①★				Curb Idle Speed②		Fast Idle Speed		Fuel Pump Pressure
	Type	Gap	Firing Order Fig. ▲	Man. Trans.	Auto. Trans.	Mark Fig.	Man. Trans.	Auto. Trans.	Man. Trans.	Auto. Trans.	
CAMARO											
1975											
6-250 Exc. Calif.	R46TX	.060	H	10°	10°	B	425/850	425/550D	1800③	1700③	3½–4½
6-250 Calif.	R46TX	.060	H	—	10°	B	—	425/600D	—	1700③	3½–4½
V8-350 2 Barrel	R44TX	.060	C	6°	6°	B	800	600D	—	—	7–8½
V8-350 4 Barrel Exc. Calif.	R44TX	.060	C	6°	8°	B	800	600D	1600④	1600④	7–8½
V8-350 4 Barrel Calif.	R44TX	.060	C	6°	4°	B	800	600D	1600④	1600④	7–8½
1976											
6-250 Exc. Calif.	R46TS	.035	H	6°	6°	B	425/850	425/550D	2100⑤	2100⑤	3½–4½
6-250 Calif.	R46TS	.035	H	—	6°	B	—	425/600D	—	1700③	3½–4½
V8-305 Exc. Calif.	R45TS	.045	C	6°	8°	B	800	600D	—	—	7–8½
V8-305 Calif.	R45TS	.045	C	—	TDC	B	—	600D	—	—	7–8½
V8-350 2 Barrel	R45TS	.045	C	—	6°	B	—	600D	—	—	7–8½
V8-350 4 Barrel Exc. Calif.	R45TS	.045	C	—	8°	B	—	600D	—	1600⑤	7–8½
V8-350 4 Barrel Calif.	R45TS	.045	C	—	6°	B	—	600D	—	1600⑤	7–8½
1977											
6-250 Exc. Calif. & High Alt.	R46TS	.035	H	6°	8°	B	⑥	⑦	2000	2000	4–5
6-250 Calif.	R46TS	.035	H	—	⑧	B	—	⑦	—	1800	4–5
6-250 High Alt.	R46TS	.035	H	—	10°	B	—	425/600D	—	2000	4–5
V8-305 Exc. Calif.	R45TS	.045	C	8°	8°	B	600/700	500/650D	—	—	7½–9
V8-305 Calif.	R45TS	.045	C	—	6°	B	—	500/650D	—	—	7½–9
V8-350 Exc. High Alt.	R45TS	.045	C	8°	8°	B	700	500/650D	1300⑤	1600⑤	7½–9
V8-350 High Alt.	R45TS	.045	C	—	8°	B	—	600/650D	—	1600⑤	7½–9
1978											
6-250 Exc. Calif.	R46TS	.035	H	6°	10°	B	425/800	425/550D	2000	2100	4–5
6-250 Calif.	R46TS	.035	H	—	6°	B	—	400/600D	—	2000	4–5
V8-305 Exc. Calif.	R45TS	.045	C	4°	4°	B	600	500D	—	—	7½–9
V8-305 Calif.	R45TS	.045	C	—	8°	B	—	500/600D	—	—	7½–9
V8-350 Exc. Calif. & High Alt.	R45TS	.045	C	6°	6°	B	700	500/600D	1300	1600	7½–9
V8-350 Calif.	R45TS	.045	C	—	8°	B	—	500/600D	—	1600	7½–9
V8-350 High Alt.	R45TS	.045	C	—	⑨	B	—	500/650D	—	1600	7½–9
1979											
6-250 Exc. Calif.	R46TS	.035	H	12°	8°	B	800	675D	1800	2000	4–5
6-250 Calif.	R46TS	.035	H	—	6°	B	—	600D	—	2000	4–5
V8-305 Exc. Callf.	R45TS	.045	C	4°	4°	B	600/700	500/600D	1300	1600	7½–9
V8-305 Calif.	R45TS	.045	C	—	4°	B	—	600/650D	—	1950	7½–9
V8-350 Exc. Calif. & High Alt.	R45TS	.045	C	6°	6°	B	700	500/600D	1300	1600	7½–9
V8-350 Calif.	R45TS	.045	C	—	8°	B	—	500/600D	—	1600	7½–9
V8-350 High Alt.	R45TS	.045	C	—	8°	B	—	600/650D	—	1750	7½–9

Continued

TUNE UP SPECIFICATIONS—Continued

Year & Engine	Spark Plug Type	Spark Plug Gap	Firing Order Fig. ▲	Ignition Timing BTDC①★ Man. Trans.	Ignition Timing BTDC①★ Auto. Trans.	Mark Fig.	Curb Idle Speed② Man. Trans.	Curb Idle Speed② Auto. Trans.	Fast Idle Speed Man. Trans.	Fast Idle Speed Auto. Trans.	Fuel Pump Pressure
CAMARO—Continued											
1980											
V6-229	R45TS	.045	F	8°	10°	G	700/800	600/675D	1300	1750	4½–6
V6-231⑩	R45SX	.060	D	—	15°	E⑪	—	600D	—	2200	3 Min.
V8-267	R45TS	.045	C	—	4°	B	—	500/600D	—	1850	7½–9
V8-305 Exc. Calif.	R45TS	.045	C	4°	4°	B	700	500/600D	1500	1850	7½–9
V8-305 Calif.㉕	R45TS	.045	C	—	4°	B	—	550/650D	—	2200	7½–9
V8-305 Calif.㉖	R45TS	.045	C	—	—	B	—	550/650D	—	—	7½–9
V8-350	R45TS	.045	C	6°	6°	B	700	500/600D	1500	1850	7½–9
CHEVELLE, MALIBU & MONTE CARLO											
1975											
6-250 Exc. Calif.	R46TX	.060	H	10°	10°	B	850	550D	1800③	1700③	3½–4½
6-250 Calif.	R46TX	.060	H	—	10°	B	—	600D	—	1700③	3½–4½
V8-350 2 Barrel	R44TX	.060	C	8°	8°	B	800	600D	—	—	7–8½
V8-350 4 Barrel Exc. Calif.	R44TX	.060	C	6°	8°	B	800	600D	1600④	1600④	7–8½
V8-350 4 Barrel Calif.	R44TX	.060	C	4°	6°	B	—	600D	1600④	1600④	7–8½
V8-400	R44TX	.060	C	—	8°	B	—	600D	—	1600④	7–8½
V8-454	R44TX	.060	C	—	16°	B	—	600D	—	1000④	7–8½
1976											
6-250 Exc. Calif.	R46TS	.035	H	6°	6°	B	425/850	425/550D	2100⑤	2100⑤	3½–4½
6-250 Calif.	R46TS	.035	H	—	6°	B	—	425/600D	—	1700③	3½–4½
V8-305	R45TS	.045	C	—	8°	B	—	600D	—	—	7–8½
V8-350 2 Barrel	R45TS	.045	C	—	6°	B	—	600D	—	—	7–8½
V8-350 4 Barrel	R45TS	.045	C	—	6°	B	—	600D	—	1600⑤	7–8½
V8-400	R45TS	.045	C	—	8°	B	—	600D	—	1600⑤	7–8½
1977											
6-250 Exc. Calif. & High Alt.	R46TS	.035	H	6°	8°	B	⑥	⑦	2000	2000	4–5
6-250 Calif.	R46TS	.035	H	—	6°	B	—	425/550D	—	1800	4–5
6-250 High Alt.	R46TS	.035	H	—	10°	B	—	425/600D	—	2000	4–5
V8-305	R45TS	.045	C	—	8°	B	—	500/650D	—	—	7½–9
V8-350 Exc. High Alt.	R45TS	.045	C	—	8°	B	—	500/650D	—	1600⑤	7½–9
V8-350 High Alt.	R45TS	.045	C	—	8°	B	—	500/650D	—	1600⑤	7½–9
1978											
V6-200	R45TS	.045	F	8°	8°	G	700	600D	1300	1600	4½–6
V6-231⑩	R46TSX	.060	D	15°	15°	E⑪	600/800	600/670D	—	—	3 Min.
V8-305 Exc. Calif. & High Alt.	R45TS	.045	C	4°	4°	B	600	500D	—	—	7½–9
V8-305 Calif.	R45TS	.045	C	—	6°	B	—	500/600	—	—	7½–9
V8-305 High Alt.	R45TS	.045	C	—	8°	B	—	600/700D	—	—	7½–9
V8-350 Exc. Calif. & High Alt.	R45TS	.045	C	—	6°	B	—	500/600D	—	1600	7½–9
V8-350 Calif.	R45TS	.045	C	—	8°	B	—	500/600D	—	1600	7½–9
V8-350 High Alt.	R45TS	.045	C	—	8°	B	—	500/650D	—	1600	7½–9

Continued

TUNE UP SPECIFICATIONS—Continued

Year & Engine	Spark Plug Type	Gap	Ignition Timing BTDC①★ Firing Order Fig.▲	Man. Trans.	Auto. Trans.	Mark Fig.	Curb Idle Speed② Man. Trans.	Auto. Trans.	Fast Idle Speed Man. Trans.	Auto. Trans.	Fuel Pump Pressure
CHEVELLE, MALIBU & MONTE CARLO—Continued											
1979											
V6-200	R45TS	.045	F	8°	12°	G	700/800	600/700D	1300	1600	4½–6
V6-231 Exc. Calif. & High Alt.⑩	R45TSX	.060	D	—	15°	E⑪	—	⑫	—	2200	3 Min.
V6-231 Calif. & High Alt.⑩	R45TSX	.060	D	—	15°	E⑪	—	600D	—	2200	3 Min.
V8-267	R45TS	.045	C	4°	8°	B	600/700	500/600D	1300	1600	7½–9
V8-305 Exc. High Alt.	R45TS	.045	C	4°	4°	B	700	500/600D	1300	1600	7½–9
V8-305 High Alt.	R45TS	.045	C	—	8°	B	—	600/650D	—	1750	7½–9
V8-350	R45TS	.045	C	—	8°	B	—	600/650	—	1750	7½–9
1980											
V6-229	R45TS	.045	F	8°	12°	G	700/800	600/675D	1300	1750	4½–6
V6-231 Exc. Calif.⑳	R45TSX	.060	D	—	15°	E⑪	—	560/670D	—	2200	4¼–5¾
V6-231 Calif.⑳	R45TSX	.060	D	—	15°	E⑪	—	600D	—	2200	4¼–5¾
V6-231 Exc.Calif.㉑	R45TS	.040	D	—	15°	E⑪	—	550D	—	2200	5
V6-231 Exc.Calif.㉑	R45TS	.040	D	—	15°	E⑪	—	600D	—	2200	5
V8-267	R45TS	.045	C	—	4°	B	—	500/600D	—	1850	7½–9
V8-305 Exc. Calif.	R45TS	.045	C	4°	4°	B	700	500/600D	1500	1850	7½–9
V8-305 Calif.	R45TS	.045	C	—	4°	B	—	550/650D	—	2200	7½–9
CHEVY NOVA											
1975											
6-250 Exc. Calif.⑬	R46TX	.060	H	8°	8°	B	850	600D	1800③	1800③	3½–4½
6-250 Exc. Calif.⑭	R46TX	.060	H	10°	10°	B	850	550D	1800③	1700③	3½–4½
6-250 Calif.⑭	R46TX	.060	H	—	10°	B	—	600D	—	1700③	3½–4½
V8-262	R44TX	.060	C	8°	8°	A	800	600D	—	—	7–8½
V8-350 2 Barrel	R44TX	.060	C	6°	6°	B	800	600D	—	—	7–8½
V8-350 4 Barrel Exc. Calif.	R44TX	.060	C	6°	8°	B	800	600D	1600④	1600④	7–8½
V8-350 4 Barrel Calif.	R44TX	.060	C	4°	6°	B	—	600D	1600④	1600④	7–8½
1976											
6-250 Exc. Calif.⑬	R46TS	.035	H	—	8°	B	—	425/600D	—	2200⑤	3½–4½
6-250 Exc. Calif.⑭	R46TS	.035	H	6°	6°	B	425/850	425/550D	2100⑤	2100⑤	3½–4½
6-250 Calif.⑭	R46TS	.035	H	—	6°	B	—	425/600D	—	1700③	3½–4½
V8-305 Exc. Calif.	R45TS	.045	C	6°	8°	B	800	600D	—	—	7–8½
V8-305 Calif.	R45TS	.045	C	—	TDC	B	—	600D	—	—	7–8½
V8-350 2 Barrel	R45TS	.045	C	—	6°	B	—	600D	—	—	7–8½
V8-350 4 Barrel Exc. Calif.	R45TS	.045	C	8°	8°	B	800	600D	1600	1600	7–8½
V8-350 4 Barrel Calif.	R45TS	.045	C	—	6°	B	—	600D	—	1600	7–8½
1977											
6-250 Exc. Calif. & High Alt.	R46TS	.035	H	6°	8°	B	⑥	⑦	2000	2000	4–5
6-250 Calif.	R46TS	.035	H	—	6°	B	—	⑦	—	1800	4–5
6-250 High Alt.	R46TS	.035	H	—	10°	B	—	425/600D	—	2000	4–5
V8-305 Exc. Calif.	R45TS	.045	C	8°	8°	B	600/700	500/650D	—	—	7½–9
V8-305 Calif.	R45TS	.045	C	—	6°	B	—	500/650D	—	—	7½–9
V8-350 Exc. High Alt.	R45TS	.045	C	8°	8°	B	700	500/650D	1300⑤	1600⑤	7½–9
V8-350 High Alt.	R45TS	.045	C	—	8°	B	—	600/650D	—	1600⑤	7½–9

Continued

TUNE UP SPECIFICATIONS—Continued

Year & Engine	Spark Plug Type	Spark Plug Gap	Ignition Timing BTDC①★ Firing Order Fig. ▲	Ignition Timing BTDC①★ Man. Trans.	Ignition Timing BTDC①★ Auto. Trans.	Ignition Timing BTDC①★ Mark Fig.	Curb Idle Speed② Man. Trans.	Curb Idle Speed② Auto. Trans.	Fast Idle Speed Man. Trans.	Fast Idle Speed Auto. Trans.	Fuel Pump Pressure
CHEVY NOVA—Continued											
1978											
6-250 Exc. Calif.	R46TS	.035	H	6°	10°⑮	B	425/800	425/550D	2000	2100	4–5
6-250 Calif.	R46TS	.035	H	—	6°	B	—	400/600D	—	2000	4–5
V8-305 Exc. Calif.	R45TS	.045	C	4°	4°	B	600	500D	—	—	7½–9
V8-305 Calif.	R45TS	.045	C	—	6°	B	—	500/600D	—	—	7½–9
V8-350	R45TS	.045	C	—	8°	B	—	⑯	—	1600	7½–9
1979											
6-250 Exc. Calif.	R46TS	.035	H	12°	8°	B	800	675D	1800	2000	4–5
6-250 Calif.	R46TS	.035	H	—	6°	B	—	600D	—	2000	4–5
V8-305 Exc. Calif.	R45TS	.045	C	4°	4°	B	600/700	500/600D	1300	1600	7½–9
V8-305 Calif.	R45TS	.045	C	—	4°	B	—	600/650D	—	1950	7½–9
V8-350 Calif.	R45TS	.045	C	—	8°	B	—	500/600D	—	1600	7½–9
V8-350 High Alt.	R45TS	.045	C	—	8°	B	—	600/650D	—	1750	7½–9
CHEVROLET											
1975											
V8-350 2 Barrel	R44TX	.060	C	—	6°	B	—	600D	—	—	7–8½
V8-350 4 Barrel	R44TX	.060	C	—	6°	B	—	600D	—	1600④	7–8½
V8-400	R44TX	.060	C	—	8°	B	—	600D	—	1600④	7–8½
V8-454	R44TX	.060	C	—	16°	B	—	600D	—	1000④	7–8½
1976											
V8-350 2 Barrel	R45TS	.045	C	—	6°	B	—	600D	—	—	7–8½
V8-350 4 Barrel Exc. Calif.	R45TS	.045	C	—	8°	B	—	600D	—	1600⑤	7–8½
V8-350 4 Barrel Calif.	R45TS	.045	C	—	6°	B	—	600D	—	1600⑤	7–8½
V8-400	R45TS	.045	C	—	8°	B	—	600D	—	1600⑤	7–8½
V8-454	R45TS	.045	C	—	12°	B	—	550D	—	1600⑤	7–8½
1977											
6-250 Exc. Calif. & High Alt.	R46TS	.035	H	—	8°	B	—	⑦	—	2000	4–5
6-250 Calif.	R46TS	.035	H	—	6°	B	—	⑦	—	1800	4–5
6-250 High Alt.	R46TS	.035	H	—	10°	B	—	425/600D	—	2000	4–5
V8-305 Exc. Calif.	R45TS	.045	C	—	8°	B	—	500/650D	—	—	7½–9
V8-305 Calif.	R45TS	.045	C	—	6°	B	—	500/650D	—	—	7½–9
V8-350 Exc. High Alt.	R45TS	.045	C	—	8°	B	—	500/650D	—	1600⑤	7½–9
V8-350 High Alt.	R45TS	.045	C	—	8°	B	—	600/650D	—	1600⑤	7½–9
1978											
6-250 Exc. Calif.	R46TS	.035	H	—	⑰	B	—	425/550D	—	2100	4–5
6-250 Calif.	R46TS	.035	H	—	6°	B	—	400/600D	—	2000	4–5
V8-305 Exc. Calif.	R45TS	.045	C	—	4°	B	—	500D	—	—	7½–9
V8-305 Calif.	R45TS	.045	C	—	6°	B	—	500/600D	—	—	7½–9
V8-350 Exc. Calif. & High Alt.	R45TS	.045	C	—	6°	B	—	500/600D	—	1600	7½–9
V8-350 Calif.	R45TS	.045	C	—	8°	B	—	500/600D	—	1600	7½–9
V8-350 High Alt.	R45TS	.045	C	—	8°	B	—	500/650D	—	1600	7½–9

Continued

TUNE UP SPECIFICATIONS—Continued

Year & Engine	Spark Plug Type	Gap	Firing Order Fig. ▲	Ignition Timing Man. Trans.	Auto. Trans.	Mark Fig.	Curb Idle Speed② Man. Trans.	Auto. Trans.	Fast Idle Speed Man. Trans.	Auto. Trans.	Fuel Pump Pressure
CHEVROLET—Continued											
1979											
6-250 Exc. Calif.	R46TS	.035	H	—	8°	B	—	675D	—	2000	4–5
6-250 Calif.	R46TS	.035	H	—	6°	B	—	600D	—	2000	4–5
V8-305 Exc. Calif.	R45TS	.045	C	—	4°	B	—	500/600D	—	1600	7½–9
V8-305 Calif.	R45TS	.045	C	—	4°	B	—	600/650D	—	1950	7½–9
V8-350 Exc. Calif. & High Alt.	R45TS	.045	C	—	6°	B	—	500/600D	—	1600	7½–9
V8-350 Calif.	R45TS	.045	C	—	8°	B	—	600/650D	—	1750	7½–9
V8-350 High Alt.	R45TS	.045	C	—	8°	B	—	500/600D	—	1600	7½–9
1980											
V6-229	R45TS	.045	—	—	10°	—	—	—	—	—	4½–6
V6-231⑩	—	—	D	—	—	E⑪	—	—	—	—	4¼–5¾
V8-267	R45TS	.045	C	—	㉓	B	—	—	—	—	7½–9
V8-305 Exc. Calif.	R45TS	.045	C	—	4°	B	—	500/600D	—	—	7½–9
V8-305 Calif.	R45TS	.045	C	—	4°	B	—	550/650D	—	—	7½–9
V8-350 Diesel㉒	—	—	—	—	—	—	—	575/750D	—	—	5½–6½
CORVETTE											
1975											
V8-350 Exc. Calif.	R44TX	.060	C	6°	6°	B	800	600D	1600④	1600④	7–8½
V8-350 Calif.	R44TX	.060	C	4°	6°	B	800	600D	1600④	1600④	7–8½
1976											
V8-350 Exc. Calif. & High Perf.	R45TS	.045	C	8°	8°	B	800	600D	1600⑤	1600⑤	7–8½
V8-350 Calif. Exc. High Perf.	R45TS	.045	C	—	6°	B	—	600D	1600⑤	1600⑤	7–8½
V8-350 High Perf.	R45TS	.045	C	12°	12°	B	1000	700D⑱	1600⑤	1600⑤	7–8½
1977											
V8-350 Exc. High Alt. & High Perf.	R45TS	.045	C	8°	8°	B	700	500/650D	1300⑤	1600⑤	7½–9
V8-350 High Alt. Exc. High Perf.	R45TS	.045	C	—	8°	B	—	600/650D	—	1600⑤	7½–9
V8-350 High Perf.	R45TS	.045	C	12°	12°	B	800	700/800D	1300⑤	1600⑤	7½–9
1978											
V8-350 Exc. Calif. & High Perf.	R45TS	.045	C	6°	6°	B	700	⑲	1300	1600	7½–9
V8-350 Calif. Exc. High Perf.	R45TS	.045	C	—	8°	B	—	500/600D	—	1600	7½–9
V8-350 High Perf.	R45TS	.045	C	12°	12°	B	900	700/800D	1600	1600	7½–9
1979											
V8-350 Exc. High Alt. & High Perf.	R45TS	.045	C	6°	6°	B	700	500/600D	1300	1600	7½–9
V8-350 Exc. High Alt. & High Perf.	R45TS	.045	C	—	8°	B	—	600/650D	—	1750	7½–9
V8-350 High Perf.	R45TS	.045	C	12°	12°	B	900	700/800D	1300	1600	7½–9
1980											
V8-305 Calif.	R45TS	.045	C	—	6°	B	—	500D	—	1600	7½–9
V8-350 High Alt. & High Perf.	R45TS	.045	C	6°	6°	B	700	500/600D	1300	1600	7½–9
V8-350 High Alt. Exc. High Perf.	R45TS	.045	C	—	8°	B	—	600/650D	—	1750	7½–9
V8-350 High Perf.	R45TS	.045	C	12°	12°	B	900	500/600D	1300	1600	7½–9

Continued

TUNE UP NOTES

①—BTDC—Before top dead center.
②—Idle speed on man. trans. vehicles is adjusted in Neutral and on auto. trans. equipped vehicles is adjusted in Drive unless otherwise specified. Where two idle speeds are listed, the higher speed is with A/C or idle solenoid energized.
③—With cam follower tang on high step of fast idle cam, distributor vacuum advance & EGR vacuum hoses disconnected & plugged & A/C off.
④—With cam follower on high step of fast idle cam.
⑤—With cam follower tang on high step of fast idle cam, EGR vacuum hose disconnected & plugged & A/C off.
⑥—Less A/C, 425/750 RPM; with A/C, 425/800 RPM.

⑦—Less A/C, 425/550D RPM; with A/C, 425/600D RPM.
⑧—Except distributor No. 1110725, 6° BTDC; distributor No. 1110725, 8° BTDC.
⑨—Except engine code CHU, 8° BTDC; engine code CHU, 6° BTDC.
⑩—Buick-built engine.
⑪—The harminic balancer on these engines has two timing marks. The timing mark measuring 1/16 in. is used when setting timing with a hand held timing light. The mark measuring 1/8 in. is used when setting timing with magnetic timing equipment.
⑫—Less idle solenoid, 500D RPM; with idle solenoid, 560/670D RPM.
⑬—Less integral intake manifold.
⑭—With integral intake manifold.
⑮—Nova 4 dr. sedan with A/C, set at 8° BTDC.

⑯—Except high altitude, 500/600D RPM; high altitude, 500/650D RPM.
⑰—Less A/C, 10° BTDC; with A/C, 8° BTDC.
⑱—If equipped with A/C, adjust carburetor idle screw to 700D RPM with A/C off, then turn A/C on & adjust solenoid to 700D RPM.
⑲—Except high altitude, 500/600D RPM; high altitude, 600/650D RPM.
⑳—Except turbocharged engine.
㉑—Turbocharged engine.
㉒—Oldsmobile-built engine.
㉓—Except Calif., 550D. Calif., 600D.
㉔—Injection timing at 800 RPM.
㉕—Exc. Z28.
㉖—Z28.

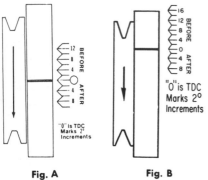

Fig. A   Fig. B

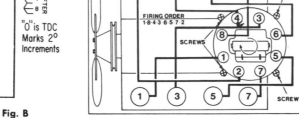

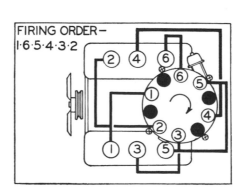

Fig. C

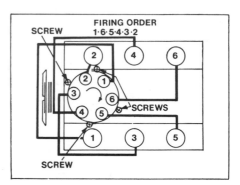

Fig. D

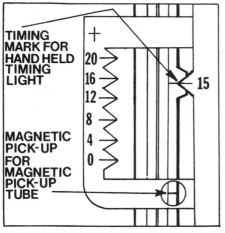

Fig. E

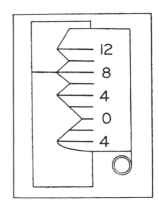

Fig. F   Fig. G

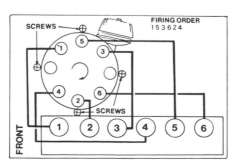

Fig. H

COOLING SYSTEM & CAPACITY DATA

Year	Model or Engine	Cooling Capacity, Qts.		Radiator Cap Relief Pressure, Lbs.	Thermo. Opening Temp. [1]	Fuel Tank Gals.	Engine Oil Refill Qts. [2]	Transmission Oil			Rear Axle Oil Pints
		Less A/C	With A/C					3 Speed Pints	4 Speed Pints	Auto. Trans. Qts. [3]	
CAMARO											
1975	6-250	12½	12½	15	195	21	4	3	—	4[5]	4¼
	8-350	15½	16½	15	195	21	4	3	3	4[5]	4¼
	8-350, Z28	15½	16½	15	180	21	4	—	3	4[5]	4¼
1976	6-250	15	16	15	195	21	4	3	—	[5]	4¼
	8-305	17½	18½	15	195	21	4	3	—	[5]	4¼
	8-350	17½	18½	15	195	21	4	—	3	[5]	4¼
1977	6-250	14.6	14.7	15	195	21	4	3	—	[5]	4¼
	8-305	17.2	17.9	15	195	21	4	3	—	[5]	4¼
	8-350	17.3	18.0	15	195	21	4	—	3	[5]	4¼
1978	6-250	15	16	15	195	21	4	3	—	[11]	4¼
	8-305	17.5	18.5	15	195	21	4	—	3	[11]	4¼
	8-350	17.5	18.5	15	195	21	4	—	3	[11]	4¼
1979	6-250	14.5	14.5	15	195	21	4	3	—	[11]	4¼
	8-305	17[13]	18	15	195	21	4	—	3	[11]	4¼
	8-350	17[13]	18	15	195	21	4	—	3	[11]	4¼
1980	V6-229	14.5	14.5	15	195	21	4[16]	3	—	[20]	4¼
	V6-231	12	12	15	195	21	4[16]	—	—	[20]	4¼
	8-267	15	15	15	195	21	4	—	—	[20]	4¼
	8-305	15	15	15	195	21	4	—	3	[20]	4¼
	8-350	16	16	15	195	21	4	—	3	[20]	4¼
CHEVELLE, MALIBU & MONTE CARLO											
1975	6-250	12½	12½	15	195	22	4	3	—	4[5]	[4]
	8-350	16	17	15	195	22	4	3	—	4[5]	[4]
	8-400	16	17	15	195	22	4	—	—	4[5]	[4]
	8-454	23	24	15	195	22	4	—	—	4½[5]	[4]
1976	6-250	15	17	15	195	22	4	3	—	[5]	4¼
	8-305	17½	18½	15	195	22	4	—	—	[5]	4¼
	8-350	17½	18½	15	195	22	4	—	—	[5]	4¼
	8-400	17½	18½	15	195	22	4	—	—	[5]	4¼
1977	6-250	15	17	15	195	22	4	3	—	[5]	4
	8-305	17½	18½	15	195	22	4	—	—	[5]	4
	8-350	17½	18½	15	195	22	4	—	—	[5]	4
1978	6-200	15	17	15	195	17.5	4	3	3	[11]	3¼
	6-231	15	17	15	195	17.5	4	3	3	[11]	3¼
	8-305	18	20	15	195	17.5	4	—	3	[11]	3¼
	8-350	18	20	15	195	17.5	4	—	—	[11]	3¼
1979	6-200	18.5	18.5	15	195	18.1	4	3	—	[11]	3¼
	6-231	15.5	15.5	15	195	18.1	4	—	—	[11]	3¼
	8-267	21	21	15	195	18.1	4	—	3	[11]	3¼
	8-305	19	19	15	195	18.1	4	—	3	[11]	3¼
	8-350	19.5	19.5	15	195	18.1	4	—	—	[11]	3¼
1980	V6-229	18.5	18.5	15	195	18.1	4[16]	3	—	[20]	3¼
	V6-231	15.5	15.5	15	195	18.1	4[16]	—	—	[20]	3¼
	8-267	21.0	21.0	15	195	18.1	4	—	—	[20]	3¼
	8-305	19.0	19.0	15	195	18.1	4	—	3	[20]	3¼

Continued

COOLING SYSTEM & CAPACITY DATA—Continued

Year	Model or Engine	Cooling Capacity, Qts.		Radiator Cap Relief Pressure, Lbs.	Thermo. Opening Temp. [1]	Fuel Tank Gals.	Engine Oil Refill Qts. [2]	Transmission Oil			Rear Axle Oil Pints
		Less A/C	With A/C					3 Speed Pints	4 Speed Pints	Auto. Trans. Qts. [3]	
CHEVY NOVA											
1975	6-250	12½	12½	15	195	21	4	3	—	4[5]	4¼
	8-262	—	—	15	195	21	4	3	—	4[5]	4¼
	8-350	15½	16½	15	195	21	4	3	—	4[5]	4¼
1976	6-250	14	15	15	195	21	4	3	—	[5]	4¼
	8-305	17	18	15	195	21	4	3	—	[5]	4¼
	8-350	17	18	15	195	21	4	3	3	[5]	4¼
1977	6-250	14	15	15	195	21	4	3	—	[9]	[10]
	8-305	17	18	15	195	21	4	3	—	[9]	[10]
	8-350	17	18	15	195	21	4	—	3	[9]	[10]
1978–79	6-250	14	15	15	195	21	4	3	—	[11]	[10]
	8-305	16	17	15	195	21	4	—	3	[11]	[10]
	8-350	16	17	15	195	21	4	—	—	[11]	[10]
CHEVROLET											
1975	8-350	16	17	15	195	26[13]	4	—	—	4[5]	[4]
	8-400	16½	17½	15	195	26[13]	4	—	—	4½[5]	[4]
	8-454	23	24	15	195	26[13]	4	—	—	4½[5]	[4]
1976	8-350	18	18	15	195	26[13]	4	—	—	[5]	[4]
	8-400	18	18	15	195	26[13]	4	—	—	[5]	[4]
	8-454	23	25	15	195	26[13]	4	—	—	[5]	[4]
1977	6-250	15	16	15	195	21[13]	4	—	—	4[8]	[10]
	8-305	18	20	15	195	21[13]	4	—	—	4[8]	[10]
	8-350	18	20	15	195	21[13]	4	—	—	4[8]	[10]
1978–79	6-250	14	15	15	195	21[13]	4	—	—	[11]	[10]
	8-305	16½[13]	17½	15	195	21[13]	4	—	—	[11]	[10]
	8-350	16½[13]	17½	15	195	21[13]	4	—	—	[11]	[10]
1980	V6-229	14.25	14.25	15	195	25[15]	4[16]	—	—	[20]	[10]
	V6-231	11.75	11.75	15	195	25[15]	4[16]	—	—	[20]	[10]
	8-267	[17]	[17]	15	195	25[15]	4	—	—	[20]	[10]
	8-305	15.5	15.5	15	195	25[15]	4	—	—	[20]	[10]
	8-350[18]	18.3	18.0	15	195	25[15]	7[19]	—	—	[20]	[10]
CORVETTE											
1975	8-350	18	18	15	180	18	4	—	3	4[6]	4
1976	8-350	21	21	15	195[12]	17	4	—	3	11	4
1977	8-350	21	21	15	195	17	4	—	3	[6]	3¾
1978	8-350	21	21	15	195	23.7	4	—	3	10	3¾
1979	8-350	21	21[14]	15	195	24	4	—	3	[7]	3¾
1980	8-305	21.5	22.9	15	195	24	4	—	—	[7]	3¾
	8-350	21.6	21.6	15	195	24	4	—	3½	[7]	3¾

[1]—For permanent type anti-freeze.
[2]—Add one quart with filter change.
[3]—Approximate. Make final check with dipstick.
[4]—4¼ pts. for 8⅛" and 8½" ring gears and 4.9 pts. for 8⅞" ring gear.
[5]—THM 200, 250 & 350 total capacity 10 qts. THM 400 total capacity 11 qts.
[6]—THM 350, 10 qts.; THM 400, 11 qts.
[7]—Oil pan only, 3 qts. Total capacity, 10 qts.
[8]—Refill capacity.
[9]—Refill capacities: THM 200, 8¼ qts. THM 350, 6¾ qts.
[10]—3¼ pts. for 7½" ring gear. 4 pts. for 8½" and 8¾" ring gears.
[11]—THM 200 oil pan only, 3½ qts. Total capacity, 5 qts., CBC 350 oil pan only, 3 qts. Total capacity, 10 qts.
[12]—Optional 350 engine, 180°.
[13]—With heavy duty cooling system, add 1 qt.
[14]—With auto. trans., add 1 qt.
[15]—Sta. Wag., 22 gals.
[16]—With or without filter change.
[17]—Exc. Sta. Wag. Standard cooling, 16.75 qts.; Sta. Wag. with standard cooling, 15.5 qts.
[18]—Diesel.
[19]—With filter change. Use recommended diesel engine oil, designated SE/CC.
[20]—THM 200, oil pan only 3½ qts., total capacity 5 qts. THM 250, oil pan 2½ qts., total capacity 10 qts. THM 350, oil pan only 3 qts., total capacity 10 qts.

SERIAL NUMBER LOCATION

On top of instrument panel, left front.

ENGINE NUMBER LOCATION

On pad at right side of cylinder block, below No. 1 spark plug.

ENGINE IDENTIFICATION CODE

Engines are identified in the following table by the code letter or letters immediately following the engine serial number.

Year	Engine	Code	Year	Engine	Code	Year	Engine	Code
1976	4-85	CDD, CDS, CDT		4-97	CNR, CNS, CNT		4-97	ZTT, ZTU, ZTW
	4-85	CDU, CVA, CVB		4-97	CNU		4-97	ZTX
	4-97	CNA, CNB, CYC		4-97	CYC, CYD, CYF	1979	4-97	DBA, DBB, DBC
	4-97	CYD, CYJ, CYK		4-97	CYH, CYY, CYZ		4-97	DBD, DBF, DBH
	4-97	CYW, CYX	1978	4-97	CYA, CYB, CYJ		4-97	DBJ, DBK, DBL
1977	4-85	CDS, CVA, CVB		4-97	CYK, CYL, CYM		4-97	DBM, DBR, DBS
	4-97	CNA, CNB, CNC		4-97	CYR, CYS, CYT		4-97	DBT, DBU, DBW
	4-97	CND, CNF, CNH		4-97	CYU, CYW, CYX		4-97	DBX, DBY, DBZ
							4-97	DSA, DSB
						1980	4-97	CKA, CKB, CKC
							4-97	CKF, CKH, CKJ, CKK
							4-97	CKL, CKM
							4-97	CKR, CKS

GENERAL ENGINE SPECIFICATIONS

Year	Engine	Carburetor	Bore and Stroke	Piston Displacement, Cubic Inches	Compression Ratio	Maximum Brake H.P. @ R.P.M.	Maximum Torque Lbs. Ft. @ R.P.M.	Normal Oil Pressure Pounds
1976–77	52 Horsepower① 4-85 1400 c.c.	1 Barrel	3.228 × 2.606 82.0 × 66.2 mm.	85 1.4 ltr.	8.5 —	52 @ 5300 —	67 @ 3400 97 Joules @ 3400	36–46 —
	60 Horsepower① 4-97 1600 c.c.	1 Barrel	3.228 × 2.980 82.0 × 75.7 mm.	97.6 1.6 ltr.	8.5 —	60 @ 5300 —	77 @ 3200 104 Joules @ 3200	36–46 —
1978	63 Horsepower① 4-97 1600 c.c.	1 Barrel	3.228 × 2.980 82.0 × 75.7 mm.	97.6 1.6 ltr.	8.5 —	63 @ 4800 —	82 @ 3200 —	34–42 —
	68 Horsepower① 4-97② 1600 c.c.	1 Barrel	3.228 × 2.980 82.0 × 75.7 mm.	97.6 1.6 ltr.	8.5 —	68 @ 5000 —	84 @ 3200 —	34–42 —
1979	70 Horsepower① 4-97 1600 c.c.	2 Barrel	3.228 × 2.980 82.0 × 75.3 mm.	97.6 1.6 ltr.	8.5 —	70 @ 5200 —	82 @ 2400 —	55 —
	74 Horsepower① 4-97② 1600 c.c.	2 Barrel	3.228 × 2.980 82.0 × 75.7 mm.	97.6 1.6 ltr.	8.5 —	74 @ 5200 —	88 @ 2800 —	55 —
1980	70 Horsepower① 4-97 1600 c.c.	2 Barrel	3.228 × 2.980 82.0 × 75.7 mm.	97.6 1.6 ltr.	8.6 —	70 @ 5200 —	82 @ 2400 —	55 —
	74 Horsepower① 4-97② 1600 c.c.	2 Barrel	3.228 × 2.980 82.0 × 75.7 mm.	97.6 1.6 ltr.	8.6 —	74 @ 5200 —	88 @ 2800 —	55 —

①—Ratings are net—as installed in vehicle.   ②—High output engine.

CHEVROLET CHEVETTE

TUNE UP SPECIFICATIONS

The following specifications are published from the latest information available. This data should be used only in the absence of a decal affixed in the engine compartment.

★ When using a timing light, disconnect vacuum hose or tube at distributor and plug opening in hose or tube so idle speed will not be affected.

● When checking compression, lowest cylinder must be within 80 percent of highest.

▲ Before removing wires from distributor cap, determine location of the No. 1 wire in cap, as distributor positikn may have been altered from that shown at the end of this chart.

Year & Engine	Spark Plug		Ignition Timing BTDC★				Curb Idle Speed②		Fast Idle Speed		Fuel Pump Pressure
	Type	Gap	Firing Order Fig. ▲	Man. Trans.	Auto. Trans.	Mark Fig.	Man. Trans.	Auto. Trans.	Man. Trans.	Auto. Trans.	
1976											
4-85 Exc. Calif.	R43TS	.035	A	10°	10°	B	600/800	③	2000④	2200④	5–6½
4-85 Calif.	R43TS	.035	A	10°	10°	B	600/1000	600/850D	2000⑤	2000⑤	5–6½
4-97.6 Exc. Calif.	R43TS	.035	A	8°	10°	B	600/800	③	2000④	2200④	5–6½
4-97.6 Calif.	R43TS	.035	A	8°	10°	B	600/1000	⑥	2000⑤	2000⑤	5–6½
1977											
4-85	R43TS	.035	A	12°	12°	B	600/800	600/800D	2300④	2400④	5–6½
4-97.6 Exc. Calif. & High Alt.	R43TS	.035	A	8°	8°	B	600/800	⑦	2300④	2400④	5–6½
4-97.6 Calif. & High Alt.	R43TS	.035	A	8°	8°	B	800	⑦	—	2400④	5–6½
1978											
4-97.6 Exc. Calif. & High Alt.	R43TS	.035	A	8°	8°	B	600/800	⑦⑧	④⑨	2400④	5–6½
4-97.6 Calif. & High Alt.	R43TS	.035	A	8°	8°	B	800	⑦⑧	—	2400④	5–6½
1979											
4-97.6 Exc. Calif.	R42TS	.035	A	12°	18°	B	800/1150	750/1150	2500⑤	2500⑤	2½–6½
4-97.6 Calif.⑩	R42TS	.035	A	12°	16°	B	800/1150	750/1150	2500⑤	2500⑤	2½–6½
4-97.6 Calif.⑪	R42TS	.035	A	12°	12°	B	800/1150	750/1150	2500⑤	2500⑤	2½–6½
1980											
4-97.6	R42TS	.035	A	12°	18°	B	800	⑫	2500⑤	2500⑤	5–6½

①—BTDC—Before top dead center.
②—Idle speed on man. trans. vehicles is adjusted in Neutral & on auto, trans. equipped vehicles is adjusted in Drive unless otherwise specified. Where two idle speeds are listed, the higher speed is with the A/C or idle solenoid energized.
③—Less A/C, 700/800D RPM; with A/C, 800/950D RPM.
④—With stop screw on high step of fast idle cam & A/C off.
⑤—With stop screw on high step of fast idle cam, EGR vacuum line disconnected & plugged & A/C off.
⑥—Less A/C, 600/850D RPM; With A/C, 850/950D RPM.
⑦—Less A/C, 600/800D RPM; with A/C, 800/950D RPM.
⑧—With A/C on, ckipressor clutch wires disconnected.
⑨—Except high output engine, 2300 RPM; high output engine, 2400 RPM.
⑩—Exc. high output engine.
⑪—High output engine.
⑫—Exc. Calif., 700/800D RPM; Calif., 750/850D RPM.

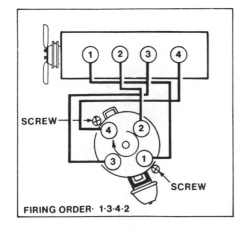

FIRING ORDER 1·3·4·2

Fig. A

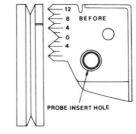

PROBE INSERT HOLE

Fig. B

COOLING SYSTEM & CAPACITY DATA

Year	Model or Engine	Cooling Capacity, Qts.		Radiator Cap Relief Pressure, Lbs.	Thermo. Opening Temp.	Fuel Tank Gals.	Engine Oil Refill Qts.	Transmission Oil			Rear Axle Oils Pints
		Less A/C	With A/C					3 Speed Pints	4 Speed Pints	Auto. Trans. Qts. ①	
1976–77	All	8½ 8 ltr.	9 8.5 ltr.	15 —	190 —	13 49.2 ltr.	4 3.8 ltr.	— —	3 1.5 ltr.	②	2 .9 ltr.
1978	All	8.5 8 ltr.	9.0 8.5 ltr.	15 —	190 —	12.5 47.3 ltr.	4 3.8 ltr.	— —	3 1.5 ltr.	5 4.6 ltr.	2 .92 ltr.
1979	All	9.0 8.5 ltr.	9.25 8.8 ltr.	15 —	190 —	12.5 47.3 ltr.	4 3.8 ltr.	— —	3 1.5 ltr.	5 4.6 ltr.	1.75 .83 ltr.
1980	All	9.0 8.5 ltr.	9.25 8.8 ltr.	15 —	190 —	12.5 47.3 ltr.	4 3.8 ltr.	— —	3.4 1.6 ltr.	③	1.75 .83 ltr.

①—Approximate. Make final check with dip-stick.   ②—1976, 6.5 qts.; 1977, 5 qts.   ③—Drain and refill, 3 qts. (2.7 ltr.).

SERIAL NUMBER LOCATION

On top of instrument panel, left front.

ENGINE NUMBER LOCATION

On 4-151 engine, the engine code stamping is located on pad at left front of cylinder block below cylinder head. On V6-173, the engine code label is located at front and rear of left rocker arm cover.

ENGINE IDENTIFICATION CODE

4-151 engine are identified by code letters on pad. V6-173 are identified by code letters immediately following the engine number.

Year	Engine	Code
1980	4-151 ①②	WA, WB
	4-151 ①③	XA, XB
	4-151 ②④	AC, AU
	4-151 ③④	Z4, Z6, Z9
	V6-173 ①②	CNF, CNH
	V6-173 ①③	CNJ, CNK

V6-173 ②④	CNL, CNM
V6-173 ③④	CNR, CNS
V6-173	DDB, DCZ

①—Except Calif.
②—Man. trans.
③—Auto. trans.
④—California.

GENERAL ENGINE SPECIFICATIONS

Year	Engine	Carburetor	Bore and Stroke	Piston Displacement, Cubic Inches	Compression Ratio	Maximum Brake H.P. @ R.P.M.	Maximum Torque Lbs. Ft. @ R.P.M.	Normal Oil Pressure Pounds
1980	90 Horsepower① 4-151	2 Barrel	4.0 × 3.0	151	8.25	90 @ 4000	134 @ 2400	36—41
	115 Horsepower① V6-173	2 Barrel	3.5 × 3.0	173	8.5	115 @ 4800	150 @ 2000	30—45

①—Ratings are net (as installed in vehicle).

TUNE UP SPECIFICATIONS

The following specifications are published from the latest information available. This data should be used only in the absence of a decal affixed in the engine compartment.

★ When using a timing light, disconnect vacuum hose or tube at distributor and plug opening in hose or tube so idle speed will not be affected.

● When checking compression, lowest cylinder must be within 80 percent of highest.

▲ Before removing wires from distributor cap, determine location of the No. 1 wire in cap, as distributor position may have been altered from that shown at the end of this chart.

Year & Engine	Spark Plug		Firing Order Fig. ▲	Ignition Timing BTDC①★			Curb Idle Speed②		Fast Idle Speed		Fuel Pump Pressure
	Type	Gap		Man. Trans.	Auto. Trans.	Mark Fig.	Man. Trans.	Auto. Trans.	Man. Trans.	Auto. Trans.	
1980											
4-151 Exc. Calif.	R43TSX	.060	A	10°	10°	B	1000/1300	650/900D	2200	2600	6½—8
4-151 Calif.	R43TSX	.060	A	10°	10°	B	1000/1200	650/900D	2200	2600	6½—8
V6-173 Exc. Calif.	R44TS	.045	C	2°	6°	D	750/1200	③	1900	2250	6—7½
V6-173 Calif.	R44TS	.045	C	6°	10°	D	750	④	2000	2000	6—7½

①—BTDC—Before top dead center.
②—Idle speed on man. trans. vehicles is adjusted in Neutral & on auto. trans. equipped vehicles is adjusted in Drive unless otherwise specified. Where two idle speeds are listed, the higher speed is with the A/C or idle solenoid energized.

③—Less A/C, 700D RPM; with A/C, 700/850D RPM.
④—Less A/C, 700D RPM; with A/C, 700/800D RPM.

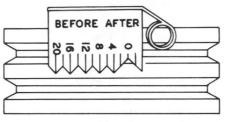

Fig. B

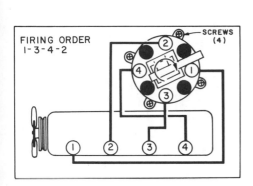

Fig. A

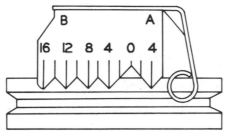

Fig. D

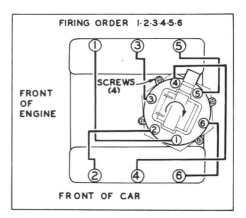

Fig. C

COOLING SYSTEM & CAPACITY DATA

Year	Model or Engine	Cooling Capacity, Qts.		Radiator Cap Relief Pressure, Lbs.	Thermo. Opening Temp.	Fuel Tank Gals.	Engine Oil Refill Qts.	Transaxle Oil	
		Less A/C	With A/C					Manual Transaxle Pts.	Auto. Transaxle Qts. ①
1980	Citation 4-151	9½	9¾	15	195	14	3②	6	③
	Omega 4-151	8½	8¾	15	195	14	3②	6	③
	Phoenix 4-151	8.3④	8.6④	15	195	14	3②	6	③
	Skylark 4-151	8.3⑤	8.6⑤	15	195	14	3②	6	③
	Citation V6-173	11½	11¾	15	195	15	4②	6	③
	Omega V6-173	10¼⑥	10¾⑥	15	195	14	4②	6	③
	Phoenix V6-173⑦	10.2⑧	10.6⑧	15	195	14	4②	6	③
	Phoenix V6-173⑨	10.5⑧	10.8	15	195	14	4②	6	③
	Skylark	10.2⑧	10.6⑧	15	195	14	4②	6	③

①—Approximate make final check with dipstick.
②—With or without filter change.
③—Oil pan capacity, 4 qts.; total capacity, 6 qts.
④—With heavy duty cooling system, man. trans. 8.7 qts., auto. trans., 9.3 qts.
⑤—With heavy duty cooling system, 8.7 qts.
⑥—With heavy duty cooling system, 11 qts.
⑦—Exc. Calif.
⑧—Heavy duty cooling system, 10.8 qts.
⑨—California.

SERIAL NUMBER LOCATION

On top of instrument panel, left front.

ENGINE NUMBER LOCATION

4-140 Cyl: On pad at right side of cylinder block, above starter.

4-151 Exc. Crossflow Engine: On pad at right front side by distributor shaft hole.

4-151 Crossflow Engine: On pad at left front corner of engine above water pump.

V6 & V8: On pad at front right hand side of cylinder block.

ENGINE IDENTIFICATION CODE

4-140 & Chevrolet V8 engines are identified by the code letters immediately following the engine number. 4-151 engines are identified by the code letters immediately preceding the engine number. V6 engines are identified by the code letters on the pad. V6 engines are identified by the code letters immediately preceding the engine number.

Monza

Year	Engine	Code
1975	4-140	CAM, CAR, CAS
	4-140	CAT, CBB, CBC
	V8-262 Std. Tr.	CZA, CZB, CZC
	V8-262 Std. Tr.	CZD, CZT, CZU
	V8-262 Auto. Tr.	CZE, CZG
	V8-262 Auto. Tr.	CGA, CGJ, CGK
	V8-350	CHY
	4-122	ZCA
1976	4-140	CAY, CAZ, CBK, CBL
	4-140	CBS, CBT, CBU, CBW
	4-140	CBX, CBY, CBZ
	V8-262	CGA, CGB, CGL, CZU, CZT
	4-140	CAA, CAB
1977	4-140	CAY, CAZ, CBK, CBL
	4-140	CBS, CBT, CBU, CBW
	4-140	CBX, CBY, CBZ
	V8-305	CPK, CPL, CPU, CPX
	V8-305	CRC, CRD
1978	4-151	WB, WD, WH
	4-151	XL, XN
	4-151	AC, AD
	4-151	ZA, ZB, ZC, ZD, ZF
	4-151	ZH, ZJ, ZK, ZL, ZN
	V6-196	PC, PD
	V6-231	OC, OD, OE, OF
	V8-305	CTA, CTB, CTC, CTD, CTF
1979	4-151	AB, AC, AD, AF, AM
	4-151	WD, WJ, XJ, XK
	4-151	ZA, ZB, ZP, ZR
	V6-196	FC, FD
	V6-231	NA, NB, NC, NF
	V8-305	DNA, DNB, DNC, DND
	V8-305	DTK, DTL
1980	4-151	A7, A9
	4-151	XC, XD
	4-151	WD, WJ
	4-151	ZA, ZB
	V6-231	EX, EY, EZ
	V6-231	OA, OB, OC

Skyhawk

Year	Engine	Code
1975	V6-231	AD
1976	V6-231 Std. Tr.①	FH
	V6-231 Std. Tr.②	FO
	V6-231 Auto. Tr.①	FI
	V6-231 Auto. Tr.②	FJ
1977	V6-231	SA, SB, SD
	V6-231	SO, SX, SY
1978	V6-231	OA, OB, OC
	V6-231	OD, OE, OF
	V6-231	OG
1979	V6-231	NA, NB, NC
	V6-231	N3, NG, NH
	V6-231	NM

Star fire

Year	Engine	Code
1975	V6-231 Std. Tr.①	FP
	V6-231 Auto. Tr.①	FR
	V6-231 Auto. Tr.②	FS
1976	4-140 Std. Tr.①	BS
	4-140 Std. Tr.②	BK
	4-140 Auto. Tr.①	BT
	4-140 Auto. Tr.②	BL

Year	Engine	Code
1977	4-140 Std. Tr.①	CAY, CBS
	4-140 Std. Tr.②	CAZ, CBK
	4-140 Auto. Tr.①	CBT
	4-140 Auto. Tr.②	CBL
	4-140 Std. Tr.③	CBS
	4-140 Auto. Tr.③	CBT
	V6-231 Std. Tr.①	SA
	V6-231 Std. Tr.②	SB
	V6-231 Auto. Tr.①	SD, SW
	V6-231 Auto. Tr.②	SE, SY
	V6-231 Auto. Tr.③	SF
	V6-231 Std. Tr.①	FH
	V6-231 Std. Tr.②	FO
	V6-231 Auto. Tr.①	FI
	V6-231 Auto. Tr.②	FJ
	V6-231	SQ, SR
	V8-305 Auto. Trans.①	CRL
	V8-305 Auto. Trans.②	CRM, CRS
	V8-305 Auto. Trans.③	CRT
	V8-305	CPX, CPY
1978	4-151 Auto. Trans.①	XL, XN
	4-151 Man. Trans.①	WD, WH
	4-151 Auto. Trans.②	ZK, ZJ
	4-151	WB, ZA, ZB
	V6-231 Man. Trans.①	OA
	V6-231 Auto. Trans.①	ED, OB
	V6-231 Man. Trans.②	OD
	V6-231 Auto. Trans.②	OE
	V6-231 Man. Trans.③	OF
	V6-231 Auto. Trans.③	OC
	V6-231	OH
	V8-305 Man. Trans.①	CTA
	V8-305 Man. Trans.②	CTB
	V8-305 Man. Trans.③	CTF
	V8-305 Man. Trans.④	CTD
1979	4-151 Auto. Trans.④	XJ, XK
	4-151 Man. Trans.④	WJ, WM
	4-151 Auto. Trans.④	ZP, ZR
	4-151 Man. Trans.②	AF, AH
	V6-231 Auto. Trans.④	NB, NM
	V6-231 Auto. Trans.②	NH
	V6-231 Man. Trans.②	NA
	V6-231 Auto. Trans.②	NC
	V6-231 Auto. Trans.③	NE
	V6-231 Auto. Trans.④	SM, SS
	V8-305 Auto. Trans.④	DTL
	V8-305 Man. Trans.④	DTK
	V8-305 Auto. Trans.②	DND
1980	4-151 Auto. Trans.①	XC, XD
	4-151 Man. Trans.①	WD, WJ
	4-151 Auto. Trans.①	ZA, ZB
	4-151 Man. Trans.②	A7, A9
	V6-231 Auto. Trans.①	EZ, OA
	V6-231 Man. Trans.①	EX
	V6-231 Auto. Trans.①	OB, OC
	V6-231 Man. Trans.②	EY

Sunbird

Year	Engine	Code
1976	4-140 Std. Tr.①	AY, BH, BS
	4-140 Std. Tr.①	BW, BX, BZ
	4-140 Std. Tr.①	AZ, BK, BY
	4-140 Auto. Tr.①	BJ, BT, BU
	4-140 Auto. Tr.②	BL
	V6-231 Std. Tr.①	FH

Year	Engine	Code
1977	4-140 Std. Tr.①	CAY, CBS, CBZ
	4-140 Std. Tr.①	CAZ, CBK, CBV
	4-140 Std. Tr.③	CBS, CBZ
	4-140 Auto. Tr.①③	CBT
	4-140	CAK, CBL, CBU
	4-140	CBW, CBX, CBY
	4-151 Std. Tr.①	WC, WD
	4-151 Auto. Tr.①	YL, YM
	4-151 Auto. Tr.②	ZH, ZJ
	4-151	ZD, ZF, ZN, ZP
	V6-231 Std. Tr.①	SA
	V6-231 Std. Tr.②	SB
	V6-231 Auto. Tr.①	SD
	V6-231 Auto. Tr.②	SY
	V6-231 Auto. Tr.③	SX
	V6-231	SO
1978	4-151 Man. Trans.①	WB, WD, WH
	4-151 Auto. Trans.①	XN, XL
	4-151 Auto. Trans.②	ZJ, ZK
	4-151	AC, AD
	4-151	ZA, ZB, ZC, ZD
	4-151	ZH, ZF, ZL, ZN
	V6-231 Auto. Trans.①	ED
	V6-231 Man. Trans.①	OA
	V6-231 Auto. Trans.②	EK, EL, EE, OE, EG
	V6-231 Man. Trans.②	OD
	V6-231 Man. Trans.③	OC
	V6-231 Man. Trans.③	OF
	V6-231	OE, OB
1979	4-151 Man. Trans.②	AF, AH
	4-151 Man. Trans.④	WJ, WM
	4-151 Auto. Trans.④	XJ, XK
	4-151 Auto. Trans.④	ZP, ZR
	V6-231 Man. Trans.②	NA, NG, RA
	V6-231 Auto. Trans.②	NC
	V6-231 Man. Trans.③	NE
	V6-231 Auto. Trans.④	NK, NL, NM
	V6-231 Auto. Trans.②	RG, RH, RW, RY
	V8-305 Auto. Trans.④	DND
	V8-305 Auto. Trans.④	DNJ, DTL
	V8-305 Man. Trans.④	DTK, DTM
	4-151 Auto. Trans.④	XC, XD
	4-151 Man. Trans.①	WD, WJ
	4-151 Auto. Trans.②	ZA, ZB
	4-151 Man. Trans.②	A7, A9
	V6-231 Auto. Trans.①	EB, EC, EO, EP
	V6-231 Auto. Trans.①	EZ, OA, OK, OL
	V6-231 Man. Trans.①	EA, EJ, OX
	V6-231 Auto. Trans.②	EF, EG, ES, ET
	V6-231 Auto. Trans.②	OB, OC, OM, ON
	V6-231 Man. Trans.②	EY
1980	4-151	A7, A9
	4-151	WD, WJ
	4-151	XC, XD
	4-151	ZA, ZB
	V6-231	EX, EY, EZ
	V6-231	OA, OB, OC

①—Except California.
②—California.
③—High altitude.
④—Exc. High altitude & Calif.

MONZA • SKYHAWK • STARFIRE • SUNBIRD

GENERAL ENGINE SPECIFICATIONS

Year	Engine	Carburetor	Bore and Stroke	Piston Displacement, Cubic Inches	Compression Ratio	Maximum Brake H.P. @ R.P.M.	Maximum Torque Lbs. Ft. @ R.P.M.	Normal Oil Pressure Pounds
1975	78 Horsepower① 4-140	1 Barrel	3.501 × 3.625	140	8.0	78 @ 4200	120 @ 2000	40
	80 Horsepower① 4-140	2 Barrel	3.501 × 3.625	140	8.0	80 @ 4400	116 @ 2800	40
	87 Horsepower① 4-140	2 Barrel	3.501 × 3.625	140	8.0	87 @ 4400	122 @ 2800	40
	110 Horsepower① V6-231	2 Barrel	3.80 × 3.40	231	8.0	110 @ 4000	175 @ 2000	37
	110 Horsepower① V8-262	2 Barrel	3.67 × 3.10	262	8.5	110 @ 3600	200 @ 2000	32-40
	125 Horsepower① V8-350	2 Barrel	4.00 × 3.48	350	8.5	125 @ 3600	235 @ 2000	32-40
1976	70 Horsepower① 4-140	1 Barrel	3.501 × 3.625	140	8.0	70 @ 4400	107 @ 2400	40-45
	79 Horsepower① 4-140	2 Barrel	3.501 × 3.625	140	8.0	79 @ 4400	109 @ 2800	40-45
	84 Horsepower① 4-140	2 Barrel	3.501 × 3.625	140	8.0	84 @ 4400	109 @ 2800	40-45
	110 Horsepower① V6-231	2 Barrel	3.80 × 3.40	231	8.0	110 @ 4000	175 @ 2000	37
	110 Horsepower① V8-262	2 Barrel	3.671 × 3.100	262	8.5	110 @ 3600	195 @ 2000	32-40
	140 Horsepower① V8-305	2 Barrel	3.736 × 3.48	305	8.5	140 @ 3800	245 @ 200	32-40
1977	84 Horsepower① 4-140	2 Barrel	3.501 × 3.625	140	8.0	84 @ 4400	117 @ 2400	36-45
	87 Horsepower① 4-151	2 Barrel	4.00 × 3.00	151	8.3	87 @ 4400	128 @ 2400	36-41
	105 Horsepower① V6-231	2 Barrel	3.80 × 3.40	231	8.0	105 @ 3200	185 @ 2000	37
	145 Horsepower① V8-305	2 Barrel	3.736 × 3.48	305	8.5	145 @ 3800	245 @ 2400	32-40
1978	85 Horsepower① 4-151	2 Barrel	4.00 × 3.00	151	8.3	85 @ 4400	123 @ 2800	36-41
	86 Horsepower① V6-196	2 Barrel	3.50 × 3.40	196	8.0	86 @ 3600	160 @ 2000	37
	103 Horsepower① V6-231	2 Barrel	3.80 × 3.40	231	8.0	103 @ 3800	180 @ 2000	37
	135 Horsepower① V8-305	2 Barrel	3.736 × 3.48	305	8.5	135 @ 3800	240 @ 2000	32-40
	145 Horsepower① V8-305	2 Barrel	3.736 × 3.48	305	8.5	145 @ 3800	245 @ 2400	32-40
1979	85 Horsepower① 4-151	2 Barrel	4.00 × 3.00	151	8.3	85 @ 4400	123 @ 2800	36-41
	90 Horsepower① 4-151	2 Barrel	4.00 × 3.00	151	8.3	90 @ 4400	128 @ 2400	36-41
	105 Horsepower① V6-196	2 Barrel	3.50 × 3.40	196	8.0	105 @ 4000	160 @ 2000	37
	115 Horsepower① V6-231	2 Barrel	3.80 × 3.40	231	8.0	115 @ 3800	190 @ 2000	37
	130 Horsepower① V8-305	2 Barrel	3.736 × 3.48	305	8.4	130 @ 3200	245 @ 2000	32-40
1980	90 Horsepower①② 4-151	2 Barrel	4.00 × 3.00	151	8.2	90 @ 4000	134 @ 2400	36-41
	86 Horsepower①③ 4-151	2 Barrel	4.00 × 3.00	151	8.2	86 @ 4000	128 @ 2400	36-41
	110 Horsepower① V6-231	2 Barrel	4.00 × 3.00	231	8.0	110 @ 3800	190 @ 1600	37

①—Ratings are net—As installed in vehicle.
②—Less electronic fuel controls.
③—With electronic fuel controls.

TUNE UP SPECIFICATIONS

The following specifications are published from the latest information available. This
data should be used only in the absence of a decal affixed in the engine compartment.

★ When using a timing light, disconnect vacuum hose or tube at distributor and plug opening in hose or tube so idle speed will not be affected.

● When checking compression, lowest cylinder must be within 80 percent of highest.

▲ Before removing wires from distributor cap, determine location of No. 1 wire in cap, as distributor position may have been altered from that shown at the end of this chart.

Year & Engine	Spark Plug Type	Spark Plug Gap	Firing Order Fig. ▲	Ignition Timing BTDC①★ Man. Trans.	Ignition Timing BTDC①★ Auto. Trans.	Mark Fig.	Curb Idle Speed② Man. Trans.	Curb Idle Speed② Auto. Trans.	Fast Idle Speed Man. Trans.	Fast Idle Speed Auto. Trans.	Fuel Pump Pressure
1975											
4-140 1 Barrel	R43T5X	.060	A	8°	10°	B	700	550/750D	2000③	2200③	3-4½
4-140 2 Barrel	R43T5X④	.060④	A	10°	12°⑥	B	700	600/750D	1600⑤	1600⑤	3-4½
V6-231	R44SX	.060	C	12°	12°	D	600/800	500/650D	—	—	3-4½
V8-262	R44TX	.060	E	8°	8°	F	800	600D	—	—	7-8½
V8-350	R44TX	.060	E	—	6°	G	—	600/650D	—	—	7-8½

Continued

TUNE UP SPECIFICATIONS—Continued

Year & Engine	Spark Plug		Ignition Timing BTDC(1)★				Curb Idle Speed(2)		Fast Idle Speed		Fuel Pump Pressure
	Type	Gap	Firing Order Fig.▲	Man. Trans.	Auto. Trans.	Mark Fig.	Man. Trans.	Auto. Trans.	Man. Trans.	Auto. Trans.	
1976											
4-140 1 Barrel	R43TS	.035	A	8°	10°	B	750/1200	550/750D	1500(3)	2200(3)	3–4½
4-140 2 Barrel Exc. Calif.	R43TS	.035	A	(7)	(8)	B	700(9)	600/750D	2200(3)	2200(3)	3–4½
4-140 2 Barrel Calif.	R43TS	.035	A	(7)	(8)	B	700/1000	600/750D	2200(3)	2200(3)	3–4½
V6-231	R44SX	.060	C	12°	12°	D(10)	600/800	600D	—	—	3–4½
V8-262 Exc. Calif.	R45TS	.045	E	8°	8°	F	800	600D(11)	—	—	7–8½
V8-305 Exc. Calif.	R45TS	.045	E	—	8°	G	—	600D(11)	—	—	7–8½
V8-305 Calif.	R45TS	.045	E	—	TDC	G	—	600D(11)	—	—	7–8½
1977											
4-140 Exc. Calif. & High Alt.	R43TS	.035	A	TDC	2°	B	700/1250	650/850D	2500(3)	2500(3)	3–4½
4-140 Calif.	R43TS	.035	A	(12)	TDC	B	800/1250	650/850D	2500(3)	2500(3)	3–4½
4-140 High Alt.	R43TS	.035	A	TDC	2°	B	800/1250	700/850D	2500(3)	2500(3)	3–4½
4-151 Exc. Calif.	R44TSX	.060	H	14(13)	14°	I	(14)	(15)	2200(3)	2400(3)	4–5½
4-151 Calif.	R44TSX	.060	H	—	12°	I	—	(15)	—	2400(3)	4–5½
V6-231 (16)	(17)	(17)	J	12°	12°	K(18)	600/800	600D	—	—	3–4½
V6-231 (19)	R46TSX	.060	L	—	15°	M(18)	—	600/670D	—	—	3–4½
V8-305 Exc. Calif. & High Alt.	R45TS	.045	E	8°	8°	G	600/700	500/700D	—	—	7½–9
V8-305 Calif.	R45TS	.045	E	—	6°	G	—	500/700D	—	—	7½–9
V8-305 High Alt.	R45TS	.045	E	—	(20)	G	—	600/700D	—	—	7½–9
1978											
4-151 Exc. Calif.	R43TSX	.060	H	14°(13)	12°(13)	I	(21)	(15)	2200(3)	2200(3)	4–5½
4-151 Calif.	R43TSX	.060	H	—	14°(13)	I	—	(15)	—	2400(3)	4–5½
V6-196	R46TSX	.060	L	15°	15°	M(18)	600/800	600D	—	—	3–4½
V6-231	R46TSX	.060	L	15°	15°	M(18)	600/800	600/670D	—	—	3–4½
V8-305 Exc. Calif. & High Alt.	R45TS	.045	E	4°	4°	G	600	500D	—	—	7½–9
V8-305 Calif.	R45TS	.045	E	—	6°	G	—	500D	—	—	7½–9
V8-305 High Alt.	R45TS	.045	E	—	8°	G	—	600D	—	—	7½–9
1979											
4-151 Exc. Calif.	R43TSX	.060	H	12°	12°	I	(22)	(15)	2200	2400	4–5½
4-151 Calif.	R43TSX	.060	H	14°(13)	14°(13)	I	(10)	(15)	2000	2400	4–5½
V6-196	(23)	.060	L	15°	15°	M(18)	600/800	550/670D	2200	2200	3–4½
V6-231	(23)	.060	L	15°	15°	M(18)	600/800	(24)	2200	2200	3–4½
V8-305 Exc. Calif.	R45TS	.045	E	4°	4°	G	600	500/600D	1300	1600	7½–9
V8-305 Calif.	R45TS	.045	E	—	2°	G	—	600/650D	—	1600	7½–9
1980											
4-151 Exc. Calif.	R44TSX	.060	N	12°	12°	I	(25)	(21)	2600	2600	4–5½
4-151 Calif.	R44TSX	.060	N	12°	12°	I	(27)	(26)	2400	2600	4–5½
V6-231 Exc. Calif.	R45TSX	.060	L	15°	15°	M(18)	600/800	(28)	2200	2000	3–4½
V6-231 Calif.	R45TSX	.060	L	15°	15°	M(18)	800	(29)	2200	2200	3–4½

Continued

TUNE UP NOTES

①—BTDC—Before top dead center.

②—Idle speed on man. trans. vehicles is adjusted in Neutral & on auto. trans. equipped vehicles is adjusted in Drive unless otherwise specified. Where two idle speeds are listed, the higher speed is with the A/C or idle solenoid energized.

③—On high step of fast idle cam with A/C off.

④—If cold weather starting problems are encountered, use R43TS spark plug gapped at .035".

⑤—On 2nd step of fast idle cam with vacuum advance hose disconnected and plugged & A/C off.

⑥—On California models starting with engine date code 476, set at 10°BTDC.

⑦—Monza & Starfire, 12°BTDC; Sunbird, 8°BTDC.

⑧—Monza & Starfire, 12°BTDC; Sunbird, 10°BTDC.

⑨—With A/C override switch disconnected & A/C on, solenoid is adjusted to 1200 RPM in Neutral.

⑩—These engines use two different harmonic balancers. The harmonic balancer used on late models has two timing marks. The mark measuring 1/16 inch is used when setting timing with a conventional timing light. The mark measuring 1/8 inch is used when setting timing with magnetic timing equipment.

⑪—With A/C on & solenoid fully extended, curb idle speed is 650 RPM in Drive.

⑫—2°ATDC, after top dead center.

⑬—At 1000 RPM.

⑭—Less A/C, 500/1000 RPM; with A/C, 500/1200 RPM.

⑮—Less A/C, 500/650D RPM; with A/C, 650/850D RPM.

⑯—Except even fire engine.

⑰—On early models, use R46TS gapped at .040"; on late models, use R46TSX gapped at .060".

⑱—The harmonic balancer on these engines has two timing marks. The mark measuring 1/16 inch is used when setting timing with a conventional timing light. The mark measuring 1/8 inch is used when setting timing with magnetic timing equipment.

⑲—Even fire engine.

⑳—Except engine code CPU, 8°BTDC; engine code CPU, 6°BTDC.

㉑—Less A/C, 500/1000 RPM; with A/C, 900/1200 RPM.

㉒—Less A/C, 500/900 RPM; with A/C, 900/1250 RPM.

㉓—R45TSX or R46TSX.

㉔—Less idle solenoid, 600D RPM; with idle solenoid, 550/670D RPM.

㉕—Less A/C, 550/1000 RPM; with A/C, 1000/1250 RPM.

㉖—Less A/C, 550/650D RPM; with A/C, 650/850D RPM.

㉗—Less A/C, 500/1000 RPM; with A/C, 1000/1200 RPM.

㉘—Less idle solenoid, 550D RPM; with idle solenoid, 550/670D RPM.

㉙—Less idle solenoid, 550D RPM; with idle solenoid, 550/620D RPM.

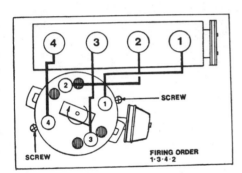

Fig. A

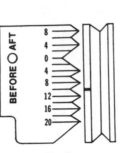

Fig. B

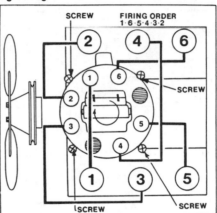

Fig. C

FIRING ORDER 1·6·5·4·3·2

Fig. D

"0" Is TDC Marks 2° Increments

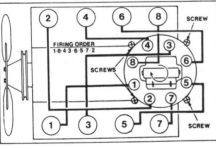

Fig. E

FIRING ORDER 1·8·4·3·6·5·7·2

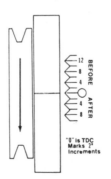

Fig. F

"0" is TDC Marks 2° Increments

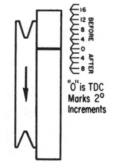

Fig. G

"0" is TDC Marks 2° Increments

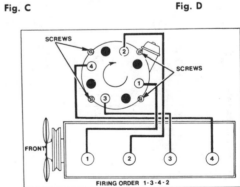

Fig. H

FIRING ORDER 1·3·4·2

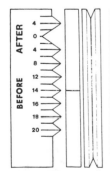

Fig. I

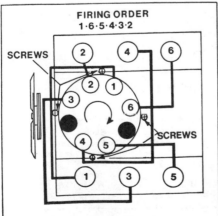

FIRING ORDER 1·6·5·4·3·2

Fig. J

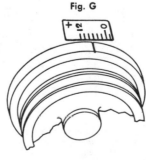

Fig. K

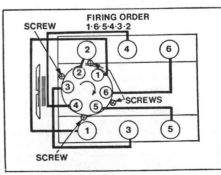

FIRING ORDER 1·6·5·4·3·2

Fig. L

Continued

TUNE UP NOTES—Continued

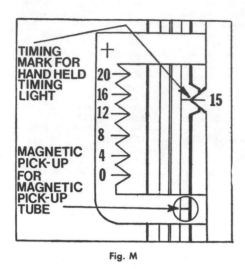

Fig. M

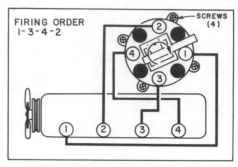

Fig. N

COOLING SYSTEM & CAPACITY DATA

Year	Model or Engine	Cooling Capacity, Qts. Less A/C	Cooling Capacity, Qts. With A/C	Radiator Cap Relief Pressure, Lbs.	Thermo. Opening Temp.	Fuel Tank Gals.	Engine Oil Refill Qts. ①	Transmission Oil 3 Speed Pints	Transmission Oil 4 Speed Pints	Transmission Oil 5 Speed Pints	Transmission Oil Auto. Trans. Quts. ②	Rear Axle Oil Pints
1975	4-140	8	8	15	195	18½	3	2.4	2.4	—	④	2¼
	V6-231	13¼	13¾	15	190	18½	4	2.4	⑤	—	④	2¼
	V8-262, 350	18	18	15	195	18½	4	2.4	2.4	3½	④	2¼
1976	4-140	8½	8½	15	195	18½	3½	3	3	3	⑥	2¾
	V6-231	13½	14	15	195	18½	4	—	⑦	⑧	⑥	⑨
	V8-262	18½	18½	15	195	18½	4	—	3	3	④	2¾
1977	4-140	8	8	15	195	18½	3	—	2.4	3½	④	3.5
	4-151	12	12	15	195	18½	3	—	2.4	3½	④	3.5
	V6-231	⑪	⑪	15	195	18½	4	—	2.4	3½	④	⑩
	V8-305	18	18	15	195	18½	4	—	2.4	3½	④	2.8
1978–79	4-151	10.7	10.7	15	195	⑫	3	—	3	3½	④	3½ ③
	V6-196	12	12	15	195	⑫	4	—	3	3½	④	3½ ③
	V6-231	12	12	15	195	⑫	4	—	3	3½	④	3½ ③
	V8-305	16.6	18.0	15	195	⑫	4	—	3	3½	④	3½ ③
1980	Monza 4-151	11.5	11.6	15	195	18½	3	—	3.4	—	3¾	3½
	Starfire 4-151	11	11.5	15	195	18½	3	—	3.12	—	3	3½
	Sunbird 4-151	10.9	—	15	195	18½	3	—	3	—	4	3½
	Monza V6-231	11.9	11.9	15	195	18½	4	—	3.4	—	3½	3½
	Skyhawk V6-231	12.3	12.3	15	195	18½	4	—	—	—	—	3½
	Starfire V6-231	11.9	12.4	15	195	18½	4	—	3.12	—	3	3½
	Sunbird V6-231	12.3	12.3	15	195	18½	4	—	3	—	—	3½

①—Add 1 qt. with filter change.
②—Approximate. Make final check with dip stick.
③—3¾ qts. on Skyhawk.
④—Refill 3 qts., total capacity 10 qts.
⑤—Exc. Skyhawk, 2½ pts.; Skyhawk, 3½ pts.

⑥—Exc. Sunbird, refill 3 qts., total capacity 10 qts.; Sunbird, refill 2½ qts.; total capacity 10½ qts.
⑦—Skyhawk, 3½ pts.; Starfire, 2½ pts.; Sunbird, 3 pts.
⑧—Exc. Sunbird, 3½ pts.; Sunbird, 3 pts.
⑨—Exc. Sunbird, 3½ pts.; Sunbird, 2¾ pts.

⑩—Skyhawk; 2.8. Sunbird; 3.5.
⑪—Exc. Sunbird, 12 qts.; Sunbird 13 qts.
⑫—Exc. Sunbird Station Wagon, Monza "S" Coupe & Station Wagon 18½; Sunbird Station Wagon 16; Monza "S" Coupe & Station Wagon 15.

SERIAL NUMBER LOCATION

On top of instrument panel, left front.

ENGINE NUMBER LOCATION

4-140, On pad at right side of cylinder block below No. 3 spark plug at cylinder head parting line.
4-151, On distributor mounting pad.

ENGINE IDENTIFICATION CODE

Engines are identified in the following table by the code letter or letters immediately following the engine serial number.

Code			Code			Code		
CAM	4-140	1975	CBU	4-140	1976	CBS	4-140	1977
CAR	4-140	1975	CBW	4-140	1976	CBT	4-140	1977
CAS	4-140	1975	CBX	4-140	1976	CBU	4-140	1977
CAT	4-140	1975	CBY	4-140	1976	CBV	4-140	1977
CBB	4-140	1975	CBZ	4-140	1976	CBW	4-140	1977
CBC	4-140	1975	ZCB	4-122	1976	CBX	4-140	1977
ZCA	4-122	1975	CAA	4-140	1977	CBY	4-140	1977
CAY	4-140	1976	CAB	4-140	1977	CBZ	4-140	1977
CAZ	4-140	1976	CAC	4-140	1977	WC	4-151	1977
CBK	4-140	1976	CAY	4-140	1977	WD	4-151	1977
CBL	4-140	1976	CAZ	4-140	1977	YL	4-151	1977
CBS	4-140	1976	CBK	4-140	1977	YM	4-151	1977
CBT	4-140	1976	CBL	4-140	1977	ZH	4-151	1977
						ZJ	4-151	1977

GENERAL ENGINE SPECIFICATIONS

Year	Engine	Carburetor	Bore and Stroke	Piston Displacement, Cubic Inches	Compression Ratio	Maximum Brake H.P. @ R.P.M.	Maximum Torque Lbs. Ft. @ R.P.M.	Normal Oil Pressure Pounds
1975	78 Horsepower① 4-140	1 Barrel	3.500 × 3.625	140	8.00	78 @ 4200	120 @ 2000	40
	87 Horsepower① 4-140	2 Barrel	3.500 × 3.625	140	8.00	87 @ 4400	122 @ 2800	40
	110 Horsepower① 4-122	②	3.500 × 3.160	122	8.50	110 @ 5600	107 @ 4800	40
1976	70 Horsepower① 4-140	1 Barrel	3.500 × 3.625	140	8.00	70 @ 4400	107 @ 2400	27–41
	79 Horsepower①③ 4-140	2 Barrel	3.500 × 3.625	140	8.00	79 @ 4400	109 @ 2800	27–41
	84 Horsepower① 4-140	2 Barrel	3.500 × 3.625	140	8.00	84 @ 4400	113 @ 3200	27–41
	110 Horsepower① 4-122	②	3.500 × 3.160	122	8.00	110 @ 5600	107 @ 4800	27–41
1977	84 Horsepower① 4-140	2 Barrel	3.500 × 3.625	140	8.00	84 @ 4400	117 @ 2400	36–45
	87 Horsepower① 4-151	2 Barrel	4.00 × 3.00	151	8.25	88 @ 4400	128 @ 2400	36–41

①—Ratings Net—as installed in the vehicle.
②—Fuel Injection.
③—California.

CHEVROLET VEGA • PONTIAC ASTRE

TUNE UP SPECIFICATIONS

The following specifications are published from the latest information available. This data should be used only in the absence of a decal affixed in the engine compartment.

★ When using a timing light, disconnect vacuum hose or tube at distributor and plug opening in hose or tube so idle speed will not be affected.

● When checking compression, lowest cylinder must be within 80 percent of highest.

▲ Before removing wires from distributor cap, determine location of the No. 1 wire in cap, as distributor position may have been altered from that shown at the end of this chart.

Year & Engine	Spark Plug		Firing Order Fig. ▲	Ignition Timing BTDC ★①		Mark Fig.	Curb Idle Speed②		Fast Idle Speed		Fuel Pump Pressure
	Type	Gap Inch		Std. Trans.	Auto. Trans.		Std. Trans.	Auto. Trans.	Std. Trans.	Auto. Trans.	
1975											
4-122	R43LTSX	.060	E	12°③	—	F	600	—	—	—	④
4-140 1 bbl.	R43TSX	.060	A	8°	10°	B	700/1200	550/750	2000	2200	3–4½
4-140 2 bbl.	R43TSX⑤	.060	A	10°	12°	B	⑥	600/750	1600	1600	3–4½
1976											
4-122	R43LTS	.035	E	12°③	—	F	600	—	—	—	④
4-140 1 bbl.	R43TS	.035	A	8°	10°	B	750/1200	550/750	—	—	3–4½
4-140 Astre 2 bbl.	R43TS	.035	A	8°	10°	B	⑦	600/750	2200	2200	3–4½
4-140 Vega 2 bbl.	R43TS	.035	A	10°	12°	B	⑦	600/750	2200	2200	3–4½
1977											
4-140 Exc. Calif & Hi. Alt.	R43TS	.035	A	TDC	2°	B	700/1250	650/850	2500	2500	3–4½
4-140 Calif.	R43TS	.035	A	2°ATDC	TDC	B	800/1250	650/850	2500	2500	3–4½
4-140 Hi. Alt.	R43TS	.035	A	TDC	2°	B	800/1250	700/850	2500	2500	3–4½
4-151 Less A/C	R43TSX	.060	C	⑧	⑧	D	500/1000	500/650	2200	2400	3–4½
4-151 With A/C	R43TSX	.060	C	⑧	⑧	D	500/1200	650/850	2200	2400	3–4½

①—BTDC—Before top dead center.
②—Idle speed on manual trans. vehicles is adjusted in Neutral and on auto. trans. equipped vehicles is adjusted in Drive unless otherwise specified. Where two idle speeds are listed, the higher speed is with the A/C or idle solenoid energized.
③—At 1600 RPM.
④—In-tank fuel pump, 7–8½; external fuel pump, 39.
⑤—If cold weather starting problems are encountered, use R43TS spark plug, gapped at .035 inch.
⑥—Exc. Calif., 700; Calif., 700/1200.
⑦—Exc. Calif., 700/1200; Calif., 700/1000.
⑧—Exc. Calif., 14° BTDC; Calif., 12° BTDC.

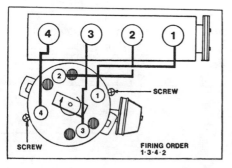

Fig. A

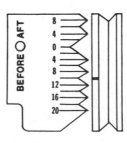

Fig. B

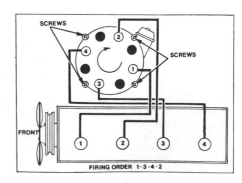

Fig. C

Continued

TUNE UP NOTES—Continued

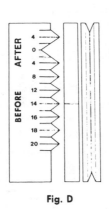

Fig. D

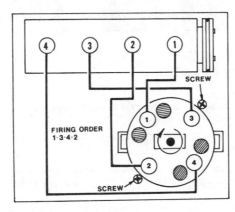

FIRING ORDER 1-3-4-2

SCREW

SCREW

Fig. E

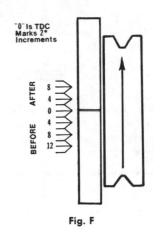

"0" Is TDC Marks 2° Increments

Fig. F

COOLING SYSTEM & CAPACITY DATA

Year	Model or Engine	Cooling Capacity, Qts.		Radiator Cap Relief Pressure, Lbs.		Thermo. Opening Temp.	Fuel Tank Gals.	Engine Oil Refill Qts. ①	Transmission Oil				Rear Axle Oil Pints
		With Heater	With A/C	With A/C	No A/C				3 Speed Pints	4 Speed Pints	5 Speed Pints	Auto. Trans. Qts. ②	
1975	4-140	7	7	15	15	195	16	3	2.4	2.4	—	⑤	2¼
1975–76	4-122	6.8	6.8	15	15	195	16	3½	—	3	—	—	2¼
1976	4-140⑦	7	7½	15	15	195	16	3½⑥	2.4	2.4	3.5	⑤	2¼
	4-140③	8	8	15	15	195	16	3½⑥	3	3	3	⑤	2¾
1977	4-140⑦	8.8	8.8	15	15	195	16	3½⑥	—	2.4	3.5	④	2.8
	4-140③	8	8	15	15	195	16	3½⑥	—	3	3	④	2¾
	4-151	11.2	11.2	15	15	195	16	3	—	2.4	3.5	④	2¾

①—Add 1 quart with filter change.
②—Approximate; make final check with dipstick.
③—Vega.
④—Turbo Hydra-Matic 200, refill 3 qts., total capacity 9.6 qts. Turbo Hydra-Matic 250, refill 2½ qts., total capacity 10 qts.
⑤—Refill 2½ qts. Total capacity 10 qts.
⑥—Add ½ quart with filter change.
⑦—Astre.

CHRYSLER • DODGE • IMPERIAL • PLYMOUTH

VEHICLE NUMBER LOCATION

1975–80: On plate attached to dash pad and visible through windshield.

ENGINE NUMBER LOCATION

1975–80 Six: Right front of block below cylinder head.

1975–80 318, 360: Left front of block below cylinder head.

1975–80 V8-400, 1975 V8-440: Upper right front of cylinder block.

1976–78 V8-440: Top of block left bank next to front tappet rail.

ENGINE IDENTIFICATION CODE

1975–80 engines are identified by the cubic inch displacement found within the engine number stamped on the pad.

GENERAL ENGINE SPECIFICATIONS

Year	Engine	Carburetor	Bore and Stroke	Piston Displacement, Cubic Inches	Compression Ratio	Maximum Brake H.P. @ R.P.M.	Maximum Torque Lbs. Ft. @ R.P.M.	Normal Oil Pressure Pounds
CHRYSLER & IMPERIAL								
1975	135 Horsepower①...... V8-318④	2 Barrel	3.91 × 3.31	318	8.5	135 @ 3600	245 @ 1600	30–80
	150 Horsepower①...... V8-318③	2 Barrel	3.91 × 3.31	318	8.5	150 @ 4000	255 @ 1600	30–80
	180 Horsepower①...... V8-360③	2 Barrel	4.00 × 3.58	360	8.4	180 @ 4000	290 @ 2400	30–80
	190 Horsepower①...... V8-360④	4 Barrel	4.00 × 3.58	360	8.4	190 @ 4000	270 @ 3200	30–80
	165 Horsepower①...... V8-400③	2 Barrel	4.34 × 3.38	400	8.2	165 @ 4000	295 @ 3200	30–80
	175 Horsepower①...... V8-400③	2 Barrel	4.34 × 3.38	400	8.2	175 @ 4000	300 @ 2400	30–80
	185 Horsepower①...... V8-400④	4 Barrel	4.34 × 3.38	400	8.2	185 @ 4000	285 @ 3200	30–80
	190 Horsepower①...... V8-400③	4 Barrel	4.34 × 3.38	400	8.2	190 @ 4000	290 @ 3200	30–80
	195 Horsepower①...... V8-400④	4 Barrel	4.34 × 3.38	400	8.2	195 @ 4000	285 @ 3200	30–80
	235 Horsepower①②.... V8-400③	4 Barrel	4.34 × 3.38	400	8.2	235 @ 4000	320 @ 3200	30–80
	215 Horsepower①....... V8-440	4 Barrel	4.32 × 3.75	440	8.2	215 @ 4000	330 @ 3200	30–80
1976	140 Horsepower①...... V8-318④	2 Barrel	3.91 × 3.31	318	8.6	140 @ 3600	250 @ 2000	30–80
	150 Horsepower①...... V8-318③	2 Barrel	3.91 × 3.31	318	8.6	150 @ 4000	255 @ 1600	30–80
	170 Horsepower①...... V8-360③	2 Barrel	4.00 × 3.58	360	8.4	170 @ 4000	280 @ 2400	30–80
	175 Horsepower①...... V8-360④	4 Barrel	4.00 × 3.58	360	8.4	175 @ 4000	270 @ 1600	30–80
	175 Horsepower①...... V8-400③	2 Barrel	4.34 × 3.38	400	8.2	175 @ 4000	300 @ 2400	30–80
	185 Horsepower①...... V8-400④	4 Barrel	4.34 × 3.38	400	8.2	185 @ 3600	285 @ 3200	30–80
	210 Horsepower①...... V8-400③	4 Barrel	4.34 × 3.38	400	8.2	210 @ 4000	305 @ 3200	30–80
	240 Horsepower①②.... V8-400③	4 Barrel	4.34 × 3.38	400	8.2	240 @ 4400	325 @ 3200	30–80
	200 Horsepower①...... V8-440④	4 Barrel	4.32 × 3.75	440	8.2	200 @ 3600	310 @ 2400	30–80
	205 Horsepower①...... V8-440③	4 Barrel	4.32 × 3.75	440	8.2	205 @ 3600	320 @ 2000	30–80
1977	135 Horsepower①...... V8-318④	2 Barrel	3.91 × 3.31	318	8.6	135 @ 3600	235 @ 1600	30–80
	145 Horsepower①........ V8-318	2 Barrel	3.91 × 3.31	318	8.6	145 @ 4000	245 @ 1600	30–80
	155 Horsepower①...... V8-360③	2 Barrel	4.00 × 3.58	360	8.4	155 @ 3600	275 @ 2000	30–80
	170 Horsepower①...... V8-360④	4 Barrel	4.00 × 3.58	360	8.4	170 @ 4000	270 @ 1600	30–80
	190 Horsepower①........ V8-400	4 Barrel	4.34 × 3.38	400	8.2	190 @ 3600	305 @ 3200	30–80
	185 Horsepower①...... V8-440⑥	4 Barrel	4.32 × 3.75	440	8.2	185 @ 3600	310 @ 2400	30–80
	195 Horsepower①...... V8-440③	4 Barrel	4.32 × 3.75	440	8.2	195 @ 3600	320 @ 2000	30–80
1978	100 Horsepower①........ 6-225	1 Barrel	3.40 × 4.12	225	8.4	100 @ 3600	170 @ 1600	30–70
	110 Horsepower①........ 6-225	2 Barrel	3.40 × 4.12	225	8.4	110 @ 3600	180 @ 2000	30–70
	140 Horsepower①.... V8-318③⑦	2 Barrel	3.91 × 3.31	318	8.5	140 @ 4000	245 @ 1600	30–80
	145 Horsepower①.... V8-318⑧	2 Barrel	3.91 × 3.31	318	8.5	145 @ 4000	245 @ 1600	30–80
	155 Horsepower①.... V8-318⑥⑦	4 Barrel	3.91 × 3.31	318	8.5	155 @ 4000	245 @ 1600	30–80
	155 Horsepower①...... V8-360③	2 Barrel	4.00 × 3.58	360	8.4	155 @ 3600	270 @ 2400	30–80
	170 Horsepower①...... V8-360⑥	4 Barrel	4.00 × 3.58	360	8.4	170 @ 4000	270 @ 1600	30–80
	190 Horsepower①........ V8-400	4 Barrel	4.34 × 3.38	400	8.2	190 @ 3600	305 @ 3200	30–80
	185 Horsepower①...... V8-440⑥	4 Barrel	4.32 × 3.75	440	8.2	185 @ 3600	310 @ 2400	30–80
	195 Horsepower①...... V8-440③	4 Barrel	4.32 × 3.75	440	8.2	195 @ 3600	320 @ 2000	30–80

GENERAL ENGINE SPECIFICATIONS—Continued

Year	Engine	Carburetor	Bore and Stroke	Piston Displacement, Cubic Inches	Compression Ratio	Maximum Brake H.P. @ R.P.M.	Maximum Torque Lbs. Ft. @ R.P.M.	Normal Oil Pressure Pounds
CHRYSLER & IMPERIAL—Continued								
1979	100 Horsepower①........6-225	1 Barrel	3.40 × 4.12	225	8.4	100 @ 3600	165 @ 1600	30–70
	110 Horsepower①........6-225	2 Barrel	3.40 × 4.12	225	8.4	110 @ 2000	180 @ 2000	30–70
	135 Horsepower①......V8-318③	2 Barrel	3.91 × 3.31	318	8.5	135 @ 4000	250 @ 1600	30–80
	155 Horsepower①......V8-318④	4 Barrel	3.91 × 3.31	318	8.5	155 @ 4000	245 @ 1600	30–80
	150 Horsepower①......V8-360③	2 Barrel	4.00 × 3.58	360	8.4	150 @ 3600	265 @ 2400	30–80
	170 Horsepower①......V8-360④	4 Barrel	4.00 × 3.58	360	8.4	170 @ 4000	270 @ 1600	30–80
	195 Horsepower①........V8-360	4 Barrel	4.00 × 3.58	360	8.0	195 @ 4000	280 @ 2400	30–80
1980	90 Horsepower① 6-225	1 Barrel	3.40 × 4.12	225	8.4	90 @ 3600	160 @ 1600	30–70
	120 Horsepower① V8-318	2 Barrel	3.91 × 3.31	318	8.5	120 @ 3600	245 @ 1600	30–80
	155 Horsepower① V8-318⑬	4 Barrel	3.91 × 3.31	318	8.5	155 @ 4000	240 @ 2000	30–80
	130 Horsepower① V8-360	2 Barrel	4.00 × 3.58	360	8.4	130 @ 3200	255 @ 2000	30–80
	185 Horsepower① V8-360②	4 Barrel	4.00 × 3.58	360	8.0	185 @ 4000	275 @ 2000	30–80
DODGE								
1975	90 Horsepower①........6-225④	1 Barrel	3.40 × 3.64	225	8.4	90 @ 3600	165 @ 1600	30–70
	95 Horsepower①........6-225③	1 Barrel	3.40 × 3.64	225	8.4	95 @ 3600	170 @ 1600	30–70
	135 Horsepower①......V8-318④	2 Barrel	3.91 × 3.31	318	8.5	135 @ 3600	245 @ 1600	30–80
	140 Horsepower①......V8-318③	2 Barrel	3.91 × 3.31	318	8.5	140 @ 3600	255 @ 1600	30–80
	145 Horsepower①......V8-318③	2 Barrel	3.91 × 3.31	318	8.5	145 @ 4000	255 @ 1600	30–80
	150 Horsepower①......V8-318③	2 Barrel	3.91 × 3.31	318	8.5	150 @ 4000	255 @ 1600	30–80
	180 Horsepower①......V8-360③	2 Barrel	4.00 × 3.58	360	8.4	180 @ 4000	290 @ 2400	30–80
	190 Horsepower①......V8-360④	4 Barrel	4.00 × 3.58	360	8.4	190 @ 4000	270 @ 3200	30–80
	230 Horsepower①②....V8-360③	4 Barrel	4.00 × 3.58	360	8.4	230 @ 4200	320 @ 3200	30–80
	165 Horsepower①......V8-400③	2 Barrel	4.34 × 3.38	400	8.2	165 @ 4000	295 @ 3200	30–80
	175 Horsepower①......V8-400③	2 Barrel	4.34 × 3.38	400	8.2	175 @ 4000	300 @ 2400	30–80
	185 Horsepower①......V8-400④	4 Barrel	4.34 × 3.38	400	8.2	185 @ 4000	285 @ 3200	30–80
	190 Horsepower①......V8-400③	4 Barrel	4.34 × 3.38	400	8.2	190 @ 4000	290 @ 3200	30–80
	195 Horsepower①......V8-400④	4 Barrel	4.34 × 3.38	400	8.2	195 @ 4000	285 @ 3200	30–80
	235 Horsepower①②....V8-400③	4 Barrel	4.34 × 3.38	400	8.2	235 @ 4200	320 @ 3200	30–80
	240 Horsepower①②....V8-400③	4 Barrel	4.34 × 3.38	400	8.2	240 @ 4400	325 @ 3200	30–80
	215 Horsepower①......V8-440③	4 Barrel	4.32 × 3.75	440	8.2	215 @ 4000	330 @ 3200	30–80
	250 Horsepower①②....V8-440③	4 Barrel	4.32 × 3.75	440	8.2	250 @ 4000	350 @ 3200	30–80
	260 Horsepower①②....V8-440③	4 Barrel	4.32 × 3.75	440	8.2	260 @ 4400	355 @ 3200	30–80
1976	90 Horsepower①........6-225④	1 Barrel	3.40 × 4.12	225	8.4	90 @ 3600	165 @ 1600	30–70
	100 Horsepower①......6-225③	1 Barrel	3.40 × 4.12	225	8.4	100 @ 3600	170 @ 1600	30–70
	140 Horsepower①......V8-318④	2 Barrel	3.91 × 3.31	318	8.6	140 @ 3600	250 @ 2000	30–80
	150 Horsepower③......V8-318③	2 Barrel	3.91 × 3.31	318	8.6	150 @ 4000	225 @ 1600	30–80
	170 Horsepower①......V8-360③	2 Barrel	4,00 × 3.58	360	8.4	170 @ 4000	280 @ 2400	30–80
	175 Horsepower①......V8-360④	4 Barrel	4.00 × 3.58	360	8.4	175 @ 4000	270 @ 1600	30–80
	220 Horsepower①②....V8-360③	4 Barrel	4.00 × 3.58	360	8.4	220 @ 4400	280 @ 3200	30–80
	175 Horsepower①......V8-400③	2 Barrel	4.34 × 3.38	400	8.2	175 @ 4000	300 @ 2400	30–80
	185 Horsepower①......V8-400④	4 Barrel	4.34 × 3.38	400	8.2	185 @ 3600	285 @ 3200	30–80
	210 Horsepower①......V8-400③	4 Barrel	4.34 × 3.38	400	8.2	210 @ 4000	305 @ 3200	30–80
	240 Horsepower①②....V8-400③	4 Barrel	4.34 × 3.38	400	8.2	240 @ 4400	325 @ 3200	30–80
	200 Horsepower①......V8-440③	4 Barrel	4.32 × 3.75	440	8.2	200 @ 3600	310 @ 2400	30–80
	205 Horsepower①......V8-440③	4 Barrel	4.32 × 3.75	440	8.2	205 @ 3600	320 @ 2000	30–80
	250 Horsepower①②....V8-440④	4 Barrel	4.32 × 3.75	440	8.2	250 @ 4000	350 @ 3200	30–80
	255 Horsepower①②....V8-440③	4 Barrel	4.32 × 3.75	440	8.2	225 @ 4400	355 @ 3200	30–80
1977	90 Horsepower①........6-225④	1 Barrel	3.40 × 4.12	225	8.4	90 @ 3600	170 @ 1600	30–70
	100 Horsepower①......6-225③	1 Barrel	3.40 × 4.12	225	8.4	100 @ 3600	170 @ 1600	30–70
	110 Horsepower①........6-225	2 Barrel	3.40 × 4.12	225	8.4	110 @ 3600	180 @ 2000	30–70
	135 Horsepower①......V8-318④	2 Barrel	3.91 × 3.31	318	8.6	135 @ 3600	235 @ 1600	30–80
	145 Horsepower①........V8-318	2 Barrel	3.91 × 3.31	318	8.6	145 @ 4000	245 @ 1600	30–80
	155 Horsepower①......V8-360③	2 Barrel	4.00 × 3.58	360	8.4	155 @ 3600	275 @ 2000	30–80
	170 Horsepower①......V8-360④	4 Barrel	4.00 × 3.58	360	8.4	170 @ 4000	270 @ 1600	30–80

GENERAL ENGINE SPECIFICATIONS—Continued

Year	Engine	Carburetor	Bore and Stroke	Piston Displacement, Cubic Inches	Compression Ratio	Maximum Brake H.P. @ R.P.M.	Maximum Torque Lbs. Ft. @ R.P.M.	Normal Oil Pressure Pounds
DODGE—Continued								
1977	175 Horsepower①...... V8-360⑤	4 Barrel	4.00 × 3.58	360	8.0	175 @ 4000	275 @ 2000	30–80
	190 Horsepower①....... V8-400	4 Barrel	4.34 × 3.38	400	8.2	190 @ 3600	305 @ 3200	30–80
	185 Horsepower①..... V8-440⑥	4 Barrel	4.32 × 3.75	440	8.2	185 @ 3600	310 @ 2400	30–80
	195 Horsepower①....... V8-440	4 Barrel	4.32 × 3.75	440	8.2	195 @ 3600	320 @ 2000	30–80
	230 Horsepower①... V8-440④⑤	4 Barrel	4.32 × 3.75	440	7.8	230 @ 4000	330 @ 3200	30–80
	245 Horsepower①... V8-440③⑤	4 Barrel	4.32 × 3.75	440	7.8	245 @ 4000	350 @ 3200	30–80
1978	90 Horsepower①...... 6-225⑬	1 Barrel	3.40 × 4.12	225	8.4	90 @ 3600	160 @ 1600	30–70
	100 Horsepower①...... 6-225③	1 Barrel	3.40 × 4.12	225	8.4	100 @ 3600	170 @ 1600	30–70
	110 Horsepower①......... 6-225	2 Barrel	3.40 × 4.12	225	8.4	110 @ 3600	180 @ 2000	30–70
	140 Horsepower①....... V8-318	2 Barrel	3.91 × 3.31	318	8.5	140 @ 4000	245 @ 1600	30–80
	155 Horsepower①..... V8-318④	4 Barrel	3.91 × 3.31	318	8.5	155 @ 4000	245 @ 1600	30–80
	155 Horsepower①..... V8-360	2 Barrel	4.00 × 3.58	360	8.4	115 @ 3600	270 @ 2400	30–80
	155 Horsepower①.... V8-360③⑨	2 Barrel	4.00 × 3.58	360	8.0	115 @ 3600	270 @ 2400	30–80
	155 Horsepower①.... V8-360③⑩	2 Barrel	4.00 × 3.58	360	8.4	115 @ 3600	270 @ 2400	30–80
	160 Horsepower①..... V8-360⑥	4 Barrel	4.00 × 3.58	360	8.0	160 @ 3600	265 @ 1600	30–80
	170 Horsepower①..... V8-360④	4 Barrel	4.00 × 3.58	360	8.4	170 @ 3600	265 @ 1600	30–80
	170 Horsepower①.... V8-360③⑬	4 Barrel	4.00 × 3.58	360	8.4	170 @ 4000	270 @ 2400	30–80
	175 Horsepower①....... V8-360	4 Barrel	4.00 × 3.58	360	8.0	175 @ 4000	260 @ 2400	30–80
	190 Horsepower①....... V8-400	4 Barrel	4.34 × 3.38	400	8.2	190 @ 3600	305 @ 3200	30–80
1979	90 Horsepower①...... 6-225④	1 Barrel	3.40 × 4.12	225	8.4	90 @ 3600	170 @ 1600	30–70
	100 Horsepower①...... 6-225③	1 Barrel	3.40 × 4.12	225	8.4	100 @ 3600	160 @ 1600	30–70
	110 Horsepower①...... 6-225③	2 Barrel	3.40 × 4.12	225	8.4	110 @ 3600	180 @ 2000	30–70
	135 Horsepower①..... V8-318③	2 Barrel	3.91 × 3.31	318	8.5	135 @ 4000	250 @ 1600	30–80
	155 Horsepower①..... V8-318④	4 Barrel	3.91 × 3.31	318	8.5	155 @ 4000	245 @ 1600	30–80
	150 Horsepower①..... V8-360③	2 Barrel	4.00 × 3.58	360	8.4	150 @ 3600	265 @ 2400	30–80
	170 Horsepower①..... V8-360④	4 Barrel	4.00 × 3.58	360	8.4	170 @ 4000	270 @ 1600	30–80
	190 Horsepower①..... V8-360④	4 Barrel	4.00 × 3.58	360	8.0	190 @ 3600	275 @ 1600	30–80
	195 Horsepower①..... V8-360③	4 Barrel	4.00 × 3.58	360	8.0	195 @ 4000	280 @ 2400	30–80
1980	90 Horsepower①........ 6-225	1 Barrel	3.40 × 4.12	225	8.4	90 @ 3600	160 @ 1600	30–70
	120 Horsepower①...... V8-318	2 Barrel	3.91 × 3.31	318	8.5	120 @ 3600	245 @ 1600	30–80
	155 Horsepower①...... V8-318	4 Barrel	3.91 × 3.31	318	8.5	155 @ 4000	240 @ 2000	30–80
	130 Horsepower①...... V8-360	2 Barrel	4.00 × 3.58	360	8.4	130 @ 3200	255 @ 2000	30–80
	185 Horsepower①..... V8-360②	4 Barrel	4.00 × 3.58	360	8.0	185 @ 4200	275 @ 2200	30–80
PLYMOUTH								
1975	90 Horsepower①....... 6-225④	1 Barrel	3.40 × 4.12	225	8.4	90 @ 3600	165 @ 1600	30–70
	95 Horsepower①...... 6-225③	1 Barrel	3.40 × 4.12	225	8.4	95 @ 3600	170 @ 1600	30–70
	135 Horsepower①..... V8-318④	2 Barrel	3.91 × 3.31	318	8.5	135 @ 3600	245 @ 1600	30–80
	140 Horsepower①..... V8-318④	2 Barrel	3.91 × 3.31	318	8.5	140 @ 3600	255 @ 1600	30–80
	145 Horsepower①..... V8-318③	2 Barrel	3.91 × 3.31	318	8.5	145 @ 4000	255 @ 1600	30–80
	150 Horsepower①..... V8-318③	2 Barrel	3.91 × 3.31	318	8.5	150 @ 4000	255 @ 1600	30–80
	180 Horsepower①..... V8-360③	2 Barrel	4.00 × 3.58	360	8.4	180 @ 4000	290 @ 2400	30–80
	190 Horsepower①..... V8-360④	4 Barrel	4.00 × 3.58	360	8.4	190 @ 4000	270 @ 3200	30–80
	230 Horsepower①②.... V8-360③	4 Barrel	4.00 × 3.58	360	8.4	230 @ 4400	300 @ 3600	30–80
	165 Horsepower①..... V8-400③	2 Barrel	4.34 × 3.38	400	8.2	165 @ 4000	295 @ 3200	30–80
	175 Horsepower①..... V8-400③	2 Barrel	4.34 × 3.38	400	8.2	175 @ 4000	300 @ 2400	30–80
	185 Horsepower①..... V8-400④	4 Barrel	4.34 × 3.38	400	8.2	185 @ 4000	285 @ 3200	30–80
	190 Horsepower①..... V8-400③	4 Barrel	4.34 × 3.38	400	8.2	190 @ 4000	290 @ 3200	30–80
	195 Horsepower①..... V8-400④	4 Barrel	4.34 × 3.38	400	8.2	195 @ 4000	285 @ 3200	30–80
	235 Horsepower①②.... V8-400③	4 Barrel	4.34 × 3.38	400	8.2	235 @ 4200	320 @ 3200	30–80
	240 Horsepower①②.... V8-400③	4 Barrel	4.34 × 3.38	400	8.2	250 @ 4400	325 @ 3200	30–80

Continued

GENERAL ENGINE SPECIFICATIONS—Continued

Year	Engine	Carburetor	Bore and Stroke	Piston Displacement, Cubic Inches	Compression Ratio	Maximum Brake H.P. @ R.P.M.	Maximum Torque Lbs. Ft. @ R.P.M.	Normal Oil Pressure Pounds
PLYMOUTH—Continued								
	215 Horsepower①........ V8-440	4 Barrel	4.32 × 3.75	440	8.2	215 @ 4000	330 @ 3200	30–90
	250 Horsepower①②.... V8-440④	4 Barrel	4.32 × 3.75	440	8.2	250 @ 4000	350 @ 3200	30–80
	260 Horsepower①②.... V8-440③	4 Barrel	4.32 × 3.75	440	8.2	260 @ 4400	355 @ 3200	30–80
1976	90 Horsepower①...... 6-225④	1 Barrel	3.40 × 4.12	225	8.4	90 @ 3600	165 @ 1600	30–70
	100 Horsepower①..... 6-225③	1 Barrel	3.40 × 4.12	225	8.4	100 @ 3600	170 @ 1600	30–70
	140 Horsepower①..... V8-318④	2 Barrel	3.91 × 3.31	318	8.6	140 @ 3600	250 @ 2000	30–80
	150 Horsepower①..... V8-318③	2 Barrel	3.91 × 3.31	318	8.6	150 @ 4000	255 @ 1600	30–80
	170 Horsepower①..... V8-360③	2 Barrel	4.00 × 3.58	360	8.4	170 @ 4000	280 @ 2400	30–80
	175 Horsepower①..... V8-360④	4 Barrel	4.00 × 3.58	360	8.4	175 @ 4000	270 @ 1600	30–80
	220 Horsepower①②.... V8-360③	4 Barrel	4.00 × 3.58	360	8.4	220 @ 4400	280 @ 3200	30–80
	175 Horsepower①..... V8-400③	2 Barrel	4.34 × 3.38	400	8.2	175 @ 4000	300 @ 2400	30–80
	185 Horsepower①..... V8-400④	4 Barrel	4.34 × 3.38	400	8.2	185 @ 3600	285 @ 3200	30–80
	210 Horsepower①..... V8-400③	4 Barrel	4.34 × 3.38	400	8.2	210 @ 4000	305 @ 3200	30–80
	240 Horsepower①②.... V8-400③	4 Barrel	4.34 × 3.38	400	8.2	240 @ 4400	325 @ 3200	30–80
	200 Horsepower①..... V8-440④	4 Barrel	4.32 × 3.75	440	8.2	200 @ 3600	310 @ 2400	30–80
	205 Horsepower①..... V8-440③	4 Barrel	4.32 × 3.75	440	8.2	205 @ 3600	320 @ 2000	30–80
	250 Horsepower①②.... V8-440④	4 Barrel	4.32 × 3.75	440	8.2	250 @ 4000	350 @ 3200	30–80
	255 Horsepower①②.... V8-440③	4 Barrel	4.32 × 3.75	440	8.2	255 @ 4400	355 @ 3200	30–80
1977	90 Horsepower①...... 6-225④	1 Barrel	3.40 × 4.12	225	8.4	90 @ 3600	170 @1600	30–70
	100 Horsepower①..... 6-255③	1 Barrel	3.40 × 4.12	225	8.4	100 @ 3600	170 @ 1600	30–70
	110 Horsepower①........ 6-255	2 Barrel	3.40 × 4.12	225	8.4	110 @ 3600	180 @ 2000	30–70
	135 Horsepower①..... V8-318④	2 Barrel	3.91 × 3.31	318	8.6	135 @ 3600	235 @ 1600	30–80
	145 Horsepower①..... V8-318③	2 Barrel	3.91 × 3.31	318	8.6	145 @ 4000	245 @ 1600	30–80
	155 Horsepower①...... V8-360	2 Barrel	4.00 × 3.58	360	8.4	155 @ 3600	275 @ 2000	30–80
	170 Horsepower①...... V8-360	4 Barrel	4.00 × 3.58	360	8.4	170 @ 4000	270 @ 1600	30–80
	175 Horsepower①..... V8-360⑤	4 Barrel	4.00 × 3.58	360	8.0	175 @ 4000	275 @ 2000	30–80
	190 Horsepower①...... V8-400	4 Barrel	4.34 × 3.38	400	8.2	190 @ 3600	305 @ 3200	30–80
	185 Horsepower①..... V8-440⑥	4 Barrel	4.32 × 3.75	440	8.2	185 @ 3600	310 @ 2400	30–80
	195 Horsepower①...... V8-440	4 Barrel	4.32 × 3.75	440	8.2	195 @ 3600	320 @ 2000	30–80
	230 Horsepower①.. V8-440④⑤	4 Barrel	4.32 × 3.75	440	7.8	230 @ 4000	330 @ 3200	30–80
	245 Horsepower①.. V8-440③⑤	4 Barrel	4.32 × 3.75	440	7.8	245 @ 4000	350 @ 3200	30–80
1978	90 Horsepower①..... 6-225⑬	1 Barrel	3.40 × 4.12	225	8.4	90 @ 3600⑬	160 @ 1600	30–70
	100 Horsepower①....... 6-225	1 Barrel	3.40 × 4.12	225	8.4	100 @ 3600	170 @ 1600	30–70
	110 Horsepower①....... 6-225	2 Barrel	3.40 × 4.12	225	8.4	110 @ 3600	180 @ 2000	30–70
	140 Horsepower①.. V8-318③⑪	2 Barrel	3.91 × 3.31	318	8.5	140 @ 4000	245 @ 1600	30–80
	145 Horsepower①.. V8-318③⑫	2 Barrel	3.91 × 3.31	318	8.5	145 @ 4000	245 @ 1600	30–80
	155 Horsepower①..... V8-318⑥	4 Barrel	3.91 × 3.31	318	8.5	155 @ 4000	245 @ 1600	30–80
	155 Horsepower①...... V8-360	2 Barrel	4.00 × 3.58	360	8.4	155 @ 3600	270 @ 2400	30–80
	175 Horsepower①....... V8-360	4 Barrel	4.00 × 3.58	360	8.4	175 @ 4000	260 @ 2400	30–80
	190 Horsepower①...... V8-400	4 Barrel	4.34 × 3.38	400	8.2	190 @ 3600	305 @ 3200	30–80
1979	100 Horsepower①........ 6-225	1 Barrel	3.40 × 4.12	225	8.4	100 @ 3600	165 @ 1600	30–70
	110 Horsepower①...... 6-225③	2 Barrel	3.40 × 4.12	225	8.4	110 @ 3600	180 @ 2000	30–70
	135 Horsepower①..... V8-318③	2 Barrel	3.91 × 3.31	318	8.5	135 @ 4000	250 @ 1600	30–80
	155 Horsepower①..... V8-318④	4 Barrel	3.91 × 3.31	318	8.5	155 @ 4000	245 @ 1600	30–80
	195 Horsepower①...... V8-360	4 Barrel	4.00 × 3.58	360	8.0	195 @ 4000	280 @ 2400	30–80
1980	90 Horsepower①........ 6-225	1 Barrel	3.40 × 4.12	225	8.4	90 @ 3600	160 @ 1600	30–70
	120 Horsepower①....... V8-318	2 Barrel	3.91 × 3.31	318	8.5	120 @ 3600	160 @ 1600	30–80
	155 Horsepower①..... V8-318⑬	4 Barrel	3.91 × 3.31	318	8.5	155 @ 4000	240 @ 2000	30–80
	130 Horsepower①...... V8-360	2 Barrel	4.00 × 3.58	360	8.4	130 @ 3200	255 @ 2000	30–80

①—Ratings are NET—as installed in the vehicle.
②—With dual exhausts.
③—Exc. California.
④—California.

⑤—High Performance.
⑥—California and high altitude.
⑦—LeBaron.
⑧—Cordoba.
⑨—Exc. Aspen coupe & sedan.

⑩—Aspen coupe & sedan.
⑪—Fury.
⑫—Volaré.
⑬—High Altitude.

TUNE UP SPECIFICATIONS

The following specifications are published from the latest information available. This data should be used only in the absence of a decal affixed in the engine compartment.

★ When using a timing light, disconnect vacuum hose or tube at distributor and plug opening in hose or tube so idle speed will not be affected.

● When checking compression, lowest cylinder must be within 80 percent of highest.

▲ Before removing wires from distributor cap, determine location of the No. 1 wire in cap, as distributor position may have been altered from that shown at the end of this chart.

Year & Engine	Spark Plug		Ignition Timing BTDC①★				Curb Idle Speed		Fast Idle Speed		Fuel
	Type	Gap	Firing Order Fig. ▲	Man. Trans.	Auto. Trans.	Mark Fig.	Man. Trans.	Auto. Trans.②	Man. Trans.	Auto. Trans.	Pump Pressure
CHRYSLER & IMPERIAL											
1975											
V8-318③	N13Y④	.035	H	—	2°⑤	B	—	900N	—	1500⑥⑦	5–7
V8-318 Exc. Calif.⑧	N13Y④	.035	H	—	2°	B	—	750N	—	1500⑦	5–7
V8-318 Calif.⑧	N13Y④	.035	H	—	⑨	B	—	750N	—	1500⑦	5–7
V8-360 2 Barrel	N12Y④	.035	H	—	6°	B	—	750N	—	1600⑦	5–7
V8-360 4 Barrel	N12Y④	.035	H	—	6°	B	—	⑩	—	1600⑦	5–7
V8-400 2 Barrel	J13Y④	.035	J	—	10°	F	—	750N	—	1600①	6–7½
V8-400 4 Barrel	J13Y④	.035	J	—	8°	F	—	750N	—	1800⑦	⑪
V8-400 High Perf.	RJ87P④	.035	J	—	6°	F	—	750N	—	1800⑦	⑪
V8-440	RJ87P④	.040	J	—	6°	D	—	⑩	—	1600⑦	⑫
1976											
V8-318③	RN12Y④	.035	H	—	2°⑤	B	—	900N	—	1250⑦	5–7
V8-318 Exc. Calif.⑧	RN12Y④	.035	H	—	2°	B	—	750N	—	1200⑦	5–7
V8-318 Calif.⑧	RN12Y④	.035	H	—	TDC	B	—	750N	—	1500⑦	5–7
V8-360 2 Barrel	RN12Y④	.035	H	—	6°	B	—	700N	—	1600⑦	5–7
V8-360 4 Barrel	RN12Y④	.035	H	—	6°	B	—	⑩	—	1700⑦	5–7
V8-400 2 Barrel	RJ13Y④	.035	J	—	10°	F	—	700N	—	1600⑦	5–7
V8-400 4 Barrel	RJ13Y④	.035	J	—	8°	F	—	750N	—	1800⑦	5–7
V8-400 High Perf.	RJ86P④	.035	J	—	6°	F	—	850N	—	1800⑦	5–7
V8-440	RJ13Y④	.035	J	—	8°	D	—	750N	—	1600⑦	5–7
1977											
V8-318 Exc. Calif. & High Alt.⑬	RN12Y④	.035	H	—	8°	B	—	700N	—	1400⑦	5–7
V8-318 Calif. & High Alt.⑬	RN12Y④	.035	H	—	TDC	B	—	850N	—	1500⑦	5–7
V8-318 Exc. Calif.⑭	RN12Y④	.035	H	—	6°	B	—	700N	—	1300⑦	5–7
V8-318 Calif.⑭	RN12Y④	.035	H	—	8°	B	—	750N	—	1500⑦	5–7
V8-360 2 Barrel	RN12Y④	.035	H	—	10°	B	—	700N	—	1700⑦	5–7
V8-360 4 Barrel⑬	RN12Y④	.035	H	—	6°	B	—	750N	—	1700⑦	5–7
V8-360 4 Barrel⑭	RN12Y④	.035	H	—	10°	B	—	750N	—	1500⑦	5–7
V8-400⑭	④⑮	.035	J	—	10°	F	—	750N	—	1400⑦	5–7
V8-440⑬	RJ13Y④	.035	J	—	8°	D	—	750N	—	1200⑦	5–7
V8-440 Exc. Calif. & High Alt.⑭	RJ13Y④	.035	J	—	12°	D	—	750N	—	1400⑦	5–7
V8-440 Calif. & High Alt.⑭	RJ13Y④	.035	J	—	8°	D	—	750N	—	1600⑦	5–7
1978											
6-225 Exc. Calif. & High Alt.	RBL16Y④	.035	G	12°	12°	K	750	750N	1500	1600⑦	3½–5
6-225 Calif. & High Alt.	RBL16Y④	.035	G	—	8°	K	—	750N	—	⑦⑯	3½–5
V8-318 2 Barrel	RN12Y④	.035	H	16°	16°	C	700	750N	1400	⑦⑰	5–7

Continued

TUNE UP SPECIFICATIONS—Continued

Year & Engine	Spark Plug Type	Gap	Firing Order Fig. ▲	Ignition Timing BTDC① ★ Man. Trans.	Auto. Trans.	Mark Fig.	Curb Idle Speed Man. Trans.	Auto. Trans.②	Fast Idle Speed Man. Trans.	Auto. Trans.	Fuel Pump Pressure
CHRYSLER & IMPERIAL—Continued											
1978											
V8-318 4 Barrel	RN12Y④	.035	H	—	10°	C	—	750N	—	1600⑦	5–7
V8-360 2 Barrel	RN12Y④	.035	H	—	20°	C	—	750N	—	1600⑦	5–7
V8-360 4 Barrel Exc. Calif.⑭⑱	RN12Y④	.035	H	—	16°	C	—	750N	—	1500⑦	5–7
V8-360 4 Barrel Calif.⑬㉗	RN12Y④	.035	H	—	⑲	C	—	750N	—	1500⑦	5–7
V8-400	④⑳	.035	J	—	㉑	E	—	750N	—	1500⑦	5–7
V8-440 Exc. Calif. & High Alt.	OJ13Y④	.035	J	—	㉒	C	—	750N	—	1400⑦	5–7
V8-440 Calif. & High Alt.	OJ13Y④	.035	J	—	8°	C	—	750N	—	1600⑦	5–7
1979											
6-225 1 Barrel Exc. Calif.	RBL16Y④	.035	G	12°	12°	K	675	675N	1400⑦	1600⑦	3½–5
6-225 1 Barrel Calif.	RBL16Y④	.035	G	—	8°	K	—	750N	—	1500⑦	3½–5
6-225 2 Barrel	RBL16Y④	.035	G	—	12°	K	—	725N	—	1600⑦	3½–5
V8-318 2 Barrel	RN12Y④	.035	H	—	16°	C	—	730N	—	1600⑦	5–7
V8-318 4 Barrel⑱	RN12Y④	.035	H	—	16°	C	—	750N	—	1600⑦	5–7
V8-318 4 Barrel㉘	RN12Y④	.035	H	—	16°	C	—	850N	—	1600⑦	5–7
V8-360 2 Barrel	RN12Y④	.035	H	—	12°	C	—	750N	—	1600⑦	5–7
V8-360 4 Barrel	RN12Y④	.035	H	—	16°	C	—	750N	—	1600⑦	5–7
1980											
6-225 Exc. Calif.	RBL16Y④	.035	G	—	12°	K	—	725N	—	1600⑦	3½–5
6-225 Calif.	RBL16Y④	.035	G	—	12°	K	—	750N	—	1400⑦	3½–5
V8-318 2 Barrel	RN12Y④	.035	H	—	12°	C	—	700N	—	1500⑦	5–7
V8-318 4 Barrel	RN12Y④	.035	H	—	16°	C	—	700N	—	1600⑦	5–7
V8-360 2 Barrel	RN12Y④	.035	H	—	12°	C	—	700N	—	1500⑦	5–7
V8-360 4 Barrel	RN12Y④	.035	H	—	16°	C	—	750N	—	1600⑦	5–7
DODGE											
1975											
6-225	BL13Y④	.035	G	TDC	TDC	A	800	750N	1700⑦	1600⑦	3½–5
V8-318③	N13Y④	.035	H	—	2°⑤	B	—	750N	—	1500⑥⑦	5–7
V8-318 Exc. Calif.⑧	N13Y④	.035	H	2°	2°	B	750	750N	1500⑦	1500⑦	5–7
V8-318 Calif.⑧	N13Y④	.035	H	—	⑨	B	—	750N	—	1500⑦	5–7
V8-360 2 Barrel	N12Y④	.035	H	—	6°	B	—	750N	—	1600⑦	5–7
V8-360 4 Barrel	N12Y④	.035	H	—	6°	B	—	⑩	—	1600⑦	5–7
V8-360 High Perf.	N12Y④	.035	H	—	2°	B	—	850N	—	1600⑦	5–7
V8-400 2 Barrel	J13Y④	.035	J	—	10°	F	—	750N	—	1600⑦	6–7½
V8-400 4 Barrel	J13Y④	.035	J	—	8°	F	—	750N	—	1800⑦	⑪
V8-400 High Perf.	RJ87P④	.035	J	—	6°	F	—	850N	—	1800⑦	⑪
V8-440	RJ87P④	.040	J	—	6°	D	—	750N	—	1600⑦	⑫
V8-440 High Perf.	J11Y④	.035	J	—	10°	D	—	750N	—	㉔	6½–7
1976											
6-225 Exc. Calif.	RBL13Y④	.035	G	6°	2°	A	750	750N	1700⑦	1600⑦	3½–5
6-225 Calif.	RBL13Y④	.035	G	4°	2°	A	800	750N	—	1700⑦	3½–5
V8-318③	RN12Y④	.035	H	—	2°⑤	B	—	900N	—	1250⑦	5–7
V8-318 Exc. Calif.⑧	RN12Y④	.035	H	2°	2°	B	750	750N	1500⑦	1200⑦	5–7
V8-318 Calif.⑧	RN12Y④	.035	H	—	TDC	B	—	750N	—	1500⑦	5–7
V8-360 2 Barrel	RN12Y④	.035	H	—	6°	B	—	700N	—	1600⑦	5–7
V8-360 4 Barrel	RN12Y④	.035	H	—	6°	B	—	750N	—	1700⑦	5–7
V8-360 High Perf.	RN12Y④	.035	H	—	2°	B	—	850N	—	1700⑦	5–7

Continued

TUNE UP SPECIFICATIONS—Continued

Year & Engine	Spark Plug Type	Gap	Firing Order Fig. ▲	Ignition Timing BTDC[1]★ Man. Trans.	Auto. Trans.	Mark Fig.	Curb Idle Speed Man. Trans.	Auto. Trans.[2]	Fast Idle Speed Man. Trans.	Auto. Trans.	Fuel Pump Pressure
DODGE—Continued											
1976											
V8-400 2 Barrel	RJ13Y[4]	.035	J	—	10°	F	—	700N	—	1600[7]	5–7
V8-400 4 Barrel	RJ13Y[4]	.035	J	—	8°	F	—	750N	—	1600[7]	5–7
V8-400 High Perf.	RJ86P[4]	.035	J	—	6°	F	—	850N	—	1800[7]	5–7
V8-440	RJ13Y[4]	.035	J	—	8°	D	—	750N	—	1600[7]	5–7
V8-440 High Perf.	RJ11Y[4]	.035	J	—	[25]	D	—	750N	—	1600[7]	6–7½
1977											
6-225 1 Barrel[26]	RBL15Y[4]	.035	G	12°	12°	A	700	700N	1700[7]	1700[7]	3½–5
6-225 1 Barrel Exc. Calif.[18][27]	RBL15Y[4]	.035	G	6°	2°	A	700	700N	1400[7]	1700[7]	3½–5
6-225 1 Barrel Calif.[27][28]	RBL15Y[4]	.035	G	8°	8°	A	750	750N	1600[7]	1700[7]	3½–5
6-225 2 Barrel Exc. Calif.	RBL15Y[4]	.035	G	12°	12°	A	750	750N	1500[7]	1600[7]	3½–5
6-225 2 Barrel Calif.	RBL15Y[4]	.035	G	4°	4°	A	850	850N	1600[7]	1700[7]	3½–5
V8-318 Exc. Calif. & High Alt.[13]	RN12Y[4]	.035	H	8°	8°	B	700	700N	1400[7]	1400[7]	5–7
V8-318 Calif. & High Alt.[13]	RN12Y[4]	.035	H	—	TDC	B	—	850N	—	1500[7]	5–7
V8-318 Exc. Calif.[14]	RN12Y[4]	.035	H	—	6°	B	—	700N	—	1300[7]	5–7
V8-318 Calif.[14]	RN12Y[4]	.035	H	—	8°	B	—	750N	—	1500[7]	5–7
V8-360 2 Barrel	RN12Y[4]	.035	H	—	10°	B	—	700N	—	1700[7]	5–7
V8-360 4 Barrel[13]	RN12Y[4]	.035	H	—	6°	B	—	750N	—	1700[7]	5–7
V8-360 4 Barrel[14]	RN12Y[4]	.035	H	—	10°	B	—	750N	—	1500[7]	5–7
V8-400[14]	[4][15]	.035	J	—	10°	F	—	750N	—	1400[7]	5–7
V8-440[13]	RJ13Y[4]	.035	J	—	8°	D	—	750N	—	1200[7]	5–7
V8-440 Exc. Calif. & High Alt.[14]	RJ13Y[4]	.035	J	—	12°	D	—	750N	—	1400[7]	5–7
V8-440 Calif. & High Alt.[14]	RJ13Y[4]	.035	J	—	8°	D	—	750N	—	1200[7]	5–7
V8-440 High Perf.[14]	RJ11Y[4]	.035	J	—	8°	D	—	750N	—	1600[7]	6–7½
1978											
6-225 1 Barrel Exc. Calif.[18]	RBL16Y[4]	.035	G	12°	12°	K	700	700N	1400[7]	1600[7]	3½–5
6-225 1 Barrel Calif.[28]	RBL16Y[4]	.035	G	—	8°	K	—	750N	—	[7][16]	3½–5
6-225 2 Barrel	RBL16Y[4]	.035	G	12°	12°	K	750	750N	1500[7]	1600[7]	3½–5
V8-318 2 Barrel	RN12Y[4]	.035	H	—	16°	C	—	750N	—	[7][17]	5–7
V8-318 4 Barrel	RN12Y[4]	.035	H	—	10°	C	—	750N	—	1600[7]	5–7
V8-360 2 Barrel	RN12Y[4]	.035	H	—	20°	C	—	750N	—	1600[7]	5–7
V8-360 4 Barrel Exc. Calif.[14][18]	RN12Y[4]	.035	H	—	16°	C	—	750N	—	1500[7]	5–7
V8-360 4 Barrel Calif.[13][28]	RN12Y[4]	.035	H	—	[19]	C	—	750N	—	1500[7]	5–7
V8-400	[4][20]	.035	J	—	[21]	E	—	750N	—	1500[7]	5–7
V8-440 Exc. Calif. & High Alt.	[4][20]	.035	J	—	8°	C	—	750N	—	1600[7]	[29]
V8-440 Calif. & High Alt.	[4][20]	.035	J	—	16°	C	—	750N	—	[30]	[29]

Continued

TUNE UP SPECIFICATIONS—Continued

Year & Engine	Spark Plug Type	Gap	Ignition Timing BTDC[1]★ Firing Order Fig. ▲	Man. Trans.	Auto. Trans.	Mark Fig.	Curb Idle Speed Man. Trans.	Auto. Trans.[2]	Fast Idle Speed Man. Trans.	Auto. Trans.	Fuel Pump Pressure
DODGE—Continued											
1979											
6-225 1 Barrel Exc. Calif.	RBL16Y[4]	.035	G	12°	12°	K	675	675N	1400[7]	1600[7]	3½–5
6-225 1 Barrel Calif.	RBL16Y[4]	.035	G	—	8°	K	—	750N	—	1500[7]	3½–5
6-225 2 Barrel	RBL16Y[4]	.035	G	—	12°	K	—	725N	—	1600[7]	3½–5
V8-318 2 Barrel	RN12Y[4]	.035	H	—	16°	C	—	730N	—	1600[7]	5–7
V8-318 4 Barrel[18]	RN12Y[4]	.035	H	—	16°	C	—	750N	—	1600[7]	5–7
V8-318 4 Barrel[28]	RN12Y[4]	.035	H	—	16°	C	—	850N	—	1600[7]	5–7
V8-360 2 Barrel	RN12Y[4]	.035	H	—	12°	C	—	750N	—	1600[7]	5–7
V8-360 4 Barrel	RN12Y[4]	.035	H	—	16°	C	—	750N	—	1600[7]	5–7
1980											
6-225 Exc. Calif.	RBL16Y[4]	.035	G	12°	12°	K	725	725N	—	1600[7]	3½–5
6-225 Calif.	RBL16Y[4]	.035	G	—	12°	K	—	750N	—	1400[7]	3½–5
V8-318 2 Barrel	RN12Y[4]	.035	H	—	12°	C	—	700N	—	1500[7]	5–7
V8-318 4 Barrel	RN12Y[4]	.035	H	—	16°	C	—	700N	—	1600[7]	5–7
V8-360 2 Barrel	RN12Y[4]	.035	H	—	12°	C	—	700N	—	1500[7]	5–7
V8-360 4 Barrel	RN12Y[4]	.035	H	—	16°	C	—	750N	—	1600[7]	5–7
PLYMOUTH											
1975											
6-225	BL13Y[4]	.035	G	TDC	TDC	A	800	750N	1700[7]	1600[7]	3½–5
V8-318[3]	N13Y[4]	.035	H	—	2°[5]	B	—	750N	—	1500[7]	5–7
V8-318 Exc. Calif.[8]	N13Y[4]	.035	H	2°	2°	B	750	750N	1500[7]	1500[7]	5–7
V8-318 Calif.[8]	N13Y[4]	.035	H	—	[9]	B	—	750N	—	1500[7]	5–7
V8-360 2 Barrel	N12Y[4]	.035	H	—	6°	B	—	750N	—	1600[7]	5–7
V8-360 4 Barrel	N12Y[4]	.035	H	—	6°	B	—	[10]	—	1600[7]	5–7
V8-360 High Perf.	N12Y[4]	.035	H	—	2°	B	—	850N	—	1600[7]	5–7
V8-400 2 Barrel	J13Y[4]	.035	J	—	10°	F	—	750N	—	1600[7]	6–7½
V8-400 4 Barrel	J13Y[4]	.035	J	—	8°	F	—	750N	—	1800[7]	[11]
V8-400 High Perf.	RJ87P[4]	.035	J	—	6°	F	—	850N	—	1800[7]	[11]
V8-440	RJ87P[4]	.040	J	—	6°	D	—	750N	—	1600[7]	[12]
V8-440 High Perf.	J11Y[4]	.035	J	—	10°	D	—	750N	—	[24]	6½–7
1976											
6-225 Exc. Calif.	RBL13Y[4]	.035	G	6°	2°	A	750	750N	1700[7]	1600[7]	3½–5
6-225 Calif.	RBL13Y[4]	.035	G	4°	2°	A	800	750N	—	1700[7]	3½–5
V8-318[3]	RN12Y[4]	.035	H	—	2°[5]	B	—	900N	—	1250[7]	5–7
V8-318 Exc. Calif.[8]	RN12Y[4]	.035	H	2°	2°	B	750	750N	1500[7]	1200[7]	5–7
V8-318 Calif.[8]	RN12Y[4]	.035	H	—	TDC	B	—	750N	—	1500[7]	5–7
V8-360 2 Barrel	RN12Y[4]	.035	H	—	6°	B	—	700N	—	1600[7]	5–7
V8-360 4 Barrel	RN12Y[4]	.035	H	—	6°	B	—	750N	—	1700[7]	5–7
V8-360 High Perf.	RN12Y[4]	.035	H	—	2°	B	—	850N	—	1700[7]	5–7
V8-400 2 Barrel	RJ13Y[4]	.035	J	—	10°	F	—	700N	—	1600[7]	5–7
V8-400 4 Barrel	RJ13Y[4]	.035	J	—	8°	F	—	750N	—	1600[7]	5–7
V8-400 High Perf.	RJ86P[4]	.035	J	—	6°	F	—	850N	—	1800[7]	5–7
V8-440	RJ13Y[4]	.035	J	—	8°	D	—	750N	—	1600[7]	5–7
V8-440 High Perf.	RJ11Y[4]	.035	J	—	[25]	D	—	750N	—	1600[7]	6–7½

Continued

TUNE UP SPECIFICATIONS—Continued

Year & Engine	Spark Plug		Ignition Timing BTDC [1] ★				Curb Idle Speed		Fast Idle Speed		Fuel
	Type	Gap	Firing Order Fig. ▲	Man. Trans.	Auto. Trans.	Mark Fig.	Man. Trans.	Auto. Trans. [2]	Man. Trans.	Auto. Trans.	Pump Pressure
PLYMOUTH—Continued											
1977											
6-225 1 Barrel[31]	RBL15Y[4]	.035	G	12°	12°	A	700	700N	1700[7]	1700[7]	3½-5
6-225 1 Barrel Exc. Calif.[18][32]	RBL15Y[4]	.035	G	6°	2°	A	700	700N	1400[7]	1700[7]	3½-5
6-225 1 Barrel Calif.[28][32]	RBL15Y[4]	.035	G	8°	8°	A	750	750N	1600[7]	1700[7]	3½-5
6-225 2 Barrel Exc. Calif.	RBL15Y[4]	.035	G	12°	12°	A	750	750N	1500[7]	1600[7]	3½-5
6-225 2 Barrel Calif.	RBL15Y[4]	.035	G	4°	4°	A	850	850N	1600[7]	1700[7]	3½-5
V8-318 Exc. Calif. & High Alt.	RN12Y[4]	.035	H	8°	8°	B	700	700N	1400[7]	1400[7]	5-7
V8-318 Calif. & High Alt.	RN12Y[4]	.035	H	—	TDC	B	—	850N	—	1500[7]	5-7
V8-360 2 Barrel	RN12Y[4]	.035	H	—	10°	B	—	700N	—	1700[7]	5-7
V8-360 4 Barrel[13]	RN12Y[4]	.035	H	—	6°	B	—	750N	—	1700[7]	5-7
V8-360 4 Barrel[14]	RN12Y[4]	.035	H	—	10°	B	—	750N	—	1500[7]	5-7
V8-400[14]	[4][15]	.035	J	—	10°	F	—	750N	—	1400[7]	5-7
V8-440[13]	RJ13Y[4]	.035	J	—	8°	D	—	750N	—	1200[7]	5-7
V8-440 Exc. Calif. & High Alt.[14]	RJ13Y[4]	.035	J	—	12°	D	—	750N	—	1400[7]	5-7
V8-440 Calif. & High Alt.[14]	RJ13Y[4]	.035	J	—	8°	D	—	750N	—	1200[7]	5-7
V8-440 High Perf.[14]	RJ11Y[4]	.035	J	—	8°	D	—	750N	—	1600[7]	6-7½
1978											
6-225 1 Barrel Exc. Calif.[18]	RBL16Y[4]	.035	G	12°	12°	K	700	700N	1400[7]	1600[7]	3½-5
6-225 1 Barrel Calif.[28]	RBL16Y[4]	.035	G	—	8°	K	—	750N	—	[7][16]	3½-5
6-225 2 Barrel	RBL16Y[4]	.035	G	12°	12°	K	750	750N	1500[7]	1600[7]	3½-5
V8-318 2 Barrel	RN12Y[4]	.035	H	—	16°	C	—	750N	—	[7][17]	5-7
V8-318 4 Barrel	RN12Y[4]	.035	H	—	10°	C	—	750N	—	1600[7]	5-7
V8-360 2 Barrel	RN12Y[4]	.035	H	—	20°	C	—	750N	—	1600[7]	5-7
V8-360 4 Barrel Exc. Calif.[14][18]	RN12Y[4]	.035	H	—	16°	C	—	750N	—	1500[7]	5-7
V8-360 4 Barrel Calif.[13][28]	RN12Y[4]	.035	H	—	[19]	C	—	750N	—	1500[7]	5-7
V8-400[14]	[4][20]	.035	J	—	[21]	E	—	750N	—	1500[7]	5-7
V8-440 Exc. Calif. & High Alt.	[4][20]	.035	J	—	8°	C	—	750N	—	1600[7]	[29]
V8-440 Calif. & High Alt.	[4][20]	.035	J	—	16°	C	—	750N	—	[30]	[29]
1979											
6-225 1 Barrel Exc. Calif.	RBL16Y[4]	.035	G	12°	12°	K	675	675N	1400[7]	1600[7]	3½-5
6-225 1 Barrel Calif.	RBL16Y[4]	.035	G	—	8°	K	—	750N	—	1500[7]	3½-5
6-225 2 Barrel	RBL16Y[4]	.035	G	—	12°	K	—	725N	—	1600[7]	3½-5
V8-318 2 Barrel	RN12Y[4]	.035	H	—	16°	C	—	730N	—	1600[7]	5-7
V8-318 4 Barrel[18]	RN12Y[4]	.035	H	—	16°	C	—	750N	—	1600[7]	5-7
V8-318 4 Barrel[28]	RN12Y[4]	.035	H	—	16°	C	—	850N	—	1600[7]	5-7
V8-360 2 Barrel	RN12Y[4]	.035	H	—	12°	C	—	750N	—	1600[7]	5-7
V8-360 4 Barrel	RN12Y[4]	.035	H	—	16°	C	—	750N	—	1600[7]	5-7

Continued

TUNE UP SPECIFICATIONS—Continued

| Year & Engine | Spark Plug | | Ignition Timing BTDC①★ | | | | Curb Idle Speed | | Fast Idle Speed | | Fuel |
	Type	Gap	Firing Order Fig. ▲	Man. Trans.	Auto. Trans.	Mark Fig.	Man. Trans.	Auto. Trans.②	Man. Trans.	Auto. Trans.	Pump Pressure
PLYMOUTH—Continued											
1980											
6-225 Exc. Calif.	RBL16Y④	.035	G	12°	12°	K	725	725N	—	1600⑦	3½–5
6-225 Calif.	RBL16Y④	.035	G	—	12°	K	—	750N	—	1400⑦	3½–5
V8-318 2 Barrel	RN12Y④	.035	H	—	12°	C	—	700N	—	1500⑦	5–7
V8-318 4 Barrel	RN12Y④	.035	H	—	16°	C	—	700N	—	1600⑦	5–7
V8-360 2 Barrel	RN12Y④	.035	H	—	12°	C	—	700N	—	1500⑦	5–7
V8-360 4 Barrel	RN12Y④	.035	H	—	16°	C	—	750N	—	1600⑦	5–7

①—BTDC—Before top dead center.
②—N: Neutral.
③—Models equipped with air pump.
④—Champion.
⑤—ATDC—After top dead center.
⑥—Carburetor models No. 8077S, set to 1250 RPM.
⑦—With stop screw on second highest step of fast idle cam.
⑧—Models with catalytic converter.
⑨—Early production, TDC; late production, 2° ATDC.
⑩—Except Calif., 850N RPM; California, 750N RPM.
⑪—Except Calif., 3½–5 psi.; California, 6–7½ psi.

⑫—Except Calif., 4–5½ psi.; California, 6–7½ psi.
⑬—Except Electronic Lean Burn engines.
⑭—Electronic Lean Burn engines.
⑮—Except high perform, engine, RJ13Y; high perf. engine, RJ11Y.
⑯—Except high altitude, 1500 RPM; high altitude, 1700 RPM.
⑰—Except high altitude, 1600 RPM; high altitude, 1700 RPM.
⑱—Except high altitude.
⑲—Distributor No. 3874115, 6° BTDC; distributor No. 3874858, 8° BTDC.
⑳—Except high perf., OJ13Y; high perf., OJ11Y.
㉑—Engine code E-64, 4500 lbs. vehicle curb

weight, 24° BTDC; all other 20° BTDC.
㉒—Except Cordoba, 12° BTDC; Cordoba, 16° BTDC.
㉓—Mopar.
㉔—Except Calif., 1600 RPM; California, 1800 RPM.
㉕—Except Calif., 10° BTDC; California, 8° BTDC.
㉖—Aspen.
㉗—Monaco.
㉘—High altitude.
㉙—Except high perf., 5–7 psi.; high perf., 6–7½ psi.
㉚—Carburetor No. 9109S, 1400 RPM; carburetor No. 9112S, 1200 RPM.
㉛—Volare.
㉜—Fury.

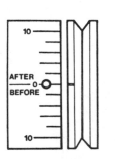

Fig. A

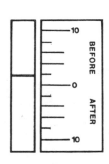

Fig. B

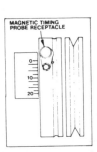

Fig. C

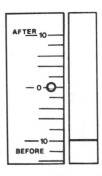

Fig. D

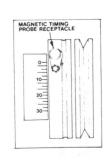

Fig. E

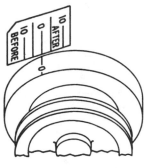

Fig. F

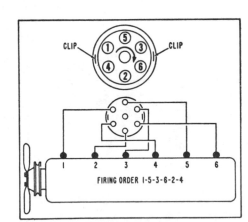

Fig. G

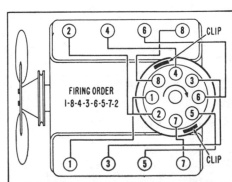

Fig. H

Continued

TUNE UP SPECIFICATIONS—Continued

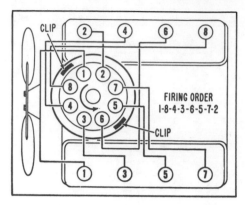

Fig. J

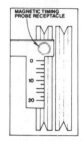

Fig. K

COOLING SYSTEM & CAPACITY DATA

Year	Model or Engine	Cooling Capacity, Qts, Less A/C	Cooling Capacity, Qts, With A/C	Radiator Cap Relief Pressure, Lbs.	Thermo. Opening Temp.	Fuel Tank Gals.	Engine Oil Refill Qts. ①	Transmission Oil 3 Speed Pints	Transmission Oil 4 Speed Pints	Transmission Oil Auto. Trans. Qts. ②	Rear Axle Oil Pints
CHRYSLER											
1975	V8-318	16½	18½	16	195	25½	4	—	—	8½⑥	4½
	V8-360	16	16	16	195	⑤	4	—	—	9½	4½
	V8-400	16½	16½	16	195	㉕	4	—	—	9½	4½
	V8-440	16	16	16	195	26½⑬	4⑭	—	—	9½	4½
1976	V8-318	16	18	16	195	⑤	4	—	—	9½	4½
	V8-360	16	16	16	195	⑤	4⑭	—	—	⑯	4½
	V8-400	16½	16½	16	195	⑤	4⑭	—	—	⑯	4½
	V8-440	16	16	16	195	⑤	4⑭	—	—	⑯	4½
1977	V8-318	16½	18	16	195	⑤	4	—	—	8½	4½
	V8-360	16	16	16	195	⑤	4	—	—	8½③	4½
	V8-400	16½	16½	16	195	⑤	4	—	—	8¼	4¼
	V8-440	16	16	16	195	⑤	4	—	—	8¼	4½
1978	6-225	12	14	16	195	19½	4	—	—	8½	2
	V8-318	16	17½	16	195	⑪	4	—	—	8½	4½
	V8-360	16	16	16	195	⑪	4	—	—	8¼	4½
	V8-400	16½	16½	16	195	⑪	4	—	—	8¼	4½
	V8-440	16½	16½	16	195	⑪	4	—	—	8¼	4½
1979	6-225	11.5	㉑	16	195	⑫	4	—	7	8½	⑳
	V8-318	15	㉒	16	195	⑲	4	—	7	8½	⑳
	V8-360	㉓	㉓	16	195	⑲	4	—	7	8½	⑳
1980	LeBaron 6-225	11½	12½	16	195	18	4	—	—	8.15	④
	LeBaron V8-318	15	15½	16	195	18	4	—	—	8.15	④
	Cordoba 6-225	11½	12½	16	195	21	4	—	—	8.15	4½
	Cordoba V8-318	15	15½	16	195	21	4	—	—	8.15	4½
	Cordoba V8-360	14	14	16	195	21	4	—	—	8.15	4½
	Newport, New Yorker 6-225	11½	14½	16	195	21	4	—	—	8.15	4½
	Newport, New Yorker V8-318	15	17½	16	195	21	4	—	—	8.15	4½
	Newport, New Yorker V8-360	16	16	16	195	21	4	—	—	8.15	4½
IMPERIAL											
1975	All	16	16	16	195	26½	4	—	—	9½	4½

Continued

COOLING SYSTEM & CAPACITY DATA—Continued

Year	Model or Engine	Cooling Capacity, Qts.		Radiator Cap Relief Pressure, Lbs.	Thermo. Opening Temp.	Fuel Tank Gals.	Engine Oil Refill Qts. ①	Transmission Oil			Rear Axle Oil Pints
		Less A/C	With A/C					3 Speed Pints	4 Speed Pints	Auto. Trans. Qts. ②	

DODGE

Year	Model or Engine	Less A/C	With A/C	Radiator Cap	Thermo.	Fuel Tank	Engine Oil	3 Speed	4 Speed	Auto. Trans.	Rear Axle
1975	Dart 6-225	13	14	16	195	16	4	3½	—	8½	2.1
	Dart 8-318	16	17½	16	195	16	4	4¾	7	8½⑥	4½
	Dart 8-360	16	16	16	195	16	4	4¾		8¼	4½
	Coronet 6-225	13	—	16	195	25½	4	4¾	—	8½	4½
	Coro., Charger 8-318	16½	18	16	195	25½⑨	4	4¾	—	8½⑥	4½
	Coro., Charger 8-360	16	16	16	195	25½⑨	4	—	—	9½	4½
	Coro., Charger 8-400	16	16	16	195	25½⑨	4	—	—	9½	4½
	Coronet 8-440	16	16	16	195	25½⑨	4⑭	—	—	8¼	4½
	Monaco 8-318	17½	17½	16	195	26½⑬	4	—	—	8½⑥	4½
	Monaco 8-360	16	16	16	195	26½⑬	4	—	—	9½	4½
	Monaco 8-400	16½	16½	16	195	26½⑬	4	—	—	9½	4½
	Monaco 8-440	16	16	16	195	26½⑬	4⑭	—	—	9½	4½
1976	Aspen, Dart 6-225	13	14	16	195	㉔	4	⑮	7	8½	4
	Aspen, Dart 8-318	16	17	16	195	㉔	4	4¾	7	8½	4
	Aspen 8-360	16	16	16	195	㉔	4	4¾	7	8½	4
	Charger, Coronet 6-225	13	14½	16	195	25½⑨	4	4¾	—	8½	4½
	Charger, Coronet 8-318	16½	18	16	195	25½⑨	4	4¾	—	8½	4½
	Charger, Coronet 8-360	16	16	16	195	25½⑨	4	4¾	—	8½	4½
	Charger, Coronet 8-400	16½	16½	16	195	25½⑨	4	4¾	—	⑯	4½
	Coronet 8-440	16	16	16	195	25½⑨	4	4¾	—	⑯	4½
	Monaco 8-318	17½	17½	16	195	26½⑬	4	—	—	9½	4½
	Monaco 8-360	16	16	16	195	26½⑬	4	—	—	9½	4½
	Monaco 8-400	16½⑰	16½⑰	16	195	26½⑬	4⑭	—	—	⑯	4½
	Monaco 8-440	16⑰	16⑰	16	195	26½⑬	4⑭	—	—	⑯	4½
1977	Aspen 6-225	12	14	16	195	18⑦	4	4¾	7	8½	2
	Aspen 8-318	16	17½	16	195	20	4	4¾	7	8½	4½
	Aspen 8-360	16	17½	16	195	20	4	—	—	8½	4½
	Charger 8-318	16½	18	16	195	25½	4	—	—	8½	4½
	Charger 8-360	16	16	16	195	25½	4	—	—	8½③	4½
	Charger 8-400	16½	16½	16	195	25½	4	—	—	8¼	4½
	Monaco 6-225	13	14½	16	195	25½⑦	4	4¾	—	8½	4½
	Monaco 8-318	16½	18	16	195	25½⑦	4	4¾	—	8½	4½
	Monaco 8-360	16	16	16	195	25½⑦	4	—	—	8½③	4½
	Monaco 8-400	16½	16½	16	195	25½⑦	4	—	—	8¼	4½
	Monaco 8-440	16	16	16	195	20½	4	—	—	8½	4½
	Royal Monaco 8-318	17½	17½	16	195	20½	4	—	—	8½③	4½
	Royal Monaco 8-360	16	16	16	195	26½⑬	4	—	—	8½③	4½
	Royal Monaco 8-400	16½	16½	16	195	26½⑬	4	—	—	8½③	4½
	Royal Monaco 8-440	16	16	16	195	20½	4	—	—	8½③	4½

Continued

COOLING SYSTEM & CAPACITY DATA—Continued

Year	Model or Engine	Cooling Capacity, Qts, Less A/C	Cooling Capacity, Qts, With A/C	Radiator Cap Relief Pressure, Lbs.	Thermo. Opening Temp.	Fuel Tank Gals.	Engine Oil Refill Qts. ①	Transmission Oil 3 Speed Pints	Transmission Oil 4 Speed Pints	Transmission Oil Auto. Trans. Qts. ②	Rear Axle Oil Pints
DODGE—Continued											
1978	Diplomat	16	17½	16	195	19½	4	—	—	8½	4½
	Aspen 6-225	12	14	16	195	⑩	4	4¾	7	8½	2
	Aspen V8-318	16	17½	16	195	⑩	4	4¾	7	8½	2
	Aspen V8-360	16	16	16	195	⑩	4	4¾	7	8½	4½
	Charger V8-318	16½	18	16	195	25½	4	—	—	8½	4½
	Charger V8-360	16	16	16	195	25½	4	—	—	8¼	4½
	Charger V8-400	16½	16½	16	195	25½	4	—	—	8¼	4½
	Diplomat 6-225	12	14	16	195	19½	4	—	7	8½	2
	Diplomat V8-318	16	17½	16	195	19½	4	—	7	8½	2
	Diplomat V8-360	16	16	16	195	19½	4	—	7	8½	4½
	Monaco 6-225	13	14½	16	195	20½	4	4¾	—	8½	4½
	Monaco V8-318	16½	18	16	195	25½⑦	4	4¾	—	8½	4½
	Monaco V8-360	16	16	16	195	25½⑦	4	4¾	—	8½	4½
	Monaco V8-400	16½	16½	16	195	25½⑦	4	4¾	—	8¼	4½
1979	Aspen 6-225	11.5	12.5	16	195	⑩	4	4.8	7	8½	④
	Aspen V8-318	15	16.5	16	195	19.5	4	4.8	7	8½	④
	Aspen V8-360	15	15	16	195	19.5	4	4.8	7	8½	④
	Diplomat 6-225	12.5	12.5	16	195	⑩	4	—	7	8½	④
	Diplomat V8-318	15	16.5	16	195	19.5	4	—	7	8½	④
	Diplomat V8-360	15	15	16	195	19.5	4	—	7	8½	④
	Magnum XE V8-318	15	17.5	16	195	21	4	—	—	8½	4.5
	Magnum XE V8-360	16	16	16	195	21	4	—	—	8½	4.5
	St. Regis 6-225	11.5	14.5	16	195	21	4	—	—	8½	4.5
	St. Regis V8-318	15	17.5	16	195	21	4	—	—	8½	4.5
	St. Regis V8-360	16	16	16	195	21	4	—	—	8½	4.5
1980	Aspen, Diplomat 6-225	11½	12½	16	195	18	4	4¾	—	8.15	④
	Aspen, Diplomat V8-318	15	15½	16	195	18	4	—	—	8.15	④
	Aspen V8-360	14	14	16	195	18	4	—	—	8.15	④
	Mirada 6-225	11½	12½	16	195	21	4	—	—	8.15	4½
	Mirada V8-318	15	15½	16	195	21	4	—	—	8.15	4½
	Mirada V8-360	14	14	16	195	21	4	—	—	8.15	4½
	St. Regis 6-225	11½	14½	16	195	21	4	—	—	8.15	4½
	St. Regis V8-318	15	17½	16	195	21	4	—	—	8.15	4½
	St. Regis V8-360	16	16	16	195	21	4	—	—	8.15	4½

Continued

COOLING SYSTEM & CAPACITY DATA—Continued

Year	Model or Engine	Cooling Capacity, Qts,		Radiator Cap Relief Pressure, Lbs.	Thermo. Opening Temp.	Fuel Tank Gals.	Engine Oil Refill Qts. ①	Transmission Oil			Rear Axle Oil Pints
		Less A/C	With A/C					3 Speed Pints	4 Speed Pints	Auto. Trans. Qts. ②	
PLYMOUTH											
1975	Fury 6-225	13	—	16	195	25½	4	4¾	—	8½	4½
	Fury 8-318	16½	18	16	195	25½⑨	4	4¾	—	⑧	4½
	Fury 8-360	16	16	16	195	25½⑨	4	—	—	9½	4½
	Fury 8-400	16½	16½	16	195	25½⑨	4	—	—	9½	4½
	Fury 8-440	16	16	16	195	25½⑨	4⑭	—	—	8¼	4½
	Gran Fury 8-318	17½	17½	16	195	26½⑬	4	—	—	⑥	4½
	Gran Fury 8-360	16	16	16	195	26½⑬	4	—	—	9½	4½
	Gran Fury 8-400	16½	16½	16	195	26½⑬	4	—	—	9½	4½
	Gran Fury 8-440	16	16	16	195	26½⑬	4⑭	—	—	9½	4½
1976	Fury 6-225	13	14½	16	195	25½⑨	4	4¾	—	8½	4½
	Fury 8-318	16½	18	16	195	25½⑨	4	4¾	—	8½	4½
	Fury 8-360	16	16	16	195	25½⑨	4	4¾	—	8½	4½
	Fury 8-400	16½	16½	16	195	25½⑨	4	4¾	—	⑯	4½
	Fury 8-440	16	16	16	195	25½⑨	4	4¾	—	⑯	4½
	Gran Fury 8-318	17½	17½	16	195	19½⑨	4	—	—	9½	4½
	Gran Fury 8-360	16	16	16	195	26½⑬	4	—	—	9½	4½
	Gran Fury 8-400	16½⑰	16½⑰	16	195	26½⑬	4	—	—	⑯	4½
	Gran Fury 8-440	16⑰	16⑰	16	195	26½⑬	4	—	—	⑯	4½
1977	Fury 6-225	13	14½	16	195	25½⑦	4	4¾	—	8½	4½
	Fury 8-318	16½	18	16	195	25½⑦	4	4¾	—	8½	4½
	Fury 8-360	16	16	16	195	25½⑦	4	—	—	8½	4½
	Fury 8-400	16½	16½	16	195	25½⑦	4	—	—	8¼	4½
	Fury 8-440	16	16	16	195	20½	4	—	—	8½	4½
	Gran Fury 8-318	17½	17½	16	195	20½	4	—	—	8½③	4½
	Gran Fury 8-360	16	16	16	195	26½⑬	4	—	—	8½③	4½
	Gran Fury 8-400	16½	16½	16	195	26½⑬	4	—	—	8½③	4½
	Gran Fury 8-440	16	16	16	195	26½⑬	4	—	—	8½③	4½
1978	Fury 6-225	13	14½	16	195	25½⑦	4	4¾	—	8½	4½
	Fury V8-318	16½	18	16	195	25½⑦	4	4¾	—	8½	4½
	Fury V8-360	16	16	16	195	25½⑦	4	4¾	—	8½	4½
	Fury V8-400	16½	16½	16	195	25½⑦	4	4¾	—	8¼	4½
1980	Gran Fury 6-225	11½	14½	16	195	21	4	—	—	8.15	4½
	Gran Fury V8-318	15	17½	16	195	21	4	—	—	8.15	4½
	Gran Fury V8-360	16	16	16	195	21	4	—	—	8.15	4½

Continued

COOLING SYSTEM & CAPACITY DATA—Continued

Year	Model or Engine	Cooling Capacity, Qts,		Radiator Cap Relief Pressure, Lbs.	Thermo. Opening Temp.	Fuel Tank Gals.	Engine Oil Refill Qts. ①	Transmission Oil			Rear Axle Oil Pints
		Less A/C	With A/C					3 Speed Pints	4 Speed Pints	Auto. Trans. Qts. ②	
VALIANT & VOLARÉ											
1975	Valiant 6-225	13	14	16	195	16	4	3½	—	8½	2.1
	Valiant V8-318	16	17½	16	195	16	4	4¾	7	8½⑥	4½
	Valiant V8-360	16	16	16	195	16	4	—	—	8¼	4½
1976	Valiant, Volaré 6-225	13	14	16	195	⑱	4	⑮	7	8½	2
	Valiant, Volaré V8-318	16	17	16	195	⑱	4	4¾	7	8½	4½
	Valiant, Volaré V8-360	16	16	16	195	⑱	4	4¾	7	8½	4½
1977	Volaré 6-225	12	14	16	195	18⑦	4	4¾	7	8½	2
	Volaré 8-318	16	17½	16	195	20	4	4¾	7	8½	4½
	Volaré 8-360	16	17½	16	195	20	4	—	—	8½	4½
1978	Volaré 6-225	12	14	16	195	⑩	4	4¾	7	8½	2
	Volaré V8-318	16	17½	16	195	⑩	4	4¾	7	8½	2
	Volaré V8-360	16	16	16	195	⑩	4	4¾	7	8½	4½
1979	Volaré 6-255	12.5	12.5	16	195	⑩	4	4.8	7	8½	④
	Volaré V8-318	15	16.5	16	195	19.5	4	—	—	8½	④
	Volaré V8-360	15	15	16	195	19.5	4	—	—	8½	④
1980	Volaré 6-225	11½	12½	16	195	18	4	4¾	—	8.15	④
	Volaré V8-318	15	15½	16	195	18	4	—	—	8.15	④
	Volaré V8-360	14	14	16	195	18	4	—	—	8.15	④

①—Add one qt. with filter change.
②—Approximate. Make final check with dipstick.
③—With A-727 transmission (heavy duty), 8¼ qts.
④—With 7¼ inch ring gear, 2 pts.; 8¼ inch ring gear, 4½ pts.
⑤—Cordoba 25½ gals.; Chrysler 26½ gals.; Wagon 24 gals.
⑥—With 727 transmission (heavy duty), 9½ qts.
⑦—Wagons, 20 gals.
⑧—With 727 transmission (heavy duty), 9½ qts.; Roadrunner models 8¼ qts.

⑨—Wagon 20 gals., Sedan Models with dual exhaust 20½ gals.
⑩—6 cyl. exc. Station Wag. 18 gal.; 8 cyl. & Station Wag., 19½ gals.
⑪—LeBaron, 19½; Cordoba, 25½; Chrysler, 26½.
⑫—Exc. LeBaron, 21 gal.; LeBaron exc. Wag, 18 gal.; LeBaron Wagon, 19½ gals.
⑬—Wagons, 24 gals.
⑭—High performance engine, 5 qts.
⑮—Exc. floor shift, 3.6 pts.; floor shift, 4¾ pts.
⑯—Exc. High Perf., 9½ qts.; High Perf., 8¼ qts.
⑰—Add one qt. with maximum cooling or trailer

towing package.
⑱—Volaré, 18 gal.; Valiant, 16 gals.
⑲—Exc. LeBaron, 21 gals.; LeBaron, 19.5 gals.
⑳—Exc. LeBaron, 4½ pts.; LeBaron, 7¼ inch ring gear, 2 pts.; 8¼ & 9¼ inch ring gear, 4½ pts.
㉑—Exc. LeBaron, 14.5 qts.; LeBaron, 12.5 qts.
㉒—Exc. LeBaron, 17.5 qts.; LeBaron, 16.5 qts.
㉓—Exc. LeBaron, 16 qts.; LeBaron, 15 qts.
㉔—Aspen, 16 gals.; Dart, 16 gals.
㉕—Chrysler exc. Wag., 26½ gals.; Wagon, 24 gals.; Cordoba exc. dual exhaust, 25½ gals.; dual exhaust, 20.5 gals.

DODGE OMNI • PLYMOUTH HORIZON

GENERAL ENGINE SPECIFICATIONS

Year	Engine	Carburetor	Bore and Stroke Inch (Millimeters)	Piston Displacement, Cubic Inches	Compression Ratio	Maximum Brake H.P. @ R.P.M.	Maximum Torque Ft. Lbs. @ R.P.M.	Normal Oil Pressure Pounds @ 2000 RPM
1978	4-105 70 Horsepower①②........ 1700cc	2 Barrel	3.13 × 3.40 (79.5 × 86.4)	105 1.7 ltr.	8.2	70 @ 5600 —	85 @ 3200	60–90
	75 Horsepower①③........ 4-105 1700cc	2 Barrel	3.13 × 3.40 (79.5 × 86.4)	105 1.7 ltr.	8.2	75 @ 5600 —	90 @ 3200	60–90
1979	4-105 65 Horsepower①②........ 1700cc	2 Barrel	3.13 × 3.40 (79.5 × 86.4)	105 1.7 ltr.	8.2	65 @ 5200	85 @ 2800	60–90
	70 Horsepower①③........ 4-105 1700cc	2 Barrel	3.13 × 3.40 (79.5 × 86.4)	105 1.7 ltr.	8.2	70 @ 5200	85 @ 2800	60–90
1980	4-105 65 Horsepower①②........ 1700cc	2 Barrel	3.13 × 3.40 (79.5 × 86.4)	105 1.7 ltr.	8.2	65 @ 5200	85 @ 2400	60–90
	65 Horsepower①③........ 4-105 1700cc	2 Barrel	3.13 × 3.40 (79.5 × 86.4)	105 1.7 ltr.	8.2	65 @ 5200	85 @ 2400	60–90

①—Ratings are net—as installed in vehicle.   ②—California & high altitude.   ③—Except California & high altitude.

TUNE UP SPECIFICATIONS

The following specifications are published from the latest information available. This data should be used only in the absence of a decal affixed in the engine compartment.

▲ Before removing wires from distributor cap, determine location of the No. 1 wire in cap, as distributor position may have been altered from that shown at the end of this chart.

● When checking compression, lowest cylinder must be within 25 PSI of the highest.

Year & Engine	Spark Plug		Ignition Timing BTDC①★				Curb Idle Speed		Fast Idle Speed		Fuel Pump Pressure
	Type	Gap Inch	Firing Order Fig. ▲	Man. Trans.	Auto. Trans.	Mark Fig.	Man. Trans.	Auto. Trans.	Man. Trans.	Auto. Trans.	
1978											
4-105 Man. Trans.	RN12Y	.035	A	15°	—	B	900	—	1100	—	4–6
4-105 Auto. Trans.	RN12Y	.035	A	—	15°	C	—	900	—	1100	4–6
1979											
4-105 Man. Trans.	RN12Y	.035	A	15°	—	B	900	—	1400	—	4–6
4-105 Auto. Trans.	RN12Y	.035	A	—	15°	C	—	900	—	1700	4–6
1980											
4-105 Man. Trans.②	RN12Y	.035	A	12°	—	B	900	1400	1400	—	4–6
4-105 Man. Trans.③	RN12Y	.035	A	10°	—	B	900	—	1400	—	4–6
4-105 Auto. Trans.②	RN12Y	.035	A	—	12°	C	—	900	—	1700	4–6
4-105 Auto. Trans.③	RN12Y	.035	A	—	10°	C	—	900	—	1700	4–6

①—BTDC-Before top dead center.   ②—Exc. California   ③—California

Continued

DODGE OMNI • PLYMOUTH HORIZON

TUNE UP NOTES—Continued

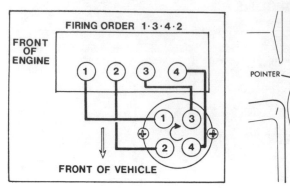

Fig. A

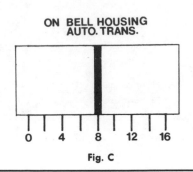

Fig. B

Fig. C

COOLING SYSTEM & CAPACITY DATA

Year	Model or Engine	Cooling Capacity		Radiator Cap Relief Pressure, Lbs.	Thermo. Opening Temp. Degrees F. (Centigrade)	Fuel Tank Gals. (Litres)	Engine Oil Refill Qts. (Litres)	Transmission Oil		Final Drive Pints (Litres) ②
		Less A/C Qts. (Litres)	With A/C Qts. (Litres)					4 Speed Pints (Litres)	Auto. Trans. Qts. (Litres) ①	
1978	All	6.5 (6.2)	6.5 (6.2)	16	195 (90.6)	13 (49)	4 (3.8)	2.8 (1.25)	7.3③ (6.8)	2.4 (1.1)
1979–80	All	6.0 (5.6)	6.0 (5.6)	16	195 (90.6)	13 (49)	4 (3.8)	2.8 (1.25)	7.3③ (6.8)	2.4 (1.1)

①—Approximate. Make final check with dipstick. ②—Automatic trans. only. ③—Drain and refill, 2.5 qts.

ENGINE & SERIAL
NUMBER LOCATION

Plate On Left Front Door Pillar

ENGINE IDENTIFICATION

★Serial number on Vehicle Warranty Plate
Engine code for 1975–80 is the last letter in the serial number.

Year	Engine	Engine Code★
1975–76	V8-351M②	Q
	V8-400	S
	V8-460	A
1977–78	V8-302	F
	V8-351W①	H
	V8-351M②	Q
	V8-400	S
	V8-460	A
1979–80	V8-302	F
	V8-351W①	H

①—Windsor engine.
②—Modified engine.

GENERAL ENGINE SPECIFICATIONS

Year	Engine	Carburetor	Bore and Stroke	Piston Displacement, Cubic Inches	Compression Ratio	Maximum Brake H.P. @ R.P.M.	Maximum Torque Ft. Lbs. @ R.P.M.	Normal Oil Pressure Pounds
FORD								
1975	148 Horsepower①④..... V8-351M	2 Barrel	4.00 × 3.50	351	8.0	148 @ 3800	243 @ 2400	50–75
	150 Horsepower①④..... V8-351M	2 Barrel	4.00 × 3.50	351	8.0	150 @ 3800	244 @ 2800	50–75
	158 Horsepower①........ V8-400	2 Barrel	4.00 × 4.00	400	8.0	158 @ 3800	276 @ 2000	50–75
	144 Horsepower①........ V8-400	2 Barrel	4.00 × 4.00	400	8.0	144 @ 3600	255 @ 2200	50–75
	218 Horsepower①........ V8-460	4 Barrel	4.36 × 3.85	460	8.0	218 @ 4000	369 @ 2600	40–65
1976	152 Horsepower①④..... V8-351M	2 Barrel	4.00 × 3.50	351	8.0	152 @ 3800	274 @ 1600	50–75
	180 Horsepower①........ V8-400	2 Barrel	4.00 × 4.00	400	8.0	180 @ 3800	336 @ 1800	50–75
	202 Horsepower①........ V8-460	4 Barrel	4.36 × 3.85	460	8.0	202 @ 3800	352 @ 1600	40–65
1977	135 Horsepower①........ V8-302	2 Barrel	4.00 × 3.00	302	8.4	—	—	40–65
	161 Horsepower①②④ .. V8-351M	2 Barrel	4.00 × 3.50	351	8.0	161 @ 3600	285 @ 1800	50–75
	149 Horsepower①②⑤ .. V8-351W	2 Barrel	4.00 × 3.50	351	8.3	149 @ 3200	291 @ 1600	40–65
	173 Horsepower①②...... V8-400	2 Barrel	4.00 × 4.00	400	8.0	173 @ 3800	326 @ 1600	50–75
	168 Horsepower①③...... V8-400	2 Barrel	4.00 × 4.00	400	8.0	168 @ 3800	323 @ 1600	50–75
	197 Horsepower①........ V8-460	4 Barrel	4.36 × 3.85	460	8.0	197 @ 4000	353 @ 2000	35–65
1978	134 Horsepower①........ V8-302	2 Barrel	4.00 × 3.00	302	8.4	134 @ 3400	248 @ 1600	40–65
	145 Horsepower①④..... V8-351M	2 Barrel	4.00 × 3.50	351	8.3	145 @ 3400	273 @ 1800	50–75
	144 Horsepower①⑤..... V8-351W	2 Barrel	4.00 × 3.50	351	8.0	144 @ 3200	277 @ 1600	40–65
	160 Horsepower①........ V8-400	2 Barrel	4.00 × 4.00	400	8.0	160 @ 3800	314 @ 1800	50–75
	— Horsepower①⑥ V8-460	4 Barrel	4.36 × 3.85	460	8.0	—	—	40–65
	202 Horsepower①⑦...... V8-460	4 Barrel	4.36 × 3.85	460	8.0	202 @ 4000	348 @ 2000	40–65
1979	129 Horsepower①②...... V8-302	2 Barrel	4.00 × 3.00	302	8.4	129 @ 3600	223 @ 2600	40–65
	130 Horsepower①③...... V8-302	2 Barrel	4.00 × 3.00	302	8.4	130 @ 3600	226 @ 2200	40–65
	142 Horsepower①②⑤ .. V8-351W	2 Barrel	4.00 × 3.50	351	8.3	142 @ 3200	286 @ 1400	40–65
	138 Horsepower①③⑤ .. V8-351W	2 Barrel	4.00 × 3.50	351	8.3	138 @ 3200	260 @ 2200	40–65
1980	130 Horsepower①........ V8-302	2 Barrel	4.00 × 3.00	302	8.4	130 @ 3600	230 @ 1600	40–60
	140 Horsepower①⑤..... V8-351W	2 Barrel	4.00 × 3.50	351	8.3	140 @ 3400	265 @ 2000	40–60

Continued

GENERAL ENGINE SPECIFICATIONS—Continued

Year	Engine	Carburetor	Bore and Stroke	Piston Displacement, Cubic Inches	Compression Ratio	Maximum Brake H.P. @ R.P.M.	Maximum Torque Lbs. Ft. @ R.P.M.	Normal Oil Pressure Pounds
MERCURY								
1975	148 Horsepower①④ V8-351M	2 Barrel	4.00 × 3.50	351	8.0	148 @ 3800	243 @ 2400	50–75
	150 Horsepower①④ V8-351M	2 Barrel	4.00 × 3.50	351	8.0	150 @ 3800	244 @ 2800	50–75
	144 Horsepower① V8-400	2 Barrel	4.00 × 4.00	400	8.0	144 @ 3600	255 @ 2200	50–75
	158 Horsepower① V8-400	2 Barrel	4.00 × 4.00	400	8.0	158 @ 3800	276 @ 2000	50–75
	218 Horsepower① V8-460	4 Barrel	4.36 × 3.85	460	8.0	218 @ 4000	369 @ 2600	40–65
1976	152 Horsepower①④ V8-351M	2 Barrel	4.00 × 3.50	351	8.0	152 @ 3800	274 @ 1600	50–75
	180 Horsepower① V8-400	2 Barrel	4.00 × 4.00	400	8.0	180 @ 3800	336 @ 1800	50–75
	202 Horsepower① V8-460	4 Barrel	4.36 × 3.85	460	8.0	202 @ 3800	352 @ 1600	40–65
1977	173 Horsepower①② V8-400	2 Barrel	4.00 × 4.00	400	8.0	173 @ 3800	326 @ 1600	50–75
	168 Horsepower①③ V8-400	2 Barrel	4.00 × 4.00	400	8.0	168 @ 3800	323 @ 1600	50–75
	197 Horsepower① V8-460	4 Barrel	4.36 × 3.85	460	8.0	197 @ 4000	353 @ 2000	35–65
1978	145 Horsepower①④ V8-351M	2 Barrel	4.00 × 3.50	351	8.0	145 @ 3400	273 @ 1800	50–75
	160 Horsepower① V8-400	2 Barrel	4.00 × 4.00	400	8.0	160 @ 3800	314 @ 1800	45–75
	— Horsepower①⑥ V8-460	4 Barrel	4.36 × 3.85	460	8.0	—	—	35–65
	202 Horsepower①⑦ V8-460	4 Barrel	4.36 × 3.85	460	8.0	202 @ 4000	348 @ 2000	35–65
1979	129 Horsepower①② V8-302	2 Barrel	4.00 × 3.00	302	8.4	129 @ 3600	223 @ 2600	40–65
	130 Horsepower①③ V8-302	2 Barrel	4.00 × 3.00	302	8.4	130 @ 3600	226 @ 2200	40–65
	138 Horsepower①⑤ V8-351W	2 Barrel	4.00 × 3.50	351	8.3	138 @ 3200	260 @ 2200	40–65
1980	130 Horsepower① V8-302	2 Barrel	4.00 × 3.00	302	8.4	130 @ 3600	230 @ 1600	40–60
	140 Horsepower①⑤ V8-351W	2 Barrel	4.00 × 3.50	351	8.3	140 @ 3400	265 @ 2000	40–60

① —Ratings are NET—as installed in the vehicle.
② —Exc. Calif.
③ —Calif. only.
④ —Modified engine.
⑤ —Windsor engine.
⑥ —Police Interceptor
⑦ —Exc. Police Interceptor

TUNE UP SPECIFICATIONS

The following specifications are published from the latest information available. This data should be used only in the absence of a decal affixed in the engine compartment.

★ When using a timing light, disconnect vacuum hose or tube at distributor and plug opening in tube or hose so idle speed will not be affected.

● When checking compression, lowest cylinder must be within 75% of the highest.

▲ Before removing wires from distributor cap, determine location of the No. 1 wire in cap, as distributor position may have been altered from that shown at the end of this chart.

Year & Engine	Spark Plug Type	Gap	Firing Order Fig. ▲	Ignition Timing BTDC① ★ Man. Trans.	Auto. Trans.	Mark Fig.	Curb Idle Speed② Man. Trans.	Auto. Trans.	Fast Idle Speed Man. Trans.	Auto. Trans.	Fuel Pump Pressure
1975											
V8-351M③	ARF-42	.044	A	—	14°	C	—	700D	—	1350④	5–7
V8-400	ARF-42	.044	A	—	12°	C	—	625D	—	1500④	5–7
V8-460	ARF-52	.044	B	—	14°	C	—	650D	—	1350④	5.7–7.7
1976											
V8-351M Exc. Calif.③	ARF-52	.044	A	—	12°	C	—	650D	—	1350④	6–8
V8-351M Calif.③	ARF-52	.044	A	—	8°	C	—	650D	—	1150④	6–8
V8-400 Exc. Calif.	ARF-52	.044	A	—	10°	C	—	650D	—	1350④	6–8
V8-400 Calif.	ARF-52	.044	A	—	10°	C	—	625D	—	1400④	6–8
V8-460 Exc. Calif.	ARF-52	.044	B	—	8°	C	—	650D	—	1350④	6.7–8.7
V8-460 Calif.	ARF-52	.044	B	—	14°	C	—	650D	—	1350④	6.7–8.7

Continued

TUNE UP SPECIFICATIONS—Continued

Year & Engine	Spark Plug Type	Gap	Firing Order Fig. ▲	Ignition Timing BTDC[1]★ Man. Trans.	Auto. Trans.	Mark Fig.	Curb Idle Speed[2] Man. Trans.	Auto. Trans.	Fast Idle Speed Man. Trans.	Auto. Trans.	Fuel Pump Pressure
1977											
V8-302	ARF-52	.050	E	—	8°	C	—	650D	—	2000[5]	6–8
V8-351W[6]	ARF-52	.050	D	—	4°	C	—	625D	—	2100[5]	6–8
V8-351M[3][7][8]	ARF-52	.050	D	—	10°	C	—	650D	—	1350[4]	6–8
V8-351M[3][7][9]	ARF-52	.050	D	—	9°	C	—	650D	—	1350[4]	6–8
V8-351M[3][7][10]	ASF-52	.050	D	—	8°	C	—	500/600D	—	1350[4]	6–8
V8-400 Exc. Calif.[7][11]	ARF-52	.050	D	—	8°	C	—	[12]	—	1350[4]	6–8
V8-400 Exc. Calif.[7][13]	ARF-52	.050	D	—	12°	C	—	600D	—	1350[4]	6–8
V8-400 Exc. Calif.[7][14]	ARF-52	.050	D	—	10°	C	—	600D	—	1350[4]	6–8
V8-400 Exc. Calif.[7][15]	ARF-52	.050	D	—	6°	C	—	600D	—	1350[4]	6–8
V8-400 Calif.	ARF-52-6	.060	D	—	6°	C	—	500/600D	—	1350[4]	6–8
V8-460 Exc. High Alt.[7][16]	ARF-52	.050	E	—	16°	C	—	525/650D	—	1350[4]	5.7–6.7
V8-460 Exc. High Alt.[7][17]	ARF-52	.050	E	—	10°	C	—	[18]	—	1350[4]	5.7–6.7
V8-460 High Alt.	ARF-52	.050	E	—	18°	C	—	500/600D	—	1350[4]	5.7–6.7
1978											
V8-302	ARF-52	.050	E	—	14°	C	—	500/600D	—	2100[5]	6–8
V8-351W[6]	ARF-52	.050	D	—	14°	C	—	600/675D[19]	—	2100[5]	6–8
V8-351M[3][7][20]	ASF-52	.050	D	—	9°	C	—	600/675D[19]	—	1350[4]	6–8
V8-351M[3][7][21]	ASF-52	.050	D	—	12°	C	—	600/675D[19]	—	1350[4]	6–8
V8-400 Exc. Calif. & High Alt.	ASF-52	.050	D	—	13°	C	—	575/650D[19]	—	1350[4]	6–8
V8-400 Calif.	ASF-52	.050	D	—	16°	C	—	600/650D[19]	—	1350[4]	6–8
V8-400 High Alt.	ASF-52	.050	D	—	8°	C	—	650D	—	2100[5]	6–8
V8-460[7][22]	ARF-52	.050	E	—	16°	C	—	580/650D[19]	—	1350[4]	5.7–7.7
V8-460[7][23]	ARF-52	.050	E	—	10°	C	—	580/650D[19]	—	1350[4]	5.7–7.7
1979											
V8-302 Exc. Calif.[7][24]	[25]	.050	E	—	8°	C	—	600/675D[19]	—	2100[5]	6–8
V8-302 Exc. Calif.[7][26]	[25]	.050	E	—	6°	C	—	550/625D[19]	—	1750[5]	6–8
V8-302 Calif.[7][27]	[28]	.060	E	—	12°	C	—	600/675D[19]	—	1800[5]	6–8
V8-302 Calif.[7][29]	[28]	.060	E	—	6°	C	—	550/625D[19]	—	1800[5]	6–8
V8-351W Exc. Calif.[6][30][31]	[25]	.050	D	—	15°	C	—	600/650D[19]	—	2100[5]	6–8
V8-351W Exc. Calif.[6][30][32]	[25]	.050	D	—	10°	C	—	600/650D[19]	—	2200[5]	6–8
V8-351W Exc. Calif.[6][33]	[25]	.050	[34]	—	[35]	C	—	550/640D[19]	—	2000[5]	6–8
V8-351W Calif.[6][33]	[25]	.050	[34]	—	[35]	C	—	620D	—	2100[5]	6–8
1980											
V8-302 Exc. Calif.[30]	ASF-52	.050	E	—	6°	C	—	500D	—	1850[4]	6–8
V8-302 Calif.[33]	ASF-52	.050	[36]	—	[35]	C	—	500/650D	—	2000[37]	6–8
V8-351W[6][33]	ASF-52	.050	[34]	—	[35]	C	—	550/640D	—	1650[37]	6–8

Continued

TUNE UP NOTES—Continued

①—B.T.D.C.—Before top dead center.
②—Idle speed on manual trans. vehicles is adjusted in Neutral & on auto. trans. equipped vehicles is adjusted in Drive unless otherwise specified. Where two idle speeds are listed, the higher speed is with the A/C or throttle solenoid energized. On models equipped with vacuum release brake, whenever adjusting ignition timing or idle speed, vacuum line to brake release mechanism must be disconnected & plugged to prevent parking brake from releasing when selector lever is moved to Drive.
③—Modified engine.
④—On kickdown step of cam.
⑤—On high step of fast idle cam.
⑥—Windsor engine.
⑦—Refer to engine calibration code on engine identification label located at rear of left valve cover. The calibration code is located on the label after the engine code number and preceded by the letter C and the revision code is located below the calibration code and is preceded by the letter R.

⑧—Calibration code 7-14B-R1.
⑨—Calibration codes 7-14B-R10 & 7-14C-R11.
⑩—Calibration code 7-34B-R0.
⑪—Calibration codes 7-17B-R1 & 7-37A-R0.
⑫—Calibration code 7-17B-R1, 600D RPM; 7-37A-R0, 500/650D RPM.
⑬—Calibration code 7-17B-R15.
⑭—Calibration code 7-17B-R16.
⑮—Calibration codes 7-17C-R1 & 7-17C-R11.
⑯—Calibration codes 7-19A-R1 & 7-19A-R17.
⑰—Calibration codes 7-19A-R2 & 7-19A-R3.
⑱—Calibration codes 7-19A-R2, 525/650D RPM; 7-19A-R3, 550/650D RPM.
⑲—With throttle solenoid energized. Higher idle speed is with A/C on, compressor clutch de-energized, if equipped.
⑳—Calibration code 8-14B-R0.
㉑—Calibration codes 8-14B-R13 & 8-14B-R22.
㉒—Calibration code 8-19A-R1.
㉓—Calibration codes 8-19C-R11 & 8-19C-R14.
㉔—Calibration codes 9-11B-R0, 9-11C-R1A, 9-11C-R1N & 9-11J-R0.
㉕—ASF-52 or ARF-52.
㉖—Calibration codes 9-11E-R1 & 9-11F-R1.

㉗—Calibration codes 9-11N-R0, 9-11R-R0, 9-11S-R0 & 9-11V.
㉘—ASF-52-6 or ARF-52-6.
㉙—Calibration code 9-11Q-R0.
㉚—Models less Electronic Engine Control (EEC) System.
㉛—Models less variable venturi carburetor.
㉜—Models with variable venturi carburetor.
㉝—Models with Electronic Engine Control (EEC) System.
㉞—Firing order, 1-3-7-2-6-5-4-8. Cylinder numbering (front to rear): Right bank 1-2-3-4, left bank 5-6-7-8. Refer to Fig. F for spark plug wire connections at distributor.
㉟—Engine cranking reference timing 10 BTDC. Ignition timing is not adjustable.
㊱—Firing order, 1-5-4-2-6-3-7-8. Cylinder numbering (front to rear): Right bank 1-2-3-4, left bank 5-6-7-8. Refer to Fig. F for spark plug wire connections at distributor.
㊲—On 2nd highest step of fast idle cam.

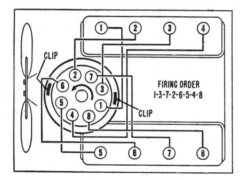

Fig. A

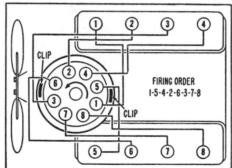

Fig. B

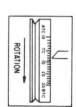

Fig. C

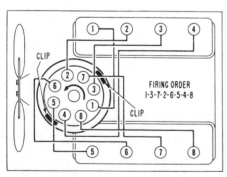

Fig. D

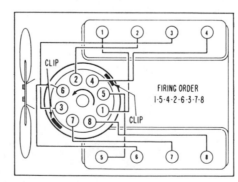

Fig. E

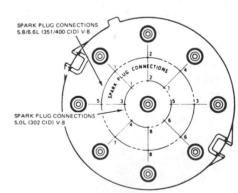

Fig. F

COOLING SYSTEM & CAPACITY DATA

Year	Model or Engine	Cooling Capacity, Qts. Less A/C	Cooling Capacity, Qts. With A/C	Radiator Cap Relief Pressure, Lbs.	Thermo. Opening Temp.	Fuel Tank Gals.	Engine Oil Refill Qts. ①	Transmission Oil 3 Speed Pints	Transmission Oil 4 Speed Pints	Transmission Oil Auto. Trans. Qts. ②	Rear Axle Oil Pints
FORD											
1975	V8-351	17.1	17.6	13–19	191	24.2④	4	—	—	⑬	⑤
	V8-400	17.1	17.6	13–19	191	24.2④	4	—	—	⑬	⑤
	V8-460	18.5	18.5⑮	13–19	191	24.2④	4⑫	—	—	⑬	⑤
1976	V8-351	17.1	17.6	13–19	191	24.2④	4	—	—	⑬	⑤
	V8-400	17.1	17.6	13–19	191	24.2④	4	—	—	⑬	⑤
	V8-460	18.5	18.5⑮	13–19	191	24.2④	4⑫	—	—	12¼	⑤
1977	V8-351	17.1	17.2	13–19	191	24.2④	4	—	—	⑬	⑤
	V8-400	17.1	17.2	13–19	191	24.2④	4	—	—	⑬	⑤
	V8-460	18.5	18.5	13–19	191	24.2④	4	—	—	⑬	⑤
	V8-460	19.0	19.0	13–19	191	24.2④	6	—	—	⑬	⑤
1978	V8-302	14.7	15.2	14–18	191	24.2⑭	4	—	—	10	⑥
	V8-351⑨	15.9	16.3	14–18	191	24.2⑭	4	—	—	11	⑥
	V8-351⑩	17.0	17.0	14–18	191	24.2⑭	4	—	—	11	⑥
	V8-400	17.0	17.0	14–18	191	24.2⑭	4	—	—	11	⑥
	V8-460③	19.7	19.7	14–18	191	24.2⑭	6	—	—	12½	⑥
	V8-460⑦	18.6	18.6	14–18	191	24.2⑭	4	—	—	12½	⑥
1979	V8-302	13.3⑧	13.8⑧	16	196	19⑯	4	—	—	11.8	⑰
	V8-351W⑨	14.6⑪	15.2⑪	16	196	19⑯	4	—	—	11.0	⑰
1980	V8-302	13.3	13.4	16	196	19⑯	4	—	—	⑱	⑲
	V8-351W⑨	14.4	14.5	16	196	19⑯	4	—	—	⑱	⑲
MERCURY											
1975	V8-351	17.1	17.6	13–19	191	24.2④	4	—	—	⑬	⑤
	V8-400	17.1	17.6	13–19	191	24.2④	4	—	—	⑬	⑤
	V8-460	18.5	18.5⑮	13–19	191	24.2④	4⑫	—	—	⑬	⑤
1976	V8-351	17.1	17.6	13–19	191	24.2④	4	—	—	⑬	⑤
	V8-400	17.1	17.6	13–19	191	24.2④	4	—	—	⑬	⑤
	V8-460	18.5	18.5⑮	13–19	191	24.2④	4⑫	—	—	12¼	⑤
1977	V8-400	17.1	17.2	13–19	191	24.2⑥	4	—	—	⑬	⑤
	V8-460	18.5	18.5	13–19	191	24.2④	4	—	—	⑬	⑤
	V8-460	19.0	19.0	13–19	191	24.2④	6	—	—	⑬	⑤
1978	V8-351	16.3	17.0	14–18	191	24.2⑭	4	—	—	⑬	⑥
	V8-400	17.0	17.5	14–18	191	24.2⑭	4	—	—	11	⑥
	V8-460③	19.7	19.7	14–18	191	24.2⑭	6	—	—	12½	⑥
	V8-460⑦	18.6	18.6	14–18	191	24.2⑭	4	—	—	12½	⑥
1979	V8-302	13.3⑧	13.8⑧	16	196	19⑯	4	—	—	11.8	⑰
	V8-351W⑨	14.6⑪	15.2⑪	16	196	19⑯	4	—	—	11.0	⑰
1980	V8-302	13.3	13.4	16	196	19⑯	4	—	—	⑱	⑲
	V8-351W⑨	14.4	14.5	16	196	19⑯	4	—	—	⑱	⑲

① —Add one quart with filter change.
② —Approximate. Make final check with dipstick.
③ —Police models.
④ —Station wagons 21 gals. Add 8 gals. with auxiliary tank.
⑤ —WER axles 4, all others 5.
⑥ —Exc. models with 460 engine, locking or optional axles, 4 pts.; Models with 460 engine, locking or optional axles, 5 pts.
⑦ —Exc. police models.
⑧ —Police, 14.2.
⑨ —Windsor engine.
⑩ —Modified engine.
⑪ —Police, Trailer tow, 15.6.
⑫ —Police Models 6½ qts.
⑬ —FMX 11 qts., C6 12¼ qts. C4 10¼ qts.
⑭ —Station wagons, 21 gals.
⑮ —Medium duty 19 qts., Heavy duty and Police 20 qts.
⑯ —Station wagon, 20 gal.
⑰ —Axle code WGZ, 4 pts.; Axle code WGY, 3.5 pts.
⑱ —C4, 9½ qts.; FMX, 11 qts.; Overdrive auto. trans., 12 qts.
⑲ —7½" ring gear, 3½ pts.; 8½" ring gear, 4 pts.

ENGINE & SERIAL NUMBER LOCATION:

Vehicle warranty plate on rear face of left front door.

ENGINE IDENTIFICATION:

Engine code is last letter in serial number on vehicle warranty plate.

Year	Engine	Engine Code
1975–77	6-200	T
	6-250	L
	8-302	F
	8-351	H
	8-400	S
	8-460	A
	8-460①	C
1978	8-400	S

Year	Engine	Engine Code
1978–80	4-140	Y
	6-200	T
	6-250	L
	8-302	F
	8-351	H
1980	4-140②	W

①—Police Interceptor.
②—Turbo charged engine.

GENERAL ENGINE SPECIFICATIONS

Year	Engine	Carburetor	Bore and Stroke	Piston Displacement, Cubic Inches	Compression Ratio	Maximum Brake H.P. @ R.P.M.	Maximum Torque Lbs. Ft. @ R.P.M.	Normal Oil Pressure Pounds
1975	70 Horsepower②........6-200	1 Barrel	3.68 × 3.13	200	8.3	—	—	30–50
	70 Horsepower②⑤.......6-250	1 Barrel	3.68 × 3.91	250	8.0	70 @ 2800	175 @ 1400	40–60
	72 Horsepower②④.......6-250	1 Barrel	3.68 × 3.91	250	8.0	72 @ 2900	180 @ 1400	40–60
	122 Horsepower②⑥.....V8-302	2 Barrel	4.00 × 3.00	302	8.0	122 @ 3800⑥	208 @ 1800⑦	40–60
	129 Horsepower②⑧.....V8-302	2 Barrel	4.00 × 3.00	302	8.0	129 @ 3800⑧	220 @ 1800⑨	40–60
	148 Horsepower②④⑱...V8-351	2 Barrel	4.00 × 3.50	351	8.0	148 @ 3800	243 @ 2400	50–75
	150 Horsepower②⑤⑱...V8-351	2 Barrel	4.00 × 3.50	351	8.0	150 @ 3800	244 @ 2800	50–75
	143 Horsepower②⑩㉑...V8-351	2 Barrel	4.00 × 3.50	351	8.1	143 @ 3600⑩	255 @ 2200⑪	40–65
	154 Horsepower②⑫㉑...V8-351	2 Barrel	4.00 × 3.50	351	8.1	154 @ 3800⑫	268 @ 2200	40–65
	144 Horsepower②⑤.....V8-400	2 Barrel	4.00 × 4.00	400	8.0	144 @ 3600	255 @ 2200	50–65
	158 Horsepower②④.....V8-400	2 Barrel	4.00 × 4.00	400	8.0	158 @ 4000	276 @ 2000	50–65
	216 Horsepower②④.....V8-460	4 Barrel	4.36 × 3.85	460	8.0	216 @ 4000	366 @ 2600	40–65
	217 Horsepower②⑤.....V8-460	4 Barrel	4.36 × 3.85	460	8.0	217 @ 4000	365 @ 2600	40–65
1976	78 Horsepower②④⑬.....6-200	1 Barrel	3.68 × 3.13	200	8.3	78 @ 3300	152 @ 1600	30–50
	81 Horsepower②④⑭.....6-200	1 Barrel	3.68 × 3.13	200	8.3	81 @ 3400	151 @ 1700	30–50
	76 Horsepower②⑤⑬⑮...6-250	1 Barrel	3.68 × 3.91	250	8.0	76 @ 3000	179 @ 1300	40–60
	78 Horsepower②④⑬⑮...6-250	1 Barrel	3.68 × 3.91	250	8.0	78 @ 3000	187 @ 1200	40–60
	78 Horsepower②⑤⑬⑰...6-250	1 Barrel	3.68 × 3.91	250	8.0	78 @ 3000	183 @ 1400	40–60
	81 Horsepower②④⑬⑰...6-250	1 Barrel	3.68 × 3.91	250	8.0	81 @ 3000	192 @ 1200	40–60
	87 Horsepower②④⑭⑮...6-250	1 Barrel	3.68 × 3.91	250	8.0	87 @ 3000	187 @ 1900	40–60
	90 Horsepower②④⑭⑰...6-250	1 Barrel	3.68 × 3.91	250	8.0	90 @ 3000	190 @ 2000	40–60
	130 Horsepower②⑤⑬⑮..V8-302	2 Barrel	4.00 × 3.00	302	8.0	130 @ 3600	238 @ 1600	40–60
	133 Horsepower②④⑬⑮..V8-302	2 Barrel	4.00 × 3.00	302	8.0	133 @ 3600	243 @ 1800	40–60
	134 Horsepower②④⑭⑮..V8-302	2 Barrel	4.00 × 3.00	302	8.0	134 @ 3600	242 @ 2000	40–60
	137 Horsepower②⑬⑰...V8-302	2 Barrel	4.00 × 3.00	302	8.0	137 @ 3600	⑳	40–60
	138 Horsepower②④⑭⑰..V8-302	2 Barrel	4.00 × 3.00	302	8.0	138 @ 3600	245 @ 2000	40–60
	140 Horsepower②⑤⑬㉑.V8-351	2 Barrel	4.00 × 3.50	351	8.0	140 @ 3400	276 @ 1600	45–65
	143 Horsepower②④⑬㉑.V8-351	2 Barrel	4.00 × 3.50	351	8.0	143 @ 3200	285 @ 1600	46–65
	152 Horsepower②⑱......V8-351	2 Barrel	4.00 × 3.50	351	8.0	152 @ 3800	274 @ 1600	45–75
	154 Horsepower②④⑲㉑.V8-351	2 Barrel	4.00 × 3.50	351	8.0	154 @ 3400	286 @ 1800	45–65
	180 Horsepower②........V8-400	2 Barrel	4.00 × 4.00	400	8.0	180 @ 3800	336 @ 1800	45–75
	202 Horsepower②........V8-460	4 Barrel	4.36 × 3.85	460	8.0	202 @ 3800	352 @ 1600	35–65
1977	96 Horsepower②④⑭......6-200	1 Barrel	3.68 × 3.13	200	8.5	96 @ 4400	151 @ 2000	30–50
	97 Horsepower②④⑬......6-200	1 Barrel	3.68 × 3.13	200	8.5	97 @ 4400	153 @ 2000	30–50
	86 Horsepower②⑤⑬......6-250	1 Barrel	3.68 × 3.91	250	8.1	86 @ 3000	185 @ 1800	40–60
	98 Horsepower②④⑬......6-250	1 Barrel	3.68 × 3.91	250	8.1	98 @ 3600	190 @ 1400	40–60
	98 Horsepower②④⑭......6-250	1 Barrel	3.68 × 3.91	250	8.1	98 @ 3400	182 @ 1800	40–60
	122 Horsepower②⑤⑬....V8-302	2 Barrel	4.00 × 3.00	302	8.1	122 @ 3400	222 @ 1400	40–65

Continued

GENERAL ENGINE SPECIFICATIONS—Continued

Year	Engine	Carburetor	Bore and Stroke	Piston Displacement, Cubic Inches	Compression Ratio	Maximum Brake H.P. @ R.P.M.	Maximum Torque Lbs. Ft. @ R.P.M.	Normal Oil Pressure Pounds
	122 Horsepower②④⑭⑬.. V8-302	2 Barrel	4.00 × 3.00	302	8.4	122 @ 3200	237 @ 1600	40–65
	130 Horsepower②⑬⑯.... V8-302	2 Barrel	4.00 × 3.00	302	8.4	130 @ 3400	243 @ 1800	40–65
	134 Horsepower②④⑬⑮.. V8-302	2 Barrel	4.00 × 3.00	302	8.4	134 @ 3600	245 @ 1600	40–65
	137 Horsepower②④⑬⑰.. V8-302	2 Barrel	4.00 × 3.00	302	8.4	137 @ 3600	245 @ 1600	40–65
	135 Horsepower②④⑬⑯㉑ V8-351	2 Barrel	4.00 × 3.50	351	8.3	135 @ 3200	275 @ 1600	40–65
	149 Horsepower②④⑬⑯㉑ V8-351	2 Barrel	4.00 × 3.50	351	8.3	149 @ 3200	291 @ 1600	40–65
	161 Horsepower②④⑬⑯⑱ V8-351	2 Barrel	4.00 × 3.50	351	8.0	161 @ 3600	285 @ 1800	50–75
	161 Horsepower②⑤⑬⑯⑱ V8-351	2 Barrel	4.00 × 3.50	351	8.0	161 @ 3600	286 @ 1800	50–75
	173 Horsepower②④⑬⑯.. V8-400	2 Barrel	4.00 × 4.00	400	8.0	173 @ 3800	326 @ 1600	50–75
	168 Horsepower②⑤⑬⑯.. V8-400	2 Barrel	4.00 × 4.00	400	8.0	168 @ 3800	323 @ 1600	50–75
1978	88 Horsepower②......... 4-140	2 Barrel	3.781 × 3.126	140	9.0	88 @ 4800	118 @ 2800	50
	85 Horsepower②......... 6-200	1 Barrel	3.68 × 3.13	200	8.5	85 @ 3600	250 @ 1600	30–50
	97 Horsepower②......... 6-250	1 Barrel	3.68 × 3.91	250	8.5	97 @ 3200	210 @ 1400	40–60
	133 Horsepower①②⑤⑬ . V8-302	2 Barrel	4.00 × 3.00	302	8.1	133 @ 3600	243 @ 1600	40–60
	134 Horsepower②④⑯.... V8-302	2 Barrel	4.00 × 3.00	302	8.4	134 @ 3400	248 @ 1600	40–60
	139 Horsepower①②④⑮.. V8-302	2 Barrel	4.00 × 3.00	302	8.4	139 @ 3600	250 @ 1600	40–60
	144 Horsepower②㉑...... V8-351	2 Barrel	4.00 × 3.50	351	8.3	144 @ 3200	277 @ 1600	40–60
	152 Horsepower②⑱...... V8-351	2 Barrel	4.00 × 3.50	351	8.0	152 @ 3600	278 @ 1800	50–75
	166 Horsepower②........ V8-400	2 Barrel	4.00 × 4.00	400	8.0	166 @ 3800	319 @ 1800	50–75
1979	88 Horsepower②......... 4-140	2 Barrel	3.781 × 3.126	140	9.0	88 @ 4800	118 @ 2800	40–60
	85 Horsepower②......... 6-200	1 Barrel	3.68 × 3.13	200	8.5	85 @ 3600	154 @ 1600	30–50
	97 Horsepower②......... 6-250	1 Barrel	3.68 × 3.91	250	8.6	97 @ 3200	210 @ 1400	40–60
	133 Horsepower②④⑯.... V8-302	2 Barrel	4.00 × 3.00	302	8.4	133 @ 3400	245 @ 1600	40–65
	137 Horsepower②④⑮.... V8-302	2 Barrel	4.00 × 3.00	302	8.4	137 @ 3600	243 @ 2000	40–65
	138 Horsepower②⑤⑬... V8-302	2 Barrel	4.00 × 3.00	302	8.4	138 @ 3800	239 @ 2200	40–65
	140 Horsepower①②④ ... V8-302	2 Barrel	4.00 × 3.00	302	8.4	140 @ 3600	250 @ 1800	40–65
	143 Horsepower①②⑤ ... V8-302	2 Barrel	4.00 × 3.00	302	8.4	143 @ 3600	243 @ 2200	40–65
	135 Horsepower②③④㉑. V8-351	2 Barrel	4.00 × 3.50	351	8.3	135 @ 3200	286 @ 1400	40–65
	149 Horsepower②⑤⑯⑱. V8-351	2 Barrel	4.00 × 3.50	351	8.0	149 @ 3800	258 @ 2200	50–75
	151 Horsepower②④⑯⑱. V8-351	2 Barrel	4.00 × 3.50	351	8.0	151 @ 3600	270 @ 2200	50–75
1980	88 Horsepower①②㉒..... 4-140	2 Barrel	3.781 × 3.126	140	9.0	88 @ 4600	119 @ 2600	40–60
	89 Horsepower①②⑤㉒...4-140	2 Barrel	3.781 × 3.126	140	9.0	89 @ 4800	122 @ 2600	40–60
	94 Horsepower①②④ 6-200	1 Barrel	3.68 × 3.13	200	8.6	94 @ 4000	157 @ 2000	40–60
	91 Horsepower①②⑤ 6-200	1 Barrel	3.68 × 3.13	200	8.6	91 @ 3800	160 @ 1600	40–60
	90 Horsepower②⑮....... 6-250	1 Barrel	3.68 × 3.91	250	8.6	90 @ 3200	194 @ 1600	40–60
	115 Horsepower②㉔..... V8-255	2 Barrel	3.68 × 3.00	255	8.8	115 @ 3800	191 @ 2000	40–60
	117 Horsepower②⑤⑮ ...V8-255	2 Barrel	3.68 × 3.00	255	8.8	117 @ 3800	193 @ 2000	40–60
	119 Horsepower①② V8-255	2 Barrel	3.68 × 3.00	255	8.8	119 @ 3800	194 @ 2200	40–60
	131 Horsepower②④㉔ ...V8-302	2 Barrel	4.00 × 3.00	302	8.4	131 @ 3600	231 @ 1600	40–60
	132 Horsepower②⑤㉔ ...V8-302	2 Barrel	4.00 × 3.00	302	8.4	132 @ 3600	232 @ 1400	40–60
	133 Horsepower②④㉕ ...V8-302	2 Barrel	4.00 × 3.00	302	8.4	133 @ 3400	245 @ 1600	40–60
	134 Horsepower②④⑮ ...V8-302	2 Barrel	4.00 × 3.00	302	8.4	134 @ 3600	232 @ 1600	40–60
	149 Horsepower②⑤㉕ .. V8-351M	2 Barrel	4.00 × 4.50	351	8.0	149 @ 3800	258 @ 2200	40–60
	151 Horsepower②④㉕ .. V8-351M	2 Barrel	4.00 × 3.50	351	8.0	151 @ 3600	270 @ 2200	40–60

①—Fairmont & Zephyr.
②—Ratings are NET—as installed in the vehicle.
③—Cougar XR-7
④—Except California.
⑤—California.
⑥—Comet & Maverick, California vehicles rated at 115 H.P. @ 3600 RPM.
⑦—California vehicles rated at 203 @ 1400 RPM.
⑧—Granada & Monarch, California vehicles rated at 115 H.P. @ 3600 RPM.
⑨—California vehicles rated at 203 @ 1800 RPM.
⑩—Granada, Monarch, Torino & Elite, California vehicles rated at 153 H.P. @ 3400 RPM.
⑪—California vehicles rated at 270 @ 2400 RPM.
⑫—Cougar & Montego, not available in California.
⑬—With auto. trans.
⑭—With manual trans.
⑮—Granada & Monarch.
⑯—LTD II & Cougar.
⑰—Comet & Maverick.
⑱—Modified engine.
⑲—Montego & Torino.
⑳—Exc. Calif.; 246 @ 1800. Calif.; 247 @ 1800.
㉑—Windsor engine.
㉒—Non-Turbocharged.
㉓—Turbocharged.
㉔—Cougar XR-7.
㉕—LTD II.

TUNE UP SPECIFICATIONS

The following specifications are published from the latest information available. This data should be used only in the absence of a decal affixed in the engine compartment.

★ When using a timing light, disconnect vacuum hose or tube at distributor and plug opening in hose or tube so idle speed will not be affected.

● When checking compression, lowest cylinder must be within 75% of the highest.

▲ Before removing wires from distributor cap, determine location of the No. 1 wire in cap, as distributor position may have been altered from that shown at the end of this chart.

Year & Engine	Spark Plug Type	Gap	Firing Order Fig. ▲	Ignition Timing BTDC ① ★ Man. Trans.	Auto. Trans.	Mark Fig.	Curb Idle Speed ② Man. Trans.	Auto. Trans.	Fast Idle Speed Man. Trans.	Auto. Trans.	Fuel Pump Pressure
1975											
6-200	BRF-82	.044	D	6°	6°	A	750	600D	1700③	1700③	4–6
6-250	BRF-82	.044	G	6°	6°	A	750	600D	1700③	1700③	4–6
V8-302	ARF-42	.044	E	6°	6°	B	900	650D	2000④	2100④	5–7
V8-351W⑤	ARF-42	.044	F	—	12°	B	—	650D	—	1400③	5–7
V8-351M⑥	ARF-42	.044	F	—	12°	B	—	650D	—	1350③	5–7
V8-400	ART-42	.044	F	—	12°	B	—	650D	—	1500③	5–7
V8-460	ARF-42	.044	E	—	14°	B	—	650D	—	1350③	5.7–7.7
1976											
6-200	BRF-82	.044	D	6°	6°	A	800	650D	1700③	1700③	5–7
6-250 Exc. Calif.	BRF-82	.044	G	4°	6°	A	850	600D	1700③	1700③	5–7
6-250 Calif.	BRF-82	.044	G	6°	8°	A	850	600D	1700③	1700③	5–7
V8-302 Exc. Calif.⑦	ARF-42	.044	E	4°	8°	B	750	650D	2000④	2100④	6–8
V8-302 Exc. Calif.⑧	ARF-42	.044	E	4°	6°	B	750	650D	2000④	2100④	6–8
V8-302 Calif.⑦	ARF-42	.044	E	—	8°	B	—	700D	—	2100④	6–8
V8-302 Calif.⑧	ARF-42	.044	E	—	4°	B	—	700D	—	2100④	6–8
V8-351W⑤	ARF-42	.044	F	—	10°	B	—	650D	—	⑨	6–8
V8-351M⑥	ARF-42	.044	F	—	8°	B	—	650D	—	③⑩	6–8
V8-400 Exc. Calif.	ARF-42	.044	F	—	⑪	B	—	650D	—	1350③	6–8
V8-400 Calif.	ARF-42	.044	F	—	⑪	B	—	625D	—	1400③	6–8
V8-460 Exc. Calif.	ARF-52	.044	E	—	10°	B	—	650D	—	1350③	6.7–8.7
V8-460 Calif.	ARF-52	.044	E	—	14°	B	—	650D	—	1350③	6.7–8.7
1977											
6-200	BRF-82	.050	L	6°	6°	C	800	650D	1700③	1700③	5–7
6-250 Exc. Calif.⑫⑬	BRF-82	.050	L	4°	6°	A	⑭	⑮	1700③	1700③	5–7
6-250 Exc. Calif.⑧⑫⑯	BRF-82	.050	L	TDC	—	A	800	—	1700③	—	5–7
6-250 Calif.	BRF-82	.050	L	—	8°	A	—	500/600D	—	2100③	5–7
V8-302 Exc. Calif. & High Alt.⑦	ARF-52	.050	J	—	6°	B	—	700D	—	2100④	6–8
V8-302 Exc. Calif. & High Alt.⑧	ARF-52	.050	J	6°	2°	B	800	650D	2100④	2100④	6–8
V8-302 Exc. Calif. & High Alt.⑰	ARF-52	.050	J	—	2°	B	—	500/600D	—	2100④	6–8
V8-302 Calif.⑦	ARF-52-6	.060	J	—	12°	B	—	500/600D	—	1900④	6–8
V8-302 High Alt.⑫⑱	ARF-52-6	.060	J	—	12°	B	—	500/600D	—	1900④	6–8
V8-302 High Alt.⑫⑲	ARF-52	.050	J	—	12°	B	—	500/650D	—	④⑳	6–8
V8-351W⑤⑧	ARF-52	.050	K	—	4°	B	—	625D	—	2100④	6–8
V8-351W⑤⑫⑰㉑	ARF-52	.050	K	—	14°	B	—	550/625D	—	2100④	6–8
V8-351W⑤⑫⑰㉒	ARF-52	.050	K	—	4°	B	—	625D	—	2100④	6–8
V8-351M Exc. Calif.⑥⑫⑰㉓	ARF-52	.050	K	—	10°	B	—	650D	—	1350③	6–8

Continued

TUNE UP SPECIFICATIONS—Continued

Year & Engine	Spark Plug		Ignition Timing BTDC① ★				Curb Idle Speed②		Fast Idle Speed		Fuel Pump Pressure
	Type	Gap	Firing Order Fig. ▲	Man. Trans.	Auto. Trans.	Mark Fig.	Man. Trans.	Auto. Trans.	Man. Trans.	Auto. Trans.	
1977—Continued											
V8-351M Exc. Calif.⑥⑫⑰㉔	ARF-52	.050	K	—	9°	B	—	650D	—	1350③	6–8
V8-351M Exc. Calif.⑥⑫⑰㉕	ASF-52	.050	K	—	8°	B	—	500/650D	—	1350③	6–8
V8-351M Calif.⑥⑫⑰㉖	ARF-52-6	.060	K	—	8°	B	—	500/600D	—	1350③	6–8
V8-351M Calif.⑥⑫⑰㉗	ARF-52-6	.060	K	—	6°	B	—	500/600D	—	1350③	6–8
V8-400 Exc. Calif.⑫⑰㉘	ARF-52	.050	K	—	8°	B	—	600D	—	1350③	6–8
V8-400 Exc. Calif.⑫⑰㉙	ARF-52	.050	K	—	12°	B	—	600D	—	1350③	6–8
V8-400 Exc. Calif.⑫⑰㉚	ARF-52	.050	K	—	10°	B	—	600D	—	1350③	6–8
V8-400 Exc. Calif.⑫⑰㉛	ARF-52	.050	K	—	6°	B	—	600D	—	1350③	6–8
V8-400 Exc. Calif.⑫⑰㉜	ARF-52	.050	K	—	8°	B	—	500/650D	—	1350③	6–8
V8-400 Calif.⑰	ARF-52-6	.060	K	—	6°	B	—	500/600D	—	1350③	6–8
1978											
4-140	AWSF-42	.034	H	6°	20°	I	850	800D	1600③	2000④	5–7㉝
6-200 Exc. Calif. & High Alt.	BSF-82	.050	L	10°	10°	C	800	650D	1700③	1700③	5–7
6-200 Calif.	BSF-82	.050	L	—	6°	C	—	650D	—	1700③	5–7
6-200 High Alt.⑫㉞	BSF-82	.050	L	—	12°	C	—	650D	—	1700③	5–7
6-200 High Alt.⑫㉟	BSF-82	.050	L	—	10°	C	—	650D	—	1700③	5–7
6-250 Exc. Calif.	BSF-82	.050	L	4°	14°	A	800	600/700D㊱	1700③	1700③	5–7
6-250 Calif.	BSF-82	.050	L	—	6°	A	—	600/700D㊱	—	2000③	5–7
V8-302 Exc. Calif. & High Alt.㊲	ARF-52	.050	J	—	6°	B	—	600/675D㊱	—	④⑫㊳	6–8
V8-302 Exc. Calif. & High Alt.⑧	ARF-52	.050	J	—	2°	B	—	600/675D㊱	—	2100④	6–8
V8-302 Exc. Calif. & High Alt.⑰	ARF-52	.050	J	—	14°	B	—	600D	—	2100④	6–8
V8-302 Calif.	ARF-52-6	.060	J	—	12°	B	—	600D	—	1800④	6–8
V8-302 High Alt.	ARF-52	.050	J	—	14°	B	—	650/725D㊱	—	2000④	6–8
V8-351W⑤	ARF-52	.050	K	—	14°	B	—	600/675D㊱	—	2100④	6–8
V8-351M Exc. Calif. & High Alt.⑥⑫㊴	ASF-52	.050	K	—	8°	B	—	650D	—	1350③	6–8

Continued

TUNE UP SPECIFICATIONS—Continued

Year & Engine	Spark Plug		Ignition Timing BTDC(1)★				Curb Idle Speed(2)		Fast Idle Speed		Fuel Pump Pressure
	Type	Gap	Firing Order Fig. ▲	Man. Trans.	Auto. Trans.	Mark Fig.	Man. Trans.	Auto. Trans.	Man. Trans.	Auto. Trans.	
1978—Continued											
V8-351M Exc. Calif. & High Alt.(6)(12)(40)	ASF-52	.050	K	—	14°	B	—	(36)(41)	—	1350(3)	6–8
V8-351M Exc. Calif. & High Alt.(6)(12)(42)	ASF-52	.050	K	—	12°	B	—	600/675D(36)	—	1350(3)	6–8
V8-351M Exc. Calif. & High Alt.(6)(12)(43)	ASF-52	.050	K	—	9°	B	—	600/675D(36)	—	1350(3)	6–8
V8-351M Calif.	ASF-52	.050	K	—	16°	B	—	600/650D(36)	—	2300(4)	6–8
V8-351M High Alt.	ASF-52	.050	K	—	12°	B	—	650D	—	2200(4)	6–8
V8-400 Exc. Calif. & High Alt.(44)	ASF-52	.050	K	—	13°	B	—	575/650D(36)	—	1350(3)	6–8
V8-400 Exc. Calif. & High Alt.(45)	ASF-52	.050	K	—	14°	B	—	600/675D(36)	—	1350(3)	6–8
V8-400 Calif.	ASF-52	.050	K	—	14°	B	—	600/675D	—	2300(4)	6–8
V8-400 High Alt.	ASF-52	.050	K	—	8°	B	—	650D	—	2100(4)	6–8
1979											
4-140 Exc. Calif.	AWSF-42	.034	H	6°	20°	I	850/1300(36)	600/800D	(3)(12)(51)	2000(3)	5–7(33)
4-140 Calif.	AWSF-42	.034	H	6°	17°	I	850	600/750D	1800(3)	1800(3)	5–7(33)
6-200 Exc. Calif.	(52)	.050	L	8°	10°	C	700/850(36)	650D	1600(3)	1700(3)	5–7
6-200 Calif.	(52)	.050	L	—	6°	C	—	600/650D	—	2150(3)	5–7
6-250 Exc. Calif.	(52)	.050	L	—	10°	A	—	600/700D	—	1700(3)	5–7
6-250 Calif.	(52)	.050	L	—	6°	A	—	600/700D	—	2300(3)	5–7
V8-302 Exc. Calif.	(46)	.050	J	12°	8°	B	800/850(36)	600/675D	2300(3)	2100(4)	6–8
V8-302 Calif.	(53)	.060	J	—	12°	B	—	600/675D	—	1800(4)	6–8
V8-351 W Exc. Calif.(5)(12)(49)	(46)	.050	K	—	15°	B	—	600/650D	—	2100(4)	6–8
V8-351W Exc. Calif.(5)(12)(50)	(46)	.050	K	—	10°	B	—	600/650D	—	2200(4)	6–8
V8-351M Exc. Calif.(6)	(46)	.050	K	—	12°	B	—	600/650D	—	2200(4)	6–8
V8-351M Calif.(6)	(46)	.050	K	—	14°	B	—	600/650D	—	2300(4)	6–8
1980											
4-140 Exc. Calif.(47)	AWSF-42	.034	H	6°	6°	I	850	750D	1800(3)	2000(3)	5–7(4)
4-140 Calif.(47)	AWSF-42	.034	H	6°	12°	I	850	750D	2000(3)	2000(3)	5–7(4)
4-140 Exc. Calif.(48)	AWSF-32	.034	H	—	8°	I	—	800D	—	—	2.5–3
4-140 Calif.(48)	AWSF-32	.034	H	—	2°	I	—	600D	—	—	2.5–3
6-200 Exc. Calif.	BSF-82	.050	L	(54)	(55)	C	(56)	550/700D	1600(3)	2000(3)	5–7
6-200 Calif.	BSF-82	.050	L	—	10°	C	—	600/700D	—	2300(3)	5–7
6-250	BSF-82	.050	L	4°	10°	A	700/800	550/650D	1700(3)	1700(3)	5–7
V8-255 Exc. Calif.(12)(57)	ASF-42	.050	J	—	6°	B	—	500/650D	—	2000(4)	6–8
V8-255 Exc. Calif.(12)(58)	ASF-42	.050	J	—	8°	B	—	550/700D	—	1800(4)	6–8
V8-255 Calif.(12)(59)	ASF-42	.050	J	—	6°	B	—	500/650D	—	2100(4)	6–8
V8-255 Calif.(12)(60)	ASF-42	.050	J	—	6°	B	—	550/700D	—	1800(4)	6–8
V8-302 Exc. Calif.(61)	ASF-52	.050	J	—	8°	B	—	500/650D	—	2000(4)	6–8
V8-302 Exc. Calif.(62)	ASF-52	.050	J	—	10°	B	—	500/650D	—	2000(4)	6–8
V8-302 Calif.	ASF-52	.050	J	—	6°	B	—	500/650D	—	2100(4)	6–8

Continued

TUNE UP NOTES—Continued

① —B.T.D.C.—Before top dead center.
② —Idle speed on manual trans. vehicles is adjusted in Neutral & on auto. trans. equipped vehicles is adjusted in Drive unless otherwise specified. Where two idle speeds are listed, the higher speed is with the A/C or throttle solenoid energized. On models equipped with vacuum release brake, whenever adjusting ignition timing or idle speed, vacuum line to brake release mechanism must be disconnected & plugged to prevent parking brake from releasing when selector lever is moved to Drive.
③ —On kickdown step of cam.
④ —On high step of fast idle cam.
⑤ —Windsor engine.
⑥ —Modified engine.
⑦ —Comet & Maverick.
⑧ —Granada & Monarch.
⑨ —Except Granada & Monarch California models, 1400 RPM see note 3; Granada & Monarch California models, 2000 RPM see note 4.
⑩ —Except Calif., 1350 RPM; California, 1150 RPM.
⑪ —Cougar, 10 BTDC; Elite, Montego & Torino, 12 BTDC.
⑫ —Refer to engine calibration code on engine identification label, located at rear of left valve cover on V6 & V8 engines, on front of valve cover on in line 4 & 6 cyl. engines. The calibration code is located on the label after the engine code number and is preceded by the letter C and the revision code is located below the calibration code and is preceded by the letter R.

⑬ —Calibration codes, man. trans. 7-8A-R2, 7-8A-R3 & 7-8A-R10; auto. trans. 7-29A-R1, 7-29A-R3 & 7-29A-R15.
⑭ —Calibration code 7-8A-R2, 850 RPM; 6-8A-R3 & 7-8A-410, 800 RPM.
⑮ —Calibration codes 7-29A-R1 & 7-29A-R3, 600D RPM; 7-29A-R15, less A/C 600D RPM, with A/C 700D RPM.
⑯ —Calibration code 7-8A-R12.
⑰ —LTD II & Cougar.
⑱ —Calibration codes, Comet & Maverick 7-11Z-RO; Granada & Monarch, 7-11Y-R2.
⑲ —Calibration codes, 7-11Z-R4 & 7-11Z-R6; Granada & Monarch, 7-11Y-R4 & 7-11Y-R6.
⑳ —Except calibration code 7-11Z-R4, 2000 RPM; calibration code 7-11Z-R4, 2100 RPM.
㉑ —Calibration code 7-32B-R1.
㉒ —Calibration codes 7-32B-R10 & 7-32B-R12.
㉓ —Calibration codes 7-14A-R1 & 7-14B-R1.
㉔ —Calibration codes, 7-14A-R10, 7-14B-R10 & 7-14C-R11.
㉕ —Calibration codes 7-34A-RO & 7-34B-RO.
㉖ —Calibration codes 7-14N-RO & 7-14N-R12.
㉗ —Calibration codes 7-14N-R13 & 7-14N-R17.
㉘ —Calibration code 7-17B-R1.
㉙ —Calibration code 7-17B-R15.
㉚ —Calibration code 7-17B-R16.
㉛ —Calibration code 7-17C-R1.
㉜ —Calibration codes 7-37A-RO & 7-37A-R1.
㉝ —With pump to fuel tank return line pinched off & a new fuel filter installed.
㉞ —Calibration code 8-7Z-RO.
㉟ —Calibration code 8-7Z-R2.
㊱ —With throttle solenoid energized. Higher idle speed is with A/C on & compressor clutch de-energized, if equipped.

㊲ —Fairmont & Zephyr.
㊳ —Calibration code 8-31B-RO, 1900 RPM; 8-11M-RO & 8-11M-R16, 2100 RPM.
㊴ —Calibration code 8-14H-RO.
㊵ —Calibration codes 8-14A-R12 & 8-34A-RO.
㊶ —Calibration code 8-14A-R12, 600/675D RPM; 8-34A-RO, 600/650D RPM.
㊷ —Calibration code 8-14A-R22.
㊸ —Calibration code 8-14A-RO.
㊹ —Calibration codes 8-17A-RO & 8-17C-RO.
㊺ —Calibration code 8-37A-RO.
㊻ —ASF-52 or ARF-52.
㊼ —Except turbocharged engine.
㊽ —Turbocharged engine.
㊾ —Calibration code 9-12E-RO.
㊿ —Calibration code, 9-12G-RO.
51 —Calibration codes 9-2A-RO & 9-2B-RO 1800 RPM; calibration codes 9-2C-RO & 9-2D-RO, 1600 RPM.
52 —BSF-82 or BRF-82.
53 —ASF-52-6 or ARF-52-6.
54 —Models less A/C, 10° BTDC; models with A/C, 12° BTDC.
55 —Models less Thermactor air pump, 7° BTDC; models with Thermactor air pump, 10° BTDC.
56 —Models less A/C, 700D RPM; models with A/C, 700/900D RPM.
57 —Calibration code, 0-16C-RO.
58 —Calibration code, 0-16C-R13.
59 —Calibration code, 0-16S-RO.
60 —Calibration code, 0-16S-R10.
61 —Except Cougar XR7 models equipped w/automatic overdrive transmission.
62 —Cougar XR7 models equipped w/automatic overdrive transmission.

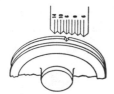

Fig. A

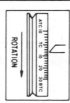

Fig. B

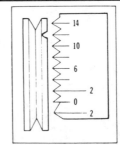

Fig. C

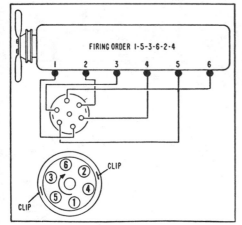

Fig. D

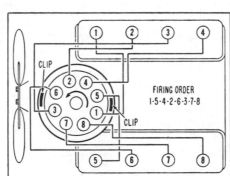

Fig. E

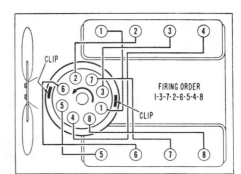

Fig. F

Continued

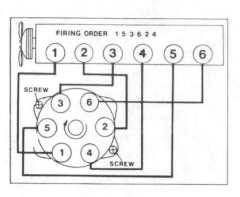

Fig. G

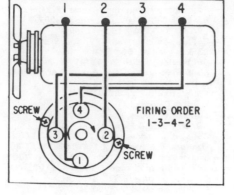

Fig. H

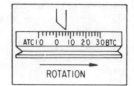

Fig. I

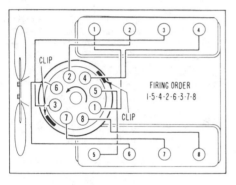

Fig. J

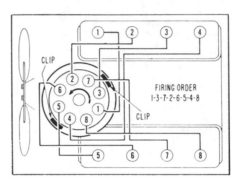

Fig. K

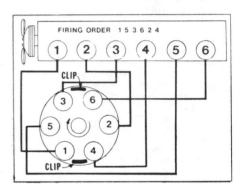

Fig. L

COOLING SYSTEM & CAPACITY DATA

Year	Model or Engine	Cooling Capacity Qts.		Radiator Cap Relief Pressure, Lbs.	Thermo. Opening Temp.	Fuel Tank Gals.	Engine Oil Refill Qts. ①	Transmission Oil			Rear Axle Oil Pints
		Less A/C	With A/C					3 Speed Pints	4 Speed Pints	Auto. Trans. Qts. ②	
1975	6-200③	8.7	8.9	13	191	19.2	4	3½	—	7¾	4
	6-200④	9.9	9.9	16	191	19.2	4	3½	—	7¾	4
	6-250③	9.7	9.7	13	191	19.2	4	3½	—	8¾	4
	6-250④	10.5	10.7	16	191	19.2	4	3½	—	8¾	4
	V8-302③	13.5	14.1	13	191	19.2	4	3½	—	8¾	4
	V8-302④	14.4	14.6	16	191	19.2	4	3½	—	8¾	4
	V8-351W④⑤	15.7	16.7	16	191	19.2	4	—	—	8¾	4
	V8-351W⑤⑥	15.9	16.2	16	191	⑦	4	—	—	⑧	5
	V8-351M⑥⑨	17.1	17.5	16	191	⑦	4	—	—	⑧	5
	V8-400⑥	17.1	17.6	16	191	⑦	4	—	—	⑩	5
	V8-460⑥	19.2	19.7	16	191	⑦	6	—	—	12¼	5
1976	6-200③	9	9	13	191	19.2	4	3½	—	7¾	4
	6-200④	9.9	9.9	16	191	⑪	4	3½	—	8¾	⑫
	6-250③	9.7	9.7	13	191	19.2	4	3½	—	8¾	4
	6-250④	10.5	10.7	16	191	⑪	4	3½	—	8¾	⑫
	V8-302③	13.5	14.1	13	191	19.2	4	3½	—	8¾	4
	V8-302④	14.4	14.6	16	191	⑪	4	3½	—	8¾	⑫

Continued

COOLING SYSTEM & CAPACITY DATA—Continued

Year	Model or Engine	Cooling Capacity Qts.		Radiator Cap Relief Pressure, Lbs.	Thermo. Opening Temp.	Fuel Tank Gals.	Engine Oil Refill Qts. (1)	Transmission Oil			Rear Axle Oil Pints
		Less A/C	With A/C					3 Speed Pints	4 Speed Pints	Auto. Trans. Qts. (2)	
	V8-351W(4)(5)	15.7	16.7	16	191	(11)	4	—	—	10¼	(12)
	V8-351W(5)(6)	15.9	16.2	16	191	(7)	4	—	—	(8)	5
	V8-351M(6)(9)	17.1	17.5	16	191	(7)	4	—	—	(8)	5
	V8-400(6)	17.1	17.5	16	191	(7)	4	—	—	(10)	5
	V8-460(6)	19.2	19.7	16	191	(7)	4	—	—	12¼	5
1977	6-200(3)	8.7	8.7	13	191	19.2	4	3½	—	7¼	4½
	6-200(4)	9.9	9.9	16	191	19.2	4	3½	5	8¼	(13)
	6-250(3)	9.6	9.6	13	191	19.2	4	3½	—	8¼	4½
	6-250(4)	10.5	10.7	16	191	19.2	4	—	5	8¼	(13)
	V8-302(3)	13.5	14.1	13	191	19.2	4	3½	—	10¼	4½
	V8-302(4)	14.4	14.6	16	191	19.2	4	—	—	8¼	(13)
	V8-302(14)	14.8	15.1	16	191	(7)	4	—	—	10¼	5
	V8-351W(4)(5)	15.7	16.7	16	191	19.2	4	—	—	10¼	(13)
	V8-351W(5)(14)	15.9	16.2	16	191	(7)	4	—	—	(8)	5
	V8-351M(9)(14)	17.1	17.5	16	191	(7)	4	—	—	(8)	5
	V8-400(14)	17.1	17.1	16	191	(7)	4	—	—	(10)	5
1978	4-140(15)	8.7	9.1	(16)	191	16	4	—	2.8	8	3.5
	6-200(15)	8.7	8.9	(16)	191	16	4	3½	—	(17)	3.5
	6-250(4)	10.5	10.6	16	191	18	4	—	5	8¼	(18)
	V8-302(15)	13.5	14.1	(16)	191	16	4(32)	—	—	10	3½
	V8-302(4)	14.2	14.3	16	191	18	4	—	5	8¼	(18)
	V8-302(14)	14.3	14.6	16	191	21	4	—	—	10¼	5
	V8-351W(5)(14)	15.4	15.7	16	191	21	4	—	—	(8)	5
	V8-351M(9)(14)	16.5	16.5	16	191	21	4	—	—	(8)	5
	V8-400(14)	16.5	16.5	16	191	21	4	—	—	(8)	5
1979	4-140(15)	8.6	10.3	(16)	191	16	4	—	2.8	8	3½
	6-200(15)	9	9	16	191	16	4	—	4½	(19)	3½
	6-250(4)	(20)	(21)	16	191	18	4	—	4½	(22)	4½
	V8-302(15)	13.9	14	16	195	16	4	—	4½	10	3½
	V8-302(4)	14.2	14.3	16	195	18	4	—	4½	10	4½
	V8-302(14)	14.3	14.6	16	195	21(23)	4	—	—	10	5
	V8-351W(5)(14)	15.4	15.7	16	195	21(23)	4	—	—	(24)	5
	V8-351M(9)(14)	16.5	16.5	16	195	21(23)	4	—	—	(24)	5
1980	4-140(25)	8.6	10.0	(16)	191	14	4	—	2.8	8	(27)
	4-140(26)	10.2	10.2	(16)	191	12.7	4.5	—	—	(30)	(27)
	6-200	9	9	(16)	191	14	4	—	4.5	(30)	(27)
	6-250	10.5	10.6	16	196	18	4	—	4.5	10	4.5
	V8-255	14.2	14.3	16	196	(28)	4(32)	—	—	9.5	(29)
	V8-302	14.2	14.3	16	196	(28)	4(33)	—	—	(31)	(29)

(1)—Add 1 qt. with filter change.
(2)—Approximate. Make final check with dipstick.
(3)—Comet & Maverick.
(4)—Granada & Maverick.
(5)—Windsor engine.
(6)—Elite, Cougar, Montego & Torino.
(7)—Except sta. wag., 26½ gals.; sta. wag., 21¼ gals.
(8)—C4, 10¼ qts.; FMX, 11 qts.; C6, 12¼ qts.
(9)—Modified engine.
(10)—FMX, 11 qts.; C6, 12¼ qts.
(11)—Except fuel economy models, 19.2 gals.; fuel economy models, 18.1 gals.
(12)—Less 4 wheel disc brakes, 4 pts.; w/4 wheel disc. brakes, 5 pts.
(13)—Models w/8 in. ring gear, 4½ pts.; models w/8.7" ring gear, 4 pts.; models w/4 wheel disc brakes, 5 pts.
(14)—Cougar & LTD II.
(15)—Fairmont & Zephyr.
(16)—Less A/C, 13 psi.; with A/C 16 psi.
(17)—C3, 8 qts.; C4, 6.7 qts.
(18)—Models w/2.47 rear axle ratio, 4 pts.; models w/3.00 rear axle ratio, 4½ pts.; models w/4 wheel disc brakes, 5 pts.
(19)—C3, 8 qts.; C4, 7½ qts.
(20)—Except Calif. 10.5 qts.; California, 10.7 qts.
(21)—Man. trans. 10.6 qts.; auto. trans. 10.8 qts.
(22)—C4, 8¼ qts.; Jatco, 8½ qts.
(23)—W/optional fuel tank, 27.5 gals.
(24)—C4, 10 qts.; FMX, 11 qts.
(25)—Non-turbocharged engine.
(26)—Turbocharged engine.
(27)—With 7.5 inch ring gear, 3.5 pts.; with 6.75 ring gear, 2.5 pts.
(28)—Cougar 17.5 gals.; Fairmont & Zephyr, 18 gals.; Granada & Monarch, 18 gals.
(29)—Cougar, 3.5 pts.; Granada & Monarch, 4.5 pts.; Fairmont & Zephyr with 7.5 inch ring gear, 3.5 pts., with 6.75 ring gear, 2.5 pts.
(30)—C3, 8 qts; C4, 9.5 qts.
(31)—C4, 9.5 qts; FIOD, 12 qts.
(32)—Dual sump oil pan. Remove both drain plugs to fully drain oil. One drain plug located at front of oil pan. Second drain plug located at left side of oil pan.
(33)—Dual sump oil pan, Cougar only. See note (32).

FORD MUSTANG & PINTO · MERCURY BOBCAT & CAPRI

ENGINE & SERIAL NUMBER LOCATION:

Vehicle warranty plate on rear face of left front door.

ENGINE IDENTIFICATION:

Engine code is last letter in serial number on vehicle warranty plate.

Year	Engine	Engine Code
1975–80	4-140(3)(1)	Y
1979–80	4-140(3)(2)	W
1975–79	V6-171(4)	Z
1979-80	6-200	T
1975-79	V8-302	F
1980	V8-255	D

(1)—Non-turbocharged
(2)—Turbocharged
(3)—2300 cc engine
(4)—2800 cc engine

GENERAL ENGINE SPECIFICATIONS

Year	Engine	Carburetor	Bore and Stroke	Piston Displacement, Cubic Inches	Compression Ratio	Maximum Brake H.P. @ R.P.M.	Maximum Torque Ft. Lbs. @ R.P.M.	Normal Oil Pressure Pounds
1975	4-140 (3)(5)	2 Barrel	3.781 × 3.126	140(5)	8.4	85.5 @ 4800	113 @ 2600	40–60
	V6-171 (3)(6)	2 Barrel	3.66 × 2.70	171(6)	8.2	110 @ 5000	135 @ 3200	40–60
	V8-302 (3)(7)	2 Barrel	4.00 × 3.00	302	8.0	140 @ 3800	228 @ 2600	40–60
1976	4-140(3)(5)	2 Barrel	3.781 × 3.126	140(5)	9.0	92 @ 5000	121 @ 5000	40–60
	V6-171(3)(6)(8)	2 Barrel	3.66 × 2.70	171(6)	8.7	(9)	(10)	40–60
	V6-171(3)(6)(11)	2 Barrel	3.66 × 2.70	171(6)	8.7	(12)	(13)	40–60
	V8-302(3)(7)	2 Barrel	4.00 × 3.00	302	8.0	134 @ 3600	(14)	40–60
1977	4-140(3)(5)(15)	2 Barrel	3.781 × 3.126	140(5)	9.0	89 @ 4800	120 @ 3000	40–60
	4-140(3)(5)(16)	2 Barrel	3.781 × 3.126	140(5)	9.0	(17)	119 @ 3000	40–60
	V6-171(3)(6)(19)	2 Barrel	3.66 × 2.70	171(6)	8.7	90 @ 4200	139 @ 2600	40–55
	V6-171(3)(6)(20)	2 Barrel	3.66 × 2.70	171(6)	8.7	90 @ 4000	139 @ 2600	40–55
	V6-171(3)(6)(21)	2 Barrel	3.66 × 2.70	171(6)	8.7	88 @ 4000	138 @ 2600	40–55
	V6-171(3)(6)(18)	2 Barrel	3.66 × 2.70	171(6)	8.7	93 @ 4200	140 @ 2600	40–55
	V8-302(3)(7)(23)	2 Barrel	4.00 × 3.00	302	8.4	129 @ 3400	242 @ 2000	40–60
	V8-302(3)(7)(24)	2 Barrel	4.00 × 3.00	302	8.1	132 @ 3600	228 @ 1600	40–60
	V8-302(3)(7)(22)	2 Barrel	4.00 × 3.00	302	8.4	139 @ 3600	247 @ 1800	40–60
1978	4-140(3)	2 Barrel	3.781 × 3.126	140(5)	9.0	88 @ 4800	118 @ 2800	50
	V6-171(6)	2 Barrel	3.66 × 2.70	171(6)	8.7	90 @ 4200	143 @ 2200	40–55
	V8-302(7)	2 Barrel	4.00 × 3.00	302	8.4	(25)	(26)	40–60
1979	4-140(5)(1)	2 Barrel	3.781 × 3.126	140(5)	9.0	88 @ 4800	118 @ 2800	40–60
	4-140(5)(2)	2 Barrel	3.781 × 3.126	140(5)	9.0	—	—	40–60
	V6-171(6)	2 Barrel	3.66 × 2.70	171(6)	8.7	102 @ 4400	138 @ 3200	40–60
	6-200(22)(7)(4)	1 Barrel	3.68 × 3.13	200	8.5	85 @ 3600	154 @ 1600	30–50
	V8-302(7)	2 Barrel	4.00 × 3.00	302	8.4	140 @ 3600	250 @ 1800	40–65
1980	4-140(1)(3)(5)(23)	2 Barrel	3.781 × 3.126	140	9.0	88 @ 4600	119 @ 2600	50
	4-140(1)(3)(5)(22)	2 Barrel	3.781 × 3.126	140	—	90 @ 4800	125 @ 2600	50
	4-140(1)(3)(5)	2 Barrel	3.781 × 3.126	140	9.0	89 @ 4800	122 @ 2600	50
	4-140(2)(3)(5)	2 Barrel	3.781 × 3.126	140	9.0	—	—	55
	6-200(2)(3)(11)	1 Barrel	3.68 × 3.126	200	8.6	91 @ 3800	160 @ 1600	30–50
	6-200(3)(4)(22)	1 Barrel	3.68 × 3.126	200	8.6	94 @ 4000	157 @ 2000	30–50
	V8-225(3)(15)	2 Barrel	3.68 × 3.00	255	8.8	119 @ 3800	194 @ 2200	40–60
	V8-255(3)(16)	2 Barrel	3.68 × 3.00	255	8.8	117 @ 3800	193 @ 2000	40–60

(1)—Non-turbocharged.
(2)—Turbocharged.
(3)—Net Rating—as installed in vehicle.
(4)—3.3 litre engine.
(5)—2300 cc engine.
(6)—2800 cc engine.
(7)—Refer to the Ford & Mercury—Compact & Intermediate Chapter for Service procedures on this engine.
(8)—Bobcat, Mustang and Pinto with auto. trans.
(9)—Exc. Calif.; 100 @ 4600 Calif.; 100 @ 4400.
(10)—Exc. Calif.; 143 @ 2600. Calif.; 144 @ 2200.
(11)—Mustang with manual trans.
(12)—Exc. Calif.; 103 @ 4400. Calif.; 99 @ 4400.
(13)—Exc. Calif.; 149 @ 2800. Calif.; 144 @ 2200.
(14)—Exc. Calif.; 247 @ 1800. Calif.; 243 @ 1800.
(15)—Exc. Calif.
(16)—Calif. only.
(17)—Sedan 88 @ 4800; Station wagon 85 @ 4800.
(18)—Sedans, exc. Calif.
(19)—Station Wagons exc. Calif.
(20)—Sedans Calif. only.
(21)—Station wagons Calif. only.
(22)—Auto. trans. exc. Calif.
(23)—Man. trans. exc. Calif.
(24)—Auto. trans. Calif. only.
(25)—Exc. Calif.; 139 @ 3600. Calif.; 133 @ 3600.
(26)—Exc. Calif.; 250 @ 1600. Calif.; 243 @ 1600.
(27)—4.2 litre engine.

FORD MUSTANG & PINTO • MERCURY BOBCAT & CAPRI

TUNE UP SPECIFICATIONS

The following specifications are published from the latest information available. This data should be used only in the absence of a decal affixed in the engine compartment.

★ When using a timing light, disconnect vacuum hose or tube at distributor and plug opening in hose or tube so idle speed will not be affected.

● When checking compression, lowest cylinder must be within 75 percent of highest.

▲ Before removing wires from distributor cap, determine location of the No. 1 wire in cap, as distributor position may have been altered from that shown at the end of this chart.

| Year & Engine | Spark Plug | | Ignition Timing BTDC①★ | | | | Curb Idle Speed② | | Fast Idle Speed | | Fuel Pump Pressure |
	Type	Gap	Firing Order Fig. ▲	Man. Trans.	Auto. Trans.	Mark Fig.	Man. Trans.	Auto. Trans.	Man. Trans.	Auto. Trans.	
1975											
4-140, 2300 cc Exc. Calif.	AGRF-52	.034	G	6°	6°	E	850	750D	1800③	1800③	3.5–5.5④
4-140, 2300 cc Calif.	AGRF-52	.034	G	6°	10°	E	850	750D	1800③	1800③	3.5–5.5④
V6-171, 2800 cc Exc. Calif.	AGR-42	.034	H	6°	10°	F	800	700D	1600③	1600③	3.5–5.5
V6-171, 2800 cc Calif.	AGR-42	.034	H	6°	8°	F	800	700D	1600③	1600③	3.5–5.5
V8-302	ARF-42	.044	I	—	6°	C	—	700D	—	2100⑤	5–7
1976											
4-140, 2300 cc	AGRF-52	.034	G	6°	20°	E	750	650D	1500③	③⑥	5–7④
V6-171, 2800 cc Exc. Calif.	AGR-42	.034	H	10°	12°	F	850	700D	1700③	1600③	3.5–5.8
V6-171, 2800 cc Calif.	AGR-42	.034	H	8°	6°	F	850	700D	1700③	1600③	3.5–5.8
V8-302 Exc. Calif.	ARF-42	.044	I	—	6°	C	—	700D	—	2100⑤	6–8
V8-302 Calif.	ARF-42	.044	I	—	8°	C	—	700D	—	2100⑤	6–8
1977											
4-140, 2300 cc Exc. Calif. High Alt.	AWRF-42	.034	G	6°	20°	E	850	600/800D	③⑦⑧	2000③	5–7④
4-140, 2300 cc Calif.	AWRF-42	.034	G	6°	20°	E	⑦⑨	600/750D	1800③	1800③	5–7④
4-140, 2300 cc High Alt.	AWRF-42	.034	G	6°	20°	E	550/850	⑦⑩	1800③	⑦⑪	5–7④
V6-171, 2800 cc Exc. Calif.⑦⑫	AWRF-42	.034	H	10°	—	F	850	—	1700③	—	3.5–6
V6-171, 2800 cc Exc. Calif.⑦⑬	AWSF-42	.034	H	12°	12°	F	850	700/750D	1700③	1600③	3.5–6
V6-171, 2800 cc Calif.	AWRF-42	.034	H	—	6°	F	—	600/750D	—	1800⑤	3.5–6
V8-302 Exc. Calif. & High Alt.	ARF-52	.050	D	8°	4°	C	850	700D	2000⑤	2100⑤	6–8
V8-302 Calif.	ARF-52-6	.060	D	—	12°	C	—	500/700D	—	1900⑤	6–8
V8-302 High Alt.⑦⑭	ARF-52-6	.060	D	—	12°	C	—	500/700D	—	1900⑤	6–8
V8-302 High Alt.⑦⑮	ARF-52	.050	D	—	12°	C	—	500/650D	—	2000⑤	6–8
1978											
4-140, 2300 cc Exc. Calif. & High Alt.⑦⑯	AWSF-42	.034	G	6°	20°	E	⑰	800D	1600③	2000③	5–7④
4-140, 2300 cc Exc. Calif. & High Alt.⑦⑱	AWSF-42	.034	G	6°	20°	E	850	600/800D	1800③	2000③	5–7④
4-140, 2300 cc Calif.⑦⑲	AWSF-42	.034	G	6°	20°	E	⑳	750D	1800③	1800③	5–7④
4-140, 2300 cc Calif.⑦㉑	AWSF-42	.034	G	6°	17°	E	850	750D	1850③	1850③	5–7④

Continued

TUNE UP SPECIFICATIONS—Continued

Year & Engine	Spark Plug		Ignition Timing BTDC ①★				Curb Idle Speed ②		Fast Idle Speed		Fuel Pump Pressure
	Type	Gap	Firing Order Fig. ▲	Man. Trans.	Auto. Trans.	Mark Fig.	Man. Trans.	Auto. Trans.	Man. Trans.	Auto. Trans.	
1978—Continued											
4-140, 2300 cc High Alt.	AWSF-42	.034	G	6°	20°	E	550/850	550/800D	1800③	2000③	5–7④
V6-171, 2800 cc Exc. Calif.	AWSF-42	.034	H	10°	12°	F	700/850	650/750D㉒	1700③	1600③	3–6
V6-171, 2800 cc Calif.	AWSF-42	.034	H	10°	6°	F	600/800	750D	1600⑤	1750⑤	3–6
V8-302 Exc. Calif. & High Alt.	ARF-52	.050	D	10°	4°	C	⑦㉒㉓	⑦㉒㉔	2000⑤	2100⑤	6–8
V8-302 Calif.	ARF-52-6	.060	D	—	10°	C	—	700D	—	1900⑤	6–8
V8-302 High Alt.	ARF-52	.050	D	—	14°	C	—	650/725D㉒	—	2000⑤	6–8
1979											
4-140, 2300 cc Exc. Calif㉕	AWSF-42	.034	G	6°	20°	E	850/1300㉒	600/800D	③③㉙	2000③	5–7④
4-140, 2300 cc Calif.㉕	AWSF-42	.034	G	6°	17°	E	850	600/750D	③㉚	③㉚	5–7④
4-140, 2300 cc㉖	AWSF-32	.034	G	2°	—	E	900/1300㉒	—	③㉛	—	5–7④
V6-171, 2800 cc Exc. Calif.	AWSF-42	.034	H	10°	⑦㉞	F	850	650/750D	1300③	1600③	3–6
V6-171, 2800 cc Calif.	AWSF-42	.034	H	—	6°	F	—	700D	—	1750⑤	3–6
6-200 Exc. Calif.	BSF-82	.050	A	8°	10°	B	700/850㉒	650D	1600③	1700③	5–7
6-200 Calif.	BSF-82	.050	A	—	6°	B	—	600/650D	—	2150③	5–7
V8-302 Exc. Calif.	㉗	.050	D	12°	8°	C	800/875㉒	600/675D	2300⑤	2100⑤	6–8
V8-302 Calif.	㉘	.060	D	—	12°	C	—	600/675D	—	1800⑤	6–8
1980											
4-140, 2300 cc Exc. Calif.㉕	AWSF-42	.034	G	6°	6°	E	850	750D	1800③	2000③	5–7④
4-140, 2300 cc Calif㉕	AWSF-42	.034	G	6°	12°	E	850	750D	2000③	2000③	5–7④
4-140, 2300 cc Exc. Calif.㉖	AWSF-32	.034	G	6°	10°	E	850	800D	1800③	—	㊵
4-140, 2300 cc Calif.㉖	AWSF-32	.034	G	2°	2°	E	900	600D	—	—	㊵
6-200 Exc. Calif.㉟	BSF-82	.050	A	—	7°	B	—	550/700D	—	2000③	5–7
6-200 Exc. Calif.㊱	BSF-82	.050	A	㊲	10°	B	700/900	550/700D	1600③	2000③	5–7
6-200 Calif.	BSF-82	.050	A	—	10°	B	—	600/700D	—	2300③	5–7
V8-255 Exc. Calif.⑦㊳	ASF-42	.050	D	—	6°	C	—	500/650D	—	2000⑤	6–8
V8-255 Exc. Calif.⑦㉝	ASF-42	.050	D	—	8°	C	—	550/700D	—	1800⑤	6–8

①—B.T.D.C.—Before top dead center.
②—Idle speed on manual trans. vehicles is adjusted in Neutral & on auto. trans. equipped vehicles is adjusted in Drive unless otherwise specified. Where two idle speeds are listed, the higher speed is with the A/C or throttle solenoid energized.
③—On kickdown step of cam.
④—With pump to fuel tank line pinched off & a new fuel filter installed.
⑤—On high step of fast idle cam.
⑥—Except Calif. 2000 RPM; California, 1800 RPM.
⑦—Refer to engine calibration code on engine identification label located at rear of left valve cover on V6 & V8 engines, on front of valve cover on inline 4 & 6 cyl. engines. The calibration code is located on the label after the engine codes number & is preceded by the letter C & the revision code is located below the calibration code is preceded by the letter R.
⑧—Except calibration code 7-2B-R16, 1600 RPM; calibration code 7-2B-R16, 1800 RPM.
⑨—Except calibration code 7-2N-R1, 800/850 RPM; calibration code 7-2N-R1, 650/850 RPM.
⑩—Calibration code 7-1X-RO, 550/750D RPM; 7-1X-R10, 550/800D RPM.
⑪—Calibration code 7-1X-RO, 1800 RPM; 7-1X-R10, 2000 RPM.
⑫—Calibration code 7-3A-R2.
⑬—Calibration codes, man. trans. 7-3A-R10; auto, trans., 7-4A-R2.
⑭—Calibration code 7-11X-R2.

Continued

FORD MUSTANG & PINTO · MERCURY BOBCAT & CAPRI

⑮—Calibration codes 7-11X-R4 & 7-11X-R6.
⑯—Calibration codes, man. trans. 8-2A-RO & 8-2A-R10; auto. trans. 8-1A-RO & 8-1B-R10.
⑰—Calibration code 8-2A-R0, 850 RPM; 8-2A-R10, 900 RPM.
⑱—Calibration codes, man. trans., 8-2B-RO; auto. trans., 8-21B-RO & 8-21B-R11.
⑲—Calibration codes, man. trans., 8-2N-RO & 8-2N-R11; auto. trans., 8-1N-RO.
⑳—Calibration code 8-2N-RO, 650/900 RPM; 8-2N-R11, 600/850 RPM.
㉑—Calibration codes, man. trans. 8-2P-RO & 8-2T-RO; auto. trans., 8-1R-R1.
㉒—With throttle solenoid energized. Higher idle speed is with A/C on & compressor clutch de-energized, if equipped.
㉓—Calibration code 8-10A-RO, 900/975 RPM; 8-10A-R10, 800/875 RPM.
㉔—Calibration code 8-31A-RO, 700/775D RPM; 8-31A-R10, 700/825 RPM.
㉕—Except turbocharged engine.
㉖—Turbocharged engine
㉗—ASF-52 or ARF-52.
㉘—ASF-52-6 or ARF-52-6.
㉙—Calibration codes 9-2A-RO & 9-2B-RO, 1800 RPM; calibration codes 9-2C-RO & 9-2D-RO, 1600 RPM.
㉚—Except Bobcat & Pinto, 1800 RPM; Bobcat & Pinto, 1850 RPM.
㉛—Except Calif., 1800 RPM; California, 1850 RPM.
㉜—Man. trans, 5–7 Psi; auto trans, 2.5–3 Psi.
㉝—Calibration code 0-16A-R12.
㉞—Calibration code 9-4A-RO, 9° BTDC; calibration codes 9-4A-R10A & 9-4A-R10N, 6° BTDC.
㉟—Models less Thermactor Air Pump.
㊱—Models with Thermactor Air Pump.
㊲—Less A/C, 10° BTDC; with A/C, 12° BTDC.
㊳—Calibration code 0-16A-RO.

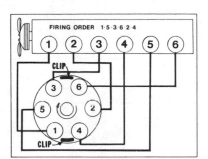

Fig. A

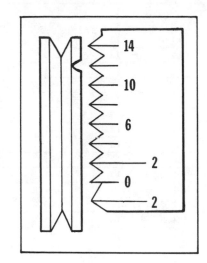

Fig. B

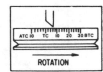

Fig. C

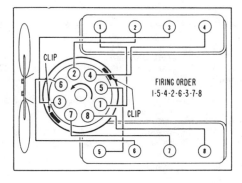

Fig. D

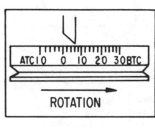

Fig. E

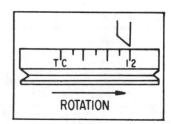

Fig. F

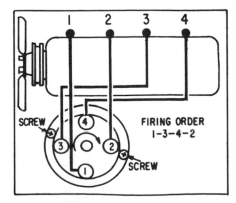

Fig. G

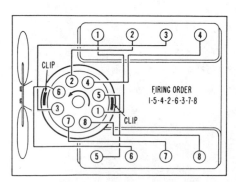

Fig. I

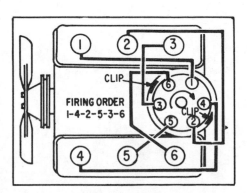

Fig. H

FORD MUSTANG & PINTO · MERCURY BOBCAT & CAPRI

COOLING SYSTEM & CAPACITY DATA

Year	Model or Engine	Cooling Capacity, Qts.		Radiator Cap Relief Pressure, Lbs.	Thermo. Opening Temp.	Fuel Tank Gals.	Engine Oil Refill Qts.	Transmission Oil			Rear Axle Oil Pints
		Less A/C	With A/C					3 Speed Pints	4 Speed Pints	Auto. Trans. Qts. (1)	
1975	4-140	(9)	9	13	191	(4)	5(8)	—	(5)	(6)	(7)
	V6-171	(11)	13¼	13	191	(4)	5(8)	—	(5)	(6)	(7)
	V8-302	16.3	16.3	13	191	16½	5(8)	—	—	8¾	4
1976	4-140	(9)	9	13	191	(4)	5(8)	—	(5)	(6)	(7)
	V6-171	(11)	13.2	13	191	(4)	5(2)	—	(5)	(6)	(7)
	V8-302	16.3	16.3	13	191	16½	5(8)	—	—	8¾	4
1977	4-140	(9)	9.1	13	191	(12)	5(8)	—	(5)	(6)	(7)
	V6-171	(10)	9.2	13	191	(4)	5(2)	—	(5)	(6)	(7)
	V8-302	16.3	16.3	13	191	16.5	5(8)	—	(5)	(6)	4
1978	4-140(13)	8.6	9.0	13	191	(16)	5(8)	—	2.8	(17)	(18)
	4-140(14)	8.8	9.1	13	191	13	5(8)	—	3.5	(17)	(18)
	V6-171(13)	8.5	9.2	13	191	(16)	5(2)	—	2.8	(17)	(18)
	V6-171(14)	(15)	9.0	13	191	13	5(2)	—	3.5	(17)	(18)
	V8-302	14.6	14.6	13	191	16.5	5(8)	—	3.5	7	(18)
1979	4-140(13)	8.6	9.0	13	191	(22)	5(8)	—	2.8	(17)	2.5
	4-140(19)(20)	8.8	9.1	13	191	11.5	4½(2)	—	2.8	(17)	2.5
	4-140(19)(21)	8.8	10.2	13	191	12.2	4½(2)	—	4.5	(17)	3.5
	V6-171(13)	8.5	9.1	13	195	(22)	5(2)	—	2.8	(17)	4.5
	V6-171(19)	8.6	9.1	16	195	12.2	5(2)	—	4.5	(17)	3.5
	6-200	9.0	9.0	16	191	16	5(8)	—	—	(14)	3.5
	V8-302	14	14.6	16	195	12.2	5(8)(26)	—	4.5	(3)	3.5
1980	4-140(13)	8.6	9.0	16	191	(22)	5(8)	—	2.8	(17)	(23)
	4-140(19)(20)	8.6	10.0	16	191	11.5(24)	5.0(8)	—	2.8	(17)	(23)
	4-140(19)(21)	10.2	10.2	16	191	12.5(25)	5.5(8)	—	3.5	(17)	(23)
	6-200	9.0	9.0	16	191	12.5	5.0(8)	—	4.5	6	(23)
	V8-255	14.2	14.3	16	197	12.5	5.0(8)(26)	—	—	6	(23)

(1)—Approximate. Make final check with dipstick.
(2)—Includes ½ qt. for filter.
(3)—C3 trans., 8 qts.; C4 trans., 10 qts.
(4)—Exc. Sta. Wag., 13 gals.; Sta. Wag. 14 gals. Add 3½ gals. with auxiliary fuel tank.
(5)—Bobcat & Pinto, 2.8 pts.; Mustang, 3½ pts.
(6)—C3 trans., 8 qts.; C4 trans., 7¼ qts.
(7)—With 6¾" ring gear Bobcat & Pinto, 2.2 pts.; Mustang, 3 pts.; units with 8 inch ring gear, 4 pts.
(8)—Includes 1 qt. for filter.
(9)—Bobcat & Pinto, 8.7 qts.; Mustang, 8.5 qts.
(10)—Bobcat & Pinto, 8.5 qts.; Mustang w/man. trans., 8.3 qts.; Mustang w/auto. trans., 8.8 qts.

(11)—Bobcat & Pinto, 12.5 qts.; Mustang, 12.3 qts.
(12)—Bobcat Calif. 11.7 gals.; Exc. Sta. Wag., 13 gals.; Sta. Wag., 14 gals. Add 3½ gals. with auxiliary fuel tank.
(13)—Bobcat & Pinto.
(14)—Mustang.
(15)—Man. trans., 8.3 qts.; Auto. trans., 8.8 qts.
(16)—Exc. Sta. Wag., 13 gals.; Sta. Wag., 14 gals.
(17)—C3 trans., 8 qts.; C4 trans., 7 qts.
(18)—6¾" axle—Pinto & Bobcat 2.2 pts., Mustang, 3 pts., 8" axle 4 pts.

(19)—Capri & Mustang.
(20)—Non-turbocharged.
(21)—Turbocharged.
(22)—Exc. Sta. Wag. & Calif. auto. sedan, 13 gals.; Calif. auto. sedan, 11.7 gals.; Sta. Wag., 14 gals.
(23)—6¾ inch axle, 2.5; 7½ inch axle, 3.5; 8 inch axle, 4.5.
(24)—A/C, 12.5 gal.
(25)—Automatic transmission, 11.9 gal.
(26)—Dual sump oil. When draining oil, it is necessary to remove both drain plugs. One drain plug is located at front of oil pan. The second plug is located on left side of oil pan.

FORD THUNDERBIRD

ENGINE & SERIAL NUMBER LOCATION

Vehicle Warranty Plate On Left Front Door Pillar.

ENGINE IDENTIFICATION

*Serial number on vehicle
Warranty Plate.

Year	Engine	Engine Code
1975–76	V8-460	A
1977–78	V8-400	S
1977–79	V8-351	H
1977–80	V8-302	F
1980	V8-255	D

GENERAL ENGINE SPECIFICATIONS

Year	Engine	Carburetor	Bore and Stroke	Piston Displacement, Cubic Inches	Compression Ratio	Maximum Brake H.P. @ R.P.M.	Maximum Torque Lbs. Ft. @ R.P.M.	Normal Oil Pressure Pounds
1975	216 Horsepower① V8-460	4 Barrel	4.36 × 3.85	460	8.0	216 @ 4000	366 @ 2600	40–65
1976	202 Horsepower① V8-460	4 Barrel	4.36 × 3.85	460	8.0	202 @ 3800	352 @ 3800	40–65
1977	130 Horsepower① V8-302	2 Barrel	4.00 × 3.00	302	8.4	130 @ 3400	243 @ 1800	40–60
	149 Horsepower① V8-351W②	2 Barrel	4.00 × 3.50	351	8.3	149 @ 3200	291 @ 1600	40–60
	161 Horsepower① V8-351M②	2 Barrel	4.00 × 3.50	351	8.0	161 @ 3600	285 @ 1800	50–75
	161 Horsepower① V8-351M③	2 Barrel	4.00 × 3.50	351	8.0	161 @ 3600	286 @ 1800	50–75
	161 Horsepower① V8-351M④	2 Barrel	4.00 × 3.50	351	8.0	161 @ 3600	285 @ 1800	50–75
	173 Horsepower① V8-400②	2 Barrel	4.00 × 4.00	400	8.0	173 @ 3800	326 @ 1600	45–75
	168 Horsepower① V8-400③	2 Barrel	4.00 × 4.00	400	8.0	168 @ 3800	323 @ 1600	45–75
	173 Horsepower① V8-400④	2 Barrel	4.00 × 4.00	400	8.0	173 @ 3800	326 @ 1600	45–75
1978	134 Horsepower① V8-302②	2 Barrel	4.00 × 3.00	302	8.4	134 @ 3400	248 @ 1600	40–60
	144 Horsepower① V8-351W②	2 Barrel	4.00 × 3.50	351	8.3	144 @ 3200	277 @ 1600	40–60
	152 Horsepower① V8-351M②	2 Barrel	4.00 × 3.50	351	8.0	152 @ 3600	278 @ 1800	50–75
	166 Horsepower① V8-351M③	2 Barrel	4.00 × 3.50	351	8.0	152 @ 3600	278 @ 1800	50–75
	152 Horsepower① V8-351M④	2 Barrel	4.00 × 3.50	351	8.0	152 @ 3600	278 @ 1800	50–75
	166 Horsepower① V8-400②	2 Barrel	4.00 × 4.00	400	8.0	166 @ 3800	319 @ 1800	35–65
	166 Horsepower① V8-400③	2 Barrel	4.00 × 4.00	400	8.0	166 @ 3800	319 @ 1800	35–65
	166 Horsepower① V8-400④	2 Barrel	4.00 × 4.00	400	8.0	166 @ 3800	319 @ 1800	35–65
1979	133 Horsepower① V8-302	2 Barrel	4.00 × 3.00	302	8.4	133 @ 3400	245 @ 1600	40–60
	135 Horsepower① V8-351W	2 Barrel	4.00 × 3.50	351	8.3	135 @ 3200	286 @ 1400	40–60
1980	119 Horsepower V8-255②	2 Barrel	3.68 × 3.00	255	8.8	119 @ 3800	194 @ 2200	40–60
	117 Horsepower V8-255③	2 Barrel	3.68 × 3.00	255	8.8	117 @ 3800	193 @ 2000	40–60
	132 Horsepower V8-302②	2 Barrel	4.00 × 3.00	302	8.4	132 @ 3600	232 @ 1400	40–60
	131 Horsepower V8-302③	2 Barrel	4.00 × 3.00	302	8.4	131 @ 3600	231 @ 1600	40–60

①—Ratings are NET—as installed in the vehicle. ②—Except Calif. & high altitude. ④—High altitude.
③—Calif.

FORD THUNDERBIRD

TUNE UP SPECIFICATIONS

The following specifications are published from the latest information available. This data should be used only in the absence of a decal affixed in the engine compartment.

★ When using a timing light, disconnect vacuum hose or tube at distributor and plug opening in hose or tube so idle speed will not be affected.

● When checking compression, lowest cylinder must be within 75 percent of highest.

▲ Before removing wires from distributor cap, determine location of the No. 1 wire in cap, as distributor position may have been altered from that shown at the end of this chart.

Year & Engine	Spark Plug		Ignition Timing BTDC① ★				Curb Idle Speed②		Fast Idle Speed		Fuel Pump Pressure
	Type	Gap	Firing Order Fig. ▲	Man. Trans.	Auto. Trans.	Mark Fig.	Man. Trans.	Auto. Trans.	Man. Trans.	Auto. Trans.	
1975											
V8-460	ARF-52	③	A	—	14°	C	—	650D	—	1350④	5.7–7.7
1976											
V8-460 Exc. Calif.	ARF-52	.044	A	—	8°	C	—	650D	—	1350④	6.7–8.7
V8-460 Calif.	ARF-52	.044	A	—	14°	C	—	650D	—	1350④	6.7–8.7
1977											
V8-302	ARF-52	.050	D	—	2°	C	—	500/600D	—	2100⑤	6.8
V8-351W⑥⑦⑧	ARF-52	.050	B	—	14°	C	—	550/625D	—	2100⑤	6–8
V8-351W⑥⑦⑨	ARF-52	.050	B	—	4°	C	—	625D	—	2100⑤	6–8
V8-351M Exc. Calif.⑦⑩⑪	ARF-52	.050	B	—	10°	C	—	650D	—	1350④	6–8
V8-351M Exc. Calif.⑦⑩⑫	ARF-52	.050	B	—	9°	C	—	650D	—	1350④	6–8
V8-351M Exc. Calif.⑦⑩⑬	ASF-52	.050	B	—	8°	C	—	500/650D	—	1350④	6–8
V8-351M Calif.⑦⑩⑭	ARF-52-6	.050	B	—	8°	C	—	500/600D	—	1350④	6–8
V8-351M Calif.⑦⑩⑮	ARF-52-6	.050	B	—	6°	C	—	500/600D	—	1350④	6–8
V8-400 Exc. Calif.⑦⑯	ARF-52	.050	B	—	8°	C	—	⑰	—	1350④	6–8
V8-400 Exc. Calif.⑦⑱	ARF-52	.050	B	—	12°	C	—	600D	—	1350④	6–8
V8-400 Exc. Calif.⑦⑲	ARF-52	.050	B	—	10°	C	—	600D	—	1350④	6–8
V8-400 Exc. Calif.⑦⑳	ARF-52	.050	B	—	6°	C	—	600D	—	1350④	6–8
V8-400 Calif.	ARF-52-6	.060	B	—	6°	C	—	500/600D	—	1350④	6–8
1978											
V8-302	ARF-52	.050	D	—	14°	C	—	500/600D	—	2100⑤	6–8
V8-351W⑥	ARF-52	.050	B	—	14°	C	—	600/675D㉑	—	2100⑤	6–8
V8-351M Exc. Calif. & High Alt.⑦⑩㉒	ASF-52	.050	B	—	14°	C	—	㉑ ㉓	—	1350④	6–8
V8-351M Exc. Calif. & High Alt.⑦⑩㉔	ASF-52	.050	B	—	12°	C	—	600/675D㉑	—	1350④	6–8
V8-351M Exc. Calif. & High Alt.⑦⑩㉕	ASF-52	.050	B	—	9°	C	—	600/675D㉑	—	1350④	6–8
V8-351M Calif.⑩	ASF-52	.050	B	—	16°	C	—	600/650D㉑	—	2300⑤	6–8
V8-351M High Alt.⑩	ASF-52	.050	B	—	12°	C	—	650D	—	2200⑤	6–8
V8-400 Exc. Calif. & High Alt.⑦㉖	ASF-52	.050	B	—	13°	C	—	575/650D㉑	—	1350④	6–8
V8-400 Exc. Calif. & High Alt.⑦㉗	ASF-52	.050	B	—	14°	C	—	600/675D㉑	—	1350④	6–8
V8-400 Calif.	ASF-52	.050	B	—	14°	C	—	600/675D㉑	—	2300⑤	6–8
V8-400 High Alt.	ASF-52	.050	B	—	8°	C	—	650D	—	2100⑤	6–8

Continued

TUNE UP SPECIFICATIONS—Continued

Year & Engine	Spark Plug		Ignition Timing BTDC①★				Curb Idle Speed②		Fast Idle Speed		Fuel Pump Pressure
	Type	Gap	Firing Order Fig. ▲	Man. Trans.	Auto. Trans.	Mark Fig.	Man. Trans.	Auto. Trans.	Man. Trans.	Auto. Trans.	
1979											
V8-302 Exc. Calif.	㉘	.050	D	—	8°	C	—	600/675D	—	2100⑤	6—8
V8-302 Calif.	㉙	.060	D	—	12°	C	—	600/675D	—	1800⑤	6—8
V8-351W⑥⑦㉜	㉘	.050	B	—	15°	C	—	600/650D	—	2100⑤	6—8
V8-351W⑥⑦㉝	㉘	.050	B	—	10°	C	—	600/650D	—	2200⑤	6—8
V8-351M Exc. Calif.⑩	㉘	.050	B	—	12°	C	—	600/650D	—	2200⑤	6—8
V8-351M Calif.⑩	㉘	.050	B	—	14°	C	—	600/650D	—	2300⑤	6—8
1980											
V8-255 Exc. Calif.⑦㉚	ASF-42	.050	D	—	6°	C	—	500/650D	—	2000⑤	6—8
V8-255 Exc. Calif.⑦㉛	ASF-42	.050	D	—	8°	C	—	550/700D	—	1800⑤	6—8
V8-255 Calif.⑦㉞	ASF-42	.050	D	—	6°	C	—	550/600D	—	2100⑤	6—8
V8-255 Calif.⑦㉟	ASF-42	.050	D	—	6°	C	—	550/700D	—	1800⑤	6—8
V8-302 Exc. Calif.㊱	ASF-52	.050	D	—	8°	C	—	500/650D	—	2000⑤	6—8
V8-302 Exc. Calif.㊲	ASF-52	.050	D	—	10°	C	—	500/650D	—	2000⑤	6—8
V8-302 Calif.	ASF-52	.050	D	—	6°	C	—	500/650D	—	2100⑤	6—8

①—B.T.D.C.—Before top dead center.
②—Idle speed on manual trans. vehicles is adjusted in Neutral & on auto. trans. equipped vehicles is adjusted in Drive unless otherwise specified. Where two idle speeds are listed, the higher speed is with the A/C or throttle solenoid energized. On models equipped with vacuum release brake, whenever adjusting ignition timing or idle speed, vacuum line to brake release mechanism must be disconnected & plugged to prevent parking brake from releasing when selector lever is moved to Drive.
③—Except Calif., .044"; California, .054".
④—On kickdown step of cam.
⑤—On high step of fast idle cam.
⑥—Windsor engine.
⑦—Refer to engine calibration code on engine identification label, located at rear of left valve cover. The calibration code is located on the label after the engine code number and is preceded by the letter C and the revision code is located below the calibration code and is preceded by the letter R.
⑧—Calibration code 7-32B-R1.
⑨—Calibration codes 7-32B-R10 & 7-32B-R12.
⑩—Modified engine.
⑪—Calibration code 7-14B-R10.
⑫—Calibration codes 7-14B-R10 & 7-14B-R11.
⑬—Calibration codes 7-34A-R0 & 7-34B-R0.
⑭—Calibration codes 7-14N-R0 & 7-14N-R13.
⑮—Calibration code 7-14N-R13.
⑯—Calibration codes 7-17B-R1 & 7-37A-R0.
⑰—Calibration code 7-17B-R1, 600D RPM; 7-37A-R0, 500/650D RPM.
⑱—Calibration code 7-17B-R15.
⑲—Calibration code 7-17B-R16.
⑳—Calibration code 7-17C-R1.
㉑—With throttle solenoid energized. Higher idle speed is with A/C on, compressor clutch de-energized, if equipped.
㉒—Calibration codes 8-14A-R12 & 8-34A-R0.
㉓—Calibration codes 8-14A-R12, 600/675D RPM; 8-34A-R0, 600/650D RPM.
㉔—Calibration code 8-14A-R22.
㉕—Calibration code 8-14A-R0.
㉖—Calibration codes 8-17A-R0 & 8-17C-R0.
㉗—Calibration code 8-37A-R0.
㉘—ASF-52 or ARF-52.
㉙—ASF-52-6 or ARF-52-6.
㉚—Calibration code, 0-16C-RO.
㉛—Calibration code 0-16C-R13.
㉜—Calibration code 9-12E-RO.
㉝—Calibration code 9-12G-RO.
㉞—Calibration code 0-16S-RO.
㉟—Calibration code 0-16S-R10.
㊱—Without automatic overdrive transmission.
㊲—With automatic overdrive transmission.

FORD THUNDERBIRD

TUNE UP NOTES—Continued

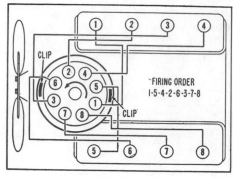

Fig. A

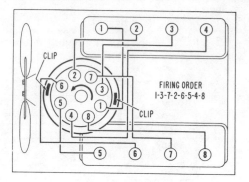

Fig. B

Fig. C

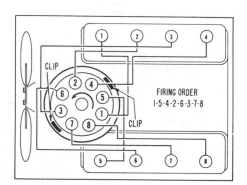

Fig. D

COOLING SYSTEM & CAPACITY DATA

Year	Model or Engine	Cooling Capacity, Qts.		Radiator Cap Relief Pressure, Lbs.	Thermo. Opening Temp.	Fuel Tank Gals.	Engine Oil Refill Qts. ①	Transmission Oil			Rear Axle Oil Pints
		With A/C	With A/C					3 Speed Pints	4 Speed Pints	Auto. Trans. Qts. ②	
1975–76	V8-460	19.3	19.3	16	191	26½	4	—	—	12½	5
1977	V8-302	14.8	15.1	16	191	26	4	—	—	10.3	5
	V8-351④	15.9	16.2	16	191	26③	4	—	—	⑤	5
	V8-351⑥	17.1	17.1	16	191	26④	4	—	—	⑤	5
	V8-400	17.1	17.1	16	191	26	4	—	—	⑦	5
1978	V8-302	14.3	14.6	16	191	21	4	—	—	10¼	5
	V8-351④	15.4	15.7	16	191	21	4	—	—	11	5
	V8-351⑥	16.5	16.5	16	191	21	4	—	—	11	5
	V8-400	16.5	16.5	16	191	21	4	—	—	12½	5
1979	V8-302	14.3	14.6	16	196	21	4	—	—	10	5
	V8-351④	15.4	15.7	16	196	21	4	—	—	⑧	5
	V8-351⑥	16.5	16.5	16	196	21	4	—	—	⑧	5
1980	V8-255	14.2	14.3	16	195	17.5	4	—	—	9.5	3.75
	V8-302	14.2	14.3	16	195	17.5	4	—	—	⑨	3.75

① —Add one quart with filter change.
② —Approximate. Make final check with dipstick.
③ —Calif, 22 gals.
④ —Windsor engine.
⑤ —C4, 10.3 qts.; FMX, 11 qts.; C6, 12.2 qts.
⑥ —Modified engine.
⑦ —FMX, 11 qts.; C6, 12.2 qts.
⑧ —C4, 10 qts.; FMX, 11 qts.
⑨ —C4, 9.5 qts; FIOD, 12 qts.

SERIAL & ENGINE
NUMBER LOCATION

Vehicle Warranty Plate on Left Front Door Pillar

ENGINE IDENTIFICATION

*Serial number on vehicle Warranty Plate.

Engine code for 1975–80 is the last letter in the serial number.

Year	Engine	Engine Code*
1975–78	V8-460	A
1975–79	V8-400	S
1977 & 1980	V8-351W	H
1977–80	V8-302	F

GENERAL ENGINE SPECIFICATIONS

Year	Engine	Carburetor	Bore and Stroke	Piston Displacement, Cubic Inches	Compression Ratio	Maximum Brake H.P. @ R.P.M.	Maximum Torque Lbs. Ft. @ R.P.M.	Normal Oil Pressure Pounds
1975	216 Horsepower①........V8-460	4 Barrel	4.362 × 3.850	460	8.0	216 @ 4400	386 @ 2600	40–65
1976	202 Horsepower①........V8-460	4 Barrel	4.362 × 3.850	460	8.0	202 @ 3800	352 @ 1600	40–65
1977	122 Horsepower..........V8-302	2 Barrel	4.00 × 3.00	302	8.1	122 @ 3400	222 @ 1400	40–60
	135 Horsepower..........V8-351	2 Barrel	4.00 × 3.50	351	8.1	135 @ 3200	275 @ 1600	45–65
	179 Horsepower①②......V8-400	2 Barrel	4.00 × 4.00	400	8.0	179 @ 4000	329 @ 1600	45–75
	181 Horsepower①③......V8-400	2 Barrel	4.00 × 4.00	400	8.0	181 @ 4000	331 @ 1600	45–75
	208 Horsepower①........V8-460	4 Barrel	4.362 × 3.850	460	8.0	208 @ 4000	356 @ 2000	35–65
1978	133 Horsepower①........V8-302	2 Barrel	4.00 × 3.00	302	8.1	133 @ 3600	243 @ 1600	40–60
	166 Horsepower①........V8-400	2 Barrel	4.00 × 4.00	400	8.0	166 @ 3800	319 @ 1800	50–75
	210 Horsepower①........V8-460	4 Barrel	4.362 × 3.850	460	8.0	210 @ 4200	357 @ 2200	35–65
1979	130 Horsepower①②......V8-302	2 Barrel	4.00 × 3.00	302	8.4	130 @ 3600	237 @ 1600	40–65
	133 Horsepower①③......V8-302	2 Barrel	4.00 × 3.00	302	8.4	133 @ 3600	236 @ 1400	40–65
	159 Horsepower①........V8-400	2 Barrel	4.00 × 4.00	400	8.0	159 @ 3400	315 @ 1800	50–75
1980	129 Horsepower①⑤......V8-302	2 Barrel④	4.00 × 3.00	302	8.4	129 @ 3600	231 @ 2000	40–60
	132 Horsepower①⑥......V8-302	2 Barrel⑦	4.00 × 3.00	302	8.4	132 @ 3600	232 @ 1400	40–60
	140 Horsepower①......V8-351W	2 Barrel⑦	4.00 × 3.50	351	8.3	140 @ 3400	265 @ 2000	40–60

①—Ratings are NET—as installed in the vehicle.
②—Exc. Calif.
③—Calif. only.
④—Electronic fuel injection

⑤—Exc. Versailles.
⑥—Versailles.
⑦—Variable Venturi carburetor.

LINCOLN CONTINENTAL & VERSAILLES

TUNE UP SPECIFICATIONS

The following specifications are published from the latest information available. This data should be used only in the absence of a decal affixed in the engine compartment.

★ When using a timing light, disconnect vacuum hose or tube at distributor and plug opening in hose or tube so idle speed will not be affected.

● When checking compression, lowest cylinder must be within 75 percent of highest.

▲ Before removing wires from distributor cap, determine location of No. 1 wire in cap, as distributor position may have been altered from that shown at the end of this chart.

Year & Engine	Spark Plug		Ignition Timing BTDC① ★				Curb Idle Speed②		Fast Idle Speed		Fuel Pump Pressure
	Type	Gap	Firing Order Fig. ▲	Man. Trans.	Auto. Trans.	Mark Fig.	Man. Trans.	Auto. Trans.	Man. Trans.	Auto. Trans.	
1975											
V8-460	ARF-52	.044	A	—	14°	B	—	650D	—	1350③	5.7–7.7
1976											
V8-460 Exc. Mark IV & Calif.	ARF-52	.044	A	—	8°	B	—	650D	—	1350③	6.7–8.7
V8-460 Calif. Exc. Mark IV	ARF-52	.044	A	—	14°	B	—	650D	—	1350③	6.7–8.7
V8-460 Mark IV	ARF-52	.044	A	—	10°	B	—	650D	—	1350③	6.7–8.7
1977											
V8-302 Calif.	ARF-52	.050	D	—	12°	B	—	700D	—	—	6–8
V8-302 High Alt.	ARF-52	.050	D	—	12°	B	—	500/650D	—	2000④	6–8
V8-351W⑤	ARF-52	.050	E	—	4°	B	—	625D	—	2100④	6–8
V8-400 Calif.	ARF-52-6	.060	E	—	6°	B	—	500/600D	—	1350③	6–8
V8-460 Exc. Calif. & High Alt.⑥⑦	ARF-52	.050	D	—	16°	B	—	525/650D	—	1350③	5.7–7.7
V8-460 Exc. Calif. & High Alt.⑥⑧	ARF-52	.050	D	—	10°	B	—	⑨	—	1350③	5.7–7.7
V8-460 High Alt.	ARF-52	.050	D	—	18°	B	—	500/600D	—	1350③	5.7–7.7
1978											
V8-302⑩	ARF-52	.050	⑪	—	30°⑫	B	—	625D	—	1900④	6–8
V8-400 Exc. Calif. & High Alt.	ASF-52	.050	E	—	13°	B	—	575/650D⑬	—	1350③	6–8
V8-400 Calif.	ASF-52	.050	E	—	16°	B	—	600/650D⑬	—	2300④	6–8
V8-400 High Alt.	ASF-52	.050	E	—	8°	B	—	650D	—	2100④	6–8
V8-460 Exc. Calif. & High Alt.⑥⑭	ARF-52	.050	D	—	16°	B	—	580/650D⑬	—	1350③	5.7–7.7
V8-460 Exc. Calif. & High Alt.⑥⑮	ARF-52	.050	D	—	10°	B	—	580/650D⑬	—	1350③	5.7–7.7
1979											
V8-302 Exc. Calif.⑩	⑯	.050	⑪	—	30°⑫	B	—	625D	—	1900④	6–8
V8-302 Calif.⑩	⑯	.050	⑪	—	15°⑫	B	—	625D	—	2100④	6–8
V8-400 Exc. Calif.	⑯	.050	E	—	14°	B	—	600/675D	—	2200④	6–8
V8-400 Calif.⑥⑱	⑲	.060	E	—	14°	B	—	600/650D	—	2200④	6–8
V8-400 Calif.⑥⑳	⑯	.050	E	—	16°	B	—	600/650D	—	2300④	6–8
1980											
V8-302 Versailles⑩	ASF-52	.050	⑪	—	6°	B	—	550/700D⑬	—	2100④	6–8
V8-302 Exc. Versailles⑩	ASF-52	.050	⑪	—	⑰	B	—	550D	—	2100④	—
V8-351W⑤⑩	ASF-52	.050	⑪	—	⑰	B	—	550/640D	—	1650㉑	6–8

Continued

TUNE UP NOTES

①—B.T.D.C.—Before top dead center.

②—Idle speed on manual trans. vehicles is adjusted in Neutral & on auto. trans. equipped vehicles is adjusted in Drive unless otherwise specified. Where two idle speeds are listed, the higher speed is with the A/C or throttle solenoid energized. On models equipped with vacuum release brake, whenever adjusting ignition timing or idle speed, vacuum line to brake release mechanism must be disconnected & plugged to prevent parking brake from releasing when selector lever is moved to Drive.

③—On kickdown step of cam.

④—On high step of fast idle cam.

⑤—Windsor engine.

⑥—Refer to engine calibration code on engine identification label, located at rear of left valve cover. The calibration code is located on the label after the engine code number and is preceded by the letter C and the revision code is located below the calibration code and is preceded by the letter R.

⑦—Calibration codes 7-19A-R1 & 7-19A-R17.

⑧—Calibration codes 7-19A-R2 & 7-19A-R3.

⑨—Calibration code 7-19A-R2, 525/650D RPM; 7-19A-R3, 550/650D RPM.

⑩—Models equipped with Electronic Engine Control (EEC) System.

⑪—Firing order 1-3-7-2-6-5-4-8. Cylinder numbering (front to rear): Right bank 1-2-3-4, left bank 5-6-7-8. Refer to Fig. C for spark plug wire connections at distributor.

⑫—At 625 RPM. Ignition timing is not adjustable.

⑬—With throttle solenoid energized. Higher idle speed is with A/C on, compressor clutch de-energized, if equipped.

⑭—Calibration code 8-19A-R1.

⑮—Calibration codes 8-19B-R11 & 8-19B-R14

⑯—ASF-52 or ARF-52.

⑰—Models equipped with Electronic Engine Control (EEC) System & Electronic Fuel Injection (EFI).

⑱—Calibration code 9-17P-R0A.

⑲—ASF-52-6 or ARF-52-6.

⑳—Calibration code 9-17Q-R0.

㉑—EEC timing is not adjustable.

㉒—On second step of fast idle cam.

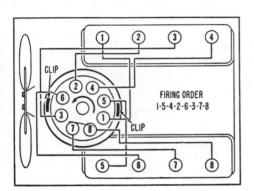

Fig. A

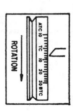

Fig. B

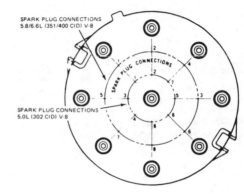

Fig. C

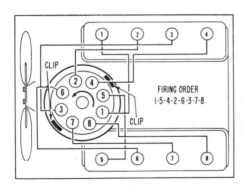

Fig. D

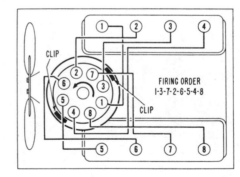

Fig. E

COOLING SYSTEM & CAPACITY DATA

Year	Model or Engine	Cooling Capactiy, Qts.		Radiator Cap Relief Pressure, Lbs.	Thermo. Opening Temp.	Fuel Tank Gals.	Engine Oil Refill Qts. ①	Transmission Oil			Rear Axle Oil Pints
		Less A/C	With A/C					3 Speed Pints	4 Speed Pints	Auto. Trans. Qts. ②	
1975	Lincoln	—	19¾	16	191	24¼	4	—	—	12½	5
	Mark IV	—	20	16	191	26½	4	—	—	12½	5
1976	Lincoln	—	19.7	16	191	24¼④	4	—	—	12½	5
	Mark IV	—	19.8	16	191	26½	4	—	—	12½	5
1977	Lincoln	⑥	⑥	16	191	24.2⑦	4	—	—	⑤	5
	Mark V	⑨	⑨	16	191	24.2⑦	4	—	—	⑤	5
	Versailles	⑧	⑧	16	191	19.2	4	—	—	10	5
1978	Lincoln	⑩	⑩	16	191	24.2	4	—	—	12½	5
	Mark V	③	③	16	191	25	4	—	—	12½	5
	Versailles	14.3	14.3	16	191	19.2	4	—	—	10¼	5
1979	Lincoln	—	16.9	16	196	24.2	4	—	—	11.8	5
	Mark V	—	16.9	16	196	25	4	—	—	11.8	5
	Versailles	—	14.3	16	196	19.2	4	—	—	10.0	5
1980	Lincoln	—	13.4⑪	16	196	18⑫	4⑭	—	—	12.0	⑬
	Mark VI	—	13.4⑪	16	196	18⑫	4⑭	—	—	12.0	⑬
	Versailles	—	14.4	16	196	19.2	4	—	—	9.6	5.25

①—Add one quart with filter change.
②—Approximate. Make final check with dipstick.
③—V8-400, 16.9; V8-460, 18.9.
④—Add 8 gals. with auxiliary tank.
⑤—FMX, 11 qts.; C6, 12.2 qts.
⑥—V8-400, 17.1; V8-460, 18.5.

⑦—Calif. V8-400, 20.0.
⑧—V8-302, 14.6; V8-351, 15.7.
⑨—V8-400, 17.5; V8-460, 19.4.
⑩—V8-400, 16.9; V8-460, 18.7.
⑪—V8-351W, 14.5 qt.
⑫—V8-351W, 20 gal.
⑬—7.5 inch axle, 3.75 pts; 8.5 inch axle, 4.25

pts.
⑭—Duel sump oil pan. When draining oil, it is necessary to remove both drain plugs. One drain plug is located at front of oil pan. The second drain plug is located on left side of oil pan.

Exc. Starfire & 1980 Omega—OLDSMOBILE

VEHICLE IDENTIFICATION PLATE:

1975–80 on left upper dash.

ENGINE NUMBER LOCATION

Buick built engines have the distributor located at the front of the engine. On 1979–80 models, the engine production code is located on front of right hand valve cover and top of left hand valve cover. On 1976–78 models, the engine production code is located on the right front of block. On 1975 models, the fifth digit in the VIN denotes the engine code.

On Chevrolet built 6-250 engines, the code is located on the cylinder block next to the distributor. Chevrolet built V8 engines have the distributor located at the rear of the engine with clockwise rotor rotation. On 1979–80 V8 engines, the engine production code is located front of right hand valve cover. On 1977–78 V8 engines, the code is stamped on the right hand side of engine.

Oldsmobile built engines have the distributor located at the rear of the engine with counterclockwise rotor rotation and right side mounted fuel pump. The engine production code is located on the oil filler tube on 1975 thru early 1978 engines or on the left side valve cover on late 1978 & 1979–80 engines.

Pontiac built V8 engines have the distirbutor located at the rear of the engine with counterclockwise rotor rotation and left side mounted fuel pump. On 1979–80 V8 engines, the engine production code is located on front of both left and right hand valve covers. On 1975 V8-400 engines, the production code is located on the right front of the cylinder block.

ENGINE IDENTIFICATION CODE

Year	Engine	Engine Prefix
1975	6-250 Man. Tr.①⑥	CJU
	6-250 Auto. Tr.①⑥	CJT
	6-250 Auto. Tr.②⑥	CJL
	V8-260 Man. Tr.①	QA, QK
	V8-260 Man. Tr. a/c①	QD, QN
	V8-260 Auto. Tr.①⑦⑧	QE
	V8-260 Auto. Tr.①⑦⑨	QB
	V8-260 Auto. Tr. a/c①⑦⑧	QJ
	V8-260 Auto. Tr. a/c①⑦⑨	QC
	V8-260 Auto. Tr.①⑩	QP
	V8-260 Auto. Tr. a/c①⑩	QT
	V8-260 Auto. Tr.②	TE, TJ, TP, TT
	V8-350 Auto. Tr.①⑦⑪	RS
	V8-350 Auto Tr. a/c①⑦⑪⑫	RT
	V8-350 Auto. Tr.⑦⑪⑬	RW
	V8-350 Auto. Tr. a/c⑦⑪⑬	RX
	V8-350 Auto. Tr.①	QL, QU
	V8-350 Auto. Tr. a/c①	QO, QX
	V8-350 Auto. Tr.②	TL, TU, TY
	V8-350 Auto. Tr. a/c②	TO, TW, TX
	V8-400 Auto. Tr.①⑬⑭	YH
	V8-400 Auto. Tr.①⑬⑭	YL, YM, YT
	V8-455 Auto. Tr. ①⑮	UB, UE
	V8-455 Auto. Tr. a/c①⑮	UC, UD
	V8-455 Auto. Tr.②⑮	VB, VE
	V8-455 Auto. Tr. a/c②⑮	VC, VD
	V8-455 Auto. Tr.①⑯	UP
	V8-455 Auto. Tr.②⑯	VP
1976	6-250 Man. Tr.①⑥	CCD, CCJ
	6-250 Auto. Tr.①⑥	CCF, CCH
	6-250 Auto. Tr.②⑥	CCC
	V8-260 Man. Tr.①	QA, QD, QK, QN
	V8-260 Man. Tr.②	TA, TD, TK, TN
	V8-260 Auto. Tr.①⑧	TE, TJ, TP, TT
	V8-260 Auto. Tr.①⑨	T2, T3
	V8-260 Auto. Tr.①⑨	T4, T5, T7, T8
	V8-350 Auto. Tr.①⑦⑪⑫	PA, PB
	V8-350 Auto. Tr.①⑦⑪⑬	PE, PF
	V8-350 Auto. Tr.②⑦⑪⑬	PM, PN
	V8-350 Auto. Tr.①	Q2, Q3, Q5
	V8-350 Auto. Tr.①⑰	Q4, Q6
	V8-350 Auto. Tr.②	TL, TO, TX, TW, TY
	V8-455 Auto. Tr. ①⑮	UB, UC, UD, UE
	V8-455 Auto. Tr.①⑮	U3, U5
	V8-455 Auto. Tr.①⑮⑰	U6, U7, U8
	V8-455 Auto. Tr.②⑮	VB, VD, VE, V3, V5
	V8-455 Auto. Tr.①⑯	U4
	V8-455 Auto. Tr.②⑯	V4
1977	V6-231 Man. Tr.④⑪	SG
	V6-231 Man. Tr.②⑪	SU
	V6-231 Auto. Tr.④⑪	SI
	V6-231 Auto. Tr.②⑪	SK, SL
	V6-231 Auto. Tr.③⑪	SM, SN
	V8-260 Man. Tr.④	OS, OT
	V8-260 Auto. Tr.④	QC, QD, QE, QJ
	V8-260 Auto. Tr.④	QU, QV

Year	Engine	Engine Prefix
	V8-305 Man. Tr.④⑥	CPA
	V8-305 Auto. Tr.④⑥	CPY
	V8-350 Auto. Tr.④⑥	CHY, CUB
	V8-350 Auto. Tr.②⑥	CKR
	V8-350 Auto. Tr.③⑥	CKM
	V8-350 Auto. Tr.④	QK, QI, QN, QO
	V8-350 Auto. Tr.④	QP, QQ
	V8-350 Auto. Tr.③	Q2, Q3
	V8-350 Auto. Tr.③	Q6, Q7, Q8, Q9
	V8-350 Auto. Tr.②	TB, TC, TU, TV
	V8-350 Auto. Tr.②	TN, TO, TX, TY
	V8-403 Auto. Tr.④⑮	UJ, UK, UL, UN
	V8-403 Auto. Tr.③⑮	U2, U3
	V8-403 Auto. Tr.②⑮	VA, VB, VJ, VK
	V8-403 Auto. Tr.④⑯	UE
	V8-403 Auto. Tr.③⑯	U6
	V8-403 Auto. Tr.②⑯	VE
1978	V6-231 Man. Tr.④⑪	EA, ET
	V6-231 Auto. Tr.④⑪	EB, EC, EH, OH
	V6-231 Auto. Tr.④⑪	EI, EJ, EM, EN
	V6-231 Auto. Tr.③⑪	EG
	V6-231 Auto. Tr.②⑪	EE, EK, EL, OK
	V8-260 Auto. Tr.④	QJ, QK, QX, QY
	V8-260 Auto. Tr.④	QL, QN, QT, QU
	V8-260 Auto. Tr.④	QD, QE
	V8-260 Auto. Tr.③	Q4, Q5
	V8-260 Auto. Tr.②	TJ, TK, TX, TY
	V8-305 Man. Tr.④⑥⑫	CTH, CRW
	V8-305 Auto. Tr.④⑥⑫	CTJ
	V8-305 Auto. Tr.③⑥⑫	CPZ
	V8-305 Auto. Tr.②⑥⑫	CRY, CRZ
	V8-305 Auto. Tr.④⑥⑬	DAC, AG, AJ, AK
	V8-305 Auto. Tr.④⑥⑬	CAJ, AM, AR
	V8-305 Auto. Tr.④⑥⑬	CPE, AH
	V8-350 Auto. Tr.③⑥	CHL, CMC
	V8-350 Auto. Tr.②⑥	CHJ
	V8-350 Auto. Tr.④	QO, QP, QQ, QS
	V8-350 Auto. Tr.④	Q2, Q3
	V8-350 Auto. Tr.②	TO, TP, TT, TU
	V8-350 Auto. Tr.②	TQ, TS, TV, TW
	V8-350 Auto. Tr.⑤⑱	QB, QC, QV, QW
	V8-350 Auto. Tr.③	Q6, Q7
	V8-403 Auto. Tr.④⑮	UA, UB, UD, UE
	V8-403 Auto. Tr.③⑮	U2, U3
	V8-403 Auto. Tr.②⑮	VA, VB, VJ, VK
	V8-403 Auto. Tr.④⑯	UC
	V8-403 Auto. Tr.③⑯	U4
	V8-403 Auto. Tr.②⑯	VC
1979	V6-231 Man. Tr.④⑪	NG, RA
	V6-231 Auto. Tr.④⑪	NJ, SJ, RB, SO
	V6-231 Auto. Tr.④⑪	NL, RX, SL, SR
	V6-231 Auto. Tr.④⑪	NK, RC, SK, SP
	V6-231 Auto. Tr.③⑪	RJ
	V6-231 Auto. Tr.②⑪	RG, RW
	V8-260 Man. Tr.④	UC, UD
	V8-260 Auto. Tr.④	UE, UJ, UK, UL

Year	Engine	Engine Prefix
	V8-260 Auto. Tr.④	UN, UO
	V8-260 Auto. Tr.③	U5
	V8-260 Auto. Tr.②	VC
	V8-260 Man. Tr.⑤⑱	UW, UX, V8, V9
	V8-260 Auto. Tr.⑤⑱	UP, UQ, V2, V7
	V8-301 Auto. Tr.④⑭	PXP, PYF
	V8-305 Auto. Tr.④⑥⑫	DTM
	V8-305 Auto. Tr.④⑥⑫	DNJ
	V8-305 Man. Tr.④⑥⑬	DNS
	V8-305 Auto. Tr.④⑥⑬	DNT, DNW, DTX
	V8-305 Auto. Tr.③⑥⑬	DTA
	V8-305 Auto. Tr.②⑥⑬	DNX, DNY
	V8-350 Auto. Tr.③⑥	DRX, DRY
	V8-350 Auto. Tr.②⑥	DRJ
	V8-350 Auto. Tr.④⑮	QO, QN, UT, US
	V8-350 Auto. Tr.④⑮	UU, UV
	V8-350 Auto. Tr.③⑮	U9, TY
	V8-350 Auto. Tr.②⑮	VE, VK
	V8-350 Auto. Tr.④⑯	TW
	V8-350 Auto. Tr.③⑯	TY
	V8-350 Auto. Tr.②⑯	TX
	V8-350 Auto. Tr.⑤⑬⑱	VO, VN, T2, T3
	V8-350 Auto. Tr.⑤⑮⑱	QQ, QP, QS, QT
	V8-350 Auto. Tr.⑤⑱	VO, VN, VQ
	V8-350 Auto. Tr.⑤⑱	V4, V6
	V8-350 Auto. Tr.⑤⑯⑱	QU, T6
	V8-350 Auto. Tr.③⑯⑱	QY, U3
	V8-403 Auto. Tr.④	QB
	V8-403 Auto. Tr.③	Q3
	V8-403 Auto. Tr.②	TB
1980	V6-231 Man. Tr.①⑪	EA
	V6-231 Auto. Tr.①⑪	EB, EC, EO, EP
	V6-231 Auto. Tr.①⑪	EM
	V6-231 Auto. Tr.②⑪	ES, ET
	V8-260 Auto. Tr.①	QAC, QAD, QAF, QAH
	V8-260 Auto. Tr.①⑱	VBK, VBL
	V8-265 Auto. Tr.①⑭	X6
	V8-305 Auto. Tr.①⑥	CEA, CMC, CMD, CMF
	V8-305 Auto. Tr.②⑥	CEC, CMM
	V8-307 Auto. Tr.①⑬	TAA, TAB, TAR, TAS
	V8-307 Auto. Tr.①⑬	TAJ, TAK, TAM
	V8-307 Auto. Tr.①⑯	TAN
	V8-350 Auto. Tr.①⑮	UAA, UAB, UAC
	V8-350 Auto. Tr.①⑮	UAN, UAR
	V8-350 Auto. Tr.②⑮	UAD, UAF
	V8-350 Auto. Tr.①⑯	UAC, UAN
	V8-350 Auto. Tr.②⑯	UAH
	V8-350 Auto. Tr.①⑮⑱	VBM, VBN, VBP, VBR
	V8-350 Auto. Tr.①⑮⑱	VBS, VBT, VCM
	V8-350 Auto. Tr.①⑯⑱	VCD, VCF
	V8-350 Auto. Tr.①⑯⑱	VBU
	V8-350 Auto. Tr.②⑯⑱	VCH

①—Except California.
②—California.
③—High altitude.
④—Exc. Calif. & High altitude.
⑤—Exc. high altitude.
⑥—Chevrolet built engine.
⑦—Omega.
⑧—Early production.
⑨—Late production.
⑩—Cutlass.
⑪—Buick built engine.
⑫—2 barrel carb.
⑬—4 barrel carb.
⑭—Pontiac Built engine.
⑮—Except Toronado.
⑯—Toronado.
⑰—Models w/2.41 rear axle ratio.
⑱—Diesel engine.

GENERAL ENGINE SPECIFICATIONS

Year	Engine	Carburetor	Bore and Stroke	Piston Displacement, Cubic Inches	Compression Ratio	Maximum Brake H.P. @ R.P.M.	Maximum Torque Ft. Lbs. @ R.P.M.	Normal Oil Pressure Pounds
1975	105 Horsepower①........6-250②	1 Barrel	3.87 × 3.53	250	8.25	105 @ 3800	185 @ 1200	36–41
	110 Horsepower①........V8-260	2 Barrel	3.50 × 3.385	260	8.5	110 @ 3400	205 @ 1600	30–45
	165 Horsepower①......V8-350③	4 Barrel	3.80 × 3.85	350	8.0	165 @ 3800	260 @ 2200	37
	170 Horsepower①........V8-350	4 Barrel	4.057 × 3.385	350	8.5	170 @ 3800	275 @ 2400	30–45
	190 Horsepower①........V8-400④	4 Barrel	4.1212 × 3.75	400	7.6	190 @ 3400	350 @ 2000	55–60
	190 Horsepower①........V8-455⑤	4 Barrel	4.126 × 4.25	455	8.5	190 @ 3600	350 @ 2400	30–45
	215 Horsepower①........V8-455⑥	4 Barrel	4.126 × 4.25	455	8.5	215 @ 2600	370 @ 2400	30–45
1976	105 Horsepower①........6-250②	1 Barrel	3.87 × 3.53	250	8.25	105 @ 3800	185 @ 1200	36–41
	110 Horsepower①........V8-260	2 Barrel	3.50 × 3.385	260	8.5	110 @ 3400	205 @ 1600	30–45
	140 Horsepower①........V8-350③	2 Barrel	3.80 × 3.85	350	8.0	140 @ 3200	280 @ 1800	37
	155 Horsepower①........V8-350③	4 Barrel	3.80 × 3.85	350	8.0	155 @ 3400	280 @ 1800	37
	170 Horsepower①........V8-350	4 Barrel	4.057 × 3.385	350	8.5	170 @ 3800	275 @ 2400	30–45
	190 Horsepower①........V8-455⑤	4 Barrel	4.126 × 4.25	455	8.5	190 @ 3400	350 @ 2000	30–45
	215 Horsepower①........V8-455⑥	4 Barrel	4.126 × 4.25	455	8.5	215 @ 3600	370 @ 2400	30–45
1977	105 Horsepower①........V6-231⑨	2 Barrel	3.80 × 3.40	231	8.0	105 @ 3400	185 @ 2000	37
	110 Horsepower①........V8-260	2 Barrel	3.50 × 3.385	260	8.0	110 @ 3400	205 @ 1600	30–45
	145 Horsepower①........V8-305②	2 Barrel	3.736 × 3.48	305	8.5	145 @ 3800	245 @ 2400	32–40
	170 Horsepower①........V8-350	4 Barrel	4.057 × 3.385	350	8.0	170 @ 3800	275 @ 2000	30–45
	170 Horsepower①........V8-350⑦	4 Barrel	4.057 × 3.385	350	8.0	170 @ 3800	275 @ 2400	30–45
	170 Horsepower①....V8-350②⑧	4 Barrel	4.00 × 3.48	350	8.5	170 @ 3800	270 @ 2400	32–40
	185 Horsepower①........V8-403⑤	4 Barrel	4.351 × 3.385	403	8.0	185 @ 3600	320 @ 2000	30–45
	200 Horsepower①........V8-403⑥	4 Barrel	4.351 × 3.385	403	8.0	200 @ 3600	330 @ 2400	30–45
1978	105 Horsepower①........V6-231⑨	2 Barrel	3.80 × 3.40	231	8.0	105 @ 3400	185 @ 2000	37
	110 Horsepower①........V8-260	2 Barrel	3.50 × 3.385	260	7.5	110 @ 2400	205 @ 1800	30–45
	145 Horsepower①........V8-305	2 Barrel	3.736 × 3.48	305	8.5	145 @ 3800	245 @ 2400	32–40
	160 Horsepower①........V8-305	4 Barrel	3.736 × 3.48	305	8.5	160 @ 4000	235 @ 2400	32–40
	160 Horsepower①........V8-350②	4 Barrel	4.00 × 3.48	350	8.5	160 @ 3800	260 @ 2400	32–40
	170 Horsepower①........V8-350	4 Barrel	4.057 × 3.385	350	8.0	170 @ 3800	275 @ 2000	30–45
	120 Horsepower①........V8-350⑩	Fuel Inj.	4.057 × 3.385	350	22.5	120 @ 3600	220 @ 1600	30–45
	185 Horsepower①........V8-403⑤	4 Barrel	4.351 × 3.385	403	8.0	185 @ 3600	320 @ 2200	30–45
	190 Horsepower①........V8-403⑥	4 Barrel	4.351 × 3.385	403	8.0	190 @ 3600	325 @ 2000	30–45
1979	115 Horsepower①........V6-231⑨	2 Barrel	3.80 × 3.40	231	8.0	115 @ 3800	190 @ 2000	37
	90 Horsepower①........V8-260⑩	—	3.50 × 3.385	260	22.5	90 @ 3600	160 @ 1600	35
	105 Horsepower①........V8-260	2 Barrel	3.50 × 3.385	260	7.5	105 @ 3600	205 @ 1800	30–45
	135 Horsepower①........V8-301④	2 Barrel	4.00 × 3.00	301	8.2	135 @ 3800	240 @ 1600	35–40
	130 Horsepower①........V8-305②	2 Barrel	3.736 × 3.48	305	8.5	130 @ 3200	245 @ 2000	32–40
	160 Horsepower①........V8-305②	4 Barrel	3.736 × 3.48	305	8.5	160 @ 4000	235 @ 2400	32–40
	160 Horsepower①........V8-350②	4 Barrel	4.00 × 3.48	350	8.5	160 @ 3600	260 @ 2400	32–40
	160 Horsepower①........V8-350⑤	4 Barrel	4.057 × 3.385	350	8.0	160 @ 3600	270 @ 2000	35
	165 Horsepower①........V8-350⑥	4 Barrel	4.057 × 3.385	350	8.0	165 @ 3600	275 @ 2000	35
	125 Horsepower①........V8-350⑩	—	4.057 × 3.385	350	22.5	125 @ 3600	225 @ 1600	30–45
	175 Horsepower①........V8-403	4 Barrel	4.351 × 3.385	403	7.8	175 @ 3600	310 @ 2000	35

Continued

GENERAL ENGINE SPECIFICATIONS—Continued

Year	Engine	Carburetor	Bore and Stroke	Piston Displacement, Cubic Inches	Compression Ratio	Maximum Brake H.P. @ R.P.M.	Maximum Torque Ft. Lbs. @ R.P.M.	Normal Oil Pressure Pounds
1980	110 Horsepower① V6-231⑨	2 Barrel	3.80 × 3.40	231	8.0	110 @ 3800	190 @ 1600	37
	105 Horsepower① V88-260	2 Barrel	3.50 × 3.385	260	7.5	105 @ 3400	195 @ 1600	30—45
	120 Horsepower① V8-265④	2 Barrel	3.75 × 3.00	265	8.3	120 @ 3600	210 @ 1600	35
	155 Horsepower① .. V8-305②⑪	4 Barrel	3.736 × 3.48	305	8.6	155 @ 4000	240 @ 1600	45
	155 Horsepower① ... V8-305②⑫	4 Barrel	3.736 × 3.48	305	8.6	155 @ 4000	230 @ 1600	45
	150 Horsepower① V8-307	4 Barrel	3.80 × 3.385	307	7.9	150 @ 3600	245 @ 1600	30—45
	105 Horsepower① V8-350⑩	—	4.057 × 3.385	350	22.5	105 @ 3200	205 @ 1600	30—45
	160 Horsepower① V8-350	4 Barrel	4.057 × 3.385	350	8.0	160 @ 3600	270 @ 1600	30—45

①—All horsepower and torque ratings are net.
②—Chevrolet-built engine.
③—Omega only. Buick-built engine.
④—Pontiac-built engine.
⑤—Exc. Toronado.
⑥—Toronado.
⑦—Cutlass.
⑧—Omega.
⑨—Buick-built engine.
⑩—Diesel.
⑪—Except Calif.
⑫—California.

TUNE UP SPECIFICATIONS

The following specifications are published from the latest information available. This
data should be used only in the absence of a decal affixed in the engine compartment.

★ When using a timing light, disconnect vacuum hose or tube at distributor and plug opening in hose or tube so idle speed will not be affected.

● When checking compression, lowest cylinder must be within 80 percent of highest.

▲ Before removing wires from distributor cap, determine location of the No. 1 wire in cap, as distributor position may have been altered from that shown at the end of this chart.

Year & Engine	Spark Plug Type	Spark Plug Gap	Firing Order Fig. ▲	Ignition Timing BTDC①★ Man. Trans.	Ignition Timing BTDC①★ Auto. Trans.	Mark Fig.	Curb Idle Speed② Man Trans.	Curb Idle Speed② Auto. Trans.	Fast Idle Speed Man. Trans.	Fast Idle Speed Auto. Trans.	Fuel Pump Pressure
1975											
6-250 Exc. Calif.③	R46TX	.060	I	10°	10°	C	425/850	425/550D	1800④	1700④	3½—4½
6-250 Calif.③	R46TX	.060	I	—	10°	C	—	425/600D	—	1700④	3½—4½
V8-260 Exc. Calif.	R46SX	.080	J	16°⑤	18°⑤	G	750	550/650D⑥	900⑦	900⑦	5½—6½
V8-260 Calif.	R46SX	.080	J	—	⑧	G	—	600/650D⑥	—	900⑦	5½—6½
V8-350 Omega⑨	R45TSX	.060	K	—	12°	D	—	600D	—	1800④⑩	3 Min.
V8-350 Exc. Calif. & Omega	R46SX	.080	J	—	20°⑤	G	—	550/650D⑥	—	900⑦	5½—6½
V8-350 Calif. Exc. Omega	R46SX	.080	J	—	20°⑤	G	—	600/650D⑥	—	1000⑦	5½—6½
V8-400 2 Barrel⑪	R46TSX	.060	L	—	16°	E	—	650D	—	—	5—6½
V8-400 4 Barrel⑪	R45TSX	.060	L	—	16°	E	—	⑫	—	1800④	5—6½
V8-455 Exc. Calif.⑬	R46SX	.080	J	—	16°⑤	G	—	550/650D⑥	—	900⑦	5½—6½
V8-455 Calif.⑬	R46SX	.080	J	—	16°⑤	G	—	600/650D⑥	—	800⑦	5½—6½
V8-455 Toronado Exc. Calif.	R46SX	.080	J	—	12°⑤	G	—	550/650D⑥	—	900⑦	5½—6½
V8-455 Toronado Calif.	R46SX	.080	J	—	12°⑤	G	—	600/650D⑥	—	800⑦	5½—6½
1976											
6-250 Exc. Calif.③	R46TS	.035	I	6°	10°	C	425/850	425/550D	1800④	1700④	3½—4½
6-250 Calif.③	R46TS	.035	I	—	10°	C	—	425/600D	—	1700④	3½—4½
V8-260 Exc. Calif.	⑭	⑭	J	16°⑤	18°⑤	G	750	550/650D⑥	900⑦	900⑦	5½—6½
V8-260 Calif.	⑭	⑭	J	14°⑤	⑮	G	750	⑥⑯	1000⑦	900⑦	5½—6½
V8-350 Omega⑨	R45TSX	.060	K	—	12°	D	—	600D	—	1800④⑩	3 Min.

Continued

TUNE UP SPECIFICATIONS—Continued

Year & Engine	Spark Plug Type	Gap	Firing Order Fig. ▲	Ignition Timing BTDC① ★ Man. Trans.	Auto. Trans.	Mark Fig.	Curb Idle Speed② Man Trans.	Auto. Trans.	Fast Idle Speed Man Trans.	Auto. Trans.	Fuel Pump Pressure
1976—Continued											
V8-350 Exc. Calif. & Omega	⑭	⑭	J	—	20°⑤	G	—	550/650D⑥	—	900⑦	5½–6½
V8-350 Calif. Exc. Omega	⑭	⑭	J	—	20°⑤	G	—	600/650D⑥	—	1000⑦	5½–6½
V8-455 Exc. Calif.⑬	⑭	⑭	J	—	16°⑤⑰	G	—	550/650D⑥	—	900⑦	5½–6½
V8-455 Calif.⑬	⑭	⑭	J	—	16°⑤	G	—	600/650D⑥	—	800⑦	5½–6½
V8-455 Toronado Exc. Calif.	⑭	⑭	J	—	14°⑤	G	—	550/650D⑥	—	900⑦	5½–6½
V8-455 Toronado Calif.	⑭	⑭	J	—	12°⑤	G	—	600/650D⑥	—	800⑦	5½–6½
1977											
V6-231⑧⑱	⑲	⑲	M	12°	12°	B⑳	600/800	600/670D㉑	—	—	3 Min.
V6-231⑧㊴	R46TSX	.060	A	—	15°	F⑳	—	600/670D㉑	—	—	3 Min.
V8-260	R46SZ	.060	J	16°⑤	㉒	G	750	550/650D⑥	900⑦	900⑦	5½–6½
V8-305③	R45TS	.045	O	8°	8°	C	600	500/650D	—	—	7½–9
V8-350 Exc. Calif.③㉓	R45TS	.045	O	—	8°	C	—	㉔	—	1600④	7½–9
V8-350 Exc. Calif. & High Alt.㉕	R46SZ	.060	J	—	20°③	G	—	550/650D⑥	—	900⑦	5½–6½
V8-350 Calif.㉕	R46SZ	.060	J	—	㉖	G	—	550/650D⑥	—	1000⑦	5½–6½
V8-350 High Alt.㉕	R46SZ	.060	J	—	20°⑤	G	—	600/700D⑥	—	1000⑦	5½–6½
V8-403 Exc. Calif. & High Alt.⑬	R46SZ	.060	J	—	㉗	G	—	550/650D⑥	—	900⑦	5½–6½
V8-403 Calif. & High Alt.⑬	R46SZ	.060	J	—	20°⑤	G	—	⑥㉘	—	1000⑦	5½–6½
V8-403 Toronado	R46SZ	.060	J	—	㉙	G	—	⑥㉚	—	⑦㉛	5½–6½
1978											
V6-231	R46TSX	.060	A	15°	15°	F⑳	800	㉜	1850④	1850④	3 Min.
V8-260 Exc. Calif. & High Alt.	R46SZ	.060	J	18°⑤	20°⑤	G	650/800⑥	500/650D⑥	750⑦	800⑦	5½–6½
V8-260 Calif.	R46SZ	.060	J	—	18°⑤	G	—	500/650D⑥	—	800⑦	5½–6½
V8-260 High Alt.	R46SZ	.060	J	—	20°⑤	G	—	550/650D⑥	—	900⑦	5½–6½
V8-305 2 Barrel Exc. Calif.③㉝	R45TS	.045	O	4°	4°	C	600/700	500/600D	1600④	1600④	7½–9
V8-305 2 Barrel Calif.③㉞	R45TS	.045	O	—	8°	C	—	㉟	—	1600④	7½–9
V8-305 4 Barrel	R45TS	.045	O	—	4°	C	—	500/600D	—	1600④	7½–9
V8-350③㉓	R45TS	.045	O	—	8°	C	—	㉔	—	1600④	7½–9
V8-350 Exc. Calif. & High Alt.㉓	R46SZ	.060	J	—	20°⑤	G	—	550/650D⑥	—	900⑦	5½–6½
V8-350 Calif. & High Alt.㉕	R46SZ	.060	J	—	20°⑤	G	—	㉘	—	1000⑦	5½–6½
V8-350 Diesel	—	—	—	㊱	—	—	—	575/650D⑥	—	—	—
V8-403 Exc. Calif. & High Alt.⑬	R46SZ	.060	J	—	㊲	G	—	550/650D⑥	—	900⑦	5½–6½
V8-403 Calif. & High Alt.⑬	R46SZ	.060	J	—	20°⑤	G	—	㉘	—	1000⑦	5½–6½
V8-403 Toronado	R46SZ	.060	J	—	㉙	G	—	⑥㉚	—	⑦㉛	5½–6½

Continued

TUNE UP SPECIFICATIONS—Continued

| Year & Engine | Spark Plug | | Ignition Timing BTDC①★ | | | | Curb Idle Speed② | | Fast Idle Speed | | Fuel Pump Pressure |
	Type	Gap	Firing Order Fig. ▲	Man. Trans.	Auto. Trans.	Mark Fig.	Man Trans.	Auto. Trans.	Man. Trans.	Auto. Trans.	
1979											
V6-231 Exc. Calif. & High Alt.⑨	R46TSX	.060	A	15°	15°	F	600/800⑥	550/670D⑥	2200	2200	3 Min.
V6-231 Calif. & High Alt.⑨	R46TSX	.060	A	—	15°	F	—	600D	—	2200	3 Min.
V8-260 Exc. Calif. & High Alt.	R46SZ	.060	J	18°⑤	20°⑤	G	650/800⑥	500/625D⑥	750	800	5½–6½
V8-260 Calif.	R46SZ	.060	J	—	18°⑤	G	—	500/625D⑥	—	800	5½–6½
V8-260 High Alt.	R46SZ	.060	J	—	20°⑤	G	—	550/650D⑥	—	900	5½–6½
V8-260 Diesel	—	—	—	㊱	㊱	—	575/695	590/650D	—	—	—
V8-301⑪	R46TSX	.060	L	—	12°	N	—	500/650D⑥	—	2000	7–8½
V8-305 2 Barrel③	R45TS	.045	O	4°	4°	C	600/700	500/600D⑥	1300	1600	7½–9
V8-305 4 Barrel Exc. High Alt.③	R45TS	.045	O	4°	4°	C	700	500/600D⑥	1300	1600	7½–9
V8-305 4 Barrel High Alt.③	R45TS	.045	O	—	8°	C	—	600/650D⑤	—	1750	7½–9
V8-350 Calif.③⑳	R45TS	.045	O	—	8°	C	—	500/600D⑥	—	1600	7½–9
V8-350 High Alt.③⑳	R45TS	.045	O	—	8°	C	—	600/650D⑥	—	1750	7½–9
V8-350 Exc. Calif.㉕	R46SZ	.060	J	—	㊳	G	—	550/650D⑥	—	900	5½–6½
V8-350 Calif.㉕	R46SZ	.060	J	—	20°⑤	G	—	500/600D⑥	—	1000	5½–6½
V8-350 Diesel	—	—	—	—	㊱	—	—	575/650D	—	—	—
V8-403 Exc. Calif.	R46SZ	.060	J	—	20°⑤	G	—	550/650D⑥	—	900	5½–6½
V8-403 Calif.	R46SZ	.060	J	—	20°⑤	G	—	500/600D⑥	—	1000	5½–6½
1980											
V6-231 Exc. Calif.⑨	R45TS	.040	A	15°	15°	F	600/800	550/670D	2200	2000	4¼–5¾
V8-231 Calif.⑨	—	—	A	—	15°	F	—	—	—	—	4¼–5¾
V8-260	R46SX	.080	J	—	㊵	G	—	500/625D	—	700	5½–6½
V8-305 Exc. Calif.③	R45TS	.045	O	—	4°	C	—	500/600D	—	1850	7½–9
V8-305 Calif.③	R45TS	.045	O	—	4°	C	—	550/650D	—	2200	7½–9
V8-307	R46SX	.080	J	—	20°⑤	G	—	500/600D	—	700	5½–6½
V8-350 Exc. Calif.	R46SX	.080	J	—	18°⑤	G	—	500/600D	—	700	5½–6½
V8-350 Calif.	R46SX	.080	J	—	㊶	G	—	550/650D	—	700	5½–6½
V8-350 Diesel Exc. Calif.	—	—	—	—	7°㊱	—	—	550/650D	—	750	—
V8-350 Diesel Calif.	—	—	—	—	7°㊱	—	—	550/650D	—	750	—

Continued

OLDSMOBILE—Exc. Starfire & 1980 Omega

TUNE UP NOTES

①—BTDC Before top dead center.

②—Idle speed on man. trans. vehicles is adjusted in Neutral & on auto. trans. equipped vehicles is adjusted in Drive unless otherwise specified. Where two idle speeds are listed, the higher the speed is with the A/C or idle solenoid energized.

③—Chevrolet-built engine.

④—With cam follower or stop screw on high step of fast idle cam, EGR vacuum line disconnected & plugged & A/C off.

⑤—At 1100 RPM.

⑥—Idle speed with solenoid energized is adjusted with A/C on & compressor clutch wires disconnected.

⑦—With stop screw of low step of fast idle cam, EGR disconnected & plugged & A/C off.

⑧—Except Omega, 16°BTDC at 1100 RPM; Omega, 14°BTDC at 1100 RPM.

⑨—Buick-built engine.

⑩—4 barrel carb. models only.

⑪—Pontiac-built engine.

⑫—Early production (engine code YM), 650D RPM; late production (engine code YL), 625D RPM.

⑬—Except Toronado.

⑭—Early production, R46SX gapped at .080"; late production, R46SZ gapped at .060".

⑮—Cutlass engine codes TP, TT & Omega engine codes T2, T3, T7 & T8, set at 16°BTDC at 1100 RPM. Cutlass engine codes T4, T5 & Omega

engine codes TE & TJ, set at 14°BTDC at 1100 RPM.

⑯—Cutlass engine codes TP, TT & Omega engine codes TE & TJ, 600/650D RPM. Cutlass engine codes T4, T5 & Omega engine codes T2, T3, T7 & T8, 550/650D RPM.

⑰—On 98 models engine codes U6, U7 & U8 with 2.41 axle ratio, set at 18°BTDC at 1100 RPM.

⑱—Except even fire engine.

⑲—Early production, R46TS gapped at .040"; late production, R46TSX gapped at .060".

⑳—The harmonic balancer on these engines has two timing marks. The timing mark measuring 1/16 in. is used when setting timing with a hand held timing light. The mark measuring 1/8 in. is used when setting timing with magnetic timing equipment.

㉑—Idle speed with solenoid energized is adjusted with distributor vacuum advance hose disconnected & plugged, A/C on & compressor clutch wires disconnected.

㉒—Except Cutlass, 20°BTDC at 1100 RPM; Cutlass 18°BTDC at 1100 RPM.

㉓—Distributor located at rear of engine, rotor rotation clockwise.

㉔—Except high altitude, 500/650D RPM; high altitude, 600/650D RPM.

㉕—Distributor located at rear of engine, rotor rotation counter clockwise.

㉖—Omega & 88 except sta. wag., 18°BTDC at 1100 RPM; Cutlass, 88 sta. wag. & 98, 20°BTDC at 1100 RPM.

㉗—Cutlass except sta. wag., 88 & 98, 20°BTDC at 1100 RPM; Cutlass sta. wag., 22°BTDC at 1100 RPM.

㉘—Except high altitude, 550/650D RPM; high altitude, 600/700D RPM.

㉙—equipped with Electronic Spark Timing (EST), refer to text for procedure.

㉚—Except Calif.; high altitude, 550/650D RPM; California, 600/650D RPM; high altitude 600/700D RPM.

㉛—Except Calif. & high altitude, 900 RPM; California & high altitude, 1000 RPM.

㉜—Except 88 with A/C, 600D RPM; 88 with A/C, 600/670D RPM see note 21.

㉝—Except high altitude.

㉞—High altitude.

㉟—Except high altitude, 500/650D RPM; high altitude, 600/700D RPM.

㊱—Injection timing at 800 RPM.

㊲—88 except sta. wag. & 98, 18°BTDC at 1100 RPM; 88 sta. wag., 20°BTDC at 1100 RPM.

㊳—Except engine codes QN & QO, 20°BTDC at 1100 RPM; engine codes QN & QO, 18°BTDC at 1100 RPM.

㊴—Even fire engine.

㊵—Engine codes QAC & QAD, 20° BTDC at 1100 RPM; engine codes QAF & QAH, 18° BTDC at 1100 RPM.

㊶—Engine codes UAD & UAF, 18° BTDC at 1100 RPM; engine codes UAH, 16° BTDC at 1100 RPM.

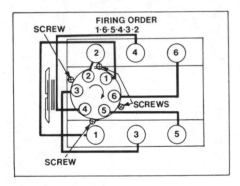

Fig. A

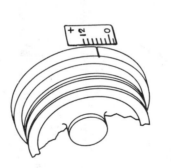

Fig. B

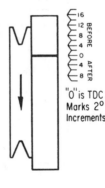

"0" is TDC Marks 2° Increments

Fig. C

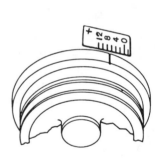

Fig. D

Fig. E

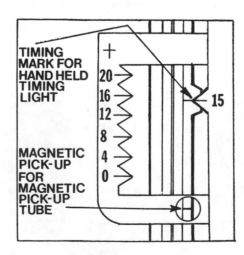

Fig. F

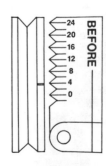

Fig. G

Continued

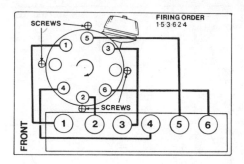

Fig. I

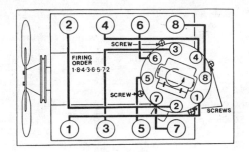

Fig. J

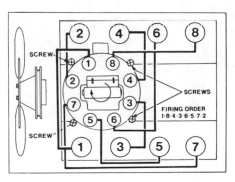

Fig. K

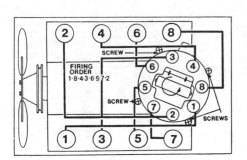

Fig. L

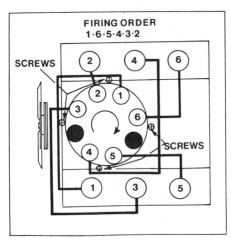

Fig. M

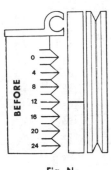

Fig. N

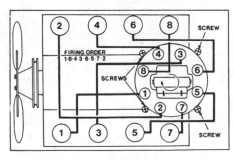

Fig. O

COOLING SYSTEM & CAPACITY DATA

Year	Model or Engine	Cooling Capacity, Qts.		Radiator Cap Relief Pressure, Lbs.	Thermo. Opening Temp. [1]	Fuel Tank Gals.	Engine Oil Refill Qts. [2]	Transmission Oil			Auto. Trans. Qts. [12]	Rear Axle Oil Pints
		Less A/C	With A/C					3 Speed Pints	4 Speed Pints	5 Speed Pints		
1975	6-250 Omega	15½	19½	15	195	21	4	3½	—	—	[10]	[9]
	6-250 Cutlass	17	17	15	195	22	4	3½	—	—	[10]	[9]
	8-260 Omega	18½	19½	15	195	21	4	3½	—	—	[10]	[9]
	8-260 Cutlass	23½	23½[4]	15	195	22	4	3½	—	—	[10]	[9]
	8-350 Omega	18½	19½	15	195	21	4	—	—	—	[10]	[9]
	8-350[7]	20	20[4]	15	195	26[8]	4	—	—	—	[10]	[9]
	8-400	21½	22[6]	15	195	26[8]	4	—	—	—	[10]	[9]
	8-455	21	21½[6]	15	195	26[8]	4	—	—	—	[10]	[9]
	Toronado	21	21½	15	195	26	5	—	—	—	[17]	4[3]
1976	6-250 Omega	15½	16½	15	195	21	4	3½	—	—	[10]	5½
	6-250 Cutlass	17	17	15	195	22	4	3½	—	3½	[10]	4¼
	8-260 Omega	18½	19½	15	195	21	4	3½	—	3½	[10]	5½
	V8-260 Cutlass	23½	23½[4]	15	195	22	4	3½	—	3½	[10]	4½
	V8-350 Omega	18½	19½	15	195	21	4	—	—	—	[10]	5½
	8-350[7]	20	20[4]	15	195	26[8]	4	—	—	—	[10]	[18]
	8-455	21	21½[6]	15	195	26[8]	4	—	—	—	[10]	[18]
	Toronado	21	21½[6]	15	195	26	5	—	—	—	[17]	4[3]
1977	6-231 Omega	12.7	13.7	15	195	21	4	3	—	—	[14]	3½
	6-231 Cutlass	16.9	17.0	15	195	22	4	3	—	—	[10]	4¼
	6-231[13]	11.5	11.4	15	195	[13][16]	4	—	—	—	[14]	3½
	8-260 Omega	16.8	17.8	15	195	21	4	—	—	3½	[14]	3½
	8-260 Cutlass	16.9	17.0	15	195	22	4	—	—	3½	[14]	4¼
	8-260[13]	15.5	15.3	15	195	[13][16]	4	—	—	—	[14]	3½
	8-305 Omega	—	—	15	195	21	4	3	—	—	[14]	3½
	8-350 Omega	15.6	16.6	15	195	21	4	—	—	—	[14]	3½
	8-350 Cutlass	15.1	15.3	15	195	22	4	—	—	—	[14]	4¼
	8-350[13]	13.8	13.7	15	195	[13][16]	4	—	—	—	[14]	4¼
	8-403 Cutlass	16.3	16.4	15	195	22	4	—	—	—	[14]	4¼
	8-403[13]	14.9	14.8	15	195	24½[16]	4	—	—	—	[14]	4¼
	8-403 Tornado	17.2	17.4	15	195	26	5	—	—	—	[17]	4[3]
1978	V6-231 Omega	12.75	12.75	15	195	21	4	3.5	—	3.5	[10]	3½
	V6-231 Cutlass	12	12	15	195	17.5[24]	4	3.5	—	3.5	[14]	4¼
	V6-231 88	12.25	12.25	15	195	25.3	4	—	—	—	[14]	[27]
	V8-260 Cutlass	16.25[19]	16.25[19]	15	195	17.5[24]	4	—	—	3.5	[14]	4¼
	V8-260 88	16.25[20]	16.25[20]	15	195	25.3	4	—	—	—	[14]	[27]
	V8-305 Omega	15.75[19]	16.0[19]	15	195	21	4	—	2.5	—	[10]	3½
	V8-305 Cutlass	15.5[21]	15.5[21]	15	195	17.5[24]	4	—	2.5	—	[14]	4¼
	V8-350 Omega	16	16.75	15	195	21	4	—	—	—	[10]	3½
	V8-350 Cutlass	15.5	16.25	15	195	17.5[24]	4	—	—	—	[14]	4¼
	V8-350 Diesel	18	18	15	195	27.25[25]	7[26][28]	—	—	—	[14]	[27]
	V8-350[13]	14	15.5	15	195	[5]	4	—	—	—	[14]	[27]
	V8-403[13]	15.75	16.5	15	195	25.3[25]	4	—	—	—	[14]	[27]
	V8-403 Toronado	17.5[23]	17.5[23]	15	195	26	5	—	—	—	[17]	4[3]

Continued

COOLING SYSTEM & CAPACITY DATA—Continued

Year	Model or Engine	Cooling Capacity, Qts. Less A/C	Cooling Capacity, Qts. With A/C	Radiator Cap Relief Pressure, Lbs.	Thermo. Opening Temp. [1]	Fuel Tank Gals.	Engine Oil Refill Qts. [2]	3 Speed Pints	4 Speed Pints	5 Speed Pints	Auto. Trans. Qts. [12]	Rear Axle Oil Pints
1979	V6-231 Omega	12.75	12.75	15	195	21	4	3	—	—	[10]	3½
	V6-231 Cutlass	13.25	13.25	15	195	18.1[24]	4	3	3	—	[14]	4¼
	V6-231 88	13.25	13.25	15	195	25	4	—	—	—	[14]	[27]
	V6-260 Cutlass	16.25[9]	16.25[19]	15	195	18.1[24]	4	—	—	3½	[14]	4¼
	V8-260 Cutlass[22]	20	20	15	195	19.8	7[25][28]	—	—	3½	[14]	4¼
	V8-260 88	16.25[20]	16.25[20]	15	195	25	4	—	—	—	[14]	[27]
	V8-301 88	20[11]	20[11]	15	195	25	5[29]	—	—	—	[14]	[27]
	V8-305 Omega	15.75[19]	16[19]	15	195	21	4	—	3	—	[10]	3½
	V8-305 Cutlass	15.5[21]	15.5[21]	15	195	18.1[24]	4	—	3	—	[14]	4¼
	V8-350 Omega	16[19]	16[19]	15	195	21	4	—	—	—	[10]	3½
	V8-350 Cutlass[30]	15.5[21]	15.5[21]	15	195	18.1[24]	4	—	—	—	[14]	4¼
	V8-350 Cutlass[31]	14.5[32]	15[32]	15	195	18.1[24]	4	—	—	—	[14]	4¼
	V8-350 Cutlass[22]	17.5	17.5	15	195	19.8	7[26][28]	—	—	—	[14]	4¼
	V8-350[13]	14.5[33]	14.5[33]	15	195	[34]	4	—	—	—	[14]	[27]
	V8-350[13][22]	18	18	15	195	27	7[26][28]	—	—	—	[14]	[27]
	V8-350 Toronado	15[35]	15[35]	15	195	20	4	—	—	—	[36]	3¼[3]
	V8-350 Toronado[22]	18.5	18.5	15	195	22.8	7[26][28]	—	—	—	[36]	3¼[3]
	V8-403[13]	15.75[37]	16.5	15	195	25[25]	4	—	—	—	[14]	[27]
1980	V6-231 Cutlass	13	13	15	195	18[24]	4	3	—	—	[38]	[27]
	V6-231 88	13	13	15	195	20¾	4	—	—	—	[38]	[27]
	V8-260 Cutlass	16	16½	15	195	18[24]	4	—	—	—	[40]	[27]
	V8-260 Cutlass[22]	19½	19½	15	195	19¾[24]	7[26][28]	—	—	—	[39]	[27]
	V8-265 88	19[41]	19[41]	15	195	25	4[29]	—	—	—	[39]	[27]
	V8-305 Cutlass	15¼[42]	15¼[42]	15	195	18[24]	4	—	—	—	[43]	[27]
	V8-307 88 & 98	15½[21]	15½[21]	15	195	20¾[44]	4	—	—	—	[45]	[27]
	V8-307 Toronado	16¼	16¼	15	195	21	4	—	—	—	[36]	3¼[3]
	V8-350 Cutlass	15	15	15	195	18	4	—	—	—	[40]	[27]
	V8-350 88 & 98	14½[33]	14½[33]	15	195	25	4	—	—	—	[46]	[27]
	V8-350 Toronado	15½[32]	15½[32]	15	195	21	4	—	—	—	[36]	3¼[3]
	V8-350 Cutlass[22]	17¼	17¼	15	195	19¾[24]	7[26][28]	—	—	—	[39]	[27]
	V8-350 88 & 98[22]	18¼	18	15	195	27	7[26][28]	—	—	—	[39]	[27]
	V8-350 Toronado[22]	18	18	15	195	23	7[26][28]	—	—	—	[36]	3¼[3]

[1]—For Permanent type anti-freeze.
[2]—Add one quart with filter change.
[3]—Final drive
[4]—With heavy duty cooling system add 2½ qts.
[5]—Delta 88 sedan & Calif. coupe, 21 gals.; Custom Cruiser, 22 gals.; all others 25.3 gals.
[6]—With heavy duty cooling system add 2 qts.
[7]—Intermediate and full size.
[8]—Intermediate and station wagons 22 gallons.
[9]—8½" ring gear 4¼ pts., 8⅞" ring gear 5½ pts., 9⅜ ring gear 5½ pts.
[10]—Oil pan only 3 qts. After overhaul 10 qts.
[11]—Trailer towing, 21 qts.
[12]—Approximate; make final check with dipstick.
[13]—Full size cars.
[14]—Turbo Hydro-matic 200: Oil pan only, 3 qts.; after overhaul, 9 qts. T.H. 250, 350 & 400: par only, 3 qts.; after overhaul, 10 qts.
[15]—Delta 88 except Calif. V8-350: 21 gals.; Calif. V8-350 & Ninety-Eight models: 24½ gals.
[16]—Custom Cruiser 22 gallons.
[17]—Oil pan only 4 qts. after overhaul 12 qts.
[18]—8½" ring gear, 4¼ pts.; 8⅞" ring gear, 5½ pts.
[19]—Heavy duty & trailer towing, 16.75 qts.
[20]—Trailer towing, 17.0 qts.; Heavy duty, 17.25 qts.
[21]—Heavy duty & trailer towing, 16.25 qts.
[22]—Diesel engine.
[23]—Trailer towing, 17.25 qts.
[24]—Cutlass Cruiser, 18.25 gals.
[25]—Custom Cruiser, 22 gals.
[26]—Includes filter.
[27]—Exc. 7.5" ring gear, 4.25 pts.; 7.5" ring gear, 3.5 pts.
[28]—Recommended diesel engine oil—1978, use oil designation SE/CD; 1979–80; use oil designated SE/CC.
[29]—With or without filter change.
[30]—Distributor located at rear of engine, clockwise rotor rotation.
[31]—Distributor located at rear of engine, counter clockwise rotor rotation.
[32]—Trailer towing, 15.25 qts.
[33]—Heavy duty & trailer towing, 15.5 qts.
[34]—Delta 88 Calif. models & models with power seats, 20.7 gals.; Custom Cruiser, 22 gals.; all other models, 25 gals.
[35]—Heavy duty, 16 qts.; trailer towing 15.5 qts.
[36]—Oil pan, 5 qts.; after overhaul, 12 qts.
[37]—Trailer towing, 16.25 qts.
[38]—T.H.M. 200 & 200C, oil pan 3½ qts., after overhaul 9½ qts., T.H.M. 350 & 350C, oil pan 3¼ qts., after overhaul 12¼ qts.
[39]—Oil pan, 3½ qts.; after overhaul, 9½ qts.
[40]—Oil pan, 3¼ qts.; after overhaul, 12¼ qts.
[41]—With heavy duty cooling system, 19¾ qts.
[42]—With heady duty cooling system, 16 qts.
[43]—T.H.M. 200 & 200C, oil pan 3½ qts.; after overhaul 9½ qts.; T.H.M. 250C, oil pan 4 qts.; after overhaul 10 qts.; T.H.M. 350 & 350C, oil pan 3¼ qts., after overhaul 12¼ qts.
[44]—98 models, 25 gals.
[45]—T.H.M. 250C, oil pan 4 qts.; after overhaul 10 qts.; T.H.M. 350 & 350C, oil pan 3¼ qts., after overhaul 12¼ qts.; T.H.M. 400, oil pan 3 qts., after overhaul 10 qts.
[46]—T.H.M. 200 & 200C, oil pan 4 qts., after overhaul 10 qts.; T.H.M. 350 & 350C, oil pan 3¼ qts., after overhaul 12¼ qts.; T.H.M. 400, oil pan 3 qts., after overhaul 10 qts.

SERIAL NUMBER LOCATION

1975–80: On plate fastened to upper left instrument panel area, visible through windshield.

ENGINE IDENTIFICATION

On Pontiac Built 4-151 engines, the engine code is located on the distributor mounting pad. On 1975–79 V8-301, 350, 400 and 455 engines, the engine code number is located on front of cylinder block below right cylinder head. On 1980 V8-265 and 301 engines, the engine code is located on labels attached to front of left and right hand valve covers.

On Buick built 1975–76 Ventura V8-350 and 1977 V6-231 engines, the engine code is located on front of block below right cylinder head. On 1978–80 V6-231 and V8-350 engines, the engine code label is located on left hand valve cover.

On Chevrolet built 6-250 engines, the engine code is stamped on a pad located at right side of cylinder block to rear of distributor. On V6-229, V8-305, and 350 engines, the engine code is located on front of block below right cylinder head.

On Oldsmobile built 1975–76 V8-260, and 1977 V8-350 and 403 engines, the engine code is located on a label attached to the oil filler tube. On 1978–79 V8-403, 1978–80 V8-350 and 1980 V8-350 Diesel engines, the engine code is located on a label attached to left hand valve cover.

ENGINE CODES

1975

CODE	TRANS.	ENGINE
JT	6	6-250[9][14]
JL	6	6-250[9][14]
QA	4	V8-260[1][12]
QD	4	V8-260[1][12]
QE	6	V8-260[1][12]
QJ	6	V8-260[1][12]
TE	6	V8-260[1][12]
TJ	6	V8-260[1][12]
RS	6	V8-350[13]
RI	6	V8-350[13]
YA	6	V8-350[1]
YB	6	V8-350[1]
RW	6	V8-350[13]
RX	6	V8-350[13]
RN	6	V8-350[13]
RO	6	V8-350[13]
WN	6	V8-350[2]
YN	4	V8-350[2]
ZP	6	V8-350[2]
YH	6	V8-400[1]
YT	6	V8-400[1]
ZT	6	V8-400[2]
YM	6	V8-400[2]
WT	4	V8-400[2]
YS	6	V8-400[2]
YW	6	V8-455[2]
YU	6	V8-455[2]
ZU	6	V8-455[2]
ZW	6	V8-455[2]
WX	5	V8-455[2]

1976

CODE	TRANS.	ENGINE
CC	6	6-250[9][14]
CD	4	6-250[9][14]
CF	6	6-250[9][14]
CH	6	6-250[9][14]
CJ	4	6-250[9][14]
QA	7	V8-260[1][12]
QB	6	V8-260[1][12]
QC	6	V8-260[1][12]
QD	7	V8-260[1][12]
QK	7	V8-260[1][12]
QN	7	V8-260[1][12]
QP	6	V8-260[1][12]
QT	6	V8-260[1][12]
TA	7	V8-260[1][12]
TD	7	V8-260[1][12]
TE	7	V8-260[1][12]
TJ	6	V8-260[1][12]
TK	7	V8-260[1][12]
TN	7	V8-260[1][12]
TP	6	V8-260[1][12]
TT	6	V8-260[1][12]
T2	6	V8-260[1][12]
T3	6	V8-260[1][12]
T4	6	V8-260[1][12]
T5	6	V8-260[1][12]
PA	6	V8-350[1][13]
PB	6	V8-350[1][13]
PO	6	V8-350[1][13]
XH	6	V8-350[1]
XN	6	V8-350[1]

CODE	TRANS.	ENGINE
YA	6	V8-350[1]
YB	6	V8-350[1]
YK	6	V8-350[1]
YL	6	V8-350[1]
YP	6	V8-350[1]
YR	6	V8-350[1]
PE	6	V8-350[2][13]
PF	6	V8-350[2][13]
PM	6	V8-350[2][13]
PN	6	V8-350[2][13]
PP	6	V8-350[2][13]
X3	6	V8-350[2]
YD	6	V8-350[2]
ZC	6	V8-350[2]
ZX	6	V8-350[2]
X3	6	V8-350[11]
XM	6	V8-350[11]
XP	6	V8-350[11]
XR	6	V8-350[11]
XU	6	V8-350[11]
XW	6	V8-350[11]
XX	6	V8-350[11]
ZF	6	V8-350[11]
ZH	6	V8-350[11]
XA	6	V8-400[1]
XB	6	V8-400[1]
XC	6	V8-400[1]
XJ	6	V8-400[1]
YC	6	V8-400[1]
YJ	6	V8-400[1]
Z8	6	V8-400[1]
WT	5	V8-400[2]
YS	6	V8-400[2]
YT	6	V8-400[2]
YY	6	V8-400[2]
YZ	6	V8-400[2]
Y6	6	V8-400[2]
Y7	6	V8-400[2]
ZA	6	V8-400[2]
ZK	6	V8-400[2]
X4	6	V8-400[11]
X6	6	V8-400[11]
X7	6	V8-400[11]
X9	6	V8-400[11]
X8	6	V8-400[11]
XS	6	V8-400[11]
XT	6	V8-400[11]
XY	6	V8-400[11]
XZ	6	V8-400[11]
ZJ	6	V8-400[11]
ZL	6	V8-400[11]
WX	5	V8-455[2]
Y3	6	V8-455[2]
Y4	6	V8-455[2]
Y8	6	V8-455[2]
ZB	6	V8-455[2]
Z3	6	V8-455[2]
Z4	6	V8-455[2]
Z6	6	V8-455[2]

1977

CODE	TRANS.	ENGINE
WF	7	4-151[1]
WH	7	4-151[1]

CODE	TRANS.	ENGINE
YR	6	4-151[1]
YS	6	4-151[1]
SG	4	V6-231[1][13]
SI	6	V6-231[1][13]
SJ	6	V6-231[1][13]
SK	6	V6-231[1][13]
SL	6	V6-231[1][13]
SM	6	V6-231[1][13]
SN	6	V6-231[1][13]
SU	4	V6-231[1][13]
HK	6	V8-301[1]
WB	5	V8-301[1]
YH	6	V8-301[1]
YW	6	V8-301[1]
YX	6	V8-301[1]
Q2	6	V8-350[2][12]
Q3	6	V8-350[2][12]
Q6	6	V8-350[2][12]
Q7	6	V8-350[2][12]
Q8	6	V8-350[2][12]
Q9	6	V8-350[2][12]
QP	6	V8-350[2][12]
QQ	6	V8-350[2][12]
TK	6	V8-350[2][12]
TL	6	V8-350[2][12]
TN	6	V8-350[2][12]
TO	6	V8-350[2][12]
TX	6	V8-350[2][12]
TY	6	V8-350[2][12]
Y9	6	V8-350[2]
YA	6	V8-350[2]
YB	6	V8-350[2]
WA	5	V8-400[2]
XA	6	V8-400[2]
Y4	6	V8-400[2]
Y6	6	V8-400[2]
Y7	6	V8-400[2]
YC	6	V8-400[2]
YD	6	V8-400[2]
YU	6	V8-400[2]
U2	6	V8-403[2][12]
U3	6	V8-403[2][12]
UA	6	V8-403[2][12]
UB	6	V8-403[2][12]
VA	6	V8-403[2][12]
VB	6	V8-403[2][12]
VJ	6	V8-403[2][12]
VK	6	V8-403[2][12]

1978

CODE	TRANS.	ENGINE
YB,YC	6	4-151[1]
EA	4	V6-231[1][13]
EC,EE,EI	6	V6-231[1][13]
EJ,EK,EL	6	V6-231[1][13]
OE,OH,OK,OR	6	V6-231[1][13]
XA,XB,XC	6	V8-301[1]
XD,XF	6	V8-301[1]
XH,XU,XW	6	V8-301[2]
CPF	6	V8-305[2][14]
CPH,CPZ,CRU	6	V8-305[1][14]
CRY,CRZ,CJJ	6	V8-305[1][14]
CTH	4	V8-305[1][14]
CTK,CTM,CTS	6	V8-305[1][14]

Continued

ENGINE CODES—Continued

1978—Cont'd

CTT,CTU,CTW	⑥	V8-305①⑭
CTX,CTY,CTZ	⑥	V8-305①⑭
MA,MB	⑥	V8-350②⑬
TO,TP,TQ	⑥	V8-350②⑫
TS,Q2,Q3	⑥	V8-350②⑫
CHJ,CHL,CMC	⑥	V8-350②⑭
CHR	⑥	V8-350②⑭
WC	④	V8-400②
XJ,XK	⑥	V8-400②
X7,X9	⑥	V8-400②
Y,YA,YH	⑥	V8-400②
YJ,YK	⑥	V8-400②
U2,U3	⑥	V8-403②
U5,U6	⑥	V8-403②⑫
VA,VB	⑥	V8-403②⑫
VD,VE	⑥	V8-403②⑫

1979

NA,NG	④	V6-231①⑩⑬
NB,NJ,NK	⑥	V6-231①⑩⑬
NC	④	V6-231①⑧⑬
NE	⑥	V6-231①⑧⑬
NH	⑥	V6-231①⑧⑬
NL,NM	⑥	V6-231①⑩⑬
RA	⑥	V6-231①⑩⑬
RB,RC,RX	⑥	V6-231①⑩⑬
RG,RW,RY	⑥	V6-231①⑧⑬

PWA,PWB	④	V8-301②⑩
PXF,PXH	⑥	V8-301①⑩
PXL,PXN,PXS	⑥	V8-301②⑩
PXP,PXR	⑥	V8-301①⑩
PXT,PXU,PXW	⑥	V8-301②⑩
PX4,PX6	⑥	V8-301②⑩
PX7,PX9	⑥	V8-301①⑩
DND,DNK	⑥	V8-305①⑧⑭
DNJ,DTL	⑥	V8-305①⑩⑭
DNX,DNY	⑥	V8-305②⑧⑭
DTA	⑥	V8-305②③⑭
DTK,DTM	⑥	V8-305①⑩⑭
SA,SC,SD	⑥	V8-350①⑩⑬
DNX,DRY	⑥	V8-350②③⑭
DRJ	⑥	V8-350②③⑧
U9	⑥	V8-350②③⑫
VK	⑥	V8-350②⑧⑫
PWH	④	V8-400②⑩
O3	⑥	V8-403②③⑫
TB,TD,TE	⑥	V8-403②⑧⑫
QB	⑥	V8-403②③⑫
QE,QL,QJ	⑥	V8-403②⑩⑫

1980

CLA	④	V6-229⑩⑭
CLB, CLC	⑥	V6-229⑩⑭

EA, EX, OJ	④	V6-231⑩⑬
EB, EC, EO, EP	⑥	V6-231⑩⑬
EZ, OA, OK, OL	⑥	V6-231⑩⑬
EF, EG, ES, ET	⑥	V6-231⑩⑬
OB, OC, OM, ON	⑥	V6-231⑧⑬
XH, XR, X6	⑥	V8-265⑩
XT, XW, X3, X9	⑥	V8-301⑩
XN, YN, YR	⑥	V8-301⑩
YL	⑥	V8-301⑮
CEC, CEL, CEM	⑥	V8-305⑧⑭
ML, MV	⑥	V8-350⑩⑬
UAD, UAF	⑥	V8-350⑧⑫

①—Two barrel carburetor.
②—Four barrel carburetor.
③—Hi Altitude.
④—Manual trans.
⑤—Four speed manual trans.
⑥—Automatic trans.
⑦—Five speed manual trans.
⑧—California.
⑨—One barrel carburetor.
⑩—Exc. California.
⑪—Does not use harmonic balancer.
⑫—See Oldsmobile chapter for service procedures.
⑬—See Buick chapter for service procedures.
⑭—See Chevrolet chapter for service procedures.
⑮—Turbocharged engine.

GENERAL ENGINE SPECIFICATIONS

Year	Engine	Carburetor	Bore and Stroke	Piston Displacement, Cubic Inches	Compression Ratio	Maximum Brake H.P. @ R.P.M.	Maximum Torque Ft. Lbs. @ R.P.M.	Normal Oil Pressure Pounds
1975	105 Horsepower① 6-250③	1 Barrel	3.87 × 3.53	250	8.25	105 @ 3800	185 @ 1200	36–41
	110 Horsepower① V8-260④	2 Barrel	3.50 × 3.385	260	8.5	110 @ 3400	205 @ 1600	30–45
	155 Horsepower① V8-350	2 Barrel	3.88 × 3.75	350	7.6	155 @ 4000	—	55–60
	175 Horsepower① V8-350	4 Barrel	3.88 × 3.75	350	7.6	175 @ 4000	—	55–60
	145 Horsepower① V8-350②⑥	2 Barrel	3.80 × 3.85	350	8.0	145 @ 3200	270 @ 3000	37
	165 Horsepower① V8-350②⑥	4 Barrel	3.80 × 3.85	350	8.0	165 @ 3800	260 @ 2200	37
	170 Horsepower① V8-400	2 Barrel	4.12 × 3.75	400	7.6	170 @ 4000	—	55–60
	185 Horsepower① V8-400	4 Barrel	4.12 × 3.75	400	7.6	185 @ 3600	—	55–60
	200 Horsepower① V8-455	4 Barrel	4.15 × 4.21	455	7.6	200 @ 3500	—	55–60
1976	110 Horsepower① 6-250③	1 Barrel	3.87 × 3.53	250	8.3	110 @ 3600	185 @ 1200	36–41
	110 Horsepower① V8-260④	2 Barrel	3.50 × 3.385	260	7.5	110 @ 3400	205 @ 1600	30–45
	160 Horsepower① V8-350	2 Barrel	3.8762 × 3.75	350	7.6	160 @ 4000	280 @ 2000	35–40
	165 Horsepower① V8-350	4 Barrel	3.8762 × 3.75	350	7.6	165 @ 4000	260 @ 2400	35–40
	140 Horsepower① V8-350②⑥	2 Barrel	3.80 × 3.85	350	8.0	140 @ 3200	280 @ 1600	37
	155 Horsepower① V8-350②⑥	4 Barrel	3.80 × 3.85	350	8.0	155 @ 3400	280 @ 1800	37
	170 Horsepower① V8-400	2 Barrel	4.1212 × 3.75	400	7.6	170 @ 4000	310 @ 1600	35–40
	185 Horsepower① V8-400	4 Barrel	4.1212 × 3.75	400	7.6	185 @ 3600	310 @ 1600	35–40
	200 Horsepower① V8-455	4 Barrel	4.1522 × 4.21	455	7.6	200 @ 3500	330 @ 2000	55–60
1977	88 Horsepower① 4-151	2 Barrel	4.00 × 3.00	151	8.3	88 @ 4400	128 @ 2400	30–45
	105 Horsepower① V6-231②	2 Barrel	3.80 × 3.40	231	8.0	105 @ 3200	185 @ 2000	37
	135 Horsepower① V8-301	2 Barrel	4.00 × 3.00	301	8.2	135 @ 4000	⑦	38–42
	145 Horsepower① V8-305③	2 Barrel	3.736 × 3.48	305	8.5	145 @ 3800	245 @ 2400	32–40
	170 Horsepower① V8-350③	4 Barrel	4.00 × 3.48	350	8.5	170 @ 3800	270 @ 2400	32–40
	170 Horsepower① V8-350	4 Barrel	3.88 × 3.75	350	7.6	170 @ 4000	280 @ 1800	55–60
	170 Horsepower① V8-350④	4 Barrel	4.057 × 3.385	350	8	170 @ 3800	275 @ 2000	37
	180 Horsepower① V8-400	4 Barrel	4.12 × 3.75	400	7.6	180 @ 3600	325 @ 1600	55–60
	200 Horsepower① V8-400⑩	4 Barrel	4.12 × 3.75	400	8.0	200 @ 3600	⑪	55–60
	185 Horsepower① V8-403④	4 Barrel	4.351 × 3.385	403	8.0	185 @ 3600	320 @ 2200	30–45

Continued

GENERAL ENGINE SPECIFICATIONS—Continued

Year	Engine	Carburetor	Bore and Stroke	Piston Displacement Cubic Inches	Compression Ratio	Maximum Brake H.P. @ R.P.M.	Maximum Torque Ft. Lbs. @ R.P.M.	Normal Oil Pressure Pounds
1978	85 Horsepower①........ 4-151	2 Barrel	4.00 × 3.00	151	8.3	85 @ 4400	123 @ 2800	36—41
	105 Horsepower①..... V6-231②	2 Barrel	3.80 × 3.40	231	8.0	105 @ 3400	185 @ 2000	37
	140 Horsepower①....... V8-301	2 Barrel	4.00 × 3.00	301	8.2	140 @ 3600	235 @ 2000	35—40
	150 Horsepower①....... V8-301	4 Barrel	4.00 × 3.00	301	8.2	150 @ 4000	240 @ 2000	35—40
	135 Horsepower①⑨.. V8-305③	2 Barrel	3.736 × 3.48	305	8.4	135 @ 3800	240 @ 2000	32—40
	145 Horsepower①⑧.. V8-305③	4 Barrel	3.736 × 3.48	305	8.4	145 @ 3800	245 @ 2400	32—40
	155 Horsepower①..... V8-350②	4 Barrel	3.80 × 3.85	350	8.0	155 @ 3400	280 @ 1800	—
	160 Horsepower①..... V8-350③	4 Barrel	4.00 × 3.48	350	8.2	160 @ 3800	260 @ 2400	32—40
	170 Horsepower①..... V8-350④	4 Barrel	4.057 × 3.385	350	7.9	170 @ 3800	275 @ 2000	30—45
	170 Horsepower①..... V8-350③	4 Barrel	4.00 × 3.48	350	8.2	170 @ 3800	270 @ 2400	32—40
	180 Horsepower①....... V8-400	4 Barrel	4.12 × 3.75	400	7.7	180 @ 3600	325 @ 1600	35—40
	220 Horsepower①..... V8-400⑩	4 Barrel	4.12 × 3.75	400	8.1	220 @ 4000	320 @ 2800	55—60
	185 Horsepower①..... V8-403④	4 Barrel	4.351 × 3.385	403	7.9	185 @ 3600	320 @ 2000	30—45
1979	115 Horsepower①..... V6-231②	2 Barrel	3.80 × 3.40	231	8.0	115 @ 3800	185 @ 2000	37
	115 Horsepower①..... V6-231②	2 Barrel	3.80 × 3.40	231	8.0	115 @ 3800	190 @ 2000	37
	135 Horsepower①..... V6-231②	2 Barrel	3.80 × 3.40	231	8.0	135 @ 3800	190 @ 2000	37
	130 Horsepower①....... V8-301	2 Barrel	4.00 × 3.00	301	8.1	130 @ 3200	245 @ 2000	35—40
	135 Horsepower①....... V8-301	2 Barrel	4.00 × 3.00	301	8.1	135 @ 3800	240 @ 1600	35—40
	150 Horsepower①....... V8-301	4 Barrel	4.00 × 3.00	301	8.1	150 @ 4000	⑤	35—40
	125 Horsepower①..... V8-305③	2 Barrel	3.736 × 3.48	305	8.4	125 @ 3200	245 @ 2000	32—40
	130 Horsepower①..... V8-305③	2 Barrel	3.736 × 3.48	305	8.4	130 @ 3200	245 @ 2000	32—40
	155 Horsepower①..... V8-305③	4 Barrel	3.736 × 3.48	305	8.4	155 @ 4000	225 @ 2400	32—40
	155 Horsepower①..... V8-350②	4 Barrel	3.80 × 3.85	350	8.0	155 @ 3400	280 @ 1800	34
	160 Horsepower①..... V8-350④	4 Barrel	4.057 × 3.385	350	7.9	160 @ 3600	270 @ 2000	30—45
	165 Horsepower①..... V8-350③	4 Barrel	4.00 × 3.48	350	8.2	165 @ 3800	260 @ 2400	32—40
	220 Horsepower①....... V8-400	4 Barrel	4.12 × 3.75	400	8.1	220 @ 4000	320 @ 2800	35—40
	175 Horsepower①..... V8-403④	4 Barrel	4.351 × 3.385	403	7.9	175 @ 3600	310 @ 2000	30—45
	185 Horsepower①..... V8-403④	4 Barrel	4.351 × 3.385	403	7.9	185 @ 3600	315 @ 2000	30—45
1980	110 Horsepower①..... V6-229③	2 Barrel	3.736 × 3.48	229	8.6	110 @ 3800	190 @ 1600	45
	115 Horsepower①..... V6-231②	2 Barrel	3.80 × 3.40	231	8.0	115 @ 3800	188 @ 2000	37
	120 Horsepower①....... V8-265	2 Barrel	3.75 × 3.00	265	8.3	120 @ 3600	210 @ 1600	35—40
	150 Horsepower①....... V8-301	4 Barrel	4.00 × 3.00	301	8.2	150 @ 4000	240 @ 2000	35—40
	170 Horsepower①..... V8-301⑫	4 Barrel	4.00 × 3.00	301	8.2	170 @ 4400	240 @ 2200	55—60
	205 Horsepower①..... V8-301⑬	4 Barrel	4.00 × 3.00	301	7.5	205 @ 4000	310 @ 2800	55—60
	150 Horsepower①..... V8-305③	4 Barrel	3.736 × 3.48	305	8.4	150 @ 3800	230 @ 2400	45
	155 Horsepower①..... V8-350②	4 Barrel	3.80 × 3.85	350	8.0	155 @ 3400	280 @ 1600	37
	160 Horsepower①..... V8-350④	4 Barrel	4.057 × 3.385	350	8.0	160 @ 3600	270 @ 1600	30—45
	105 Horsepower①.... V8-350④⑭	Fuel Inj.	4.057 × 3.385	350	22.5	105 @ 3200	205 @ 1600	30—45

①—Ratings are NET-as installed in vehicle.
②—Buick-built engine.
③—Chevrolet-built engine.
④—Oldsmobile-built engine.

⑤—Manual trans., 240 @ 2400; auto. trans., 240 @ 1600.
⑥—Ventura only.
⑦—Manual trans., 235 @ 2000. Auto. trans., 245 @ 2000.
⑧—Exc. high altitude.

⑨—High altitude.
⑩—High performance Trans Am engine.
⑪—Manual trans., 325 @ 2400; auto trans., 325 @ 2200.
⑫—E/C (electronic control) engine.
⑬—Turbocharged engine.
⑭—Diesel engine.

TUNE UP SPECIFICATIONS

The following specifications are published from the latest information available. This data should be used only in the absence of a decal affixed in the engine compartment.

★ When using a timing light, disconnect vacuum hose or tube at distributor and plug opening in tube or hose so idle speed will not be affected.

● When checking compression, lowest cylinder must be within 80% of the highest.

▲ Before removing wires from distributor cap, determine location of the No. 1 wire in cap, as distributor position may have been altered from that shown at the end of this chart.

Year & Engine	Spark Plug		Ignition Timing BTDC①★				Curb Idle Speed②		Fast Idle Speed		Fuel Pump Pressure
	Type	Gap	Firing Order Fig. ▲	Std. Trans.	Auto. Trans.	Mark Fig.	Std. Trans.	Auto. Trans.	Std. Trans.	Auto. Trans.	
1975											
6-250③	R46TX	.060	L	10°	10°	H	425/850	④	1800⑤	1800⑤	3–5
V8-260 Exc. Calif.⑥	R46SX	.080	M	16°⑦	18°⑦	J	750	550/650D	900⑧	900⑧	5½–6½
V8-260 Calif.⑥	R46SX	.080	M	—	16°⑦	J	—	600/650D	—	900⑧	5½–6½
V8-350 Ventura⑨	R45TSX	.060	N	—	12°	K	—	600D	—	1800⑤⑩	3 Min.
V8-350 2 Barrel Exc. Ventura	R46TSX	.060	O	—	16°	I	—	600D	—	1700	3–6½
V8-350 4 Barrel Exc. Calif.⑪	R46TSX	.060	O	12°	16°	I	775	650D	1800⑤	1800⑤	3–6½
V8-350 4 Barrel Calif.⑪	R46TSX	.060	O	12°	12°	I	775	625D	1800⑤	1800⑤	3–6½
V8-400 2 Barrel	R46TSX	.060	O	—	16°	I	—	650D	—	—	3–6½
V8-400 4 Barrel Exc. Calif.	R45TSX	.060	O	12°	16°	I	775	㉒	1800⑤	1800⑤	3–6½
V8-400 4 Barrel Calif.	R45TSX	.060	O	12°	12°	I	775	600D	1800⑤	1800⑤	3–6½
V8-455 Exc. Calif.	R45TSX	.060	O	—	16°	I	—	650D	—	1800⑤	3–6½
V8-455 Calif.	R45TSX	.060	O	—	10°	I	—	675D	—	1800⑤	3–6½
1976											
6-250③	R46TS	.035	L	6°	10°	H	850	⑬	1200⑤	1200⑤	3–5
V8-260 Exc. Calif.⑥	⑭	⑭	M	16°⑦	18°⑦	J	750	550D⑮	900⑧	900⑧	5½–6½
V8-260 Calif.⑥	⑭	⑭	M	14°⑦	⑯	J	750	600D	900⑧	900⑧	5½–6½
V8-350 Ventura⑨	R45TSX	.060	N	—	12°	K	—	600D	—	1800⑤⑩	3 Min.
V8-350 2 Barrel⑪	R46TSX	.060	O	—	16°	I	—	550D	—	—	3–6½
V8-350 4 Barrel⑪	R46TSX	.060	O	—	16°	I	—	600D	—	1800⑤	3–6½
V8-400 2 Barrel	R46TSX	.060	O	—	16°	I	—	550D	—	—	3–6½
V8-400 4 Barrel	R45TSX	.060	O	12°	16°	I	775	575D	1800⑤	1800⑤	3–6½
V8-455 Exc. Calif.	R45TSX	.060	O	16°	16°	I	775	550D	1800⑤	1800⑤	3–6½
V8-455 Calif.	R45TSX	.060	O	—	12°	I	—	600D	—	1800⑤	3–6½
1977											
4-151	R44TSX	.060	F	14°⑰	14	Q	⑱	⑲	2200⑤	2400⑤	4–5½
V6-231⑨⑳	㉑	㉑	G	12°	12°	C㉒	600/800	600D㉓	—	—	4¼–5¾
V6-231⑨㉔	R46TSX	.060	D	—	15°	E㉒	—	600/670D㉕	—	—	4¼–5¾
V8-301	R46TSX	.060	O	16°	12°	A	750/850	550/650D	1750	1750	7–8½
V8-305③	R45TS	.045	P	—	8°	H	—	500/650D	—	—	7½–9
V8-350㉖	R45TSX	.060	P	—	16°	H	—	575/650D	—	1800	7½–9
V8-350③㉗	R45TS	.045	P	—	8°	H	—	㉘	—	1600	7½–9
V8-350⑥㉙	R46SZ	.060	M	—	㉚	J	—	㉛	—	1000	5½–6½
V8-400	R45TSX	.060	O	18°	㉜	I	775	㉝	1800	1800	7–8½
V8-403 Exc. Calif. & High Alt.⑥	R46SZ	.060	M	—	22°⑦	J	—	550/650D	—	900	5½–6½
V8-403 Calif. & High Alt.⑥	R46SZ	.060	M	—	20°⑦	J	—	㉞	—	1000	5½–6½
1978											
4-151	R43TSX	.060	F	—	14°㉟	B	—	㊱	—	⑤㊲	4½–5
V6-231⑨	R46TSX	.060	D	15°	15°	E㉒	800	㊳	—	—	4½–5.9
V8-301 2 Barrel	R46TSX	.060	O	—	12°	A	—	550/650D	—	2200	7–8½

Continued

Exc. Astre, Sunbird & 1980 Phoenix—PONTIAC

TUNE UP SPECIFICATIONS—Continued

Year & Engine	Spark Plug		Ignition Timing BTDC①★				Curb Idle Speed②		Fast Idle Speed		Fuel Pump Pressure
	Type	Gap	Firing Order Fig. ▲	Std. Trans.	Auto. Trans.	Mark Fig.	Std. Trans.	Auto. Trans.	Std. Trans.	Auto. Trans.	
1978—Continued											
V8-301 4 Barrel	R45TSX	.060	O	—	12°	A	—	550/650D	—	2300	7–8½
V8-305 Exc. Calif. & High Alt.③	R45TS	.045	P	4°	4°	H	600/700	500/600D	1600	1600	7½–9
V8-305 Calif.③	R45TS	.045	P	—	6°	H	—	500/600D	—	1600	7½–9
V8-305 High Alt.③	R45TS	.045	P	—	8°	H	—	600/700D	—	1600	7½–9
V8-350③㉗	R45TS	.045	P	6°	8°	H	700	㊴	1300	1600	7½–9
V8-350⑥㉙	R46SZ	.060	M	—	20°⑦	J	—	550/650D	—	㊵	5½–6½
V8-350⑨㊶	R46TSX	.060	N	—	15°	E㉒	—	550D	—	1500	㊷
V8-400	R45TSX	.060	O	16°	㉜	I	775	㉝	1800	1800	7–8½
V8-403⑥	R46SZ	.060	M	—	20°⑦	J	—	㉛	—	1000	5½–6½
1979											
V6-231⑨	R46TSX	.060	D	15°	15°	E㉒	600/800	㊸	2200	2200	4½–5.9
V8-301 2 Barrel	R46TSX	.060	O	—	12°	A	—	500/650D	—	2000	7–8½
V8-301 4 Barrel	R45TSX	.060	O	14°	12°	A	700/800	500/650D	2000	2200	7–8½
V8-305 2 Barrel Exc. Calif.③	R45TS	.045	P	4°	4°	H	600/700	500/600D	1300	1600	7½–9
V8-305 2 Barrel Calif.③	R45TS	.045	P	—	4°	H	—	600/650D	—	1950	7½–9
V8-305 4 Barrel③	R45TS	.045	P	—	4°	H	—	500/600D	—	1600	7½–9
V8-350③㉗	R45TS	.045	P	—	8°	H	—	㊴	—	1600	7½–9
V8-350⑥㉙	R46SZ	.060	M	—	20°⑦	J	—	500/600D	—	1000	5½–6½
V8-350⑨㊶	R46TSX	.060	N	—	15°	E㉒	—	550D	—	1550	㊷
V8-400	R45TSX	.060	O	18°	—	I	775	—	1800	—	7–8½
V8-403⑥	R46SZ	.060	M	—	20°⑦	J	—	500/600D	—	1000	5½–6½
1980											
V6-229 Exc. Calif.③	R45TS	.045	Q	8°	10°	R	700/800	600/670D	1300	1750	4½–6
V6-231 Exc. Calif.⑨	R45TSX	.040	D	15°	15°	E㉒	600/800	550/670D	2200	2000	4¼–5¾
V6-231 Calif.⑨	—	—	D	—	—	E㉒	—	—	—	—	4¼–5¾
V8-265	R45TSX	.060	—	—	10°	—	—	525/625D	—	2000	7–8½
V8-301㊹	R45TSX	.060	O	—	12°	A	—	500/650D	—	2500	7–8½
V8-301㊺	R45TSX	.060	O	—	12°	A	—	550/650D	—	2500	7–8½
V8-301㊻	R45TSX	.060	O	—	8°	A	—	600/650D	—	2400	7–8½
V8-305③	R45TS	.045	P	—	4°	H	—	550/650D	—	2400	7½–9
V8-350 Exc. Calif.㊶	R45TSX	.060	N	—	15°	E㉒	—	550/670D	—	1850	6–7½
V8-350 Calif.⑥㉙	R46SX	.080	M	—	18°⑦	J	—	550/650D	—	700	5½–6½
V8-350 Diesel⑥	—	—	—	—	7°⑯	—	—	575/650D	—	750	—

①—BTDC—Before top dead center.

②—Idle speed on man. trans. vehicles is adjusted in Neutral & on auto. trans. equipped vehicles is adjusted in Drive unless otherwise specified. Where two idle speeds are listed, the higher speed is with the A/C or idle solenoid energized.

③—Chhevrolet-built engine.

④—Except Calif., 425/500D RPM; California, 425/600D RPM.

⑤—On high step of fast idle cam with A/C off.

⑥—Oldsmobile-built engine.

⑦—At 1100 RPM.

⑧—On low step of fast idle cam with EGR vacuum hose disconnected and plugged & A/C off.

⑨—Buick-built engine.

⑩—4 barrel carb. only.

⑪—Except Ventura.

⑫—Except full size sta. wag., 650D RPM; full size sta. wag., 625D RPM.

⑬—Except Calif., LeMans with A/C 575D RPM, all other models 550D RPM; California, 600D RPM.

⑭—Early models use R46SX gapped at .080"; late models use R46SZ gapped at .060".

⑮—On Grand LeMans & LeMans models, set to 575D RPM.

Continued

PONTIAC—Exc. Astre, Sunbird & 1980 Phoenix

TUNE UP NOTES—Continued

⑯—Engine codes TE, TJ, T4 & T5, set to 14° BTDC at 1100 RPM; engine codes TP, TT, T2 & T3, set to 16° BTDC at 1100 RPM.
⑰—At 1000 RPM.
⑱—Less A/C, 500/1000 RPM; with A/C, 500/1200 RPM.
⑲—Less A/C, 500/650D RPM; with A/C, 650/850D RPM.
⑳—Except Even-Fire engine.
㉑—R46TS gapped at .040" or R46TSX gapped at .060".
㉒—The harmonic balancer on these engines has two timing marks. The mark measuring 1/16 in. is used when setting timing with a hand held timing light. The mark measuring 1/8 in. is used when setting timing with magnetic timing equipment.
㉓—On Ventura, Phoenix & full size models with A/C, set to 600/670D RPM.
㉔—Even-Fire engine.
㉕—On full size models, idle speed with solenoid energized is set with A/C on.
㉖—Distributor located rear of engine, rotor rota-

tion counter clockwise. Fuel pump located left side of engine.
㉗—Distributor located rear of engine, rotor rotation clockwise.
㉘—Except high altitude 500/650D RPM; high altitude, 600/650D RPM.
㉙—Distributor located rear of engine, rotor rotation counter clockwise. Fuel located right side of engine.
㉚—Except Firebird, Phoenix & Ventura Calif. models, 20° BTDC at 1100 RPM; Firebird, Phoenix & Ventura California models, 18° BTDC at 1100 RPM.
㉛—Except high altitude, 550/650D RPM; high altitude, 600/700D RPM.
㉜—Except Firebird high performance engine (engine code Y6), 16° BTDC; Firebird high performance engine (engine code Y6), 18° BTDC.
㉝—Except Firebird high performance engine (engine code Y6), 575/650D RPM; Firebird high performance engine (engine code Y6), 600/700D RPM.

㉞—Except high altitude, 550/650D RPM; high altitude, 600/650D RPM.
㉟—At 1000 RPM.
㊱—Less A/C, 500/650D RPM; with A/C, 650/850D RPM.
㊲—Engine code YB, 2200 RPM; engine code YC, 2400 RPM.
㊳—Less idle solenoid, 600D RPM; with idle solenoid, 600/670D RPM.
㊴—Except high altitude, 500/600D RPM; high altitude, 600/650D RPM.
㊵—Except Calif., 900 RPM; California, 1000 RPM.
㊶—Distributor located at front of engine.
㊷—Less A/C, 5–6½ psi.; with A/C, 5.9–7.4 psi.
㊸—Less idle solenoid, 600D RPM; with idle solenoid, 550/670D RPM.
㊹—Except E/C (electronic control) & turbocharged engines.
㊺—E/C (electronic control) engine.
㊻—Turbocharged engine.
㊼—Injection timing at 800 RPM.

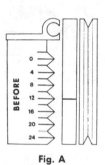

Fig. A

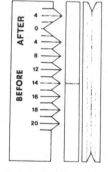

Fig. B

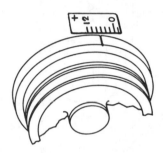

Fig. C

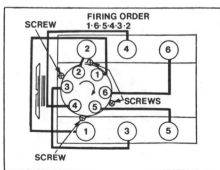

Fig. D

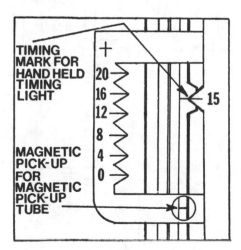

Fig. E

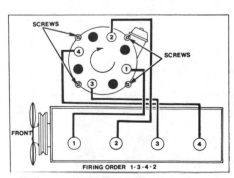

Fig. F

Continued

TUNE UP NOTES—Continued

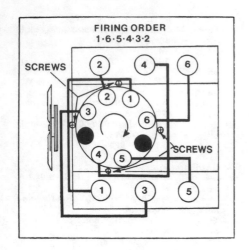

Fig. G

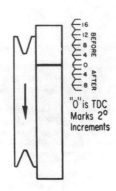

Fig. H

Fig. I

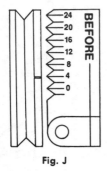

Fig. J

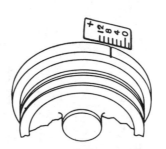

Fig. K

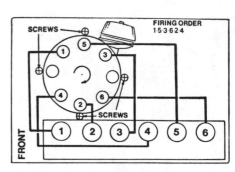

Fig. L

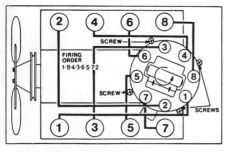

Fig. M

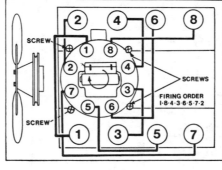

Fig. N

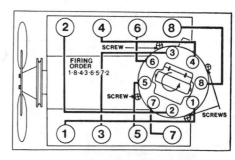

Fig. O

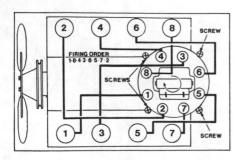

Fig. P

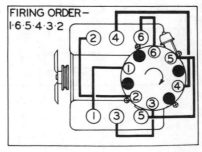

Fig. Q

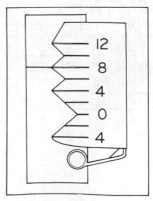

Fig. R

COOLING SYSTEM & CAPACITY DATA

Year	Model or Engine	Cooling Capacity, Qts. Less A/C	Cooling Capacity, Qts. With A/C	Radiator Cap Relief Pressure, Lbs.	Thermo. Opening Temp. ①	Fuel Tank Gals.	Engine Oil Refill Qts. ②	Transmission Oil 3 Speed Pints	Transmission Oil 4 Speed Pints	Transmission Oil 5 Speed Pints	Auto Trans. Qts. ③	Rear Axle Oil Pints
1975	6-250 Ventura	13.1	—	14–17	195	20.5	4	3½	—	—	2½[27]	3¾
	6-250 Firebird	13.1	—	14–17	195	21.5	4	3½	—	—	4[8]	4¼
	6-250 LeMans	14.7	—	14–17	195	21	4	3½	—	—	4[8]	3[28]
	V8-260 Ventura	22.4	22.9	14–17	195	20.5	4	3½	2½	—	2½[27]	3¾
	V8-350 Ventura	20	20	14–17	195	20.5	4	—	2½	—	2½[27]	3¾
	V8-350 Firebird	22	23.3	14–17	195	21.5	5	3½	2½	—	4[27]	4¼
	V8-350 LeMans	21.3	23.6	14–17	195	21	5	—	—	—	4[27]	3[28]
	V8-400 Firebird	21.3	[9]	14–17	195	21.5	5	—	2½	—	4[27]	4¼
	V8-400 LeMans	21.3	[10]	14–17	195	21[13]	5	—	—	—	3¾[8]	3[28]
	V8-400 Grand Prix	21.5	24	14–17	195	25	5	—	—	—	3¾[8]	3[28]
	V8-400 Pontiac	21.6	22.4	14–17	195	25.8	5	—	—	—	3¾[8]	5½
	V8-455 LeMans	19.9	21.6	14–17	195	21[13]	5	—	—	—	3¾[8]	3[28]
	V8-455 Grand Prix	20.2	22.5	14–17	195	25	5	—	—	—	3¾[8]	3[28]
	V8-455 Pontiac	19.8	22.3	14–17	195	25.8[14]	5	—	—	—	3¾[8]	5½
1976	6-250 Ventura	13.0	—	14–17	195	20.5	4	3.5	—	—	2½[27]	3¾
	6-250 Firebird	13.5	—	14–17	195	21.5	4	3.5	—	—	4[8]	4¼
	6-250 LeMans	15.0	—	14–17	195	21	4	3.5	—	—	4[8]	3[28]
	V8-260 Ventura	20.6	21.3	14–17	195	20.5	4	3.5	—	3.0	2½[27]	3¾
	V8-260 LeMans	23.5	26.0	14–17	195	21	4	3.5	—	3.0	4[8]	3[28]
	V8-350 Ventura	17.3	18.0	14–17	195	20.5	4	—	—	—	2½[27]	3¾
	V8-350 Firebird	21.2	21.6	14–17	195	21.5	5	—	—	—	4[27]	4¼
	V8-350 LeMans	21.4	22.0	14–17	195	21	5	—	—	—	4[8]	3[28]
	V8-350 Grand Prix	21.6	22.0	14–17	195	25	5	—	—	—	3¾[8]	3[28]
	V8-400 Firebird	21.6	23.3	14–17	195	21.5	5	—	2.5	—	4[27]	4¼
	V8-400 LeMans	21.4	22.0	14–17	195	21[14]	5	—	—	—	3¾[8]	3[28]
	V8-400 Grand Prix	22.2	22.2	14–17	195	25	5	—	—	—	3¾[8]	3[28]
	V8-400 Pontiac	21.6	22.4	14–17	195	25.8[14]	5	—	—	—	3¾[8]	5½
	V8-455 Firebird	23.3	23.3	14–17	195	21.5	5	—	2.5	—	4[27]	4¼
	V8-455 LeMans	21.6	21.6	14–17	195	21[14]	5	—	—	—	3¾[8]	3[28]
	V8-455 Grand Prix	22.2	22.2	14–17	195	25	5	—	—	—	3¾[8]	3[28]
	V8-455 Pontiac	22.1	22.1	14–17	195	25.8[14]	5	—	—	—	3¾[8]	5½
1977	4-151 Ventura	12.4	12.4	14–17	195	21	4	3.5	2.4	3.5	3[15]	3½
	V6-231 Ventura	13.8	13.8	14–17	195	21	4	3.5	2.4	3.5	3[15]	3½
	V6-231 LeMans	14.5	14.5	14–17	195	22	4	3.5	—	—	4[8]	4.25
	V6-231 Firebird	13.2	13.2	14–17	195	21	4	3.5	2.5	—	4[8]	4.25
	V6-231 Pontiac	12.9	12.9	14–17	195	21	4	—	—	—	[16]	[17]
	V8-301 Ventura	19.8	20.2[23]	14–17	195	21	5½	3.5	2.4	3.5	3[18]	3½
	V8-301 LeMans	20.2	20.8[23]	14–17	195	22	5½	3.5	—	—	[16]	4.25
	V8-301 Firebird	19.5	19.5	14–17	195	21	5½	3.5	2.5	—	4[8]	4.25
	V8-301 Pontiac	18.6	19.8[23]	14–17	195	21	5½	—	—	—	[16]	[17]
	V8-301 Grand Prix	20.5	21.1[23]	14–17	195	25	5½	—	—	—	3¾[8]	4.25
	V8-305 Ventura	17	18	14–17	195	21	4	3.5	2.4	3.5	3[18]	3½
	V8-350 Ventura	16.6	16.6	14–17	195	21	4	3.5	2.4	3.5	3[8]	3½
	V8-350 LeMans[19]	21.7	23.9[23]	14–17	195	22	5	3.5	—	—	[16]	4.25
	V8-350 LeMans[20]	16.7	17.5[23]	14–17	195	22	4	3.5	—	—	[16]	4.25
	V8-350 Firebird[19]	20.3	23[23]	14–17	195	21	5	3.5	2.5	—	4[8]	4.25
	V8-350 Firebird[20]	16	18.2[23]	14–17	195	21	4	3.5	2.5	—	4[8]	4.25
	V8-350 Pontiac[19]	15	16.2[23]	14–17	195	21	5	—	—	—	[16]	[17]
	V8-350 Pontiac[20]	15	16.2[23]	14–17	195	21	4	—	—	—	[16]	[17]
	V8-350 Grand Prix[7]	21.9	24.1[23]	14–17	195	25	5	—	—	—	3¾[8]	4.25
	V8-350 Grand Prix[20]	17	17.8[23]	14–17	195	25	4	—	—	—	3¾[8]	4.25
	V8-400 LeMans	21.7	23.9[23]	14–17	195	22	5	3.5	—	—	[16]	4.25
	V8-400 Firebird[21]	21.1	22.9	14–17	195	21	5	3.5	2.5	—	4[8]	4.25

Continued

COOLING SYSTEM & CAPACITY DATA—Continued

Year	Model or Engine	Cooling Capacity, Qts.		Radiator Cap Relief Pressure, Lbs.	Thermo. Opening Temp. ①	Fuel Tank Gals.	Engine Oil Refill Qts. ②	Transmission Oil				Rear Axle Oil Pints
		Less A/C	With A/C					3 Speed Pints	4 Speed Pints	5 Speed Pints	Auto Trans. Qts. ③	
1977	V8-400 Firebird(22)	20.4	21.2	14–17	195	21	5	3.5	2.5	—	4(8)	4.25
	V8-400 Firebird	—	23(23)	14–17	195	21	5	3.5	2.5	—	4(8)	4.25
	V8-400 Pontiac	21.7	23.9(23)	14–17	195	21	5	—	—	—	(16)	(17)
	V8-400 Grand Prix	21.9	24.1(23)	14–17	195	25	5	—	—	—	3¾(8)	4.25
	V8-403 LeMans	17.9	18.7(23)	14–17	195	22	4	3.5	—	—	(16)	4.25
	V8-403 Firebird	17.1	19.4(23)	14–17	195	21	4	3.5	2.5	—	4(8)	4.25
	V8-403 Pontiac	16.1	17.3(23)	14–17	195	21	4	—	—	—	(16)	(17)
	V8-403 Grand Prix	18.2	19.0(23)	14–17	195	25	4	—	—	—	3¾(8)	4.25
1978	4-151 Phoenix	11.8	11.8	14–17	195	21	3	3.5	2.5	3.5	3(12)	3½
	V6-231 Phoenix	14.0	14.1	14–17	195	21	4	3.5	2.5	—	3(12)	3½
	V6-231 LeMans	14.3	14.2	14–17	195	17(5)	4	3.5	2.4	—	3(12)	3½
	V6-231 Firebird	14.0	14.0	14–17	195	21	4	3.5	2.5	—	3(4)	4¼
	V6-231 Grand Prix	14.3	14.2	14–17	195	15	4	3.5	—	—	3(12)	3½
	V6-231 Pontiac	14.2	14.1	14–17	195	21	4	—	—	—	3(12)	(17)
	V8-301 LeMans	20.3	20.2	14–17	195	15(5)	5	—	—	—	3(12)	3½
	V8-301 Grand Prix	20.3	20.2	14–17	195	15	5	—	—	—	3(12)	3½
	V8-301 Pontiac	20.2	20.1	14–17	195	21	5	—	—	—	3(12)	(17)
	V8-305 Phoenix	16.8	17.0	14–17	195	21	4	—	2.5	—	3(12)	3½
	V8-305 LeMans	17.7	17.4	14–17	195	15(5)	4	—	—	—	3(12)	3½
	V8-305 Firebird	17.2	17.2	14–17	195	21	4	—	3.5	—	3(4)	4¼
	V8-305 Grand Prix	17.7	17.4	14–17	195	15	4	—	—	—	3(12)	3½
	V8-350 Phoenix	17.1	17.8	14–17	195	21	4	—	—	—	3(12)	4¼
	V8-350 LeMans	17.7	18.1	14–17	195	15(5)	4	—	—	—	3(12)	3½
	V8-350 Firebird	17.2	17.2	14–17	195	21	4	—	3.5	—	3(4)	4¼
	V8-350 Pontiac(6)	16.6	18.5	14–17	195	21	4	—	—	—	3(12)	4¼
	V8-350 Pontiac	16.5	19.1	14–17	195	21(7)	4	—	—	—	3(12)	4¼
	V8-400 Firebird	19.7	22.0	14–17	195	21	5	—	2.4	—	3(4)	4¼
	V8-400 Pontiac	26.3	20.3	14–17	195	21	5	—	—	—	3(12)	4¼
	V8-403 Firebird	17.4	18.0	14–17	195	21	4	—	—	—	3(4)	4¼
	V8-403 Pontiac	17.7	23.0	14–17	195	21	4	—	—	—	3(12)	4¼
1979	V6-231 Phoenix	14	14	14–17	195	21	4	3.5	3.5	—	3(34)	(17)
	V6-231 LeMans	14.2	14	14–17	195	18	4	3.5	3.5	—	3(34)	3½
	V6-231 Firebird	14	14	14–17	195	21	4	3.5	2.5	—	3(34)	4¼
	V6-231 Grand Prix	14.2	14	14–17	195	18	4	3.5	3.5	—	3(34)	3½
	V6-231 Pontiac	13.9	13.9	14–17	195	21	4	3.5	2.5	—	3(34)	(31)
	V8-301 Firebird	(26)	(26)	14–17	195	21	4(33)	3.5	2.5	—	3(34)	4¼
	V8-301 LeMans	20.3(32)	20.3(32)	14–17	195	18	4(33)	3.5	3.5	—	3(34)	3½
	V8-301 Grand Prix	20.3(29)	20.3(29)	14–17	195	18	4(33)	3.5	2.5	—	3(34)	4¼
	V8-301 Pontiac	20.2	20.2	14–17	195	21	4(33)	—	—	—	3(34)	(31)
	V8-305 Phoenix	16.8(11)	17(11)	14–17	195	21	4	3.5	3.5	—	3(34)	(17)
	V8-305 LeMans	17.7(30)	18.3	14–17	195	18	4	3.5	3.5	—	3(34)	3.5
	V8-305 Firebird	17.2(11)	17.8	14–17	195	21	4	3.5	2.5	—	3(34)	4¼
	V8-305 Grand Prix	17.7(30)	18.3	14–17	195	18	4	3.5	3.5	—	3(34)	3½
	V8-350 Phoenix	17.1	17.8	14–17	195	21	4	3.5	3.5	—	3(34)	(17)
	V8-350 LeMans	17.7(30)	18.3	14–17	195	18	4	3.5	3.5	—	3(34)	3.5
	V8-350 Firebird	17.2	17.8	14–17	195	21	4	3.5	2.5	—	3(34)	4¼
	V8-350 Pontiac	17	23	14–17	195	21	4	—	—	—	3(34)	(31)
	V8-400 Firebird	19.7(24)	20.3(24)	14–17	195	21	5	3.5	2.5	—	3(34)	4¼
	V8-403 Firebird	17.4(25)	18	14–17	195	21	4	3.5	2.5	—	3(34)	4¼
	V8-403 Pontiac	17(30)	23(30)	14–17	195	21	4	—	—	—	3(34)	(31)
1980	V6-229 LeMans	18.5	18.5	15	195	18.1	4	3.5	—	—	(35)	3.5
	V6-231 LeMans	13.3	13.3	15	195	18.1	4	—	—	—	(35)	3.5

Continued

COOLING SYSTEM & CAPACITY DATA—Continued

Year	Model or Engine	Cooling Capacity, Qts. Less A/C	Cooling Capacity, Qts. With A/C	Radiator Cap Relief Pressure, Lbs.	Thermo. Opening Temp. ①	Fuel Tank Gals.	Engine Oil Refill Qts. ②	Transmission Oil 3 Speed Pints	Transmission Oil 4 Speed Pints	Transmission Oil 5 Speed Pints	Auto Trans. Qts. ③	Rear Axle Oil Pints
	V6-231 Firebird	14	14	15	195	20.8	4	3.5	—	—	㉟	4.2
	V6-231 Grand Prix	13.3	13.3	15	195	18.1	4	—	—	—	㉟	3.5
	V6-231 Pontiac	13.3	13.3	15	195	25⑭	4	—	—	—	㉟	⑰
	V8-265 LeMans	20.3	20.3	15	195	18.1	4㉝	—	—	—	㉟	3.5
	V8-265 Firebird	21.6	21.6	15	195	20.8	4㉝	—	—	—	㉟	4.2
	V8-265 Grand Prix	20.3	20.3	15	195	18.1	4㉝	—	—	—	㉟	3.5
	V8-265 Pontiac	21.1	21.1	15	195	25⑭	4㉝	—	—	—	㉟	⑰
	V8-301 LeMans	20.3	20.3	15	195	18.1	4㉝	—	—	—	㉟	3.5
	V8-301 Firebird	21.6	21.6	15	195	20.8	4㉝	—	—	—	㉟	4.2
	V8-301 Grand Prix	20.3	20.3	15	195	18.1	4㉝	—	—	—	㉟	3.5
	V8-301 Pontiac	21.1	21.1	15	195	25⑭	4㉝	—	—	—	㉟	⑰
	V8-305 LeMans	18.5	18.5	15	195	18.1	4	—	—	—	㉟	3.5
	V8-305 Firebird	17.3	17.3	15	195	20.8	4	—	—	—	㉟	4.2
	V8-305 Grand Prix	18.2	18.2	15	195	18.1	4	—	—	—	㉟	3.5
	V8-305 Pontiac	20.1	20.1	15	195	25⑭	4	—	—	—	㉟	⑰
	V8-350 Pontiac㊲	14.8	14.8	15	195	25⑭	4	—	—	—	㉟	⑰
	V8-350 Pontiac㊳	16.4	16.4	15	195	25⑭	4	—	—	—	㉟	⑰
	V8-350 Diesel Pontiac	18.2	18.2	15	195	27	7㊱	—	—	—	㉟	⑰

①—With permanent type anti freeze.
②—Add one quart with filter change.
③—Approximate. Make final check with dip-stick.
④—Oil pan only. After overhaul 10 qts.
⑤—Station Wagons, 18 gals.
⑥—Distributor located at front of engine.
⑦—Station Wagons 24 gals.
⑧—Oil pan only. After overhaul 9½ qts.
⑨—2 BBl. Carb. 22.5 qts., 4 BBl. Carb. 23.3 qts.
⑩—2 BBl. Carb. 21.9 qts., 4 BBl. Carb. 23.6 qts.
⑪—With heavy duty cooling system, 17.8 qts.
⑫—Oil pan only. After overhaul; THM 200, 9 qts. THM 350, 10 qts.
⑬—Grand Am 25 gals., Sta. Wagon 22 gals.
⑭—Station Wagons 22 gals.
⑮—Oil pan only. After overhaul 6¾ qts.

⑯—THM 200, oil pan only 3 qts.; after overhaul 8¾ qts. THM 350, oil pan only 4 qts.; after overhaul 9.6 qts. THM 400, oil pan only 3¾ qts.; after overhaul 9½ qts.
⑰—7½ inch axle 3½ pints. 8½ & 8¾ inch axle 4¼ pints.
⑱—Oil pan only. After overhaul 8¾ qts.
⑲—With fuel pump located on driver side of engine.
⑳—With fuel pump located on passenger side of engine.
㉑—Manual trans.
㉒—Auto. trans.
㉓—Vehicles equipped with A/C and/or heavy duty cooling system.
㉔—With heavy duty cooling system, 21.7 qts.
㉕—With heavy duty cooling system, 18.1 qts.
㉖—With 2 barrel carb., 19.9 qts. With 4 barrel carb., 20.5 qts. With 2 barrel carb. and

heavy duty cooling system, 20.4 qts. With 4 barrel carb. and heavy duty cooling system, 21 qts.
㉗—Oil pan only. After overhaul 10½ qts.
㉘—"C" Type 4.9 pints.
㉙—With heavy duty cooling system, 20.8 qts.
㉚—With heavy duty cooling system, 18.5 qts.
㉛—Exc. Station Wagon, 3.5 pts.; Station Wagon, 4.25 pts.
㉜—With heavy duty cooling system, 20.8 qts.
㉝—With or without filter change.
㉞—Oil pan only. After overhaul 9 qts.
㉟—THM 200 & 200C, refill 3½ qts., after overhaul 9½ qts.; THM 250C & 350C, refill 2¾ qts., after overhaul 10¼ qts.
㊱—Includes filter. Use only oil meeting manufacturers recommendations.

AMC
1975–80

Services to be done	Mileage (in thousands) ①						
	15	25	30	45	50	60	75
Engine oil—change; Filter—replace②③④⑤	124●5●—every 5,000 miles; 34○5○6—at 3,500 miles and every 5,000 miles thereafter						
Coolant—change; Cooling system—tune up⑥	6○	12345	6●				
Rear axle fluid—change			123456			123456	
Fluids—check⑦⑧	124●5●—every 5,000 miles; 34○5○6—every 7,500 miles			123456	124●5●	123456	123456
Auto transmission—drain and refill; adjust bands⑨	45		123456	45		123456	45
Body—lubricate; Brakes—inspect⑩	123456		123456	123456		123456	123456
Front suspension—check & adjust⑪	123456		123456	123456		123456	123456
Clutch—inspect, adjust, lubricate linkage	12346		123456	12346		123456	12346
Fuel filter—replace	123456□		123456□	123456□		123456□	123456□
Carburetor air cleaner element—replace⑫			123456			123456	
Chassis—lubricate⑬⑮	6⑭		123456	6⑭		123456	6⑭
Heat valve (exhaust manifold)—inspect & lubricate			1234○5○6○			1234○5○6○	
Drive belts—inspect & adjust	126—every 30,000 miles; 34—at 5, 15, and every 15,000 miles thereafter; 4●5—every 5,000 miles; 6○□—at 5, 10, 30, 45, 60, 75,000 miles; 6□—at 10, 30, 45, 60, 75,000 miles						
EGR system lines, hoses & connections—inspect⑯	4○	12	34○56□	4○	12	34○56□	124○
Manual transmission fluid—change			6			6	
PCV filter—replace			6●				
PCV filter—clean			123456			123456	
PCV valve—replace			123456□			123456□	
PCV hoses & connections—inspect			123456□			123456□	
Cylinder head—retorque; Engine valves—adjust	5●—every 5,000 miles						
Carburetor idle speeds (curb and fast)—adjust	5—every 5,000 miles						

Legend:

1—1975 models.
2—1976 models.
3—1977 models.
4—1978 models.
5—1979 models.
6—1980 models.
●—4-cylinder only.
○—except 4-cylinder.
■—California models only.
□—except California models.

Service notes:

① —1979–80 models: perform service at months and/or miles, whichever comes first. (Example: 5 months/5000 miles, 10 months/10,000 miles etc.)
② —Service more often under severe operating conditions.
③ —Service at months and/or miles, whichever comes first. (Example: 5 months/ 5000 miles.)
④ —1979 models: Heavy Duty operation—service every 2.5 months/2500 miles.
⑤ —1980 4-cylinder models: replace oil filter at 7.5, 22.5, 37.5 months/miles (thousands).
⑥ —Change coolant initially at months/miles indicated in schedule, and then at the start of each winter season.
⑦ —Check: battery, axle differentials, coolant, power steering, manual steering gear, automatic and manual transmission, brake master cylinder and hydraulic clutch (1980 4-cylinder).
⑧ —1979 models: check battery every 15 months/15,000 miles; check axle differential, manual steering gear and manual transmission every 5000 miles.
⑨ —Heavy duty operation only. Service not required under normal use.
⑩ —Complete body lubrication and brake inspection includes—
    1. Inspection and correction, as needed, of brake linings and other parts.
    2. Hood latch and hinges.

    3. Door latches, lock cylinders and door hinges.
    4. Trunk lid (or tailgate) hinges and latches.
    5. Front seat racks.
    6. Ash tray slides.
    7. Glove box door latch and hinge.
    8. Courtesy light switch buttons.
    9. Apply silicone lubricant to all door, window and trunk (or tailgate) rubber weather seals.
⑪ —Inspect the following items and correct to specifications as necessary: manual or power steering gear and linkage for leaks, looseness or wear. Springs, shock absorbers and busings for leaks, looseness or wear. Tire condition. Overall steering/suspension condition and action.
⑫ —Replace twice as often under heavy duty or dusty conditions.
⑬ —Check and lubricate: front suspension ball joints, front wheel bearings, turning radius stop plate and bracket, parking brake, manual or power steering gear and linkage, front disc brake caliper abutment surfaces.
⑭ —1980 models: also lubricate steering linkage every 15 months/15,000 miles.
⑮ —1980 models: lubricate front disc brake caliper abutment surfaces every 7.5 thousand miles.
⑯ —1978 Pacer, Concord and AMX with 8-cyl. engines also receive this service at 15, 45 & 75 thousand miles.
⑰ —If equipped.

AMERICAN MOTORS 1975–80—ADDITIONAL TUNE UP SERVICES

	Service to be done	Mileage (in thousands) ①					
		7.5	15	22.5	30	37.5	45
a	Carburetor idle mixture—check & reset		5○		123456○□		5○
b	Distributor vacuum & centrifugal advance mechanism—check				123456□		
c	Distributor rotor & cap—check				123456□		
d	Carburetor mounting bolts—check & adjust	6●			6●□		
e	Choke system—clean & lubricate	6●			123456		6●
f	Air cleaner thermostatic system (TAC)—check	6●□			123456□		
g	Fuel inlet filter at charcoal canister—replace				6●□		
h	Air inlet filter at charcoal canister—replace				123456○□		
i	Air Guard System—check				123456○□		
j	Fuel system: cap, tank, lines, hoses & connections—check		6●		123456		6●
k	Vacuum fitting, hoses & connections—check	6●□	5○		123456□		5○6●□
l	Coil & spark plug wires—check		6●		123456		6●
m	Transmission controlled spark—check⑰				12345		
n	Exhaust system—check	6●	6●	6●	6●	6●	6●
o	Ignition timing—check		5		123456□		5
p	Spark plugs—replace				123456		
q	Oxygen sensor—replace⑰				6●■6□		
r	Oxygen sensor signal—reset⑰				6●■6□		
s	Ignition points & condensor—replace		5●		5●		5●

Chrysler
1975–76 Models

Services to be done	Every 6 months	Every 6 months or 5,000 miles, whichever occurs first	Every 12 months or 10,000 miles, whichever occurs first	Every 10,000 miles	Every 12 months or 15,000 miles, whichever occurs first	Every 15,000 miles	Every 24 months or 30,000 miles, whichever occurs first	Every 25,000 miles	Every 30,000 miles	Every 36 months or 35,000 miles, whichever occurs first
Maintenance Interval										
Carburetor choke shaft—apply solvent	X									
Fast idle cam and pivot pin—apply solvent	X									
Exhaust system—check for leaks, missing or damaged part	X									
Brake master cylinder—check fluid level	X									
Transmission and rear axle—check fluid level	X									
Brake and power steering hoses—check for deterioration or leaks	X									
Air conditioner—check belts, sight glass and operation of controls	X									
Ball joints, steering linkage, and universal joints—inspect seals	X									
Hood lock, release mechanism and safety catch—lubricate	X									
Engine oil—change		X								
Power steering—check fluid level		X								
Drive belts—check condition and tension		X								
Upper and lower control arm bushings—inspect		X								
Cooling system—check and service as required			X							
Engine oil filter—replace	X (first time only)	X								
Tires—rotate				X						
Brake linings—inspect				X						
Cooling system—drain, flush and refill					X		X (first time only)			
EGR system—check operation and service as required							X			
Idle speed and air/fuel mixture—check and adjust							X			
PCV valve—check operation							X			
Tappet adjustment (6 cyl. engine)							X			
Underhood rubber and plastic components (emission hoses)—inspect							X			
Vapor storage canister filter element—replace							X			
Front wheel bearings—inspect								X		
Automatic transmission (severe usage only)—change fluid and filter, adjust bands								X		
Automatic choke—check and adjust									X	
Carburetor air filter—replace									X	
Crankcase inlet air cleaner—clean									X	
Fuel filter—replace									X	
Ignition cables, distributor cap and rotor—check									X	
PCV valve—replace									X	
Manifold heat control valve—apply solvent									X	
Spark plugs—inspect*									X	
Ball joints and tie rod ends—lubricate										X

*Long-life spark plugs are expected to perform satisfactorily for at least 50,000 miles.

Chrysler
1977–78 Models

Services to be done	Every oil change	Every 3 months or 3,000 miles whichever occurs first	Every 6 months	Every 6 months or 6,000 miles whichever occurs first	Every 6 months or 7,500 miles whichever occurs first	Every 9,000 miles	Every 10,000 miles	Every 12 months or 15,000 miles whichever occurs first	Every 15,000 miles	Every 22,500 miles	Every 24,000 miles	Every 36 months or 30,000 miles whichever occurs first	Every 30,000 miles	Every 24 months or 30,000 miles whichever occurs first	Every 36,000 miles
Automatic choke—check and adjust													X		
Carburetor choke shaft—apply solvent				X											
Carburetor air filter—replace													X		
Cooling system—check and service as required								X							
Cooling system—drain, flush and refill									X					X*	
Crankcase inlet air cleaner—clean													X		
Engine oil—change		○		X											
Engine oil filter—replace		○*		X*				X							
Fast idle cam pivot pin—apply solvent			X												
Fuel filter—replace													X		
Idle speed and air-fuel mixture—check and adjust								X							
Ignition cables—check and replace	As required at time of spark plug replacement														
Manifold heat control valve—apply solvent													X		
PCV valve—check and replace if necessary									X*				X		
PCV valve—replace													X		
Spark plugs (without cat. converter)—replace									X						
Spark plugs (with cat. converter)—replace													X		
Tappet adjustment 6-cylinder engine—check and adjust									X						
Rubber and plastic emission hoses—inspect and replace if necessary									X						
Vapor storage filter element—replace													X		
Power steering—check fluid level	X														
Exhaust system—check for leaks, missing or damaged parts		X													
Brake master cylinder—check fluid level		X													
Transmission—check fluid level		X													
Brake and power steering hoses—check for deterioration and leaks		X													
Air conditioner—check belts, sight glass and operation of controls		X													
Ball joints, steering linkage and universal joints—inspect seals		X													
Hood lock, release mechanism and safety catch—lubricate		X													
Drive belts—check condition and tension	X														
Upper and lower control arm bushings—inspect	X														
Tires—rotate, inspect for wear						X									
Brake linings—inspect										X					
Front wheel bearings—inspect											X				
Radiator hose clamps (2 wire)—tighten						X									
Ball joints and tie rod ends—lubricate												X			
Rear axle—replace lubricant											○				
Steering and suspension ball joints—relubricate									○						
Wheel bearings—relubricate														○	
Automatic transmission—change fluid and filter, adjust bands (1977 models)															○
Automatic transmission—change fluid and filter, adjust bands (1978 models)									○						
Manual transmission—change lubricant					○										

X Normal service operation
○ Severe service operation
X* Normal service operation (first time only)
○* Severe service operation (first time only)

Service to be done		Mileage Intervals In Thousands					
		7.5	15	22.5	30	37.5	45
Automatic choke—check & adjust as required	AT		1		B1X		1
Carburetor choke shaft—apply solvent	AT	B1X	B1X	B1X	AB12X	B1X	B1X
Carburetor air filter—replace	AT				AB12X		
Crankcase inlet air cleaner—clean	AT				BX		
Engine oil—change every 12 months	OR	AB12X	AB12X	AB12X	AB12X	AB12X	AB12X
Engine oil filter—replace at initial oil change and every 2nd oil change or 12 months thereafter	OR	AB12X		AB12X		AB12X	
Drive belts—check condition & tension & replace if necessary	AT	1	AB12X	1	AB12X	1	AB12X
Fast idle cam and pivot pin—apply solvent	AT	B1X	B1X	B1X	AB12X	B1X	B1X
Fuel filter—replace	AT	1		1	BX	1	
Idle speed and air-fuel mixture—check and adjust as required	AT		B1X		B1X		B1X
Ignition cables—check and replace as required	AT		B1X		B1X		B1X
Manifold heat control valve—apply solvent	AT				BX		
Oxygen sensor (if so equipped)—replace sensor and reset mileage counter; replace E.M.R. battery if so equipped ①	AT				A1		
Positive crankcase vent valve—check operation & replace if necessary			B1X				B1X
Positive crankcase vent valve—replace	AT				B1X		
Spark plugs (without cat. converter)—replace	AT		AB12X		AB12X		AB12X
Spark plugs (with cat. converter)—replace	AT				AB2X		
All fuel system and under hood rubber & plastic components (emission hoses)—inspect and replace if necessary	AT		B1X		B1X		B1X
Vapor storage canister filter element—replace	AT		X		BX		X
Tappet adjustment 4 & 6 cyl. engines—check and adjust as required	AT		AB12X		12		12
Ignition timing—check and adjust as required	AT		1		1		1
Front wheel bearings—inspect	AT				ABX		
Ball joints—lubricate	AT				ABX		
Cooling system—check and service as required every twelve months	OR		AB12X		AB12X		AB12X
Cooling system—drain, flush and refill at 24 months and every twelve months thereafter	OR				AB12X		AB12X
Clutch pedal free play—check and adjust as required	AT	12X	12X	12X	12X	12X	12X
Brake linings—front—inspect	AT		12		AB12X		12
Brake linings—rear—inspect ②	AT				AB12X		
Rear wheel bearings—inspect	AT				12		

Severe Service Maintenance Schedule ⑦	
Service to be done	Maintenance interval
Engine oil filter	Change every 3 months or 3000 miles
Engine oil filter	Replace at initial oil change and every 2nd oil change thereafter
Automatic transmission	Change fluid, filter and adjust bands every 15,000 miles
Manual transmission ③	Change fluid every 30,000 miles
Axle differential oil ④	Change every 36,000 miles
Brake linings	⑤
Front wheel bearings ④	Inspect & lubricate every 9000 miles
Rear wheel bearings ③	Inspect & relubricate ⑥
Ball joints ④	Lubricate every 18 months or 15,000 miles
Universal joints	Inspect at every oil change
Tie rod ends	Lubricate every 18 months or 15,000 miles

Legend:
A—Vehicles with Maintenance Schecule "A" indicated on the Vehicle Emission Control Information Label located in the engine compartment.
B—Vehicles with Maintenance Schedule "B" indicated on the Vehicle Emission Control Label.
C—1979 Omni/Horizon models.
D—1980 Omni/Horizon models.
X—All other vehicles.

Service notes:
①—1979 models except Omni/Horizon: replace at 15,000-mile intervals.
②—1980 Omni/Horizon models: also adjust if required.
③—Omni/Horizon models only.
④—Except Omni/Horizon models.
⑤—Omni/Horizon: inspect front every 6000 miles, inspect rear every 15,000 miles. All other models: inspect front & rear every 9000 miles.
⑥—1979 Omni/Horizon: service every 9000 miles, 1980 Omni/Horizon: service every 12,000 miles.
⑦—Stop and go driving in dusty conditions, extensive idling, frequent short trips, operating at sustained high speeds during temperatures above 90°F., trailer towing, taxi, police or limousine use.

Ford
1975–76 Models

Service Interval
(Number of months or thousands of miles, whichever occurs first)

Services to be done		5	6	10	12	15	18	20	24	25	30	35	36	40	42	45	48	50
Engine oil—change①②		AB	C	AB	C	AB	C	AB	C	AB	ABC	AB	C	AB	C	AB	C	AB
Oil filter—replace①②		AB	C			AB	C			AB	C	AB			C	AB		
Intake manifold bolts/nuts—torque			C⑭			B	C	A			C⑭				C⑭			
Exhaust control valve—lubricate, check③			C			C	B	C	A	C	BC		C	A	C	B	C	
Fuel system filter—replace			C			B		A										
Carburetor air cleaner element④	Check				C	B							C			B		
	Replace							A	C		B			A			C	
Emissions filter in air cleaner④	Check				C	B							C			B		
	Replace							A	C		B			A			C	
Idle fuel mixture—adjust	All except 4 cyl.		C			B		A	C		B			A		B	C	
	4 cyl.		C		C	B		A	C		B		C	A		B		
Fast idle speed—adjust	All except 4 cyl.	AB	C			B		A	C		B			A		B		
	4 cyl.	AB	C		C	B		A	C		B		C	A		B	C	
Curb idle speed—adjust		AB				B		A			B			A		B		
Curb idle speed and TSP off speed—adjust	All except 4 cyl.		C						C									
	4 cyl.		C		C				C								C	
Throttle solenoid off speed—adjust		AB																
Air cleaner temp. control and delay valve—check⑤						C	B		A	C	B		C	A		B	C	
Throttle and choke linkage and delay valve or air valve—check	All except 4 cyl.		C⑤				B		A	C⑤	B			A		B		
	4 cyl.		C⑤		C⑤	B		A	C⑤		B		C⑤	A		B		
Fuel deceleration valve—check⑤		AB⑭	C		C	B⑭		A⑭	C		B⑭		C	A⑭		B⑭	C	
Engine valve clearance (2800)—adjust					C	B		A	C		B		C	A		B	C	
Fuel vapor emissions system—inspect								A	C		B			A			C	
PCV valve—replace								A	C		B			A			C	
PCV system⑤	Check				C	B		A					C	A		B		
	Clean							A	C		B			A			C	
Initial ignition timing—adjust						B	C	A			B		C	A		B		
Ignition system—check⑥						B		A			B			A		B		
Distributor cap and rotor—inspect⑦						B	C	A			B		C	A		B		
Spark plugs—replace①⑧						B	C	A			B		C	A		B		
Spark plug wires—check⑨						B	C	A			B		C	A		B		
Crankcase breather cap (if so equipped)—check⑮						C			C					C			C	
Spark control system and delay valve—check⑤						C	B		A	C	B		C	A		B	C	
Thermactor system—check⑤							B		A	C	B			A		B	C	
Evaporative emissions canister—inspect⑤⑩	All except 4 cyl.							A	C		B			A			C	
	4 cyl.					C		A	C		B		C	A			C	
EGR system and delay valve—check⑤⑪						C			C		C						C	
Drive belt tension—check			C					B	A									
Drive belt condition—check						C			C		B		C	A		B	C	
Belt-driven accessories (4 cyl.)—check⑫						C	B		A	C	B		C	A		B	C	
Coolant condition and protection—check⑬						C	B		A	C						B	C	
Coolant—replace												B	C	A				
Cooling system hoses and clamps—check									C		AB						C	
Exhaust system heat shield—inspect⑯		AB				AB					AB					AB		
Transmission fluid level—check		AB	C			AB	C				ABC				C	AB		
Rear axle fluid level—check		AB	C			AB	C				ABC				C	AB		
Brake master cylinder fluid level—check		AB	C		C	AB	C		C		ABC		C		C	AB	C	
Clutch linkage and free play—inspect		AB	C		C	AB	C		C		ABC		C		C	AB	C	
Steering linkage (looseness and seals)—inspect						C	AB		C		AB		C			AB	C	
Automatic transmission band—adjust⑰	Normal svc.					C	AB											
	Severe svc.	AB				C	AB		C		AB		C			AB	C	
Brake linings, hoses, front wheel bearing lubrication—inspect									C	AB				C				AB
Front suspension and steering linkage—lubricate											AB							
Front suspension ball joints—lubricate													C					
Automatic transmission (continuous service only)—replace fluid											AB							
Exhaust system—inspect⑱						C			C				C				C	

NOTES:

Three maintenance schedules, identified by the letters A, B and C, are specified in the chart. The schedule applying to the particular vehicle is identified on a decal on the glove box door which displays either an A, B or C.

①—For A and B rated cars—when operating the vehicle under severe service conditions, change engine oil every 2½ months or 2,500 miles. Change oil filter the first oil change and every 5 months or 5,000 miles thereafter. Check, clean and regap spark plugs every 5,000 miles.

For C rated cars—when operating the vehicle under severe service conditions, change oil every 2 months or 3,000 miles and the oil filter every 4 months or 6,000 miles. Clean and regap spark plugs every 4 months or 6,000 miles.

Severe service conditions include:
- Extended periods of idling or low-speed operation.
- Driving short distances (less than 10 miles) while outside temperature remains below 10° F for 60 days or more.
- Excessive dust conditions.

②—For C rated cars—normal oil change is at every 6,000 miles or 4 months, whichever occurs first. Normal oil filter change is at first 6,000 miles or 4 months and at alternative oil change periods thereafter.

③—Lubricate and free up at each oil change (C rated cars only).

④—Replace more often if operated in severe dust conditions.

⑤—Adjust, repair or replace as required.

Maintenance Interval

⑥—For A rated cars—check with scope (recheck after any maintenance or repair).

⑦—Clean or replace as indicated by scope check.

⑧—If not replaced at 12,000 or 18,000 mile intervals, replace complete set at time of plug malfunction.

⑨—Repair or replace wires as indicated by scope check and verified by continuity check.

⑩—Replace canister if contaminated by water, oil, etc.

⑪—Check exhaust passages in EGR valve, carburetor spacer, and intake manifold.

⑫—Check and torque to specifications.

⑬—If coolant is dirty or rusty in appearance, the system should be drained, cleaned and refilled with the prescribed solution of cooling system fluid and water.

⑭—Four-cylinder and V-6 only.

⑮—More often if operated in severe dust conditions.

⑯—Remove accumulated debris or replace shield as required. Perform each 5,000 miles for severe service usage over unpaved roadways or off-road applications.

⑰—Severe service operation (see note 1 for definition of "severe service.")

⑱—Perform each 6,000 miles for severe service usage over unpaved roadways or off-road applications.

Ford
1977 4-Cylinder and V6 Models

Services to be done	5	6	7.5	10	12	15	18	20	22.5	24	30	36	37.5	40	42	45	48	50
Engine oil—change ①		C	AB	C		C	AB		C	ABC	C		AB	C		C	C	AB
Oil filter—replace ①		C	AB			C	AB			ABC			AB	C				AB
Intake manifold bolts/nuts—torque		C			C					C				C				
Exhaust control valve—lubricate, check ③		C		C		C			C	C	C			C				
Fuel system filter—replace		C																
Carburetor air cleaner element ④ — Check					C						C							
Carburetor air cleaner element ④ — Replace										C	AB						C	
Emissions filter in air cleaner—replace ④										C	AB						C	
Idle fuel mixture—adjust ⑪ — V6 only		C							A	C	B							
Idle fuel mixture—adjust ⑪ — 4 cyl. only		C			C			A		C	B	C					C	
Fast idle speed—adjust — V6 only		C	AB								C							
Fast idle speed—adjust — 4 cyl. only	A	C		B	C					C		C					C	
Curb idle speed—adjust ⑪	A			B			A				B							
Curb idle speed and TSP off speed—adjust — V6 only	A	C		B							C							
Curb idle speed and TSP off speed—adjust — 4 cyl. only	A	C		B	C					C		C					C	
Air cleaner temp. control and delay valve—check ⑤				C						C	B	C		A			C	
Throttle and choke linkage and delay valve or air valve—check ⑤ — V6 only		C									C							
Throttle and choke linkage and delay valve or air valve—check ⑤ — 4 cyl. only		C			C						C	C					C	
Choke system—check								A			AB			A				
Fuel deceleration valve—check ⑤		C			C					C	C						C	
Fuel vapor emissions system—inspect ⑤										C	B			A			C	
PCV valve—replace ⑪								A		C	B						C	
PCV system ⑤ — Check					C							C						
PCV system ⑤ — Clean											C						C	
Initial ignition timing—adjust ⑪	A			B		C					C							
Engine valve clearance (2.8L V6 engine only)—adjust	A			B				A			B			A				
Distributor cap and rotor—inspect ⑤						C						C						

Service Interval (Number of months or thousands of miles, whichever occurs first)

Services to be done	5	6	7.5	10	12	15	18	20	22.5	24	30	36	37.5	40	42	45	48
Spark plugs—replace ② ⑥ with use of low lead or unleaded fuel						C	A		B	C			A				
with use of leaded fuel				C					C	C					C		
Spark control system and delay valve—check ⑤ ⑦				C					C	C					C		
Belt driven accessory mounting hardware (4 cyl. only)—check ⑧				C					C	C					C		
Coolant condition and protection—check ⑨ A and B rated cars									Annually								
C rated cars				C					C	C					C		
Coolant—replace ⑫										C	AB						
Cooling system hoses and clamps—check ⑬									C		AB				C		
Drive belt tension—check ⑤	C		B				A		B				A				
Drive belt condition—check ⑤	C			C					C	C					C		
Exhaust system heat shield—inspect ⑮ ⑯						C	AB			C	AB			AB			
Brake master cylinder fluid level—check									ABC								
Clutch linkage and free play—inspect ⑤ ⑯		AB		C	AB		AB	C	AB	C	AB			AB		C	
Brake linings, hoses, front wheel bearing lubrication—inspect ⑤ ⑯									ABC								
Front suspension and steering linkage—lubricate									AB	C							
Automatic transmission (severe or continuous service only) replace fluid ⑰						C	AB			C				AB			
Spark plug wires—check ② ⑥ with use of low lead or unleaded fuel						C				C					C		
with use of leaded fuel				C					C	C					C		
Thermactor system—check ⑤ ⑭							A		C	B			A		C		
Evaporative emissions canister—inspect ⑤ V6 only									C						C		
4 cyl. only				C					C	C					C		
EGR system and delay valve—check ⑤ ⑦				C					C	C					C		

Ford
1977 V8 Models

Services to be done	Service Interval (Number of months or thousands of miles, whichever occurs first)																
	5	6	7.5	10	12	15	18	20	22.5	24	30	36	37.5	40	42	45	48
Engine oil—change ①	C	AB		C	AB	C			AB	C	ABC	C	AB		C	AB	C
Oil filter—replace ①	C	AB			C				AB	C			AB		C		
Intake manifold bolts/nuts—torque	C				C					C					C		
Exhaust control valve—lubricate, check ③	C			C		C				C	C	C			C		
Fuel system filter—replace	C																
Carburetor air cleaner element ④ Check					C								C				
Replace										C	AB						C
Emissions filter in air cleaner—replace ④										C	AB						C
Idle fuel mixture—adjust ⑪	C								A	C	B						
Fast idle speed—adjust	C	AB								C							
Curb idle speed—adjust ⑪		AB							A		B						
Curb idle speed and TSP off speed—adjust	C	AB								C							
Air cleaner temp. control and delay valve—check ⑤						C				C	B	C					C
Throttle and choke linkage and delay valve or air valve—check ⑤	C									C							
Choke system—check									A		B					A	
Fuel deceleration valve—check ⑨	C				C					C		C					C
Fuel vapor emissions system—inspect ⑤										C	B					A	C
PCV valve—replace ⑪									A	C	B						C
PCV system ⑤ Check					C								C				
Clean											C						C
Initial ignition timing—adjust ⑪		AB				C							C				
Distributor cap and rotor—inspect ⑤						C							C				
Spark plugs—replace ② ⑥ with use of low lead or unleaded fuel						C			A		B	C				A	
with use of leaded fuel					C					C	C						C
Spark control system and delay valve—check ⑤ ⑦					C					C	C						C

Services to be done	Service Interval (Number of months or thousands of miles, whichever occurs first)																
	5	6	7.5	10	12	15	18	20	22.5	24	30	36	37.5	40	42	45	48
Coolant condition and protection—check ⑨ A and B rated cars	Annually																
C rated cars					C				C		C						C
Coolant—replace ⑫											C					AB	
Cooling system hoses and clamps—check ⑬										C						AB	C
Drive belt tension—check ⑤	C	B							A	B						A	
Drive belt condition—check ⑤	C				C				C		C						C
Exhaust system heat shield—inspect ⑮ ⑯							C		AB		C	AB				AB	
Brake master cylinder fluid level—check									ABC								
Clutch linkage and free play—inspect ⑤ ⑯			AB	C	AB		AB	C	AB	C	AB					AB	C
Brake linings, hoses, front wheel bearing lubrication—inspect ⑤ ⑯									ABC								
Front suspension and steering linkage—lubricate											AB	C					
Automatic transmission (severe or continuous service only) replace fluid ⑰						C	AB					C				AB	
Spark plug wires—check ② ⑥ with use of low lead or unleaded fuel							C					C					
with use of leaded fuel					C					C	C						C
Thermactor system—check ⑤ ⑭								A	C		B					A	C
Evaporative emissions canister—inspect ⑤										C							C
EGR system and delay valve—check ⑤ ⑦					C					C	C						C

NOTES:

Three maintenance schedules, identified by the letters A, B and C, are specified in the chart. The schedule applying to the particular vehicle is identified on a decal on the glove box door which displays either an A, B or C.

①—For A and B rated V8 cars—when operating the vehicle under normal service conditions, change the engine oil every 7,500 miles or 6 months. Replace oil filter at first oil change and at alternate oil changes thereafter.

When operating the vehicle under severe service conditions, change the engine oil every 3,000 miles or 3 months. Replace oil filter at first oil change and at alternate oil changes thereafter.

For A and B rated 4-cyl. and V6 cars—when operating the vehicle under normal service conditions, change the engine oil and replace the oil filter at 10,000 miles or 6 months. If the vehicle mileage is less than 7,500 miles each 6 months, change engine oil every 7,500 miles or 6 months and replace the oil filter at first oil change and at alternate oil changes thereafter.

When operating under severe service conditions, change engine oil every 3,000 miles or 3 months and replace oil filter at alternate oil changes.

For C rated cars—when operating under normal service conditions, change the engine oil every 6,000 miles or 4 months. Oil filter change is at first 6,000 miles or 4 months and at alternate oil changes thereafter.

When operating under severe service conditions, change engine oil every 3,000 miles or 2 months. Change the oil filter every 6,000 miles or 4 months. Severe service conditions include:
- Extended periods of idling or low-speed operation.
- Towing trailers over 2,000 pounds gross loaded weight for long distances.
- Outside temperature remains below +10°F for 60 days or more and most trips are less than 10 miles.
- In severe dust conditions.

②—Under severe service conditions:

For A and B rated cars—check, clean and regap spark plugs every 6,000 miles. For C rated cars—check spark plug wires, and clean and regap spark plugs every 6,000 miles or 4 months.

③—Lubricate and free up at each oil change (C rated cars only).

④—Replace more often if operated in severe dust conditions.

⑤—Adjust, repair or replace as required.

⑥—C rated cars only. If not replaced at 12,000 or 18,000 mile intervals, replace complete set at time of plug malfunction.

⑦—Check exhaust passages in EGR valve, carburetor spacer, and intake manifold.

⑧—Check and torque to specifications.

⑨—If coolant is dirty or rusty in appearance, the system should be drained, cleaned and refilled with the prescribed solution of cooling system fluid and water.

⑩—More often if operated in severe dust conditions.

⑪—Refer to Vehicle Emission Control Decal.

⑫—Replace coolant every 3 years or at specified mileage, whichever occurs first.

⑬—Check every 3 years or at specified mileage. A and B rated cars.

⑭—If so equipped.

⑮—For A and B rated cars, remove accumulated debris and inspect shield and attachment. Perform each 10,000 miles for severe service usage over unpaved roadways or off-road applications.

For C rated cars, remove accumulated debris or replace shield as required. Perform each 6,000 miles for severe service usage over unpaved roadways or off-road applications.

⑯—For A and B rated cars, Mustang II with 302 V8 only serviced at all intervals. Other applicable models serviced at 15/24, 30/48 and 45/72.

⑰—For A and B rated cars, adjust bands at 7,500, 15,000 and 45,000 miles for severe service.

For C rated cars, adjust bands at 6,000, 12,000, 30,000 and 48,000 miles for severe service.

Ford
1978–80

Service to be done	Service Interval (number of months or thousands of miles, whichever occurs first)⑥					
	5	7.5	10	15	20	22.5
Engine oil—change①②		246	135	246	135	246
Oil filter—replace①②		246	135		135	246
Carburetor air cleaner element—replace③						
Idle fuel mixture—adjust⑤⑦⑧					1A3A	2A4A
Engine idle speed—adjust⑤	1⑨23⑧⑩3F45	1B6	3⑧⑪			4A⑫
Choke system—check				3F	1A3A	2A4A
PCV valve—replace⑤					1A3A	2A4A
Spark plugs—replace②⑤⑭				3F	1A⑬3A	2A4A
Crankcase emission filter—replace③⑰						
Thermactor delay valve—check				3F	1A3A	2A4A
Drive belt condition and tension—check㉑㉓	5	2B4B6	1B3B	3F	1A3A	2A4A
Coolant condition and protection—check	ANNUALLY					
Coolant—replace						
Cooling system hoses and clamps—check⑱						
Exhaust system heat shield—check						12
Brake master cylinder fluid level—check						
Clutch linkage and free play—inspect		4	33F5	1246	33F5	124
Brake linings, hoses, front wheel bearing lubrication—inspect						
Front suspension and steering linkage—lubricate						
Automatic transmission (severe or continuous service only)—replace fluid				33F5	1246	
Automatic transmission (severe service only)—adjust bands㉔	33F5	1246	33F5	1246		
Engine valve clearance (2.8L only)—check	1A		1B3B			
Traction-Lok rear axle (severe service only)—drain and refill㉕		6				

Service to be done	Service Interval (number of months or thousands of miles, whichever occurs first)⑥					
	30	37.5	40	45	50	52.5
Engine oil—change①②	123456	246	135	246	135	246
Oil filter—replace①②	135	246	135		135	246
Carburetor air cleaner element—replace③	1233F456					4A④
Idle fuel mixture—adjust⑤⑦⑧	1B2B3B4B					
Engine idle speed—adjust⑤	4B⑫56					
Choke system—check	1B2B3B3F456		1A3A4A	2A3F		
PCV valve—replace⑤	1B2B3B4B					
Spark plugs—replace②⑤⑭	1B⑬2B3B3F4B56		1A⑬3A	2A3F4A		
Crankcase emission filter—replace③⑰	13B4⑮5⑲		3A		3A5⑳	24⑯6
Thermactor delay valve—check	1B2B3B3F4B		1A3A	2A3F4A		
Drive belt condition and tension—check㉑㉓	1B2B3B3F4B56		1A3A	2A3F4A	3B	4B㉒
Coolant condition and protection—check	ANNUALLY					
Coolant—replace		4⑫			133F5	24④6
Cooling system hoses and clamps—check⑱					133F	24
Exhaust system heat shield—check	33F456	12				
Brake master cylinder fluid level—check	1233F456					
Clutch linkage and free play—inspect	1233F456	124	33F5	1246	33F5	4
Brake linings, hoses, front wheel bearing lubrication—inspect	1233F456					
Front suspension and steering linkage—lubricate	1233F456					
Automatic transmission (severe or continuous service only)—replace fluid			33F5	1246	33F5	
Automatic transmission (severe service only)—adjust bands㉔	33F456			1246		
Engine valve clearance (2.8L only)—check	1B3B		1A3A		3B	
Traction-Lok rear axle (severe service only)—drain and refill㉕						

Legend:

1—1978 4- & 6-cylinder engines.
2—1978 V8 engines.
3—1979 4- & 6-cylinder engines.
4—1979 V8 engines.
5—1980 4- & 6-cylinder engines.
6—1980 V8 engines.

A, B and F correspond to the maintenance schedule identified by a decal inside the glove box door and on the Vehicle Emission Control Information Decal, which is located on or near the engine. Maintenance operations applicable to 1978 V8 engines, Schedule A, for example, would be listed as 2A. A number listed without a letter (2), indicates that both 2A and 2B are applicable to that service. This rule applies to categories 1–6, with the exception of 3F, which is listed separately.

continued

Service notes:

① —2.3L turbocharged engine: change oil and replace oil filter every 3000 miles.

② —Severe service operation: change engine oil every 3 months/3000 miles and replace filter at alternate oil changes. Check, clean and regap spark plugs every 6000 miles. Severe service conditions include: extended periods of idling or low speed operation, towing trailers up to 1000 lbs for long distances (do not tow trailers with turbocharged vehicles), operation when outside temperature remains below 10°F and operation in severe dust conditions.

③ —More often if operated in severe dust conditions.

④ —5.0L (302 cid) engine only.

⑤ —Refer to Vehicle Emission Control Information Decal.

⑥ —Scheduled maintenance beyond 50,000 miles should be continued at the same intervals as before except as noted.

⑦ —Check idle fuel mixture after PCV valve replacement if artificial enrichment specifications are given on the engine decal (3.3L only).

⑧ —These services are required only to correct unusual engine operation after 50,000 miles.

⑨ —'78, Schedule A: all 4- and 6-cylinder except 2.3L engine with feedback carburetor (Calif.); Schedule B: 2.3L engine with feedback carburetor (Calif. only.)

⑩ —2.3L engine.

⑪ —2.8L and 3.3L engines.

⑫ —5.8L and 6.6L engines only.

⑬ —All except 3.3L engines in California.

⑭ —1978 3.3L engine (California): Replace each 50,000 miles or 30 months, whichever comes first.

⑮ —7.5L V8.

⑯ —All V8 except 7.5L.

⑰ —'79 2.3L engine: replace at 60,000 miles. '79 2.3 Turbo, and all '79 V8s: not required for first 50,000 miles; as required thereafter.

⑱ —1980 models: check annually.

⑲ —1980 6-cylinder only.

⑳ —1980 4-cylinder only.

㉑ —Serpentine drive belt: service not required.

㉒ —Except 6.6L V8.

㉓ —'79 5.0L engine: see note ⑧.

㉔ —Adjustment not required on vehicles equipped with automatic overdrive transmission.

㉕ —Severe service: service every 7500 miles.

General Motors
1975-76 Models

Services to be done	Maintenance Intervals					
	Every 6 months or 7,500 miles, whichever occurs first	Every 12 months or 15,000 miles, whichever occurs first	Every 18 months or 22,500 miles, whichever occurs first	Every 12 months	Every 30,000 miles	Every 60,000 miles
Chassis—lubricate	X					
Fluid levels—check	X					
Engine oil—change	X					
Engine oil filter, V8's and in-line 6's—replace		X (First one at 6 months or 7,500 miles				
Engine oil filter, V6—replace	X					
Tires—rotate	Bias-belted every 7,500 miles. Steel-belted radials at first 7,500 miles; then every 15,000 miles					
Differential (or final drive, front-drive cars)—change lubricant		X (Every 15,000 miles if car pulls trailer				
Air conditioning system—check charge and hose condition				X		
Cooling system—wash radiator cap and filler neck, pressure test system, inspect and tighten hoses, clean radiator core		X				
Cooling system—drain, flush and refill with new coolant					X	
Front wheel bearings (rear bearings in front drive vehicles)—clean and repack					X	
Final drive axle boots and output shaft seal—check condition					X	
Automatic transmission—change fluid and service filter					X ('75 models)	X ('76 models)
Manual steering gear—check seals					X	
Clutch cross shaft—lubricate					X	
Tires and wheels—check condition	X					
Exhaust system—check condition	X					
Drive belts—check condition and adjustment	X ('75 models)	X ('76 models)				
Front and rear suspension and steering system—check condition	X					
Brakes and power steering—check all lines and hoses	X					

Services to be done	Every 6 months or 7,500 miles, whichever occurs first	Every 12 months or 15,000 miles, whichever occurs first	Every 18 months or 22,500 miles, whichever occurs first	Every 12 months	Every 30,000 miles	Every 60,000 miles
Drum brakes and parking brake—check condition of linings; adjust parking brake		X				
Throttle linkage—check operation and condition		X				
Underbody—flush and check condition		X				
Bumpers—check condition		X				
Thermostatically controlled air cleaner—check operation	X (First service)		X			
Carburetor choke—check operation	X (First service)		X			
Engine idle speed adjustment	X (First service)		X			
EFE valve—check operation	X (First service)		X			
Carburetor—torque attaching bolts or nuts to manifold	X (First service)		X			
Vacuum advance system and hoses—check operation	X (First service—'76 models)	X ('75 models)	X ('76 models)			
Carburetor fuel inlet filter—replace		X				
PCV system—check operation		X				
PCV system—replace filter and valve					X	
Idle stop solenoid or dashpot—check operation			X			
Spark plug and ignition coil wires—inspect and clean			X			
Spark plugs—replace			X (Every 22,500 miles)			
Engine timing adjustment and distributor check			X (Every 22,500 miles)			
ECS system—check and replace filter					X (Or 24 months whichever is first)	
Fuel cap, tank and lines—check condition					X (Or 24 months whichever is first)	
Air cleaner element—replace					X	

General Motors
1977–78 Models

Services to be done	Every 3,000 miles	First 3,000 miles then every 30,000 miles	Every 6,000 miles	First 6 months/7,500 miles then every 18 months/22,500 miles	First 7,500 miles then every 15,000 miles	Every 12 months/7,500 miles whichever occurs first	Every 12 months	Every 12 months/9,000 miles whichever occurs first	Every 12 months/15,000 miles whichever occurs first	Every 15,000 miles	First 6 months/7,500 miles then every 24 months/30,000 miles	Every 22,500 miles	Every 24,000 miles	Every 24 months/30,000 miles whichever occurs first	Every 30,000 miles	Every 60,000 miles
Chassis—lubricate						12		3								
Fluid levels—check						12		3								
Engine oil—change ①	3					12										
Engine oil filter—replace ②	3			12												
Tires—rotate ③				12												
Differential (or final drive, front-drive cars)—change lubricant ④							See Notes									
Air conditioning system—check charge and hose condition ⑤						12										
Cooling system—wash radiator cap and filler neck, pressure test system, inspect and tighten hoses, clean radiator core									123							
Cooling system—drain, flush and refill with new coolant														12		
Front wheel bearings (rear bearings in front drive vehicles)— clean and repack ⑥												123				
Final drive axle boots and output shaft seal—check condition												12				
Automatic transmission—change fluid and service filter ⑦ ⑧																123
Manual steering gear—check seals												12				
Clutch cross shaft—lubricate												12				
Tires, disc brakes and wheels—check condition						12		3								
Exhaust system—check condition						12		3								
Drive belts—check condition and adjustment									123							
Front and rear suspension and steering system—check condition						12		3								
Brakes and power steering—check all lines and hoses						12		3								
Drum brakes and parking brake— check condition of linings; adjust parking brake									123							
Throttle linkage—check operation and condition									123							
Underbody—flush and check condition									123							
Bumpers—check condition									123							
Thermostatically controlled air cleaner—check operation				1							2					
Carburetor choke (except fuel injection)—check operation ⑨				1							2					
Engine idle speed adjustment	3			1							2					
EFE valve (except fuel injection)—check operation				1							2					
Carburetor (or fuel injection throttle mounting body)— torque attaching bolts or nuts to manifold				1							2					
Vacuum advance system and hoses—check operation				1					2							
Carburetor fuel inlet filter—replace ⑩									12							
PCV system—check operation									12							
PCV system—replace filter and valve ⑪															12	
Idle stop solenoid or dashpot—check operation												1			2	
Spark plug and ignition coil wires—inspect and clean									2			1				
Spark plugs—replace ⑭												1			2	
Engine timing adjustment and distributor check												1			2	

Services to be done	Every 3,000 miles	First 3,000 miles then every 30,000 miles	Every 6,000 miles	First 6 months/7,500 miles then every 18 months/22,500 miles	First 7,500 miles then every 15,000 miles	Every 12 months/7,500 miles whichever occurs first	Every 12 months	Every 12 months/9,000 miles whichever occurs first	Every 12 months/15,000 miles whichever occurs first	Every 15,000 miles	First 6 months/7,500 miles then every 24 months/30,000 miles	Every 22,500 miles	Every 24,000 miles	Every 24 months/30,000 miles whichever occurs first	Every 30,000 miles	Every 60,000 miles
														Maintenance Intervals		
ECS system—check and replace filter														12		
Carburetor vacuum brake—adjust 12												1			2	
Fuel cap, tank and lines—check condition														12		
Fuel filter—replace													3			
Air cleaner element—replace 15 16															123	
Differential vacuum delay and separator valve—check hoses, connections and operation 13 17										'77 Models 2			1		'78 Models 2	
Clutch pedal—check								12								
Oxygen sensor—change 13											12					
Crankcase ventilation breather cap, valve and filter—check			3													
Crankcase ventilation breather cap, valve assembly and flow control valve—replace															3	
Turbocharger vacuum bleed valve check (2 bbl. only) power enrichment valve check (4 bbl. only)															2	

GM NOTES:

Three maintenance schedules, identified by the numbers 1, 2 and 3 are specified in the chart. These schedules correspond with schedules I, II and III as identified on the vehicle emission control decal located on the glove box door or under the hood.

① —Change each 12 months or 7,500 miles whichever occurs first under normal driving conditions, or each 3 months or 3,000 miles when the vehicle is operated under the following conditions: a) driving in dusty conditions, b) trailer pulling, c) extensive idling or d) short-trip operation at freezing temperatures (with the engine not thoroughly warmed-up).
On turbocharged engines, change the engine oil every 3,000 miles.

② —Replace at the first oil change and every other oil change thereafter, if mileage (7,500) is the determining factor. If time (12 months) is the determining factor, change oil filter with every oil change.
On turbocharged engines, replace the oil filter every 3,000 miles.

③ —Rotate steel belted radial tires at the first 7,500 miles and then at every 15,000 miles thereafter. Rotate bias ply tires every 7,500 miles.
On 1978 Oldsmobile schedule 3 cars, rotate steel belted radial tires at the first 6,000 miles and then at every 12,000 miles thereafter. Rotate bias ply tires every 6,000 miles.

④ —Change rear axle lubricant according to the following schedule:
1977 Oldsmobile and Buick—For controlled differentials, change lubricant at the first 15,000 miles and every 7,500 miles when pulling a trailer. For standard differentials, replace lubricant every 15,000 miles when pulling a trailer.
1978 Oldsmobile (Schedule 1 and 2): For controlled differentials, change lubricant at the first 7,500 miles and every 7,500 miles when pulling a trailer. For standard differentials, change lubricant every 15,000 miles when pulling a trailer.
1978 Oldsmobile (Schedule 3): For controlled differentials, change lubricant every 6,000 miles when pulling a trailer. For standard differentials, change lubricant every 15,000 miles when pulling a trailer.
1977 and 1978 Cadillac: For controlled differentials, change lubricant at the first 15,000 miles. For standard differentials and 1978 controlled differentials, change lubricant every 15,000 miles when pulling a trailer.

1977 Pontiac: For controlled and standard differentials, change lubricant every 15,000 miles when pulling a trailer.
1977 Chevrolet: On controlled differentials, change lubricant at the first 15,000 miles. On controlled and standard differentials, change lubricant every 7,500 miles when pulling a trailer.
1978 Chevrolet, Pontiac and Buick: On controlled differentials, change lubricant at the first 7,500 miles. On controlled and standard differentials, change lubricant every 15,000 miles when pulling a trailer.

⑤ —1977 models only.

⑥ —1978 Chevrolet, Pontiac, Oldsmobile and Buick: For severe service operation, repack front wheel bearings at each brake relining or every 15,000 miles.

⑦ —On Cadillac, service every 100,000 miles.

⑧ —For severe service operation, service all except Cadillac every 15,000 miles. Service Cadillac every 50,000 miles.

⑨ —For 1978 Buick (Schedule 1 and 2) and 1977–78 Chevrolet, 1978 Pontiac, 1977–78 Oldsmobile and 1977–78 Cadillac (all Schedule 2 only) check carburetor choke, wire, linkages and hoses at 6 months or 7,500 miles, 24 months or 30,000 miles and every 12 months or 15,000 miles thereafter.

⑩ —Except fuel injection and diesel.

⑪ —Change at same interval as air cleaner element.

⑫ —Applies to: 1977 Pontiac 140 CID 2-bbl. and 301 CID V8, 1978 Pontiac 305 CID V8 engine code U, 305 CID V8 engine code H, 350 CID V8 engine code L and 301 CID V8 engine code Y; 1978 Chevrolet all 250, 305 and 350 CID engines; and 1977–78 Buick with engine families having suffix codes L and Y.

⑬ —If so equipped.

⑭ —1977 Pontiac engine family 720K4EH (350/400—4 bbl. Schedule 1) and 1978 Pontiac engine family 820N4EH (400—4 bbl.) and 1977–78 Chevrolets with L6 engines receive this service at 45,000 miles. 1977–78 Buicks with engine families having suffix H do not receive this service.

⑮ —1977–78 Chevrolet, Pontiac and Oldsmobile with L4 engine receive this service at 50,000 miles.

⑯ —More frequently when operated in dusty areas.

⑰ —1977 Oldsmobile: service at 30,000 miles; 1978 Oldsmobile (Schedule 1): service at 22,500 miles.

1979—80 GENERAL MOTORS GASOLINE AND DIESEL

Service to be done	Every 3000 miles	At first 3000 miles then every 30,000 miles	Every 6000 miles	Every 7500 miles	At first 7500 miles then every 12,000 miles	Every 12 months/7500 miles	At first 12 months/7500 miles then every 24 months/15,000 miles	First 7500 miles then every 15,000 miles	First 6 months/7500 miles then every 18 months/22,000 miles
Chassis Lubrication ①						12			
Fluid Levels Check ②						12			
Engine Oil Change ③	3					12			
Clutch Pedal Free Travel Check/Adjust						12●			
Oil Filter Change ④	3						12		
Tire Rotation (Radial Tires)					3			12	
Rear Axle Lube Change & Manual Trans. ⑤ Check (Toronado and Riviera Final Drive)				3	12●				
Cooling System Check				1					
Wheel Bearing Repack									
Final Drive Boots and Seals Check									
Manual Steering Gear Seals Check									
Clutch Cross Shaft Lubrication									
Auto. Trans. Fluid & Filter Change ⑥									
Tire, Wheel and Disc Brake Check						12			
Exhaust System Check						12			
Suspension and Steering Check						12			
Brake and Power Steering Check						12			
Drive Belt Check									
Drum Brake and Parking Brake Check									
Throttle Linkage Check									
Bumper Check									
Thermo Controlled Air Cleaner Check									1A
Carburetor Choke & Hoses Check									1A
Engine Idle Speed Adjustment			3						1A
EFE System Check (If so equipped)									1A
Vacuum Advance System & Hoses Check									1A
Fuel Filter Replacement									
PCV System Check ⑦									
PCV Valve & Filter Service ⑦									
Oxygen Sensor Change (If so equipped) ⑪									
Vacuum Differential Valve and Differential Vacuum Delay and Separator Valve—3.8 Litre (231 CID) V6 Engine with A.I.R.									
Spark Plug Wires Check				3					
Idle Stop Solenoid and/or Dashpot Check									
Spark Plug Replacement ⑫									
Engine Timing Adjust. & Distrib. Check									
Carburetor Vacuum Break Check ⑬									
ECS System Check & Filter Replacement									
Fuel Cap, Tank and Lines Check									
Air Cleaner Element Replacement ⑭									
Carburetor or Fuel Injection Throttle Body Mounting Torque									1A
Cat. Converter Catalyst Change—V6 only ⑮									

Legend:

1—1979 gasoline engine.
2—1980 gasoline engine.
3—1979–80 diesel engine.
●—California models only.
○—Except California models.
A—Emission Control Maintenance Schedule I*
B—Emission Control Maintenance Schedule II*

*—Refer to vehicle Emission Control Label located under the hood near the radiator.

Service notes:

①—Lubricate all grease fittings in front suspension, and steering linkage. Lubricate transmission shift linkage, hood latch, hood and door hinges, parking brake cable guides, underbody contact points and linkage.
②—Check level in brake master cylinder, power steering pump, radiator, axle, transmission and winshield washer.
③—Change every 7,500 miles or 12 months, whichever comes first under normal driving conditions. Change each 3,000 miles or 3 months under these conditions: (a) dusty conditions, (b) trailer pulling, (c) frequent idling, (d) short-trips where engine does not thoroughly warm up. Change oil and filter as soon as you can after driving in a dust storm. Turbocharged V6 engine, change oil every 3,000 miles.
④—Replace at the first oil change, and then every second oil change if mileage (7,500 miles) determines oil change. If time (12 months) determines oil

Service to be done	First 6 months/7500 miles then every 24 months/30,000 miles	Every 12 months/9000 miles	Every 12 months/15,000 miles	Every 15,000 miles	Every 22,500 miles	Every 24,000 miles	Every 24 months/30,000 miles	Every 30,000 miles	Every 100,000 miles
Chassis Lubrication ①		3							
Fluid Levels Check ②		3							
Engine Oil Change ③									
Clutch Pedal Free Travel Check/Adjust.		3							
Oil Filter Change ④									
Tire Rotation (Radial Tires)									
Rear Axle Lube Change & Manual Trans. ⑤ Check (Toronado and Riviera Final Drive)									
Cooling System Check			123						
Wheel Bearing Repack								12●3	
Final Drive Boots and Seals Check								123	
Manual Steering Gear Seals Check								12	
Clutch Cross Shaft Lubrication								12●	
Auto. Trans. Fluid & Filter Change ⑥									123
Tire, Wheel and Disc Brake Check		3							
Exhaust System Check		3							
Suspension and Steering Check		3							
Brake and Power Steering Check		3							
Drive Belt Check			123						
Drum Brake and Parking Brake Check			123						
Throttle Linkage Check			123						
Bumper Check			123						
Thermo Controller Air Cleaner Check	1B2								
Carburetor Choke & Hoses Check	1B⑧2○							2●	
Engine Idle Speed Adjustment	1B2								
EFE System Check (If so equipped)	1B2								
Vacuum Advance System & Hoses Check	2		1B						
Fuel Filter Replacement			1		2	3			
PCV System Check ⑦			1					2	
PCV Valve & Filter Service ⑦				1				2●⑨	
Oxygen Sensor Change (If so equipped) ⑪						1A		1B	
Vacuum Differential Valve and Differential Vacuum Delay and Separator Valve—3.8 Litre (231 CID) V6 Engine with A.I.R.					1B2	1A		2	
Spark Plug Wires Check						1A		1B2	
Idle Stop Solenoid and/or Dashpot Check						1A		1B	
Spark Plug Replacement ⑫						1A		1B2	
Engine Timing Adjust. & Distrib. Check						1A		1B	
Carburetor Vacuum Break Check ⑬							1	2	
ECS System Check & Filter Replacement							1		
Fuel Cap Tank and Lines Check			2					12⑩3	
Air Cleaner Element Replacement ⑭									
Carburetor or Fuel Injection Throttle Body Mounting Torque	1B2								
Cat. Converter Catalyst Change—V6 only ⑮								2○	

change, or if you change the oil at 3,000 miles or 3 months, replace filter at each oil change. Turbocharged V6 engine, change filter every 3,000 miles.

⑤—Change lubricant every 7500 miles when used for trailer towing.

⑥—Change the transmission fluid and change the filter (or service the screen) every 15,000 miles if the car is mainly driven under one or more of these hot conditions: In heavy city traffic where the outside temperature regularly reaches 90°F, in hill or mountain areas, frequent trailer pulling, uses such as taxi, police car or delivery service.

⑦—Check that system works properly and clean filter, if it is on the valve cover, each 15,000 miles. Each 30,000 miles replace the valve. Replace worn or plugged hoses. Replace filter if it is in the air cleaner at each 30,000 miles. Filter service does not apply to 1.6 Litre—L4 Engine or California 2.5 Litre—L4 Engine.

⑧—Also requires service at 45,000 miles.

⑨—Not required for engine families with suffix "Z".

⑩—Chevrolet L4—1.6L engines: service at 50,000-mile intervals.

⑪—Engine families with suffix "J"—change sensor at 30,000-mile intervals.

⑫—Engine families with suffix "H"—change plugs at 45,000-mile intervals.

⑬—Only GM engines assembled by Chevrolet or GM of Canada, which have the number "1" or "7" in the second digit of the engine family designation, have this service.

⑭—1.6L—L4 and 2.5L L4 engines: replace air cleaner assembly at 50,000-mile intervals.

⑮—Applies only to GM engine family 01C2EY.

GLOSSARY
Glossary of Automotive Terminology

ABDC   After Bottom Dead Center.

accelerator   The floor pedal used to control, through linkage, the throttle valve in the carburetor.

accelerator pump   A small pump, located in the carburetor, that sprays additional gasoline into the air stream during acceleration.

Ackerman principle   Bending the outer ends of the steering arms slightly inward so when the car is making a turn, the inside wheel will turn more sharply than the outer wheel. This principle produces toe-out on turns.

additive   Some solution, powder, etc., added to gasoline, oil, grease, etc., to improve the characteristics of the original product.

adjuster (cam)   A device by which brake shoe-to-drum clearance may be adjusted to compensate for lining wear and to maintain minimum travel during brake application and no drag when brakes are not applied.

advance   Setting the ignition timing so a spark occurs earlier or more degrees before Top Dead Center (TDC).

AIR   Air Injection Reaction system. This emission control system reduces objectionable exhaust emissions.

air conditioner   A device used in the control of temperature, humidity, cleanness, and movement of air.

air conditioning   The control of the temperature, humidity, cleanness, and movement of air.

air duct   A tube which carries air from one location to another such as the carburetor preheat air duct on most late-model engines.

air filter   A device used to filter out harmful impurities from the air drawn into the engine.

air-fuel ratio   The ratio, by weight or volume, between the air and gasoline that make up the engine fuel mixture.

air gap (spark plugs)   The distance between the center and side electrodes.

air horn   The top portion of the air passageway through the carburetor; or, a warning horn operated by compressed air.

air pollution   Contamination of the earth's atmosphere by various natural and man-made pollutants such as smoke, gases, dust, etc.

air suspension   An automotive suspension system wherein conventional steel springs are replaced by chambers filled with compressed air which support the car's weight.

alignment   The process of positioning separate objects (such as wheels) in a correct relationship to one another.

alternator   A device similar to the generator but producing AC. The AC must be changed to DC before reaching the car's electrical system.

alternating current (AC)   An electrical current that first flows one way in a circuit and then the other.

ammeter   An instrument used to measure the rate of current flow in amperes.

ampere   A unit of measurement of the rate of flow of an electrical current, named after Andre Marie Ampere, French electrical research physicist.

ampere hour capacity   A measurement of storage battery ability to deliver a specified current over a specified length of time.

anchor   Some point, such as a pin or slotted plate, at which brake shoes are prevented from rotating when applied against the rotating drum surface. The anchor may be fixed or adjustable, depending on brake design.

anode   The positive pole in an electrical circuit.

antibackfire valve   The valve used in the air injection reaction (exhaust emission control) system to prevent backfiring during the period immediately following sudden deceleration.

anti-brake-dip feature   Arrangement of the front suspension geometry, made possible by the use of ball joints in an independent front suspension, which counters the front-end lowering effects of the apparent forward weight transfer on braking.

antifreeze   A chemical added to the cooling system to prevent the coolant from freezing in cold weather.

antifreeze hydrometer   An instrument for measuring the specific gravity of a coolant, and thus its antifreeze content.

antipercolator   A device for venting vapors from the main discharge tube, or the well, of a carburetor.

antistall dashpot   A device that keeps an engine from stalling by preventing the throttle from closing too rapidly.

arcing   Electricity leaping the gap between two electrodes.

armature   A rotating core, usually composed of soft iron laminations, around which is wound a coil of wire that is moved through a magnetic field in a generator or motor.

asymmetrical rear springs   A form of rear leaf spring in which the rear axle is mounted ahead of the center of the spring. The forward portion of the spring is relatively rigid to give superior control over spring windup while the longer rear portion is more supple to provide most of the springing action.

ATDC   After Top Dead Center.

atmospheric valve   The valve in a power brake system which controls the input of outside air to the apply side of the power brake diaphragm in proportion to the pedal pressure applied.

atomization (vaporization) In the carburetor and intake manifold, a fine dispersal of liquid gasoline in droplets so small and light they remain airborne. This results from the design of the fuel nozzles in the carburetor, which discharge gasoline in a spray, and the heat of the manifold, which maintains the dispersal.

automatic choke A heat-sensing device which automatically controls the choke plate in the carburetor to enrich the fuel-and-air mixture sufficiently to keep an engine going properly until it reaches operating temperature.

axis A line or point denoting the center around which something turns or pivots.

axle REAR GEARS: the two gears, one per axle, splined to the inner ends of the drive axles. They mesh with and are driven by the spider gears.
FULL-FLOATING: an axle used to drive the rear wheels. It does not hold them on or support them.
SEMI- OR ONE-QUARTER FLOATING: an axle used to drive the wheels, hold them on, and support them.
THREE-QUARTER FLOATING: an axle used to drive the rear wheels as well as hold them on. It does not support them.
SHAFT: solid metal rod, extending from the differential, that transfers power to a car's drive wheel.

backfire INTAKE SYSTEM: burning of the fuel mixture in the intake manifold. May be caused by faulty timing, crossed plug wires, leaky intake valve, etc.
EXHAUST SYSTEM: passage of the unburned fuel mixture into the exhaust system where it is ignited and causes an explosion (backfire).

backlash The amount of play between two parts. In the case of gears, it refers to how much one gear can be moved back and forth without moving the gear into which it is meshed.

back pressure This refers to the resistance to the flow of exhaust gases through the exhaust system.

baffle An obstruction used to slow down or divert the flow of gases, liquids, sounds, etc.

ballast resistor An electrical resistor in the primary circuit which is bypassed to permit a full 12-volt surge of current to facilitate engine starting, and brought into the circuit to reduce voltage when the engine is running at lower speeds.

ball joint A device composed of a spherical part which bears against and is retained by a matching socket, used to join two structural members. It permits rotational movement in any plane between the two joined members. Ball joints are used in front suspension control arms to support the steering knuckles, and at the ends of tie-rods to connect them to the steering arms and the center link.

ball joint steering knuckle A steering knuckle that pivots on ball joints rather than on a kingpin.

ball joint rocker arms Rocker arms mounted on a ball-shaped device at the end of a stud, rather than on a shaft.

band (brake band) A flexible metal strip lined with a suitable friction material, which encircles the outer diameter of a drum. When applied, the band contracts to bring the lining material to bear against the drum, giving a braking effect similar to that of a shoe and lining assembly.

barrels (bore) The air passage or passages in the carburetor through which air flows to the intake manifold, and in which fuel is added to the air.

battery A component of the car's electrical system which stores electrical energy for use in the system. A battery consists of a connected group of cells in a rectangular casing, and an acid electrolyte which supports a reversible electrochemical reaction. When electrical energy is drawn from the battery, it is discharging. When electrical current from the alternator is directed through the battery, the reaction is reversed and the battery is charging.

battery charging The process of renewing the battery by passing an electrical current through it in a reverse direction.

battery hydrometer An instrument for measuring the specific gravity of a battery's electrolyte solution and thus its state of charge.

battery posts Round lead posts protruding from a battery to which the battery cables are attached.

bearing A device used to support a moving component, allowing the part to move with a minimum of friction. Bearings used in automotive engines are of the ball, roller, or plain type. Lubrication between moving bearing surfaces is essential to prevent metal-to-metal contact and resulting high friction.

bearing clearance The amount of space left between a shaft and the bearing surface. This space is for lubricating oil to enter.

BBDC Before Bottom Dead Center.

BDC Bottom Dead Center.

bell housing (clutch housing) The metal covering around the flywheel and clutch, or torque converter assembly.

belts Layers of material reinforced with steel or fabric within some tires that strengthen the tread and resist puncturing by sharp objects.

bendix-type starter drive A self-engaging starter drive gear, which engages when the starter begins spinning and automatically disengages when the starter stops.

bezel The crimped edge of metal securing a glass face to an instrument.

BHP See Brake Horsepower.

bias-belted tire A tire with the basic body structure of a bias-ply tire that has an additional two or more layers (or belts) of material reinforced with steel or fabric between the body plies and the tread.

bias-ply tire A tire in which the reinforcing cords in the body plies run in alternating directions at an angle (or bias) to the centerline of the tread.

bimetal   A bonded strip of two metals having appreciably different expansion characteristics under heat. Because of the dissimilar rates of expansion, the strip will change configuration with any change in temperature.

bleeding the brakes   The removal of air from the hydraulic system. Bleeder screws are loosened at each wheel cylinder, one at a time, and brake fluid is forced from the master cylinder through the lines until all air is expelled.

block   That part of the engine containing the cylinders.

blow-by   Leakage of combustion fumes past piston rings and into the crankcase due to high combustion chamber pressures produced during the compression and power strokes.

boiling point   The temperature at which a liquid changes to a vapor.

bonded brake lining   A brake lining attached to the brake shoe by an adhesive.

booster   A device incorporated in a car system, such as the brakes or steering, to increase the pressure output or decrease the amount of effort required to operate it, or both.

boot   Any flexible cover used to protect working parts from contamination by foreign materials.

bore   This may refer to the cylinder itself or to the diameter of the cylinder.

bore diameter   The diameter of the cylinder.

boring   Renewing the cylinders by cutting them out to a specified size. A boring bar is used to make the cut.

boring bar   A machine used to cut engine cylinders to a specific size.

boxed rod   A connecting rod in which the I-beam section has been stiffened by welding plates on each side of it.

brake anchor   A steel stud on which one end of the brake shoe is either attached or rests against. The anchor is firmly affixed to the backing plate.

brake backing plate   A rigid steel plate to which the brake shoes are attached. The braking force applied to the shoes is absorbed by the backing plate.

brake band   A band, faced with brake lining, that encircles a brake drum. It is used on several parking brake installations.

brake bleeding   See bleeding the brakes.

brake cylinder   See wheel cylinder.

brake   DISC-TYPE: a braking system using a steel disc with a caliper-type lining, rather than the conventional brake drum with internal brake shoes. When the brakes are applied, a section of lining on each side of the spinning disc is forced against the disc, thus imparting a braking force. This type of brake is very resistent to brake fade. DRUM: a braking system using a cast-iron or aluminum housing, bolted to the wheel, that rotates around the brake shoes. When the shoes are expanded, they rub against the machined inner surface of the drum and exert a braking effect upon the wheel.

brake drum lathe   A machine used to refinish the inside of a brake drum.

brake fade   A reduction in braking force due to loss of friction between brake shoes and drum, caused by heat buildup.

brake fluid   A special fluid in hydraulic brake systems.

brake flushing   Cleaning the brake system by flushing it with alcohol or brake fluid. This is done to remove water, dirt, or any other contaminant. Flushing fluid is placed in the master cylinder and forced through the lines and wheel cylinders where it exits at the cylinder bleed screws.

brake horsepower (BHP)   A measurement of the actual usable horsepower delivered at the crankshaft. It is commonly computed by using an engine dynamometer.

brake lining   A friction material fastened to the brake shoes. The brake lining presses against the rotating brake drum and stops the car.

brake, parking   A brake used to hold the car in position while parked. One type applies the rear brake shoes by mechanical means; the other type applies a brake band to a drum installed in the drive train.

brakes, power   A conventional hydraulic brake system utilizing engine vacuum to operate a vacuum power piston. The power piston applies pressure to the brake pedal, or in some cases, directly to the master cylinder piston. This reduces the amount of pedal pressure the driver must exert to stop the car.

brake pull (pull)   A sudden, sometimes unpredictable tendency of the car to swerve when the brakes are applied. This can be caused by contaminated linings or other malfunctions within the brake, or by any of a number of factors not directly related to the brake system.

brake shoe grinder   A grinder used to grind the brake shoe lining so it will be square to and concentric with the brake drum.

brake shoe heel   That end of the brake shoe adjacent to the anchor bolt or pin.

brake shoe toe   The free end of the shoe, not attached to or resting against an anchor pin.

brake shoes   That part of the brake system, located at the wheels, to which the brake lining is attached. When the wheel cylinders are actuated by hydraulic pressure, they force the brake shoes apart and bring the lining into contact with the drum.

brake warning switch   A unit warning the driver that one of the hydraulic systems has failed. As pressure falls in the front or rear system, the other system's normal pressure forces the piston to the inoperative side, contacting the switch terminal and illuminating a red warning light on the instrument panel.

breaker arm   The movable arm on which one of the breaker points is affixed.

breaker points   Components of the distributor which momentarily break the current flow in the primary ignition circuit to create an induced high voltage current in the secondary ignition circuit. The points themselves are two small discs of metal, usually with a high tungsten content. One is attached to a stationary arm, the other to a cam-actuated moving arm which alternately opens and closes the gap between the two points.

break-in   The period of operation between the installation of new or rebuilt parts and the time the parts are worn to the correct fit. Or, driving at a reduced and varying speed for a specified mileage to permit parts to wear to the correct fit.

breather pipe   A pipe opening into the interior of the engine, used to assist in ventilation. It usually extends downward to a point just below the engine so the passing air stream will form a partial vacuum.

brush   An electrical circuit component, usually composed of graphite or carbon, used to complete the circuit between a stationary component and a moving component on an electrical part such as an alternator, generator, or motor.

BTDC   Before Top Dead Center.

BUDC   Before Upper Dead Center. Same as BTDC.

bushing   A bearing for a shaft, spring shackle, piston pin, etc., of one-piece construction, which may be removed from the part.

butterfly valve   A valve in the carburetor so named because of its resemblance to the insect of the same name.

bypass filter   An oil filter that constantly filters a portion of the oil flowing through the engine.

bypass valve   A valve that can open and allow a fluid to pass through in other than its normal channel.

cable equalizer   A device in the system of cables linking the parking brake control with the rear wheel brakes. It divides the applying force equally between the two rear wheel brakes for a more positive brake application.

calibrate   With reference to test instruments, adjusting the dial needle to the correct zero or load setting.

caliper   An adjustable tool for measuring outside or inside dimensions. Also see disc brake caliper.

cam   An eccentric or lobe-shaped rotating device having one or more smoothly-contoured protrusions that cause movement of an adjacent component which bears upon the cam's surface.

cam angle (dwell)   The number of degrees the breaker cam rotates from the time the breaker points close until they open again.

cam ground   A piston that is ground slightly egg-shaped. When it is heated, it becomes round.

camber   The characteristic curved appearance of automotive leaf springs; tilting from the vertical of a wheel-and-tire assembly when viewed from the front of a car. If it leans outward, away from the car, at the top, the wheel is said to have positive camber. If it leans inward, it is said to have negative camber. Camber is one of the factors in front end alignment.

camshaft   In the valve train of a car engine, a rotating shaft turning at one-half of the engine speed and including integral cams that actuate the intake and exhaust valves. The camshaft drives other engine components such as the distributor and fuel pump.

camshaft gear   A gear used to drive the camshaft.

can tap   A device used to pierce, dispense, and seal small cans of refrigerant.

carbonize   The building up of carbon on objects such as spark plugs, pistons, heads, etc.

carbon monoxide   A deadly, colorless, odorless, and tasteless gas found in the engine exhaust. Formed by incomplete burning of hydrocarbons.

carburetor   A fuel-and-air metering and mixing device. Automotive carburetors are of the float-type, in which air is metered by a venturi and fuel is metered by properly-sized restrictions in the fuel passages. The amount of the fuel-and-air mixture delivered to the engine is controlled by the throttle plate(s) in the carburetor.

carburetor circuits   A series of passageways and units designed to perform a specific function—idle circuit, full power circuit, etc.

carburetor icing   The formation of ice on the throttle plate or valve. As the fuel nozzles feed fuel into the air horn it turns to a vapor. This robs heat from the air and when weather conditions are just right—fairly cold and quite humid—ice may form.

carrier bearings   The bearings on which the differential case is mounted.

caster   Tilting of the steering axis forward and backward. The relationship of the axis about which a steering wheel swivels or pivots (the steering axis or king pin axis) and the point of contact between the wheel and its supporting surface (the road). Positive caster, with the axis ahead of the point of contact, will tend to pull the wheel in the direction of travel, adding directional stability. Negative caster, with the axis behind the point of contact, will tend to push the wheel to one side—an unstable condition. Caster is a factor in front end alignment.

castle or castellated nut   A nut having a series of slots cut into one end into which a cotter pin may be passed to secure it.

catalytic converter   A device that chemically reduces harmful emissions of automobile exhaust.

cell (battery)   The individual (separate) compartments in the battery containing positive and negative plates suspended in electrolyte. A six-volt battery has three cells, a 12-volt battery six cells.

cell connector   The lead strap or connection between battery cell groups.

center link   A steering system utilizing two tie-rods connected to the steering arms and to a central idler arm. The idler arm is operated by a center link connected to the Pitman arm.

centrifugal advance   A unit designed to advance and retard the ignition timing through the action of centrifugal force.

centrifugal clutch   A clutch utilizing centrifugal force to expand a friction device on the driving shaft until it is locked to a drum on the shaft.

charcoal canister   A container which stores gasoline vapor in order to prevent air pollution. It is part of the emission control system.

charcoal canister filter (charcoal canister)   A powder-puff shaped filter which filters the air entering the charcoal canister.

charge (battery)   Passing an electrical current through a battery to restore it to the active state.

charging   The act of placing a charge of refrigerant or oil into the air-conditioning system.

chassis   Generally, chassis refers to the frame, engine, front and rear axles, springs, steering system, and gas tank. It includes everything but the body.

chassis dynamometer   See dynamometer.

chatter   A low-frequency vibration caused by a rapidly changing coefficient of friction between the drums and the linings when braking at high speeds. This is usually caused by heat spots—small areas of the brake drums which have been drastically overheated to the point where their molecular structure has been changed from cast iron to that of steel. Steel has a different coefficient of friction than cast iron.

choke   In a carburetor, a plate near the top of the air passage through the carburetor which can be closed fully or partially to restrict the amount of air admitted to the carburetor and thus cause engine vacuum to draw a richer flow of fuel from it.

choke stove   A heating compartment in or on the exhaust manifold from which hot air is drawn to the automatic choke device.

CID   Cubic Inch Displacement.

circuit   The complete path of an electrical current, including the generating apparatus, or a distinct segment of the complete path.

circuit breaker   A device in an electrical circuit incorporating a bimetallic spring which, when overheated by current flow in excess of specifications, will separate two contact points and break the circuit to prevent damage. Some circuit breakers will reset themselves automatically when the bimetal cools, while others must be reset manually.

clearance   A given amount of space between two parts—between piston and cylinder, bearing and journal, etc.

clockwise   Rotation to the right.

cluster or counter gear   The cluster of gears that are all cut on one long gear blank. The cluster gears ride in the bottom of the transmission and provide a connection between the transmission input and output shafts.

clutch   A device used to connect or disconnect the flow of power from one unit to another.

clutch diaphragm spring   A round, dish-shaped piece of flat spring steel used to force the pressure plate against the clutch disc in some clutches.

clutch disc   That part of the clutch assembly splined to the transmission clutch or input shaft. It is faced with friction material. When the clutch is engaged, the disc is squeezed between the flywheel and the clutch pressure plate.

clutch field   This consists of many windings of wire and is fastened to the front of the compressor. When current is applied, a magnetic field is set up that pulls the armature in to engage the clutch.

clutch housing (bell housing)   A cast iron or aluminum housing surrounding the flywheel and clutch mechanism.

clutch pedal free travel   The specific distance the clutch pedal may be depressed before the throw-out bearing actually contacts the clutch release fingers.

clutch pilot bearing   A small bronze bushing, or in some cases a ball bearing, placed in the end of the crankshaft or in the center of the flywheel, depending on the car, used to support the outboard end of the transmission input shaft.

clutch pressure plate   The part of a clutch assembly that through spring pressure squeezes the clutch disc against the flywheel, thereby transmitting a driving force through the assembly. To disengage the clutch, the pressure plate is drawn away from the flywheel via linkage.

clutch semi-centrifugal release fingers   Clutch release fingers having a weight attached to them so that at high revolutions per minute, the release fingers place additional pressure on the clutch pressure plate.

clutch throw-out fork   The device or fork that straddles the throw-out bearing and forces it against the clutch release fingers.

coil   A specialized form of electrical transformer which boosts the voltage supplied by the car's electrical system to an extremely high level adequate for the high-voltage requirements of the spark plugs.

coil spring   A form of spring used in automotive suspension systems. It is a steel rod wound in a cylindrical shape, resulting in continuous coils that do not touch. Under a load, the coils draw closer together, subjecting the rod to both flexing and twisting forces.

combustion   Burning. The chemical reaction of combining oxygen with another substance, resulting in the release of heat energy.

combustion chamber   The portion of an engine's cylinders where combustion takes place. In general usage, the recessed portion of the cylinder head which fits over the cylinder is referred to as the combustion chamber. To be completely accurate, the head of the piston and, in some cases, the upper extreme of the cylinder, should also be considered parts of the combustion chamber.

combustion chamber volume   The volume of the combustion chamber (the space above the piston with the piston on top dead center), measured in cubic centimeters (cc).

commutator   An axially-mounted cylindrical element at the end of an armature of a motor or generator. The cylinder is composed of copper segments separated by a thin layer of insulating material. Each segment serves as the terminal point for a coil winding of the armature. Stationary brushes contact the commutator to conduct the induced voltage from the windings to the car's electrical system.

compensating port   A small hole in a brake master cylinder which permits fluid to return to the reservoir.

compensator valve   On an automatic transmission, a valve designed to increase the pressure on the brake band during heavy acceleration.

compression   In an internal combustion engine, compressing the combustible mixture into a smaller volume within the cylinders to extract more power from the combustion that follows.

compression check   Testing the compression in all the cylinders at cranking speed. All plugs are removed, a compression-gauge is placed in one plugged hole, the throttle is wide open, and the engine is cranked until the gauge no longer climbs. A compression check determines the condition of the valves, rings, and cylinders.

compression gauge   A gauge used to test the compression in the cylinders.

compression ignition engine   A type of engine (diesel engine) which depends on compression of the fuel-and-air charge in the cylinder to generate heat sufficient to ignite the fuel spontaneously.

compression ratio   The ratio of the volumes between the piston head and the top of the cylinder at bottom dead center and top dead center. Generally, the higher the compression ratio (in other words, the greater the compression), the more usable power will be extracted from the fuel.

compressor   A component of the refrigeration system that pumps refrigerant and increases the pressure of the refrigerant vapor.

compressor shaft seal   An assembly consisting of springs, snap rings, O rings, a shaft seal, a seal seat, and gaskets, mounted on the compressor crankshaft, which permits the shaft to be turned without loss of refrigerant or oil.

condensation   Moisture, from the air, deposited on a cool surface.

condense   Turning a vapor back into a liquid.

condenser   The unit in an air-conditioning system that cools the hot compressed refrigerant and turns it from a vapor into a liquid.

condenser   A device in the ignition distributor which absorbs the surge of current resulting when the breaker points open, and then discharges back into the primary circuit. This action protects the points from arcing and burning, and prolongs the discharge of high-voltage current to the spark plugs.

conductor   Any material through which an electrical current will flow. All materials are conductors, to a degree. In common usage, however, only those which conduct electricity with relatively little resistance are classified as conductors.

connecting rod   An engine component, usually of forged steel, which forms a structural link between the piston and the crankshaft.

constant mesh gears   Gears that are always in mesh with each other, driving or not.

constant velocity universal joint   A universal joint designed to effect a smooth transfer of torque from the driven shaft to the driving shaft without any fluctuations in the speed of the driven shaft.

contact points (breaker points)   Two movable points or areas that, when pressed together, complete a circuit. These points are usually made of tungsten, platinum, or silver.

continuity light   A testing instrument with a sharp probe that can penetrate wire insulation. It is used to determine whether or not current is flowing in a circuit.

control arms   Structural parts of independent front suspension systems which form moving links between the car's underbody structure and the king pin or ball joints upon which the steering knuckle pivots.

control unit   A unit consisting of electronic circuitry which when triggered by the pickup coil causes the power-switching transistor to interrupt the primary circuit of the ignition coil.

coolant   Liquid in the cooling system.

cords   Heavy, wound strands of reinforcing material (nylon, rayon, polyester) in the body of a tire.

counterbalance   A weight attached to some moving part so the part will be in balance.

counterbore   Enlarging a hole to a certain depth.

counterclockwise   Rotation to the left as opposed to that of clock hands.

countersink   To make a counterbore so the head of a screw may set flush, or below, the surface.

counterweight   On a crankshaft, a mass of metal of a precise weight located opposite the connecting rod journals to balance out and minimize unbalanced forces causing vibrations when the engine is running.

cowl   The part of the car body between the engine firewall and the front of the dash panel.

crankcase   That part of the engine surrounding the crankshaft.

crankcase dilution   An accumulation of unburned gasoline in the crankcase. An excessively rich fuel mixture or poor combustion will allow a certain amount of gas to pass down between the pistons and cylinder walls.

crankcase ventilation system   A system designed to remove combustion fumes and other contaminants from the crankcase and other enclosed portions of the engine.

crankshaft   The power-transmitting component of an engine that converts the reciprocating motion of the pistons and connecting rods to a rotary motion by means of crank throws—segments offset from the center of the crankshaft rotation, to which the connecting rod is attached.

crankshaft gear   A gear mounted on the front of the crankshaft, used to drive the camshaft gear.

cross shaft   The shaft in the steering gearbox that engages the steering shaft worm. The cross shaft is splined to the Pitman arm.

crude oil   Petroleum in its raw or unrefined state. It forms the basis of gasoline, engine oil, diesel oil, kerosene, etc.

cubes   Cubic inches, or the cubic inch displacement of an engine.

current   The movement of electricity through the linked conductors of a circuit. An instantaneous displacement of electrons of the conductor from the negative pole to the positive pole, caused by the introduction of free electrons into the circuit by an electrical power source.

cylinder (bore)   The hollow, cylindrical component of an engine, usually machined in the engine's cylinder block, in which the piston is seated. Cylinder walls support and guide the piston, confine the pressures of combustion, and conduct combustion heat to engine coolant.

cylinder block (engine block)   The main framework of a liquid-cooled engine, usually of cast iron, which contains the cylinders, water jacket, crankcase, passages for engine oil and coolant, engine mounting fittings, and many other components.

cylinder head   The casting and related parts used to seal the tops of an engine's cylinders. The cylinder head contains coolant passages, spark plug ports, and in the case of valve-in-head engines, the intake and exhaust valves and ports, rocker arms, and associated parts.

cylinder hone   A tool using an abrasive to smooth out and bring to exact measurements engine cylinders, wheel cylinders, bushings, etc.

cylinder sleeve   A replaceable cylinder made of a pipe-like section either pressed or pushed into the block.

damping   In a hydraulic-type shock absorber, the physical control of unwanted spring vibrations caused by resistance to a forced flow of confined fluid through passages in the piston and base of the shock absorber.

dashboard   That part of the body containing the driving instruments, switches, etc.

dashpot   A unit that retards or slows down the movement of some part.

DC   Direct Current

dead axle   An axle that does not rotate but merely forms a base upon which to attach the wheels.

dead center   The point at which the piston reaches its uppermost or downmost position in the cylinder. The rod crank journal would be at 12 o'clock upper dead center, or 6 o'clock lower dead center.

de dion   A rear axle setup in which the driving wheels are attached to a curved dead axle in turn attached to the frame by a central pivot. The differential unit is bolted to the frame and con-

nected to the driving wheels by drive axles utilizing universal joints.

deflection   In a spring, the initial movement in response to any force acting on the spring. Deflection may take the form of flexing, as with a leaf spring, or twisting, as with a torsion bar.

deglazer   An abrasive tool used to remove the glaze from cylinder walls so a new set of rings will seat.

degree $\frac{1}{360}$ part of a circle.

degree wheel   A wheel-like unit attached to the engine crankshaft, used to time the valves to a high degree of accuracy.

detent ball and spring   A spring-loaded ball that snaps into a groove or notch to hold some sliding object in position.

detergent   A chemical added to the engine oil to improve its characteristics (sludge control, non-foaming, etc.).

detonation (knocking, pinging)   A virtually instantaneous combustion of fuel in the combustion chamber, resulting in the instant release of heat energy, usually with the generation of excessive pressures which can damage adjacent engine components.

dial gauge or indicator   A precision micrometer-type instrument that indicates a reading via a needle moving across a dial face.

diaphragm-type pump   A fluid-moving device consisting of a sealed chamber with one wall formed by a flexible diaphragm. As the diaphragm is moved out to enlarge the chamber, fluid enters past an inlet check valve. Then the diaphragm is moved inward, squeezing the fluid out of the chamber past an outlet check valve.

die   A device for cutting out or stamping.

die casting   Formation of an object by forcing molten metal, plastic, etc., into a die.

diesel engine   An internal combustion engine using diesel oil for fuel. The true diesel does not use an ignition system, but injects diesel oil into the cylinders when the piston has compressed the air so tightly that it is hot enough to ignite the fuel without a spark.

dieseling   When fuel continues to burn after the ignition has been turned off.

differential   A unit that drives both rear axles at the same time, but allows them to turn at different speeds when negotiating turns.

differential case   The steel unit to which the ring gear is attached. The case drives the spider gears and forms an inner bearing surface for the axle and gears.

dimmer switch   A two-way switch mounted on the car's floor where it can be conveniently operated by the pressure of the driver's foot to select the high- or low-beam headlight circuit.

diode   A cylindrical, solid-state electrical device which allows the passage of an electrical current in one direction but prevents it in the other. It is used in the alternator to convert alternating current to direct current.

dipstick   A graduated metal rod passing into a container to determine the depth or quantity of liquid.

direct current (DC) An electrical current which flows in only one direction. The polarity of the circuit does not change.

direct drive. As in high gear when the crankshaft and drive shaft revolve at the same speed.

directional stability The ability of a car to move forward in a straight line with a minimum of driver control. A car with good directional stability will not be unduly affected by side wind, road irregularities, etc.

disc brake (See brake. Disc-type:)

disc-brake caliper A mechanism that straddles a brake disc and contains the brake pads.

discharge (battery) Drawing electrical current from the battery.

disc wheel A wheel constructed of stamped steel.

displacement (piston displacement, cubes) The volume of the fuel-and-air mixture an engine is theoretically capable of drawing into all cylinders during one operating cycle, or the space swept through by the pistons in moving from one end of a stroke to the other. (The formula for determining displacement: cylinder diameter times cylinder diameter times 0.7854 times length of stroke times number of cylinders; or bore times bore times 0.7854 times stroke times cylinders.)

distribution tubes Tubes used in the engine cooling area to guide and direct the flow of coolant to vital areas.

distributor A unit designed to make and break the ignition primary circuit, and to distribute the resultant high voltage to the proper cylinder at the correct time.

distributor cap An insulated cap containing a central terminal with a series (one per cylinder) of terminals evenly spaced in a circular pattern around the central terminal. The secondary voltage travels to the central terminal where it is then channeled to one of the outer terminals by the rotor.

diverter valve A valve in the AIR (air emission reaction) system which prevents engine backfiring on deceleration.

DOHC This refers to an engine with double (two) overhead camshafts.

double flare The end of some tubing, especially brake tubing, which has a flare so made that its area utilizes two wall thicknesses. This makes a much stronger joint.

dowel pin A steel pin, passed through or partly through, two parts to provide proper alignment.

downdraft carburetor A carburetor in which the air passes downward into the intake manifold.

dragging brakes A constant, relatively light contact between the linings and the drum when the brakes are not applied, resulting in excessive lining wear and other possible damage. This condition is usually due to overadjustment or other mechanical problems.

drag link See center link.

drill A tool used to bore holes.

drill press A nonportable machine used for drilling.

drive belt Any of several V-shaped belts that transfer power by means of pulleys from the crankshaft to various units such as the fan and the power-steering pump.

drive-fit A fit between two parts when they must be literally driven together.

drive or propeller shaft safety strap A metal strap or straps surrounding the drive shaft to prevent it from falling to the ground in the event of a universal joint or shaft failure.

drive pulley A vee pulley attached to the crankshaft of a car which drives the compressor clutch pulley by use of a belt.

drive shaft The shaft connecting the transmission output shaft to the differential pinion shaft.

drop center rim The center section of the tire rim is lower than the two outer edges, allowing the bead of the tire to be pushed into the low area on one side while the other side is pulled over and off the flange.

drop-forged A part formed by heating a steel blank red hot and pounding it into shape with a powerful drop hammer.

drum The circular outer shell of the car brake, which rotates with the wheel and transmits braking force to the wheel and tire when the brake shoe and lining assemblies are pressed against the inside surface of the drum rim.

drum runout A term denoting the measurement of the degree of concentricity, eccentricity, or ovality of the drum braking surface with the rotational axis of the drum.

dry cell or dry battery Like a flashlight battery, using no liquid electrolyte.

dry-charged battery A battery with the plates charged but lacking electrolyte. When ready for use, the electrolyte is added.

dry sleeve A cylinder sleeve which is supported in the block metal over its entire length. The coolant does not touch the sleeve itself.

dual brakes A tandem or dual master cylinder which provides a separate brake system for both the front and rear of the car.

dual breaker points A distributor using two sets of breaker points to increase the cam angle so that at high engine speeds sufficient spark will be produced to fire the plugs.

duals Two sets of exhaust pipes and mufflers, one for each bank of cylinders.

dwell See cam angle.

dwell meter A precision electrical instrument used by professional mechanics to measure the cam or dwell angle of the distributor cam as it rotates.

dynamic balance A condition of stability in a moving body where no unbalanced forces are created to disturb the direction of movement. A car wheel-and-tire assembly is said to be in dynamic balance if it will revolve rapidly without showing any tendency to wobble.

dynamo Another word for generator.

dynamometer A machine used to measure the engine horsepower output. An engine dynamometer measures horsepower at the crankshaft and a chassis dynamometer measures horsepower output at the wheels.

eccentricity (drum runout) In a brake drum, an undesirable quality causing braking vibrations and noise.

economizer valve A fuel-flow control device within the carburetor.

EGR Exhaust Gas Recirculation. An emission control system device which reduces engine emissions of exhaust gases such as nitric oxides (NOx).

EGR valve A valve which controls the EGR system by the use of a vacuum.

electrical circuit The complete path taken by electricity as it flows from a source to an electrical device, then back to the source through a ground.

electricity An unbalanced distribution of electrons which seek to return to a balanced condition and in so doing, release usable energy.

electrochemical The chemical (battery) production of electricity.

electrochemical energy Energy available in an electrical current created by a chemical reaction.

electrode The center rod passing through the insulator forms one electrode in a spark plug; the rod welded to the shell forms another. They are referred to as the center and side electrodes.

electrolyte The sulphuric acid-and-water solution in the battery.

electronic ignition system An ignition system with a distributor using no breaker points.

element A group of plates in a battery. There are three elements in a six-volt and six in a 12-volt battery. The elements are connected in series.

engine block The main part of an internal-combustion engine containing the cylinders.

engine breathing A general term referring to an engine's ability to draw in, use, and discharge air.

engine displacement The volume of the space through which the head of the piston moves in the full length of its stroke multiplied by the number of cylinders in the engine. The result is given in cubic inches.

engine lubrication system An interconnected system, consisting of a reservoir, pump, filters, and passages which conveys oil to most moving parts requiring lubrication within the engine and then returns the oil to the reservoir. A few engine parts, such as the water pump and distributor cam, are lubricated directly, not by the engine lubrication system.

engine timing Determining the correct time, to achieve optimum ignition, for high voltage to be delivered to a spark plug in relation to its piston position.

EP lubricant A lubricant compounded to withstand very heavy loads imposed on the gear teeth.

ethyl gasoline Gasoline to which ethyl fluid has been added to improve its resistance to knocking. It slows down the burning rate, thereby creating a smooth pressure curve allowing the gasoline to be used in high compression engines.

ethylene glycol A chemical solution added to the cooling system to protect against freezing.

evacuate To create a vacuum within a system and remove all traces of air and moisture.

evaporation Changing from a liquid to a vapor.

evaporation control A pollution-control device employing a vapor separator to collect fumes from the fuel tank and a charcoal canister to store them for burning in the engine.

evaporator The unit in an air-conditioning system used to transform refrigerant from a liquid to a gas. It is at this point that cooling takes place.

exhaust gas analyzer An instrument used to check the exhaust gases to determine combustion efficiency.

exhaust manifold A component of the exhaust system which routes the flow of burned gases from individual exhaust ports to a common point that connects with the rest of the exhaust system.

exhaust manifold heat control valve A thermostatically-controlled valve in the exhaust system that temporarily diverts hot exhaust gases through a passage in the intake manifold to warm it before the engine reaches its normal operating temperature.

exhaust pipe The pipe connecting the exhaust manifold to the muffler.

exhaust valve The valve through which the burned fuel charge passes on its way from the cylinder to the exhaust manifold.

expansion tank A tank at the top of a car radiator which provides room for heated coolant to expand and give off any air that may be trapped in it. It also holds a reserve supply of coolant for the cooling system.

eyes Open cylindrical shapes formed at the ends of the main leaf of a spring to accommodate attaching parts, usually bolts and bushings, that link the spring to the car's underbody.

Fahrenheit A thermometer scale using 32 degrees as the freezing point of water.

fan A device with two or more blades, attached to the shaft of a motor mounted in the evaporator, which causes air to pass over it. A device with four or more blades, mounted on the water pump, which causes air to pass through the radiator and condenser.

feeler gauge A precision-machined piece of thin, hardened steel used by professional mechanics to measure breaker point gap as well as other critical distances.

fiberglass A mixture of glass fibers and resin that when cured (hardened) produces a very light and strong material. It is used for car bodies, tires, and to repair damaged areas.

field The area covered or filled with a magnetic force.

field coil Closely spaced, coil windings of

insulated wire used in certain electrical devices to create a magnetic field. A specialized form of electromagnet.

filament   A component of an incandescent light bulb, normally composed of malleable tungsten, capable of providing such high resistance to current flow that the heat created causes it to glow and thus produce light.

filler tube   A tube leading from the radiator, fuel tank, and either the valve cover or the crankcase with a removable cap designed to provide a means of checking and/or replenishing the engine's supply of coolant, fuel, and oil.

filter   A device designed to remove foreign substances from air, oil, gasoline, water, etc.

finishing stone (hone)   A fine stone used for final finishing during honing.

firewall   The metal partition between the driver's compartment and the engine compartment.

firing order   The order in which cylinders must be fired—one, five, three, six, two, four, etc.

fit   The contact area between two parts.

fixed caliper   The type of disc brake incorporating four small pistons, two on either side of the disc, to provide the braking effect.

flare   A flange or cone-shaped end applied to a piece of tubing to provide a means of fastening it to a fitting.

flasher unit   A specific type of automatic resetting circuit breaker in the turn signal/emergency signal circuit. It periodically interrupts the current causing the signal lights to blink on and off when the circuit is actuated.

flat head   An engine with all the valves in the block.

flat spot   This refers to a spot during an acceleration period where the engine seems to lose power for a second or so and then begins to pull again.

float bowl   That part of the carburetor acting as a reservoir for gasoline and in which the float is placed.

floating caliper   The type of disc brake incorporating only one large piston acting on one side of the disc to provide the braking effect.

float level   The height of the fuel in the carburetor float bowl. It also refers to the specific float setting that will produce the correct fuel level.

flooding   When the fuel mixture is overly rich or an excessive amount has reached the cylinders. Starting is difficult and sometimes impossible until the condition is corrected.

fluid   A liquid, gas, or vapor.

fluid coupling   A unit that transfers engine torque to the transmission input shaft through the use of two vaned units (called torus) operating closely together in a bath of oil. The engine drives one torus, causing it to throw oil outward and into the other torus, which then begins to turn the transmission input shaft. A fluid coupling cannot increase torque above that produced by the crankshaft.

flush   To remove solid particles such as metal flakes or dirt.

flux (soldering)   An ingredient placed on metal being soldered to remove and prevent the formation of surface oxidation which would make soldering difficult.

flywheel   A relatively large wheel attached to the crankshaft to smooth out the firing impulses. It provides inertia to keep the crankshaft turning smoothly during the periods when no power is being applied. It also forms a base for the starter ring gear and, in many instances, for the clutch assembly.

flywheel ring gear   A gear on the outer circumference of the flywheel. The starter drive gear engages the ring gear and cranks the engine.

foot pound   A measurement of the work involved in lifting one pound one foot; or, a one-pound pull one foot from the center of an object.

forge   To force a piece of hot metal into the desired shape by hammering.

four-banger, six-banger, etc.   A four- or six-cylinder engine, etc.

four-on-the-floor   A four-speed manual transmission with floor-mounted shift.

four-stroke cycle (Otto cycle)   The four strokes, intake, compression, power, and exhaust, which a car engine's piston moves through to complete one power-producing cycle.

four-stroke cycle engine   An engine requiring two complete revolutions of the crankshaft to fire each piston once.

frame   A structural unit in a car chassis supported on the axles and supporting the rest of the chassis and the body.

freewheel   This usually refers to the action of a car on a downgrade when the overdrive overrunning clutch is slipping with a resultant loss of engine braking power. This will only occur after the overdrive unit is engaged but before the balk ring has activated the planetary gearset.

freezing point   The temperature at which a given liquid will solidify. Water will freeze at 32 degrees Fahrenheit.

Freon-12   A gas used as the cooling medium in air-conditioning and refrigeration systems.

friction bearing   A bearing made of babbitt, bronze, etc. There are no moving parts and the shaft that rests in the bearing merely rubs against the friction material in it.

front end alignment   The systematic procedure for checking and adjusting certain steering system elements to specifications, using a special machine designed for this purpose. Camber, caster, and toe-in are set to specifications by simple adjustments, but toe-out on turns and steering axis inclination or king pin slant can be corrected only by replacing faulty parts.

fuel-and-air mixture ratio   A numerical ratio denoting the relative proportions of fuel and air by weight mixed in the carburetor and delivered to the engine.

fuel injection   A system which replaces the

conventional carburetor with devices that spray fuel under pressure directly into the cylinders or into the airflow just as it enters each individual cylinder.

fuel mixture   A mixture of gasoline and air. An average mixture, by weight, would contain 16 parts of air to one part of gasoline.

fuel pump   A pump, usually of the diaphragm type, which supplies fuel to the carburetor.

full-floating axle   A rear-drive axle that does not hold the wheel on, in line, or support any weight. It merely drives the wheel, and is used primarily on trucks.

full-time 4-wheel drive   A system in which the 4-wheel drive is always engaged and there is no shift lever.

fuse   A device in an electrical circuit which protects against an excessive flow of current overheating and damage the circuit. A fuse is a strip of soft metal that will melt at a fairly low temperature. All current in the circuit flows through this strip of metal and if the current flow rises above the number of amperes the fuse is rated for, the heat created will cause the strip to melt, breaking the circuit. To restore it, a new fuse must be inserted in place of the burned-out one.

fuse block   A special device for holding the electrical fuses found in cars. It is available in single or multiple arrangements.

fusible link   A fuse wire used to protect the main wiring harness against overload damage. If this fuse burns out, all electrical circuits in the car are rendered inoperative.

fusion   The act of melting.

gap   SPARK: also known as the spark plug gap. It is the distance the spark current jumps from the center spark plug electrode (positive) to the side electrode (ground).
BREAKER POINTS: the amount of space between the ignition point contact surfaces when they are separated to open the primary circuit.

gas   A vapor having no particles or droplets of liquid.

gasket   A material placed between two parts to insure proper sealing.

gas turbine engine   An engine in which fuel is burned continually in the combustion chambers. It utilizes the force of the escaping burned gases to rotate a turbine wheel that drives a compressor to feed more air to the engine, making it self-sustaining.

gasoline   A liquid blend of volatile hydrocarbons extracted from crude oil, with certain other ingredients added to improve its qualities for use as a car engine fuel.

gauge set   Two or more instruments attached to a manifold and used for measuring or testing pressure.

gear-type pump   A fluid-moving device using the rotating teeth of two meshed gears as vanes to propel fluid through a close-fitting annular passage around the perimeter of both gears.

gear ratio   The relationship between the number of turns made by a driving gear to complete one full turn of the driven gear. If the driving gear turns four times to turn the gear once, the gear ratio would be 4 to 1.

generator   A device in which voltage and current are induced in the windings of a revolving armature by a magnetic field created by surrounding stationary field coils. Alternating current is generated in the armature windings, but is converted to direct current by the manner in which it is picked up by the brushes on the commutator.

glass pack muffler   A straight-through (no baffles) muffler utilizing fiberglass packing around a perforated pipe to deaden exhaust sound.

glaze   A highly smooth, glossy finish on the cylinder walls.

glow plugs   Tiny electrical heaters in diesel engines which take the place of spark plugs in the conventional gasoline engine.

governor   A device designed to automatically control the speed, pressure, or temperature.

grabbing brakes   A sudden increase in braking, out of proportion to pedal pressure, usually caused by contaminated linings which have an unreliable coefficient of friction.

grid   The lead screen or plate to which the battery plate active material is affixed.

grind   To remove metal from an object by means of a revolving abrasive wheel, disc, or belt.

ground   In a CAR: using the metal structure of the body, engine, etc. to serve as a return path to the battery to complete the electrical circuits. The name was derived from the practice of using the earth as a return conductor for electric telegraph circuits.
BATTERY: the negative terminal of the battery connected to the metal framework of the car.

gum   Oxidized portions of fuel that form deposits in the fuel system or engine parts.

halide leak detector   A device consisting of a tank of acetylene gas, a stove, a chimney, and a search hose, used to detect leaks by visual means.

harmonic balancer   See vibration damper.

headers   Special exhaust manifolds that replace stock manifolds. They are designed with smooth flowing lines to prevent back pressure caused by sharp bends, rough castings, etc.

heat crossover   A passage from one exhaust manifold up, over, and under the carburetor to the other manifold. This crossover provides heat to the carburetor during engine warm-up.

heat range   This refers to the operating temperature of a given-style spark plug. Plugs are made to operate at different temperatures depending on the thickness and length of the porcelain insulator.

heat riser   An area, surrounding a portion of the intake manifold, through which exhaust gases can pass to heat the fuel-and-air mixture during warm-up.

heat riser valve (heat riser)   A valve located in the exhaust manifold of the engine controlling the heat of exhaust gases during engine warm-up.

heel   BRAKES: the end of the brake shoe which rests against the anchor pin.

GEAR TOOTH: the wide end of a tapered gear tooth such as those found in differential gears.

helical gear   A gear with the teeth cut at an angle to its centerline.

hemi   An engine using hemispherically-shaped combustion chambers.

hemispherical combustion chamber   A round, dome-shaped combustion chamber. The hemispherical shape lends itself to the use of large valves for improved breathing and suffers somewhat less heat loss than other shapes.

high compression head   A cylinder head with a smaller combustion chamber area which raises the compression. It can be custom-built or a stock head milled (cut) down.

high lift rocker arms   Custom rocker arms designed so a standard lift of the push rod will depress or open the valve somewhat more than the stock lifter.

high load condition   When an air conditioner must operate continuously at maximum capacity to provide the cool air required.

hone   To remove metal with a fine grit abrasive stone to precise tolerances.

horizontal-opposed engine   An engine with two banks of cylinders placed flat or 180 degrees apart.

horsepower   A unit of measurement of mechanical power or the rate at which work is done. One horsepower equals 33,000 foot pounds per minute.

hotchkiss drive   The method of connecting the transmission output shaft to the differential pinion by using open drive shafts. The driving force of the rear wheels is transmitted to the frame through the rear springs or through link arms connecting the rear axle housing to the frame.

hot wire   A wire connected to the battery or to some part of the electrical system with a direct connection to the battery. A current-carrying wire.

howl   A continuous brake noise, lower in pitch but higher in volume than brake squeal.

hub   The unit to which the wheel is bolted.

hyatt roller bearing   Similar to a conventional roller bearing except that the rollers are hollow and split lengthwise in a spiral fashion.

hydraulic brakes   Brakes operated by hydraulic pressure transmitted via steel tubing to the wheel cylinders which in turn apply the brake shoes to the drums.

hydraulic lifter   A valve lifter utilizing hydraulic pressure from the engine's oiling system to keep it in constant contact with both the camshaft and the valve stem. It automatically adjusts to any variation in valve stem length.

hydrocarbon   A mixture of hydrogen and carbon.

hydrocarbon, unburned   Hydrocarbons not burned during the normal engine combustion process. Unburned hydrocarbons make up about 0.1 percent of the engine exhaust emission.

hydrocarbons   The combination of hydrogen and carbon atoms. All petroleum-based fuels (gasoline, kerosene, etc.) consist of hydrocarbons.

hydrometer   A float device for determining the specific gravity of the electrolyte in a battery. This will determine the state of charge.

hydroplaning   A driving phenomenon in which a car's tires ride up on a wedge of water and lose contact with the road surface.

hypoid gearing   A system of gearing in which the pinion gear meshes with the ring gear below the centerline of the ring gear. This allows a somewhat lower driveline, thus reducing the hump in the floor of the car. For this reason, hypoid gearing is used in the differential on many cars.

idle-circuit nozzle   The aperture through which the fuel from the idle circuit enters the carburetor barrel.

idle-mixture screw   The device that adjusts the idle-circuit nozzle to control the amount of fuel reaching the cylinders during idling.

idler arm   See symmetrical idler arm.

idle valve or idle needle   A needle used to control the amount of fuel-and-air reaching the cylinders during idling. It, or they, may be adjusted by turning the exposed head.

ignition system   The components which comprise two electrical circuits—the ignition primary circuit and the ignition secondary circuit. Included are the battery, coil, condenser, breaker points, distributor, spark plugs, plus the interconnecting wires and ground.

ignition system   That portion of a car's electrical system designed to produce a spark within the cylinders to ignite the fuel charge. It consists of the battery, key switch, resistor, coil, distributor, points, condenser, spark plugs, and wiring.

impact wrench   An air- or electrically-driven wrench that tightens or loosens nuts, cap-screws, etc., with a series of sharp, rapid blows.

impeller   A wheel-like device on which fins are attached. It is whirled to pump water, move and slightly compress air, etc.

incandescent electric bulb   An electrically-energized light source consisting of a filament enclosed with an airtight glass glove with practically all the air exhausted from its interior. When an electrical current passes through the filament, the high resistance heats it so it glows brightly.

inch pound   The unit of energy required to raise one pound one inch.

included angle   The angle formed by centerlines drawn through the steering axis (kingpin inclination) and the center of the wheel (camber angle) as viewed from the front of the car. It combines both the steering axis and the camber angles.

independent suspension   A suspension system allowing each wheel to move up and down without undue influence on the other wheels.

indicated horsepower (IHP)   Indicated horsepower is a measure of the power developed by fuel burning within the cylinders.

inhibitor   A substance added to oil, water, gas, etc., to prevent foaming, rusting, etc.

injector   Component of a fuel injection system that squirts or injects a measured amount of gasoline into the intake manifold in the vicinity of the intake valve. In the diesel engine, fuel is injected directly into the cylinder; or, the nozzle and related parts used to spray a metered amount of fuel under pressure into a cylinder of a compression ignition engine.

inlet port   A vertical passage at the bottom of the master cylinder reservoir, positioned to allow brake fluid to enter the cylinder between the primary and secondary cups. From there, it flows through a small passage in the head of the piston, past a check valve, and into the forward end of the cylinder when needed. When the piston moves forward, the pressure generated ahead of it holds the valve closed, preventing any return flow.

in-line engine   An engine with all its cylinders arranged in one row.

input shaft   A shaft delivering power to a mechanism. The shaft from the clutch to the transmission is called the transmission input shaft.

insert bearing   A removable, precision-made bearing insuring a specified clearance between a bearing and a shaft.

insulator   A unit made of a material that will not readily conduct electricity or heat.

intake manifold   An engine component, usually a casting, which distributes the fuel-and-air mixture from the carburetor to the intake ports of all engine cylinders.

intake valve   The valve through which the fuel-and-air mixture is admitted to the cylinder.

intermediate gear   Any gear in the transmission between first and high.

internal combustion engine   An engine that burns fuel inside its cylinders to produce power.

jet   A small hole or orifice used to control the flow of gasoline in various parts of the carburetor.

journal   That part of a rotating shaft or similar device which turns in a bearing.

keyless entry   A system permitting entry to a car by pushing buttons on the outside of the driver's door.

kick-down switch   An electrical switch causing a transmission to shift down to a lower gear. It is often used to achieve fast acceleration.

kilometer   A metric measurement equivalent to $\frac{5}{8}$ of a mile.

kinetic energy   The energy of motion.

kingpin   A pin-like component placed in a nearly vertical position, around which the steering knuckle, or the front axle of single-kingpin cars, can pivot to steer the front wheels.

kingpin slant   See steering axis inclination.

knocking   A noise created by movement in a loose or worn bearing; or, a condition accompanied by an audible noise, occuring when the

gasoline in the cylinders burns too quickly. This is also referred to as detonation.

knuckle (steering knuckle)   A front suspension component that acts as a hinge to support a front wheel and permit it to be turned to steer the car. The knuckle pivots on ball joints fitted into the outer ends of the upper and lower control arms. The wheel spindle, which provides an axle for the front wheel to rotate around, is an integral part of the knuckle. The knuckle is bolted to the front wheel brake backing plate, keeping it stationary against braking loads.

knurl   To roughen the surface of a piece of metal by pressing a series of cross-hatch lines into it, thus raising the area between the lines.

lacquer   A fast-drying automotive body paint.

laminated   Something made up of many layers.

lands   Part of the power steering system, these are collar-like rings on both ends of the sliding spool which open and close the power chamber fluid ports as the steering wheel is turned; or, the piston metal between the ring grooves.

lead-acid battery   The type of battery used almost universally in cars.

leads   The wires, lines, or cables in an electrical circuit. Although all these terms mean essentially the same thing, there can be a shade of difference between them. Leads are generally the portions of wire that connect directly or lead to another electrical component. Lines are usually relatively long stretches of wire. Cables are heavy wires or conductors used to handle high amperage or high voltage.

leaf spring   A suspension device composed of several superimposed strips of flat spring steel held to the frame at one end by a shackle.

letter drills   A series of drills in which each drill size is designated by a letter of the alphabet.

limited-slip differential   A differential unit designed to provide superior traction by transferring driving torque, when one wheel is spinning, to the wheel that is not slipping.

lining   A high-friction material attached by rivets or a bonding process to a brake shoe.

linkage   Any series of metal rods or levers transmitting motion from one unit to another.

liter   A metric measurement of capacity equivalent to 2.11 pints. Five liters equals 1.32 gallons.

live axle   An axle on which the wheels are firmly affixed. The axle drives the wheels.

live wire   See hot wire.

locking ring   An adjustable ring on the end of the steering column that allows the driver to preset the steering wheel position according to his seating comfort.

long and short arm suspension   A suspension system using an upper and lower control arm. The upper arm is shorter than the lower to allow the wheel to deflect in a vertical direction with a minimum change in camber.

longitudinal leaf spring A leaf spring mounted so it is parallel to the length of the car.

louver Ventilation slots sometimes found in the hood of a car.

low brake pedal When the brake pedal depresses too close to the floorboard before actuating the brakes.

low pivot swing axle A rear axle setup in which the differential housing is attached to the frame by a pivot mount. A conventional type of housing and axle extend from the differential to one wheel. The other side of the differential is connected to the other wheel by a housing and axle pivoted at a point in line with the differential-to-frame pivot point.

lubricant A friction-reducing substance placed between moving parts.

lug To cause the engine to labor by failing to shift to a lower gear when necessary.

manifold The pipe connecting a series of outlets to a common opening.

manifold gauge A calibrated instrument used for measuring pressures.

manifold gauge set A manifold complete with gauges and charging hoses.

manifold heat control valve A valve placed in the exhaust manifold, or in the exhaust pipe, that deflects a certain amount of hot gas around the base of the carburetor to aid in engine warm-up.

manifold vacuum Air at less than atmospheric pressure within the intake valve port, intake manifold, and lower portion of the carburetor. It is created by the restriction of airflow to the cylinders, primarily by the throttle plate or venturi in the carburetor.

master cylinder The unit in a hydraulic brake system that forces brake fluid to the wheel cylinders.

metering rod A movable rod used to vary the opening area through a carburetor jet.

metering valve A valve in the disc brake system that cuts off pressure to the front brakes in order to reduce front wheel braking on slippery or icy surfaces. It is sometimes called a hold-off valve.

metric size Units made to metric system measurements.

micrometer A precision measuring tool giving readings accurate to within one thousandth of an inch.

mill To remove metal through the use of a rotating, toothed cutter.

millimeter A metric measurement equivalent to .039370 of an inch.

milling machine A machine using a variety of rotating cutter wheels to cut splines, gears, keyways, etc.

misfiring The failure of a fuel charge to ignite in an engine cylinder.

modulator A pressure control or adjusting valve used in the hydraulic system of an automatic transmission.

motor An electrically-driven power unit (electric motor). This term is often incorrectly applied to an internal combustion engine.

mph Miles per hour.

muffler A device, usually with an oval or round cross section, containing tubes and baffles designed to slow the rush of exhaust gases and absorb some of their heat as they flow through it.

multiple disc clutch A clutch with several discs.

multiple filament bulb An incandescent light bulb in which more than one filament is enclosed. Separate contacts on the base of the bulb allow any of the filaments to be energized selectively to provide the desired degree of illumination. Current is returned through the base of the bulb, which serves as a common ground for all filaments.

multiviscosity oils Engine oils with flow characteristics to provide adequate lubrication at both high and low temperatures.

needle bearing A roller-type bearing in which the rollers have a very narrow diameter in relation to their length.

negative The name for one pole of a magnet or one terminal of any electrical device. In an electrical current, electrons flow from the negative pole toward the positive pole.

nitrogen oxides In the combustion process, nitrogen from the air combines with oxygen to form nitrogen oxides.

number drills A series of drills in which each size is designated by a number (zero to 80).

nut rack A component of the steering gear which rides on the worm shaft and converts rotational movement of the steering wheel to linear movement which is then applied to the sector gear by means of the rack gear teeth.

octane rating A number representing a particular gasoline's ability to resist knocking, determined by the quantity of antiknock substances blended into it.

odometer An instrument, set in the speedometer, that registers the total distance traveled by a car.

ohm A unit of measurement used to indicate the amount of resistance to the flow of electricity in a given circuit.

ohmmeter An instrument used to measure the amount of resistance in a given unit or circuit, in ohms.

oil bath air cleaner An air cleaner using a pool of oil to remove impurities from the air entering the carburetor.

oil burner An engine consuming an excessive quantity of oil.

oil, combination splash and pressure system An engine oiling system using both pressure and splash oiling for lubrication.

oil filter A replaceable part that removes foreign particles from the circulating oil.

oil, full pressure system An engine oiling system forcing oil, under pressure, to the moving parts of the engine.

oil gallery   Pipes or bored passageways in an engine carrying oil from one area to another.

oil pump   A mechanism that forces lubricating oil, under pressure, through the engine.

oil pumping   When an excessive quantity of oil passes the piston rings and is consumed in the combustion chamber.

oil seal   A device used to prevent oil leakage past a certain area.

oil, splash system   An engine oiling system depending on the connecting rods to dip into troughs and splash oil on all moving parts.

open circuit   A break or opening in an electrical circuit prohibiting the passage of current.

orifice   A passage between two chambers, generally precisely-sized and finished, which restricts the flow of a fluid forced through it.

oscilloscope   An electronic testing instrument that translates electrical-circuit performance into a pattern visible on a cathode-ray tube, used to check ignition systems.

outlet port (compensating port)   A restricted passage at the bottom of the master cylinder reservoir, positioned to allow brake fluid to return to the reservoir when the brake is released, thus compensating for the expansion of fluid in the lines.

output shaft   Any shaft delivering power from within a mechanism (a transmission output shaft).

ovality   In a brake drum, an undesirable elliptical contour of the drum braking surface which can cause low-speed pulsation and other problems.

overdrive   A gear in some manual transmissions that, when actuated, allows the drive shaft to turn faster than the crankshaft, resulting in higher speeds with less engine effort and lower fuel consumption.

overhead camshaft   A camshaft mounted above the cylinder head and driven by a long timing chain.

overhead valves   Valves located in the head.

overhead valve engine   An engine with the intake and exhaust valves mounted in the cylinder head(s) directly above the cylinders.

overrunning clutch   A clutch mechanism that drives in one direction only. If driving torque is removed or reversed, the clutch slips.

overrunning clutch starter drive   A starter drive that is mechanically engaged. When the engine starts, the overrunning clutch operates until the drive is mechanically disengaged.

oversquare engine   An engine in which the bore diameter is larger than the length of the stroke.

oversteer   A built-in characteristic of certain types of rear suspension causing the rear wheels to slide toward the outside of the turn.

oxides of nitrogen   Exhaust gas formed by high combustion temperatures.

oxidize   The formation of crust on certain metals due to the action of heat and oxygen.

pan   The metal part bolted to the bottom of a crankcase or automatic transmission that holds oil or fluid.

paper air cleaner   An air cleaner using special paper through which the air to the carburetor is drawn.

parallelogram steering linkage   A steering system using two short tie-rods connected to the steering arms and to a long center link. The link is supported on one end on an idler arm and the other end is attached directly to the Pitman arm. The arrangement forms a parallelogram shape.

parking brake   A hand-operated brake which prevents vehicle movement while parked by locking the rear wheels or the transmission output shaft.

pawl   An arm pivoted so its free end can engage the teeth of a shaft or gear and lock it to prevent movement.

PCV   Positive crankcase ventilation. An emission control system device in which engine crankcase gases are drawn into the carburetor or intake manifold for reburning in order to reduce pollution.

PCV valve   The valve controlling the flow of engine crankcase gases.

penetrating oil   A special oil used to free rusted parts so they can be removed.

petroleum   The raw material from which gasoline, kerosene, lube oils, etc., are made. It consists of hydrogen and carbon.

Phillips head screw   A screw with cross slots instead of the single slot used in conventional screws.

pickup coil   The coil in which voltage is induced resulting from the interaction of the reluctor and the permanent magnet.

pilot shaft   A dummy shaft placed in a mechanism as a means of aligning the parts. It is then removed and the regular shaft installed.

pinging   A metallic, rattling sound produced by the engine during heavy acceleration when the ignition timing is too far advanced for the grade of fuel being burned.

pinion carrier   That part of the rear axle assembly supporting and containing the pinion gear shaft.

pipes   Exhaust system pipes.

piston   A solid cylindrical component of an engine. Its head forms the lower extreme of the combustion chamber and it is linked by the connecting rod to the crankshaft to transmit the forces of combustion to it.

piston boss   The built-up area around the piston pin hole.

piston collapse   A reduction in the diameter of the piston skirt caused by heat and constant impact stresses.

piston displacement   The amount (volume) of air displaced by a piston when moved through the full length of its stroke.

piston head   That portion of the piston above the top ring.

piston lands   That portion of the piston between the ring grooves.

piston pin (wrist pin)   A round, usually hollow, steel pin that is passed through the piston and used as a base upon which to fasten the upper end of the connecting rod.

piston ring   A split ring installed in a groove in the piston. The ring contacts the sides of the ring groove and also rubs against the cylinder wall, thus sealing the space between the piston and the wall.
With reference to compression, a ring designed to seal the burning fuel charge above the piston. Generally there are two compression rings per piston and they are located in the two top ring grooves.
With reference to oil control, a piston ring designed to scrape oil from the cylinder wall. The ring allows the oil to pass through it and then through holes or slots in the groove. In this way the oil is returned to the pan. There are many shapes and special designs used on oil control rings.

piston ring end gap   The distance left between the ends of the ring when installed in the cylinder.

piston ring expander   See ring expander.

piston ring groove   The slots or grooves cut in the piston head to receive the piston rings.

piston ring side clearance   The space between the sides of the ring and the ring lands.

piston skirt   That portion of the piston below the rings. (Some engines have an oil ring in the skirt area.)

piston skirt expander   A spring device placed inside the piston skirt to produce an outward pressure which increases its diameter.

pitching   A fore-and-aft rocking motion of a car as the front end rises and the rear end falls and vice-versa.

Pitman arm   A short lever arm splined to the steering gear cross shaft which transmits the steering force from the cross shaft to the steering linkage.

planet carrier   That part of a planetary gearset on which the planet gears are affixed. The gears are free to turn on hardened pins set into the carrier.

planet gears   Those gears in a planetary gearset in mesh with both the ring and sun gear. They are referred to as planet gears because they orbit or move around the central or sun gear.

planetary gearset   A gearing unit consisting of a ring gear with internal teeth, a sun or central pinion gear with external teeth, and a series of planet gears meshed with both the ring and sun gear.

plate   A component of a lead-acid battery cell composed of sponge lead which is reacted on by electrolyte to produce electric voltage.

plate strap   An electrical conductor used to connect two cells of a battery to continue the circuit through the battery.

plates   Thin sections of lead peroxide or porous lead in the battery. There are two kinds of plates—positive and negative. They are arranged in groups called elements, and are completely submerged in the electrolyte.

play   Movement between two parts.

plies   Layers of rubber-coated cords constituting the carcass of a tire.

plug gapping   Adjusting the side electrode on a spark plug to provide the proper air gap between it and the center electrode.

ply rating   An indication of tire strength (load-carrying capacity). It does not necessarily indicate the actual number of plies. A 2-ply/4-ply-rated tire would have the load capacity of a four-ply tire of the same size but with only two actual plies.

points   See breaker points.

polarity   This indicates if a battery terminal is positive or negative (plus or minus, + or −). With reference to the generator, polarity indicates if the pole shoes are magnetized to make current flow in a direction compatible with the direction of flow set by the battery.
Polarity may indicate if the end of a magnet is the north or south pole (N or S).
Polarity also refers to the process of sending a quick surge of current through the field windings of the generator in a direction that will cause the pole shoes to assume the correct polarity.

pole   One of two points at which opposite electrical qualities are concentrated, as in the two poles of a magnet.

pole piece   In an electronic ignition system, a metal bracket around which the pickup coil is wound.

pole shoes   Metal pieces about which the field coil windings are placed. When current passes through the windings, the shoes become powerful magnets. Pole shoes are found, for example, in a generator or starter motor.

poppet valve   The valve used to open and close the valve port entrances to the engine cylinders.

ports   Openings in engine cylinder blocks for the exhaust and intake valves and water connections.

positive   The name for a pole of a magnet or a terminal of an electrical device. In an electrical current, electrons flow toward the positive pole from the negative pole.

positive terminal   That terminal, as on the battery, to which the current flows.

post, terminal   In a battery or other electrical device, a cylindrical protrusion at either end of the electrical circuit.

power   See horsepower.

power chambers   In a power steering system, the design of the piston divides the power cylinder into two chambers—one to provide power assist on left turns, the other for right turns.

power steering   A system using a hydraulic pressure booster to augment the steering force.

preignition   An undesirable early ignition of the fuel-and-air mixture, usually due to glowing carbon deposits in the combustion chamber, which can be damaging to adjacent engine components.

pre-loaded ball joint Tightness between the ball and socket in this type of joint.

pre-loading Adjusting the antifriction bearing so it is under mild pressure. This prevents loose bearings under driving stress.

press-fit The fit or contact between two parts requiring pressure to force the parts together. Also referred to as drive or force-fit.

pressure bleeder A device forcing brake fluid, under pressure, into the master cylinder so that by opening the bleeder screws at the wheel cylinders, all air will be removed from the brake system.

pressure cap A special cap for the radiator which maintains a predetermined amount of pressure on the water in the cooling system, enabling the water to run hotter without boiling.

pressure relief valve A valve designed to open at a specific pressure, preventing pressure in a system from exceeding certain limits.

pressure-vent cooling system A cooling system operating at atmospheric pressure under normal conditions, but becoming pressurized for more efficient cooling when high engine loads require greater cooling.

primary cell (dry cell) An electrochemical power source using dry ingredients to generate electricity. A flashlight battery is an example of a primary cell.

primary ignition circuit The circuit in the ignition system that operates under the regular electrical system voltage (approximately 12 volts) to induce an extremely high voltage in the coil for use at the spark plugs.

primary piston The rear piston in the tandem master cylinder actuated directly by the brake pedal or power booster.

primary shoe The forward shoe of the servo-contact brake assembly. It absorbs some of the rotating force of the drum and transmits it to the secondary shoe, forcing it against the drum when the brakes are applied. This reduces the pedal effort needed for braking.

primary winding The outer winding of relatively heavy wire in an ignition coil. This winding carries the 12-volt flow of current from the battery before it is induced into the high-tension secondary winding.

primary wires The wiring serving the low-voltage part of the ignition system (the wiring from the battery to the switch, resistor, coil, and distributor points).

proportioning valve This unit operates by restricting, at a given ratio, hydraulic pressure to the rear brakes when the brake system pressure reaches a certain point. On light pedal application, the valve allows full brake hydraulic pressure to the rear brakes.

printed circuit An electrical circuit made by connecting the units with electrically-conductive lines printed on a panel. This eliminates actual wire and the task of monitoring it.

prony brake A device using a friction brake to measure the horsepower output of an engine.

propeller shaft The shaft connecting the transmission output shaft to the differential pinion shaft.

psi Pounds per square inch.

pull (brake pull) Unbalanced braking at the front wheels, causing a car to swerve when the brakes are applied.

pulsation During braking at low speeds, an out-of-round brake drum causes a varying rate of deceleration. The driver will feel a pulsating sensation in the car.

pulsation damper A device used to smooth out the pulsations of fuel from the fuel pump to the carburetor.

pump The compressor. It also refers to the vacuum pump.

pumping the gas pedal Forcing the accelerator up and down in an endeavor to feed extra gasoline to the cylinders. This is often the cause of flooding.

push rod The rod connecting the valve lifter to one end of the rocker arm. Used on valve-in-head installations.

quadrant The gearshift selector indicator marked PRNDL.

rack-and-pinion gearbox A type of steering gear using a pinion gear on the end of the steering shaft. The pinion engages a long rack (a bar with a row of teeth cut along one edge), which is connected directly to the steering arms by rods.

rack-and-sector gear Component parts of the steering gear. The rack is a series of gear teeth arranged in a straight line on the rack nut. The sector is a segment of a conventional circular gear which meshes with the teeth on the rack. Linear motion of the rack is translated into rotating motion of the sector.

radial engine An engine with various numbers of cylinders so arranged to form a circle around the crankshaft centerline.

radial tire A tire in which the body cords run at right angles (radially) to the centerline of the tread, with two or more belts to strengthen the tread.

radiator The unit dissipating engine coolant heat to the outside air by passing the fluid through finned core pipes.

radius rods Rods attached to the axle and pivoted on the frame, used to keep the axle at right angles to the frame and yet permit an up-and-down motion.

Rankine-cycle engine An external combustion engine using the energy of expanding gases (such as steam) to drive a piston or turbine.

ratchet A mechanism employing a particular type of pawl to allow movement of its associated gear in one direction while preventing movement in the opposite direction.

rate A term denoting the load required to move a spring or a suspended wheel a given distance, expressed in pounds per inch. It is an indicator of the softness or firmness.

ratio A fixed relationship between things in number, quantity, or degree. For example, if the fuel-and-air mixture contains 15 parts of air to one part of gas, the ratio is 15 to one.

rear axle housing Banjo type: a rear axle housing from which the differential unit may be removed while the housing remains in place on the car. The housing is solid from side-to-side. Split type: a rear axle housing made up of several pieces and bolted together. The housing must be split apart to remove the differential.

rebound The movement of a wheel downward from its normal position, usually due to uncontrolled overtravel of a spring as it returns after reacting to a road shock, the sudden drop of a wheel into a depression in the road, or a weight transfer away from the wheel.

receiver A container for the storage of liquid refrigerant.

receiver dehydrator A combination container for the storage of liquid refrigerant and a desiccant.

reciprocating action Back-and-forth movement, like the action of pistons inside cylinders.

recirculating ball worm and nut A type of steering gear using a series of ball bearings that feed through, around, and back through the grooves in the worm and nut.

red line The top recommended engine revolutions per minute (RPM) for a car. If a tachometer is used, it will have a red mark indicating the maximum RPM.

refrigerant The liquid used in refrigeration systems to remove the heat from the evaporator coils and carry it to the condenser.

refrigerant-12 The name of the refrigerant generally used in automotive air-conditioning systems.

regulator A device used to control generator voltage and current output, or to control gas or liquid pressure.

relay An electromagnetic switch which switches a large amount of current by using a small amount of current, such as a horn or starter relay.

relief valve This valve limits the power steering pump output and protects the system against excessive pressure buildup.

reluctor In an electronic ignition, a wheel-like rotor whose eight iron teeth vary the magnetic flux generated by the permanent magnet and act as a bridge between the permanent magnet and the pickup coil for the magnetic flux.

resistance A measure of a conductor's ability to retard the flow of electricity.

resistor A device used in an electrical circuit to deliberately introduce added resistance to it.

resistor spark plug A spark plug containing a resistor designed to shorten both the capacitive and inductive phases of the spark, suppressing ratio interference and lengthening electrode life.

resonator A small, muffler-like device in the exhaust system near the end of the tailpipe, used to provide additional silencing.

retard To set the ignition timing so a spark occurs later or less degrees before top dead center.

returnability The natural tendency of certain front end alignment conditions, especially steering axis inclination, to bring the front wheels back to their straight-ahead position and hold them there following a turn.

return spring A spring designed to return some component to its original position after the force which moved it has been released. In the brake system, return springs are used on brake shoes, the master cylinder piston, the brake pedal mechanism, and the parking brake mechanism.

reverse flush Cleaning the cooling system by pumping a powerful cleaning agent through it in a direction opposite to the normal flow.

reverse idler gear A gear used in the transmission to produce a reverse rotation of the transmission output shaft.

rheostat A wire bound variable resistor used in the control of current.

riding the clutch This refers to a driver resting his foot on the clutch pedal while the car is in operation.

ring A ring, the outer edge of which has a thin layer of chrome plate.

ring expander A spring device placed under piston rings to hold them snugly against the cylinder wall.

ring gear This may refer to the large gear attached to the differential carrier or to the outer gear in a planetary gear setup.

ring grooves The grooves cut into the piston to accept the rings.

ring job Reconditioning the cylinders and installing new rings.

ring ridge That portion of the cylinder above the top limit of ring travel. In a worn cylinder, this area is of a smaller diameter than the remainder of the cylinder and has a ledge or ridge that must be removed.

rivet A metal pin used to hold two objects together. One end of the pin has a head and the other end is set or peened over.

rocker arm A form of lever designed to transmit linear motion in a reverse direction and actuate a component, as in the valve train and the fuel pump.

rocker arm shaft The shaft on which the rocker arms are mounted.

rocker panel That section of the car body between the front and rear fenders and beneath the doors.

rodding the radiator The top, and sometimes the bottom tank, of the radiator is removed, and the core is then cleaned by passing a cleaning rod down through the tubes. This is done when radiators are clogged with rust, scale, and various mineral deposits.

roll The tendency of a car to lean outward, away from the direction of a turn, due to the transfer of weight toward the outside wheels caused by centrifugal force.

roller bearing   A bearing with a series of straight, cupped, or tapered rollers engaging an inner and outer ring or race.

roller clutch   A clutch with a series of rollers placed in ramps that provides power in one direction but will slip or freewheel in the other.

rotary engine   A piston engine in which the crankshaft is fixed and the cylinders rotate around it.

rotary engine (Wankel)   An internal combustion engine which is not of a reciprocating (piston) engine design. One or more three-sided rotors revolve in specially-shaped chambers. In every revolution, each side of the rotor performs the functions of a four-stroke cycle engine.

rotary flow (torque converter)   The movement of the oil as it is carried around by the pump and the turbine. The rotary motion is not caused by the oil passing through the pump, to the turbine, the stator, etc., as is the case with vortex flow. Rotary flow is at right angles to the centerline of the converter whereas vortex flow is parallel, depending on the ratio between the speeds of the pump and the turbine.

rotor   The portion of the alternator that revolves and carries the alternator field windings. The ignition distributor also has a rotor which directs high-tension current to the spark plug cable terminals.
A rotating conductor mounted on the distributor cam carrying secondary voltage to the distributor cap electrodes.

rotor-type pump   A fluid-moving device consisting of an inner and an outer rotor, turning on eccentric centers. As the two rotors turn, the space between their lobes expands and contracts. Fluid is introduced in the space as it expands, and discharged as it contracts.

rpm   Revolutions per minute.

running fit   A fit in which sufficient clearance is provided to enable parts to turn freely and receive lubrication.

SAE   Society of Automotive Engineers.

SAE or rated horsepower   A simple formula used to determine what is commonly referred to as the SAE or rated horsepower. The formula is:

$$\frac{\text{bore diameter}^2 \times \text{number of cylinders}}{2.5}$$

This formula is used primarily for licensing purposes and is not a very accurate means of determining actual brake horsepower.

safety rim   A tire rim with two safety ridges, one on each lip, to prevent the tire beads from entering the drop center area in the event of a blowout. This feature keeps the tire on the rim.

scale   The accumulation of rust and minerals in the cooling system.

schematic drawing   A drawing of an electrical circuit in the simplest, most easily-understood form.

Schrader valve   A spring-loaded valve, similar to a tire valve, located inside the service valve fitting and used on some control devices to hold

refrigerant in the system. Special adapters must be used with the gauge hose to allow access to the system.

score   A scratch or groove on a finished surface.

screen   A metal mesh located in the receiver, expansion valve, and compressor inlet to prevent particles of dirt from circulating through the system.

screw extractor   A device used to remove broken bolts, screws, etc., from holes.

sealed-beam headlight   A headlight in which the lens, reflector, and filament are fused together to form a single unit.

sealed bearing   A bearing lubricated at the factory and then sealed. It cannot be lubricated during regular maintenance.

seat   A surface on which another part rests or seats.

seat   Minor wearing of the piston ring surface during initial use. Rings then fit or seat properly against the cylinder wall.

secondary ignition circuit   The electrical circuit in the ignition system that delivers the high-voltage current from the coil to the spark plugs.

secondary, reverse, or trailing brake shoe   The brake shoe installed facing the rear of the car.

secondary piston   The piston at the front of the tandem master cylinder which, in normal operation, is hydraulically operated by the primary piston.

secondary winding   The inner winding of fine wire in an ignition coil, in which a secondary or high-tension voltage is created by induction.

secondary wire   The high-voltage wire from the coil to the distributor tower and from the tower to the spark plugs.

sector shaft   Part of the power train in the power steering gear assembly, the sector shaft is connected by the steering arm to the steering linkage. Its teeth mate with the teeth on the power piston. The sector shaft initiates a right or a left turn as the piston is moved upward for a left or downward for a right turn.

sediment   An accumulation of matter which settles to the bottom of a fluid.

selector forks   Devices that move the synchronizing rings in a transmission.

self-energizing   A brake shoe which, when applied, develops a wedging action that actually assists the braking force applied by the wheel cylinder.

semi-floating axle   The type of axle commonly used in modern cars. The outer end turns the wheel and supports the weight of the car; the inner end, which is splined, floats in the differential gear.

sensor   A device which operates when subjected to temperature, vacuum, pressure, or air flow, usually used to control exhaust gas recirculation and such systems.

servo   An oil-operated device used to push or pull another part.

servo action   Brakes with one end of the primary shoe bearing against the end of the secondary shoe. When the brakes are applied, the primary shoe attempts to move in the direction of the rotating drum and in so doing applies force to the secondary shoe. This action, called servo action, makes less brake pedal pressure necessary, and is widely used in brake construction.

shackle   A short connecting link, usually a flat plate, used to form a flexible connection between the eye of a leaf spring and the spring mounting point on the car's underbody. The flexibility is needed because a leaf spring's length changes as it flexes under deflection.

shear pins   Connecting inserts formed by injecting a plastic material into openings. Their purpose is to hold connected and interacting parts of an assembly in alignment under normal operating conditions, and to give way when abnormal pressure or strain is applied. In the telescoping gearshift tube, for example, if an accident causes the steering column to compress, the gearshift tube components telescope within the column.

shift forks   The devices straddling slots cut in sliding gears. The fork is used to move the gear back and forth on the shaft.

shift point   This refers to the point, either in engine revolutions per minute or road speed, at which the transmission should be shifted to the next gear.

shift rails   Sliding rods on which the shift forks are attached, used for shifting automatic transmissions.

shim   A thin, flat piece of metal, used to separate two parts by a given distance determined by the thickness of the shim or shims placed between them.

shimmy   A fairly violent vibration of the car's front end, sometimes strong enough to shake the steering wheel back and forth, caused by front wheels wobbling as they rotate. This condition is usually due to loose steering linkage parts, poor front end alignment, or unbalanced tires.

shock absorber   A hydraulic mechanism that dampens oscillation in the suspension system.

shoe   A curved part supporting the friction material, or brake lining. It also absorbs and transmits braking forces.

shoe knock or slap   A knocking noise during braking, with a frequency related to wheel speed. This can be caused by spiral cutting tool marks on the drum braking surface. During braking, these fine marks pull the shoes on the left-hand brakes out until they snap back against the support plate. This occurs only on newly-machined drums, since usage soon wears the marks down.

short circuit   A malfunctioning of an electrical circuit or a portion thereof, in which the current finds a low resistance path to ground through damaged insulation or some other condition. In effect, the current takes a short cut, bypassing the higher resistance components beyond the damage or short. When this occurs,

current flow is usually so high because of the greatly reduced resistance that the fuse or circuit breaker overheats and shuts off the current.

short finder   A special testing device that pinpoints the location of a short circuit in a conductor without penetrating the insulation. The short finder detects the presence or lack of a magnetic field around a conductor.

shrink-fit   A fit between two parts so tight the outer or encircling piece must be expanded by heating to fit over the inner piece. In cooling, the outer part shrinks and grasps the inner part securely.

side-draft carburetor   A carburetor in which the air passes into the intake manifold in a horizontal plane.

sight glass   In the air-conditioning system, a window in the liquid line or in the top of the drier to observe the liquid refrigerant flow.

silencer   Muffler.

single-barrel, double-barrel and four-barrel carburetors   This refers to the number of throttle openings or barrels from the carburetor to the intake manifold.

skid   The sudden movement of a car, due to loss of tire traction, in which the driver loses control and the automobile slips sideways on the road.

skirt   A cover for the rear fender cutout.

slant engine   This is an in-line engine in which the cylinder block has been tilted from a vertical plane.

slave cylinder   A cylinder that converts hydraulic pressure generated by the master cylinder into a mechanical force. Automotive brake wheel cylinders are slave cylinders.

sliding gear   A transmission gear splined to the shaft which may be moved back and forth for shifting.

sliding spool   Part of the power steering valve. Its sliding action controls oil flow from the oil pump.

slip angle   The angle formed during a turn between the direction a tire is pointed and the direction it is actually moving. This is not an indication of tire slippage, since the tire tread flexes and twists slightly so it moves sideways in a turn.

slip joint   A joint transferring driving torque from one shaft to another while allowing longitudinal movement between the two shafts.

slip rings   In an alternator, ring-like components of the rotor which take field current from brushes and convey it to the rotor field windings.

sludge   Black, mushy deposits throughout the interior of the engine, caused by a mixture of dust, oil, and water being whipped together by the moving parts.

smog   Fog made darker and heavier by chemical fumes and smoke.

snap ring   A split ring snapped into a groove in a shaft or a hole. It is used to hold bearings, thrust washers, gears, etc., in place.

snow tire   A tire with an open-tread pattern and deep grooves to provide extra traction.

SOHC   Single Overhead Camshaft.

soldering   Joining two pieces of metal together with a lead-and-tin mixture. Both pieces of metal must be heated to insure proper adhesion of the melted solder.

solenoid   An electrically-operated magnetic device used to produce mechanical movement. A movable iron core is placed inside a coil. When current flows through the coil, it will attempt to center itself. In so doing, it will exert considerable force on anything connected to it.

solenoid valve   An electromagnetic valve remotely controlled by energizing and de-energizing a coil.

solvent   A liquid used to dissolve or thin another material. Alcohol thins shellac; gasoline dissolves grease.

spark   The bridging or jumping of a gap between two electrodes by electrical current.

spark advance   Causing the spark plug to fire earlier by altering the position of the distributor breaker points in relation to the distributor shaft.

spark gap   The space between the center and side electrode tips on a spark plug.

spark knock   See preignition.

spark plug   An electrical assembly used in the ignition system to provide a high-tension voltge spark for igniting the compressed fuel-and-air mixture in the engine cylinder.

specific gravity   The relative weight of a given volume of a specific material as compared to the weight of an equal volume of water.

speedometer   An instrument used to determine the forward speed of a car.

spider gears   Small gears, mounted on a shaft pinned to the differential case, which mesh with, and drive, the axle and gears.

spindle   A stub axle for a front wheel, which protrudes from the steering knuckle.

spiral bevel gear   A ring-and-pinion setup widely used in differentials. The teeth of both the ring and the pinion are tapered and cut on a spiral so they are at an angle to the centerline of the pinion shaft.

splined joint   A joint between two parts in which each part has a series of splines cut along the contact area. The splines on one part slide into the grooves between the splines on the other.

spongy pedal   When there is air in the brake lines, or shoes not properly centered in the drums, the brake pedal will have a springy or spongy feeling when the brakes are applied. The pedal normally will feel hard when applied.

spool balance valve   A hydraulic valve that balances incoming oil pressure against spring control pressure to produce a steady pressure to some control unit.

spot weld   Fastening parts together by fusing at various points. A heavy surge of electricity is passed through the parts held in firm contact by electrodes.

sprag clutch   A clutch that allows rotation in one direction but locks up and prevents any movement in the other.

springs   The primary components of automotive suspension systems which absorb the force of road shocks by flexing or twisting.

spring booster   A device used to beef up sagging springs or to increase the load capacity of standard springs.

spring windup   The curved shape assumed by the rear leaf springs during acceleration or braking.

sprung weight   This refers to the weight of all parts of the car supported by the suspension system.

spur gear   A gear on which the teeth are cut parallel to the shaft.

spurt   A small hole in the large end of the connecting rod that indexes (aligns) with the oil hole in the crank journal. When the holes index, oil spurts out to lubricate the cylinder walls.

square engine   An engine in which the bore diameter and stroke are of equal dimensions.

squeak   A high-pitched brake noise of short duration.

squeal   A continuous, high-pitched, low-volume, piercing brake noise.

stabilizer bar   A special form of torsion bar linking both sides of an independent front suspension. It resists side sway on turns by transferring some of the added load on the suspension for one front wheel to the suspension for the other. However, it also transfers road shock and vibration from one wheel to the other.

stamping   A sheet metal part formed by being pressed between metal discs.

starter   A compact, powerful electric motor that drives the engine crankshaft flywheel by means of a gear engaging mating teeth on the rim of the flywheel. It is the most powerful electric motor on the car and draws the most current.

static balance   A condition of stability in a stationary body. A wheel-and-tire assembly is in static balance if its weight is evenly distributed around the wheel hub axis so it will remain in whatever position it is placed.

static pressure   A certain amount of pressure that always remains in the brake lines, even with the brake pedal released. Static pressure is maintained by a check valve.

stator   A small hub, upon which a series of vanes are affixed in a radial position. Oil leaving the torque converter turbine strikes the stator vanes and is redirected into the pump at an angle conducive to high efficiency. The stator makes torque multiplication possible. Torque multiplication is highest at stall when the engine speed is at its highest and the turbine is standing still.

steel pack muffler   A straight-through (no baffles) muffler utilizing metal shavings surrounding a perforated pipe.

steering arm   An arm protruding from the steering knuckle connected to the tie-rod. It turns the knuckle in response to tie-rod movement.

steering axis inclination   Tipping the tops of the kingpins inward towards each other. This places the centerline of the steering axis nearer the center of the tire-and-road contact area.

steering gear The gear, mounted on the lower end of the steering column, used to carry the rotary motion of the steering wheel to the car wheels.

steering gear arm (Pitman arm) The arm linking the cross shaft in the steering gear with the steering linkage.

steering geometry The various angles assumed by the components making up the front wheel turning arrangement (camber, caster, toe-in, etc.). It is also used to describe the related angles assumed by the front wheels when the car is negotiating a curve.

steering knuckle A device pivoted by the steering mechanism, causing the wheels to turn.

steering knuckle angle The angle formed between the steering axis and the centerline of the spindle, sometimes referred to as the included angle.

stick shift This refers to a transmission shifted manually through the use of various forms of linkage. It often refers to the upright gearshift stick that protrudes through the floor.

stirling-cycle engine An external combustion engine using gas that is alternately heated and cooled within a closed system to drive the pistons.

stock car A car as built by the factory.

stratified-charge engine A modification of the combustion chamber in the piston engine in which both lean and rich fuel mixtures are simultaneously supplied to each cylinder.

stroboscope See timing light.

stroke The distance a piston travels from top dead center to bottom dead center.

strut In the controlled-expansion type of aluminum piston, a steel segment cast into the piston to restrain its expansion with heat to nearly equal the expansion of the cast-iron cylinder and maintain a more constant piston-to-cylinder wall clearance.

stud A headless bolt with threads on both ends.

stud puller A tool used to install or remove studs.

suction See vacuum.

sump That part of the oil pan containing the oil.

sun gear The center gear around which the planet gears revolve.

supercharger An air compressor used on some high-performance engines to increase volumetric efficiency by forcing a greater quantity of air into the cyclinders on each intake stroke.

support plate A component of the brake attached to the car's underbody which supports all other brake parts except the drum.

suppressor-type cable A wire or cable used for spark plug wires that resists or suppresses certain electrical signals produced in ignition systems so radio and TV signals will not be interrupted.

suspension The components of a car which cushion the body from the reactions of the wheels to irregularities of the surface over which it travels.

sweat The use of a soft solder to join two pieces of tubing or fitting by the use of heat.

sweat fitting A fitting designed to be used in sweating.

swing axle An independent rear suspension system in which each driving wheel can move up or down independently of the other. The differential unit is bolted to the frame and various forms of linkage are used on which to mount the wheels. Drive axles, utilizing one or more universal joints, connect the differential to the drive wheels.

switch An electrical device used to control the flow of electrical current. Switches normally are used either to turn current on or off, or to route current to one of a number of related circuits.

symmetrical idler arm A steering linkage supporting the right side of the steering center link that operates the two tie-rods. The symmetrical idler arm is a geometric duplicate of the steering gear arm.

synchromesh transmission A transmission using a device that synchronizes the speed of the gears being shifted together. This prevents gear grinding. Some transmissions use a synchromesh on all gears, while others only synchronize second and high.

synchronize Timing causing two or more events to occur simultaneously, such as a plug firing or a valve opening when the piston is in the correct position.

synchronizing rings Devices in a synchromesh transmission that bring up the speed of the driven gear to that of the driving gear and lock the driven gear to the output shaft of the transmission, avoiding gear clash.

tachometer A device used to indicate the speed of the engine in revolutions per minute.

tailpipe The exhaust pipe running from the muffler to the rear of the car.

tap To cut threads in a hole; or, the fluted tool used to cut the threads.

tap and die set A set of taps and dies for internal and external threading.

tapered roller bearing A bearing utilizing a series of tapered, hardened steel rollers operating between an outer and inner hardened steel race.

tappet A plunger that rides on a camshaft lobe and transfers the lobe action to the pushrod or valve stem.

tappet noise Noise caused by the lash or clearance between the valve stem and the rocker arm or between the valve stem and the valve lifter.

TDC Top Dead Center.

terminal A connecting point in an electrical circuit. When referring to the battery, it means the two battery posts.

thermistor A heat-sensing device in the diesel engine.

thermostat A temperature-sensitive device used in cooling systems to control the flow of coolant.

third brush A generator in which a third

movable brush is used to control current output.

throttle valve A valve in the carburetor used to control the amount of the fuel-and-air mixture that reaches the cylinders.

throw The offset portion of the crankshaft designed to accept the connecting rod.

throwing a rod When an engine throws a connecting rod from the crankshaft.

thrust bearing The engine's main bearing designed to resist side pressure of the crankshaft.

thrust washer A bronze or hardened steel washer placed between two moving parts. It prevents longitudinal movement and provides a bearing surface for the thrust surfaces of the parts.

tie-rod A rod connecting the steering arms. When the tie-rod is moved, the wheels pivot.

timing chain A chain that operates the camshaft by engaging sprockets on the camshaft and the crankshaft.

timing gears Gears attached to the camshaft and to the crankshaft to provide a means of driving the camshaft.

timing light A type of stroboscope used for adjusting the timing of the ignition spark. One lead of the light is connected to the battery and the other to the high tension wire of the number one cylinder.

timing marks Marks, usually located on the vibration damper, used to snychronize the ignition system so the plugs will fire at the correct time.

timing marks One tooth on either the camshaft or the crankshaft gear is marked with an indentation or some other mark. Another mark will be found on the other gear between two of the teeth. The two gears must be meshed so the marked tooth meshes with the marked spot on the other gear.

timing the ignition A tune-up procedure in which spark plug firing is adjusted to occur at the correct instant of a given piston's cycle.

tire balance See dynamic balance and static balance.

tire bead The reinforced portion of a tire holding the tire on the wheel rim.

tire casing The main body of the tire exclusive of the tread.

tire patch area The small portion of tire tread, roughly oval in shape, providing the only contact the car has with the road at a given instant. All directional, starting, and stopping control is concentrated in the tire patch areas of the four tires.

tire profile The ratio between a tire's tread-to-bead height and its sidewall-to-sidewall width.

tire plies The layers of nylon, rayon, etc., used to form the tire casing. Most car tires are 2-ply with a 4-ply rating. Two-ply indicates two layers of cloth.

tire rotation Moving the front tires to the rear and the rear to the front to equalize wear.

tire sidewall That portion of the tire between the tread and the bead.

tire tread That part of the tire that contacts the road.

toe The comparison of the distance between the extreme front of both tires and the distance between the extreme rear of both tires, measured at the front wheels. If the front wheel tires are closer together at the front than at the rear, it is called toe-in. If farther apart at the front than at the rear, it is called toe-out. And if the distance is exactly equal at the front and rear, so the wheels run parallel, it is called zero toe.

toe-out on turns A built-in characteristic of automotive steering systems, in which toe-out of the front wheels is increased in proportion to the angle they are turned away from the straight-ahead position. This is necessary because the inside wheel on a turn follows a path that is a tighter circle than the path of the outside wheel. Toe-out on turns is one of the elements in front end alignment.

toggle switch A switch actuated by flipping a small lever either up or down or from side to side.

tolerance The amount of variation permitted from an exact size or measurement. The actual amount from the smallest acceptable dimension to the largest acceptable dimension.

Top Dead Center (TDC) The point at which a piston reaches the top of its travel in a cylinder.

top off Fill a container to full capacity.

torque A turning or twisting force such as that imparted on the driveline by the engine. It is expressed as the force times the distance of a moment arm in foot pounds or meter kilograms.

torque converter A unit, quite similar to the fluid coupling, that transfers engine torque to the transmission input shaft. Unlike the fluid coupling, the torque converter can multiply engine torque. This is accomplished by installing one or more stators between the torus members. In the torque converter, the driving torus is referred to as the pump and the driven torus as the turbine.

torque multiplication Increasing engine torque through the use of a torque converter.

torque tube drive The method of connecting the transmission output shaft to the differential pinion shaft by using an enclosed drive shaft. The drive shaft is bolted to the rear axle housing on one end and pivoted through a ball joint to the rear of the transmission on the other. The

torque wrench A wrench used to draw nuts, cap screws, etc., up to a specified tension by measuring the torque being applied.

torsion See torque.

torsional vibration A twisting and untwisting action developed in a shaft. It is caused either by intermittent applications of power or load.

torsion bar A long, spring steel rod attached in such a way that one end is anchored while the other is free to twist. If an arm is attached, at right angles, to the free end, any movement of the arm will cause the rod or bar to twist. The bar's resistance to twisting provides a spring action. The torsion bar replaces both coil and leaf springs in some suspension systems.

track   The distance between the front wheels or the distance between the rear wheels. They are not always the same.

traction   The ability of a tire to grip the road surface, which determines the degree of effectiveness steering, driving, and braking forces have on the car's motion.

traction differential   See limited-slip differential.

tramp   A hopping motion of the front wheels.

transaxle   A drive setup in which the transmission and differential are combined into a single unit.

transformer   An electrical device used to increase or decrease voltage. A car ignition coil transforms the voltage from 12 volts to nearly 20,000 volts.

transistor ignition   A relatively new form of ignition, this system utilizes transistors and a special coil. The conventional distributor and point setup is used. With the transistor unit, the voltage remains constant, thus permitting high engine revolutions per minute without causing engine miss. Point life is greatly extended because the transistor system passes a very small amount of current through the points.

transmission   A device using gearing or torque conversion to effect a change in the ratio between engine revolutions per minute (RPM) and driving wheel RPM. When engine RPM goes up in relation to wheel RPM, more torque but less speed is produced. A reduction in engine RPM in relation to wheel RPM produces a higher road speed but delivers less torque to the driving wheels.

transmission   Automatic: a transmission that automatically effects gear changes to meet varying road and load conditions. Gear changing is done through a series of oil-operated clutches and bands.
Standard, manual, conventional: a transmission that must be shifted manually.

transmission adapter   A unit that allows a different make or year transmission to be bolted to the original engine.

transverse leaf spring   A leaf spring mounted so it is at right angles to the length of the car.

tread   The distance between the two front or two rear wheels; or, that portion of the tire contacting the roadway.

tread-wear indicators   Horizontal bands molded into a tire tread that appear across the tread grooves when only $\frac{1}{16}$ of an inch of tread remains.

trip odometer   An auxiliary odometer that may be reset to zero at the option of the driver.

troubleshooting   Diagnosing engine, transmission, and other problems.

tube cutter   A tool used to cut tubing by passing a sharp wheel around and around it.

tune-up   The process of checking, repairing, and adjusting the carburetor, spark plugs, points, belts, timing, etc., in order to obtain maximum performance from the engine.

turbine   A wheel on which a series of angled vanes are affixed so a moving column of air or liquid will cause the wheel to turn and produce power.

turbine engine   An engine utilizing burning gases to spin a turbine, or series of turbines, as a means of propelling a car.

turbocharger   A high speed fan or blower that blows the fuel-and-air mixture into the compression chamber, thus giving greater power.

turbulence   The violent, broken movement or agitation of a fluid or gas. The swirling motion imparted to the fuel-and-air mixture entering the cylinder.

turning radius   The diameter of the circle transcribed by the outer front wheel when making a full turn.

TV rod   This refers to the throttle valve rod extending from the foot throttle linkage to the throttle valve in an automatic transmission.

twist drill   A metal-cutting drill with spiral flutes (grooves) to permit the exit of chips while cutting.

two-stroke cycle engine   An engine requiring one complete revolution of the crankshaft to fire each piston once.

undercoating   The soft, deadening material sprayed on the undersides of a car, under the hood, trunk lid, etc., to prevent corrosion.

understeer   The tendency for a car, when negotiating a turn, to resist and continue straight ahead.

undersquare engine   An engine in which the bore diameter is smaller than the length of the stroke.

unitized body design (unit body)   A method of body construction which combines body and frame structures into one integrated, welded assembly, instead of bolting the body to a separate frame.

unit body   A car body in which the body itself acts as the frame.

universal joint   A flexible joint permitting changes in the driving angle between the driving and driven shaft.

unsprung weight   The weight of that portion of the car not supported by the springs (the wheels, tires, brakes, rear axle, steering knuckles, and control arms).

updraft carburetor   A carburetor in which the air passes upward into the intake manifold.

vacuum   Technically, a true vacuum exists only in a space where there is absolutely no matter. However, in general usage, the word is used to mean a partial vacuum.

vacuum advance   A unit designed to advance and retard the ignition timing through the action of partial vacuum in the intake manifold.

vacuum booster A small diaphragm vacuum pump, generally in combination with the fuel pump, used to bolster engine vacuum during acceleration so the vacuum-operated devices will continue to work.

vacuum gauge A gauge used to determine the amount of vacuum existing in a chamber.

vacuum pump A diaphragm-type pump used to produce a vacuum.

vacuum run-out point The point when a vacuum brake power piston has built up all the braking force of which it is capable with the vacuum available.

vacuum tank A tank in which a vacuum exists. It is generally used to provide vacuum to a power brake installation when there is no engine vacuum. The tank will supply several brake applications before the vacuum is exhausted.

valve A device—of which there are many different types— used either to open or close an opening.

valve duration The length of time, measured in degrees of engine crankshaft rotation, a valve remains open.

valve face The outer lower edge of the valve head. The face contacts the valve seat when the valve is closed.

valve float When the valves in the engine are forced back open before they have had a chance to seat. Usually brought about by extremely high revolutions per minute.

valve grinding Renewing the valve face area by grinding on a special grinding machine.

valve guide The hole through which the stem of the poppet valve passes, designed to keep the valve in proper alignment. Some guides are pressed into place and others are merely drilled in the block or in the head metal.

valve-in-head engine An engine in which both intake and exhaust valves are mounted in the cylinder head and driven by push rods or by an overhead camshaft.

valve lash Valve tappet clearance or total clearance in the valve operating train with the cam follower on the camshaft base circle.

valve lift The distance a valve moves from the fully-closed to the fully-opened position.

valve lifter The unit contacting the end of the valve stem and the camshaft. The follower rides on the camshaft and when the cam lobes move it upward, it opens the valve.

valve margin The width of the edge of the valve head between its top and the edge of its face. Too narrow a margin results in preignition and valve damage through overheating.

valve oil seal A neoprene rubber ring placed in a groove in the valve stem to prevent excess oil entering the area between the stem and the guide. There are also other types of valve seals.

valve overlap The interval at the end of the exhaust stroke and the beginning of the following intake stroke when both the intake and exhaust valves are open.

valve port The opening, through the head or block, from the intake or exhaust manifold to the valve seat.

valve rotator A unit placed on the end of the valve stem so when the valve is opened and closed, it will rotate a small amount, providing longer valve life.

valve seat The area on which the face of the poppet seats when closed. The two common angles for this seat are 45 and 30 degrees.

valve seat grinding Renewing the valve seat area by grinding it with a stone mounted on a special mandrel.

valve seat insert A hardened steel valve seat that may be removed and replaced.

valve spring The coil spring used to keep the valves closed.

valve tappet An adjusting screw to obtain the specified clearance at the end of the valve stem (tappet clearance). The screw may be in the top of the lifter, in the rocker arm, or in the case of the ball joint rocker arm, the nut on the mounting stud acts in place of a tappet screw.

valve timing Adjusting the positioning of the camshaft in relation to the crankshaft so the valves will open and close at the proper time.

valve train A system of components within an engine, designed to actuate the intake and exhaust valves of each cylinder in the proper order. The valve train includes the camshaft, tappets, valves, and springs, and in the case of valve-in-head engines, the push rods and rocker arms.

valve umbrella A washer-like unit placed over the end of the valve stem to prevent the entry of excess oil between the stem and the guide. Used in valve-in-head installations.

vaporization Changing a liquid into vapor, usually by addition of heat.

vapor lines Lines used to carry refrigerant gas or vapor.

vapor lock Boiling or vaporizing of the fuel in the lines from excess heat. The boiling will interfere with the movement of the fuel and will in some cases completely stop the flow.

vapor separator A device used on cars equipped with air conditioning to prevent vapor lock by feeding vapors back to the gas tank via a separate line.

variable pitch stator A stator with vanes that may be adjusted to various angles depending on load conditions. The vane adjustment will increase or decrease the efficiency of the stator.

varnish A deposit on the interior of the engine caused by the engine oil breaking down under prolonged heat and use. Portions of the oil deposit themselves in hard coatings of varnish.

vee pulley Used to drive the water pump, generator, alternator, and power steering units, as well as some accessories.

venturi In the carburetor, a streamlined constriction in the air horn for the movement of gasoline into the passing air.

vibration damper A round, weighted device attached to the front of the crankshaft to minimize the torsional vibration.

viscosimeter A device used to determine the vicosity of a given sample of oil. The oil is heated to a specific temperature and then allowed to flow through a set orifice. The length of time required for a certain amount to flow determines the oil's viscosity.

viscosity A term denoting the ability of a fluid to flow readily. A fluid with high viscosity will flow sluggishly, while one with low viscosity will flow much more rapidly.

viscosity index A measure of an oil's ability to resist changes in viscosity when heated.

volatile Easily evaporated.

volatility The property of gasoline, alcohol, etc., to evaporate quickly and at relatively low temperatures.

volt A unit of measurement of electrical pressure. One volt is defined as the pressure or potential needed to push a current of one ampere through a resistance of one ohm.

voltage drop The lowering of voltage due to excess length of wire, undersize wire, or resistance.

voltage regulator See regulator.

voltmeter An instrument used to measure the voltage in a given circuit.

volume The measurement of the space within a certain object or area. The capacity of a container.

volumetric efficiency A comparison between the actual volume of the fuel-and-air mixture drawn in on the intake stroke and what would be drawn in if the cylinder were to be completely filled.

vortex flow (torque converter) The whirling motion of the oil as it moves from the pump, through the turbine, through the stator, and back into the pump.

V-type engine An internal combustion engine in which the cylinders are arranged in two banks at an angle to each other.

wallowing The slow, pitching motion of a car driven over a smooth road with only slight undulations or crosswise tar strips at regular intervals. One cause of this may be shock absorbers with too little control over minor spring deflections.

wander An unstable steering condition in which the car tends to steer itself slightly to both right and left, requiring repeated steering corrections. This usually means the front end needs realignment.

Wankel engine See rotary engine.

water jacket The area around the cylinders and valves left hollow so water may be admitted for cooling.

water valve A shut-off valve, mechanically- or vacuum-operated, for stopping the flow of hot water to the heater.

wedge An engine using a wedge-shaped combustion chamber.

wedge combustion chamber A widely-used and efficient combustion chamber utilizing a wedge shape.

weight distribution The portion of the car's weight that rests on each of the four wheels. In early cars, as much as 70 percent of the weight was on the rear wheels. Modern cars are designed with the weight distribution falling nearly equally on all four wheels.

weld To join two pieces of metal together by raising the area to be joined to a temperature hot enough for the two sections to melt and flow together. Additional metal is usually added by melting small drops from the end of a metal rod.

wet sleeve A cylinder sleeve application in which the water in the cooling system contacts a major portion of the sleeve itself.

wheel aligner A device used to check camber, caster, toe-in, etc.

wheel balancer A machine used to check the wheel-and-tire assembly for static and dynamic balance.

wheelbase The distance between the center of the front wheels and the center of the rear wheels.

wheel cylinder The part of the hydraulic brake system receiving pressure from the master cylinder and in turn appling the brake shoes to the drums.

wheel hop A hopping action of the rear wheels during heavy acceleration.

wheel lug (lug) The bolts used to fasten the wheel to the hub.

wide treads Wide tires. The tire height, bead-to-tread surface, is about 70 percent of the tire width across the outside of the casing.

winding the engine Running the engine at top revolutions per minute.

wiring diagram A drawing showing the various electrical units and their correct wiring arrangements.

worm gear A coarse, spiral-shaped gear cut on a shaft. It is used to engage with and drive another gear or portion of a gear. As used in the steering gearbox, it often engages the cross shaft via a roller or by a tapered pin.

worm and roller A type of steering gear utilizing a worm gear on the steering shaft. A roller on one end of the cross shaft engages the worm.

worm and sector A type of steering gear utilizing a worm gear engaging a sector (a portion of a gear) on the cross shaft.

worm and taper pin A type of steering gear utilizing a worm gear on the steering shaft. The end of the cross shaft engages the worm via a taper pin.

wormshaft A shaft in the steering gear coupled to the shaft from the steering wheel.

wrist pin A round steel pin inserted through a piston to which a connecting rod is fastened.

X-body cars A front-wheel drive, chassis-body combination in which the engine is mounted in the front, with the cylinders in line across the car.

Index

B

C

E

F

G

H

I

M

N

O

P

R

S

T